A Guidance Approach for the Encouraging Classroom

Fifth Edition

Dan Gartrell, Ed.D.
Bemidji State University

 WADSWORTH
CENGAGE Learning

Australia • Brazil • Japan • Korea • Mexico • Singapore • Spain • United Kingdom • United States

WADSWORTH
CENGAGE Learning™

A Guidance Approach for the Encouraging Classroom, Fifth Edition
Dan Gartrell

Executive Editor: Linda Schreiber-Ganster

Assistant Editor: Caitlin Cox

Editorial Assistant: Linda Stewart

Associate Media Editor: Ashley Cronin

Marketing Manager: Kara Kindstrom

Marketing Assistant: Dimitri Hagnéré

Marketing Communications Manager: Martha Pfeiffer

Content Project Manager: Samen Iqbal

Creative Director: Rob Hugel

Art Director: Maria Epes

Print Buyer: Paula Vang

Rights Acquisitions Account Manager, Text: Bob Kauser

Rights Acquisitions Account Manager, Image: Leitha Etheridge-Sims

Production Service: Pre-PressPMG

Photo Researcher: Pre-PressPMG

Copy Editor: Deborah Bader

Cover Designer: Bartay Studios

Cover Image: © Ariel Skelley / Blend Images / Corbis

Compositor: Pre-PressPMG

For product information and technology assistance, contact us at
Cengage Learning Customer & Sales Support, 1-800-354-9706

For permission to use material from this text or product, submit all requests online at **www.cengage.com/permissions**
Further permissions questions can be emailed to **permissionrequest@cengage.com**

Library of Congress Control Number: 2009930828

ISBN-13: 978-1-4283-6096-9

ISBN-10: 1-4283-6096-4

Wadsworth
20 Davis Drive
Belmont, CA 94002
USA

Cengage Learning is a leading provider of customized learning solutions with office locations around the globe, including Singapore, the United Kingdom, Australia, Mexico, Brazil, and Japan. Locate your local office at **www.cengage.com/global**

Cengage Learning products are represented in Canada by Nelson Education, Ltd.

To learn more about Wadsworth, visit **www.cengage.com/wadsworth**

Purchase any of our products at your local college store or at our preferred online store **www.cengagebrain.com**

Printed in the United States of America
2 3 4 5 6 7 15 14 13 12 11

Contents

Preface ix

Acknowledgments xiv

Part One: Foundations of a Guidance Approach 1

Preview... 1

Chapter 1: The Guidance Tradition 3

Guiding Questions 3

Key Concepts.. 3

Pioneers of the Guidance Tradition 4

Mid-20th-Century Influences: The Developmental and
   Self Psychologists.. 11

The 1980s: Guidance or Obedience-Based Discipline? 20

Beyond Discipline to Guidance 22

Parent-Teacher Relations in the Guidance Tradition 27

Summary.. 32

Follow-Up Activities 33

Recommended Readings 35

Guidance Matters: The Case of Jeremiah 35

Chapter 2: Child Development and Guidance........................... 39

Guiding Questions 39

Key Concepts... 39

Piaget: A Foundation for the Study of Child Development 41

Vygotsky: How the Adult Guides Development 47

Erikson: Personal Development and the Classroom 53

Gardner's Multiple Intelligences: Guidance for Healthy Development 62

Emotional Intelligence: Defining the Central Guidance Issue 68

The Contributions of Brain Research 72

A Climate for Partnerships with Families 76

Summary 80

Follow-Up Activities 82

Recommended Readings 85

*Guidance Matters Column: Competition: What Place in
    Our Programs* 85

*Chapter 3: Mistaken Behavior: Understanding Conflicts, Agression, and
    Challenging Behavior* 89

Guiding Questions 89

Key Concepts 89

Beyond Misbehavior 90

The Concept of Mistaken Behavior 92

*Relational Patterns: A Model for Social-Emotional Development
    in the Classroom* 94

Three Levels of Mistaken Behavior 97

Mistaken Behavior, Aggression, and Challenging Behavior 111

Communicating with Parents about Mistaken Behavior 118

Summary 121

Follow-Up Activities 123

Recommended Readings 126

Guidance Matters: Swearing and Words That Hurt—Three Anecdotes 126

Chapter 4: Guidance in the Classroom 129

Guiding Questions 129

Key Concepts 129

A Professional, Not a Technician 130

The Need for Positive Teacher-Child Relationships 132

Reducing Mistaken Behavior 139

Taking a Solution Orientation 145

Liberation Teaching 153

Building Partnerships with Parents 156

Summary 157

Follow-Up Activities 159

Recommended Readings 161

Guidance Matters: "He Did It on Purpose" 162

Part Two: Creating the Encouraging Classroom 165

Preview 165

Chapter 5: Organizing the Encouraging Classroom 167

Guiding Questions 167

Key Concepts 167

Reducing School Anxiety: The Encouraging Classroom 168

Developmentally Appropriate Practice Today 170

Learning Centers in the Encouraging Classroom 182

Building the Classroom for Prosocial Development 192

Encouraging Classroom Volunteers 194

Summary 198

Follow-Up Activities 200

Recommended Readings 202

Guidance Matters: Promote Physical Activity—It's Proactive Guidance 203

Chapter 6: Managing the Encouraging Classroom 207

Guiding Questions 207

Key Concepts 207

The Daily Program 208

The Limits of Large Groups 218

Managing Transitions 230

Routines in the Encouraging Classroom: A Teacher's Perspective 235

Guidance Means Teamwork with Other Adults 237

Encouraging Family Members and Other Classroom Volunteers 241

Summary 247

Follow-Up Activities 249

Recommended Readings 251

Guidance Matters: A Concerned Director Writes 252

Chapter 7: Leadership Communication with the Group 255

Guiding Questions 255

Key Concepts 255

Establishing Leadership 256

Guidelines, Not Rules. 259

Encouragement. 264

Discussing Inclusively 270

Class Meetings: Sustaining the Encouraging Classroom .272

Encouraging Friendliness. 283

Leadership Communication with Parents. 287

Summary. 295

Follow-Up Activities 297

Recommended Readings 299

Guidance Matters: Class Meetings 299

Chapter 8:Leadership Communication with the Individual. 303

Guiding Questions 303

Key Concepts. 303

Listening Techniques 304

Contact Talk 312

The Compliment Sandwich. 317

Friendly Humor 318

Friendly Touch 321

Be There for the Children, Be There for Yourself 324

Leadership Communication in the Parent-Teacher Conference. 326

Summary. 329

Follow-Up Activities 331

Recommended Readings 333

Guidance Matters: Build Relationships through Talk. 334

Part Three: Solving Problems in the Encouraging Classroom. 337

Preview. 337

Chapter 9: Conflict Management. 339

Guiding Questions 339

Key Concepts. 339

Basics of Conflict Management. 340

Developmental Considerations in Conflict Management 346

The Five-Finger Formula..349

Teaching Conflict Management Skills..354

Understanding Diversity in Family Structures......................................361

Summary...366

Follow-Up Activities..367

Recommended Readings 369

Guidance Matters: Conflict Mediation 370

Chapter 10: Problem Solving Mistaken Behavior...................................373

Guiding Questions...373

Key Concepts..373

The Decision to Intervene...374

Four Quick Intervention Strategies...382

Behaviors Reported By Other Children 390

Intervention Strategies When Follow-Up Is Needed 392

Why Take the Time? 398

Building Cooperation with Today's Diverse Families 402

Summary...407

Follow-Up Activities..409

Recommended Readings 411

Guidance Matters: Boys and Men Teachers..411

Chapter 11: Guidance Through Intervention 415

Guiding Questions...415

Key Concepts..415

When Boys have Conflicts 417

Conditions that Make Intervention Necessary.....................................421

Crisis Management 424

Comprehensive Guidance/The Individual Guidance Plan...........................434

When Teachers Feel Anger...445

When Teachers and Parents Disagree 450

Summary...454

Follow-Up Activities..456

Recommended Readings 458

Guidance Matters: Comprehensive Guidance 459

Chapter 12: Liberation Teaching: A Guidance Response
*   to Violence In Society*..463
Guiding Questions..463
Key Concepts...463
Societal Violence and the Classroom.....................................464
Liberation Teaching: The Guidance Response..............................470
The Guidance Response to Bullying.......................................477
Liberation Teaching and Related Educational Practices...................483
Liberation Teaching and Parent Involvement..............................490
Summary...495
Follow-Up Activities..497
Recommended Readings..499
Guidance Matters: Understand Bullying...................................500

Appendices..505
*A. The NAEYC*Code of Ethical Conduct*....................................505
B. Sample Greeting Letters and Surveys to Children and Their Families...515
C. Sample Guidebook: The Education Program in Our Class.................523
D. Developmentally Appropriate Guidance of Young Children...............531
E. Individual Guidance Plan Worksheet...................................555

Glossary..557

References..565

Index...579

Dedication

In Memory of Three Education Professors

Ben Thompson of Antioch College, Yellow Springs, Ohio

Maurice Lucas of the University of North Dakota, Grand Forks and

Bill "Doc" McDowall of Bemidji State University Bemidji, Minnesota

Preface

One outstanding new feature highlights this fifth edition of *A Guidance Approach for the Encouraging Classroom*. Each chapter concludes with a reprinted "Guidance Matters" column from the National Association for the Education of Young Children journal, *Young Children*. I wrote the columns for *YC* between November of 2005 and May of 2008 and have selected columns that focus on such issues as:

▶ swearing

▶ competition

▶ "he did it on purpose"

▶ class meetings

▶ boys and men teachers

▶ conflict mediation

▶ comprehensive guidance

▶ bullying

The columns personalize the content of each chapter by building practical but referenced discussions around lead-in anecdotes of actual situations from early childhood classrooms. In some cases the columns pick up on and enlighten topics from the chapters. Other columns take the reader on new paths generated by the chapter content. I wish to thank NAEYC for their generous permission to use the Guidance Matters columns. Readers can download all of the columns at http://danielgartrell1.efoliomn2.com.

The fifth edition retains other features important to users of the text.

Part One presents the foundations of guidance, including history of the approach and theoretical considerations that empower the paradigm shift from conventional discipline to guidance. Part One also introduces concepts and considerations vital in the use of guidance, such as the construct of *mistaken behavior,* and discusses implications of the pushdown of academics into early childhood education. Some content features important in *Part One* are:

▶ Extended coverage of *emotional intelligence* as defining the central guidance issue.

▶ Comparison of current thought about the term *challenging behavior* with the text concept of *strong unmet needs mistaken behavior.*

▷ Discussion of the contributions of multiple intelligence theory and brain development research to the practices of guidance.

▷ An analysis of forms of *aggression,* and how aggression shows itself in different levels of mistaken behavior.

▷ Discussion of the "accountability shove-down" and increasing academic pressures on teachers and young children, which cause stressful classrooms and mistaken behavior.

Part Two details the dynamics of building an *encouraging classroom,* the physical and social *learning community* in which all children are accepted as worthwhile, contributing members. This part develops the premise that the most effective guidance is preventive, by the use of developmentally appropriate practice in schedule, room arrangement, instructional method, and leadership communication. Featured content in *Part Two* discusses:

▷ Organization of the encouraging classroom to promote prosocial development, the learning of democratic life skills by every child.

▷ The argument for physically active programming for young children, not just during set periods, but also throughout the day.

▷ The need for teachers to balance developmentally appropriate programming with teaching and assessing for the attainment of standards.

▷ Vital guidance-leadership techniques that the teachers uses with groups and individual children in the encouraging classroom.

▷ Skills for building relationships with children that include the use of: intentional listening techniques, contact talks, compliment sandwiches, friendly humor, and friendly touch.

▷ Part Two makes the case that encouraging classrooms are places of significant learning, but learning that supports the uniqueness and autonomy of each child in a friendly community environment.

Part Three presents intervention methods, ranging from guidance talks to comprehensive guidance, that empower the teacher to respond to classroom conflicts in ways that teach rather than punish. A new feature of *Part Three* is the lead-off section in Chapter Eleven titled "Considerations for When Boys Have Conflicts." The section builds upon findings from recent studies indicating that whereas most early childhood teachers are female, most children who receive strict discipline and are expelled from preschool programs are boys. The section explores intervention strategies practiced by both women and men teachers that convey respect for the young boy, while at the same time guiding toward productive behaviors. Other key features of *Part Three* include:

▷ New classroom examples that illustrate a workable strategy for conflict mediation with young children.

▷ A section that explores two diverse family structures that are on the increase: single-father families and grandparent-led families.

▶ An updated discussion of *quick intervention techniques* that de-escalate classroom conflicts.

▶ Practical considerations for using *crisis management techniques when children have lost control and there is a danger of harm to the child or others.*

▶ A thorough treatment of the use of *comprehensive guidance* for when children experience frequent and extreme conflicts in the classroom.

▶ A discussion of the effects of indirect and direct violence on young children in the classroom, including resiliency mentoring with children suffering from post-traumatic stress syndrome.

▶ A thorough section on the guidance response to bullying, including how bullying shows itself in three levels of mistaken behavior and how the teacher works with the class, the child, staff, and families to prevent and resolve bullying behavior.

▶ A discussion of liberation teaching as a unifying concept that links socially responsive teaching practices such as antibullying education, guidance, antibias teaching, and peace education.

A feature kept in the fifth edition is a concluding section in each chapter focusing on **families.** Guidance is best seen as a three-way partnership of teachers, children, and family members. In fact, works on guidance that do not include building relationships with families are to me just plain incomplete. Many parents in our society (though certainly not all) have had school experiences that were more unhappy than happy. Also, some have had experiences in their upbringing and adult lives that keep them from being the "ideal" parents that educators would like them to be.

As readers are aware, the "ideal" family structure lauded in the past represents a small percentage of American families today. Many children have parents who are separated, divorced, not married, single, and/or often not present. Families that are headed by biological parent-substitutes—such as grandparents, aunts and uncles, foster parents, or adoptive parents—are on the increase. These custodial caregivers, if not biological parents, need special recognition and support for their difficult but crucial role in children's lives.

To remind readers of the trend toward family diversity, I use the term *family members* alternately with the term *parents* in the text. A guiding principle with families is, according to a friend who is a longtime successful kindergarten teacher in a Native American community, "Be friendly first and then stay that way."

Formatting Features

1. A *preview section* begins each of the three parts of the text.

2. Each chapter starts with five to seven *guiding questions* that organize the main chapter headings, the chapter summary, and follow-up student application activities.

3. Each chapter now begins with *key concepts* that are bolded in the text and defined in the Glossary. The key concepts are terms important both in the guidance tradition and in progressive education in general over the last 150 years.

4. Because of their increasing acceptance, guidance terms originating in my writings continue in the new edition, terms such as *mistaken behavior, levels of mistaken behavior, contact talks, guidance talks, the five-finger formula (for conflict mediation),* and *liberation teaching.* When not bolded, signifying inclusion in the Glossary, important guidance terms are italicized in the text.

5. More than 100 classroom anecdotes offer a practical insight into concepts discussed, most provided by former students, many new in this edition.

6. End-of-chapter "follow-up" activities are discussion questions for the class and application activities for individual students. The application activities include both observation and interview options. Each follow-up activity asks students to "integrate theory and practice" by inter-relating specifics from the observation or interview with specifics from the chapter.

7. Now moved to the "end matter" before the index, a thorough list of chapter references is provided, many updated for this edition. (However, when "classic" references have kept their relevance, they have been retained.) The numerous references document the established guidance tradition in early childhood education through time and across the age span of preschool through the primary grades.

Supplements

A team of people has assisted in updating supplements for the fifth edition.

The book-specific Web site at www.cengage.com/education/gartrell offers students a variety of study tools and useful resources such as tutorial quizzes for each chapter, guiding questions, flash cards, case studies, Internet exercises, and links that both provide a concise overview of key ideas from each chapter and connect the reader to resources that extend text material. The instructor area of the Book Companion Web site offers access to password-protected resources such as an Instructor's Manual and PowerPoint slides.

An updated *Instructor's Manual and Test Bank* is keyed both to each chapter in the text and to the companion website.

A new supplement, the PowerLecture, is a one-stop digital library and presentation tool that includes preassembled Microsoft® PowerPoint® lecture slides by Dan Gartrell, in addition to a full Instructor's Manual and Test Bank. It also includes ExamView® testing software with all the test items from the the Instructor's Manual Test Bank in electronic format, enabling you to create customized tests in print or online.

WebTutor™ Toolbox for WebCT™ or Blackboard® provides access to all the content of this text's rich Book Companion Web site from within your course management system. Robust communication tools—such as a course calendar, asynchronous discussion, real-time chat, a whiteboard, and an integrated e-mail system—make it easy for your students to stay connected to the course.

Age Range Addressed

Readers know that individual timetables for development in children vary. Still, there is general agreement that by about age three, 36 months, children have emerged from toddlerhood into the early childhood period. By around age eight, or 96 months, children have exited from early childhood into middle childhood. Some readers have requested that the text address children younger than three years. Others have requested, for institutional reasons, that the age cut-off be before or after kindergarten.

So much happens during the five years between ages three and eight—both developmentally, within the child's mind and body, and from without, due to the child's exposure to increasingly complex social forces and educational expectations. With respect to the diversity of opinion on this matter, the age range of three to eight years retains its legitimacy for me as the developmental focus.

Aim and Purpose

The text is used in capstone (final) courses of two-year college programs, upper-division baccalaureate programs, and even graduate classes. It is comprehensive enough to stand as a primary text in courses that integrate content in group management, learning environment, developmentally appropriate practice, child guidance, and parent-teacher partnerships*. A little like the children's classic *Are You My Mother*, the text has developmental flexibility—spanning the two-year college to –graduate–level scope of practice.

The fifth edition of *A Guidance Approach* contains well over 300 references to the works of others. While maintaining the scholarship required of a postsecondary textbook, I have made frequent use of classroom anecdotes and photos to make the text accessible.

Moreover, I have used a writing style that does not talk down to students, but is at times informal. In these pages the discerning reader will find an occasional colloquialism, the hint of a joke, or the rare use of a first-person reference. Intentionally as well, when the point of an anecdote warranted it, I have let stand the idioms used by young children, such as "foots" and "Me going too, Teacher." Their expressions will become more conventional with age, but in the meantime, I have tried to portray realistically how young children do talk and act.

Further, if a child in a classroom anecdote used an expletive, and the expletive was central to the anecdote, I included it, with or without ellipses for strategic letters.

---

* *For a more concise, less comprehensive treatment of guidance in early childhood, readers might consider The Power of Guidance: Teaching Social:Emotional Skills in Early Childhood Classrooms. This 2004 collections of writings is a joint publication of Wadsworth Cengage Learning and the National Association for the Education of Young Children.*

In early childhood classrooms young children do on occasion "swear"—even if they don't always get the pronunciation right or know what the word really means. In my view prospective teachers need to face expletive use head on and develop a response strategy that (on occasion) is not without a tinge of humor. (See the Guidance Matters column, "Swearing and Words That Hurt," at the end of Chapter Three.)

I accept any criticism about informality in the writing style. The challenge of the text has been to introduce terms and concepts that are important for a paradigm shift away from traditional discipline practices—while at the same time making the material readable for a broad range of students and (dare I say it in regards to a textbook) interesting.

In this text, I (as always) advocate for the use of guidance—discipline that teaches without punishment—bringing numerous references to the material to vouch for this tradition in early childhood education. This text is from my heart as well as my mind, and I am pleased to include moments of "real life" humor and passion that hopefully help the ideas come to life.

Acknowledgments

Many persons have helped to make this fifth edition possible. First, as always, appreciation goes to the memory of my mother, Beth Goff, who raised me this way, and to my wife, Julie Jochum Gartrell, for ongoing assistance and support—*especially* with the electronic supplements. Thanks are due to the many students over the years who have contributed anecdotes and otherwise inspired me with their guidance teaching, sometimes even as practicum students and student teachers before graduation. These former students provide continuous renewal for me as a teacher and author.

Thanks so much to those special teachers over the years with whom I have had the opportunity to be a colleague. Some of them have contributed anecdotes or to sections of the text, but all have taught me so much: Susan Bailey, Robin Bakken, Joyce Duffney, Lynn Gerhke, Sharon Hoverson, Terry Leinbach, Bryan Nelson, Leah Pigatti, Pat Sanford, Kathleen Sonsteng, and Pam Stowe. In addition I would like to thank staff members of Bi-County Head Start (Bemidji and Blackduck), Campus Childcare, Mahube Head Start, and Schoolcraft Learning Community. Their positive practices have contributed to the guidance ideas in this text.

Further, I wish to express appreciation to the colleagues and many former students who contributed classroom anecdotes. The following shared multiple or "featured" anecdotes from their classrooms: Robin Bakken, Kelly Grunenwald, Sharon Hoverson, Julie Curb, Kevin Helgren, Karen Palubicki, Ben Roland, Pat Sanford, Kathleen Sonsteng, and Marta Underthun. To the many others as well who gave permission to use their stories, I extend my gratitude.

Special acknowledgment is continued to Dr. Steven Harlow for his important concept of *levels of social relations*. His construct has given rise to my concept of mistaken behavior, a featured concept in the text.

A figure bigger than his life, Haim Ginott has particularly imbued the text with his message and spirit.

Thanks are sent out for production assistance locally, including Monte Draper of *The Bemidji Pioneer* for photos, and Julie Jochum Gartrell and Mina Blyly-Strauss for developing the electronic supplement. Appreciation is extended to Cengage staff for key photos in the book, and to reviewers of Cengage Learning who gave helpful feedback and suggestions for the fifth edition. They are:

Tamara B. Calhoun, Schenectady County Community College

Martha Lash, Kent State University

Donna Rafanello, Long Beach City College

Veronica Getskow, Los Angeles Community College District

Judith Gifford, University of Wisconsin–Stout

Tracy Keyes, Kutztown University

Alice D. Beyrent, Hesser College

Thanks to Caitlin Cox who provided leadership in developmental editing for the fifth edition, to Marie Desrosiers, project editor, and the staff of Cengage Learning for competence and enthusiasm in the complex production process.

Finally, appreciation is expressed to those instructors at a range of postsecondary levels who have continued to use *A Guidance Approach* as their textbook, sometimes even modifying course formats in order to fully utilize the book. As well, I extend a welcome to new instructors adopting the text for the first time. May the text and supplements serve you well. To all, feel free to contact me with questions, comments, and suggestions.

Dan Gartrell, Ed.D.
Bemidji State University
Bemidji, Minnesota 56601
dgartrell@bemidjistate.edu

About the Author

During the 1960s, Dan Gartrell was a teacher for an inner-city elementary school in Ohio and the Head Start Program of the Red Lake Band of Ojibwe in Minnesota. In the early 1970s, Dan earned a master's degree at Bemidji State University in northern Minnesota. At Bemidji State, Dan became a field advisor, CDA trainer,

and then director of the Child Development Training Program. Dan completed his doctorate at the University of North Dakota's Center for Teaching and Learning in 1977. He is currently Professor of Early Childhood and Elementary Education and Director of the Child Development Training Program at Bemidji State University. As a teacher, CDA trainer, and student teaching supervisor, Dan has been working with students and teachers (and observing children) in early childhood classrooms for 40 years.

Dan has led more than 300 presentations, trainings, and keynote addresses on guidance in many states and in Germany and Mexico. He has written nine pieces that have appeared in *Young Children,* the journal of NAEYC, along with his column, "Guidance Matters." In 2004 Cengage Learning and NAEYC jointly published a compilation of Dan's writing, *The Power of Guidance: Teaching Social-Emotional Skills in Early Childhood Classrooms.* The book was selected as a comprehensive membership benefit to NAEYC members in 2004.

Dan is an amateur photographer who especially enjoys nature photography. He and his wife, Dr. Julie Jochum, have a blended family that includes five children and eleven grandchildren. (He brings grandkid photos to all events.)

Part 1

Foundations of a Guidance Approach

Preview

One—The Guidance Tradition

Chapter One provides historical overview of the guidance tradition. Direct quotes by pioneers in the field are included to document their own thoughts about education and the role of guidance. Mid-20th-century influences of the developmental and self psychologists are traced. The trend away from punishment and toward guidance in the 1980s and 1990s is presented. The tradition of parent-teacher partnerships within the guidance approach is explored.

Two—Child Development and Guidance

Chapter Two explores child development theories of the last 70 years and discusses the relation of each to guidance principles. The developmental theories are those of Piaget, Vygotsky, Erikson, Gardner, and Goleman. An overview of important findings from brain research and attachment theory, and the implications for guidance of each is provided. The conclusion that guidance is the approach to children's behavior that comes closest to the essence of our growing understanding about child development is presented.

Three—Mistaken Behavior: Understanding Conflicts, Aggression, and Challenging Behavior

Chapter Three presents a concept in line with the work of the self psychologists for understanding young children's behavior: that behavior traditionally considered as misbehavior is more constructively viewed as mistaken behavior. Three levels of mistaken behavior are analyzed. The term "challenging behavior" is set within the context of mistaken behavior. Considerations for acquainting parents with the concept of mistaken behavior are discussed.

Four—Guidance in the Classroom

Chapter Four develops four principles of a guidance approach: that it means teachers are professionals, not technicians; builds from positive teacher-child relations; reduces the need for mistaken behavior; takes a solution orientation; includes liberation teaching; and involves parent-teacher partnerships.

Chapter 1 — The Guidance Tradition

Guiding Questions

- *Who were the pioneers of the guidance tradition?*
- *Who were mid-20th-century influences in the guidance tradition?*
- *What was the significance of discipline trends in the 1980s?*
- *What is the state of the guidance tradition today?*
- *What is the importance of parent-teacher relations in the guidance tradition?*

© Cengage Learning

Key Concepts

- *Autonomy*
- *Conflict management*
- *Constructivist education*
- *Democratic life skills*
- *Developmentally appropriate practice (DAP)*
- *Discipline*
- *Encouraging classroom*
- *Guidance*
- *No Child Left Behind*
- *Obedience-based discipline*
- *Parent-teacher partnerships*
- *Self-psychology*

Here in the 21st century, we want citizens to think intelligently and ethically and to solve problems cooperatively by the use of words. *A Guidance Approach for the Encouraging Classroom* explores the teaching and learning of these democratic life skills in early childhood education.

The **guidance** approach has its roots in the history of Western education and is tied to the thoughts of progressive educators over the last two centuries. The basis of guidance, the empowering of productive human activity, lies in the view that human nature has the potential for good. In this view, the role of the adult is not to "discipline the child away from evil" but to guide the child to develop the personal strength and understanding necessary to make ethical, intelligent decisions. This capacity, which Piaget (1932/1960) termed **autonomy**, is a primary goal in the guidance approach. A companion goal is to guide children in the use of **conflict management**, the ability to think intelligently and ethically in order to prevent and, if necessary, peaceably resolve conflicts. These companion goals serve as themes throughout the text, sometimes directly addressed and sometimes implied, but always there.

In recent years a growing number of educators consider the term **discipline** to be controversial. These educators have observed that discipline too often slides into *punishment,* a practice not used in guidance (Gartrell, 2004; Reynolds, 2000). For this reason, guidance goes beyond usual classroom discipline, which is the use of rewards and punishments to make children obedient to the "educational program" (Gartrell, 2004; Kohn, 1999; Montessori, 1912/1964). Guidance is education for democracy—it is teaching social and emotional skills through all classroom situations.

The kind of classroom in which children learn these social and emotional skills is the **encouraging classroom**. In the encouraging classroom, all children feel they are able learners and worthy members of the class. The teacher builds an encouraging classroom through positive leadership with the children, their families, and the community. In the encouraging classroom, guidance practices merge with developmentally appropriate practices and together become the everyday curriculum (Reineke, Sonsteng, & Gartrell, 2008, p. 92).

For the teacher in the encouraging classroom, unique human characteristics— differing styles, cultural backgrounds, appearances, temperaments, and behavior patterns—become sources of mutual affirmation and respect. Within the confines of a caring community, the right of each child to fully develop his or her potential is basic. The teacher uses guidance to nurture that potential.

Part One provides the foundations of the guidance approach. This first chapter documents that over the years progressive educators frequently have called for an integrated education model, one that links the positive potential of the child, the interactive nature of an appropriate curriculum, and the guiding role of the teacher. Chapter One traces the guidance tradition in Western educational thought.

Pioneers of the Guidance Tradition

A principle in the guidance tradition is that the management of behavior cannot be separated from the curriculum, and that both are tied to the teacher's views of human nature (Gartrell, 2004). This three-way relationship is no recent occurrence and can be seen in the 17th century in the writings of the educators

Guidance is based on the view that human nature has the potential for good.

of the time—the clergy. Osborn's (1991) informative chronology, *Early Childhood Education in Historical Perspective*, frames a fundamental disagreement about the nature of childhood that still impacts education and management practice today. Osborn documents that within the clergy two contrasting reasons were given for the importance of education. The 1621 treatise, *A Godly Form of Household Government*, states:

> *The young child which lieth in the cradle is both wayward and full of affection; and though his* body be small, yet he hath a wrongdoing heart and is inclined to evil. . . . If this spark be suffered to increase, it will rage over and burn down the whole house. For we are changed and become good, not by birth, but by education. (p. 24)*

An opposing point of view portrayed the child as a *tabula rasa* (blank slate). This point of view can be seen in Earle's *Microcosmography* (1628):

> *The child is a small letter, yet the best copy of Adam. . . . His soul is yet a white paper un-scribbled with observations . . . and he knows no evil. (p. 22)*

For centuries among Western countries, acceptance of the first view of human nature meant that teachers commonly relied on strict discipline, including corporal punishment, to enforce obedience (Berger, 2007; deMause, 1974). Although the use of corporal punishment is now widely rejected, punishment as an "educational tool" remains an issue in most American schools. Progress toward humane educational practice has been made, of course, and some teachers of the attitude expressed by Earle have always used guidance. The following discussion

---

* *For purposes of accuracy, masculine pronouns are retained in quotes. Otherwise, the author has sought to reduce and balance gender-specific pronoun use. In odd chapters teacher is referred to as "she" and child as "he." Reverse occurs in even chapters.*

Believing that children tended toward evil, schoolmasters of previous times "beat the devil" out of children—corporal punishment that would be considered child abuse today.

of pioneers in the guidance tradition comes in part from the research of Jennifer Wolfe in *Learning from the Past: Historical Voices in Early Childhood Education* (2002).

John Comenius

A clergyman who lived between 1592 and 1670, John Comenius spent over half his life in forced exile from his home in eastern Europe. He nonetheless became known throughout the continent for his farsighted contributions to education. Comenius wrote the first illustrated children's book, which schoolchildren in Europe and North America used for almost 200 years! He recognized the importance of early childhood education and saw parents as the first educators. He taught that the interests and senses of the child, rather than the rule of the teacher, should guide the education process. He thought that education was truly productive when it is in tune with the natural order of development in the child.

Comenius believed that all children, from whatever social circumstances, were deserving of an education, and that girls as well as boys should attend school. He saw the classroom as a safe and happy place, where corporal punishment was forbidden. In his work, *The Great Didactic*, Comenius stated:

> *The desire to learn can be excited by teachers, if they are gentle and persuasive and do not alienate their pupils from them by roughness, but attract them by fatherly sentiments and words. (Wolfe, 2002, p. 56)*

Many of these same ideas about instruction and child guidance can be seen in progressive social thinkers who followed Comenius over the centuries, including Pestalozzi, Owen, Froebel, Montessori, Dewey, and Piaget.

Johann Pestalozzi and Robert Owen

From the late 18th century into the 19th, Pestalozzi, along with Owen, Friedrich Froebel, and others, fundamentally reformed Western educational practice. Pestalozzi (1746–1827) advocated an integrated education that addressed the "hand, heart, and mind." He observed that children learn by interactions with the physical and social world and by organizing their experiences around these interactions. He asserted that teachers teach best by interacting with children rather than talking at them. He argued that punishments and even rewards distracted children from their natural course of development. In Pestalozzi's view, teachers need to continually monitor their methods in order to keep children interested and involved in learning experiences.

Both Robert Owen and Friedrich Froebel studied with Pestalozzi and carried forward Pestalozzi's ideas (Wolfe, 2002). Owen was an enlightened business leader who established planned industrial communities in New Lanark, Scotland, and later in New Harmony, Indiana. Owen was one of the first to demonstrate that workers would be more productive if they were respected and treated well. He took the position, controversial at the time, that young children should be cared for and educated before becoming industrial workers. Owen established early school/child care centers, which were to follow seven key (and farsighted) principles:

▸ Children were not punished.

▸ Teachers must be kind.

▸ Instruction was based on children's experiences.

▸ Dance, rhymes, singing, and music were a large part of the program.

▸ Children's questions were to be answered in respectful and kindly ways.

▸ Outdoor time was for when children grew fatigued, not just for set periods.

▸ Curriculum included learning about the out-of-doors, not just academic subjects.

Owen believed that children would naturally strive to fulfill their natures, and that punishment would undermine the child's natural course of development. Of children in his schools he stated: "Punishment . . . will never be required, and should be avoided as much as giving poison in their food" (Owen, 1967).

Friedrich Froebel

Born in eastern Germany in 1782, Friedrich Froebel was the originator of the kindergarten ("child's garden"), intended to serve children aged three to six. The purpose of the kindergarten was to provide an extension of the family life that Froebel thought all children should have. Education for Froebel was positive guidance, so that "the innate impulses of the child" could harmoniously develop through play and playlike active experiences. Froebel's kindergarten guided children through a sequence of manipulative experiences with increasingly complex "gifts" and "occupations." An emphasis was on children expressing feelings and thoughts through "rhythm, dancing, music, language, and drawing" (Wolfe, 2002, p. 112). Important for Froebel was that children see connections in life, and nature study—outside the classroom as well as in—was an emphasis in his kindergarten curriculum.

Froebel championed several forward-looking practices, such as:

▶ respect for the development of each child

▶ boys and girls together in classrooms

▶ "hands-on" rather than recitation-based instruction

▶ the training and use of women teachers

▶ home visits

▶ and mothers meetings.

In 1851, finding these practices too radical, the Prussian government outlawed Froebel's kindergartens and his training programs for teachers. In the face of this repression, emigrant families from Germany began taking the kindergarten idea with them to many countries, most notably the United States and Canada. Growing from the first kindergarten in Wisconsin in 1856, 3,000 kindergartens flourished across the country by 1890 (Osborn, 1991).

Froebel believed that the developing nature of the child was essentially good and that "faults" were the result of particular experiences. In *Friedrich Froebel: A Selection from His Writings* (1967), Lilley quotes the educator:

There are many faults . . . which arise simply through carelessness. When children act on an impulse which in itself may be harmless or even praiseworthy, they can become so entirely absorbed that they have no thought for the consequences, and indeed from their own limited experience can have no knowledge of them. . . .

Moreover, it is certainly true that as a rule the child is first made bad by some other person, often by the educator himself. This can happen when everything which the child does out of ignorance or thoughtlessness or even from a keen sense of right and wrong is attributed to an intention to do evil. Unhappily there are among teachers those who always see children as mischievous, spiteful . . . whereas others see at most an over exuberant sense of life or a situation which has got out of hand. (p. 135)

In his views about children and their behavior, Froebel showed clear understanding of the need for a guidance approach to children's behavior.

Maria Montessori

Maria Montessori was a landmark transition figure between education dominated by the religious philosophy of the 19th century and the social sciences of the twentieth. Maria Montessori was the first woman physician in Italy, and the difficulty of this achievement is shown by this fact: As a medical student, Montessori was required to wait until all male students entered lecture halls before she was allowed to be seated (Wolfe, 2002). Montessori specialized in pediatrics, bringing the independence of her thinking and learning to this field. When other authorities dismissed children with special needs as uneducable, Montessori organized teams of teachers and doctors who worked successfully with the children (Wolfe, 2002): Montessori believed that "mental deficiency" was more a problem of teaching and learning than a strictly medical matter (Montessori, 1912/1964).

In 1907, Montessori's chief contribution to early childhood education materialized in the "Casa dei Bambini" (children's houses) of Rome. These early childhood centers, designed for the children of factory workers, provided an important model for the elevation of child care from the custodial to the educational. Points of emphasis were the teaching of practical life skills, and sensory-based manipulative materials at increasing levels of complexity. Montessori believed that children learn through responsible decision making in a "prepared environment," designed to further each child's development. Directresses (teachers) worked quietly but firmly with children to assist them to make appropriate decisions about the learning materials available—which usually had prescribed uses.

The particular mix of freedom and structure that is the Montessori approach has always been controversial, first welcomed in the United States, then for many years ostracized by American educators. Since the 1960s in North America, Montessori schools have seen a resurgence. "Orthodox" and "Americanized" branches of Montessori education each have found a niche, with families and educators gravitating to one or the other.

Throughout her career Montessori maintained a fundamental principle, that "the child is in a continual state of growth and metamorphosis, whereas the adult has reached the norm of the species" (Standing, 1962). Education must be attuned to, and designed to further, the individual child's development. Montessori—as well as her American contemporary, John Dewey—protested traditional education practices, with children planted behind desks and expected to recite lessons of little meaning in their lives. Both criticized approaches to discipline based on this pervasive schooling practice. In her comprehensive *The Montessori Method* (1912/1964), the educator asserted:

> *We know only too well the sorry spectacle of the teacher who, in the ordinary schoolroom, must pour certain cut and dried facts into the heads of the scholars. In order to succeed in this barren task, she finds it necessary to discipline her pupils into immobility and to force their attention. Prizes and punishments are ever-ready and efficient aids to the master who must force into a given attitude of mind and body those who are condemned to be his listeners. (p. 21)*

Montessori (1912/1964) devoted a full chapter of her text to a modified discipline approach that was more respectful of the child's development. For

Montessori the purpose of education and discipline is the same: to encourage the development of responsible decision making and *self*-discipline.

John Dewey

John Dewey is considered the architect of progressive education in the United States. Over a 60-year period, Dewey raised the nation's understanding about the kind of education needed in an industrial society. Like Montessori, Dewey viewed discipline as differing in method depending on the curriculum followed. In the 1900 monograph *The School and Society,* Dewey commented:

> *If you have the end in view of forty or fifty children learning certain set lessons, to be recited to the teacher, your discipline must be devoted to securing that result. But if the end in view is the development of a spirit of social co-operation and community life, discipline must grow out of and be relative to such an aim . . . There is a certain disorder in any busy workshop; there is not silence; persons are not engaged in maintaining certain fixed physical postures; their arms are not folded; they are not holding their books thus and so. They are doing a variety of things, and there is the confusion, the bustle that results from activity. Out of the occupation, out of doing things that are to produce results, and out of doing these in a social and cooperative way, there is born a discipline of its own kind and type. Our whole conception of discipline changes when we get this point of view. (Dewey, 1900/1969, pp. 16–17)*

Dewey's advocacy of progressive education has made clear to generations of educators to this day the clear connection between curriculum, teaching methods, and the form of discipline practiced. In the later years of his career, critics attacked Dewey's approach as too "child-centered"—children having too much freedom of choice in the classroom (Wolfe, 2002). With the broader context that time allows, thoughtful readers of Dewey's works see that he always regarded the teacher as in charge. The nature of the adult's leadership, as the quote above suggests, was interactive rather than dictatorial—in keeping with the views of other progressive educational reformers.

Dewey's emphasis on the project method—in which children in small groups engage in active study of topics of meaning to them—indicates the balance of the individual and the group that Dewey emphasized in his classroom "workshops." Dewey's view of discipline, as essentially a tool for maintaining a spirit of cooperation amid the bustle of the classroom, is similar to what his predecessors, going back to the 17th century, also envisioned. Dewey's unique gift was his philosophical connection of the dynamics of the classroom with the promise of democracy that societies are still striving to attain. Emphasis on the development of democratic life skills in this text is a nod to Dewey's major contribution.

A synopsis of the views of the pioneers in the guidance tradition in the field of education is provided in Table 1-1.

Table 1-1 *Pioneers of the Guidance Tradition from the Field of Education*	
John Comenius 1592–1670	The desire to learn can be excited by teachers, if they are gentle and persuasive and do not alienate their pupils from them by roughness. Rods and blows should never be used in schools.
Johann Pestalozzi 1746–1827	Teachers need to look first at the system if there are behavioral problems. Positive behavior is a natural outgrowth when children are involved in engaging activities that meet their needs.
Robert Owen 1771–1858	Punishment is never required, and should be avoided as much as giving poison in their food. Teachers are to use kindness in tone, look, word, and action.
Friedrich Froebel 1782–1852	The teacher should see the natural impulses of the child not as a tendency toward evil but as the source and motivation for human development that with guidance leads to character in the adult.
Maria Montessori 1870–1952	The child is in a process of dynamic development, which the adult has attained. Children educate themselves through absorption in meaningful tasks. In this process they learn both self-discipline and responsible decision making.
John Dewey 1859–1952	Out of the occupation, out of doing things that are to produce results, and out of doing these things in a social and cooperative way, there is born a discipline of its own kind and type.

Mid-20th-Century Influences: The Developmental and Self Psychologists

By the mid-20th century, two distinct branches of psychology were contributing to the progressive education movement and the guidance tradition. In Europe, Jean Piaget brought together his distinct scholarship in the fields of biology and child study to provide the foundations of modern developmental psychology. In the United States, a group of psychologists integrated neo-Freudian thought and American humanistic psychology into a new branch of study, *self-concept* psychology, shortened in the present text to **self-psychology**. These two distinct psychological fields gave articulation to many of the practices of today's guidance approach. Piaget's contributions are introduced here and returned to in Chapter Two.

Jean Piaget

Clinical (rather than classroom centered) in his orientation, Jean Piaget was the preeminent developmental psychologist of the 20th century. Writing in French, the Swiss psychologist shared with Montessori the viewpoint that the

When the classroom becomes a "busy workshop," our conception of discipline changes.

© Cengage Learning

© Cengage Learning

© Cengage Learning

developing child learns most effectively by interacting with the environment. Further, Piaget shared with Dewey the view that education must be a cooperative endeavor and that discipline must respect and respond to this fact. In *The Moral Judgment of the Child* (1932/1960), Piaget stated:

> It is . . . the essence of democracy to replace the unilateral respect of authority by the mutual respect of autonomous wills. So that the problem is to know what will best prepare the child for the task of citizenship. Is it the habit of external discipline gained under the influence of unilateral respect and of adult constraint, or is it the habit of internal discipline, of mutual respect and of "self government"? . . . If one thinks of the systematic resistance offered by pupils to the authoritarian method, and the admirable ingenuity employed by children the world over to evade disciplinary constraint, one cannot help regarding as defective a system which allows so much effort to be wasted instead of using it in cooperation. (pp. 366–367)

Generations of psychologists and educators have been influenced by Piaget's studies of how children develop. In the last few years, "neo-Piagetian" writers have focused on **constructivist education** (DeVries & Zan, 1995). In the constructivist perspective, the child builds knowledge by interacting with the social and physical environment. Knowledge is not a commodity "given" to the learner "ready-made," but is constructed by the child as a result of ongoing experiences. From experiences the child constructs meaning.

The project method is one model for how constructivist education is practiced. Another expression is found in the Reggio Emilia of Italy (Gandini, 1993; Wurm, 2005). These schools have become a beacon for the creative process at the heart of constructivist education. Teachers and children create together, building from interesting topics to generate multimedia projects that have redefined what young children may be capable of learning and expressing. (See Recommended Readings: *Working in the Reggio Way: A Beginner's Guide for American Teachers* [Wurm, 2005].)

Whatever the model of constructivist education, the locus of construction of knowledge is within the child, as shown in this situation:

Classroom Anecdote	*A parent wanted very much for his four-year-old son, Abraham, to be able to print his name. The teacher explained (more than once) that with daily exposure to his name on classroom charts, and with daily encouragement to write his name as best he could, Abraham would teach himself this skill in time.*
	For two months into the preschool year, Abraham wrote only an uppercase A and a short line of personal script. His father remained dubious. One day, while the teacher was reading Abraham a book, the boy pointed to a b and said, "There's my name." Before the book was over, he picked out two other letters, r and m, as also being "his name." The next day on his picture the boy wrote "Abrm." The teacher asked if it would be easier just to print, "Abe" and showed him how. The boy shook his head and said, "My name is Abraham." Within two weeks, he was printing all of the letters. Within a month he was printing all of the letters in order: "Abraham." (The teacher again had to remind Dad to be patient with the last name, "Abdumanni.")

In order to construct knowledge—and so find personal meaning in the experience—the child's development and education must be aligned. This is the girding insight behind developmentally appropriate practice (Copple & Bredekamp, 2008).

By redefining education from a *constructivist* perspective, developmental educators are challenging the way professionals in the field look at teaching, learning, the curriculum, and discipline. This developmental and interactive view of the educational process blends well with the guidance tradition (DeVries, 1994).

Alfred Adler and The Self Psychologists

Alfred Adler, an Australian-born psychiatrist who came to the United States in 1927, was a formative figure in the positive psychology that has leant so much to the guidance approach. Adler believed that healthy development of the child resulted in an adult ability for interconnectedness with social groups, to the benefit of both society and the individual (Marcus & Rosenberg, 1998). He saw the first five years as crucial in development, with encouragement by caring adults as essential. A key life task to Adler was the individual's effort to overcome the "inferior" life position of the child without developing an "inferiority complex" on the one hand or "overcompensating" by a hypercompetitive style of life on the other. Adler saw adult guidance that was encouraging without being permissive or dictatorial as central, leading to adults able to actualize their individual potentials.

Adler influenced an entire generation of American psychologists. Among them were Abraham Maslow, whom he mentored, and Theodore Dreikurs, who brought the principles of Adlerian psychology into the classroom (discussed later in the chapter).

The Self Psychologists. During the 1960s and 1970s, the writings of such psychologists as Combs (1962), Erikson (1963), Maslow (1962), Purkey (1970), and Rogers (1961) brought attention to the developing self as the primary dynamic in human behavior. Combs' work furthered the idea that reality for the individual is what he or she perceives. This "perceptual field theory" pressed the need for educators to be responsive to the feelings of children in the class. The **self psychologists** developed an idea that Adler earlier had held: to the extent children felt safe in their circumstances and valued as members of the group, they would see themselves positively and not need to act out against the world. These psychologists conducted numerous studies of self-image (the collection of feelings about who one is) and self-concept (the conscious picture of who one is). Collected in works by Purkey (1970) and Hamachek (1971), the trend in these studies was that children who felt better about themselves got along better with others and did better in school. Moreover, the studies found a high correlation between schooling practices and heightened or lowered self-esteem. Purkey stated:

> *The indications seem to be that success or failure in school significantly influence the ways in which students view themselves. Students who experience repeated success in*

school are likely to develop positive feelings about their abilities, while those who encounter failure tend to develop negative views of themselves. (p. 26)

Purkey discussed schooling practices that reinforced failure and frustration:

Traditionally, the child is expected to adjust to the school rather than the school adjusting to the child. To ensure this process, the school is prepared to dispense rewards and punishments, successes and failures on a massive scale. The child is expected to learn to live in a new environment and to compete for the rewards of obedience and scholarship ... Unfortunately a large number of schools employ a punitive approach to education. Punishment, failure, and depreciation are characteristic. In fact, Deutsch argues that it is often in the school that highly charged negative attitudes toward learning evolve. The principle that negative self-concepts should be prevented is ignored by many schools. (p. 40)

The self psychologists provided insights that supported the articulation of developmentally appropriate practice and the use of guidance. A shared position of the self psychologists was that threat has no place in the classroom. From decades of brain research, we are learning more about why: Threat in the classroom causes stress in children. Healthy brain development is impeded when children experience stress over time (Shonkoff & Phillips, 2000). A message of the self psychologists still relevant today is that while "intense anticipation" is important for learning, teacher-induced stress is detrimental to it. (If educators are going to "challenge" children to learn, they need to *support* children in the learning process.) Dreikurs (1968) and Ginott (1972) were two noted psychologists who adapted principles from self-psychology for general classroom use, principles that are still studied and used today.

Rudolph Dreikurs

Mentored by Adler, Theodore Dreikurs advocated the application of social science principles to classroom management. He contributed much to the movement toward "positive discipline." An early contribution is Dreikurs' insistence that teachers need to be "leaders rather than bosses" (1968). This emphasis on working with students, rather than being in opposition to them, is fundamental to a guidance approach. The idea of "teacher as leader" corresponds to the interactive view central to progressive education.

A second contribution of Dreikurs is the distinction between encouragement and praise (Dreikurs, Grunwald, & Pepper, 1982). Teachers who are leaders recognize the importance of specific acknowledgment of a child's efforts and progress. Such encouragement is more authentic than praise, which serves as a quick mental shortcut for the teacher—"good job"—and sometimes to manipulate the group—"Missy and Ryan are sitting nicely." Praise tends to offer a "final judgment" about the child's products, often without explanation. Encouragement gives information that assists the child to carry on: "You are really working hard on that puzzle. It's almost done." Encouragement is a valued technique with teachers who use guidance. Two kinds of encouragement, public and private, are discussed in Chapter Seven.

Many believe that Dreikurs' most substantial contribution is his explanation of the "goals" of misbehavior (Dreikurs, Grunwald, & Pepper, 1982). Building on his background in Adlerian theory, Dreikurs emphasized that all behavior is goal directed and that the preeminent goal of behavior is social acceptance.

> *Behavior is purposive or goal-directed. . . . Humans are social beings with the over riding goal of belonging or finding a place in society. . . . The child's behavior indicates the ways and means by which he tries to be significant. If these ways and means are antisocial and disturbing, then the child did not develop the right idea about how to find his place. The antisocial ways or "mistaken goals". . . reflect an error in the child's judgment and in his comprehension of life and the necessities of social living. To understand a child, we must understand the child's purpose of behavior, a purpose of which the child may be unaware. (p. 9)*

In books such as *Psychology in the Classroom* (1968), Dreikurs developed a theory, using four levels, for why children misbehave. A clear synopsis of the "four mistaken goals of misbehavior" is provided in *Building Classroom Discipline* (1996) by C. M. Charles:

> *Dreikurs identifies four mistaken goals to which students turn when unable to satisfy the genuine goal [of social acceptance]: (1) getting attention, (2) seeking power, (3) seeking revenge, and (4) displaying inadequacy. . . . The goals are usually, though not always, sought in the order listed. If unable to feel accepted, individuals are likely to try to get attention. If they fail in that effort, they turn to seeking power. If thwarted there, they attempt to get revenge. And if that fails, they withdraw into themselves and try to show that they are inadequate to accomplish what is expected of them. (pp. 90–91)*

As important as Dreikurs' theory is, it has not received scrutiny for consistency with ideas about personality development contributed by the self psychologists. In Dreikurs' writings, the "overriding goal" of children's behavior is acceptance by others. This view differs from theory based on developmental research and the writing of psychologists like Maslow and Combs (and even Adler). In the view of these psychologists, social acceptance *is* a significant factor in children's behavior, but it is regarded more as a foundation for healthy development than an end in itself (Gartrell, 2004).

Between three and eight years, children make tremendous strides in brain development and thinking processes, the communication of ideas and feelings,

© Cengage Learning

Repeated success experiences help children build positive feelings about their abilities.

perceptual-motor skills, self-concept development, cultural identity, and social responsiveness. They are engaged in a process of *total development*. Yet with the natural insecurities of childhood and limited ability to understand the needs of others, children make mistakes in their behavior. Social acceptance of each child, even while the teacher addresses mistaken behavior, sustains *healthy personal development,* the primary goal in human behavior (Maslow, 1962; Purkey, 1970; Rogers, 1961).

In his insistence that adults can understand the purposes of mistaken behavior, Dreikurs nonetheless has made a vital contribution to the guidance tradition in educational thought. Dreikurs' writings argue persuasively that conflicts are the result of mistakes that children make in the "purposeful" goal of social acceptance (Dreikurs, 1968; Dreikurs, Grunwald, & Pepper, 1982).

To reach a child's mind, a teacher must capture a child's heart.

Dreikurs raised the level of discussion about discipline from teacher judgments concerning children's morality to strategies for helping children learn acceptable social behaviors.

Haim Ginott

If Dreikurs has contributed to the theory of the guidance tradition, Ginott has contributed to its articulation. The opening lines from the chapter "Congruent Communication" in his book, *Teacher and Child* (1972), illustrate the eloquent phrasing in Ginott's "psychology of acceptance":

Where do we start if we are to improve life in the classroom? By examining how we respond to children. How a teacher communicates is of decisive importance. It affects a child's life for good or for bad. Usually we are not overly concerned about whether one's response conveys acceptance or rejection. Yet to a child this difference is fateful, if not fatal.

Teachers who want to improve relations with children need to unlearn their habitual language of rejection and acquire a new language of acceptance. To reach a child's mind a teacher must capture his heart. Only if a child feels right can he think right. (p. 69)

Table 1-2 *Pioneers in the Guidance Tradition from the Fields of Developmental and Self Psychology*

Jean Piaget 1896–1980	The modern ideal is cooperation—respect for the individual and for general opinion as elaborated in free discussion. Children come to this spirit of democracy through the modeling of cooperation by adults who are able to make autonomous (intelligent and ethical) decisions themselves.
The Constructivists (Contributions 1980s–present)	Sampling: Elkind, Bredekamp and Copple (on behalf of the National Association for the Education of Young Children), DeVries & Zan, Gandini. The child constructs knowledge (builds meaning) through ongoing interactions with others and the physical environment. Guidance enables all children to develop at their own rates and learn in their own ways through the personal construction of knowledge.
Alfred Adler (1870–1937)	Healthy development of the child results in an adult ability for interconnectedness with social groups, to the benefit of both society and the individual. Guidance that is encouraging without being permissive or dictatorial is central, leading to adults able to actualize their individual and social potentials.
Self Psychologists (Contributions: 1960s–1970s)	Sampling: Arthur Combs, Erik Erikson, Abraham Maslow, Carl Rogers, William Purkey. The developing self is the dynamic in human behavior. Schools must address not just academics, but also the self-concepts of learners. Students experiencing successful involvement in education feel positively about themselves, have little need to act out, and are able to engage in significant learning.
Rudolph Dreikurs 1897–1972	Teachers need to be leaders, not bosses. When their attempts to achieve social acceptance fail, children show antisocial behavior for a purpose, to achieve any of four mistaken goals. Teachers should use techniques such as encouragement and logical consequences instead of punishment to help the child find social acceptance.
Haim Ginott 1922–1973	The "psychology of acceptance" means that the teacher's task is to build and maintain positive relations with each child. The teacher uses techniques such as "I" messages, the "cardinal principle" (address the behavior, accept the child), and nonjudgmental acknowledgment to support relationships and solve problems.

Virtually all early childhood education texts written in the last 20 years have emphasized a need for management methods that respect the feelings and dignity of the individual child. Although Ginott's writings do not address the early childhood age group per se, they speak to adult-child relations at all levels and elevate the tone and philosophy of the guidance approach. Ginott's writings nurture the caring spirit that infuses the guidance tradition.

A synopsis of the pioneers in the guidance tradition from the fields of developmental and self psychology is provided in Table 1-2.

The 1980s: Guidance or Obedience-Based Discipline?

During the 1980s, many of the criticisms of traditional education made by Montessori, Dewey, Ginott, and others took on a new urgency. With the "back to the basics" emphasis of the late 1970s and 1980s, curriculum and teaching methods became more prescribed. Though the emphasis clashed directly with increased understanding about how young children learn (Bredekamp & Copple, 1987), the prescriptive academic influence meant increasing numbers of young children at school spending long hours in their seats, following directions passively, and completing endless work sheets and workbook pages.

In some kindergarten and many primary classrooms, the prescribed academic program was not new—classrooms had always been run this way. However, on a broad scale, more kindergarten programs were expected to become academic, and preschool programs felt pressures to "get children ready for kindergarten." The emphasis on academic programming with younger children lent itself to tightly controlled classrooms (Elkind, 1987). Except for the occasional teacher who made human relations a priority, the interactive nature of the guidance approach did not fit the regimen of the prescribed, academic classroom. As educational priorities shifted, discipline systems changed as well. With the need to keep normally active young learners in their seats and on-task, new obedience-driven discipline systems became popular (Canter & Canter, 1976).

Assertive Discipline

Looking for methods to increase student compliance, administrators and teachers embraced new, "more effective" **obedience-based discipline** systems. Predominant among these programs was Canter's assertive discipline, "a take-charge approach for today's educator" (Canter & Canter, 1976). A psychologist who worked with special education students in a clinical setting, Lee Canter actively marketed his discipline program for classroom use, and the program gained widespread popularity in school systems across the country (Canter, 1989).

Canter argued that assertive discipline clearly establishes the authority of the teacher and the role of the student. The model teaches students to choose between the rewards of compliance and the consequences of disobedience. The system makes clear to students a sequence of punishments that result from repeated conflicts. It provides a consistent system of rewards and punishments within a classroom and across a school or district. Through contracts sent home, assertive discipline also involves families. In the eyes of Canter and his adherents, his system "works" (Canter, 1989).

Critics, including Brewer (1995), Curwin and Mendler (1989), Gartrell (1987), and Hitz (1988), argued that assertive discipline has negative implications for children, teachers, and parents.

Effects on Children. Because rules and their consequences are cut in stone, the model does not allow for individual circumstances. Children who may make innocent mistakes suffer. The tendency toward public identification of "culprits" causes humiliation and can begin a process of negative self-fulfilling prophecy. Students who become stigmatized by the punishments grow immune to the system and may form unwelcome "out-groups" in the classroom and school (Render, Padilla, & Krank, 1989).

Although the system includes positive recognition for compliance, even the public rewards set up "winners" and "losers" within the class. Classrooms in which teachers have become entrenched in the negative aspects of the system are unpleasant, anxious places to be. The emphasis on obedience in the assertive-discipline classroom inadequately prepares children to function in a democracy (Curwin & Mendler, 1989; Render, Padilla, & Krank, 1989). Directing their comments to early childhood, Gartrell (1987) and Hitz (1988) assert that the Canter model is inappropriate for use with children during their most impressionable years.

Effects on Teachers. A second criticism is that the system seriously reduces the teacher's ability to use professional judgment (Gartrell, 1987). Because of the "obedience or consequences" emphasis, the teacher cannot easily react to the uniqueness of individual situations or individual children's needs. Neither can the teacher accommodate background, developmental, or learning style differences that manifest themselves in behaviors outside of acceptable limits (Hitz, 1988). Because the model is essentially authoritarian, it cannot adapt to democratic, interactive teaching styles necessary for developmentally appropriate practice. Where schools or districts have mandated the system, teachers are expected to use it even if they are uncomfortable with it. The danger is that teachers may become technicians rather than professionals, unhappy with the social climate of the classrooms they are expected to enforce (Curwin & Mendler, 1989; Gartrell, 1987; Render, Padilla, & Krank, 1989).

Effects on Parents. In some situations, parents who disagree with the terms of the family "contracts" find themselves at odds with teachers and administrators charged with soliciting parental compliance. During these years, parents from several states expressed to the author frustrations at being helpless to affect what they regard as negative education policy (unpublished correspondence and discussions with the author). Often, parents who object to assertive discipline are the very ones who might otherwise become productively involved in school affairs.

Beyond Discipline to Guidance

During the 1980s, two separate fields kept classroom guidance alive: early childhood education and the conflict resolution movement. The guidance tradition in early childhood had always been strong. By the end of the 1980s, this tradition received renewed attention by writers who spoke directly about it and by a new emphasis from the National Association for the Education of Young Children (NAEYC) on the use of **developmentally appropriate practice (DAP) (1987, 1997, 2008)**.

The Contribution of Early Childhood Educators

At the same time that obedience-based discipline systems were taking hold in many school systems, other forces were at work. Inspired by the nursery school movement earlier in the century and the work of the developmental psychologists, writers at the preschool level were declaring their independence from the conventional practices of classroom discipline. Textbooks in the nursery school tradition, such as Read (1950, tenth edition 1997), phrased the setting of the preschool as a "human relations laboratory" in which the teacher models positive guidance skills.

In the writings of the time by Stone (1978), Shickedanz and Schickedanz (1981), Cherry (1983), Marion (1998/2006), Clewett (1988), and Greenberg (1988), careful distinction was drawn between positive and negative discipline practices. Teachers using negative discipline relied on punishment to enforce compliance or impose retribution (Clewett, 1988). Teachers using positive discipline, in contrast, worked to prevent problems and, when they occurred, intervened in ways respectful of the child's self-esteem (Stone, 1978; Greenberg, 1988; Wichert, 1989).

The Switch to Guidance. In the early childhood literature, discomfort with the very term *discipline* has emerged. Despite the claim that discipline is "value neutral" and an "umbrella term" (Marion, 1998/2006), *discipline* still carries the baggage of negative connotations. The term to *discipline a child* suggests

The guidance approach addresses children's behaviors in ways that support self-esteem.

punishment, a practice rejected in the guidance approach. Gartrell (2004) points out that in problem situations, teachers tend to blur the distinction between punishment and discipline, and not to think about "guidance." He comments that unless handled so that a logical consequence is logical from the child's point of view, the child tends to perceive the act of discipline as punishment. For this reason, the teacher needs to emphasize guidance, which involves carefully teaching children behavior alternatives.

In *Guiding Young Children* (2006), Reynolds provides a problem-solving approach that begins with setting up the environment and includes specific communication and problem-solving strategies and techniques. Reynolds argues that the problem-solving approach precludes the necessity of the term *discipline*. She does not use the term in order to avoid confusion and misinterpretation. For some teachers, unless the connection between the two terms is made, they may tend to think of *guidance* in one set of circumstances and *discipline*, perhaps lapsing into punishment, in another. This fifth edition of the present text continues the position that one can address any situation with the use of guidance. The present text is in line with the well-regarded text by Kaiser and Sklar-Rasminsky, *Challenging Behavior in Young Children* (2006), which also does not use the term *discipline*.

Developmentally Appropriate Practice

In 1987, NAEYC first published *Developmentally Appropriate Practice in Early Childhood Programs Serving Children from Birth Through Age 8,* (Copple & Bredekamp, 1987). Significant is the fact that chapters in the work are supported by 600 separate references to authorities in the child development and early childhood fields. The NAEYC position document, updated in 1997 and again in 2008 (Copple & Bredekamp, 1997, 2008), advocates educational practices that allow for an interactive approach to learning and teacher-child relations. Clearly espousing the guidance tradition, the document cites positive guidance techniques that encourage the teacher to:

- establish routines and expectations understandable to children
- use methods such as modeling and encouraging expected behavior
- redirect behavior toward acceptable activity
- set clear limits (Copple & Bredekamp, 1997, p. 129).

The work emphasizes that "teachers' expectations match and respect children's developing capabilities" (Copple & Bredekamp, 1997, p. 129). In addition:

Teachers ensure that classrooms or groups of young children function as caring communities. They help children learn how to establish positive, constructive relationships with adults and other children. (Copple & Bredekamp, 1997, p. 123)

Teachers provide many opportunities for children to learn to work collaboratively with others and to socially construct knowledge as well as develop social skills, such as cooperating, helping, negotiating, and talking with others to solve problems. (Copple & Bredekamp, 1997, p. 129)

According to the NAEYC document, *inappropriate* discipline practices are these:

Teachers spend a great deal of time punishing unacceptable behavior, demeaning children who misbehave, repeatedly putting the same children who misbehave in time-out or some other punishment unrelated to the action. . . . Teachers do not set clear limits and do not hold children accountable to standards of behavior. . . . Teachers do not help children set and learn important rules of group behavior and responsibility. (Copple & Bredekamp, 1997, p. 129)

DAP and No Child Left Behind. High academic expectations on young children in classrooms have resurfaced in the country with the No Child Left Behind law. Evolved through reauthorizations of the Elementary and Secondary Act of 1968, No Child Left Behind, with its emphasis on accountability through standardized testing, became law during the George W. Bush administration. The intent of the law was noble, to close the educational achievement gap between students of mainstream American and students facing social and economic disadvantages. The means to the end, however, has been political pressure toward a largely one-dimensional instructional approach, focused on standardized assessments. In states across the country, published Annual Yearly Progress (AYP) indexes, based heavily on the test scores, provide public notice of schools' relative success with the AYP.

The rising complaint of educators about No Child Left Behind is that it reduces the teaching role to test preparation. In primary, kindergarten, and even preschool classrooms, some educators are implementing curricula and teaching methods that are inappropriate for young children, methods that are facilitated by the use of teacher-imposed extrinsic rewards (Elkind, 2005; Gough, 2002; Kamii, 1990; Jalongo, 2007).

Guidance Defined

The NAEYC document, pertaining to children from birth to eight, concretely contrasts *guidance* with discipline practices based on rewards and punishments, which are developmentally inappropriate (Renike, Sonsteng, & Gartrell, 2008). Building from this landmark document, a picture of guidance emerges.

▶ Guidance means teaching children to learn from their mistakes, rather than punishing children for making mistakes.

▶ Guidance means teaching children to solve their problems rather than punishing children for having problems they cannot solve.

© Cengage Learning

Teachers facilitate the development of positive social skills at all times.

- Guidance empowers the encouraging classroom in which all children feel fully accepted as capable members and learners.

- Guidance facilitates an interactive learning environment in which the adult functions as responsive leader and the child engages in an ongoing process of constructing meaning through developmentally appropriate activities.

- Guidance assists children to take pride in their developing personal and cultural identities and to view differing human qualities as sources of affirmation and learning.

- Guidance places healthy emotional, social, and cultural development on a par with cognitive development in the curriculum (teaching the whole child).

- Guidance links together teacher, parent, and child as an interactive team.

The Goals of Guidance: Democratic Life Skills.

Because so much of educational practice is now "outcome based," specific goals in the use of guidance have become essential. A guidance approach teaches children democratic life skills—the skills individuals need to function as productive citizens and healthy individuals. Democratic life skills include the ability to:

- *see oneself as a worthy individual and capable member of the group*

- *express strong emotions in nonhurting ways*

- *make decisions ethically and intelligently*

- *work cooperatively in groups to recognize and resolve common problems*

- *be understanding of human qualities and characteristics in others.*

Guidance and the Conflict Resolution Movement

From the country's beginnings, a peace tradition has been part of American thought, most often associated with the religious views of the Quakers. During the Vietnam conflict, peace groups such as the Fellowship of Reconciliation in Nyack, New York, held a visible profile in the society. Following the conflict, in response to growing awareness of what the Surgeon General termed "the epidemic of violence" in our society, peace groups began to turn attention to child rearing and the schools.

As early as 1973, the Children's Creative Response to Conflict Program trained teachers in the New York area to both teach conflict resolution skills to children and create a classroom atmosphere modeling the friendly community (Prutzman, 1988). In Miami, the Grace Contrino Abrams [Peace Education] Foundation also began working with teachers at about this time. Other groups followed, including the Community Board Program in San Francisco; Educators for Social Responsibility in Cambridge, Massachusetts; and School Mediation Associates in Belmont,

California. The National Institute for Dispute Resolution, now merged with the National Association for Mediation in Education, became a national clearinghouse for conflict management materials.

Over the first half of the 20th century, John Dewey (1900, 1944) fundamentally altered the views of many about education. Dewey advocated that society should practice its democratic ideals by making the classroom a "microcosm" of democracy. Democracy in the classroom (with the teacher as leader) remains a goal of educators who espouse the guidance tradition. Using a similar philosophy, groups working for a nonviolent society see the peaceable classroom as the crucial first step. In the book *The Friendly Classroom for a Small Planet*, Prutzman (1988) states:

> *We find that children develop positive self-concepts and learn to be open, sharing, and cooperative much more effectively when they become part of a [classroom] community in which these attributes are the norm. (p. 2)*

The conflict resolution movement in American schools has established these important principles, which are that are still gaining in acceptance today:

1. Each individual in the classroom, both child and adult, is to be treated with friendly respect.
2. All individuals, including young children, can learn to prevent and resolve problems by using words in peaceable ways.
3. Teachers create friendly classrooms by both modeling and teaching conflict management and by a philosophy of peace education throughout the entire school program

With these principles and active training programs during the 1980s, the conflict resolution organizations served as a countertrend to obedience-based discipline prevalent in so many schools. Today, the conflict resolution movement continues to complement the guidance tradition. Perhaps the movement's foremost contribution is this reminder, that outside of the home the primary vehicle for learning democratic life skills is interaction by children with each other, facilitated by the teacher in the peaceful classroom (Swick, 2001).

Parent-Teacher Relations in the Guidance Tradition

Positive parent-teacher relations contribute at a fundamental level to the success of the guidance approach. **Parent-teacher partnerships** have a tradition in early childhood education that goes back at least as far as Froebel's kindergartens. Over the years, Montessori programs, the British/American nursery school movement, and the national Head Start program have sustained this trend.

Froebel's Kindergartens

Froebel's first kindergartens during the 1840s in Germany called for cooperation between parents and teachers. As Lilley (1967) indicates, Froebel recognized the importance of the family in the education of the child:

> *The child fully develops his driving need for creative activity only if the family, which is the vehicle of his existence, makes it possible for him to do so. (p. 94)*

Home visits were a part of the first kindergarten programs, and Froebel included parents in his vision of early childhood education:

> *The plan [for the kindergarten]: is primarily to provide games and means of occupation such as meet the needs of parent and child, educator and pupil, and possess interest and meaning for adults as they share children's play or observe children sympathetically and intelligently. (p. 98)*

In his writing Froebel called upon the mothers of Germany to take leadership in organizing kindergartens nationwide (Lilley, 1967). The original kindergartens, in Germany and then other countries, relied on parent involvement, perhaps facilitated by the large numbers of women who became kindergarten teachers. The first kindergartens in America were run by immigrants who wanted the kindergarten experience for their own children. As the traditional beginning point for public school education, kindergartens have enjoyed relatively high levels of parent interest, allowing the opportunity for productive parent-teacher relations to this day.

Montessori's Children's Houses

Like Froebel, Montessori (1912/1964) encouraged parent involvement in the "Casa dei Bambini" (Children's Houses) of Italy. Perhaps due to her standing as a Catholic physician, educator, and philosopher, Montessori saw the directress (teacher) as a consummate professional, providing a model for children and parents alike. Montessori's Children's Houses were located in tenement buildings and were attended by the children of the residents. Directresses lived in the tenements in which they worked. In the translation of her definitive work, *The Montessori Method* (1912/1964), Montessori described the "modeling" role of the directress:

> *The directress is always at the disposition of the mothers, and her life, as cultured and educated person, is a constant example to the inhabitants of the house, for she is obliged to live in the tenement and to be therefore a co-habitant with the families of all her little pupils. This is a fact of immense importance. (pp. 61–62)*

Despite a professional-client distinction in the relationship, an element of partnership was also present. The parent and directress met each week to discuss the child's progress at school and home. Moreover, Montessori reported that the parents felt a sense of "collective ownership" toward the Children's Houses, which she discussed this way:

> The parents know that the "Children's House" is their property, and is maintained by a portion of the rent they pay. The mothers may go at any hour of the day to watch, to admire, or to meditate upon the life there. (pp. 63–64)

Nursery School

Between 1890 and the 1930s, a child study movement in Europe and the United States sparked new interest in humane child-rearing practices and child-oriented education. Cooperative nursery schools, administered by parents, began in Chicago in 1916 and continue with few major changes on a nationwide basis today. The nursery school model, with parent governing boards and close parent-teacher relations, has proven popular in other types of early childhood programs, private "alternative" schools, and a growing number of public charter schools as well.

Head Start

By the 1960s, new knowledge about the importance of the early years in development began to impact government policy. In 1965, Project Head Start began nationally, designed to provide comprehensive education and social services for low-income preschool children and their families. From the beginning, parent involvement became an integral part of its operations. Head Start encourages family involvement at several levels. In the home-based option, home visitors work with individual parents and children on a regular basis. In the center-based and home/center combination options, besides regular conferences with staff and periodic home visits, parents are encouraged to volunteer in the classroom.

Under all options, parents are given active policy roles on a local, agency-wide and regional basis. In Minnesota, approximately 30% Head Start staff began as parents having children in the program. In response to the rise in low-income working parents in recent years, Head Start nationally is putting new emphasis on serving pregnant moms, infants and toddlers (Early Head Start) and supporting affiliated family and center child care programs. Because the families served by Head Start are low-income, and/or have children with special needs, the contribution of Head Start to parent involvement, and to parenting competence, has been significant (Gage & Workman, 1994). A frequent report of parents is that they enrolled their children thinking the children alone would benefit, but the parents ended up benefiting themselves. Nationwide, many parents are more involved in their children's K 12 education as a result of participating in Head Start.

The Public Schools

Aside from early childhood initiatives, public school personnel traditionally have assumed an authority-client relationship with parents. Between the end of the Civil War and 1920, the population of the United States more than doubled with many new citizens being non-English-speaking immigrants. Universal education got its start during this time. To "Americanize the aliens" (Weber, 1919), kindergarten teachers especially were requested to make home visits and start mothers' groups. The practice of the Bureau of Education in the Department of the Interior (with the encouragement of business leaders) was to reach children in the school and mothers in the home so that immigrant and other nonmainstream families could be made "good citizens" (Locke, 1919). Although now somewhat outdated, this "melting pot" idea long was a part of American education.

With the advent of compulsory attendance laws, over time American schools have assumed a powerful role in their communities, as the institutions charged with socializing children to American society. One result of the schools' growing institutional power is that the opportunity for real parent input became limited, especially for parents "out of the mainstream" (Greenberg, 1989). Although the parents of children with disabilities have led the way, the determination and confidence necessary to advocate for one's child at school remains for many a daunting task. In most school districts, the individual teacher must build cooperative parent-teacher relations largely on her own time. (An exception is charter schools, many of which have policies and practices friendly to parent involvement.) Indeed, individual teachers can make a difference, and teachers and parents together can change school policy.

Later Generation Preschool Programs. As Head Start approaches 50 years, a later generation of early childhood programs is having a positive influence on parent-teacher relations. In many states early childhood special education personnel now establish contact with parents before the infant has left the hospital. Teachers in early childhood special education work with families in some cases for years before a child with a disability begins kindergarten. Parent-teacher collaboration is a hallmark of successful special education at all levels; the foundation often is being set by early childhood special education teachers.

In the last 25 years, new parent and child programs run through public schools are beginning to change the face of parent involvement. One national model is a statewide program in Minnesota that features weekly parenting classes held at the same time as preschool activities. Minnesota's Early Childhood Family Education is available at no or low cost in every school district, and in 2004 served nearly 300,000 children and parents. Another approach to bringing parents and teachers together is the "universal" school-based program for four-year-olds, now available in several states. On a smaller scale, "even start" and "school readiness" programs now operate in many parts of the country. Later generation preschool programs do well to follow the Head Start model with its comprehensive involvement by families—and not just provide classroom time for children.

Historically, many parents from low-income and minority-group backgrounds have felt ill at ease at building relationships with K–12 educators. (Many of these parents had unhappy K–12 classroom experiences themselves.) Head Start, early childhood special education, and school-based child and parent programs are helping to raise parent confidence at communicating with teachers. Increased parent involvement in children's education after preschool is the result.

© Cengage Learning

Parent-teacher partnerships are accepted practice in all types of early childhood education.

Parents and Developmentally Appropriate Practice

The NAEYC position document on DAP (Copple & Bredekamp, 1997, 2008) is significant because it ties together research about child development and appropriate teaching practice. As shown, discipline methods are those in the guidance tradition. A vital dimension of developmentally appropriate guidance is close, cooperative relations between parents and teachers. The NAEYC document identifies characteristics of parent-teacher relations that continue the guidance tradition:

> *Teachers work in partnerships with parents, communicating regularly to build mutual understanding and ensure that children's learning and developmental needs are met. Teachers listen to parents, seek to understand their goals and preferences for their children, and respect cultural and family differences.... Teachers and parents work together to make decisions about how best to support children's development and learning.... Parents are always welcome in the program and home visits are encouraged. (p. 134)*

For the guidance approach to be effective, the teacher develops a team relationship that includes the teacher, the family, and the child. *Parent-teacher partnerships* are an essential component in developmentally appropriate practice, and of the guidance tradition.

Summary

1. Who were the pioneers of the guidance tradition?

Guidance has its roots in the history of Western education and is tied to the thoughts of progressive educators over the last 350 years. Comenius led the way in the early 17th century with progressive ideas about who should be educated and how, paying new attention to children's development. Two hundred years later Pestalozzi and Owen followed, refining and implementing the ideas of Comenius: educating girls and boys together and using progressive, humane discipline practices. Later in the 19th century, Froebel considered the child to be "unfolding" (developing) toward goodness but vulnerable to the negative influences of others. For Maria Montessori, self-discipline was an extension of education itself—the purpose of which is to educate for the development of responsible decision making on the part of the child. For Dewey, the classroom should be "a busy workshop," with teachers not enforcing silence, but teaching cooperation.

2. Who were mid-20th-century influences in the guidance tradition?

As the foremost developmental theorist of the 20th century, Piaget argued that only when all members of the group share authority can autonomous moral thought develop. Influenced by transitional psychologist Alfred Adler, several *self psychologists* demonstrated the importance of supporting self-esteem in the classroom. Among them was Dreikurs, who introduced the idea that children misbehave not because they are immoral, but because they adopt mistaken goals of behavior out of a need for social acceptance. Ginott's position that teachers must show acceptance of the child even while they address unacceptable behavior is at the heart of the guidance approach.

3. What was the significance of discipline trends in the 1980s?

During the 1980s many school systems placed an emphasis on "back to the basics," even at the early primary and preschool levels. To enforce compliance with these practices, schools began using new obedience-based discipline systems at all levels of education. Proponents argued that such systems as *assertive discipline* permitted "the teacher to teach and the *student to learn*"; critics charged that these systems were inappropriately harsh, especially with younger children. By the end of the 1980s, vigorous debate about the use of obedience-based discipline in the nation's schools was occurring. Even now, No Child Left Behind continues to push teachers toward academics and discipline methods developmentally inappropriate for young learners.

4. What is the state of the guidance tradition today?

A landmark NAEYC publication (1987, 1997, 2008) focused national attention on the need for education to be "developmentally appropriate"—responsive to the stage and needs of each child. Guidance rather than punishment empowered the active learning advocated by the NAEYC work. Some authors maintained that because of the punitive connotations attributed to the term *discipline*, it should be replaced with *guidance*, or at least used with qualifiers. Authors generally agree that interactive, developmentally appropriate teaching techniques and guidance go together.

5. What is the importance of parent-teacher relations in the guidance tradition?

Parent-teacher partnerships long have been a part of the guidance tradition. Over the years progressive nursery schools, Head Start, and a later generation early childhood programs have demonstrated the value of close parent-teacher relations. The "professionalization" of the public schools earlier in the 20th century gave rise to paternalistic attitudes toward parent-teacher relations in many school systems (Greenberg, 1989). New awareness of the importance of parent-teacher partnerships, in part inspired by the charter school movement, is serving to change the mind-set of K–12 educators. The view that the child, teacher, and parent are on the same team, working together, is integral to the guidance approach.

FOLLOW-UP ACTIVITIES

Note: *An element of being a professional teacher is to respect the children, parents, and educators you are working with by maintaining confidentiality—keeping identities private. In completing follow-up activities, please respect the privacy of all concerned.*

Discussion Activity

Think about a teacher at any stage of your education who most embodied guidance in her teaching. What qualities or skills characterize the teacher's approach? What is a main insight you have gained from the teacher who is assisting you in your professional development? How does this insight relate to what the chapter says about guidance and its use in the classroom?

Application Activities

Application activities allow students to interrelate material from the text with real-life situations. The observations imply access to practicum experiences; the interviews, access to teachers or parents. To inter-relate theory and experience, students compare or contrast observations and interviews with referenced ideas from the chapter.

1. Pioneers of the guidance tradition

   a. Each of the pioneers advocated teaching practices that empower children to be active, involved learners. Observe a classroom in which such teaching is in practice. What kind of guidance practices do you see in use? Relate specifics to your observation to the words of one of the pioneers from the chapter. Which pioneer did you choose? Why?

   b. Interview an early childhood teacher or college professor who has studied the work of Froebel, Montessori, Dewey, or Piaget. What does the person believe to be significant about how the pioneer educator thought about discipline issues? Relate comments from the interview to the words of the identified pioneer from the chapter.

2. Mid-20th-century influences in the guidance tradition

   a. An emphasis of the self psychologists is support of the child's self-esteem. Observe an instance in the classroom when an adult supported a child's self-esteem. What did the teacher say and do? How did the child respond? How did specifics from your observation relate to the ideas of one or more of the self psychologists?

   b. Interview a teacher who values the ideas of either Dreikurs or Ginott. What is important to the teacher in the psychologist's writings? Relate comments from the interview with the words of the identified psychologist from the chapter.

3. Discipline trends in the 1980s

   a. Observe an instance in a classroom when a teacher intervened to stop a conflict or disruptive situation. Respecting privacy, how did the adult teach or fail to teach more appropriate social skills through the intervention? Referring to ideas from the chapter, did the teacher use guidance or traditional discipline? Why do you think so?

   b. One issue raised in the debate of the obedience discipline systems of the | 1980s is the role of punishment. Interview a teacher about what she considers to be the difference between guidance, discipline, and punishment. When, if ever, does the teacher believe punishment is justified? How do the teacher's thoughts about each term compare to ideas from the chapter?

4. The guidance tradition today

   a. Developmentally appropriate practice responds to the level of development and the needs of each child. Observe an instance of developmentally appropriate practice in a classroom. What are typical behaviors of the children? How does the teacher handle any problems that may arise? How do the teacher's actions compare to developmentally appropriate guidance practices identified by NAEYC in the chapter?

   b. Interview two teachers at the prekindergarten to third-grade level who are familiar with the term *developmentally appropriate practice*. How are the teachers' comments similar? How are the comments different? How do each teacher's comments compare to the discussion of DAP in the text?

5. Parent-teacher partnerships in the guidance tradition

   a. Observe an instance of productive parent-teacher relations at work. What seem to be the benefits of the productive relationship for the family? For the teacher? Compare your thoughts to what the chapter says about the benefits of parent-teacher relations.

   b. Interview a teacher who has taught for five or more years. Talk with the teacher about how her views have changed or stayed the same regarding parent-teacher relations. Compare the teacher's comments with ideas about parent-teacher relations in the chapter.

Note to readers: In this edition, each chapter concludes with one of the Guidance Matters columns that I wrote for the journal, *Young Children*, between November of 2005 and May of 2008.

Recommended Readings

Copple, C., & Bredekamp, S. (2005). Basics of developmentally appropriate practice. Washington, D.C.: Natural Association for the Education of Young Children.

Elkind, D. (2005). Viewpoint. Early childhood amnesia: Reaffirming children's need for developmentally appropriate programs. *Young Children, 60*(4), 38–40.

Geist, E., & Baum, A. C. (2005). Yeah *but's* that keep teachers from embracing an active curriculum: Overcoming the resistance. *Young Children, 60*(4), 28–36.

National Association for the Education of Young Children. (2005). Resources on developmentally appropriate practice in 2005: Updates from the field. *Young Children, 60*(4), 55–56.

Schiller, P. & Willis, C. A. (2008). Using brain-based teaching strategies to create supportive early childhood environments that address learning standards. *Young Children, 63*(5), 52–55.

Vartuli, S. (2005). Research in review. Beliefs: The heart of teaching. *Young Children, 60*(5), 76–85.

Wurm, P. (2005). *Working in the Reggio way: A beginner's guide for American teachers.* St. Paul, MN: Redleaf Press.

Guidance Matters

The Case of Jeremiah

January, 2006

Jeremiah was almost three when I started teaching at the center. He was one of those very physical kids, whose feelings and thoughts always moved through his body *first. He'd had a turbulent life and when I came to the center, he was living mostly with his mom, and some with his dad. They were separated and neither made very much money. Jeremiah was curious about and interested in everything. He loved stories and connected with others with his whole heart. He knew much about the natural world and was observant and gentle with animals, insects, and plants. When I first started working with Jeremiah, he had a lot of angry outbursts. The center used time-out at that point (the dreaded "green chair") and Jeremiah spent considerable time there. While I was at the center, we moved away from using time-outs. Instead we introduced a system called "peer problem solving." By the time Jeremiah graduated to kindergarten, we had been using the system for three years, and he was one of the experts. One day, I overheard a fracas in the block corner. I stood up to see what was going on, ready to intervene. The youngest child in the room, who was just two and only talking a little bit, and one of the four-year-olds were in a dispute over a truck. I took a step forward, ready to go to their aid, and then I saw Jeremiah approach them. "What's going on?" he asked (my standard opening line). He proceeded to facilitate a discussion between the two children that lasted for five minutes. He made sure both kids got a chance to speak; he interpreted for the little one. "Jordan, what do you think of that idea?" he asked. Jordan shook his head and clutched the truck tighter. "I don't think Jordan's ready to give up the truck yet," he told the four-year-old. It was amazing. Jeremiah helped the kids negotiate an agreement, and then he walked away with a cocky tilt to his head I'd never seen before. His competence was without question; his pride was evident.*

Reprinted with permission from the National Association for the Education of Young Children. All rights reserved.

In 2005, a National Prekindergarten Study of nearly 4,000 prekindergarten classrooms was published by the Yale University Child Study Center. One recently released report from the study includes this sobering summary: "Results indicated that 10.4 percent of prekindergarten teachers reported expelling at least one preschooler in the past 12 months. Nationally, 6.67 preschoolers were expelled per 1,000 enrolled . . . 3.2 times the rate for K–12 students. Rates were highest for older preschoolers and African-Americans, and boys were over 4 1/2 times more likely to be expelled than were girls" (Gilliam, 2005, p. 1).

The Yale study, together with the case of Jeremiah and other children and teachers I've known, keeps bringing me to this question: What is it in the dynamics of teacher-child relations that allows a child with "a lot of angry outbursts" to become a peer mediator in one program while in another program he might be expelled? Early childhood professionals cannot expect to love, perhaps even like, every child in their groups. Most feel guilty about this, but early childhood teachers are human, not angels. If they are truly professionals, however, they learn to build positive relationships with every child—whatever their personal feelings. When a teacher gives up on a child—sees "a lot of angry outbursts" and decides, consciously or unconsciously, that "this child does not belong here"—the young child's fate is sealed.

When teachers reach the point of mental rejection, it is evident to the child—and to the others in the group. Soon enough, the child gets verbal and nonverbal messages. He begins to see himself as not okay, as not belonging in the group. The child feels stressed and may have more conflicts than before being labeled. Because of his behavior and the aura of teacher rejection around him, the child will also be rejected by other children. He now has become stigmatized. Often from there, in a matter of time, it is out the door. While the classroom may run more smoothly—and staff may be relieved—the child and his family must deal with the emotional aftermath. As noted in the Yale study, "Expulsion is the most severe disciplinary sanction that an educational program can impose" (Gilliam, 2005, p. 1).

The teacher in the anecdote accepted Jeremiah. She chose to see him as a child who possessed more assets than were visible during conflicts. Her vital lesson to us is: Know the child beyond the behavior exhibited during a conflict; from friendly relationships much else becomes possible. When we consider children like Jeremiah not as impediments to our program, but as what our programs essentially are about, we avoid becoming part of the child's problem. We commit ourselves to trying to free the child from his vulnerabilities.

For a while our group may have to suffer a bit with us—and this is hard on any teacher. But we must keep in mind that the experience can teach other children important life lessons about redemption and the acceptance of others—lessons they will be deprived of if we give up on the child. Mental health resources for children and families *are* essential. Some states, like Michigan and Connecticut, are making real progress in this direction (Gilliam, 2005), but more progress in all states is needed. Early childhood professionals also need personal resources and support, both within the program and at home.

The challenges of working with some young children clearly are tremendous. But look at the benefits for educators, the group, families, and the child: "His competence was without question; his pride was evident" (and the two-year-old got to keep the truck).

To increase your knowledge:

Locate books and articles and consult Internet resources to learn more about working with children who have frequent conflicts. One useful site is the Center for Evidence-Based Practice: Young Children with Challenging Behavior (http://challengingbehavior.fmhi.usf.edu/), which offers many positive, evidence-based practices to help children with challenging behaviors. Talk with colleagues about techniques you find particularly promising. Together, work for mastery using these ideas.

Try These Techniques with Children You Find Challenging

1. Welcome new children and families.

Use phone calls, greeting meetings, positive notes home, conferences, and even home visits to let the family and the child know you welcome them as members of the classroom community. When children begin to have conflicts, working with parents you know is preferable to coping with parents you have not yet developed a relationship with.

2. Use contact talks.

Contact talks are moments of quality time outside of conflict situations between the teacher and individual child. The teacher finds the time and makes the talks happen by becoming a willing, active listener. Through regular talks, the teacher gets to know the child and

the child gets to know the teacher. Trust builds and conflicts become less severe. Finding quality time upon arrival can really reduce conflicts during the day.

3. Offer compliment sandwiches.

With the child and the family, use the coaching technique of compliment sandwiches to show you are working with—and not against—them: **Compliment:** Clearly recognize efforts and progress the child has shown. **Behavior:** Address a challenging behavior and direct the child or family to a specific alternative behavior the child can use next time. **Compliment:** Again, comment on the child's effort and progress. Watch for signs of progress you can continue to acknowledge.

4. Keep interventions private and respectful.

Embarrassment can result in lifelong, emotionally painful memories. Move to the conflict so you can address the situation privately. Compose yourself, then help the child to calm down. Keep your voice low and be firm and friendly, not firm and harsh. Ask the child to share his view of what happened. Respect his feelings and perceptions. Teach a specific alternative behavior the child can use next time. Have him repeat back to you the behavior to use. Do not force an apology, but ask the child what he can do to help the other person feel better.

5. Build your own support system.

It is okay to discuss (and vent) your frustrations with trusted others, as long as you do not use real names and everyone understands that the information shared is confidential. Remember that the purpose is not to reinforce negative attitudes about the child but to lessen your own anger and frustration. After honest venting, children sometimes don't seem so challenging ☺☺

6. Engage others in using a comprehensive approach.

Involve the family, classroom staff, nonclassroom personnel, and outside professionals in developing a comprehensive plan. Implement, review, and modify the plan as needed. Respecting issues of personal dignity and confidentiality, a plan sometimes might include class meetings to help other children understand or conferences with parents to explain your approach. (This is a tough decision; give it thought.) Only after comprehensive approach strategies are fully tried should the team discuss the future of the child in your class. (A comprehensive approach may bring together the resources you need to make expulsion unnecessary.)

A step you can take:

Read the Yale study and discuss reactions in your class. Find out what your state is doing to increase mental health resources for young children. Together with others, advocate for these services.

Column References

Gilliam, W. S. (2005). *Prekindergarteners left behind: Expulsion rates in state prekindergarten systems*. New Haven, CT: Yale University Child Study Center. Online: http://www.fcd-us.org/PDFs/NationalPreKExpulsion Paper03.02_new.pdf.

For additional information on using the guidance approach in the encouraging classroom, visit our website at www.cengage.com/education/gartrell.

Chapter 2

Child Development and Guidance

Guiding Questions

▶ *How do Piaget's ideas provide a foundation for the study of child development?*

▶ *How do Vygotsky's ideas describe the adult's role in guiding development?*

▶ *Why is Erikson's work a link between child development and guidance in the classroom?*

▶ *How does Gardner's theory of multiple intelligences support the guidance approach?*

▶ *How does the concept of emotional intelligence define the central guidance issue?*

▶ *What are the implications of brain development for guiding personal development?*

▶ *How does the teacher create a climate for partnerships with families?*

© Cengage Learning

Key Concepts

▶ *Attachment theory*

▶ *Conditional acceptance*

▶ *Developmental egocentrism*

▶ *Disequilibrium*

▶ *Emotional intelligence (EI)*

▶ *Equilibrium*

▶ *Executive function*

▶ *Multiage classrooms*

▶ *Multiple intelligences (MI)*

(Thanks to Lynn Gehrke for assistance with the section on Lev Vygotsky.)

 ⟩ *Peer scaffolding*

 ⟩ *Personal development*

 ⟩ *Private speech*

 ⟩ *Problem of the match*

 ⟩ *Scaffolding*

 ⟩ *Separation anxiety*

 ⟩ *Table talk*

 ⟩ *Zone of proximal development*

At least since Socrates, thoughtful observers have studied the developmental dynamic that transforms infants into adults. The process of human development is universal, altered only somewhat by culture and time. For each individual, though, the course of development is unique—a continuous interplay of genes, environment, brain growth, and emerging consciousness—distinct for each human.

Over the last half century, psychologists have made great strides in assisting teachers to understand and guide developmental processes. This chapter looks at the contributions of a group of well-known psychologists, three of the last century and two of this. The focus of the discussion is what each has contributed to our knowledge of those broadly educational processes that together lead to adults who are healthy individuals and productive citizens. Working from the standpoint of Alfred Adler and the self psychologists, we see the purpose of education to be healthy personal development, recognizing that the term addresses both intrapersonal health and interpersonal responsiveness.

Unfortunately, modern life has its share of individuals who use their intelligence with little regard for those around them. Educating children to be "intelligent," without at the same time being *ethical* (responsive to the common good), is building for the 22nd century without the lessons of the 20th and the 21st. Healthy personal development includes the ability to use information intelligently *and* ethically, the only "sustainable" educational outcome for a democratic society. As Piaget (1932/1960) wrote, for moral development (the growing understanding of right from wrong) to emerge together with cognitive skills, education needs to address both.

Our discussion begins with three mid-20th-century psychologists: Jean Piaget, Lev Vygotsky, and Erik Erikson. To bring the major contributions of these writers up-to-date, interpretations of a "second generation" of developmental psychologists—notably Charlesworth (2007), Crain (2005), Elkind (1987, 1993, 2005), Schickedanz et al. (2001), and Trawick-Smith (2006)—have been included, along with references to the psychologists' original works. A discussion then follows of two contemporary psychologists, Howard Gardner and Daniel Goleman, who bring unique 21st-century viewpoints to matters of intelligence, brain function, and development.

Piaget: A Foundation for the Study of Child Development

Jean Piaget's clinical studies with his own and other children brought developmental theory into the forefront of 20th-century psychology. Piaget discovered that in the process of growing and learning, each person passes through "a biologically determined sequence of stages" (Charlesworth, 2007). Piaget identified four major stages of development. The typical age span for each is included, although individual children may take more or less time to pass through the stages.

▶ Sensorimotor (birth to two)

▶ Preoperations (two to seven)

▶ Concrete operations (seven to eleven)

▶ Formal operations (eleven to adulthood).

In Piaget's view, the way a child responds to a situation is linked to her stage of development. Although a child's mode of thinking is limited by the psychological characteristics of the developmental stage, the process of learning is always active. The child constructs knowledge (derives meaning) through interacting with the environment. As each new stage is reached, the old ways of thinking are not lost but are integrated into the new ways (Charlesworth, 2007).

Charlesworth's interpretation of Piaget is helpful in understanding the development of thought. Cognitive development begins during the sensorimotor stage as the infant forms schemata, or sensory impressions, of what she perceives. By the beginning of the preoperational stage, the toddler is linking similar schemata into preconcepts (Charlesworth, 2007).

Preconcepts represent the start of symbolic thought and often contain *overgeneralizations*, such as calling all four-legged animals "kiki" (for kitty), and *overspecializations* (Charlesworth, 2007), such as expressing shock at seeing "the Easter Bunny" get into a car. During the preoperational stage, the child forms new preconcepts and refines existing concepts to increasingly accommodate the outside world.

Pat Sanford, a "case study" kindergarten teacher in Chapter Six, tells this story about a five-year-old in her class that illustrates a child's contending with *overspecialization*:

> One Sunday my husband and I were ushers at church. Following the service, the mother of one of my kindergarten students said that her son had been so excited to see me in that capacity that he said, "I can't believe it! Pat's a gusher today!" Both Mom and I complimented Eric for noticing that his kindergarten teacher was also an "usher." (Gartrell, 2000)

The child constructs knowledge through interacting with the environment.

Until about age seven when most children have begun concrete operations, their perceptions are limited by a tendency to focus on the outstanding elements of what is perceived. The young child does not yet have the ability to comprehend the complexities of situations (or the accuracy of terms). In the anecdote on previous page, both parent and teacher complimented the child's perceptiveness at noticing that the teacher also could be an usher. Noting his progress at moving beyond overspecialization, the adults modeled the conventional wording; the child's word mix-up was secondary.

From Piaget's perspective, the role of the teacher is not to correct beginning concepts. Instead, the teacher supports the child's interactions with objects and people—and the construction of knowledge that results from these transactions. Within the limits of conceptual ability, the child notices and processes information with efficiency and often creativity.

Classroom Anecdote	*In a Midwestern Native American community, a Head Start class returned early from a trip to the beach on a very windy day. They were discussing why they had to leave early when the teacher asked, "What makes the wind blow anyway?"*
	A four-year-old named Virgil exclaimed, "Don't you know, teacher? The trees push the air." With a perplexed smile the teacher commented, "Virgil, how do you know that?" Amused at the teacher's obvious lack of knowledge, Virgil explained, "'Cause the leaves is fans, of course."

Undoubtedly Virgil's understanding of what makes the wind blow has changed since that experience. (Children's concepts become more conventional as they mature.) But to this day the teacher (who is the author) remains impressed with the boy's perceptive preoperational stage thinking.

Through experiences with others and objects, the learner encounters new, often conflicting information. The child learns by mentally processing this information and building personal meaning from it. The need to reach **equilibrium**, harmony between perceptions and understanding, out of **disequilibrium**, dissonance between perceptions and understanding, is intrinsic. Piaget believed that the disequilibrium felt by the child is a primary source of the intrinsic motivation to learn (Charlesworth, 2007). However, too much disequilibrium can be stressful. Making disequilibrium intriguing but not threatening is a big part of the teacher's job.

Classroom Anecdote	*Jinada and Lorenzo were playing house. Jinada commented, "I'm the momma so I'll get breakfast."*
	Lorenzo retorted, "Poppas get breakfast, so I will get breakfast." A heated exchange followed.
	Hearing the argument, the teacher intervened, "Jinada, you have a momma in your house and she makes breakfast. Lorenzo, you have a poppa in your house, and your poppa makes breakfast. Since you two are a momma and a poppa in the same house, maybe you can make the breakfast together."
	Jinada said, "Yeah, and I will make the toast and the cereal." Lorenzo added, "I will put them dishes and spoons on the table." The two children proceeded to "make" and "eat" breakfast. Afterward, the teacher was amused to hear Jinada say, "But we got to go to work so we'll clean up later." Lorenzo says, "Yeah," and the two went off to work.

Early childhood teachers are at their best when they help children understand another way to view a situation. With lowered stress, learners usually can take it from there.

© Cengage Learning

The motivation to do puzzles and matching games lies in the need to create equilibrium through putting the pieces in place from the disequilibrium of the missing pieces.

Developmental Egocentrism

In Piaget's theory, a key idea is that young children show what the present author terms **developmental egocentrism**. Piaget observed that young children show egocentrism as a result of their limited development. By this observation, he meant that young children understand events from their own perspectives and have difficulty accommodating the viewpoints of others. Egocentrism in the developmental sense refers to the inability of young children to understand the complexity of social situations.

DeVries and Zan (1996) state the matter this way:

Young children often appear selfish when, for example, they grab objects from others and demand to be first in line or first in a game. This behavior often happens because young children have difficulty understanding others' points of view. Such selfishness in young children is not the same as selfishness in older children and adults. (p. 266)

Classroom Anecdote	*Two student teachers organized a game of musical chairs with 12 preschoolers. To their amazement, the first child "put out" began to cry, the second moped, and the third swept a book off a shelf. The two noticed that as the remaining children left the game, none looked happy. The last child out complained that the winner pushed and "It's not fair."*
	After discussing with their supervisor, the student teachers realized that the children were developmentally unable to comprehend the rules of the game. The children probably thought they were being punished by being put out and felt hurt, frustrated, and angry.
	Not to give up, the student teachers organized the game on another day, but with different rules. The children helped to write and tape their names to chairs. They were then asked to suggest the names of animals and came up with "chickens," "dolphins," and "elephants." When the music stopped, the children proceeded to their special chairs, moving each time like the animal selected. The game continued for 40 minutes, all of the children participated, and all—including the student teachers—had a good time.

Again, young children see the world from their own perspectives—often blaming themselves or becoming upset when they do not understand the full set of social dynamics. The task of the early childhood teacher is to adapt the curriculum so that *all* children can engage in experiences successfully. The student teachers went from one child winning and everyone else bothered, to everyone winning—because all the children could successfully participate. As the anecdote suggests, adult-structured competition should come later in childhood (Elkind, 1987). The young child wins by noncompetitive group participation, building individual strength to manage the many competitive situations to come.

Prosocial Preschoolers. Critics of Piaget's conclusions about egocentrism cite evidence that children in the preoperational stage are capable of "prosocial" acts. The capability is there, of course, but this criticism is a misinterpretation of egocentrism in the young child. Take the situation of a toddler who becomes terrified when a grasshopper lands on his shoulder. A second young child hears his screams, brushes the grasshopper off, and pats him on the back. The second child likely did not respond from high-level empathetic analysis but from the discomfort she felt at the first child's distress. (She happened to notice the main elements of the situation, which were the first child's screams and "the big grasshopper.")

The second child was being prosocial, but from reasoning that was developmentally egocentric. Still, the acknowledgment that the second child receives for being helpful is just the kind of reinforcement that makes social responsiveness a more conscious part of her behavior (DeVries & Zan, 1996). With meaningful social experiences, the child gradually outgrows the egocentrism of early childhood.

Piaget's Concept of Autonomy

To Piaget, the challenge in development is for the child to build the dual capacity for social understanding and intelligent decision making. Piaget referred to the individual's ability to make intelligent, ethical decisions as *autonomy* (Piaget,

1932/1960). For educators who agree with Piaget's viewpoint, autonomy is another way of stating the central goal of education (Kamii, 1984). Autonomy means being governed by oneself—as opposed to **heteronomy**, or being governed by others. For Piaget, as well as Dewey, individual autonomy is essential to democratic society. (The present chapter includes autonomy as a key dimension in healthy personal development—autonomy is a key democratic life skill.)

Writing about autonomy, Kamii (1984) states:

> *Autonomy enables children to make decisions for themselves. But autonomy is not synonymous with complete freedom.... There can be no morality when one considers only one's own point of view. If one takes the other people's views into account, one is not free to tell lies, to break promises, to behave inconsiderately. (p. 411)*

Early childhood education provides the first institutional experience for children in relation to issues of autonomy. Yet, young children's limited social

© Cengage Learning

Progress toward autonomy happens through adult guidance.

experience and developmental egocentrism make instruction for *autonomy* a sometimes exasperating part of preschool-primary instruction. Charlesworth (2007) puts the teacher's dilemma concisely:

> *How often the adult says of the young child, "I know he knows better!" And the adult is right; the child does "know better," but is not yet able to reason and act consistently with his knowledge. It is not until the child is close to six that he begins to develop standards, to generalize, and to internalize sanctions so that he acts morally not just to avoid punishment but because he should act that way. (p. 479)*

By middle childhood, the child's **executive function** is more (but still not fully) formed and she is intentionally integrating ethics into behavior. But life is complex, and it takes into adulthood for most of us to become reasonably autonomous. For developmental psychologists, knowledge is not fixed and finite, to be transferred to the minds of students who immediately "see the light." Learning in both the intellectual and the moral spheres is a *constructive process*; that is, the learner constructs meaning from experiences over time. From this viewpoint, social experience is fundamental to the education process. Through interactions with adults and classmates, the learner builds, alters, and integrates mental concepts and, in turn, contributes to the learning of others.

A legacy of Piaget, borne out by current brain research, is that children are biologically programmed to try to learn and to get along. But their cognitive equipment is limited and just developing. They perceive events and situations differently than adults. *A teacher who accepts children where they are right now helps them move to where they will be later.* A conflict over who washes a doll at this moment can become two children washing two dolls (or the one doll together) minutes later. Teachers who use guidance teach for autonomy because they have made real progress in this area themselves. They know its importance in the dynamic lives of children—and for the future of society.

Vygotsky: How the Adult Guides Development

Over the last few decades, there has been increased interest in the work of Lev Vygotsky, specifically his studies on the role of social interaction in cognitive development. Although he was a contemporary of Piaget, Vygotsky's writings were not published until after his untimely death in 1934 at age 38, and not released by the Soviet government until 1956 (Crain, 2005). The translated writings of Vygotsky bring a focus on environmental and social influences to the study of development. Of interest to early childhood educators is Vygotsky's work on the significance of interactions between the child and an adult or more experienced peer in the learning process.

While Vygotsky recognized Piaget's position that children construct knowledge by their interactions with the environment, he added that "if children's minds were simply the products of their own discoveries and inventions, their minds wouldn't advance very far" (Crain, 2005, p. 232). In Vygotsky's view, a child's actions on objects contribute to optimal development only when the actions happen in a context that includes communication with others. The interaction furthers the child's learning beyond what she could achieve on her own. The psychological "distance" between what the child can learn on her own and through interaction with others is called the zone of proximal development. The extension of learning through the zone of proximal development by interaction with an adult or more experienced peer is called scaffolding.

We now look at Vygotsky's contributions regarding the zone of proximal development and scaffolding, as well as his work on children's private speech. (Vygotsky argues that the self-talk that young children do during play, *private speech*, evolves into an internal mechanism for processing thought and building self-control as they develop.)

Zone of Proximal Development

In his theory of the *zone of proximal development,* Vygotsky attempted to give adults an explanation for how to recognize and empower a child's learning. He defined the zone as:

> The distance between the actual developmental level as determined by independent problem solving and the level of potential development as determined through problem solving under adult guidance or in collaboration with more capable peers. (Vygotsky, 1935, p. 86)

In an encouraging classroom, where all children's interests and abilities are valued, a teacher who understands the distance between what a child can do alone and with help is in an excellent position to use effective teaching strategies. The challenge for the educator is to avoid what Piaget cautions as taking charge of the child's learning. In agreement with Piaget, Vygotsky was critical of direct, teacher-centered instruction (Vygotsky, 1935). In a classroom of young children, learning activities should emphasize interaction with others, both adult—child and child—child, to promote cognitive growth. To Vygotsky, activities must be carefully planned to include interactions that are slightly higher than a child's current level of development. The teacher uses finely tuned support, such as open-ended questions, to engage the child's interests and discovery. During the interaction, the teacher relinquishes control as soon as the child begins working independently with the new information.

Scaffolding

By *scaffolding*, Vygotsky meant the effective teaching necessary to move a child through the zone of proximal development. Scaffolding involves questions and prompts that help a child actualize potential development. Scaffolding helps children think about what they are doing by describing their activity, by providing clues to finishing that activity, by modeling the activity, and/or by enlisting the aid of a peer as a "tutor" or partner in the activity. When the scaffolding has been successful, the child brings the activity to fruition and reaches her potential relative to the zone of proximal development at that time. Throughout the process, the child constructs knowledge.

Classroom Anecdote	*A child in a mixed-age preschool classroom dumps a puzzle on the floor and begins to move the pieces around in an attempt to put it back together. The teacher notices the activity and from prior observation knows the child has not completed a puzzle of this complexity before, but sees her interest in the activity. The teacher sits down next to the child and says, "You are working on a puzzle. It looks like the Barney school bus puzzle." Another child joins the two on the floor. The teacher knows this second child is a capable puzzle solver and acknowledges that this child has done the puzzle before.*
	"I wonder if that piece with the bus tire fits here with the other part of the tire; see where the curves match?" asks the teacher.
	"Yes," replies the puzzle expert. The young girl tries the suggested move and yells, "It fits! Let's do this one." She picks up another piece. This time the teacher asks what she sees on the piece. She replies, "Another tire."
	"Do you see that round space there? Do you think the round tire will fit in that space?" The teacher points as he asks.
	Again, the puzzle expert offers, "Yes, it does, I know it fits."
	After successfully placing the piece, the teacher suggests that the two work together as he watches. The teacher's knowledge of the "expert's" ability to help and not take over is critical here. The "beginner" puzzle builder and the "expert" complete the puzzle and immediately agree to "do it again." The teacher backs out to let them work but continues to observe from a distance.

This anecdote illustrates how a teacher helps a child achieve at a level higher than she could do on her own. The perceptive support from this teacher provides the "scaffold" needed. The teacher relinquishes assistance as soon as the child, working with a peer, demonstrates her new skill of fitting the puzzle pieces together. According to Crain (2005),

> *[Educators who follow Vygotsky's ideas] oppose the view of human development as a lone venture in which the child must figure everything out on her own. Instead, society has a responsibility to provide the child with instruction and assistance. To develop their minds children need the help of adults and more capable peers. (p. 243)*

Private Speech

In his writings, Vygotsky regarded children's **private speech** as a guide to development in behavior and thinking. In fact, when children talk to themselves, they are trying out new ideas, actually acting as their own "teacher." Vygotsky said that private speech helps children plan and complete activities, in other words to solve problems (Vygotsky, 1935). The link to *scaffolding* is that when children work with an adult who supports their activity, they use more private speech after the adult leaves than if the adult had not given assistance.

Piaget had his own name for this kind of self-talk, which he called "egocentric speech." The difference in view between Piaget and Vygotsky over private speech is well documented. Piaget's work suggests that children's egocentric speech will fade away, as they progress through the preoperational stage toward concrete operations. Vygotsky disagreed and argued that self-talk does not fade away, but becomes inner speech, the kind of discussions we often have with ourselves when we try to solve problems (Crain, 2005). "It is like saying that the child stops counting when he ceases to use his fingers and starts adding in his head" (Vygotsky, 1934, p. 230).

Classroom Anecdote	*A preschooler was alone in the home living center of her classroom busily caring for a baby doll. "You need some breakfast." "I'm going to cook breakfast for you." "You sit in your high chair while I cook, don't cry now." The narration continues as she acts out this drama, talking to the doll and describing her actions.*

The anecdote illustrates what many early childhood professionals have observed. By the use of private speech, the child is creating a play scenario, solving problems in her head, and even dealing with the "baby's" emotions. Vygotsky's position is that language, through private speech and social interaction, is the primary dynamic in a child's learning (Berk & Winsler, 1995). The debate continues as to whether language helps children learn, rather than being only the product of learning (Schickedanz, Schickedanz, Forsyth, & Forsyth, 2001). Many see the issue as not yet resolved. Nonetheless, Vygotsky's theory of private speech has contributed greatly to thought about the role of language in the learning process of young children.

Vygotsky's Work Considered

Some critics of Vygotsky argue that the zone of *proximal development* and *scaffolding*, as primary instructional strategies, make children passive recipients of teacher-directed instruction. The strategies can be construed to mean that education is a lockstep process of assessing what a "group" knows, teaching to "the next level," testing the group to determine "achievement," and again defining the next level of instruction. Vygotsky and his interpreters made clear that this viewpoint is incorrect (Berk & Winsler, 1995). Each child perceives, integrates, and expresses new information differently—in a way unique from any other child. Hence, teachers follow a diagnosis—teaching-assessment sequence that is different for each child. Because of its lack of responsiveness to the individual, teacher-directed, group-focused instruction in early childhood education tends to be stressful to some young children, boring to many, and intriguing only to a few (Schickedanz, Schickedanz, Forsyth & Forsyth, 2001). (For all but the few, the scaffolding process has gone askew.)

When scaffolding is skillfully done, there is a pleasant partnership between teacher and child. As in the anecdote about the puzzle, the situation in which scaffolding occurs is often child-selected activity. As Berk and Winsler (1995) write,

> *During this collaboration the adult supports the child's autonomy by providing sensitive and contingent assistance, facilitating children's representational and strategic thinking, and prompting children to take over more responsibility for the task as their skill increases. (p. 32)*

The Role of Peers. Another concern about Vygotsky's theory is his emphasis on scaffolding by peers *who are more capable.* When a teacher keeps the practice informal and "situation-based," children gain from peer scaffolding. An example of situation-based peer scaffolding is when the "puzzle expert" joined the activity with the other child and teacher. Concerns arise, however, when the "more capable/less capable" strategy becomes formalized, as in some elementary school "peer reader" programs. The concern is that the teacher may establish a core of "more capable peers" to help another identified group of "less capable peers" (Shickedanz et al., 2001). Some in the class gain the reputation—and self-label—of *academic winners*, while others see themselves as *academic losers*—class "stars" and "asteroids." Teachers then find it difficult to maintain a sense of worth among all members of the class—a goal in the encouraging classroom.

Shickedanz and her colleagues (2001) suggest a strategy to address this dilemma: cross-age peer assistance. One-room schoolteachers traditionally relied on older learners to help younger learners. Montessori teachers, preschool teachers who utilize family groups, and probably most family child care providers all use cross-age assistance. Schools that organize by multiage classrooms—having children of different ages/grades in the same class—often cite cross-age peer assistance as a key teaching strategy. Piaget (1932/1960) documented the readiness of younger children to accept the authority of older children. A third grader with reading problems can still read a picture book with a kindergarten child. The younger child will gain cognitively and affectively from the experience. And the older child is likely to gain at least affectively—a boost in self-esteem from the experience.

Teachers can avoid *more gifted/less gifted labeling* by intentionally using the social nature of classroom learning:

- Through informal table talk, children exchange ideas and challenge each other to solve problems.
- Interest centers promote interaction and spontaneous peer-assisted learning.
- Small groups formed by criteria other than "learning ability" promote continuous "nonstratified" sharing and mutual scaffolding (Schickedanz et al., 2001).

For many teachers the question of who is the novice and who is the expert is less important than how the learning of each is scaffolded by the other.

Besides, the interactive nature of a developmentally appropriate classroom often raises the question of who is the expert and who is the novice. In a kindergarten class during attendance, a teacher held up Rita's name card and announced to the class it was Renee's (who was absent). When Rita immediately corrected the teacher, he said with a smile that he was just testing to see if the children could read their names—to which Rita replied, "Yeah, right." Another time, while reading a book to Rita, the teacher called an alligator a crocodile. After Rita raised the question, they looked up the difference—Rita was right. (Sometimes the child is the teacher, and the teacher is the learner.) A friendly sense of humor is a valuable scaffolding asset.

As new teachers quickly realize, scaffolding often proves more difficult than they anticipated. When they scaffold, teachers need to take care not to impose heteronomy (reliance on external authority) in the learning situation. Teachers are attentive and collaborative in learning situations, ever responsive to extending children's learning. Effective scaffolding takes *personalization* of the educational program, careful listening, and thoughtful response to each child—which Vygotsky clearly maintained.

© Cengage Learning

When older children play with younger children, both benefit from the experience.

Private Speech and Emotions Management. In addition to his emphasis on a collaborative relationship between child and teacher, Vygotsky made a direct contribution to guidance in the area of private speech. For Vygotsky, private speech serves as a vehicle for social-emotional problem solving, no less than for cognitive learning. Children who receive warm care and responsive support are more effective in the use of private speech (Crain, 2005). By scaffolding children through their zones of *social-emotional development*, a teacher helps children learn to self-regulate their behavior—a primary goal in guidance. In these situations private speech becomes an aid in developing skills such as self-awareness, handling strong feelings, empathy, and social competence. Just as these abilities in children constitute democratic life skills, the teaching practices that underline them constitute guidance. One can imagine Benita's private speech before and after the guidance talk with her teacher in this situation:

Classroom Anecdote	*Terry, a three-year-old, was riding a trike. Benita, a five-year-old, took it from him. Terry lay down on the sidewalk and wailed. Benita looked over her shoulder, turned the trike around, and rode back to Terry. She got off the trike and gave it to him. Benita said to the teacher who was kneeling by Terry, "He needed it more than me and he was crying harder."* *The teacher helped Terry get back on the trike, then asked Benita to come sit by her. The two talked about how Benita was able to recognize Terry's feelings and also what Benita could do next time instead of taking the trike.*

Erikson: Personal Development and the Classroom

The noted psychologist, Erik Erikson, framed an elegant theory of human development across the life span in his much quoted work, *Childhood and Society* (1963). Erikson believed that healthy personal development comes from the resolution of universal inner conflicts (Trawick-Smith, 2006). Throughout life, Erikson wrote, each individual faces eight stage-based crises, with mental health impacted by the ability to reconcile a fundamental conflict faced at each stage. From birth through the primary years, children go through four stages, and face four conflicts, as shown in Table 2-1.

Trust versus Mistrust—Birth to 18 Months

When an infant receives secure, warm, and responsive care during the first 18 months, she has a good chance of finding the world reliable and worthy of trust. The security from this foundation allows the child to venture into life with openness toward learning. On the other hand, without stable and loving relationships, the infant is unable to develop trust in the world, and all subsequent development will be affected.

Table 2-1	
Erikson's Four Childhood Stages	**Life Conflict**
1. Infancy/Birth to 18 months	Trust versus mistrust
2. Toddlerhood/18 months to 42 months	Autonomy versus shame and doubt
3. Preprimary/42 months to 6 years	Initiative versus guilt
4. Primary/6 to 12 years (Adapted from Erikson, 1963)	Industry versus inferiority

An updated depiction of the first life conflict, trust versus mistrust, is found in **attachment theory** (Trawick-Smith, 2006). During the first months of life, infants develop a long-term emotional bond (attachment) with primary caregivers—mothers, fathers, and other close family members such as grand-parents. With secure attachments, the infant senses that the world is reliable and feels relatively safe about venturing forth: "Securely attached infants tend to be more friendly and competent and have more positive views of themselves in later childhood" (Trawick-Smith, 2006, p. 178). If attachments are unhealthy—inconsistent, erratic, abusive, neglectful—the infant experiences deep unmet needs and may find future relationships difficult to form and future conflicts difficult to resolve (Raikes, H. H., & Pope Edwards, Carolyn, 2009).

Separation Anxiety. Trawick-Smith cites studies that indicate that roughly 70% of infants in the United States form relatively secure attachments with one or more adults. Between six and eight months, though, all infants begin to recognize who is and who is not a primary caregiver, and they begin to experience stranger concern and **separation anxiety**. Early experiences of short-term absence from primary caregivers and short stays with familiar other adults—such as extended family members—tend to reduce these anxieties (Trawick-Smith, 2006). Family members aggravate separation fears when they show anxiety themselves and prolong transitions through lingering one-on-one contact.

Research by Weinraub and Lewis (1977) and Lollis (1990) found that two-year-olds showed less upset at family members' departure during child care drop-off when the separation was explained to them clearly ahead of time. Separation was also found to be smoother if the departing family member suggested activities for the child to engage in during separation (Trawick-Smith, 2006). At child care drop-off, family members and teachers often form a team, with family members setting the scene for the transition and suggesting activities. Teachers then follow through with individual support and getting the children involved.

Transition times are easier for parents and children when teachers take the lead.

For most children *separation anxiety* reaches its peak at about 14 months, and for most it decreases in the following months (Trawick-Smith, 2006). With some children, though, a combination of the child's temperament and the pattern of adult—child interaction causes separation anxiety to become a learned behavior. In this case teamwork among the adults becomes necessary, to nudge the child toward independence (while sustaining secure attachments). By helping very young children to form positive attachments outside of the immediate family, the adult may be assisting them to develop confidence in social situations for the long term (Kagan, 1997).

At separation—especially when care away from home is involved—many family members experience strong feelings: guilt about their parenting, worry about the child, and a sense of lost control. In the early childhood classroom, the teacher orients family members about the transition process and takes the lead at separation to assist the family member and the child. An important task of the early childhood teacher is to help young children and their family members feel that the classroom is a natural extension of their home lives.

Classroom Anecdote	At 8 A.M. children and their family members were filing into the classroom. One two-and-a-half-year-old, Scott, and his dad came in. Scott resisted entering the classroom, and his dad was saying things like, "Come on, Scott, it's just like the other day. Daddy has to go to class." Scott's dad looked at his watch and said, "Scott, give me a hug and then I have to go. I'm late for class." Scott gave his dad a hug and cried, holding on tightly to his dad.
	The teacher walked over, took Scott from his dad, and said, "We will be just fine." The dad left Scott crying and went to class. The teacher sat down on a chair with Scott and held him. She said, "Don't worry, Scott, your dad will be back after his classes." Another child came over to try to comfort him, and Scott hid his face. The teacher asked the girl in a friendly tone to find something to play with while she talked to Scott for a minute. She proceeded to tell Scott, "I know you're embarrassed about crying, but that's okay; everyone misses their mom and dad sometimes, even teachers. She was just trying to help and tell you that it was okay. It really is okay to be sad when your dad leaves, but you know that he will come back as soon as his classes are over."
	She paused and Scott nodded. She said, "Would you like to sit here and cuddle for a little bit?" Scott nodded his head again. He sat there for about two minutes and then slid off of the teacher's lap and went to go play with the girl who had come over to him (Gartrell, 2000).

"Autonomy" versus Shame and Doubt— 18 Months to 42 Months

The basic issue of trust versus mistrust is reconciled to some degree (hopefully positively) during infancy. The trust–mistrust polarity is really a lifelong problem, though, one that shows itself in each of the other stages. In fact, Charlesworth (2007) reminds us that we never totally resolve the crises of any stage, but that relative success with one stage is likely to support us with the next. For the rambunctious toddler, the crucial issue remains trust versus mistrust—it is just that the individual's attempts to resolve this crisis show themselves differently now that the toddler is walking and beginning to talk. The issue transitions to "autonomy" versus shame and doubt. (For Erikson, the term "autonomy" means the beginnings of independence.)

Family members know that infants have become toddlers and a new life conflict comes on the scene when:

▶ "No!"—sometimes with a smile—becomes a mantra.

▶ A toddler sees candy in a store, and a public tantrum ensues.

▶ Any item attractive to a child becomes "hers."

▶ She washes her face, but gets soap in her eyes—and mouth.

▶ She dresses herself, but won't put on socks.

▶ She won't hold your hand, but will run ahead.

▶ She accidentally falls into Aunt Jo's herb garden after you have warned her to be careful of Auntie's plants.

▶ She expertly competes for your attention when you are on the phone.

Ah yes, toddlerhood! The challenge for family members and caregivers is to sustain the child's trust in the adult–child attachment while at the same time keep the balance between the toddler's need for independence and for safe limits. Would anyone deny that looking after toddlers is a full-time job? Trawick-Smith (2006) provides some indicators of progress during the second stage:

> *Once children are trustful of adults and know that their basic needs will be met, they are willing to venture out away from the safety of parents and family. They now wish to become individuals apart from those with whom they are bonded. In their striving for individuality, children often assert themselves, rebel against rules, and assume a negative affect when confronted with adult control. Erikson argues that the emotionally healthy toddler gradually acquires a sense of autonomy—a feeling of individuality and uniqueness apart from his or her parents. Children who are overly restricted or harshly punished for attempts at becoming individuals will come to doubt their individuality and suffer shame. Gradually, such children can become timid, lack confidence in their abilities and assume identities as mere extensions of their parents. (p. 185)*

Initiative versus Guilt—42 Months to 6 Years

The third critical stage, *initiative versus guilt*, identifies the drive in young children to explore, to create, and to discover. Healthy development during this period depends on responsiveness in the adult to these needs. The teacher structures the environment and provides guidance so that children can experience fully while learning nonpunitively about the limits of acceptable behavior. The saying, "The process is more important than the product," applies to this period, as children learn primarily from the doing and the gratification of *self-defined* results, particularly through play.

Erikson's encouragement of *initiative* in preschoolers echoes the writings of Piaget about the need for active learning on the part of the preoperational

© Cengage Learning

The development of a sense both of initiative and belonging during early childhood indicates the importance of the period.

stage child. In fact, for years a standard of high-quality programs for young children has been the inclusion of large amounts of play—an "academic" definition of which is *self-selected, self-directed, autonomous learning activity*. The importance of play in the development of children is argued anew in the most recent edition of *Developmentally Appropriate Practice in Early Childhood Programs* (Bredekamp & Copple, 2008). If we want children who are active learners, who construct their own learning, who are intrinsically motivated to learn, and who see themselves as capable learners, we must approach the teaching of young children in developmentally appropriate ways—and this means play every day.

As discussed in Chapter One, the swing of the pendulum in educational thought toward the premature introduction of academics is counter to the philosophy that a foremost characteristic of a developmentally appropriate program is play. How do classrooms devoid of active, hands-on learning affect the young learner? How does a one-dimensional, teacher-focused classroom affect the learning environment? A foremost interpreter of the writings of Erikson as well as Piaget, David Elkind (1993) puts it well in his essay, "Overwhelmed at an Early Age":

> *Unfortunately, the child does not think or say, "Hey, you dumb grown-up, I am not ready to learn these things yet; wait a couple of months, and I will gobble it up like a candy bar." What the child is likely to think and say to herself is, "These all-wise, all-knowing adults say I should be able to learn this, but I can't. I guess there must be something wrong with me; I must be dumb!" (p. 82)*

This quote captures in a nutshell the opposite of a sense of *initiative*: feelings of guilt when a young child cannot meet the expectations of adults. The uniqueness of preprimary children lies in their new awareness of how things are supposed to happen in the adult world, combined with their still limited ability to make them happen as expected. For instance, what do we make of a preprimary child who draws a purple pig? Do we criticize the absence of "realistic" colors, or do we accept that purple is an impressive color to a young child, and the pigs she saw at the farm yesterday were impressive animals? (Or, maybe purple was the first color the kid had available—and she really wanted to draw this experience.)

A difficult task for many preprimary teachers is to recognize that art—like play—needs to be self-realized. Giving children interesting materials and occasional themes—but not models or our own parallel drawing—allows them to show initiative in the graphic expression of ideas. After a snowfall, we do not have children copy our model of Frosty. We have them make their own pictures that tell what they like to do outside in the snow (Bredekamp & Copple, 2008).

Classroom Illustration	*At 42 months a child makes a snow picture by covering blue paper completely with white chalk. To the adult's comment, "You are really working hard on that picture," the child replies, "This is a bizzard and my dad is back there plowing, but you can't see him." At 72 months the same child draws a snow picture of three skiers on three hills, with another person skiing down one hill. In between the hills are four pine trees. In the sky there are clouds and a sun—all the colors are realistic. Under the story picture the child has written: "Me an my famle goin skeen its fun."*

For the preprimary child, art empowers creative thought. The young child is not restricted by the conventions of literacy. She can develop her ideas creatively and elaborately. Of course, the adult's role is paramount. It is only if we appreciate the "bizzard" that the child gains the confidence to progress to a ski picture with her family, expressed in writing as well as art.

According to Erikson the challenge is to encourage children to explore many possibilities, not to narrow their focus to the one "possibility" the teacher has in mind (Newberger, 1997). When we communicate that yes, the sky is many colors and not just blue, who knows what ideas will open in children's minds? Karen, a four-year-old Native American child once showed me a picture she drew of

Rudolph with a yellow nose. "That is so Santa can see better," she said. This Head Start child improved on the whole Rudolph concept!

Initiative and Belonging. In his books and articles, David Elkind (1987, 1993, 2005) discusses factors in schooling that affect young children's development. Elkind interprets the third critical age by referring to it as "initiative and belonging versus guilt and alienation." Elkind (1987) explains:

> *Erik Erikson describes this period as one that determines whether the child's sense of initiative will be strengthened to an extent greater than the sense of guilt. And because the child is now interacting with peers, this period is also critical in the determination of whether the child's sense of "belonging" will be greater than the sense of alienation. (p. 115)*

Elkind's inclusion of "belonging versus alienation" in the early childhood period is insightful. Studying the transition from preschool to kindergarten made by a sample of 58 children, Ladd and Price (1987) found that preschoolers who were liked by their peers had fewer adjustment problems in kindergarten.
In a second study,

> *Ladd found that the number of new friendships children formed in the first two months of the school year predicted higher levels of social and academic competence, fewer absences from school, fewer visits to the nurse, and less behavioral disruptiveness. (Bukatko & Daehler, 1992, p. 669)*

The value of friendships and the ability to make friends clearly are important skills, so important that they appear to predict school success. Given these findings, the teacher who assists a young child with limited social skills to make friends contributes in a lasting way to the child's future.

Industry versus Inferiority—6 Years to 12 Years

During the preprimary years children, hopefully, have been immersed in rich *initiative* experiences with the social and physical world. Because of these experiences, by the time they reach the next critical period, they are ready for more sophisticated social interactions and learning activities. Erikson's fourth critical period, *industry versus inferiority*, occurs mainly during the elementary grade years. A characteristic of children during this time is that they are easily affected by the judgments of others. They become fully aware, for instance, of the possibility of failing, and sensitivity in teacher feedback is critical.

The teacher who relies on competition and stresses evaluative comparisons creates social stratification among students. These teachers believe that classrooms that are cooperative in nature fail to teach children about the realities of life, such as academic competition and standardized tests. These teachers frequently practice **conditional acceptance**, approval dependent on academic achievement and deference to authority. In the mind of the teacher, and soon enough the minds of the class, some students are perceived as "winners" and others as "losers" (more gifted/less gifted labeling).

About these practices Honig and Wittmer (1996) comment:

Competitive classrooms result in some children becoming tense, fearing failure, and becoming less motivated to persist at challenging events. (p. 63)

Kohn (1999) and Reineke, Sonsteng, & Gartrell (2008) argue that children who see themselves as failures may well be hampered by this label in future learning endeavors. Elkind (1997) states that the use of conditional acceptance is a significant contributor to feelings of inferiority, the downside of the conflict that Erikson sees for this period. Erikson's model reminds us that a common tool that the teacher uses to control the class, public embarrassment, can build feelings of inferiority in students for years to come.

Teaching practices that lead to feelings of inferiority and low self-esteem include:

▶ Applying group pressure (like negative comparisons to other groups) to "prepare students" for "high-stakes" standardized testing.

▶ Showing rejection (sometimes subtle) of children who learn slowly, are unpopular, or are from nonmainstream backgrounds.

▶ Giving negative public attention to incorrect responses and classroom conflicts.

▶ Stressing competitive evaluation procedures that single out students.

▶ Using punishments routinely such as time-outs, in-school detentions, or exclusion of some children from special events.

▶ Reacting in discriminatory ways toward the families of some children.

Practices That Promote Industry. Teachers who promote industry in children tend to affirm each student's worth. They build group spirit so that all members of the class feel that they belong and can succeed. These teachers address conflicts in ways that support the dignity of all. They operate from the premise that an essential skill in a democracy is cooperation to solve mutual problems, and they lead their classrooms to model this value. They believe that education in a democracy means more than preparing for high-stakes assessments.

Just as there is general recognition of practices that lead to feelings of inferiority, a corresponding list of teaching practices that promote industry includes the following. The teacher:

▶ Emphasizes friendly relations and friendly interactions.

▶ Adapts curriculum to offer a variety of means to achieve success.

▶ Uses multidimensional grouping arrangements—informal interest groups, heterogeneous study groups.

▶ Includes older students and other adults to maximize personal attention.

▶ Gives specific, nonembarrassing feedback and evaluation.

▶ Applies a problem-solving, conflict management orientation to classroom conflicts.

As children approach middle childhood, they are greatly affected by the judgments of others.

▶ Prepares students to succeed in assessments in ways that support all in the class.

▶ Promotes involvement opportunities for family members of all children.

Teachers who nurture industry in their classrooms empower students with the tools to continue with healthy personal development. Positive feelings about oneself as a learner and group member are gifts that cannot be underestimated as children move into adolescence. The continuity in Erikson's theory reminds educators of the lifelong impact of their good works in the classroom.

Gardner's Multiple Intelligences: Guidance for Healthy Development

In his many writings Howard Gardner develops the case for a different way of thinking about mental abilities. To Gardner the notion is mistaken that an individual possesses a fixed, genetic entity called *intelligence* (Gardner, 1993, 1999). Instead, Gardner and his associates argue for multiple, separate intelligences, which have a genetic basis but can be developed. Gardner finds much that is problematic in the *assumptions* and the *social policy* of the last century regarding a fixed, one-dimensional intelligence.

In relation to *assumptions* about intelligence, Gardner argues against the following commonly held beliefs (Gardner, 1993):

▶ Intelligence is defined primarily by the individual's ability to use verbal and numerical reasoning.

▶ Intelligence is determined by heredity.

▶ Intelligence is fixed through life.

▶ Intelligence can be measured by standardized tests.

▶ "Intelligence scores" can be compared and used in "utilitarian" ways—like ability grouping in schools, the military, etc.

For Gardner and other psychologists, these assumptions have been disproved by the longitudinal research of the 1950s and 1960s, and by the findings of cognitive psychology and brain research (Gardner, 1999; Shonkoff & Phillips, 2000). The midcentury longitudinal studies demonstrated that environment has a profound effect on intelligence: Young children from enriched, caring situations were able to function more capably in youth and adulthood than were young children from deprived circumstances (Charlesworth, 2007; Schickedanz et al., 2001; Trawick-Smith, 2006). The conclusiveness of these studies gave rise to Head Start and other government programs intended to break "the culture of poverty."

As neuroscientists and cognitive psychologists became able to assess physical brain development in response to environmental influences, mounting research from these fields also supported the impact of enriched environments on intelligence (Newberger, 1997; Shonkoff & Phillips, 2000). With the assumptions about single, genetically determined intelligence debunked, new doors for discovery about mental abilities have opened (Gardner, 1999).

In relation to *social policy* resulting from a theory of fixed intelligence, the new psychologists have joined with many others to decry clearly repressive social practices. One was the *eugenics* movement, which planned "for the betterment of the human race by using various strategies for eliminating those thought to be genetically inferior" (Schickedanz et al., 2001, p. 6). Horrendous examples were in Nazi Germany, and more recently in the Balkan nations, Rwanda and Darfur, with large-scale genocide and "ethnic cleansing." Crimes of eugenics in the United States, largely before 1950, have been documented as well, ranging from the long-standing mistreatment of Native Americans to the lynching of African Americans to the sterilization of vulnerable minority group members, prisoners, and the mentally disabled. Laws in 31 states—now repealed—forbade mixed-race marriages on the presumption that resulting children would be "genetically inferior".

Other mistaken policies stemming from a notion of fixed intelligence are found in American education. Placement of students in "ability tracks"—and in special education classes—frequently was done as a result of intelligence quotient (IQ) test scores, often with little additional information (Gardner, 1993). Attempts have even been documented to end early childhood education programs like Head Start out of a false notion that not poverty but low intelligence keeps low-income populations from advancing (Schickedanz et al., 2001). In recent years with the transformation in thinking about the development and expression of intelligence, social theories based on the assumptions of fixed intelligence have gone out the window.

Multiple Intelligences: An Integrative Theory

The **multiple intelligences (MI)** theories (there are more than one) of the last 25 years reflect the developing "neuroscience" of the brain as an organ intricately affected by interactions with the environment. MI theories share a rejection of the notion that intelligence is fixed by birth (Shonkoff & Phillips, 2000). The sea change idea that especially the young physiologically develop their brains through experiences in the home, in classrooms, and in between, is common to all the MI theories. The dynamic of brain development that MI theories share has fundamental implications for early childhood education and guidance. As a reflection of these precepts, Gardner's concept of intelligence is incisive:

> *A biopsychological potential to process information that can be activated in a cultural way to solve problems or create products that are of value to a culture. (Gardner, 1999, pp. 33–34)*

Noteworthy in Gardner's definition is the interplay of culture and biology in a "potential" that is developed and expressed. For Gardner, environment fundamentally impacts the development of intelligence. Further, he broadened the arena for the expression of intelligence to more than the academic, legal, and scientific settings where the capacity to reason with words and/or numbers is paramount (Gardner, 1993, 1999). If the problems solved and the creations made are to be of value to culture, then there must be MI to develop and express ideas in the many ways that a culture might value.

A chart of Gardner's MI follows (Table 2-2). Gardner has considered adding a ninth and even a tenth intelligence, in the existential and spiritual domains (Gardner, 1999). The eight MIs listed here Gardner believes are well established. When addressed together, they relate directly to early childhood education, guidance, and personal development.

Implications for Education

Gardner's construct places an emphasis on the development of abilities in the context of culture. Different societies value some intelligences over others—logical-mathematical over musical, or interpersonal over linguistic (Gardner, 1999; Schickedanz et al., 1998). Each child is born with unique potential relative to the intelligences, and education becomes the empowering of those potentials

---

Table 2-2 *Multiple Intelligences Identified by Gardner*

1. Musical intelligence—the ability to listen to, to create, and to perform music.
2. Bodily-kinesthetic intelligence—the ability to use large and small muscle activity to express ideas, solve problems, and produce results.
3. Logical-mathematical intelligence—the ability to use reason, logic, and mathematics to solve problems.
4. Linguistic intelligence—the ability to use written and oral language.
5. Spatial intelligence—the ability to perceive, orient oneself in relation to, graphically represent, and think creatively in relation to visual and spatial phenomena.
6. Interpersonal intelligence—the ability to perceive and interpret the behaviors, motives, feelings, and intentions of others.
7. Intrapersonal intelligence—the ability to understand one's own skills and their limits, motivations, self-perceptions, emotions, temperaments, and desires (Gardner, 1993).
8. Naturalist intelligence (the eighth intelligence, added later)—the ability to perceive and understand the meaning of subtleties and distinctions in the natural "living" world (Gardner, 1999).

---

in relation to, but not limited by, cultural predispositions. We see clashes of cultural values with individual intelligences in a British miner's son who would become a poet, for instance; a daughter in Spain who would become a bullfighter, or an American child of a banker who would be a rapper.

In Gardner's view the purpose of education is progressive, to assist learners in the development and expression of their unique abilities for the benefit of culture—more than to assimilate individuals into the existing institutional traditions. Charlesworth (2007) states the matter this way:

> *Gardner's objective is to free children from the narrow standardized test perspective and help them discover their own intelligences and use the information as a guide to vocational and recreational choices so that they can find roles where they feel comfortable and productive. (p. 434)*

Adapted from the works of Charlesworth (2007), Gardner (1995, 1999), Schickedanz et al. (2001), and Shores (1995), educational principles that are compatible with MI theory follow:

- The gifted artist, athlete, carpenter, or teacher is no less intelligent than the scientist—just differently intelligent.
- Each kind of intelligence is relatively independent, engages different parts of the brain, and shows itself in different behaviors.
- Children have different potentials for development in the eight intelligences, determined by the child's genetic makeup and brain formation.
- Children make progress in developing all intelligences through those intelligences in which they are more comfortable and capable.

▸ Schooling must be opened up to educate children in each of the intelligences.

▸ Children make progress in developing their intelligences when they are intrigued (challenged positively) by learning opportunities, but not threatened by them.

▸ The teaching style for progress in the eight intelligences is encouraging and interactive, not didactic and dictatorial.

▸ As children construct meaning for themselves from activities and interactions, they make progress in the eight intelligences.

The Matter of Assessment. An overriding issue in education today is account-ability. Many critics believe the discussion of accountability has been politicized, driving classroom practice toward undue preparation for standardized tests (as in No Child Left Behind). The new psychologists argue the need to measure the performance of schools not by aggregate standardized test scores—tiny samples of performance in children's educational lives—but by the authentic assessment of children's progress in the MI that are developing within each child (Gardner, 1999). Gardner (1993) states it this way:

> *Assessment, then, becomes a central feature of an educational system. We believe that it is essential to depart from standardized testing. We also believe that standard pencil-and-paper short-answer tests sample only a small proportion of intellectual abilities and often reward a certain kind of decontextualized facility. The means of assessment we favor should ultimately search for genuine problem-solving or product-fashioning skills in individuals across a range of materials. An assessment of a particular intelligence (or set of intelligences) should highlight problems that can be solved in the materials of that intelligence. (p. 31)*

From this standpoint, assessment is for the purpose of assisting children in development of the eight diverse domains. Assessment is authentic to the everyday activity of the child and utilizes an appropriate variety of collection mechanisms.

Multiple Intelligences and Early Childhood Education

An early childhood perspective on Gardner's construct is that it is a modern effort to educate the whole child (the longtime goal of developmentally appro-priate education). The implications of MI theory for the classroom draw from the above list and have much in common with the findings of Piaget, Vygotsky, Erikson, and the constructivist educators who came after them. Particular practices these writers likely would find compatible include:

▸ developmentally appropriate curriculum that allows each child a path for individual development

▸ a focus on the individual, rather than on group instruction

▸ a priority on friendly relationships with other children and adults

⬗ many opportunities each day for child choice, cooperative activity, active play, and self-expression

⬗ teacher guidance for healthy social-emotional development.

Schickedanz and her colleagues (2001) provide a chart adapted from Gardner (1995) delineating educational practices that foster the intelligences. In modified form, that information follows (Table 2-3). Notice its overlay with widely accepted views about developmentally appropriate early childhood education.

Multiple Intelligences and Guidance

Intrapersonal Intelligence. Guidance is about teaching young children *democratic life skills*, starting with the support for personal development young children need to learn these high-level skills. As to intrapersonal intelligence,

Table 2-3 *Educational Practices That Foster Multiple Intelligences*	
Musical	Expose children to various types of music; use rhythmic and melodic instruments; encourage dancing, singing, and song composing.
Spatial	Provide opportunities for exploring spaces, varying arrangements of materials, fitting materials into spaces, frequent puzzles, mapping and charting, creative art experiences.
Linguistic	Support writing, oral expression, vocabulary development, learning other languages; read to children and encourage reading.
Logical-mathematical	Provide manipulatives for math; encourage puzzle and problem solving; encourage experimentation and prediction; work in daily practical experiences involving a number of concepts.
Bodily-kinesthetic	Encourage dancing, creative movement, making things with hands, running, climbing, practicing large and small motor skills, noncompetitive sports skills. Integrate bodily-kinesthetic activity into the curriculum.
Interpersonal	Provide opportunities for social interactions, cooperation, personal problem solving, conflict management. Play games figuring out intentions and emotions. Include frequent class meetings and small-group experiences.
Intrapersonal	Encourage expression of emotions, preferences, and thinking strategies. Help with understanding of wishes, fears, and abilities. Emphasize activities that include creativity and personal expression.
Naturalist	Nurture observation skills on field trips and in classroom activities. Encourage expression of observations through journals, artwork, discussions, and nonverbal creations. Provide firsthand experiences with plants and animals and the living world.

teachers help children to accept themselves as worthwhile individuals and members of the group (feeling that one is an acceptable group member). Teachers assist children to express strong emotions in nonhurting ways. The curriculum activities suggested in Table 2-3 under intrapersonal *plus* the teaching done around resolving conflicts fit together to assist children with intrapersonal intelligence. In Erikson's terms the adult teaches for trust, autonomy, initiative, and industry.

Interpersonal Intelligence. Teaching for ethical and intelligent decision making (Piaget's *autonomy*) coincides with the activities listed in Table 2-3 to build interpersonal intelligence. Other democratic life skills also fit perfectly under interpersonal intelligence: helping children work together to solve problems; encouraging children to accept one another whatever their unique human qualities. Integrating cultural diversity awareness into the curriculum, beginning with the children and their families, would be a priority. The notion of the encouraging classroom in which friendliness defines relations and relationships would be key.

The curriculum, learning environment, and social relationships employed by guidance teachers are exactly those of teachers working with young children for intrapersonal and interpersonal intelligence. The teacher, of course, uses conflicts to teach rather than as opportunities to punish. The congruence of guidance with teaching for interpersonal intelligence is complete.

Not surprisingly, teaching that empowers Gardner's interpersonal and intrapersonal intelligences resonates with the interactive teaching styles suggested by the other psychologists addressed in this chapter. In classrooms where MI provide the basis for curriculum, instruction, and assessment, conventional discipline becomes unnecessary and guidance emerges.

Emotional Intelligence: Defining the Central Guidance Issue

Progressive educators have always known that the essence of wisdom is healthy emotional functioning. Truly reflective thinking requires the ongoing integration of thoughts and feelings. Over centuries, progressive writers have stated that enduring education happens only when emotions are blended with, and not artificially separated from, the teaching-learning process. A quote at least 2,000 years old, variously attributed to Socrates and Plutarch, argues this case: "The mind is not a vessel to be filled, but a fire of aspirations to be kindled." The motivation to learn begins with a feeling. During learning activity, feelings sustain effort from initial exploration through mastery. Feelings after mastery impact the future significance of what has been learned.

While the impact of emotion on learning has long been studied, the references to **emotional intelligence (EI)** in the literature are fairly recent. Mayer and Salovey did early research on EI in 1990. In 2005, Salovey and Grewal gave this definition: "the ability to perceive emotion, integrate emotion to facilitate thought, understand emotions and regulate emotions to promote personal growth" (p. 6). Salovey and his colleagues took the viewpoint about EI that it is a relatively fixed capacity, somewhat like IQ, that can be assessed through standardized measures and is a function of overall intelligence (Mayer & Salovey, 1997).

In contrast, Daniel Goleman (1995) wrote of EI as a set of four constructs:

Self-awareness—the ability to read one's emotions and recognize their impact while using gut feelings to guide decisions.

Self-management—involves controlling one's emotions and impulses and adapting to changing circumstances.

Social awareness—the ability to sense, understand, and react to others' emotions while comprehending social networks.

Relationship management—the ability to inspire, influence, and develop others while managing conflict.

For Goleman, competencies within each construct are *not* a set product of heredity. Through education and training, individuals can increase skill in the competencies and perform at a higher level of EI. Goleman's books have been best-sellers (1995, 1998, 2006). Like the Salovey group, Goleman was instrumental in devising assessments for the EI competencies. The contrasts between differing EI theories have triggered much research, controversy, and in Goleman's case, commercial success.

Not so much because of the popularity of Goleman's work as for its ties to other conceptions of multi-intelligences, this section focuses on Goleman's contributions. Goleman gives credit to Gardner for the paradigm shift from a single intelligence to MI (Goleman, 1995). Goleman provides a now-famous illustration of the existence of MI. He states that both psychologists agree on the plausibility of the following scenario: a scientist with a 160 IQ working as an employee for a successful CEO with an IQ of 100. In his ability to manage and market the products of the company, the CEO must have social-emotional knowledge not measured by traditional assessments of IQ (Goleman, 1995).

Goleman's response to the Gardner construct, though, includes criticism. He believes that Gardner's presentation of inter- and intrapersonal intelligence is slanted toward cognitive thought processes. By this he means that Gardner is more concerned about the reflective understanding of one's emotions than in the consideration of emotion as a driving force in behavior (Goleman, 1995).

Goleman argues that EI explains how individuals use their emotions in their behavior. In his books, he presents studies of "Stars," successful individuals who have shown outstanding EI, and he discusses environments—settings that promote *emotional literacy* (learning about the role of emotions in behavior), and so empower *emotional intelligence* (Goleman, 1995, 1998). He argues that education about the emotions needs to be central to modern family life *and* classroom practices—and cannot begin too early. For Goleman (1998):

> *"Emotional intelligence" refers to the capacity for recognizing our own feelings and those of others, for motivating ourselves, and for managing emotions well in ourselves and in our relationships. It describes abilities distinct from, but complementary to, academic intelligence, the purely cognitive capacities measured by IQ. (p. 317)*

Because of the complexities of human emotions as a life force, there probably will not be one-dimensional assessments and scores that define emotional intelligence, or "EQ." With the faults that critics now find in the century-old notion of "IQ," this is probably just as well. But the research continues. Findings from researches about EI are already assisting, and will continue to assist, parents and educators who believe emotionally intelligent learners can benefit society. As the other psychologists in the chapter indicate, however, one cannot separate emotional from social functioning. (Goleman (2006) recognizes this too in his latest book on "social intelligence"). Infusing education with teaching that helps individuals know themselves and be responsive to others is a crucial educational goal.

Emotional Intelligence and Challenging Behavior

One can look at the components of EI as being in an order; that is, one must recognize one's emotions before being able to manage them. Further, a child (or adult) must be able to manage emotions in order to interact effectively with others. Goleman (1995), O'Neil (1996), and Kaiser and Sklar Rasminsky (2007) maintain that *management* of emotions is the central psychological dynamic to social-emotional competence. The premise that all children can make progress in developing EI follows from Goleman's construct. The main deterrent to that learning is the presence of stress in the child's life (LeDoux, 1996; Shore, 1997), which overwhelms healthy brain function with a perceived need for survival (Novik, 1998).

Based on their survey of the literature, Webster-Stratton and Reid (2004) estimate that "the prevalence of aggressive behavior problems in preschool and early school-age children is about 10%, and may be as high as 25% for socioeconomically disadvantaged children" (p. 96). Children may experience difficulty in learning to manage emotions due to a combination of physiological factors (before and after birth) and psychological factors that generate prolonged stress.

Physiological factors include prebirth conditions such as gene makeup, temperament, brain function issues (in utero drug addiction and fetal alcohol influence), pregnancy difficulties due to health conditions, and malnutrition (Kaiser & Rasminsky, 2007). After-birth physiology factors include health conditions in the child that go undiagnosed or are ineffectively treated—for example, poor diet, asthma, pervasive dental problems, chronic ear infections, vision difficulties, attention deficit-hyperactivity disorder/attention deficit disorder (ADHD/ADD), and the autism spectrum.

Psychological factors (due to environmental situations) that cause stress and make it difficult for children to manage emotions are mostly well known. Children are very likely to be at-risk when they come from family circumstances in which:

⟩ parent—child attachments are unhealthy

⟩ violence against family members occurs

⟩ mental illness and substance abuse in family members go untreated

⟩ poverty circumstances cause chronic stress

⟩ the psychological effects of untreated physiological conditions exasperate the behavioral expression of the conditions.

Environmental factors outside the family can also negatively impact children's learning to manage emotions, such as exposure to violence in the community and/or through the media, and negative social experiences in the neighborhood, on school buses and playgrounds, and in the classroom. Young children who experience difficulty in managing emotions are at-risk for life directions that may prevent them from gaining emotional literacy long term (Webster-Stratton & Reid, 2004).

Widespread acknowledgment of the importance of EI is adding to our understanding of how vulnerable young children can become healthy and contributing citizens. Three widely accepted research conclusions have already emerged:

1. Children's emotional, social, and behavioral adjustment is vital for school success. Children unable to manage their emotions and fit in socially are more likely to become educational failures (Ladd, Kochenderfer, & Coleman, 1997; Raver & Zigler, 1997; Shores & Wehby, 1999).

2. Children at-risk for emotional difficulties can substantially reduce this risk through positive attachments with, and careful teaching by, caring adults (Novik, 1998; Webster-Stratton & Reid, 2004).

3. While healthy attachment with a parent or custodial family member is crucial, children can also gain much from positive attachments with other family members, a teacher, or another caring professional (Novik, 1998; O'Neil, 1996).

In recent years, alarm about childhood obesity is generating renewed interest about the relation of physical activity and healthy mental functioning—including the reduction of stress. Programs that incorporate physical activity into early childhood curriculum and the daily schedule benefit children in many ways relative to building EI (Pica, 2006; Gartrell, 2008). Educating the whole child in early childhood classrooms means that teachers address EI together with physical intelligence; they see body and mind as one in the young child. Children groove when they move. The time of the "sit, listen, and follow directions" classroom is past.

The Contributions of Brain Research

Research on the development of the brain over the last 15 years has been exciting to follow. Neuroscience that images changes in the brain in response to experiences is affirming a new important practices in early childhood education. The psychologists in this chapter, most at work before brain study was possible, observed processes in child development that we can explain more fully because of learning about the brain. Their constructs are the more valid for what the research is suggesting.

Jean Piaget wrote of the difference in learning processes in preschoolers and older children. We know that the *executive function* is still developing in the fontal cortex of the preschool child (Shonkoff & Phillips, 2000). Before formulation of this "control panel" for problem solving and ethical thought, young children (logically) would approach problems with more naïveté and less reasoning power than when they are older. Vytgosky's contention that private speech permits elemental reasoning in the child makes sense, again, in relation to the early point of development of the executive function.

Vygotsky's insistence that adults who scaffold children's learning must maintain friendliness corresponds to research on the roles of criticism versus support in how the brain functions (Shore, 1977). Stress causes cortizol hormone secretion and alternation of neurotransmission paths within the brain that make it hard for the child to process information, to "think" (LeDoux, 1996). Stress throughout childhood drives children to falter in the various life conflicts described in Erikson's theory. Stress due to unhealthy attachments and relationships causes life pressure within the child toward mistrust, shame and doubt, guilt and alienation, and inferiority. Healthy relations with significant others brings about physiologically more healthy neurotransmission activity, and structures like the pre-frontal cortex (the locus of the executive function) gain in mass and function as a result (Shonkoff & Phillips, 2000).

With his theory formulated during the time of brain research, Gardner (1999) contends that each of his MI triggers different patterns of brain activity, an important consideration in decisions about the intelligences identified. In accord with Vygotsky, brain development and learning in relation to the intelligences would need to flow from intrigue-based rather than stress-based activities—from interest rather than imposed challenge. Challenging behavior as largely stress caused marks a key obstacle to making gains in EI. Goleman, like the other psychologists, sees education (and brain development) happening optimally in teaching and learning transactions that affirm the worth of children and their capacity to learn.

Brain Development in Young Children

Several works in the last few years, perhaps most notably *Neurons to Neighborhood: The Science of Early Childhood Development*, describe trends in research that directly impact the life of young children in the home and classroom

(Shonkoff & Phillips, 2000). Citing some of these works, the following discussion presents accepted conclusions from studies on brain research and their implications how young children develop.

1. *The brain is not fully formed and operational at birth, but develops physiologically in response to experiences throughout childhood.* With daily experience, the brain of the young child transforms perceptions into billions of new connections, called dendrites, across its neurons, the cells of the brain. Healthy development is necessary for maintenance of the dendrites and for optimum brain functioning. The child's experiences influence how these dendrites form, and the brain influences how the experiences are interpreted. The brain of the young child builds its physical structure while it simultaneously functions in relation to experiences (Wolfe & Brandt, 1998).

Within the pre-frontal cortex (the primary structure for conscious thought), the executive function is the last part of the brain to develop fully (Shonkoff & Phillips, 2000). Of the executive function, Dr. Philip Zelazo (2008), professor of neuroscience psychology at the University of Toronto, explains:

> *The executive function . . . affects many different facets of children's mental development, from their understanding of other people's points of view to their ability to focus on a task. (p. 1)*

The executive function is influenced both by the child's relations and experiences— greatly influenced—and in turn influences the sense that the child makes of the world. The executive function develops rapidly during the preschool years, but takes until adulthood to develop fully (Shonkoff & Phillips, 2000).

2. *Intelligence is not fixed at birth.* The child's environment is not neutral. Experiences either aid brain development by promoting dendrite formation, or hinder brain development by retarding dendrite formation—or even causing already formed dendrites to die off. This is why we say that mental abilities are the result of the interplay of heredity—the unique mass of brain neurons the infant is born with—and environment—the wiring of neurons with dendrites as the result of experiences (Shonkoff & Phillips, 2000). The young child's brain is about two and a half times more active than the brain of the adult. We say that the first years are the most important learning years because the child is not just processing prodigious amounts of information and making meaning of it, but building the brain cell connections necessary for further learning in the process.

3. *The brains of children develop best in enriched environments* (Diamond & Hopson, 1998; Shore, 1997). Enriched environments have particular characteristics. They include the provision of:

- consistent, positive emotional support that balances against both over- and understimulation
- nutrition and life circumstances that promote physical health
- a learning environment that is pleasurably intense (intriguing) but free of undue pressure and stress

▶ interest-based activities that encourage multiple aspects of development (physical, emotional, aesthetic, cognitive, language, social, cultural)

▶ ongoing opportunities for children to construct personal meaning and to express and share ideas

▶ ongoing opportunities for children to participate in friendly relationships and social activities that affirm their personal and social worth (Wolfe & Brandt, 1998).

4. *Abilities are acquired more easily during certain sensitive periods, or "windows of opportunity" while the individual is young.* During the period of birth to age five, hundreds of billions of dendrite connections among neurons are constantly forming. During adolescence and into adulthoods, the building process slows down but does not stop. Certain abilities such as eyesight, however, develop only during windows of opportunity very early in life, while dendrite formation for that ability is most active. These abilities cannot develop if environmental deprivation occurs during the critical time (Diamond & Hopson, 1998). For other abilities, such as second-language learning, the window of opportunity does not close as quickly or tightly. The optimum time for learning additional languages is before adolescence. A second language can be learned later in life, though usually not as easily.

5. *Emotions strongly influence learning by aiding or hindering brain development.* When heightened *but not* stressful emotions are attached to experiences, an individual forms stronger memory patterns around the experiences. Hormones generated by the positively charged experience both generate potent processing of the information and facilitate healthy dendrite formation, which fosters future learning (Wolfe & Brandt, 1998). In contrast, when children's minds are beset with stress—generated by either the classroom situation itself or pressures from outside the classroom—emotions negatively affect brain functioning.

LeDoux in *The Emotional Brain* (1996) provides an authoritative analysis of how this happens: Sensing danger, the amygdala (the brain structure that processes experiences into emotions), sends out strong stress hormones to the hippocampus (the structure that mediates emotional reactions). If the experience is severe and prolonged, the hormones actually cause damage to the dendrites of the hippocampus. Healthy communication between the hippocampus and other parts of the brain, including those that mediate thought, is then disrupted. Memory and recall processes, essential for learning, become more difficult (LeDoux, 1996).

LeDoux states that if infrequent episodes of stress are discontinued, and the stress is not too severe, the hippocampus can repair its dendrites and resume normal functioning. However, in relation to long-term stress LeDoux (1996) states, "In survivors of trauma, like victims of repeated child abuse or Vietnam veterans with post-traumatic stress disorder, the hippocampus is shrunken" (p. 242). More so than others, these individuals must struggle to perform everyday thinking processes, made more stressful by knowing they are struggling.

Emotional memories always have a strong unconscious component and often have a conscious component as well. Emotional memories of either type are difficult to extinguish on one's own (LeDoux, 1996).

Brain Research and Early Childhood Education

Almost all windows of opportunity for brain development begin during early childhood. The child is learning and simultaneously building brainpower as during no other time in life. Because early learning experiences build neural connections, it is imperative that these experiences generally be positive and developmentally appropriate. In *Rethinking the Brain*, Shore (1997) makes the point that the hallmark of quality nonparental care is not different from the quality care given by mothers and fathers: "Warm, responsive, consistent care-giving geared to the needs of individual children" (p. 59). Results of brain research indicate the following additional characteristics of quality child care:

▶ a sufficient number of adults for each child

▶ small group sizes

▶ high levels of staff education and specialized training

▶ low staff turnover and administrative stability; and

▶ high levels of staff compensation (Shore, 1997, p. 59).

Brazelton and Greenspan (2000) argue that one cannot ignore the importance of the caregiver's role in healthy development. "When there are secure, empathetic, nurturing relationships, children learn to be intimate and empathetic and eventually to communicate about their feelings, reflect on their own wishes, and develop their own relationships with peers and adults" (p. 3). These responsive and secure relationships help children develop an ability to self-regulate their emotions and behavior. The study of early relationships and brain development has given support to what many in early childhood education have known all along. The authors phrase the issue this way:

> *The notion that relationships are essential for regulating our behavior and moods and feelings as well as for intellectual development is one that needs greater emphasis as we think about the kinds of settings and priorities we want for our children. The interactions that are necessary can take place in full measure only with a loving caregiver who has lots of time to devote to a child. (p. 28)*

About 75% of children are in child care during the first five years. Yet programs are underfunded and underregulated. Speaking of the need for early intervention instead of later remediation, Wolfe and Brandt (1998) state "That with intense early intervention, we could reverse or prevent some adverse effects. They contend that the billions of dollars spent on special education services might be better spent on early intervention".

As Head Start and subsequent generations of innovative early childhood programs have demonstrated, the need for society to improve the environments of children living in poverty is generally recognized. Intervention programs that provide enriched environments can protect children from the effects of chronic stress conditions on brain development. In studies cited by Wolfe and Brandt (1998), the most effective programs started with children when they were infants and directly involved parents.

In their statement about young children, Brazelton and Greenspan (2000) also argue for small ratios in infant/toddler care, higher salaries for child care providers, and full-time child care only for children after age two. Within these parameters optimal relationships develop, followed by healthy brain development—and the self-regulatory skills, trust, autonomy, and cognitive abilities that healthy brain development engenders.

One caveat in relation to their thesis emerges, however. In this day and age, even though most family members might like to, many simply cannot stay home full-time with their infants and toddlers. Brazelton and Greenspan state that this should be the goal whenever possible and, if not, part-time care is preferential to full-time care. Even when the very young are in full-time care, however, the brain research tells us that positive attachments of children with nonparental caregivers are possible and desirable. The benefits (and real costs) of empowering positive adult—child attachments in early childhood settings need to be recognized outside of the early childhood profession.

A Climate for Partnerships with Families

Teachers, directors, principals, and child care providers are in positions that require them to create positive environments for young children. Just as crucial, for the healthy development of their children, they must find ways to build partnerships with families. The beginning point for building partnerships is when the child is about to begin a program. Steps caregivers take to lessen separation anxiety in children (and adults) create a climate for partnerships that will benefit the child and family members in the long run.

> A young child's anxiety in a new school experience may be lessened if there is not an abrupt division between home and school. Children thrive when they feel a continuity between parents and teachers that can be present only when adults have reached out in an effort to understand and respect each other. Just as a teacher's first task in relating to young children is to build a sense of trust and mutual respect, the same task is important in working with parents. (Gestwicki, 2004, p. 126)

In school-related programs, teachers use a variety of spring and summer activities to acquaint both children and family members with the new year's program. Examples include: a Head Start program that coordinates spring bus runs so that children and family members can visit kindergarten classrooms the children will be attending; transition journals that provide a dialogue between the child and family, the preschool teacher, and the kindergarten teacher; and summer kindergarten transition classes held in the classrooms children will attend in September.

In the days immediately preceding the beginning of school, teachers accelerate efforts at communicating with families. Several veteran kindergarten teachers from Minnesota have unique approaches for building partnerships with family members during this period. The following case study is a composite of the practices of a few of these teachers, combined into the approach of one teacher, "Juanita."

Before School Begins

Juanita views both the children and the parents as her "customers." Her intent is to build "happy customers." Part of her approach is to reach the family members through the children. Another part is to reach the children through the parents. A guideline that she works with is "if the children are happy, the parents will be too." Juanita knows that parents who themselves had unhappy school experiences will be more likely to accept a teacher if they know that she cares about their kids. Juanita puts this idea to work even before the first day.

About two weeks before school, Juanita sends letters to both the child and the family. To the child she says how happy she is that the child is in her class and how many fun things they will do at school. The teacher encloses an animal sticker and tells each child to watch for that animal when they get to school. The animal emblem is prominently displayed by the classroom door, and Juanita wears a replica of the emblem during the first week. (See letters in Appendix B.)

In the letter to the family, Juanita says the same things but goes on to invite them to either of two orientation meetings (one late afternoon, the other at night) to be held during the second week of school.

In addition, with permission of the principal, she offers each family the option of a home visit, "as a good way for you, your child, and I to get to know each other." She comments in the letter that not all families are comfortable with a

The results of liberation teaching often speak for themselves.

home visit, which is fine. She can make a visit later in the year, if they would like, and she will be telephoning each family a day or two before start-up to discuss any questions they might have. Juanita intentionally sends the letter "To the Family Of" to include custodial adults who may not be parents—an increasing demographic in our society. (See section on family diversity in Chapter Nine.)

After Start-Up

First Day. On the first day of school, Juanita always has a parent volunteer from the year before to help with separation problems. Juanita greets each child with a name tag as they arrive. At the request of Juanita and the other kindergarten teachers, the district allows half of each class to come in on separate days during the first week. This arrangement means that instead of 24 children attending on the two first days, 12 children attend on each day. Family members are always welcome in Juanita's class (and are put to use), although during the first two weeks or so, they are encouraged to let the children make the adjustment to school on their own, to the extent possible.

First-Night Phone Call. During the evening of the first day of school, Juanita telephones each family to make sure that children have returned home safely, to let the parents know how the child has adjusted, and to ask about any problems that may have occurred. Juanita has said that although she would rather be doing other things after the first day, like drinking a beverage and going to bed early, she regards these telephone calls as the best investment she makes all year in her relations with parents. For parents without listed telephone numbers, she makes a personal contact as soon as possible using notes or informal visits.

Settling In. Over the first days, Juanita allows a lot of exploration time, but she also gets the children used to numerous routines right away. She comments, "A lot of problems never happen if the children know and are comfortable with the routines." Juanita and the volunteer make sure that all children get on the correct buses at the end of the day. Before leaving the classroom, they have a "class meeting" to discuss how happy Juanita will be to see them the next time they come to school. Juanita gives an individual good-bye to each child as they leave, a practice she continues all year. After completing kindergarten, children receive individual letters saying how much she enjoyed having them in her class and wishing them the very best when they begin first grade next fall.

Greeting Meetings. Juanita holds two orientation meetings (which she calls "Greeting Meetings"), and families can attend either one. She gets high school students who had her as a teacher to care for children who come with the parents to the greeting meetings. At the meetings, Juanita answers questions they might have and talks about the education program. To assist in the discussion, she provides each family with a brochure titled, "The Education Program in Our Class." (See the sample brochure in Appendix C.) The brochure discusses matters such as the role of play in the program, why manipulatives are used in math, why the art is creative, why a guidance approach is used, and the importance of family involvement.

Surveys. Juanita also asks the parents to fill out a brief survey. The one-page survey includes items about their and their child's interests, the child's family background, the kinds of activities the parents can help with during the year, and other information "that would help me to understand and work with your child." Completing the survey is optional but almost all parents fill it out. The responses provide useful information to discuss at the first conference later in the year. (See Appendix B for sample letters and surveys to families.)

The teacher attributes the high level of attendance at the orientation meetings to the telephone calls, letters, and home visits at the beginning of the school year. She says the first week is exhausting, but the investment is worth it. "That telephone call the first night of school really wins them over. I remember how I felt the first time my child left for kindergarten. I still get tears when I think about it."

Juanita tries hard to communicate with family members and has even held a conference at a cocktail lounge, where a single parent worked afternoons and evenings. Juanita does have strong feelings about parents who she believes could be doing more for their children. She attempts to be friendly with these

Family members are always welcome in Juanita's class and contribute in many ways. (courtesy, The Bemidji Pioneer)

© Cengage Learning

parents nonetheless. She knows that some parents did not receive appropriate nurturing as kids and never had a chance to grow up completely themselves. She realizes that getting a family member involved may make a difference in that child's life. She knows because she has seen parents get involved and grow, and as a result their children's attitudes and behaviors change.

It is not realistic to expect teachers to like all parents. However, it is essential and possible for teachers to respect all parents for their caring and efforts. In most cases, parents do care. This belief is the basis for all teacher interaction. (Gestwicki, 2004, p. 126)

Juanita practices Gestwicki's words.

Summary

1. *How do Piaget's ideas provide a foundation for the study of child development and guidance?*

The writings of Piaget document that children interpret experiences differently over time and that their interpretations conform to the stage of development they are in. For teaching to be effective, it must accommodate the child's developmental level, base of experience, active learning nature, limited social perspective, and developmental egotism. For Piaget *autonomy*, or ethical and intelligent decision making, is the purpose of education. Guidance in the encouraging classroom is the teaching approach that leads children to develop autonomy.

2. *How do Vygotsky's ideas describe the adult's role in guiding development?*

Vygotsky studied the learning process of the child and concluded that the role of others is central to it. In any act of learning, the child has a *zone of proximal development*, which is the psychological difference between what the child can learn on her own and what she can learn with the help of a more capable other. *Scaffolding*, or sensitive interaction, guides the child through the zone. The child uses private speech, later internalized as conscious thought, to solve learning problems and self-regulate behavior. An interpretation of Vygotsky's work is that guidance is the scaffolding process by which children learn the skills of social and emotional problem solving.

3. *Why is Erikson's work a link between child development and guidance in the classroom?*

Erikson theorized that all humans go through critical periods, or stages, in each of which they face a central life conflict. Young children pass through four: During the first critical period of *trust versus mistrust*, the infant tries to develop feelings of basic trust in her world. During the second, *autonomy versus shame and doubt*, the toddler begins to develop a sense of identity—hopefully with the encouragement of reliable adult relationships. During the third period of *initiative and belonging versus guilt and alienation*, preschoolers need support in creative activities and social interactions, through which they can positively define themselves. During the primary years, the critical issue is *industry versus inferiority*. Through each of the critical periods, the approach that encourages both productive learning and positive feelings about oneself as a learner is guidance.

4. How does Gardner's theory of multiple intelligences support the guidance approach?

Gardner is among a growing number of psychologists who have debunked the idea that intelligence is a single entity, determined by heredity and fixed for life. Gardner's concept of eight *multiple intelligences* are intended to change how we look at child development, education, and social policies regarding mental abilities. To respond to the eight intelligences in the classroom, curriculum, teaching practices, and assessment methods need to be opened up and made developmentally appropriate. To assist children to develop their intrapersonal and interpersonal intelligences, teachers must model these intelligences and teach to them.

5. What are the implications of emotional intelligence for guiding personal development?

The concept of emotional intelligence (EI) was delineated by Mayer and Salovey and popularized by Goleman. In Goleman's construct, EI has four components: self-awareness, self-management, social awareness, and relationship management. Research relating to the concept has concluded that young children who lack understanding of and the ability to manage their emotions come to have high levels of academic failure. Whatever combination of factors put young children at-risk, caring adults can teach the skills of EI that increase the likelihood of school success. The caring adults should not only be family members but also can be other caregivers or teachers.

6. What are the implications of brain development for guiding personal development?

Over the last 15 years, important research findings have been made in relation to brain development. We now know that the brain changes physiologically in response to the environment, and that intelligence is not fixed at birth. Enriched environments in early childhood empower optimal brain functioning and physical brain development. Teaching that aids brain development includes many opportunities for active, social, self-realized learning—opportunities that intrigue and engage the learner but that minimize stress. Teaching that is based on guidance creates the encouraging classroom in which brain development can flourish. High-quality, comprehensive preschool programs contribute to healthy brain development. The need for such programs should be more fully recognized.

7. How does the teacher create a climate for partnerships with families?

Before and during the first days of school, the teacher does much to create a climate for partnerships with family members through the use of notes, telephone calls, home visits, and greeting meetings. Initiating partnerships eases the transition of the child from home to school. If parents know the teacher is working to build positive relations with both the child and themselves, they are more likely to become involved. Teachers cannot expect to feel positively toward every family member, but by remaining friendly and accessible, most family members will respond. Family involvement in the education program can make a lifelong difference to the child and the family.

FOLLOW-UP ACTIVITIES

Note: *An element of being a professional teacher is to respect the children, parents, and educators you are working with by maintaining confidentiality—that is, keeping identities private. In completing follow-up activities, please respect the privacy of all concerned.*

Discussion Activity

The discussion activity encourages students to interrelate their own thoughts and experiences with specific ideas from the chapter.

Think about an academic subject that you personally are quite comfortable with or feel quite uncomfortable about. Trace your memories about that subject back to your teacher(s) and try to pinpoint experiences that led to your present feelings. Analyze your thoughts, feelings, and experiences regarding the subject area in relation to the developmental ideas of one of the following: Vygotsky, Gardner, Goleman, or LeDoux's ideas about emotions and brain development.

Application Activities

Application activities allow students to inter-relate material from the text with real-life situations. The observations imply access to practicum experiences; the interviews, access to teachers or parents. To inter-relate theory and experience, students compare or contrast observations and interviews with referenced ideas from the chapter.

1. Piaget's foundation for the study of child development.

   a. Observe two small groups of children in situations where they have to share materials with others: one group ages three or "young" four; the other group ages five or six. Record the age in years and months of each child. Write down a sample conversation from each observation. What similarities and differences do you observe in the two groups in their actions and words? How much of what you observe can you attribute to developmental differences? to personality differences? Compare your findings to text material regarding Piaget's ideas.

    b. Interview an experienced teacher about the differences in what three- and four-year-olds versus five- and six-year-olds understand about *cooperating with others*. Ask how the teacher would accommodate the understanding level of each group. What are the similarities and differences in the strategies the teacher would use? Compare your findings to text material regarding Piaget's ideas.

2. Vygotsky describes the adult's role in guiding development.

    a. Closely observe a teacher using scaffolding with a young child. Record the age of the child in years and months. Write down as much actual dialogue from the interaction as you can. Hypothesize about both the child's and the adult's comfort levels during the experience. Did the scaffolding result in the learning that the adult expected? Why or why not? Compare your findings with text material regarding Vygotsky's ideas.

    b. Interview a teacher about the use of scaffolding with young children. Does the teacher use similar or different techniques with children of different ages? Why or why not? How does the teacher know when the scaffolding has been successful or unsuccessful? Compare your findings from the interview with text material regarding Vygotsky's ideas.

3. Erikson—a link between child development and guidance.

    a. Observe a child who seems to you to be clearly at one of the four of Erikson's childhood stages. Record actions and words in a fairly typical activity or situation for that child. Using the text material as a reference, analyze why you believe the child is at the stage you identify. Based on your observation, hypothesize about the child's apparent progress in dealing with the life conflict at that stage. Compare your findings with text material regarding Erikson's stage theory.

    b. Interview a teacher about two children, one the teacher believes is progressing in terms of healthy personal development, and one who is having difficulties in making progress. Assuring that privacy will be protected, learn as much as you can about each child from the teacher. Apply the findings from your interview to Erikson's ideas in the text about personal development at the stage you believe each child to be in.

4. Gardner's construct of multiple intelligences (MI) contributes to the guidance approach.

    a. Observe at least an hour in a classroom in which the children seem fully engaged in a variety of activities. Apply Gardner's construct of MI to your observation. How many of the different intelligences could you document that individual children seemed to be using/developing? Write a sentence or two of documentation for each intelligence you observed. Compare your observations to the Figure 2–3 in the chapter titled "Educational Practices That Foster Multiple Intelligences."

b. Interview a teacher about how he or she teaches to encourage development in any three of the "nonacademic" intelligences. (The teacher may refer to them as "skills areas" or "competency areas.") Compare the teacher's comments to Figure 2–3 in the chapter titled "Educational Practices That Foster Multiple Intelligences."

5. The concept of emotional intelligence (EI) defines the central guidance issue.

a. Observe a child who strikes you as having a high level of self-understanding and/or understanding of the feelings and needs of others. Record actions and words in a typical social situation for that child. Based on your observation, hypothesize about the child's use of EI. Relate your findings to EI ideas discussed in the text.

b. Interview a teacher about the idea of EI as separate from the traditional notion of "cognitive intelligence." Protecting identity, ask the teacher to discuss a child who seems to consistently make emotionally intelligent decisions. What seems to be "special" about the child in terms of personality, learning style, and home situation? Putting together your interview and your reading, discuss what you have learned about EI.

6. Brain development guides personal development.

a. In a program you believe conducive to healthy development, record observations in as much detail as you can in a time block that involves *active learning* (not just listening and following directions). Referring to the text material on brain development, what practices did you see that did or did not seem to be supporting healthy brain development in children you observed?

b. Interview a teacher about brain development. Ask the teacher's response to the idea in the text that if children experience high levels of stress over time, their brain functioning may be hindered. Ask about the teacher's approach when a child seems to be bringing high stress levels into the classroom. Compare the teacher's responses with the text material on brain development.

7. The teacher creates a climate for partnerships with families.

a. Interview a teacher about the steps he or she takes at the beginning of the year to build partnerships with families. Ask about the practices modeled by the teacher in the chapter. Compare your findings with material from the chapter about building partnerships.

b. Interview a family member about what is important for a teacher to do at the beginning of the year to create a climate for partnerships with family members. Ask about the practices modeled by the teacher in the chapter. Compare answers with material from the chapter about building partnerships.

Recommended Readings

Black, S. (2003, January). Too soon to test. *The American School Board Journal,* 13–20.

Brazelton, T. B., & Greenspan, S. (2000). *The irreducible needs of children—what every child must have to grow, learn, and flourish.* Cambridge, MA: Perseus.

Elkind, D. (2005). Viewpoint. Early childhood amnesia: Reaffirming children's need for developmentally appropriate programs. *Young Children, 60*(4), 38–40.

Raikes, H. H., & Pope Edwards, C. (2009). *Extending the dance in infant & toddler caregiving.* Baltimore, MD: Paul H. Brookes Publishing Company. Washington, DC: NAEYC.

Reineke, J., Sonsteng, K. & Gartrell. (2008). Nurturing mastery motivation: No need for rewards. *Young Children,* 65(5), 88–94.

Sapon-Shevlin, M. (2008). Learning in an inclusive community. *Educational Leadership, September 2008. 49–53.*

Turner, N. T., Broemmel, A. D., & Wooten, D. A. (2004). History through many eyes: Ten strategies for building understanding of time concepts with historical picture books. *Childhood Education, 81*(1), 20–24.

Vance, E., & Jimenez Weaver, P. (2003). Words to describe feelings. *Young Children, 58*(4), 45.

Zelazo, P. D. (2008). Executive function: A six part series. Toronto, Canada: Hospital for Sick Children, University of Toronto, http://aboutkidshealth.ca/News/SeriesArchive .aspx#ExecutvieFunction

Guidance Matters Column

(Note to readers: The following column has been adapted to reduce repetition of ideas from the chapter.)

Competition: What Place in Our Programs

March, 2007

Student teacher Sarah Laney had this learning experience with an older preschool group at a university child care center in Minnesota:

A wind chill factor below zero means the children play downstairs today and not on the playground. The basement playroom lacks the capacity for children to run and be free. I decided the restlessness in the room can be broken up by allowing small groups to go in the long hall outside the classroom and run, run, run.

Sarah: Suzzane, Johnson, Jayne, and Zack, would you four come join me at the door? (The four come running with

excitement.) Since we can't go outside today, I am going to let groups of four run down this hallway and back.

Be aware of others and be careful of anyone running behind, in front of, or alongside you.

Johnson: Sarah, you mean we can run as fast as we can?

Sarah: Exactly!

Zack: I can run really, really fast, Sarah!

Suzzane: Zack, I can run fast too.

Sarah: I am excited to see you all run and do your best!

Jayne: *I don't like to run a long time . . . (looking down at her shoes).*

Sarah: *Jayne, run as far as you would like, or you can skip or jump if you'd rather.*

Jayne: *I like to skip!*

Johnson: *Um, Teacher, how will we know when to start running?*

Sarah: *That is a good question, Johnson. I have a whistle. (The boys jostle to see who will go first.)*

Zack: *Johnson, that was not nice, you are not supposed to push.*

Johnson: *But I want to go firrrrrsssstttt!*

Sarah *(seeing the conflict): This is not a race. (She puts her whistle in her pocket.) Are you ready to just run and have fun?*

All: *Yeaaah!*

Sarah: *You can start. (The kids start running or skipping.)*

Johnson: *Teacher, look I am the first one. I am fast! (Johnson is definitely a fast runner and has broken away considerably from the group.)*

Jayne: *I am skipping, Teacher! (Jayne is doing her own thing and doing it well).*

Suzzane *(trying so hard her panting is echoing through the hallway, while her little running feet are going as fast as they possibly can): Wait, Johnson, don't go so far. Wait for us!*

Zack *(a fast runner as well; not far behind Johnson and gaining): Suzzane, c'mon, I am waiting for you. You can do it. We will run there and back together! (Zack slows his pace intentionally to allow Suzzane to catch up.)*

Sarah: *Johnson, Zack, Jayne, and Suzzane, you all ran or skipped all the way down the hall and back! (addressing Zack) Zack, I like how you waited for Suzzane and encouraged her to keep running. That was a friendly thing to do!*

Zack grins. I am excited about how he acted. Zack has had lots of problems lately, and later I tell the other teachers about his friendliness.

In this anecdote the student teacher put away her whistle. She overcame the stereotype that at school running is organized racing. Instead, Sarah met the need of the young children to run for the sake of running, not to win or lose. Intuitively, she guided the children away from competitiveness, toward cooperation. This moment of liberation empowered Zack, often competitive in activities, to slow his running pace and include Suzzane, not leave her behind.

Emotional Readiness First

The developmental egocentrism that Jean Piaget (1932/1960) documented in young children—due, we now know, to still developing brains and very limited experience—makes winning and losing hard for them to understand (unlike us adults, right?). Take the game Musical Chairs. Each time the music stops, the leader removes a chair, and the child who cannot find a seat quickly enough is out of the game. Young children do not yet have the social perspective and emotional readiness that allow them to understand "it's just a game." Judging from the emotional reactions I've seen in this activity, children who are out of the game are more apt to be feeling, "This adult doesn't like me" or "I am not worthy of playing this game" (see Hyson, 2004).

Piaget demonstrated that between the ages of three and seven, children become much more capable of understanding the rules in games. As our anecdote illustrates, perceived rules can have a great impact on the children's behavior. When an adult even benignly imposes rules, they are often beyond young children's capacities to emotionally handle and may elicit some strong reactions:

Zack: Johnson, that was not nice, you are not supposed to push.

Johnson: But, I want to go firrrrrsssstttt!

There is a difference between rules teachers impose and rules that evolve from children's activities; in the latter instances, children are more likely to understand the expectations. Child-generated rules become conventional as children approach middle childhood, but before that their rules can be interestingly preconventional.

For example, four preschoolers once played a game of cards this way: One child dealt the cards. The four picked up their hands, giggled, put their cards back down, and the same child dealt them again. Their game went on like this for 20 minutes. An adult who might have tried to teach a "real" card game probably would have then seen the children scatter. A year or two later, of course, the four children easily might play a regular game of cards.

Life's Conflicts and Resolutions

Erik Erikson (1963), the mid-20th-century psychologist, posed "eight ages." Which I refer to as "critical life conflicts," that humans face in the cycle of life, infancy through older adulthood. To the extent individuals can resolve each conflict successfully, they are likely to experience mental health. Those who can resolve the early life conflicts almost certainly struggle less to resolve the later conflicts. The life dilemmas children experience in the early years strongly point to the essential guiding role adults play in each young one's life.

A developmental psychologist who followed Erikson was David Elkind. Elkind (1987) indicates that the dilemmas faced by preschool to primary-grade children are that they need to experience healthy transactions with the world and at the same time find a place of acceptance within social groups. In an adult-organized competitive game, many young children leave feeling they are to blame for an unhappy experience and feeling alienated from the rest of the group. In contrast, when teachers guide groups to run for the sake of running (or skip for the sake of skipping) and play games for the sake of playing, they nurture a sense of both initiative and belonging in children: The players win just by participating successfully—as do both Zack and Suzzane in the anecdote.

When Winning Is Losing

But what of young children who enter the classroom with "built-in" competitiveness? Whether it is a consequence of disposition, family priorities, or both, these children seem to feel they are worthy of acceptance by others only if they are competing and winning. This mind-set makes life's future conflicts more challenging. Ironically, here is a situation in which the teacher must be tougher (in a friendly way) than the child. Each day, the teacher offers the child intentional, focused, unconditional acceptance; kindly discourages a winner—loser mentality; and presents meaningful individual and cooperative activities as clear opportunities for success. A relationship with the child is critical to this effort.

Referring to the anecdote, Sarah commented to me that she had been working hard with Zack to help him resolve conflicts less aggressively. On this day, for the first time, her supportive relationship paid off.

And what of our country's emphasis on competition? Shouldn't we prepare young children for competing? Well, yes, by following Erikson's and Elkind's ideas. We guide children to develop reasonable trust in the world, a sense of self that is good, a confidence in doing things for their own sake, and a feeling of acceptance as a member of the group. As children grow, these social-emotional qualities will fundamentally aid them to be industrious in all kinds of situations and not to feel inferior and alienated.

Elkind (2001) writes about the importance of helping young children make meaning of their childhood by celebrating them more for who they are than for how they perform. We owe a lot to Elkind (1987, 2005) for showing us that there is more to being a child than duly participating in adult-organized competitive events, including in the classroom. Forced winning and losing come to today's children too hard and too fast.

Courtesy in the face of competition, cooperation to resolve the larger dilemmas in life: these are the goals that should come first in our classrooms, not an emphasis on the hard lessons of winning and losing. Sarah sensed this when she made the running activity less competitive, and Zack responded by slowing down to let Suzzane catch up.

To Increase Your Knowledge

Seek out works by David Elkind and others, especially the following:

Elkind, D. (2001). *The hurried child: Growing up too fast too soon* (3rd ed.). Reading, MA: Addison-Wesley.

Gallagher, K. C., & Mayer, K. (2006). Teacher-child relationships at the forefront of effective practice. *Young Children, 61*(6), 44–49.

Quann, V., & Wien, C. A. (2006). The visible empathy of infants and toddlers. *Young Children, 61*(4), 22–29.

Steps You Can Take

1. Review your regular classroom practices. Identify those that reinforce children's perceptions of themselves as winners or losers. Brainstorm modifications you can make to build a more inclusive group spirit. Try your ideas and note changes in children's levels of satisfaction with that part of your program.

2. Work on your relationship with a child whose competitive behavior is causing problems for him or her and for the group. Reflect about possible sources of the child's competitiveness—personality factors? Prior experiences? Adult expectations? Use your relationship to help the child find meaning in noncompetitive, individual expression and in cooperative activities with other children.

Column References

Elkind, D. (1987). *Miseducation: Preschoolers at risk*. New York: Knopf.

Elkind, D. (2001). *The hurried child: Growing up too fast too soon* (3rd ed.). Reading, MA: Addison-Wesley.

Elkind, D. (2005). Viewpoint. Early childhood amnesia: Reaffirming children's need for developmentally appropriate programs. *Young Children, 60*(4), 38–40.

Erikson, E. H. (1963). Childhood and society (2nd ed.). New York: Norton.

Hyson, M. (2004). *The emotional development of young children: Building an emotion-centered curriculum*. New York: Teachers College Press.

Piaget, J. (1932/1960). *The moral judgment of the child*. Glencoe, IL: The Free Press.

For additional information on using the guidance approach in the encouraging classroom, visit our website at www.cengage.com/education/gartrell.

Chapter  **3** *Mistaken Behavior: Understanding Conflicts, Aggression, and Challenging Behavior*

Guiding Questions

▸ *What is inappropriate about the term misbehavior?*

▸ *What is the concept of mistaken behavior?*

▸ *What are relational patterns?*

▸ *What are the three levels of mistaken behavior?*

▸ *What are considerations in understanding mistaken behavior, aggression, and challenging behavior in young children?*

▸ *How does the teacher communicate with parents about mistaken behavior?*

© Cengage Learning

Key Concepts

▸ *Aggression*

▸ *Challenging behavior*

▸ *Compliment Sandwich*

▸ *Comprehensive guidance*

▸ *Conflict*

▸ *Experimentation (Level One) mistaken behavior*

▸ *Guidance talk*

▸ *Intentional mistaken behavior*

▸ *Intentionality*

▸ *Mistaken behavior*

▸ *Relational patterns*

▸ *Socially influenced (Level Two) mistaken behavior*

▸ *Strong unmet needs (Level Three) mistaken behavior*

▸ *Superhero syndrome*

Beyond Misbehavior

As educators shift the paradigm from traditional discipline to guidance, they need to reevaluate their use of terms related to discipline, such as *misbehavior*. As commonly used,

> *Misbehavior implies willful wrongdoing for which a child must be "disciplined" (punished). The term invites moral labeling of the child. After all, what kind of children misbehave? Children who are "naughty," "rowdy," "mean," "willful," or "not nice." Although teachers who punish misbehavior believe they are "shaming children into being good," the result may be the opposite. Because of limited development and experience, children tend to internalize negative labels, see themselves as they are labeled, and react accordingly. (Gartrell, 2004, p. 8)*

When a child has difficulties in a classroom, the teacher who uses guidance has more important tasks than to criticize (and perhaps reinforce) children's supposed character flaws. For one thing, the teacher needs to consider the reasons for the behavior—a basic guidance technique. Was the behavior a result of a mismatch of the child and the curriculum, just a "bad day" for the child, or serious trouble in the child's life? Equally important, the teacher needs to decide how she can intervene to teach the child a more acceptable way to solve the

© Cengage Learning

How to share materials, as these kindergarten children are discovering, takes time to learn.

problem. By fixating on the child's *misbehavior*, the teacher may have difficulty in carrying out these important guidance tasks.

Teachers use guidance work to free themselves of value judgments about the child. They do not view children as sometimes "good" and sometimes "bad," or being on balance "good children" or "bad children" (Greenberg, 1988). From the guidance perspective, teachers take a more positive view of human nature. They accept the findings of the developmental and brain psychologists of the last 70 years. They recognize the yet untold possibilities of optimum brain development for human development (Goleman, 2006; LeDoux, 1996). These teachers understand that only with the assistance of caring adults can children learn and grow in healthy ways (Watson, 2003). When life circumstances permit them physical and psychological health, children are able to find personal meaning in everyday experiences, develop positive self-concepts, and grow toward social responsiveness (Corso, 2003).

Yet, at the same time, conflicts about property, territory, and privilege are so common in early childhood classrooms. If it is not "misbehavior," what explains the conflicts that young children so frequently experience? Young children have *conflicts*—differing points of view that clash—because they have not yet learned to solve problems in ways that avoid the conflicts. Effective social problem solving is complicated, and takes most of us into adulthood to master. To put young children's ages into perspective, remember that even "big" six-year-olds have lived only about one-fifteenth of the modern average life span. Three-year-olds have only 36 months of life experience. Four-year-olds have been around for fewer than 60 months.

If we think of children as being just months old, we realize that they are only beginning to develop their intrapersonal and interpersonal intelligences. They have just begun the lifelong process of using democratic life skills. As they learn how to solve social problems, all children make *mistakes*. In the guidance approach, this understanding is all-important. Guidance requires teachers to look at the conflicts that children have not as misbehavior, but as mistaken behavior.

As in traditional discipline, *in a guidance approach there are consequences for when a child engages in mistaken behavior.* But, the consequences are different—for the adult as well as the child. The consequence for the adult is to teach the child socially productive responses in conflict situations. The consequence for the child is the need to learn those more productive responses. As Ginott wrote in *Teacher and Child* (1972), firmness without harshness is essential in guidance. The adult who intervenes in the face of mistaken behavior often must be firm, but is firm and friendly, not firm and harsh; the goal is to help children learn positive social skills from their mistakes.

This chapter provides a psychological basis for the guidance approach by developing the concept of mistaken behavior. It explains levels of social relations from which three levels of mistaken behavior can be understood. Teacher responses to each level of mistaken behavior—basic guidance techniques—are introduced.

The chapter also examines "hot button" issues relating to mistaken behavior. The chapter discusses:

▶ *intentionality*—the fact that mistaken behavior can be deliberate, "done on purpose."

▶ *aggression as mistaken behavior*—the idea that even this most vexing classroom problem is not "misbehavior."

▶ *challenging behavior*—the thought that mistaken behavior can add to teachers' understanding about behaviors they often find challenging.

The Concept of Mistaken Behavior

In learning new skills of any kind, children make mistakes. Under the right circumstances, errors in the cognitive domain are accepted as part of the learning experience. Correction, when given, is responsive to the child's development and experience. It is offered in the form of helpful expansion or direction, and certainly is not intended as criticism of the child's character. For example, a three-year-old child says, "Teacher, me gots itchy feets." The teacher is likely to show acceptance of the child's comments, gently model the conventional language in her response, and offer to help: "You have itchy feet? Are your socks making your feet itch? How about if we take a look?"

Perhaps because of higher emotional stakes, many adults have difficulty reacting in a similar way to children's mistakes in behavior. Missing the opportunity to teach a constructive behavioral lesson, a teacher may resort to punishment. This adult sees discipline as "teaching the child a lesson." But for the child the "lesson" is likely to be humiliation and not much else. That a different, more constructive response could be used may not occur to the teacher, unless she becomes aware of the possibility (Watson, 2003).

Classroom Anecdote	*Inez and Hector were quarreling over who would use a car on the block road they had built. Grabbing and pushing began. The teacher went to the children and declared: "You children don't know how to share the car properly, so I will put it away." As the teacher walked off with the car, Inez sat down at a table and looked sad. Hector frowned at the teacher's back, made a fist, and stuck one finger in the air. It was his index finger, but he still (graphically) expressed his anger.*

The teacher in this case was punishing the children for "misbehavior," not guiding them to learn from their mistaken behavior. As suggested by their reactions, the likely emotional message for the children was that they are incapable of playing together, solving their problems, using school materials, and meeting the teacher's expectations. Because young children are still early in the process of self-concept development, the teacher needs to avoid consequences that result in perceptions of unworthiness (Watson, 2003).

In contrast, the adult might have used guidance in this situation, specifically conflict management. Depending on the children, the teacher might use active mediation: holding the car, calming the children, coaching them to agree about the problem, and assisting them to come up with a solution. Or, the adult might have calmed the children and encouraged them to work out the problem themselves: "Look, you both want to use the same car. This is a problem. How can you solve the problem so you can get along?" (The adult then observes, ready to use active mediation if the children need assistance.)

Teachers can reduce classroom conflicts with planning and responsive teaching (like having more than one popular car available). But, adults need to recognize that when a large number of small bodies are in a fixed space for long periods, conflicts are going to happen. Conflict management is a vital guidance technique—whether the situation calls for active mediation or low-key encouragement. Conflict management teaches children that conflicts are not a source of shame, but experiences from which important life lessons need to be learned. (See more on conflict management in Chapter Nine.) Guidance means teaching children how to solve their problems rather than punishing children for having problems they cannot solve.

In candid moments teachers recognize that when conflicts occur, they sometimes hold children to standards that they themselves do not always meet. Take the matter of "losing one's temper," a not unknown emotional state to most adults.

Classroom Anecdote	*For a special first-grade cooking activity, the teacher planned to have two assistants and a parent come in, so the children could work in small groups. The principal reassigned assistants at the last minute, and the parent failed to make it. The teacher did the best she could with the whole class and later improvised when the music specialist went home with the flu. In an after-school meeting with the other first-grade staff, the teacher's proposal for more journaling and fewer worksheets was rejected. On the way home for a quick supper before an evening of parent conferences, the teacher got a speeding ticket. When she got home expecting supper to be ready, she discovered that her husband and children had forgotten to fix it. The teacher did not say, "That's OK, dear family; I'm sure you had a hard day too." (What would you say?)*

Developing the ability to manage and appropriately express strong emotions is a high-level skill. Perhaps the one skill that is more difficult is guiding children to learn it. Adults frequently operate from the misconception that children know how to behave and that their behavior is the result of a willful decision to do "wrong." In truth, the decision to act out or defy is made because the child does not yet have the cognitive and emotional resources necessary for more appropriate responses. Children gain these resources as they develop over time through modeling and teaching by caring adults (Corso, 2003).

Relational Patterns: A Model for Social-Emotional Development in the Classroom

Building from the work of the developmental and self psychologists, Steven D. Harlow (1975) has contributed a model for understanding children's social-emotional development in the classroom. Harlow's concept involves three levels of relational patterns: survival, adjustment, and encountering. Although he directed his study to special education, Harlow actually provided a perspective about social development that pertains to all learners. Harlow's concept is helpful in that it also provides a model for understanding mistaken behavior. Below selections from his monograph are presented:

As a way of viewing children's functioning in the classroom setting, it might be helpful to examine general relational patterns that individual children disclose. By relational patterns, I mean ways in which children relate to situations, persons and things in the school environment. The patterns I would like to examine are: surviving, adjusting, encountering, all of which differ in their openness to experience, maturity, and their capacity to operate freely.

The most immature and the least open of the relational patterns is that of survival. A child operating at the survival level is concerned with merely getting through time and space without disturbing his established ways of satisfying needs. For whatever reason—perhaps he has learned that his environment is a dangerous and painful place, and cannot by his efforts be mastered—the child wishes to keep things constant and reduce the amount of change in his world. Accordingly, his behavior is extremely stereotyped and rigid. When confronted by a new situation, he will ignore its special demands and treat it as if it were no different than previous situations.

The second relational pattern is that of adjustment. At this level, the child is less preoccupied with predictability and is far more open to others than was true of the survivor. The adjustor's concern is that of learning what is expected of him by others and then producing corresponding behavior. His sensitivity to a reference group's norms and expectations is characteristic of David Riesman's other-directed individual. His reinforcements and rewards come from the response of others to his behavior. . . . New ways of thinking and behaving are first sanctioned by an individual or reference group representing authority, before they are considered by the adjustor. . . .

The relational pattern of greatest maturity (and it should be added that maturity has little to do with chronological age) is that of the encounterer. Many educators and psychologists (among them Jean Piaget, Eric Erikson, and John Holt) have described the individual functioning at this level. In contrast with the adjustor and survivor, the encounterer is less concerned with security and certainty and much more occupied with what Erikson referred to as the inner mechanism that permits

The adult accepts children as worthwhile individuals who, like all of us, sometimes make mistakes.

the individual "to turn passive into active" and to maintain and regain in this world of contending forces an individual sense of centrality, of wholeness, and of initiative. (pp. 27–28)

In regard to the teacher's understanding of relational patterns, Harlow is clear that the teacher should not label children by the patterns they show. Instead, the teacher should consider how to assist children to progress to a more mature relational pattern. Harlow (1975) states:

The purpose of the paradigm is to help describe and understand a child's functioning in order to encourage him to a higher level of functioning. Rather than a label that indicates to school personnel a condition of some endurance, the typology describes functioning that is amenable to change. (p. 28)

Children at each relational level pose challenges and opportunities for teachers. The child at the *survivor level* is difficult for teachers to accept because of the nonsocial, at times antisocial, characteristics of the child's behavior. (Children at the survivor level show the most challenging behaviors.) Yet, the trust made possible by a positive adult–child relationship empowers the child to progress to a higher relational pattern (Harlow, 1975).

© Cengage Learning

Children who learn in ways that are creative and interactive learn best.

© Cengage Learning

Children at the *adjustor level* also can be challenging. Daily, teachers must respond to children, who fearing criticism, show anxiety over the completion of activities. Some children put off starting tasks or don't start at all. Others ask the teacher or a friend to do it for them—or copy. Even when they have finished, many young children show taxing persistence in pursuing the blessings of the teacher. As the following anecdote shows, teachers of young children must work hard to encourage progress from the adjustor pattern of relations.

Classroom Anecdote	*After much encouragement by her kindergarten teacher, Emily completes a creative "family day" invitation card.*

> *Emily: Did I do it good?*
> *Teacher: You worked hard, and your mother will love it.*
> *Emily: But did I do it good?*
> *Teacher: What's important is that you like it.*
> *Emily: But is it good?*
> *Teacher: Emily, I like whatever you make, just because you are you.*
> *Emily (Smiles): Now, I'm gonna do one for my sister.*

Some teachers are notorious for preferring the obedience of children at the adjustor level to the independence of children at the *encountering level*. Yet, Harlow's (1975) concept indicates that children at the encountering level are learning most effectively about themselves and the world. As psychologists ranging from Piaget (1932/1960) and Maslow (1962) to Gardner (1999) and DeVries and Zan (2003) have written, children need to interact and problem solve freely for healthy development to occur. The challenge to the teacher is to maintain harmony in the classroom at the same time that she encourages children to approach and enter the encountering level of social relations.

At any relational level, the cause of mistaken behavior in the young child is insufficient understanding about how to act maturely in the complex situations of life. With the internal need to go forward and to learn, but with limited ability to balance one's own needs with those of others, conflicts and mistaken behavior will occur. Harlow's model fits well with our current understanding of brain development. Children learn best when they can think for themselves and their minds are not beset by anxieties. They learn to function with autonomy (thinking intelligently and ethically) when they are guided and not punished for the mistakes in behavior that they make. Using Harlow's relational patterns, three levels of mistaken behavior can be seen. Knowledge of the three levels assists the teacher in understanding and working with children when classroom conflicts happen.

Three Levels of Mistaken Behavior

Mistaken behavior results from attempts by inexperienced, developmentally young children to interact within a complicated, increasingly impersonal world. When mistaken behavior occurs, adults significantly affect what children learn from the experience. Guidance responses encourage children to keep trying and learning. Guidance empowers encountering level social relations. On the other hand, punitive reactions coerce children to adopt defensive behaviors, usually in compliance with the teacher's expectations.

Continued or severe punishment even leads to unmet emotional needs and to survival level relational patterns: children who retreat from situations, show aggression, or display chronic (longtime) anxiety (Kaiser & Sklar-Rasminsky, 2003). Significant in Harlow's view, the interactions of the adult and child together determine the path of the child's behavior in the educational setting, not the child's behavior alone.

Over many years of observing young children in classrooms, the present author has noted patterns of conflict in children's behavior that parallel the levels of social relations explored by Harlow. By extending Harlow's concept, a model for understanding and addressing mistaken behavior emerges, one that treats mistaken behavior as occurring at three different levels (Gartrell, 2004):

Level One: Experimentation mistaken behavior

Level Two: Socially influenced mistaken behavior

Level Three: Strong unmet needs mistaken behavior

Common Sources of Motivation

The relationship of Harlow's relational patterns and the levels of mistaken behavior is close. The motivational sources of each are the same. At the level of encountering and experimentation mistaken behavior, the motivation is curiosity or involvement. At the level of adjusting and socially influenced mistaken behavior, the motivation is the desire to please and emulate others. At the level of the survival and strong needs mistaken behavior, the motive is unmet basic needs. When a child at any of the three relational patterns acts in a way that is disruptive to the group or harmful to self or others, the child is showing mistaken behavior at that level. In other words, mistaken behavior is an expression of the child's particular level of relational pattern in a conflict situation. The common sources of motivation between the relational patterns and levels of mistaken behavior are indicated in Table 3-1.

Harlow constructed the relational patterns around the relative mental health of the child. The same is true for the levels of mistaken behavior. The three levels of mistaken behavior indicate the degree that autonomy motivates a child's actions versus heteronomy (dependency on others for moral direction) and stress due to unmet needs. In general, the conflicts of children at Level One are not as violent, and certainly not as persistent, as the mistaken behaviors of children at Level Three. At Level Two, socially influenced mistaken behavior, young children show a lack of concern for others' feelings, but again their behaviors will not tend to show the emotional extreme of hostility.

In the chapters to follow, the levels of mistaken behavior serve as a reference for understanding children's motivations and needs when they experience conflicts. The present chapter now examines each of the three levels of mistaken behavior—and updates the construct in relation to the hot-button issues of aggression and challenging behavior.

Table 3-1 *Common Sources of Motivation: Relational Patterns and Levels of Mistaken Behavior*

Motivational Source	Relational Pattern	Level of Mistaken Behavior
Desire to explore the environment and engage in relationships and activities	Encounterer	One: Experimentation
Desire to please and identify with significant others	Adjustor	Two: Socially influenced
Inability to cope with problems resulting from health conditions and life experiences	Survivor	Three: Strong needs

Level One: Experimentation Mistaken Behavior

Level One is experimentation mistaken behavior. Level One mistaken behavior corresponds to Harlow's level one social relation of encountering. As children begin to master the social expectations of the classroom, the continuous process of making decisions results in mistaken behavior. In early childhood classrooms, children naturally do things to see what will happen, or because they are totally involved in a situation. For reasons of curiosity and involvement, all children who are responding at Harlow's encountering relational level occasionally show experimentation mistaken behavior.

Experimentation level mistaken behavior occurs, then, when the child reacts to one of two motives:

▶ *involvement*—the child unintentionally causes a conflict when a situation unexpectedly gets out of hand.

▶ *curiosity*—the child intentionally causes a conflict to see what will happen.

In a previous anecdote Hector and Inez argued about a car; this incident illustrates experimentation mistaken behavior, as a result of their total *involvement* in the situation. Another example is shown in the following:

Classroom Anecdote	*(Level One mistaken behavior as a result of involvement in a situation.)* At lunch in a Head Start classroom, three-year-old Rodney said to the teacher, "Gimme the bread." With a serious look, the teacher responded, "What are the magic words, Rodney?" Not hesitating for a moment, Rodney raised his arms, spread his fingers, and chanted, "Abra-cadabra!" Smiling about the response, the teacher passed the bread. She commented, "Those are great magic words, Rodney, but the magic words for the table are 'please' and 'thank you,' okay?" Rodney nodded, took the bread and said, "Thank you, please."

Sometimes there is an element of charm in mistaken behavior at this level. The novelty of children's responses in everyday situations is an elixir of great worth to many an early childhood teacher. The ability to understand that the child is trying to learn through experimental mistaken behavior is the hallmark of the guidance approach. A sense of humor and the avoidance of overreaction are useful guidance techniques.

The following example illustrates experimentation mistaken behavior, done with *the intentionality of a curious child*:

Classroom Anecdote	*(Level One mistaken behavior as a result of curiosity about limits.)*
	A teacher passed by a child in the back of the room apparently talking to herself. Karen was whispering, "Ship, shick, shit." She stopped at the last word and grinned. Karen then approached the teacher and said with the same grin, "Shit, Teacher."
	Realizing the child had been involved in a phonetic word recognition activity, he kneeled down, hid a smile, and responded, "I like how you are always learning new words at Head Start, Karen. Some words bother people though, and this is one of them. You keep using new words, but not that one, okay?" He looked her in the eye, and she complained a bit, but nodded. He did not hear Karen use that word again.

Some mistaken behaviors, such as the use of unacceptable words, happen at any of the three levels. The context, frequency, and intensity of this mistaken behavior identify the level for the teacher. "Swearing" provides a useful illustration of this crossover pattern, in this case Level One mistaken behavior. In the anecdote, no moral issue was made, and the child was not punished for showing curiosity about the limits of acceptability in the classroom. Instead, the teacher reinforced the limits in a matter-of-fact way without putting down Karen's efforts at vocabulary development.

Had the teacher made this more of an issue, the word's power would have been reinforced, and Karen might have used it in a situation involving Level Two or even Level Three mistaken behavior. This possibility was reduced by the teacher's respectful but firm response. In line with the guidance approach, the teacher lct Karen know that her status as a member of the group was not in question (Watson, 2003), even while he addressed Karen's experimentation level mistaken behavior.

Level Two: Socially Influenced Mistaken Behavior

Corresponding to adjustor social relations is Level Two mistaken behavior, **socially influenced mistaken behavior**. Socially influenced mistaken behavior happens when children are reinforced in an action, sometimes unintentionally, by others important to them. Examples include a child's repeating an expletive (swearword) just as someone at home might use it, being persuaded by classmates to call another child a name, or being influenced by others to join in aggressive play. A significant adult can cause Level Two mistaken behavior by unintentionally reinforcing a Level One mistaken behavior. An example would be if the teacher in the preceding anecdote had overreacted and reinforced the payoff of the swearword, rather than dampened it, in Karen's mind.

Level Two mistaken behavior is learned behavior. Typical sources of social influence that can result in Level Two mistaken behavior include:

▶ parents or other adult family members

▶ siblings or other relatives

▶ friends and neighbors

▶ other children in the center or school

A sense of humor and the ability to avoid overreaction are useful guidance techniques during displays of innocent mischief.

© Cengage Learning

- the teacher or caregiver
- other adults in the center or school
- media "superheroes" from television movies or computer games.

Classroom Anecdote	*(Level Two mistaken behavior as a result of family influence)* *Every so often Jeremy's dad got quite upset at home, especially when his handyman efforts went wrong. When dad got upset, he swore. In kindergarten, when Jeremy spilled too much glue on his paper one day, he used an expression quite familiar to him, "Damn it to hell!"* *The teacher heard the comment and saw what happened. She quietly told Jeremy that she didn't blame him for getting upset. She added that next time, he could use other words that don't bother people at school like "I'm upset" or "I spilled my glue," and she would come to him with help.*

Reality suggests that on occasion many adults use language not dissimilar to Jeremy's dad. By saying that Jeremy needs to learn words that do not bother people at school, the teacher avoided judging Jeremy's home life and perhaps putting Jeremy (and possibly his dad) in an awkward position. Instead, the teacher focused on understanding Jeremy's frustration, even if his words were inappropriate, and on teaching Jeremy alternative words to use.

If the teacher had resorted to punishment, by removing him from the group or flipping a card from green to yellow, she would have made a simple problem into something possibly more lasting and serious. Of course, additional intervention is needed if Jeremy continued to use unacceptable language. The guidance teacher is consistently friendly even if the situation dictates that she needs to be consistently firm.

The difference in teacher response to Level One and Level Two mistaken behavior is often the degree of firmness. At the experimentation level, children are in the process of learning new behaviors. Teachers need to appreciate the tentative nature of this situation and not overreact. At the socially influenced level, teachers need to recognize that learning has already occurred and that the course of the learning needs to be changed. Children, like all of us, are more able to change if they know they are accepted, their efforts are appreciated, and there are positive expectations about their capacity to learn.

Sometimes, teaching to alter socially influenced mistaken behavior consists of reminders about limits and requests for alternate responses—as happened with Jeremy. Other times, the teacher works at consciousness raising to help children become more sensitive to a child or situation. The following anecdote involves children in a prekindergarten classroom. Notice the use of a class meeting, which is the guidance intervention of choice when mistaken behavior has become public in nature, that is, involves many in the group. (Chapter Seven features a section on class meetings.)

Classroom Anecdote	*(Level Two mistaken behavior as a result of peer influence)*
	Charlie had just progressed from crutches to a new leg brace. Several children noticed that the brace squeaked. By the end of the day, they were laughing among themselves about "Squeaky Leg, Charlie."
	The next day the teacher talked with Charlie and at a class meeting announced that he had something to show everyone. With a grin, Charlie pulled up his pant leg and announced, "Look, guys, I got a new leg brace. It squeaks some, but it works pretty good." With that he invited the children to come over and look at the brace close-up. He flexed his leg for them and made the brace squeak. The teacher then explained about Charlie's leg brace and how well he could walk with it. The children were impressed; the name-calling stopped.
	The following day the teacher was absent. When she returned, the substitute called and reported, "I must tell you what happened yesterday. Just as I walked in the door, three children came up to me and said that Charlie has a new leg brace. They said it squeaks, but he gets around on it "really good."

With friendliness and a smile, the teacher can still respond firmly to a mistaken behavior.

The teacher here used a class meeting to raise children's sensitivity to a classmate and to defuse a definite instance of socially influenced mistaken behavior. Note that the guidance was aimed at the class as a whole—a necessity when socially influenced mistaken behavior "goes public." The positive outcome of the class meeting speaks for itself.

Superheroes and Socially Influenced Mistaken Behavior. One of the ironies of modern life is that children can be influenced to Level Two mistaken behavior not just by people, but also by media figures who are not even real! The superhero syndrome is well known in early childhood classrooms. Children actively identify with a current, popular media character and become overly aggressive in their play.

The superhero syndrome is not new—many generations of superheroes have entered and left the scene—the Incredible Hulk many times! In the author's childhood, a popular superhero was the Lone Ranger—on the radio! For younger adults some action figures of choice were Superman, Wonder Woman, and the Ninja Turtles. The Power Rangers, Bat Man, Spider Man, and World Wrestling Federation (WWF) professional wrestlers have had quite a long run. Current figures include the X-men, vampires, Transformers, and assorted computer game characters. (Thanks to Grandson Thomas for the update.) The following anecdote from a few years ago, submitted male student teacher, illustrates superhero-inspired mistaken behavior involving four boys. The "superheroes" are professional wrestlers "from the WWF".

Classroom Anecdote	*The older preschoolers were outside on a summer day. I was with some children in the sandbox when I heard Vernon yelling. I went around the corner to where he was. Darnell was sitting on Vernon, Rydell was trying to pull Vernon up, and Voshon was trying to pull Rydell down! Vernon was still yelling, and since Darnell was rather large, I didn't blame him.*
	I got the four separated and had them sit down, take deep breaths, and we talked.
	Me: What was happening over here? I heard somebody yelling.
	Darnell: We was playing wrestlers and Voshon and me was Earthquake and Hurricane. Rydell was Hulk Hogan and Vernon was Jesse the Body (smile)!
	Vernon: But I was not 'cause I didn't want to be no wrestler.
	Rydell: But you gotta be 'cause Hulk needs a partner!
	Me: Okay, I've got it. You three were doing team wrestling and you wanted Vernon to be Rydell's partner, right?
	Darnell: Yeah, but Vernon wouldn't wrestle.
	Me: Well, we have a problem, because of the "No wrestling with other people rule." (They knew the rule, this was why they were around the corner.) Okay, how's this? You either find something else to do that isn't wrestling, or you be one tag team and fight the invisible Phantom Wrestlers, but I don't know because they're kind of tough.
	Darnell: (Speaking as usual for the rest). Yeah, and you could too, Vernon. (I left with all four wrestling the invisible wrestlers. It was hard to say who was winning!)
	(continued)

Classroom Anecdote	*Student teacher reflection: It seems like mainly boys have to get physical in their play. You can tell them no guns, but then they'll use blocks or Lincoln logs. They're going to do it anyway, so I guess you have to figure out how they can so nobody gets dragged in or hurt. The teacher liked how I handled this. Before long the four became firefighters fighting the fire in the skyscraper (the climbing gym) (Gartrell, 2000, pp. 98–99).*

James, the student teacher in the anecdote, used informal mediation to re-inforce a previous class meeting held to resolve a media-influenced wrestling problem. To his credit James did not "discipline" the boys, but guided them to redirect their high-energy play in a less aggressive activity. In the article "Boys Will Be Boys," Kantrowitz and Kalb (1998) make the point that boys especially are susceptible to the influence of fictional superheroes and have a definite physiological need for active physical play. Levin (2003) suggests moving children beyond the narrow focus on aggressive themes in their active play, which James did here. Key in the management of active play is to minimize the aggressiveness while maximizing the "active" in the play (Levin, 2003; Gartrell & Sonsteng, 2008).

Level Three: Strong Unmet Needs Mistaken Behavior

Mistaken behavior at Level Three, strong unmet needs mistaken behavior, is close in concept to the social relations pattern of the *survivor*. Children show Level Three mistaken behavior as a reaction to difficulty and pain in their lives that is beyond their capacity to cope with. Serious mistaken behavior happens because a child is reacting to strong unmet needs, acting out against a perceived hostile and uncaring world. Level Three mistaken behavior is the most serious. Ironically, often children show Level Three mistaken behavior in the classroom because it is the safest place in their lives.

Several researchers and educators—Stone (1973), Warren (1977), Honig (1986), Erickson and Pianta (1989), Slaby et al. (1995), and Kaiser and Sklar-Rasminsky (2003)—all make the fundamental point that serious mistaken behavior is due to trouble in children's lives. At Level One, a child might experiment with a swearword to see what the reaction will be. A child at Level Two will use an expletive learned from others to express a spontaneous feeling (which passes quickly unless a teacher overreacts). At Level Three, reacting to strong unmet needs, a child might let loose a string of expletives over a simple frustration, having completely lost control. The primary signs of the strong needs level are repeated conflicts that have a definite emotional undercurrent—extreme behaviors that continue over time.

On occasion, any child (or adult) experiences a Level Three day. Anxiety, irritability, frustration, inattentiveness, hostility, withdrawal, and fatigue are common Level Three behaviors. Any of these can result from a short-term upset to an individual's physical or emotional health. With young children, Level One situations occasionally generate very strong reactions—children feel intensely about things.

The teacher needs to watch how quickly the child recovers from the upset and whether such episodes are infrequent or common. When serious mistaken behavior is repeated and continues for more than a day or two, the teacher should be alert to the possibility that basic needs of the child are not being met.

Two sources of strong unmet needs mistaken behavior operate independently or together. These sources are *physical discomfort*, due to untreated physiological conditions (health-related problems), and *emotional discomfort*, due to neglect or abuse of a child's needs.

Physiological Factors and Level Three Behaviors. Increasingly, educators recognize the effects of physiological factors for Level Three mistaken behavior. Based on genetic traits, children show individual temperaments—consistent cognitive and emotional dispositions that cause them to have distinct reaction tendencies over time (Thomas & Birch, 1977). Children with temperaments that lean toward intensity of feelings, difficulty in managing impulses, high activity levels, and low trust levels experience many more conflicts than children with "easier" temperaments.

Some neurological conditions that put children at risk for classroom conflicts are well known: attention deficit disorder (ADD), attention deficit/hyperactivity disorder (ADHD), and autism spectrum disorders. Less obvious factors include language difficulties, information-processing disabilities, and motor development delays. These neurological impairments may be separate from or in addition to "extreme temperaments" that a child may be born with (Kaiser & Sklar-Rasminsky, 2003).

Significant other sources of physiological difficulties are due to early environmental factors. The following conditions, adapted from Kaiser and Sklar-Rasminisky (2003), have been shown to make children vulnerable for Level Three mistaken behavior:

- prenatal alcohol and drug exposure
- other complications during pregnancy such as parental malnutrition or depression
- premature delivery or difficult delivery
- malnutrition during infancy

Untreated chronic health problems—such as vision and hearing deficits, perceptual-motor difficulties, respiratory, and digestive problems—can also "distress children" into serious mistaken behavior. Acute health conditions—ear infections and other untreated diseases—dramatically affect how a child feels and acts. Teachers also have become more cognizant of possible neglect- and abuse-related conditions: hunger, hygiene problems, lack of sleep, unexplained injuries, and posttraumatic stress reactions.

Significantly, none of these conditions in and of itself "destines" a child to a continuing pattern of conflicts (Kaiser & Sklar-Rasminsky, 2003). But these conditions—some of which are caused or aggravated by overwhelmed parenting—do put children at risk. Unless parents are able to build positive attachments, and through effective parenting guide them to overcome— or obtain medical assistance to treat—their behavioral vulnerabilities, these children are at greater risk for a long-term cycle of conflict and consequences in school and life (Kaiser & Sklar-Rasminsky, 2003). This is why programs like Head Start, which provides comprehensive services to the family as well as the child, and early childhood special education are such important social (as well as educational) investments.

All these conditions, with physical etiologies and emotional ramifications, affect the behavior of children at school. A review process in which mistaken behaviors are evaluated for possible health-related causes is important.

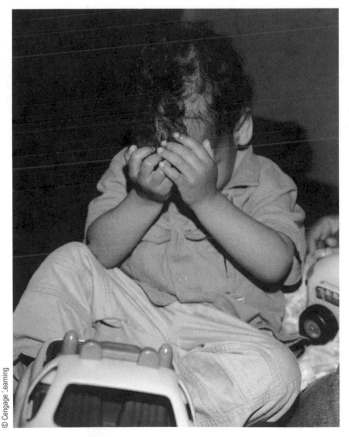

© Cengage Learning

Stress and frustration are a part of life, even for young children.

The process may be as informal as observing and asking the child a few questions, or as formal as a meeting that involves the parents, an assessment, and a resulting plan that might involve referral.

Emotional Factors and Level Three Behaviors. In the classic little book, *What About Discipline?* (1973), Jeanette Stone discussed the connection between mistaken behavior and trouble in the children's life:

> *People who persist in thinking of childhood as a time of happy innocence are fooling themselves. Every child's life includes some stress and frustration and it comes out in the child's behavior. Young children are not good at covering up their feelings or at expressing them in words.*

> *While most of these troubles fall under the category of normal stress, there are children whose lives are marked by deep unhappiness. Some children have to endure violence against themselves or other family members or the disruptive effects of drug dependency or mental illness by a family member. Children feel helpless at such times, as they do in the face of divorce, illness, and death.*

> *When people are going through trouble in their personal lives, most show it in other parts of their lives. Adults may be unable to concentrate, for example. They may brood about their problems and not see or hear what is going on around them. They may try to deny their feelings but then get into arguments or fights because they are angry or worried. It is the same with children. (pp. 8–11)*

Stone complements Harlow's discussion of the survival relational pattern. Harlow's (1975) words help the teacher to understand dynamics behind serious mistaken behavior in the classroom:

> *When problems arise, the survivor unsuccessfully attempts to meet them with generally inappropriate behavior. He may, for example, be prone to lash out destructively or withdraw completely when a problem presents itself. To the observer, it would appear that such behavior is self-defeating—and it is—but it serves the function of preventing the child from involving himself and opening himself to something in his environment that may prove overwhelming. Here, after all, is a child with little confidence in his ability to alter matters by direct action. (p. 34)*

Responding to Level Three Mistaken Behavior. When a child shows behavior that is disruptive or harmful, teachers need to enforce limits and preserve safety in the classroom. If mistaken behavior is serious, and especially if it continues over time, however, interventions alone are not enough to improve the situation (Watson, 2003). The "catch-22" with children behaving at Level Three is that although they need a helping relationship with a teacher the most, they are often the most difficult to work with and accept (Gartrell, 2004). A reminder from Watson (2003) applies here: The teacher must work to build a helping relationship with each child based on acceptance and respect.

Classroom Anecdote	*Building the relationship—which goes beyond the cliché, "catch them being good"—is essential if the teacher is to guide the child toward more productive patterns of behavior. In the effort the teacher works to understand reasons for the pattern of mistaken behavior. The common disclaimer, "He has a rough home life," serves only as the beginning point for learning about the actual circumstances affecting the child.*
	After five weeks of school, a second-grade teacher noted the following pattern in a child's behavior. During the middle of the week, Wendy showed an interest in activities and cooperated easily with fellow students and the teacher. By Friday, however, Wendy was less able to concentrate, avoided contacts with other students, and "lashed out" at the teacher. Usually, Wendy was not fully back into the swing of things until Tuesday of the following week, remaining aloof and "gloomy."
	The teacher contacted the mother, who disclosed that she and Wendy's father had separated. Until a divorce was finalized, Wendy was living with her mother during the week and with the father on weekends in a new location. Fortunately, in this case, the mother expressed confidence that the father was caring appropriately for Wendy. The teacher hypothesized that the separation and the transition from one home to the next were affecting her. The teacher encouraged each parent to help Wendy understand the situation and to assist her during the transitions. For the teacher's part, she became less judgmental about Wendy's behavior, did relationship building with her during noncrisis times, and actively communicated support for Wendy during times of greatest need. Over a few weeks, Wendy began to adjust, and she became less stressed and more responsive at the beginning and end of the week. Her mistaken behavior decreased.

As illustrated in the anecdote, the teacher seeks to understand what is going on with the child. Full understanding may not happen, but new information almost always is attainable and can help in building relations. Efforts to increase understanding should include discussions with parents, other staff, and the child. Discarding the myth that the professional teacher works alone, she needs to communicate with other personnel (that is, through teaming arrangements, staffings, and cross-agency collaborations). The more serious the mistaken behavior, the more the teacher may need to work with others to bring about a positive resolution.

Strong needs mistaken behavior that continues then requires **comprehensive guidance**, a strategy that involves a clear but flexible plan. The plan should include components for: (a) getting more information, (b) building a helping relationship with the child, (c) making the environment more manageable for the child, (d) intervening in nonpunitive ways, and (e) teaching the child acceptable behavioral alternatives. (Chapter 11 discusses comprehensive guidance more fully.)

In assisting Wendy to resolve issues causing her Level Three mistaken behavior, the teacher informally used a comprehensive guidance strategy. In fact, comprehensive guidance is often used informally, but generally has the components listed previously. Table 3-2 is a summary of how the plan was used with Wendy.

Table 3-2 *Using Comprehensive Guidance to Assist Wendy*	
a. Obtain more information.	Teacher observed carefully; contacted parents.
b. Build a relationship with child.	Teacher became more understanding of Wendy; spent quality time with her outside of conflict situations.
c. Improve environment for the child.	Parents and teachers helped child understand situation.
d. Intervene in nonpunitive ways.	Teacher actively supported and guided child during transition days.
e. Teach child alternatives.	Child was able to learn alternatives as her stress levels decreased.

When the plan is working, in Harlow's (1975) words:

What occurs then, over time, is that the survivor's need for predetermined constancy is replaced by a new network of dependable relationships, which are based upon his successful actions on, or mastery of, at least a portion of the classroom environment.... As the child begins to sense his powers of mastery, a new self-regard emerges. This self-regard enables the child to open himself to endeavors that before would have proven to be defeating. (p. 34)

The discussion of Level Three mistaken behavior has been developed in some detail for a particular reason. Children at Level Three are the most challenging for teachers. Their situations are the most complex, and responses by the teacher need to be the most comprehensive (see Chapter Eleven).

Visual Summary: Three Levels of Mistaken Behavior

Each of the levels of mistaken behaviors have distinct motivational sources. Behaviors that appear similar on the surface can be a result of differing motivations, and so be at different levels. The teacher must observe carefully to understand the motivation and the level of mistaken behavior in order to respond effectively. Table 3-3 illustrates how sample mistaken behaviors can be at different levels.

In the guidance approach, the teacher responds to children not just on the basis of the behavior shown, but on a hypothesis about the meaning of the behavior for the child. This hypothesis-making is a high-level skill that takes practice and sensitivity. The discussion to follow assists the adult in interpreting and responding to mistaken behavior in ways that enforce limits and teach alternatives, yet respect children's self-esteem.

Table 3-3 *Sample Mistaken Behaviors by Level*

Incident of Mistaken Behavior	Motivational Source	Level of Mistaken Behavior
Child uses expletive.	Wants to see teacher's reaction.	One
	Emulates important others.	Two
	Expresses deeply felt hostility.	Three
Child takes ball from another child.	Wants ball; has not learned to ask in words.	One
	Follows aggrandizement practices modeled by other children.	Two
	Feels need to act out against world by asserting power.	Three
Child refuses to join in group activity.	Does not understand or like teacher's expectations.	One
	Has developed habit of not joining in.	Two
	Is not feeling well or feels high anxiety.	Three

Mistaken Behavior, Aggression, and Challenging Behavior

Three considerations are helpful in understanding the relationships between mistaken behavior, aggression, and challenging behavior in young children.

Consideration One: Mistaken Behavior Can Be on Purpose

Students may be tempted to associate mistaken behavior with "accidents" and misbehavior with acts "done on purpose." Mistaken behavior includes both accidents and intentional actions. Let's take the example of a preschooler on a trike who runs over the toe of another child.

If the incident is an accident, the child has shown *Level One* mistaken behavior. The accident was the result of loss of control or failure to look where one is going. The accident was unintentional, but it was Level One because it was a mistake in behavior that arose from involvement. The "experiment" of trike riding got out of control.

A child may run over another's foot for a second reason related to Level One: The trike rider hits the other's foot "accidentally on purpose" to see what will happen. The lack of development of young children means that they have difficulty understanding how another child would feel under such circumstances. The act was intentional, but was done without full awareness of the consequences and is Level One mistaken behavior. The importance of the term *mistaken behavior* is that it reminds the adult that the trike rider needs guidance about human feelings and the consequences of actions, not punishment for making a mistake in judgment.

Of course, hitting another child's foot might also be a Level Two or Three mistaken behavior. At *Level Two,* one child follows another on a trike. The second rider sees the first swing close to a bystander and follows suit, hitting the bystander's toe. At Level Three, a trike rider comes to school with feelings of hostility and acts out against an innocent child.

When the teacher hypothesizes that Level Two or Level Three is involved, she reacts with increasing degrees of firmness while retaining the element of friendliness, which is at the heart of guidance. If the situation indicates strong needs mistaken behavior, the teacher follows up as suggested in the section for *Level Three.* The follow-up is important because serious mistaken behavior is shown when children are victims of life circumstances that they cannot control. The acting out may have been intentional, but the impetus behind the behavior were the child's unrecognized unmet needs. The mistaken behavior was intentional, but at the same time was (an unintentional) request for assistance.

Guidance Interventions with Intentional Mistaken Behavior. Whatever the level of mistaken behavior, the teacher responds to the immediate situation by using guidance interventions. She first gives attention to the "victim." This action shows support for the child who needs it most immediately, lets the trike rider know the teacher is aware of what happened, and may help the teacher calm down. The teacher then decides whether to use conflict mediation with the children together or a **guidance talk** with the trike rider. This decision is based on the emotional state of each child and on the teacher's idea of who needs to learn what in the situation.

If she uses *conflict mediation*, the teacher follows the five-step procedure outlined in Chapter Nine:

1. Helps all parties cool down enough to talk.

2. Asks the children to each tell their side and works for agreement on what each thought happened.

3. Encourages the children to come up with possible solutions.

4. Guides the children to select and try a solution all can live with.

5. Facilitates and monitors the resolution process. Has a follow-up guidance talk with one or both children as she sees fit.

© Cengage Learning

With trust in the environment, the child succeeds at tasks that before would have been self-defeating

© Cengage Learning

Strengths of mediation in a situation like the trike incident are that it empowers the child who was "victimized," nonpunitively teaches limits to the trike rider, leads to an honest (as opposed to teacher-forced) reconciliation, and models for both children how to solve problems using words (Wichert, 1989).

If the teacher chooses to use a *guidance talk*, she builds empathy by asking the child his viewpoint of the situation, pointing out that the trike rider hurt the other child and that the teacher cannot let anyone, including the trike rider, be hurt at school. The teacher discusses with the trike rider how that child could avoid the problem next time. Although the teacher does not force an apology, she asks how the trike rider could help the child who was hurt feel better. The teacher then assists the trike rider to return to positive activity, which often includes helping the child to make amends (Gartrell, 2004). A strength of the guidance talk is that it shows that the teacher cares enough about the trike rider to believe the child can change and conveys this message to him.

Whether the teacher decides to use conflict management with the children or a guidance talk with one, she avoids the traditional discipline reaction. The teacher does not lecture about how naughty the behavior was and automatically put the trike rider in a time-out. The teacher may or may not request the child to give up the trike, depending on the outcome of the guidance exchange. The child does need to face a consequence, but a guidance consequence: learning a non-hurting alternative behavior. The teacher works as a guidance professional, trusting her judgment as she understands the situation, and teaching the child to act and react in non-hurting ways.

It takes time, practice, and learning about individual children to make guidance responses work consistently. (Remember, in early childhood education if things go exactly as you expect, something is wrong.) Building relationships with children is central to knowing how to respond. In the following anecdote, student teacher Belinda is still learning how to work with Andy, who intentionally spills his milk.

Classroom Anecdote	It was during my first week of student teaching. Andy was sitting at a table eating his snack and drinking his milk. I looked away for a minute and when I looked back at him, his cup was tipped just enough for the milk to spill out onto the floor. There was a puddle on the floor so he had spilled more than I first thought he did. He looked right at it, then at me, and turned away. When I asked him to help me wipe up the milk, he refused and walked away. Another teacher finally got him to help clean up the spill, but not willingly.
	It seemed to me that Andy spilled the milk on purpose. He knew it was spilling, yet he didn't try to stop it. It's not like him to not cooperate, but today he sure didn't. He didn't want to clean up after lunch either. I think he was having a bad day or just wanted some attention. I was surprised that he refused to help me clean up the spill. He's usually friendly to me. I guess I haven't spent enough time with the kids to really know them all yet or how they typically behave.

Andy spilled his milk on purpose, testing how the new student teacher would respond. Sometimes young children ask for relationships with adults in peculiar ways. They need to know if an adult is "safe," and this is how Andy chose to find out. The student teacher reported that as she got to know Andy better, he stopped testing her and began to ask for her attention in more appropriate ways. Andy's act was deliberate—intentional mistaken behavior—but it still was mistaken behavior. He made a mistake in judgment that could have resulted in a fairly serious conflict. Because the lead teacher intervened and guided Andy with firm, low-key direction, he learned the consequence of spilling the milk (cleaning up the spill), and the possibility of an improved relationship between he and Belinda was sustained. The consequence was guidance, not punishment.

A premise in the guidance approach is that even "willful acts" that are done "on purpose" still constitute mistaken behavior. A child who intentionally disobeys has made a mistake in judgment. The adult who is able to approach children as worthwhile individuals are beginners and make mistakes is in a philosophically strong position to guide them toward productive behavior and healthy development.

Consideration Two: Aggression Is Serious Mistaken Behavior

Citing the definition of aggression "as behavior that is aimed at harming or injuring others," Kaiser and Sklar-Rasminsky (2003) state: "Challenging behavior isn't always aggressive—sometimes it is disruptive or antisocial or annoying. But aggressive behavior is always challenging" (p. 13).

Two *forms* of aggression are often cited in relation to young children: (a) physical aggression, which is hitting, kicking, biting—that is, using violence to assert one's will physically upon another, and (b) psychological aggression, which includes teasing, threatening rejection, ignoring or otherwise excluding, bullying, spreading rumors—that is, using psychological oppression rather than physical hostility (Dodge, 1991).

Two *uses* of aggression are instrumental aggression, using aggression to gain a goal like taking a ball or lining up first in line, and reactive aggression, hostile reactions to frustration and the perceived transgressions of others (Dodge, 1991). Very young children often use direct, instrumental aggression to get what they want, ranging from biting to tantrums. The combination of strong wants and just emerging language abilities makes the mistaken behavior of toddlers and young preschoolers often challenging to work with. During the developmental process, as young children learn language skills most find less need to use instrumental aggression. A few children, however, learn that instrumental aggression can be effective in conflict situations. By school age, children who have not learned to replace instrumental aggression with negotiation begin to experience rejection by their peers (Dodge, 1991).

Table 3-4 *Aggression in Young Children*	
Forms	**Uses**
Physical Aggression	Physical violence used to assert one's will
Psychological Aggression	Verbal or nonverbal psychological oppression used to assert one's will
Instrumental Aggression	Physical or psychological aggression to gain a goal
Reactive Aggression	Physical or psychological aggression as a reaction to frustration and perceived threat

Children who show instrumental aggression usually have not lost control of emotions. In contrast, reactive aggression happens when children feel profound frustration or perceive, sometimes by mistake, a transgression by others. They lash out as an attempt to rid themselves of the source of the provocation. Even in the preschool years, children who use reactive aggression are "invariably disliked" (Kaiser & Sklar-Rasminsky, 2003). These children experience a psychological bind, as they have come to believe that aggression is a normal part of life, at the same time that they are rejected by peers for showing aggression. Without friendly but firm guidance, these children are likely to remain in the quandary of high levels of stress and anger—and consequent outcast status in the classroom.

Aggression and Levels of Mistaken Behavior. Aggression is a vexing problem for teachers. Intuitively, children's aggression seems like "flat-out misbehavior." In fact, the levels of mistaken behavior can increase teachers' understanding about this extreme form of classroom conflict. A teacher who knows about aggression will be more effective in assisting children to move away from it. Let us consider aggression "by the levels."

Aggression at Level One. Young children making clear progress with social and emotional skills (at the social relations level of encountering) are still really only months old (four years = 48 months). They may show fledgling leadership skills through instrumental aggression, especially psychological, to achieve their objectives in day-to-day classroom life. For example, an "old four" may "flout her authority" and coerce a desired toy from a three-year-old. If the younger child tries to take it back, the older child may strike out to protect what she now perceives as her property by using reactive aggression.

The teacher does not allow aggression in the classroom, even if it is "experimental." At the same time, she recognizes that young children are still at an "emerging" level of social-emotional competence. Through mediating conflicts, she works to increase the resources and skills in children to be able to use negotiation. As children learn the language of negotiation, they have less need to use aggression as a learned behavior.

Aggression at Level Two. At the socially influenced level, children have learned that using aggression can have strategic benefits. Note, though, that they typically have not been victimized themselves by aggression to the extent that they are using violence to act out against the world. Rather, a child may just be around peers or older children who use aggressive behaviors and be influenced to copy the behaviors. The child learns that behaviors such as bullying and ostracism have dramatic effects and be reinforced to use them. Like children at Level One, the child may lash out with direct reactive aggression if her plans go awry. (These kids also have not yet learned to handle frustrations with negotiation.) Teachers have to be careful about their responses to children who show aggression at Level Two. They do not want to further reinforce an already learned behavior with overreaction. Staying calm is important. With individual children, the teacher does well to keep these discussions private.

When aggression at Level Two is "catching on"—such as several children who use psychological aggression to ostracize another child—the teacher often holds class meetings. In the meetings, the teacher raises empathy levels about the effects of aggression, establishes that this behavior is not allowed, and involves children in discussion that is inclusive of all classmates. The class may come up with two or three posted guidelines (positively stated rules) to guide in nonaggressive conflict management—example: "If we can't solve it ourselves, we get help."

<u>Aggression</u> at <u>Level</u> <u>Three</u>. At the strong unmet needs level, young children have been directly victimized, perhaps even brutalized, by violence. They have witnessed and experienced the unfortunate power of aggression firsthand. These children also have been impacted by the modeling of aggression and come to see it as a useable "life tool" (Slaby et al., 1995). In lashing out against an unfair world, they experience an adrenaline rush from using aggression and from its consequences. This emotional rush can become addicting, even for young children, as it masks the chronic stress these children feel.

The teacher must work hard to intervene in ways that prevent harm, but also teach rather than punish. Of necessity, the teacher must also work outside of conflict situations to build trust with the child. Only through a trust relationship can the child open himself to new, more gratifying, and less stressful social experiences (Harlow, 1971; Kaiser & Sklar-Rasminsky, 2003). Part Three of this book discusses the use of guidance with Level Three mistaken behaviors, including physical and psychological aggression.

Consideration Three: Mistaken Behavior or Challenging Behavior

For good reason, many educators are giving attention to strategies for dealing with **challenging behavior**. Kaiser and Sklar-Rasminsky (2003) identify behavior as challenging if it:

▶ interferes with children's learning, development, and success at play

▶ is harmful to the child, other children, or adults

▶ puts a child at high risk for later social problems or school failure. (p. 9).

Mistaken behavior at any level can at times be challenging. The focus of Kaiser and Sklar-Kaminsky, however, is on what we consider the third level of mistaken behavior: strong unmet needs mistaken behavior—frequent, serious conflicts repeated over time. One can make the case that virtually all Level Three behavior is challenging.

Likewise, the approach of teachers in the two constructs is similar. Teachers modify physical and social environments in ways that reduce the need for extreme behaviors. Teachers build supportive, trust-based relationships with the child and use guidance rather than punishment. Teachers carefully assess the pattern of the conflicts and teach targeted, alternative social-emotional skills to the child. Kaiser and Sklar-Kaminsky (2003) suggest, as in this book, that the more serious the behavior, the more comprehensive the approach that teachers take—more often than not involving families.

In my writing, I make a distinction between the concept of mistaken behavior and the concept of challenging behavior. The concept of mistaken behavior is developed from the broad philosophical perspective of using guidance to create an encouraging classroom and to teach democratic life skills for every child. The focus is not just on conflict-ridden behavior of certain children and how to deal with it, but on how to help all children develop the skills they need to be successful citizens and healthy individuals—including children with serious problems in their lives.

Kaiser and Sklar-Rasminsky seem to classify children who show challenging behavior as being of a different order than others—rather than children who are like everyone else, but who have difficult life situations to overcome. The model developed by the two authors seems to describe classrooms in which children's behavior either is challenging to teachers or it is not. There is not an apparent continuum between mental ill-health and mental health that provides the teacher with a positive context for regarding the potential of the child to heal and to grow.

With a "he is or he isn't" emphasis, my concern is that challenging behavior can too easily become a negative label not just for a child's behavior, but also for the child. At what point does the teacher decide that it is not just the child's behavior that is challenging, but the child? At that moment, the child becomes vulnerable for rejection. Possibly expulsion, but almost certainly the onset of a negative self-label, becomes more likely. Life circumstances for the child then can become worse.

Kaiser and Sklar-Rasminsky (2003) do state that a positive teacher-child relationship is fundamental to assisting children who experience frequent conflicts. The authors also recognize that if teachers label a child as challenging, they may find building a relationship more difficult. My suggestion is that for some teachers it may be easier to build attachments if they see a child not as challenging but as having strong unmet needs.

The constructs of challenging behavior and mistaken behavior both contribute to the practice of guiding for emotional and social competence in young children. In a conversation with the author, Barbara Kaiser expressed essential agreement with the following idea: The challenge to the teacher when dealing with challenging behavior is to accept the child as challenged by life circumstances and to work to help the child overcome the challenges he or she faces. This process, in the present book, is called guidance.

Communicating with Parents about Mistaken Behavior

As teachers know, families' views about their children and the subject of discipline vary a great deal: "My kid is basically a good kid who just needs some TLC." "My child can be willful and will try to get away with things unless you are right on him." Many of the expectations of parents go back to their own parents, and to the social, religious, and cultural views of their families. Once commonplace, the notion that children are to be "seen but not heard" has been replaced in many families by less authoritarian and more interactive parenting styles. Yet, some families from a variety of cultural groups still hold the view firmly that children are to be absolutely respectful and compliant toward adults. At the same time, some children come from home situations in which parents have not been able to establish consistent expectations at all.

In discussing children's behavior with families, the teacher first seeks to understand how the parent views the child. The teacher works to be sensitive to cultural and social differences that might make communication about the child more difficult. However else they differ, both teacher and family share a priority: the well-being of the child. The teacher's job is to make the most of that

Parents who feel positively about their children generally accept the concept of mistaken behavior.

common ground by remembering that whatever family values they espouse, parents want the best for their children (Gurham & Nason, 1997).

Families who have positive views about their children generally accept the concept of mistaken behavior and its three levels. Out of an adult sense of fair play, however, parents want neither their child "to get away with things" nor other children to treat their child unfairly. In explaining conflicts to parents, the teacher needs to emphasize that the child is at the beginning of a developmental process of learning acceptable behaviors, and that all children make mistakes in that process. The teacher is firm and friendly in stating the importance of providing guidance to help the children in their development. This is the teacher's job with their child.

Guidance Tips for Talking with Parents about Their Children (Using Previous Anecdote Involving Wendy)

Adults as well as children have an easier time with requests for change and improvement when the teacher recognizes their efforts, progress, and achievements. The compliment sandwich helps the teacher keep this goal in mind and is an important technique in general communication. With parents, a triple-decker **compliment sandwich** is the goal.

▶ The teacher compliments two indicators of efforts, progress, or achievement: Wendy likes books and reading and has close friends. (The compliments are discussed.)

▶ The teacher mentions the point needing discussion: We've noticed that on Mondays and Fridays she has a few difficulties concentrating and getting along. Is there anything you can think of to help us understand this pattern? (Discussion follows.)

▶ The teacher works for agreement about a follow-up action, which she summarizes.

▶ The teacher ends the conference with another compliment: Wendy is so open and honest with her feelings. We really enjoy having her in class, and like you, we want her to feel good about all she is accomplishing. This plan should really help.

Compliment sandwiches need to be sincere and should always convey the teacher's interest in working with the parent. Chapter Eight provides a more detailed discussion of conducting parent–teacher conferences and also includes information about compliment sandwiches.

Especially with more serious behaviors, the teacher must be clear to the parent that children, like all of us, make mistakes. At the same time, the child needs to learn from the mistake, and the role of the teacher is to help. Calling a hurting or disruptive behavior "a mistake" does not justify it. Guidance is not indecisive or permissive. In the terms of Haim Ginott (1972), "Helpful correction is direction." The teacher is firm but friendly with family members in conveying that when a child has classroom conflicts, it is the child's job to learn how to solve them in. The teacher's job is to teach the child how.

The goal in communicating with the parent is to convey a stance of acceptance of the child and of the need for appropriate guidance in relation to the child's behavior. The levels of mistaken behavior provide a helpful vocabulary for the teacher in working toward this goal. If a child is having problems, the teacher also needs to communicate about the efforts, progress, and achievements the child has made. Again, parents, like all of us, accept suggestions for improvement more easily when progress is recognized.

At times, parents will be more critical of the child than the teacher. Parents can express skepticism about their children's behaviors and still be nurturing parents. Occasionally, however, a teacher encounters a parent who has overly negative views about the child or unrealistic reactions to the child's mistaken behavior. One important comment needs to be made here. If a teacher believes that difficulties in parent–child communication are posing Level Three problems for the child, then the teacher needs to take a comprehensive problem-solving approach that includes collaboration with others. The teacher works with the family as well as with other professionals to solve difficult problems. Succeeding chapters discuss parent–teacher communication under these circumstances.

Summary

1. What is inappropriate about the term misbehavior?

The complexity of teaching democratic life skills leads some adults to the misconception that young children know how to behave; they just choose to "misbehave." When conflicts occur, teachers who focus on misbehavior tend to label the child's character and attempt to shame the child into better behavior. Because of a lack of development and experience, a child may internalize the negative message and act out even more. Classrooms where teachers dwell on misbehavior tend to be tension-filled and become negative learning environments for all in the class.

2. What is the concept of mistaken behavior?

Teachers who use guidance see democratic life skills as difficult to learn, and they recognize that children are just at the beginning stages of a lifelong process of learning these skills. In the process of learning any difficult skill, children, like all of us, make mistakes. These teachers recognize that when children experience conflicts it is because they have not yet developed the cognitive and emotional resources for more mature responses. The concept of mistaken behavior frees the adult from the emotional baggage of value judgment about the child. The concept allows the adult to focus fully on what the child can learn to resolve the present problem and to better solve problems in the future.

3. What are relational patterns?

Steven D. Harlow has developed a system for understanding social development in the classroom, which he calls *relational patterns*. The three relational patterns Harlow identified are *surviving*, *adjusting*, and *encountering*. Because of a perception that the environment is a dangerous place, the child at the *survival level* resorts to extreme behaviors and may act out as a means of protection from perceived harm. A child at the *adjustor level* has a primary motive of desiring to please others, especially those in authority. A child at the *encountering level—at the highest level of mental health—*is less concerned with security and approval and more occupied with exploring new ideas, materials, and experiences.

Children at each level of social relationship pose particular challenges for the teacher. In general, the teacher needs to avoid labeling children by relational pattern and assist children to progress through the differing patterns across the range of classroom experiences they share.

4. What are the levels of mistaken behavior?

Three levels of mistaken behavior correspond to the relational patterns. Level One is *experimentation mistaken behavior*, which corresponds to the relational pattern of encountering. Children show Level One mistaken behavior through curiosity and involvement. With Level One mistaken behavior, the teacher avoids overreaction but educates to more appropriate alternatives for problem solving.

Level Two is *socially influenced mistaken behavior*. Children show Level Two mistaken behavior when they are influenced toward an inappropriate act by significant others: peers, adults, or media figures. Level Two mistaken behaviors are learned behaviors. The teacher acts in a firm but friendly manner to reinforce limits, raise consciousness levels, and teach alternative behaviors.

Level Three is *strong unmet needs mistaken behavior*. Continuing serious mistaken behavior is caused by strong unmet needs that the child cannot cope with. The source of the unmet needs might be health conditions that are untreated, emotional suffering from experiences either at home or school, or a combination of the two. To deal with strong needs mistaken behavior, the teacher takes a multi-step approach called comprehensive guidance.

5. What are considerations in understanding mistaken behavior, aggression, and challenging behavior in young children?

One: Mistaken behavior can be and often is done on purpose. Without the brain development and experience to manage conflicts, young children make errors in judgment and act on the basis of feelings. Intentional acts are still mistaken behaviors made at the beginning of a lifelong social-emotional learning process.

Two: Children can show aggression at any level of mistaken behavior. Aggression is most serious when it is at Level Three and is the symptom of deep unmet needs. Forms of aggression can be expressed physically, through direct attempts at causing injury, or psychologically, through bullying and ostracism. Two uses of aggression are *instrumental*, a strategy to achieve an objective, and *reactive*, anger that is the result of frustration or a perceived threat.

Three: The causes, expressions, and responses relative to *challenging behavior* and *strong unmet needs mistaken behavior* are similar. One possible side effect of regarding behavior as "challenging" is that the teacher may come to label the child showing the behavior as challenging. Teachers who think in terms of mistaken behavior may be freer of the tendency to negatively label the child—and the consequences of child-labeling that result. Both theoretical viewpoints regard positive teacher–child relationships as central in the effort to reduce the frequency and severity of a child's classroom conflicts.

6. How does the teacher communicate with parents about mistaken behavior?

For social, religious, and cultural reasons, parents' views about their children and the subject of discipline vary greatly. In communicating with parents, the teacher first seeks to understand how the parent views the child. Parents who see their children positively generally accept the concept of mistaken behavior and its three levels. Whether the teacher uses the term or not, she needs to convey to parents that children are at the beginning of a lifelong learning process and will make mistakes. The teacher and parent just need to work together to help the child learn from mistakes.

FOLLOW-UP ACTIVITIES

Note: *An element of being a professional teacher is to respect the children, parents, and educators you are working with by maintaining confidentiality—that is, keeping identities private. In completing follow-up activities, please respect the privacy of all concerned.*

Discussion Activity

The discussion activity encourages students to interrelate their own thoughts and experiences with specific ideas from the chapter.

Think back to a classroom incident that you witnessed or were a part of when a teacher intervened. Use references from the chapter to determine what level or levels of mistaken behavior were involved. Did the teacher respond as though the incident was misbehavior or mistaken behavior? Why did you reach this conclusion? What was the result of the intervention for the child, for the teacher?

Application Activities

Application activities allow students to interrelate material from the text with real-life situations. The *observations* imply access to practicum experiences; the *interviews*, access to parents and teachers. The comparison of this information to ideas from the text prompts the student to bring together theory and experience.

1. Misbehavior, an inappropriate term

   a. Respecting privacy, observe an incident in a classroom where a teacher intervened. Do you think the teacher regarded the situation as misbehavior or mistaken behavior? What difference did the teacher's decision make for the child or children involved? For the teacher? Compare results to ideas from the chapter.

   b. Respecting privacy, interview a teacher about typical problems she sees concerning children in the classroom. To what extent does the teacher seem to think misbehavior is involved? Mistaken behavior? Compare your findings from the interview with ideas from the chapter.

2. The concept of mistaken behavior

   a. Observe a conflict situation in a prekindergarten, kindergarten, or primary-grade classroom. Analyze the situation using the concept of mistaken behavior. What lack of understanding or awareness did you perceive in the child that suggests the conflict was mistaken behavior? Compare your observations to ideas from the chapter?

   b. The concept of mistaken behavior is a new one for many teachers. Talk with a teacher about the concept. What parts of it are they comfortable with; what parts are they not sure about? Compare your findings from the interview with ideas in the text about mistaken behavior.

3. Relational patterns

   a. Observe one child who is at two different relational patterns in two differing classroom situations. Which two relational patterns seem to be operating? Discuss differences in the child's words and actions in the two situations. Compare your observations with what the text says about the two relational patterns.

   b. Briefly explain to a teacher the typical behaviors of children in each relational pattern. What for the teacher are the rewards and challenges of working with a child at each level? How do the teacher's comments compare with ideas from the text?

4. The three levels of mistaken behavior

   a. Observe an example of Level One, experimentation mistaken behavior. What did you observe that makes you think the mistaken behavior is at this level? In what ways does recognizing this level of mistaken behavior help you to understand the child? Compare your observations with ideas from the chapter.

b. Observe an example of Level Two, socially influenced mistaken behavior. What did you observe that makes you think the mistaken behavior is at this level? In what ways does recognizing this level of mistaken behavior help you to understand the child? Compare your observations with ideas from the chapter.

c. Observe an example of Level Three, strong needs mistaken behavior. What did you observe that makes you think the mistaken behavior is at this level? In what ways does recognizing this level of mistaken behavior help you to understand the child? Compare your observations with ideas from the chapter.

5. What are considerations in understanding mistaken behavior, aggression, and challenging behavior in young children?

a. Observe a conflict situation from its beginning until after it is resolved. (The conflict should include purposeful acts of aggression that might easily be called challenging.) Record in detail what the children, and an adult, said and did during the situation. Referring to pages in the text, analyze the behavior in terms of its being intentional, aggressive, and challenging. Again referring to the text, discuss why the conflict does or does not seem to you to be mistaken behavior.

b. Interview an early childhood teacher about the concept of strong unmet needs mistaken behavior as it is explained in the text. Pointing out what the book says about Level Three mistaken behavior, ask the teacher questions around this issue: Does the teacher accept the idea that challenging behavior, which is often aggressive and on purpose, can be considered mistaken behavior? Why or why not? Record in detail the dialogue from your interview. Referring to ideas from the text, compare the text ideas with the ideas of the teacher about mistaken behavior.

6. Communicating with parents about mistaken behavior

a. Talk with a teacher about the approach she uses when talking with a parent about a problem the child is having in the classroom. What is important to the teacher to convey to the parent? How does the teacher's approach relate to the concept of mistaken behavior? Compare the teacher's thoughts with ideas from the chapter.

b. Talk with a parent about the approach she would like a teacher to use if the parent's child were having a problem in the classroom. How do the parent's comments relate to the concept of mistaken behavior? Compare the teacher's thoughts with ideas from the chapter.

Recommended Readings

Bernal, G. R. (1997). How to calm children through massage. *Childhood Education, 74*(1), 9–14.

Corso, R. (2003). The Center on the Social and Emotional Foundations for Early Learning. *Young Children, 58*(4), 46–47.

Fox, L., Dunlap, G., Hemmeter, M. L., Joseph, G. E., & Strain, P. S. (2003). The teaching pyramid: A model for supportive social competence and preventing challenging behavior in young children. *Young Children, 58*(4), 48–52.

Froschl, M., & Sprung, B. (1999). On purpose: Addressing teasing and bullying in early childhood. *Young Children, 54*(2), 70–72.

Gartrell, D. J., & Sonsteng, K. (2008). Promote physical activity—it's proactive guidance. *Young Children, 53*(3), 46–49.

King, M. (2003). Building an encouraging classroom with boys in mind. *Young Children, 58*(4), 33–37.

Levin, D. E. (2003). Beyond banning war and superhero play: Meeting children's needs in violent times. *Young Children, 58*(3), 60–63.

Guidance Matters

Swearing and Words That Hurt—Three Anecdotes

November, 2007

1. Sitting alone in the book corner, Sherry is talking to herself: "Shick? Nah. Ship? Nah. Sh*t?" The teacher, overhearing, grins. He is curious about what Sherry will do next. The four-year-old gets up, walks toward him, and with a smile says, "Sh*t, Teacher." Kneeling at the child's level and looking her in the eyes (okay in Sherry's cultural group), he compliments Sherry on her use of new words, then adds, "That word bothers people in our classroom, though, so please don't use it. But you keep learning new words, okay? That is good to do." Some days later, the teacher realizes that he hasn't heard Sherry use "that" word again.

2. Kindergarten is in its second week. Thad wets his pants but ignores it and continues drawing. Before the teacher notices Thad's dilemma, Lon does. He tells other children, and they begin laughing about "Pee-Pants Thad." Many in the class overhear. While another staff member takes Thad to the bathroom to change clothes, Vicki, the teacher, calls an unscheduled class meeting.

She tells the class that when she was young, she once wet her pants at school. She says the other children—and the teacher—made fun of her, and she still feels sad about it. One boy responds by saying his sister wet her pants and he didn't make fun of her. Other children share experiences about their accidents. Thad returns to the room wearing different pants. Vicki is pleased when one of the children involved in the name-calling says, "It's okay, Thad. I wet my pants once too." Thad looks relieved and takes his seat.

3. Wayne is building with blocks by himself. He has been having a tough time lately, and the teachers work hard to help him get through each day. As Ryan hurries by, his foot knocks over part of Wayne's construction. Totally losing control, Wayne unleashes a string of swearwords (not all pronounced correctly but more than the teachers have heard from the rest of the children together all year!) and throws a block. Myra, the teacher who has worked most with Wayne, sits beside him, puts her arm around his shoulders, and quietly says, "It's all right to be upset, Wayne. It's all right." Wayne begins to cry. He leans against Myra. After a few comforting moments, Myra helps Wayne rebuild his structure. In a soothing tone, she talks with him about what happened and what he could say instead next time.

For starters, just a reminder that in this column I use the term mistaken behavior rather than misbehavior. Because the latter term carries centuries of moral baggage, when teachers view conflicts as misbehavior, they tend to slide into unhelpful judgments about the character of a child. They may make bad child/good child assumptions and discipline the child based on those assumptions.

In learning difficult skills, such as the social uses of language, we *all* make mistakes—especially young children. This column discusses swearing and hurting words as errors in judgment (mistakes) by children as they learn to use language. For me, even Wayne, who in the third anecdote swore on purpose and threw a block, did not "misbehave," but showed a mistaken behavior. As with all mistaken behaviors, children swear for different reasons. Even when an action is deliberate, the teacher who sees it as mistaken behavior is in a solid psychological position to provide guidance and will not feel the need to punish—with the negative classroom dynamics that tend to follow.

Sherry: Experimentation

Let's face it, children often hear others use expletives (swearing and other exclamations spoken in motional circumstances). For many children, like Sherry, the reactions caused by these words can be enticing.

Trying new things, including new words, is what healthy four-year-olds are about. Writers from Montessori to Erikson to Gardner have been stating for years that experimentation is how young children learn. Brain research tells us that optimal neural development occurs as children experience the intrigue of discovery without the stress of harsh evaluation (Shonkoff & Phillips, 2000). When we withhold moral judgment, we have to admit that Sherry was engaged in a high-level, phonetic word-recognition activity! The challenge to

teachers is that children's experiments sometimes take us—and them—in edgy directions.

Sherry's teacher saw her developmental need to experiment. He used a compliment sandwich to steer Sherry's experimentation within the guidelines for productive classroom behavior. The teacher knew that overreaction might prompt a child to store certain words for use in "just the right" emotional situations. Sherry did not see the need to use the word again, a sign that the teacher successfully balanced guidance and support in his classroom.

Thad: Socially Influenced Hurting Words

Children are like living sponges. They absorb information from the world around them and incorporate it into their growing beings. A child is socially influenced by adults and repeats in school words heard at home and in the community. Word experiments like "berry intelligent" make us smile without condition; a word like "sh*t," as used by Sherry, may also make us smile, but that is probably not our only reaction.

Classroom peers exert social influence on individuals, sometimes toward mistaken behaviors like a child starting a chant of "Pee-Pants Thad." The leadership style of the teacher has much to do with whether socially influenced mistaken behavior becomes a pattern or remains just a sometime thing. When mistaken behavior involves many children, as in the second anecdote, it is time for a class meeting. Vicki's meeting did what this forum does best: respectfully raises empathy levels and reminds the group that the classroom is to be encouraging for all.

Class meetings sometimes involve complicated social dynamics, including the issue of whether the child at the center of the situation should be present. In the November 2006 issue of *Young Children*, Guidance Matters addresses some of these issues in a column titled "The Beauty of Class Meetings."

Wayne: Strong Unmet Needs

When children experience frequent and severe conflict over time, they face problems that are bigger than they are. For reasons of biology, life circumstances, or a mix of the two, these children have deep unmet needs. Their behaviors are no less mistaken than those of children for whom survival is not an issue. The conflicts they cause—often so challenging to adults—are attempts to ask for help. With his stress level high and his still-developing brain geared to fight or flight, Wayne could in no way say, "Ryan, it really bothers me that you knocked down part of my building."

Wayne's blue streak of swearwords was his way of protesting that his life was overwhelming and he had lost control. From her relationship with Wayne, Myra guessed the meaning of his behavior; she knew that the swearing was a symptom of the difficult challenges Wayne faced. At NAEYC's 2007 National Institute for Early Childhood Professional Development in Pittsburgh, I shared this thought:

> Children who are challenging to adults are challenged by their own circumstances. The challenge for the teacher is to build a relationship with the child, work with fellow staff on a coordinated guidance plan, collaborate with family and other professionals to improve the situation, and, in short, rise to the challenge of the challenging behavior.

For children like Wayne, swearing is an expression of unmet needs, not an indication of their character. There are many reasons children swear and use hurting words. When we see the use of expletives as a signal to learn about and work with a child, we are on the road to being caring professional teachers.

To Increase Your knowledge

Children use swearwords and hurting language in the overall process of language development. By understanding more about language development in general, the early childhood professional can listen to and interact with children to help them develop communication skills that make the "edgy words" unnecessary. Here are two articles you can read:

Bailey, B., & Brookes, C. (2003). Thinking out loud: Development of private speech and the implications for school success and self-control. *Young Children*, 58(5), 46–52.

Bailey and Brookes discuss the stages of development of private speech from infancy through age eight and provide teachers with informal methods of assessing which stage a child is in.

Soundy, C., & Stout, N. (2002). Pillow Talk: Fostering the emotional and language needs of young learners. *Young Children*, 57(2), 20–24.

Meaningful verbal interactions are important to young children and support their language development. Soundy and Stout describe Pillow Talk, a naptime ritual in which the teacher gives every child special one-on-one attention and acknowledges the child's interests and experiences. Language is the foundation for all academic and social skills, and Pillow Talk teaches children that communicating with adults is interesting and rewarding.

A Step You Can Take

Intentionally look for the occasions when a child uses expletives or hurting words. If you need to intervene, do so, but in a firm and friendly way that involves either a guidance talk (perhaps with a compliment sandwich) or—if several children are involved—a class meeting. Brainstorm with colleagues why the child may have used the particular words. How might you use thoughts from this discussion as you continue to work with the child?

Column References

Shonkoff, J. P., & Phillips, D. A. (Eds.). (2000). *From neurons to neighborhoods: The science of early childhood development*. A report of the National Research Council and the Institute of Medicine. Washington, DC: National Academies Press.

For additional information on using the guidance approach in the encouraging classroom, visit our website at www.cengage.com/education/gartrell.

Chapter 4

Guidance in the Classroom

Guiding Questions

▶ *What are the differences between a teacher who is a professional and a teacher who is a technician?*

▶ *How are positive teacher-child relations the basis of the guidance approach?*

▶ *How does guidance reduce the need for mistaken behavior?*

▶ *What does it mean that "guidance is solution oriented"?*

▶ *Why is liberation teaching fundamental to the encouraging classroom?*

▶ *How are family-teacher partnerships important in the guidance approach?*

© Cengage Learning

Key Concepts

▶ *Academic performance*

▶ *Cardinal principle*

▶ *Class meetings*

▶ *Conflict management*

▶ *Conflict Mediation*

▶ *Crisis management techniques*

▶ *Guidance intervention practices*

▶ *Institution-caused mistaken behavior*

▶ *Labeling*

▶ *Liberation teaching*

▶ *Passive restraint*

▶ *Professional teacher*

▶ *Self-fulfilling prophecy*

▶ *Stigma*

▶ *Unconditional positive regard*

▶ *With-it-ness*

Chapter Four explains six teaching practices that define the guidance approach and set the foundation for encouraging classrooms. The six guidance practices show how the teacher:

▶ acts as a professional, not a technician

▶ builds positive teacher-child relations

▶ reduces mistaken behavior

▶ takes a solution-orientation

▶ aspires to liberation teaching

▶ works for family-teacher partnerships.

A Professional, Not a Technician

Chapter One took the position that discipline based on obedience restricts the teacher's role. Obedience-based discipline reduces teachers to the status of *technicians*, trained to follow specific sets of rules in predetermined, inflexible ways. In contrast, the guidance approach asks that the teacher be a *professional* (Almy, 1975). How the teacher responds to situations in the classroom defines the difference between the teacher as technician and as professional (Gartrell, 2004).

The professional teacher:

1. *Uses diagnostic skills to assess situations.* The technician tends to determine only whether a rule has been violated or not. The professional recognizes that each situation is different and attempts to understand what actually is occurring.

2. *Makes ongoing hypotheses and takes action based on the hypotheses.* The technician responds in an inflexible manner—X behavior happened, therefore discipline Y is called for. The professional uses a problem-solving approach. As classroom leader, he dialogues with the child in order to resolve the conflict equitably and teach the child alternative behaviors.

3. *Learns from experience.* On a daily basis, the teacher makes quick assessments, forms hypotheses, and takes positive actions. Even experienced teachers find that interventions do not always work out as intended. Being a professional means that while the teacher does not always make the "perfect" decision, he endeavors to learn from every experience to improve interactions, relations, and problem-solving abilities.

Learning While Teaching

In 1977, Kounin wrote about "with-it-ness" to describe a teacher's ability to diagnose those key situations in the classroom that need to be addressed. Discussed in Charles (2007), the term has become a staple in the literature of classroom management. From his classroom research, Kounin concluded that

Human motivations, relationships, and behaviors are complex, even when young children are concerned.

effective teachers—the ones with "eyes in the back of their heads"—have with-it-ness; less effective teachers do not.

With-it-ness, like other teaching skills, takes time to master, and even experienced teachers can be fooled. When teachers recognize that becoming fully informed is the goal, but that they must often act on less than complete information, then with-it-ness is put in its proper perspective. When teachers miscalculate a situation, then a sensible practice is to recognize both their fallibility and their potential to learn, and go on from there (Gartrell, 2004). Teachers who have the ability to learn from their mistakes are proactive rather than reactive, professionals rather than technicians. The following anecdote illustrates the challenge in becoming more professional as a teacher.

Classroom Anecdote	*A circus was set up in a large room of a child care center. Different activities were occurring in various areas, including a very popular cotton candy concession. Brian, age five, had a reputation as a "tough veteran" of the program. Brian was standing in line when he was pushed from in front. He accidentally bumped against and fell on a three-year old, who*

(continued)

Classroom Anecdote	*was hurt. A teacher arrived on the scene, helped the younger child, and told Brian to go to the end of the line for pushing. A student teacher who had seen the incident explained to the teacher what had happened. The teacher went to Brian, kneeled down at his level, and apologized. She helped Brian get back his place, second in line. The teacher was surprised to see Brian cry quiet tears as he waited his turn. The emotional roller coaster had been too much. He smiled though when he got his wand of cotton candy.*

Teachers often have difficulty knowing exactly what happened in a situation and how to intervene. An important guideline is that anytime a teacher can act more like a mediator and less like a police officer, he is improving his chances of acting as a professional. Quick judgments sometimes are necessary, but a more positive resolution may come about if the teacher delays action to hear from the children and collect her thoughts.

Especially with children who have reputations, staying open to learning has benefits. First, the teacher gains new information that may increase understanding about the child. Second, the *effort* to gain new information can improve the teacher-child relationship. The facts that Brian was wrongly blamed and cried as a result of the experience gave the teacher new information for working with the boy. From a modification in relations, a child may come to see school in a different light.

While guidance provides no magic answers for teacher-technicians, it offers practices and principles to learn about, try, and learn from. Guidance offers the promise of professional growth, which is difficult for teachers locked into the technician role. Teachers who are professionals work to empower the healthy development of the young child and of themselves. Professional teachers learn even as they teach.

A teacher friend (who is a capable **guidance professional**) once told me that it took her about five years before the guidance responses she worked so hard over at first became automatic responses in her relations with children. The good news is that guidance doesn't have to be used perfectly, so long as the children know you care. In this case the children and the teacher together grow.

The Need for Positive Teacher-Child Relationships

The early childhood teacher builds positive relationships with children based on the role that he fills. The role is different from that of the parent, whose relationship with the child is highly personal and subjective. The unique task of the early childhood teacher is to facilitate the transitions of the child between private family relationships and the more public, collectively driven relationships in the classroom (*Texas Child Care Quarterly,* 2002; Wilson, 2003). Adjustment to school is easier for children who feel positively about themselves in the school situation (Erickson & Pianta, 1989). Recent articles by Ostrosky and Jung (2003) and Gallagher and Mayer (2008) reinforce the basic guidance idea that positive teacher-child relationships make a critical difference in the ability of the child to adjust to school and to experience continuing success in school and life.

Teachers face two challenges in building relationships with children: *institutional dynamics* that may work against their efforts, and *personality dynamics* that make building relations difficult.

Institutional Dynamics That Work Against Relationships

During 2005 a national study of nearly 4,000 preschool classrooms was published, titled "Prekindergarteners Left Behind: Expulsion Rates in State Prekindergarten Systems" (Gilliam, 2005). The study included this sobering summary:

> *Results indicated that 10.4 percent of prekindergarten teachers reported expelling at least one preschooler in the past 12 months. Nationally, 6.67 preschoolers were expelled per 1,000 enrolled ... 3.2 times the rate for K–12 students. Rates were highest for older preschoolers and African-Americans, and boys were over 4 1/2 times more likely to be expelled than were girls" (p. 1)*

Gilliam found that prekindergarten programs less likely to expel children had more support resources available to teachers. Programs like Head Start, and those affiliated with school systems, fell into this category.

At the public school level, children may be *expelled* less, but a similar dynamic of institutional rejection, based on behavior, still can be found. (The common use of in-school and out of-school suspension—*temporary expulsion*—illustrates this trend. According to the Children's Defense Fund Annual Report for 2008, a student is suspended from American public schools "every second.") Sometimes, as in the kinds of preschools where young children are often expelled, the individual elementary school teacher finds himself at odds with larger institutional dynamics that make forming positive relationships difficult. In the following anecdote, the issue of "in-groups versus out-groups" involving a group of boys illustrates this situation.

Classroom Anecdote	*A first-year teacher built relations by appealing to the pride of a group of very active boys in her third-grade class. By October, she had them functioning fairly well and working fairly hard.*
	During November, the principal gave a staff training in a new discipline system he expected the whole school to use. Names were to be recorded for bad behavior, and children were to be given disciplinary referral slips for repeat offenses. The school would hold a roller skating party at the end of the winter term. Children with fewer than three disciplinary referral slips were to be included.
	The teacher felt obligated to use the system and found she was often writing the names of the group of boys on the board. A few days before the party, a popular member of the group got his third referral slip. By the day before the party, the boy's friends also had gotten their three slips; it seemed to the teacher, on purpose. Conspicuously, the group missed the party. During spring term, the teacher quietly reduced her use of the "school-wide discipline system" and worked hard to regain positive relations with the boys. By the end of the year, she felt she had almost gotten back to that point with them, but not quite.

"Out-groups that become in-groups" present difficult challenges for schools—better to make classrooms inclusive from the beginning. As a professional, the first-year teacher had to work against institutional pressures in order to regain a classroom encouraging to all of her students. The new teacher quietly minimized use of the system in her classroom—and quietly collaborated with tenured teachers to get the system changed. Within two years, the school dropped the "official" system.

Personality Dynamics

Due to the nationwide emphasis on assessment-based performance, many schools are using discipline practices that make "invisible" children who are likely to cause classroom disruption (Children's Defense Fund, 2008). Administrators can do much to make classroom environments more or less encouraging for every child. The fundamental element in this effort (as indicated in the preceding anecdote) comes down to the ability of the teacher to form positive relationships.

Self-Fulfilling Prophecy. For individual teachers who continue to use conventional discipline, children who "misbehave" have "green light–red light" cards flipped, have their names written on the board, are put into time-out, are deprived of class rewards, or are publicly embarrassed in other ways. The "argument" is that the teacher sends the message to the child that unless she behaves "properly," she will be ostracized from the group. The problem with this argument is that although the teacher believes that he is "shaming the child into being good," the result may be the opposite, due to the **self-fulfilling prophecy** (Merton, 1949/1968). "Because of limited development and experience, children tend to internalize negative labels, see themselves as they are labeled, and react accordingly" (Gartrell, 2004).

Classroom Anecdote	*Early in the kindergarten year, Jamal got upset with another child and punched her in the stomach. The teacher tended to the girl and then marched Jamal to the time-out chair. Later in the day the principal gave him a "stern lecture." Two days later, Jamal got into another argument and hit again. As the teacher came toward him, Jamal walked to the time-out chair by himself and said, "I know. I'm going to the chair 'cause I'm no good." The teacher knelt beside him and explained that he did not upset her but that his behavior did. Afterwards, she worked to improve their relationship.*

One concern about children who become stigmatized as troublemakers is that the threat of ostracism loses its power. (See the prior anecdote about the skating party.) These children not only come to see themselves negatively, but they may grow to care little about themselves in the school situation. A vicious cycle of "I am a troublemaker, therefore I misbehave, therefore I am punished" is not one educators should want to introduce (Gartrell, 2004). Realizing this possibility, the teacher in the preceding anecdote switched gears and began to build a relationship with Jamal. (In gaining information about Jamal she learned that he had recently been switched back and forth between his own home and a foster home.) In building the relationship, the teacher moved from being a technician to guidance professional.

Classroom Anecdote	*After a few weeks of Head Start, a three-year-old named Jimmy began to show a strange behavior when he arrived in the morning: He began to kick the teacher in the leg! Susan, the teacher, tried different techniques, none of which worked. But she steadfastly refused to brand Jimmy with labels. Finally, she tried a new approach. When Jimmy first walked in the door, the teacher approached him quickly, gave him a hug, and told him how happy she was to see him. After a few days of this new welcome, Jimmy would arrive, give the teacher a wide berth, and say, "Hi, Teacher."*
	Four years later, Susan received a Christmas card from Jimmy and his mother. Written on the card were these words: "Dear Teacher, I'm having a nice Christmas. I hope you are. I still remember you. Do you remember me?"

Labeling. What labels might an adult give to a child who kicks his teacher? The teacher above recognized that "labeling is disabling," and avoided what Ginott calls "teaching at its worst" (Ginott, 1972). Labeling children has two broad negative effects. *First,* as the self-fulfilling prophecy suggests, children learn to see themselves in the way they are labeled. The label is incorporated into the child's self-concept and may influence future behavior. Without fortunate counter experiences that tell the child, "I'm not like that," the child's views and feelings about self may be permanently affected (Kaiser & Sklar-Rasminsky, 2003).

Second, the label influences the teacher to believe the "problem" is totally within the child—and not a product of his relationship with the child. From this mistaken position, the teacher "watches out for" particular behaviors he has come to expect. The teacher fails to see other important patterns and qualities in the child. Every child is greater than the sample of behavior that stands out to the teacher. So much development has yet to occur that the teacher must avoid constricting that development by labeling (Watson, 2003). The ability to value the child as a still developing person who naturally will make mistakes allows for teaching responses that truly are *liberating.* Susan showed a guidance response by seeing the child beyond the behavior and by building her relationship with Jimmy.

A key understanding about labeling is that it occurs even when the adult does not specifically "call names." A teacher scolds a child by saying that what she did was "not nice." As a result of "developmental immaturity and limited experience," the child internalizes the message as "I'm not nice" (Watson, 2003). As Ginott (1972) suggests, the challenge is to convey to children that although the teacher may be bothered by what happened, he still accepts them as individuals of worth and welcome members of the group. In other words, when they intervene *teachers select their words carefully*. Assess for yourself which intervention is more supportive of children's developing selves:

"Kyle, you are being rowdy." "If you don't work quietly, I will move you."	"The talking is too loud. You choose, Kyle; work quietly or find a different seat."
"Zach, don't you be lazy. You used the blocks.	"Zach, all who used the blocks need to put them back.
If you don't put them away, you won't go outside."	As soon as they're away, we can go out."
"Class, you are being antsy again. Story time is now over; go and take your seats."	"Okay, everybody, we need a break. Let's stand up and stretch. When the music starts, let's all 'get the wiggles out.'"

In *Caring* (1977), Warren classically commented that teachers cannot feel love for each child and need not feel guilty when they realize this. Warren states, however, that the teacher does have an obligation to build a positive relationship with every child and to help each feel a sense of belonging with the group. Building relations with persons we don't feel comfortable around is hard for all human beings. The task may be especially difficult when children show Level Three mistaken behaviors, which can be extreme. In a 2008 article titled "I Just Don't Like That Kid," Grossman states that "feelings unexpressed or ignored will escape somewhere and may result in an outburst toward an undeserving child (p. 147). As Weber-Schwartz (1987) points out, seeking to understand the child is the all-important first step. Productive human relations are an essential life goal in a democratic society and an essential goal for the teacher in the classroom (Rightmyer, 2003). A key ingredient in high-quality teacher-child relationships is personal affirmation by the professional teacher, unconditional positive regard for the person of the child (Rogers, 1961).

Unconditional Positive Regard—Communicating to Protect Self Esteem

Unconditional positive regard is a venerable idea that was used in the nursery school movement of the 1920s even before Rogers coined the term (Read, Gardner, & Mahler, 1993). In 1972, Ginott gave renewed articulation to the idea with his "cardinal principle." Since relationships grow from teachers' communication skills, then effective teacher-child communication is at the heart of the guidance approach. Ginott phrased the principle this way:

> *At their best, teachers address themselves to the child's situation. At their worst, they judge his character and personality. This, in essence, is the difference between effective and ineffective communication. (p. 70)*

Unconditional positive regard means personal affirmation by the teacher.

With children who are difficult for the teacher to understand and accept, the **cardinal principle** is a reminder of the central guidance practice: effective communication affirms the worth of the child *and* seeks to help the child learn from her mistakes. Teachers who base classroom communication on this principle have turned the corner in becoming guidance professionals.

Ostrosky and Jung (2003) provide a series of teacher responses that affirm positive regard for the child. "Teachers let children know they care about them through warm, responsive, physical contact such as giving pats o the back, hugging, and holding children on their laps (p. 141)." They encourage mutual respect by listening when children speak and encouraging them to listen to others and by using "positive guidance techniques." In building positive teacher-child relations, the authors emphasize that teachers:

▶ Engage in one-to-one interactions with children

▶ Get on the child's level for face-to-face interactions

▶ Use a pleasant, calm voice and simple language

▶ Provide warm, responsive physical contact

▶ Acknowledge children for their efforts and accomplishments.

© Cengage Learning

When teachers intervene, they select their words with care.

In accepting the challenge of challenging behaviors, teachers intentionally direct these responses to the child who especially needs the relationship—whatever their personal feelings toward the child. The teacher, the child, and others in the class all benefit from improved teacher-child relationships (Ostrosky & Jung, 2003).

Classroom Anecdote	A few weeks after start-up of Head Start in a rural community, Denny, a young four-year-old, began to have difficulties transitioning into the beginning large group after he arrived on the bus. New teacher R.J. noticed the conflicts shortly after Mom stopped driving Denny to Head Start. Denny's bus route went by the new home of his dad, who was in a custody battle with Mom over the boy. Some days Denny dramatically refused to join the group. Other days, after joining group, he would pinch, shove, or kick at other children—and at R.J. when the teacher intervened. R.J. noticed too that this "very active class" resonated with Denny' mistaken behavior during group. The teacher had to conclude large group earlier than planned on more than one occasion.
	Against the preferences of the experienced assistant, R.J. decided to "get proactive." The teacher extended open center time at the beginning of the day. Daily, he made a point of

(continued)

greeting and spending quality minutes with Denny. With more transition time and the attention, Denny had an easier time joining group. (The assistant reluctantly agreed to sit with Denny during the group each day.) R.J. also reduced the time spent in large group, kept it snappy with musical movement activities, and moved the daily story to later, done in small groups. R.J. also transitioned the children from the shortened large group to a vigorous active playtime outdoors or in the "motor development room." After active play, the children went into the daily story and a follow-up in small groups—with Denny staying in R.J.'s group.

Over the next two weeks, the assistant and R.J. agreed there was a reduction in number of conflicts caused by Denny. The "very active class" also benefited, with fewer total conflicts during the day. The two staff agreed they could lengthen the large group (a bit) later in the year when the children had gained a bit in development and experience. During home visits, R.J. encouraged the family to get additional support services for the child.

Long-Term Benefits. In November of 2008, Gallagher and Mayer published a research review titled "Enhancing Development and Learning Through Teacher-Child Relationships" in young children (birth to age eight). Their review focused on the benefits of close teacher-child relationships and the implications of studies about positive relationships for teaching in infant/toddler, preschool, and primary-grade age settings. A summary of their findings was that:

> *High-quality relationships in early childhood support the development of social, emotional, and cognitive skills. When children have secure relationships with their primary caregivers, they have better language skills, more harmonious peer relationships, and fewer behavior problems. In high-quality teacher-child relationships, teachers respond to children's needs appropriately and in a timely manner. Teachers are gentle and take frequent opportunities to interact face-to-face with children. When teachers develop high-quality relationships with young children, they support children's problem solving, allowing the children to experience success without too much or too little assistance. (p.82)*

Given the benefits of high-quality relationships, and the detriments of not forming them, the teacher does well to ask: Which children need positive relationships with me the most? Which children do I find building relationships with challenging? How do I communicate within the classroom and with the child to improve teacher-child relationships?

Reducing Mistaken Behavior

Because of the biological dynamics within their brains and bodies, young children normally come to school ready to learn and grow. When children experience conflicts in the school environment, two factors tend to be involved: (1) the challenges of childhood and (2) "matching problems" between the child and the program.

The Challenges of Childhood

The first factor has to do with the particular challenges of childhood. All young children bring insecurities—the fear of abandonment, of rejection, of failure—into the early childhood classroom. These anxieties, combined with only a beginning understanding of social expectations, mean that young children make mistakes in judgment and behavior. Many mistaken behaviors are the product of the lives of young children in the classroom—not wanting to share play dough or quarreling over a pencil.

The stresses on children, plus a just beginning ability to solve social problems, means that minor conflicts sometimes escalate. While the teacher monitors these conflicts to prevent harm and serious disruption, he may not immediately jump in. Through learning to resolve everyday conflicts for themselves, children gain lifelong emotional and social skills (DeVries & Zan, 2004; Rightmyer, 2003).

So, the teacher does not seek to create a "perfect order" classroom by "ridding" the program of all conflicts. But, neither does he manufacture problems in order to "build character." (Life poses enough vexations for children without teachers' "contributions.") Working to understand the life situations of the children in his class, he strives to assist each child to find strategies to help the child get along. The following anecdote illustrates the depths, and the rewards, of these challenges for early childhood teachers.

Classroom Anecdote	

A young four-year-old, new in a Head Start class, had a high need for structure. Bernard became easily (and highly) agitated at transition times between activities and at the end of the day. Staff had approached the family members about a special education assessment, but the family was not yet ready to accept a need. The teachers became frustrated with Bernard's sometimes intense conflicts during transitions. After a staff meeting, the teachers decided on a strategy to make the transitions less threatening for Bernard. The lead teacher contacted the mother, and they discussed the staff's plan. The mother got interested and agreed.

Over the next few days the assistant teacher, comfortable with a digital camera, took many photos of the child during successful transitions and throughout the trip home. She created a laminated book called "Bernard's Day at Head Start" using the photos with printed captions. Early the next morning the lead teacher, who had developed a relationship with Bernard, read the book to him. She told him it was his book to keep with him or put in his cubby. Before each transition, the teacher located the book and went over the next part of the schedule with him.

At the end of this day, when the boy had particular difficulties, the teacher stayed with Bernard on the bus ride and shared the book with him. With its photos and captions showing Bernard getting ready to board the bus, riding, and greeting his mother at the bus stop, the book calmed Bernard. Bernard and the teacher presented the book to the mom. (Mom—and the bus driver—made sure the book came back to Head Start the next day.)

The boy valued "Bernard's Day..." and for weeks, looked through it when he needed to. Other children took interest, and Bernard and his teacher read it to them. Within a month, each child had their own book—which acquainted family members as well with the Head Start day.

In assisting young children cope with the complexities of childhood, the challenge for the teacher is to get to know each child. In the process, the teacher learns the kinds of problems a child can handle on a particular day and the kind she will need assistance with (Grossman, 2008). By allowing the child to try to solve some problems, working to prevent others, and providing assistance in the resolution of still others, the teacher empowers successful life experiences in the classroom—the kind every child needs (Watson, 2003).

The Match of the Child and the Program

A second factor that contributes to mistaken behavior lies in children's reactions to teaching practices that are developmentally *inappropriate*. One way to look at developmentally appropriate practice is that when it is present, every child in the class is able to actively engage in learning activities and construct personal meaning—attention spans grow surprisingly long at these times. The current emphasis on **academic performance** even in kindergarten and preschool tends to produce an over-reliance on teacher-directed, full-group instruction.

The activity levels and learning styles of young children mean that they are not ready to sit, listen and complete work sheets (Bredekamp & Copple, 2008). Some children, usually older and often girls, can adjust and at least give the impression of quiet involvement. Other children, usually younger and often boys, lapse into *passivity*—with the short attention spans, expressed frustrations, and "off task play," characteristic of classrooms where there is a poor child-program match.

The current preoccupation with assessment of academic performance has put pressure on teachers to be "information crammers" rather than the teachers of the whole child that most would like to be. At the preschool level, many preschool teachers feel pressure from both parents and public school educators to "get children ready for kindergarten" (Hardy, 2003).

Classroom Anecdote	*(Improving the match for emerging literacy)* Vera, a Head Start teacher, knew that recognizing beginning letter sounds was a skill area on a "kindergarten readiness assessment" used by the school district in her area. Vera dutifully followed the program of her agency—drill activities on a selected consonant sound each week. On Friday during "C week," she heard Nelda, while doing a puzzle, say to herself "K, K cat, K, K cat," and the teacher smiled. The next week, "D week," Vera overheard Nelda saying distinctly to herself, "K, K dog, K, K dog!" Another teacher might have corrected the child. Vera again smiled, but for a different reason.
	The teacher continued the consonant-drill lessons, seeing them as fun rhyming activities that (at least) sent a "phonics" message home to families. But Vera also emphasized experience-related writing activities in the new writing center. Daily she encouraged the children to draw and write stories (make story pictures) about topics that were important to them. Seven weeks later Nelda made a story picture (using paper that was blank on the top with lines on the bottom). Sadly, the picture was of a black figure that appeared to be lying down. The figure had a very red tongue. Below the picture, Nelda wrote, "M dg gt kl."

(continued)

Classroom Anecdote	*Whatever the children were or were not learning through "letter of the week," Vera recognized, that through the story–pictures she was making phonemic awareness personally significant to the children. (Notice that in her story picture Nelda showed knowledge of ending as well as beginning consonant sounds.)*

In an article titled "Accountability Shove-down: Resisting the Standards Movement in Early Childhood Education," J. A. Hatch (2002) takes the position that instruction for standards assessment is appropriate and needed, as long as it meets ten conditions. This list of the ten is adapted from Hatch's article:

1. Does not put children at risk for feeling pressured and stressed in the classroom.

2. Does not pressure teachers to abandon "the greater calling" of their mission for prescribed standards-focused instruction.

3. Does not reduce the rich learning experiences of young children to narrowly focused academic lessons.

4. Does not punish with the systematic identification of "deficiency scores"—as though public prodding will motivate programs to try harder to meet standards.

5. Does not reduce teachers from professionals—able to make informed judgments about curriculum and instruction—to technicians who doggedly follow preset programs and are not expected to make independent decisions.

6. Does not emphasize performance—snapshots of selected samples of children's work for evaluative display—over true learning that has lasting meaning in the child's development, and is more difficult to assess.

7. Does not devalue the individual dispositions, needs, learning, and self-expression styles of young children, for the sake of group compliance in teacher-directed instruction.

8. Does not emphasize sameness over diversity so that children from unique cultural backgrounds are forced to give up pride in themselves and their families.

9. Does not exaggerate the benefits of narrowly focused instruction and standardized assessment over the benefits of more developmentally appropriate education and assessment practices.

10. Does not impose a corporate mentality on the education processes of the classroom—so that "product efficiency" reduces the atmosphere to that of an assembly line (pp. 457–462).

In classrooms where teachers feel they must push children "to get them ready," children feel heightened levels of stress, anxiety, and frustration (Hardy, 2003). The normal challenges of childhood become aggravated, and **institution-caused mistaken behaviors** become frequent. The basic factor in reducing institution-caused mistaken behavior is the relevance of the educational program to the child. To further healthy development, the teacher uses programming that has meaning for all the children and at which each child can succeed. In this effort the teacher accommodates developmental characteristics, activity levels, and personal life factors by using appropriate curriculum and methods. Family backgrounds are affirmed by culturally responsive teaching practices. As a professional, the teacher works from the beginning of the year

© Cengage Learning

A factor in reducing mistaken behavior is the relevance of the educational program to the child.

© Cengage Learning

to increase the acceptance of these ideas among colleagues in the center or school and among the families of the children in the class (Bredekamp & Copple, 2008).

Improving the Match. As a professional, the teacher balances outside academic pressures with accepted early childhood guidelines for appropriate and responsive practices. He monitors, and on occasion more formally assesses, the match between the needs and experiences of the children and the education program. If children's behaviors deviate from expectations, he revises the program to improve the match. Modification of the program to heighten learner engagement is at the heart of reducing institution-caused mistaken behavior (Bredekamp & Copple, 2008). The two anecdotes that follow illustrate how two teachers fine-tuned activities to respond more appropriately to the developmental and cultural needs of their young learners. (Notice that modification of large groups is a common technique for improving the match of young children to the daily program.)

Classroom Anecdote	(#1. Improving the developmental match/Rhythm Instruments.) *A kindergarten teacher introduced rhythm instruments to her class. She held up the various instruments— tambourine, triangle, rhythm sticks, bells, blocks—and asked who wanted to use each. Many hands shot up for the "exotic" instruments; not many for the rhythm sticks. She observed that some children were crestfallen when they didn't get the choices they wanted. Others pressured those near them to trade.*
	After several minutes of getting instruments into the children's hands, the teacher got the activity explained. She would start the CD, call out the name of an instrument, and just that group would play. Unexpectedly, the class made "rhythms" at will, without much sense of either the beat or the instrument group called. Some children weren't playing at all, but still trying to trade for "better" instruments. The teacher got everyone playing but just let the whole class play the rhythms they heard. She saw that some adjustments were needed.
	For the next two weeks during afternoon center time, a music center included a set of each rhythm instrument. Small groups of children used the instruments each day while they listened to music on their headphones. (The teacher selected this center time because the next-door class was out of the room with a specialist. She also put the music center partially in a large closet.)
	After two weeks of exploration, the teacher resumed the large-group rhythm activity, but with an expanded supply of instruments borrowed from the next-door teacher. The teacher carefully spelled out what the children would be doing and when. The rhythm band played together and quickly improved its skills.

The listening, language, mathematical, social, and even scientific benefits of music make this activity so important in early childhood classrooms. ("Kids don't care if teachers sing off key, just if they don't sing.") The values of daily music with children range from enhanced brain development to the possibility of heightened cross-cultural awareness.

Classroom Anecdote	(#2. Improving cultural responsiveness with rhythm sticks.) *A teacher had been working with preschoolers using rhythm sticks for a few weeks when two Native American (Ojibwe) children joined the program. The teacher told Antoine and Cheyenne that they could participate with the group or sit and watch. The two boys watched, then noticed two extra sticks on a chair behind the teacher. They each picked up a stick, cupped one ear, and began drumming the sticks on the chair to the music. The teacher became upset, took the sticks, and told them to sit quietly for the rest of the activity.* *Afterwards, a teacher aide who was also Ojibwe explained that the children were using the sticks as their older relatives did, to "beat the drum and sing like they do at a pow-wow." Embarrassed, the teacher asked the aide's help to organize an Ojibwe singing event for the preschool. The aide got the two boys' relatives to come and bring their drum. Antoine and Cheyenne were proud to sit with the singers (their elders) and lead their teacher in the dance.*

The teacher reduces the need for mistaken behavior by using practices that are developmentally appropriate and culturally responsive.

Taking a Solution Orientation

About child-rearing practices of the past, Berger (1986) states:

> *Except for a few dissenters ... most people were much more interested in disciplining children to keep them from becoming sinners or degenerates than in nurturing them so that they would preserve their natural curiosity and enthusiasm.*

Only in the 20th century did empathy for the condition of childhood become a broad-based social value (deMause, 1974). Widespread understanding that children show mistaken behavior out of developmental immaturity and unmet basic needs is a surprisingly recent occurrence.

The guidance approach holds that children should not be punished for having problems, but they should be assisted in developing the democratic life skills necessary to solve their problems (Gartrell, 2004; Honig & Wittmer, 1996). Children's ability to make decisions intelligently and ethically cannot be built through punitive discipline (Crosser, 2002). A guidance approach empowers children to build the self-control *and* self-acceptance necessary to say yes or no "because it is the right thing to do."

Every day guidance intervention practices that the teacher uses to solve social problems, and teach children how to solve them, include: conflict management, guidance talks, class meetings, and crisis management techniques. An overview of each follows. Chapters 8–12 discuss crisis intervention practices in detail.

Conflict Management

In the guidance approach, the adult teaches techniques for *conflict management* as an ongoing part of the education program.

Conflict management includes the ability to prevent or reduce the severity of a conflict so that the problem causing the conflict can be resolved.

Conflict management skills are critical in a democracy. Logically individuals should begin to learn these skills when they are young. But, the idea that young children are capable of learning to resolve their disputes peaceably is only gaining acceptance (Noddings, 2005).

One of the first books on this topic, Wichert's *Keeping the Peace: Practicing Cooperation and Conflict Resolution with Preschoolers* (1989) provides a construct still useful for teaching young children to mediate their own problems. In Wichert's schema, children operate at one of three skill levels to resolve classroom difficulties. At *high-level adult intervention*, the teacher actively assists children to become calm, focus on the problem, and move toward resolution. In *minimal adult intervention*, "children define the problem using their own language and the adult merely clarifies when needed" (p. 56). At the level of *negotiation* children take charge, talking together to solve the problem. The teacher intentionally leads children to progress from high-level conflict mediation to low-level mediation to child negotiation.

Views differ on the practice of having children leave the place of activity in order to engage in mediation or *child negotiation*. The prospect of moving to engage in the resolution process is often incentive enough for children to quickly negotiate. A first step in mediation is always to make sure everyone is calm. Moving to another location is often part of the calming strategy. Talk-and-listen chairs, talking sticks, and peace puppets serve as props that can aid young children to resolve their problems. The anecdote that follows illustrates clearly the direction of Wichert's approach—from high adult intervention to children negotiating on their own.

Classroom Anecdote	*Two preschool teachers in northern Minnesota set up talk-and-listen chairs in their classroom to help their children learn to settle conflicts. They introduced the concept in a class meeting, and even modeled use of the chairs over a make-believe argument concerning play dough. (One talked, the other listened, and then they switched chairs and roles.) A week later two four-year-olds, Jason and Amber, pushed and shoved over use of the computer. Chelsey (one of the teachers) got the children quieted down, brought them to the chairs, and in front of a few onlookers, resolved the conflict. The two teachers consistently used the method of mediation with Amber and Jason and other children.*
	The following month, when Jason and Amber again argued over the computer, the two teachers held back to see if the children would take charge. This time Amber said, "We gotta go use them chairs!" Jason said, "Yeah." The teachers watched as the children exchanged chairs twice, settled the problem, and used the computer together.

Many methods for conducting mediation are available to teachers. The uses of the "five-finger? formula" are explained in detail in Chapter Nine.

Guidance Talks

Teachers hold guidance talks with individual children when there is a conflict between them or the teacher decides an individual talk with a child is needed. A common memory for many adults, even senior adults, is being embarrassed by a teacher in front of a class. The teacher thought she was dealing with a problem of the moment. These hurting emotional memories get etched into brains and stay with individuals for years. Can you remember such an experience? The teacher minimizes the punishing effect of public embarrassment by conducting the guidance talk as privately as possible, face-to-face, after the teacher has helped the child to cool down.

Guidance talks are not "lectures" and they are not "preaching or screeching." The teacher informally follows the steps in the five-finger formula, sometimes informally such as by blending the middle steps:

1. Calm all down, including yourself.
2. Come to agreement on each person's perceptions of the conflict.
3. Brainstorm possible solutions to the conflict.
4. Agree on a solution that best resolves the conflict.
5. Put it into effect with teacher monitoring and follow-up if needed.

Classroom Anecdote	*After outdoor time, Azra, age five, strode into the classroom, swept raincoats off hooks, pushed some table toys onto the floor, and made a beeline for the juice pitcher. Elsie, the teacher, looked up from where she was tending to another child. She caught Azra a step away from the pitcher, held him to her side, and said, "It's Okay, Azra, let's calm down." Azra tried to pull away, but Elsie held on and they walked to a corner of the room. Still holding Azra, they sat together on the floor. Elsie used soothing words to help Azra let go of his strong impulse. As he became calm, she told the rest of the class to find activities at centers "while I help Azra." The class was used to Azra's dramatic mistaken behavior and found things to do.*
	As Azra got calm, Elsie told him they would talk later about what happened. She said, "I am going to get snack ready now. You can have snack when you are ready." Azra sat on the floor until most of the children were finished, then came to his place and ate. The kindergarten children had language arts activities as centers after snack. Elsie and Azra talked:
	Elsie: You were very upset when you came in today.
	Azra: Sam [the playground attendant] said I had to get off the swing. He didn't give me the "three." (the three-minute warning Elsie frequently used with Azra)
	Elsie: He didn't give you the three? What happened then?
	Azra: I told him but he said get off now. He made me. I got mad.
	Elsie: What can we do about this?
	Azra: Tell him to give me the three and not to yell.
	Elsie: What can you do to make this better? Is there something you can say to Sam?
	(continued)

Classroom Anecdote	*Azra: Tell him sorry.*
	(Brief pause)
	Elsie: How about at lunch I will talk to Sam about the "three." When you go outside what can you do?
	Azra: Tell him sorry.
	Elsie: Anything else?
	Azra: Get off when it's time.
	Elsie: You forgot to come to me and say "I am mad" when you got in the room. Next time?
	Azra: Yeah.
	Elsie: Gyro and Marcie fixed the coats. Can you go join them at the Center? (Elsie watched Azra join the other children. She decided to talk with him again later about what he needed to remember when his impulses took control.)

If you review the guidance talk, you can see that Elsie used all five steps. Now, how can a kindergarten teacher take the time for guidance talks with individual children? Elsie, like all teachers, has to work at making the time. The first step, calming Azra down, cannot be delayed. Disruption only continues when emotions are high. Elsie postponed the other steps, and sometimes teachers need to do this. Notice, though, that the actual guidance talk took only eight exchanges, just a minute or two—though these talks seem longer. Elsie clearly had a caring relationship with Azra. Teachers start relationships on the first day of school, to build trust in children for moments like this. Notice also that the class was respectful of the situation. Elsie worked from the first day to build an encouraging classroom for all. Children who feel appreciated, appreciate others. Guidance talks do not always have to work as smoothly as this one. Like the other guidance interventions, teachers get positive, if not perfect, results when they show they are leaders and they care. More on guidance talks is found in Chapter Ten.

Class Meetings

Guidance talks are one-on-one private. **Class meetings** are public; they involve the whole class. Class meetings are part of the daily schedule in many early childhood classrooms, including with very young preschoolers. Class meetings also happen when socially influenced mistaken behavior has grown to involve several members of the class—with most or all aware of the situation. As guidance intervention, the teacher uses her leadership skills to confront the conflict head-on. Again, an informal combination of the steps in the five-finger formula often is helpful. They are handy to count off as cues to know what to say at different points of the meeting. The following anecdote illustrates a class meeting at a first-grade level.

Classroom Anecdote	*In Ms. Hollander's first grade, the research teams (two students each—assigned to different birds) were having conflicts over use of the three computers in the room. For some groups, the small timer seemed to magically reset midway through the designated ten minutes. Children were clearly frustrated at both having to stop before done and having to wait longer than they should. Disputes in the computer area were growing. Ms. Hollander called a class meeting. She reminded them of the need to be respectful of every child and to focus on what the problem was and how to solve it.*
	Team members quickly identified the problem. No names were mentioned—the class was used to the meetings. Ms. Hollander asked the class to brainstorm solutions. Several were mentioned. No large (very public) timer was available, so the class settled on a strategy suggested by the teacher. The class decided an order for using the computers based on chance. The class made a list of each team in the order decided. For the three days of information collection time for the "birds where we live" theme, each team could use a computer for the 40 minutes of "research time" during late afternoon. Not all 11 teams decided to use the computers, so the three days would be enough. Ms. Hollander wrote down and posted the agreed-to system. The research went more smoothly.

Chapter Seven examines class meetings with various age groups, even with toddlers about biting! Educational models such as Responsive Classroom rely on class meetings to set class routines and resolve group problems. Class meetings establish the inclusive nature of the encouraging classroom and uniquely prepare students for life in a democracy. Class meetings are a step (way) up from the "group punishments," which many readers are familiar with from their years in school. In using class meetings to confront and resolve public conflicts, the teacher models the effectiveness of guidance interventions that make her a positive leader and build group spirit.

Crisis Management Techniques

Young children are just beginning to understand the complexities of social situations, and they feel emotions strongly. On occasion they need to be rescued from their own behavior. The test of the teacher's use of guidance is when she must directly intervene to prevent harm or serious disruption. Although early intervention to head off a crisis is preferable, it is not always possible. When communication has broken down and physical or psychological harm becomes likely, the teacher must act. *The purpose of crisis management interventions is to lower emotions, restore safety, and set the scene for one or more of the guidance interventions in the previous section.* Sample crisis management techniques are disused as follows:

Requesting a Choice. A first **crisis management technique** is to request a choice. The teacher uses this technique to prevent an impending crisis from erupting. The teacher describes what she sees, then requests the choice. Examples are:

> "Boys, active play is fine, but vampire biting is not. Tell me what you can play on the climber instead."

Frequently, the teacher waits to see whether children can resolve a conflict on their own.

"Devon and Macabee your words are getting loud. Discuss this quietly or work separately and we will discuss it later."

"Sheila, you have a right to be upset. Use your words so we can talk about this now, or go to a cool-down place so we can talk later."

When the teacher's emotions are high, Ginott (1972) suggests a third step. As a check on what the teacher says, she uses an "I" message: (1) describe what you see; (2) *tell the children how you feel about it*; (3) request the choice. An example is: "Devon and Macabee, you are pushing and shoving. *I am concerned someone will be hurt.* Sit down here and we will talk, or move away to cool down. Then we will talk.

Calming. Simultaneously with checking for injury, the teacher uses calming techniques to lower emotions during conflicts. It is difficult even for adults to discuss emotional matters calmly. The guidance teacher needs to have a collection of calming techniques to use (with herself if needed) and the children. The teacher may use soothing words and touch, take deep breaths with the child, or have the child count to ten. A student teacher got two children to cool down by jumping up and down three times.

Classroom Anecdote	*In a Minneapolis preschool, the teacher noticed that Cody, a child who rarely initiated conversations, was using a truck. The teacher did not see exactly what happened next, but heard Cody crying and saw Shannon (a "veteran" five-year-old) pushing the truck to another part of the room. The teacher was tempted to confront Shannon, who was looking over her shoulder, but went first to Cody and quietly talked with him. When the teacher got up and walked toward Shannon, the five-year-old did not argue that she had the truck first. Instead Shannon said, "I didn't mean to." This response allowed the teacher to assist Shannon to make amends.*

By calming Cody first, the teacher also managed her own feelings about Shannon. Shannon figured out that the teacher knew what happened and had a chance to work through initial defensiveness. The teacher's with-it-ness provided for helpful calming that facilitated solving the problem.

Cool-down Time. When children cannot cool down on the spot, limited brief periods of supervised removal, as described in the anecdote with Azra, help the child to regain management of emotions. The difference between removal as punishment and as guidance is that the teacher does the removal to help the child calm down, not as a consequence of what the child has done. (See the Chapter Eleven discussion of time-out.) The purpose of the cool-down time is to make a guidance talk or conflict management possible to resolve the problem.

A technique currently having a lot of use, as in Responsive Classroom, is brief self-removal to regain control. The child feels he is going to "lose it" and takes himself out of the situation. Self-removal, as part of a strategy worked out with an individual child, indicates gains in impulse control—very much needed by some children, like Azra in the anecdote. By following up even briefly, the teacher reinforces the child in its use. Brief self-removal as standard classroom practice, especially when not followed up with individual teacher-child contact, may be more punishment than guidance. Everyone in the class is aware of who leaves the group and how often, especially at the "invitation" of the teacher. Self-removal is not an end goal, but a means to emotions management—so the child doesn't need to leave the conflict, but can use words to resolve it. For any child, if the frequency of self-removals does not decrease, the teacher needs to think again about the practice and perhaps try something else.

Passive Restraint. If a child has totally lost control, the teacher may need to use **passive restraint**—to prevent harm to the child himself or to others. **Passive restraint** is arms around arms, legs around legs. The teacher goes into a sitting posture holding the child facing away with his head to one side of the teacher or the other. The teacher immediately uses calming techniques that she thinks may work with the child—gentle words, soft singing, sitting and rocking, or just sitting—all the while holding the child. The child will not understand what the teacher is doing at first, and will attempt to break lose as a fear reaction. This is

© Cengage Learning

The teacher gains new information that assists in understanding behavior and building relations.

what makes the passive bear hug difficult and occasionally bruising for teachers. As the child calms down, which may take a few minutes, he will stop fighting and often actually nestle against the adult. The child has come to realize that the teacher has brought order to an out-of-control world. Perhaps expressed only nonverbally, the child often become grateful. He needs the continued support of the teacher, and often time, to rejoin classroom activity.

The "passive bear hug" is the crisis management technique of last resort (Slaby, Roedell, Arezzo, & Hendrix, 1995). Teachers use it only within the guidelines established by the program or school, and often with other adults present. When passive restraint is used, the teacher typically files a report and discusses the matter with a supervisor. Except with certain children who show frequent Level Three mistaken behavior, a teacher has little occasion to use the technique. As determined by policy, the adult may have to use the technique in order to prevent serious harm. Passive restraint is one of the crisis management techniques discussed more thoroughly in Chapter Eleven.

Crisis management techniques by themselves do not end mistaken behavior nor "cure" the underlying reasons for it. The techniques constitute guidance when their use enables further contact with teachers, and sometimes other professionals. Through the direct assistance that crisis management allows, the child becomes more able to resolve classrooms conflicts.

By themselves, crisis management techniques can only get teachers and children through the crisis. Together with planned prevention and intervention strategies, crisis management is essential to the comprehensive guidance, which some children need. Comprehensive guidance, the coordinated use of guidance strategies to assist children who show strong needs behavior over time, is featured in Chapter Eleven.

Liberation Teaching

Teachers have stated that their greatest challenge is working with the few children in a class who are difficult to like—or in the words of one frustrated first-grade teacher, who are "a pain in the butt." In any classroom, some children will be challenging to a teacher, who may have difficulty coping with, relating to, and understanding them. Even early childhood teachers cannot love every child. But, necessary for the encouraging classroom, the teacher needs to build a relationship with each child so that all children feel they are worthy and accepted members of the class (Grossman, 2008).

Children come into classrooms vulnerable in many ways. Some come from nontraditional family situations or from cultural or religious groups different from the mainstream. Other children may have long-recognized disabilities such as hearing loss or cerebral palsy, "less traditional" disabilities such as fetal alcohol syndrome, or less easily diagnosed conditions such as information-processing difficulties. Children may have unusual facial appearances, be distinctly short or tall, overweight or underweight, or grossly lacking in physical coordination.

Children may display unique learning styles, have experienced "everything" or very little, come from "super-enriched" or impoverished backgrounds, or show atypical developmental patterns. They may possess "extreme" dispositions that show in a high need for:

▶ attention

▶ acting on impulses

▶ opposing external control

▶ controlling the environment (Kaiser & Sklar-Rasminsky, 2003).

Young children come into classrooms with a range of behavioral styles, social attributes, cultural backgrounds, physical characteristics, learning capabilities, and levels of self-esteem, any of which can impede or enhance a child's progress in the class. The professional teacher learns how to respond positively to each child, given the mix of qualities and behaviors that comprise each child's developing personality. As the most significant adult outside the family, the teacher has great influence.

In contrast, responses that aggravate a child's need for security and acceptance and that deny growth are *stigmatizing*. In Goffman's terms (1963), receiving a **stigma** disqualifies an individual from full participation in the group and greatly diminishes self-esteem. Teacher responses that affirm the child's sense of belonging, worth, and competence empower the child toward growth. Teachers who do so liberate children from vulnerability for stigma. These adults practice **liberation teaching**.

A teacher can make a significant difference in children's lives by empowering them through activities.

Liberation teaching has its roots in the social psychology of Goffman (1963), the social commentary of authors such as Gottlieb (1973), and the practices of countless caring teachers over the years. The term *liberation* is borrowed from such disparate sources as Catholic theology and the writings of Faber and Mazlich (1974).

The self psychologist Maslow has particularly contributed to the construct with his discussion of the dual human needs for safety and growth (1962). Of the two needs, the need for safety—security, belonging, identification, love relationships, respect—is the stronger. To the extent the child feels safety needs are unmet, she becomes preoccupied with meeting safety needs and is likely to show mistaken behavior in the attempt to meet them—level three mistaken behavior.

On the other hand, as safety needs are met, the child is empowered to address the need for growth through such qualities as openness, curiosity, creativity, problem-solving ability, responsiveness, and self-actualization (Maslow, 1962). In Maslow's terms, liberation teaching is the ability to assist the child to meet safety needs and to nudge the child toward growth.

Other psychologists also have contributed to the liberation concept. In Piaget's work *liberation teaching* is assisting the child to move from heteronomy toward autonomy (Piaget, 1932/1960). Vygotsky described scaffolding as the process of a teacher taking a child where she is and actively supporting her in the developmental process, including social–emotional development. In Erikson's construct, liberation teaching is empowering the child to grow from shame, doubt, and inferiority to initiative and industry (Elkind, 1993). For Harlow, cited in Chapter Three, liberation teaching is helping the child to rise from survival and adjustment to the social relations level of encountering.

An enduring notion of the "real" teacher, sometimes attributed to Socrates, holds that she does not cram students' minds with facts, but kindles enthusiasm in students' minds by giving them an awareness of what they can become. Such descriptions clearly are not new. Why, then, use the term *liberation* when what is being described is plain old "good teaching"?

The answer lies in the power of the teacher to impact the present and the future of the child (Noddings, 2005). As the teacher "figures out" a hard-to-like child, develops a helping relationship with a child that other children reject, and assists a child in conquering mistaken behaviors to become a full member of the class, that teacher deserves to know that she is engaged in a special. Life-altering process (Gallagher & Mayer, 2008). In the practice of liberation teaching, the teacher has demonstrated not just to the child, but also to the family and the other children, that this classroom is an encouraging place, and all children in it can learn and grow.

Accepting Our Humanness

To be effectively liberating, teachers need to monitor their own feelings and retain positive consistency in their communications. They watch out for their own Level Three days, as the following anecdote illustrates.

Classroom Anecdote	*After a night of little sleep, because her infant was teething and her husband was out of town, Marissa (who happened to be suffering from a sinus headache) discovered her sick-leave days were used up. She got her infant to child care and herself to school, and modified the plans for her first-grade class. She relied more on her educational assistant, soft-pedaled expectations for individuals and the group, increased self-directed activities, and used an educational video that was scheduled for another day. The day proved long, but not as long as it might have been if she had not recognized her needs, changed her expectations, and made necessary adjustments. Her husband returned that evening and took care of their infant so she could get some much-needed rest.*

When teachers are affected by personal circumstances, they sometimes let the class know. In a caring classroom, even three-year-olds will make an effort to "help Teacher feel better." (Teachers report, however, that this practice loses its effectiveness if used on a daily basis.) Often, they may share their situation with selected other staff. Teachers who keep a list of strategies to help them through physically or emotionally rough days show an understanding about their importance in the lives of young children.

Despite the best of intentions and because they are human, teachers too make mistakes. They may misinterpret situations, overreact to a child, be punitive toward a group, or be unprofessional to an adult. Use of a guidance approach does not presume perfection. Mastering social problem-solving orientation is a long process. In guidance, a teacher has a right to make mistakes, but like the children he needs to learn from them. The professional teacher learns even while he teaches.

Building Partnerships with Parents

In a still relevant commentary in the NAEYC journal *Young Children*, Greenberg (1989) discussed roadblocks to effective parent-teacher relations, including the issues of gender bias, racism, and classism. Greenberg developed the argument that as the 20th century progressed, schools grew more "professional," and parents became less welcome in them—especially parents from cultural and income backgrounds different from school personnel. Moreover, the administrative structure of schools became male-dominated, making communication difficult for many single parents, most of whom are women, and for many women teachers of young children. Greenberg defines the resulting problem this way:

If, when they were children, parents had a great many frustrations and failure experiences in school, they may not like schools very much. This feeling can be contagious to their children. It can be true in any family. It seems to be particularly true of low-income minority families, though of course it's by no means always so. In this case, many children feel they have to choose to spurn the family and throw themselves into succeeding at school, or to spurn school success to win family approval. This is a tough spot to put a young child in! Children who have to buck school to avoid disapproval at home are often big-time discipline problems. (p. 61)

In further response to this issue, Greenberg concludes:

Conversely, children whose parents expect them to cooperate and to do their best at school, and who are proud when they do, tend to have better self-discipline. [The children] are striving to achieve family approval; to do this they must earn the teacher's approval. Encouraging a high degree of family enthusiasm for their children's public schools and child care centers is one of the best ways in which teachers can build children's self-esteem and reduce discipline problems.... (pp. 61–62)

For the reasons mentioned by Greenberg, partnerships with family members are integral to a teacher's use of guidance. Building such relations requires teachers to put aside biases and focus on what they and family members have in common, the well-being of the child (Gestwicki, 2007; Brand, 1996; Peterson, 2002; see also Recommended Resources). Exceptional teachers always have gone out of their way to make family members feel welcome and esteemed. Authorities in the field make the point that the responsibility to reach even hard-to-reach family members lies with the teacher (Gestwicki, 2007; Peterson, 2002).

Classroom Anecdote	*In a low-income, rural community in Minnesota, a principal informed a longtime third-grade teacher that she was assigned to a large first-grade class the next fall. Taken by surprise, Mindy requested that she be allowed to invite family members into the class to help with activities. The principal reluctantly agreed but told the teacher the idea would never work.*
	By the end of October, the teacher had 75% of the family members, including working parents, coming into class on a regular basis. By December, every family member had been into the classroom at least once. The principal responded warmly. She said she was sold on the idea the day a substitute had taught in mindy's first grade and offered this reaction: Between the family volunteers and the children, the classroom ran itself.

Whatever the existing practices of a school or center toward collaboration with family members, the teacher does well to note two generally accepted ideas in early childhood about parents:

⟩ There is no more important profession for which there is so little preparation as being a parent.

⟩ Parents are the primary educators of their children; teachers only help.

Writers such as Brand (1996) and Peterson (2002) echo Greenberg's call for prospective teachers to have more preparation in working with family members and for administrators to give more attention to family-teacher relations. The child is an extension of the family. The teacher who understands this and works well with the families will be more successful in guiding children's development.

Awareness of the importance of family member involvement in their children's education is growing in the society (Gestwicki, 2007; Gartrell, 2004). Despite busy schedules, many family members are willing to become involved. They need invitations, choices regarding their involvement, and support from the teacher. With increased family member participation, children learn they are supported at home *and* at school, mistaken behavior becomes less, and real progress in the learning of democratic life skills is made (Lundgren & Morrison, 2003).

Summary

1. What are the differences between a teacher who is a professional and a teacher who is a technician?

Technicians view teaching as the effective implementation of preset curriculum and discipline systems. They tend to react in rigid ways, determined by school traditions, administrative expectations, and inflexible classroom rules. Professionals use informed hypotheses formulated through continuing education and experience. They recognize that each child and each situation is unique. The teacher practices with-it-ness but recognizes that teachers usually do not know all that has happened in a situation. They adjust teaching practice on the basis of experience to improve the social and educational climate of the class. Professionals learn even as they teach.

2. How are positive teacher-child relations the basis of the guidance approach?

As a professional, the teacher works to accept each child as a welcome member of the group. While the teacher need not love every child, she understands the importance of high-quality teacher-child relationships and works to form these relationships with every child in the class. The *unconditional positive regard* the guidance professional shows does not mean that the teacher is permissive, but that she separates mistaken behaviors from the personality of the child—addressing the behaviors while affirming personal worth. To maintain positive relations, the teacher practices the *cardinal principle*, avoids labels, is firm but friendly, and affirms the worth of every child.

3. How does guidance reduce mistaken behavior?

The teacher recognizes that when children have trouble in the school environment, two factors tend to be involved. First are the challenges of childhood. The teacher accepts the fact that, due to the anxieties of life and developmental inexperience, make mistakes in the process of learning. A second factor lies in children's reactions when teaching practices are developmentally inappropriate. Current pressures for the assessment of academic performance means that teachers must work hard to keep their classrooms responsive to the activity levels and learning styles of young children. The teacher improves the match by using developmentally appropriate and culturally responsive teaching practices—and ties them to the attainment of standards by observation-based assessment.

4. What does "guidance is solution oriented" mean?

The teacher creates an environment in which problems can be resolved. She does so by practicing the guidance interventions of conflict management, guidance talks, class meetings, crisis management interventions, and comprehensive guidance. The teacher intervenes nonpunitively in crises, requesting choices and calming everyone down. She uses removal for cooling down and passive restraint only as methods of last resort. Being models to children, teachers acknowledge their mistakes and learn from them.

5. Why is liberation teaching fundamental to the encouraging classroom?

The various physical, social, cultural, cognitive, and behavioral circumstances of children put them at risk for stigma, that is, negative separation from the group. A problem many teachers face is how to work with those children they, or other children, find difficult to accept. To the extent that the teacher figures out how to assist at-risk to meet their needs for safety and to move toward growth, she is practicing liberation teaching. Liberation teaching is a necessary condition for the creation of the encouraging classroom. Liberation teaching means not giving up on any child.

6. How are family-teacher partnerships important in the guidance approach?

The teacher recognizes that being a family member is a difficult job and that many family members, for personal and cultural reasons, feel discomfort in communicating with educators. The teacher's job is to initiate relations even with hard-to-reach family members ("be nice first"). Although busy, many family members respond positively to invitations to become involved in their children's education. The need for mistaken behavior diminishes and the chance for school success increases when family members and teachers work together.

FOLLOW-UP ACTIVITIES

Note: An element of being a professional teacher is to respect the children, parents, and educators you are working with by maintaining confidentiality, that is, keeping identities private. In completing follow-up activities, please respect the privacy of all concerned.

Discussion Activity

The discussion activity encourages students to interrelate their own thoughts and experiences with specific ideas from the chapter.

Identify the guidance principle (listed at the beginning of the chapter) that is the most important to you in your professional development. Relate the principle to an experience of yours as a student either before entering your teacher preparation program or since. Why is this experience relating to the principle important to you?

Application Activities

Application activities allow students to interrelate material from the text with real-life situations. The observations imply access to practicum experiences; the interviews, access to teachers or parents. In order to integrate theory and practice, students compare or contrast observations and interviews with referenced ideas from the chapter.

1. The differences between a teacher who is a professional and a teacher who is a technician.

   a. Observe a teacher you regard as a professional as he or she responds to situations in the classroom. Record an incident that you believe was handled effectively. Talk with the teacher about his and the child(ren)'s responses. Compare findings to ideas in the chapter.

    b. Interview a teacher you believe to be a professional. Discuss decisions the teacher has made that might be construed difficult, innovative, or even controversial in order to assist a child. Ask about the teacher's reasons for the decisions. Compare findings to ideas in the chapter.

2. Positive teacher-child relations.

    a. Observe an instance in which a teacher affirmed positive regard for a child. What did the teacher say and do? What did the child say and do? How do you think the child's behavior might be influenced by such an exchange? Compare findings to ideas in the chapter.

    b. Talk with a teacher about a sensitive topic: Explain that your textbook says that teachers do not always have natural positive feelings toward every child. Ask the teacher how he builds relationships with children who are "more difficult to like or understand—challenging." Compare findings to ideas in the chapter.

3. Guidance reduces the need for mistaken behavior.

    a. Observe an instance when a teacher acted to resolve a problem (without punishment) in a firm but friendly manner. Think about what level of mistaken behavior was at work. Reflect about how the teacher showed understanding of the child or children involved. Compare results to ideas in the chapter.

    b. Observe an activity that seemed a "good match" between the levels of development of the children and what the activity asked the children to do. Discuss the amount of productive behavior and/or mistaken behavior you observed during the activity. Compare findings to ideas in the chapter.

    c. Ask a teacher to discuss a change he has made to the curriculum or schedule to improve the match between the needs of the children and the expectations of the program. How did the change make the day "go better" for the children, and for the teacher? What does the teacher think were the educational implications of the change? Compare findings to ideas in the chapter.

4. Guidance is solution oriented.

    a. Observe an instance when a teacher assisted children to peaceably resolve a problem. What did the teacher and children say and do? How was the teacher's intervention similar or different from the guidance intervention technique(s) in the chapter. Compare findings to ideas in the chapter.

    b. Ask a teacher to recall an instance when he successfully assisted one or more children to resolve a classroom problem without punishment. Ask how the teacher determined the outcome was successful. Ask the teacher his feelings about the experience. Compare findings to ideas in the chapter.

5. Liberation teaching, fundamental to the encouraging classroom.

   a. Observe an example of liberation teaching when a teacher assisted a child who otherwise might be stigmatized. Focusing on the responses of the teacher and the child in the situation, decide why you believe liberation teaching was at work. Compare findings to ideas in the chapter.

   b. Ask a teacher to share an experience when he was successful in helping a child who was at risk for stigma. Inquire about what the teacher did that supported the child. Ask how the teacher determined the outcome was successful. Ask the teacher his feelings about the experience. Compare findings to ideas in the chapter.

6. Family-teacher partnerships.

   a. Observe a situation in which a teacher is working in partnership with one or more family members. What actions on the part of the teacher(s) seem to build the relationship? How did the family member seem to respond? Compare findings to ideas in the chapter.

   b. Interview a family member about a teacher who built a partnership with the family. What did the parent think the teacher said and did to build the relationship? How did the parent feel about the relationship? Compare findings to ideas in the chapter.

Recommended Readings

Children's Defense Fund. (2008). *The state of America's children: 2008.* Washington, DC: Children's Defense Fund.

Children's Defense Fund. (2009). *The state of America's children: 2009.* Washington, DC: Children's Defense Fund.

Crosser, S. (2002, May–June). What's the difference between right and wrong: Understanding how children think. *Early Childhood News*, pp. 12–16.

Gallagher, K. C., & Mayer, K. (2008). Research in review: Enhancing development and learning through teacher-child relationships. *Young Children, 63*(6), 80–87.

Gilliam, W. S. (2005). *Prekindergarteners left behind: Expulsion rates in state prekindergarten systems.* New Haven, CT: Yale University Child Study Center. Online: http://www.fcd-us.org/PDFs/NationalPreKExpulsionPaper03.02_new.pdf

Grossman, S. (2008). "I just don't like that kid": Confronting and managing personal feelings about children. *Childhood Education, 84*(3), 147–149.

Lundgren, D., & Morrison, J. W. (2003). Involving Spanish-speaking families in early childhood programs. *Young Children, 58*(3), 88–95.

Noddings, N. (2005, September). What does it mean to educate the whole child? *Educational Leadership, 63*(1), 8–13.

Ostrosky, M. M., & Jung, E. Y. (2003). Building positive teacher-child relationships. *What Works Briefs.* Nashville, TN: The Center on the Social and Emotional Foundations of Early Learning. Vanderbilt University, http://www.vanderbilt.edu/csefel/

Guidance Matters

"He Did It on Purpose!"

September, 2007

On this day in a child care center, the lead teacher is absent as the three-year-old group has come in from the playground. A child is feeling sick, so the assistant teacher is tending to her in the quiet area. This leaves the new student teacher, Rhonda, to get the children into a large-group activity by herself.

As the children enter the room, most sit down in the group meeting area. Raffi, a quiet "younger three," sits in the circle near the door. Wade, almost four, approaches the group, then lies down and sidles along the floor toward Raffi. Wade kicks at Raffi, who turns around and protests, "Stop!"

Rhonda, busy getting the group ready for a story, doesn't seem to notice the conflict. Wade continues pushing his foot hard into Raffi's back. Holding his back, Raffi begins to cry. Rhonda leads Raffi to the other side of the circle, finds him a place to sit, and returns to reading the story.

When Wade notices Rhonda move Raffi while ignoring him, he again crawls around behind Raffi. Again Wade pushes his foot into Raffi's back. Looking exasperated, Rhonda starts to get up to deal with the situation.

But seeing what is happening, Anne, an experienced student teacher with another group, comes over, comforts Raffi, and takes Wade away to the nearby dramatic-play area. Wade scoots under a table and will not come out. Anne does not make Wade come to her, but sits on the floor near the table, apparently listening to the story. After a few minutes, Wade crawls out and sits on Anne's lap. The two listen to the rest of the story and watch the group activities. As the class transitions to center time, the assistant teacher rejoins the group. Rhonda looks relieved.

Discussion

What do teachers do when children cause conflicts on purpose? Rhonda probably ignored Wade's intentional act the first time, and simply moved Raffi the second time, because she did not want to overreact to the situation and risk losing control of the group. Especially in group situations, the decision to intervene in conflicts or to ignore them is a common and difficult dilemma.

For this reason, preventing conflicts (rather than having to react to them) is always the teacher's priority. In early childhood education, it is helpful to remember that young children and large groups are not a natural match! Children manage in large groups more easily as they grow older. So, especially in group situations, we should not underestimate the importance of teaching in teams. If available, the assistant teacher might have helped Wade join the circle, preventing the conflict. Even after an incident happens, a second adult is invaluable. Rhonda later expressed appreciation to Anne for assisting her.

Rhonda's reaction to Wade's behavior was to let the situation go and hope for the best. In contrast, some teachers automatically shift into "discipline mode" when a child intentionally causes a conflict. The problem with this reaction is that it influences teachers to jump from judging the behavior to judging the child (Gartrell, 2004). Back in 1988, Polly Greenberg criticized the practice of labeling kids as good or bad and enforcing "me against you discipline" (punishment) to increase "good behavior." This line of reasoning presumes that children, even young children, know how to behave, but they choose to be "bad." Even today, teachers who take this view consider children such as Wade to be *willful, defiant, oppositional,* or *challenging* and in need of discipline to shame them away from bad behavior.

Research now tells us that due to still-developing brains and limited social experience, most young children are just beginning to learn how to behave (Albert, 2003). The effect of punishment on a child like Wade (especially when repeated) is that instead of being shamed into being "good," he is shamed into feeling he is bad (Dreikurs, Grunwald, & Pepper, 1982/1998; Gartrell, 2004). This psychological dynamic causes the child's stress levels to go up and feelings of isolation to arise. The child needs affirmation from the teacher but perceives that the teacher regards him as unworthy. Mistakenly, the child acts out to get the human connection he needs, sometimes against the child who "caused" him to get in trouble in the first place (Dreikurs, Grunwald, & Pepper, 1982/1998; Albert, 2003).

By punishing the instigator, teachers may think that they are fixing the problem. In reality, they are probably reinforcing bullying tendencies in the disciplined child and a victim identity in the child who was bullied. Too often the automatic discipline reaction makes future classroom dynamics even worse (Albert, 2003; Gartrell, 2004).

Dreikurs' Contribution

Psychologist Rudolf Dreikurs contributed much to our understanding of how to respond to children's behavior (1968; Dreikurs, Grunwald, & Pepper, 1982/1998). Dreikurs wrote that teachers help a child learn productive behaviors only when they, in firm and friendly ways, guide the child toward finding social acceptance. Dreikurs, along with Ginott (1972) and others who followed them, argued that frustration in achieving the life goal of social acceptance is the real reason why children cause conflicts (Albert, 2003; Gartrell, 2004).

Guiding children in finding social acceptance is one of the most important parts of the early childhood teacher's job. The second student teacher in the anecdote, Anne, really helped Wade. After comforting Raffi, she quietly left with Wade and then let him sit on her lap—the right actions for that child in that situation. Anne helped Wade regain social acceptance. Later, when Wade is calm and the time is right, a teacher who

knows Wade well might have a guidance talk with him. A guidance talk means teaching and learning about

- what happened (in the situation that required teacher intervention);
- how the other child felt;
- what the child can think of to help the other child feel better (better than forcing the child to say "I'm sorry");
- what the child can do differently next time.

An alternative guidance intervention is conflict mediation, which a teacher would undertake with Raffi and Wade together. (See "Guidance Matters," March 2006, in Beyond the Journal, for a discussion of this equally important guidance technique. Go to http://journal.naeyc.org/btj/200603/GuidanceBTJ.pdf.)

In the guidance perspective, children learn from conflicts only when they have productive relationships with the teacher who intervenes. *The relationship comes first.* Teachers build productive relationships through shared quality time outside of conflict situations. Frequent acknowledgment of the child's efforts and achievements is key. We know we are building a relationship when a child comes to us in the tough times. Wade came out from under the table and sat on Anne's lap. Anne let him.

Guidance requires teachers to be firm—but firm and friendly, not firm and harsh. There are definite consequences when a child causes a conflict, for the teacher as well as the child. The consequence for the teacher is teaching—by first calming everyone down (and remembering that these young children are just beginning to learn difficult life skills). The consequence for the child is learning how to express strong emotions in non-hurtful ways, how to get along with others, and how to feel capable of learning important life skills.

The children in our classrooms are just beginning a very complex, lifelong learning process. They, like all of us, make mistakes—errors in judgment in their behaviors. Guidance means teaching children what they have not yet learned. Teaching—not punishment—is the *logical consequence* (Dreikurs' term) when a child causes conflicts.

To Increase Your Knowledge

Get a historical take on working with children's behavior. Locate a book or an article by either Rudolf Dreikurs or Haim Ginott (who famously said, "To reach a child's mind, a teacher must capture his or her heart"). What do these esteemed psychologists have to say that applies to working with children today?

A Step You Can Take

With other staff, select a child who is having frequent conflicts. Develop a plan for helping the child to feel more accepted in the group. Perhaps involve the child in more small-group activities or take turns spending quality time with the child. Actively follow the plan for one to two weeks. Discuss the following questions with your colleagues: How has your thinking changed about the child? How do you think your way of relating to the child has changed? Why do you think there have or have not been changes in the child's behavior? What might be some ways to continue helping the child to fit in with the group?

Column References

Albert, L. (2003). *Cooperative discipline*. Lebanon, IN: AGS/Pearson Globe.

Dreikurs, R. (1968). *Psychology in the classroom* (2nd ed.). New York: Harper & Row.

Dreikurs, R., Grunwald, B. B., & Pepper, F. C. (1982/1998). *Maintaining sanity in the classroom: Classroom management techniques* (2nd ed.). London: Taylor & Francis.

Gartrell, D. (2004). *The power of guidance: Teaching social-emotional skills in early childhood classrooms*. Clifton Park, NY: Thomson Delmar Learning (also Washington, DC: NAEYC).

Ginott, H. G. (1972). *Teacher and child: A book for parents and teachers*. New York: Avon.

Greenberg, P. (1988). Ideas That Work with Young children: Avoiding "me against you" discipline. Young *Children, 44*(1), 24–29.

For additional information on using the guidance approach in the encouraging classroom, visit our website at www.cengage.com/education/gartrell.

Part 2

Creating the Encouraging Classroom

Preview

Five—Organizing the Encouraging Classroom

Chapter Five investigates organization of the encouraging classroom. Topics include examination of how the encouraging classroom reduces school anxiety, the vital role of developmentally appropriate practice, physical layout of the encouraging classroom, organizing for prosocial development, and encouraging family members to volunteer.

Six—Managing the Encouraging Classroom

Chapter Six explores management of the encouraging classroom to reduce mistaken behavior. Topics include the daily program, mixing active and quiet times, the place of large groups, managing transitions, and working with volunteers in the encouraging classroom.

Seven—Leadership Communication with the Group

Chapter Seven addresses the use of leadership communication with the group, including establishing leadership at the beginning of the school year; implementing guidelines instead of rules; providing encouragement; discussing inclusively, using class meetings; and communicating with parents to maintain partnerships.

Eight—Leadership Communication with the Individual

Chapter Eight discusses leadership communication with the individual to build relationships and reduce mistaken behavior. With the individual child, the teacher uses leadership communication by listening to life experiences and having regular contact talks, and also by relying on compliment sandwiches, humor, and the friendly use of touch. In the last section, the chapter considers conferences with family members in which the teacher uses many of these same leadership communication techniques.

Chapter 5 Organizing the Encouraging Classroom

Guiding Questions

▶ *What is an encouraging classroom and how does it prevent school anxiety?*

▶ *What is the relationship of developmentally appropriate practice today and the encouraging classroom?*

▶ *What is the place of learning centers in the encouraging classroom?*

▶ *How does the teacher organize the classroom for prosocial development?*

▶ *How does the teacher encourage family members to be classroom volunteers?*

© Cengage Learning

Key Concepts

▶ *Authentic assessment*

▶ *Culturally linguistically different (CLD)*

▶ *Educational accountability*

▶ *Integrated curriculum*

▶ *Learning centers*

▶ *Mastery motivation*

▶ *Political accountability*

▶ *Process modeling/Product modeling*

▶ *Prosocial development*

▶ *School anxiety*

▶ *School readiness*

▶ *Story pictures*

▶ *Thematic instruction*

▶ *Webbing*

Reducing School Anxiety: The Encouraging Classroom

School Anxiety

If a child wants to go to school when ill, something is right; if a child does not want to go when well, something is wrong. Young children who are unhappy at school cannot easily work through anxieties with words. In some children, school anxiety shows in direct mistaken behavior (*institutionally caused mistaken behavior*)—inattentiveness, frequent frustration, defiance, and/or irritability. In others, school anxiety shows itself in physical conditions. Symptoms range from a twice-a-year stomachache to actual ulcers, from occasional headaches and nervousness to high blood pressure and depressive episodes. Gallagher makes the case that long-term school anxiety even affects brain development and function (2005).

School anxiety can result from specific situations such as the morning bus ride, being bullied on the playground, or the afternoon "power" test. The buildup to high-stakes standardized assessments is a well-known time of stress for children and teachers alike. The cause of stress can also be more pervasive—a general feeling of being:

) disliked by the teacher

) alienated from other children

) dislocated from the education program.

School anxiety is a major cause of Level Three mistaken behavior—strong unmet needs that children react to in the classroom. Educators sometimes miss school anxiety as a cause of serious mistaken behavior. In previous times some teachers rationalized frequent classroom conflicts by negatively labeling the offending child More recently, educators often attribute "a bad home life" to children who act out—and seek to provide the controls the teacher assumes are not provided at home.

Much Level Three mistaken behavior *is* caused by situations outside the school. However, teaching practice that fails to accommodate developmental levels and individual circumstances is a major cause of mistaken behavior in some situations and a contributing factor in others. For instance, young children who are culturally linguistically different (CLD)—from a non-mainstream cultural heritage and whose first language is not English—may feel rejected in underresponsive educational settings. In such situations, individual CLD children experience, and react to, the effects of repeated classroom frustrations. Where numbers of CLD learners feel similarly, the "out-group" status becomes a common bond and frequent mistaken behavior can result.

What kind of educational settings reduce the occurrence of school anxiety and institution-caused mistaken behavior? Several terms apply: inclusive classrooms, differentiated instruction classrooms, culturally responsive classrooms, developmentally appropriate classrooms, and encouraging classrooms. Advocates

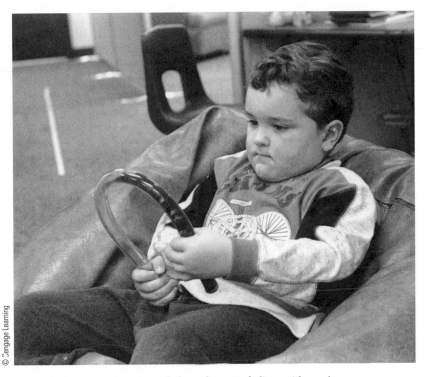

Young children cannot easily work through strong feelings with words.

of any of the terms might argue that theirs takes in the others. The term used in this book is the *encouraging classroom*, which has at its heart the use of developmentally appropriate practice—which *is* culturally responsive (Bredekamp & Copple, 2009). Wien (2004) refers to "overturning the rules and creating amiable classrooms" as the process in which encouraging classrooms come to be (p. 34). Curtis and Carter (2005) refer to the process as rethinking early childhood environments to enhance learning.

The Encouraging Classroom

As mentioned, the encouraging classroom is a place where children want to be even when they are sick—as opposed to not wanting to be there when they are well. It is a place where children feel at home when they are out of the home. A textbook definition of an encouraging classroom is:

> *The physical surrounds of a school, center or family child care program in which adults provide ongoing guidance in order to maintain an equilibrium between the needs of each developing child and the right of the learning community for mutual appreciation among its members. It involves the creation and sustenance of a caring community among children and adults for the purpose of furthering the learning and development of each member. (Gartrell, 2004, p. 75)*

The encouraging classroom begins within the minds of its teachers. In the encouraging classroom, teachers work hard to sustain the dynamic balance between the changing needs of each individual (child and adult) and the right of the community for mutual appreciation—"of each other and yourself too." The equilibrium between the individual and the group is difficult to maintain because young children, with only "months" of total development and experience, still have trouble expressing and meeting their needs. Remember that expressing and meeting individual needs in socially acceptable ways are long-term democratic life skills. We work on these skills our entire lives. Young children are just beginning this life's work.

In an encouraging classroom, a teacher guides children to a good start even, and especially, when children make mistakes in the social–emotional learning process—when they show mistaken behavior. Guidance, which is the approach teachers use to build the encouraging classroom, actively teaches children to express and meet needs acceptably, in non-hurting ways. Unlike teachers who use traditional punitive discipline, in a guidance approach teachers do not threaten the child's membership in the classroom community—such as with time-outs or suspension—to "motivate" better behavior. Instead, they build a positive relationship to ensure the child's acceptance in the class and provide freedom, within limits, to allow the child to learn and to grow. These teachers give the child positive reason to resolve problems peaceably. The child's place in the classroom community, except in rare situations that involve parents and usually other professionals, is not up for discussion (Gartrell, 2004).

Developmentally Appropriate Practice Today

A nationwide trend is for *educational accountability*, which means teachers need to be accountable for the education they are providing. Unlike more simple times in the past, educational accountability now has a place even in early childhood classrooms. Increasingly, early childhood teachers are familiar with terms like "Work Sampling," "portfolios," "authentic assessment," "performance assessment," "standards-based assessment," and "kindergarten readiness." Educational accountability is vital at all levels of education, including in early childhood. One good that has come out of this movement is developmentally appropriate practice (DAP), a priority of the National Association for the Education of Young Children (NAEYC; Bredekamp & Copple, 2009).

A danger in the trend, however, is the confusion of educational accountability with political accountability. When officials put inappropriate pressures on schools and programs to have children perform on assessments, they put both teachers and children at risk (Butzin, 2004). A main symptom of political accountability, the over emphasis on testing and test scores, has *pushed down into the early years* academic lessons and reduced child-directed learning and play (Black, 2003). As in the 1980s, teachers are again expecting too much of young children and are using forced instructional and discipline techniques (Elkind, 1997; Hatch, 2002).

Informal pairings of "neighbors" for projects is one example of multidimensional grouping.

Common inappropriate practices—such as long periods of sitting and "listening," prescribed activities done to exact standards, critical evaluation of children's work, and teacher approval based on performance—invite school anxiety and mistaken behavior. With the imposition of developmentally *in*appropriate practice, children become less able to meet teacher expectations. They experience frustration, resentment, and a sense of failure—school anxiety. An encouraging classroom obviously is difficult under these circumstances (Butzin, 2004).

In the encouraging DAP classroom, a professional teacher works to maximize children's engagement in the learning process. Such methods as learning centers, thematic instruction, emergent/**integrated curriculum**, creative art and journals (even before they can write conventional script) manipulatives-based math, diverse small-group experiences, and active, concise large-group sessions allow children—including children who are culturally linguistically different—to find meaning and success in learning experiences (Brewer, 2007). Utilizing such practices, Table 5–1 illustrates how DAP can reduce mistaken behaviors.

Table 5–1 *Increasing Appropriate Practice to Reduce Mistaken Behavior*		
Moving from Inappropriate Practice	**To Appropriate Practice**	**Reduces These Mistaken Behaviors**
Prolonged sitting and listening in large groups	Active, concise large groups; increased use of small groups	Restlessness, bothering neighbors, confrontation with adults
Prescribed activities done to exacting standards	Creative, flexible-outcome activities for varying developmental levels and diverse backgrounds	Acting out of feelings of failure, frustration, inferiority, boredom
Critical evaluation of children's work	Supportive evaluation of children's work	Mix of reactions to frustration, stress, and lowering of self-esteem
Punishment of some children due to mistaken behavior	Acceptance of all children as welcome group members	Acting out of feelings of rejection, disenfranchisement, hostility

School Readiness and Play

In response to increasing pressures on educators due to political accountability, in 1995 the NAEYC maintained the following about **school readiness**:

1. Inequities in early life experiences should be addressed so that all children have access to the opportunities that promote school success.

2. Individual differences are recognized and supported among children including linguistic and cultural differences.

3. Reasonable and appropriate expectations of children's capabilities are established upon school entry.

The recommendations, reinforced by Deyell-Gingold (2006), still pertain today.

Current knowledge of child development and learning indicates that early education should be focused on the attainment of life skills outcomes pertaining to the whole child rather than on narrowly focused academic preparation. The premature introduction of academics is counter to this philosophy (Hardy, 2003; Bredekamp & Copple 2009). *Significant* learning (when the child constructs new personal meaning from an experience) has always been at the heart of early childhood education, but we now know definitively that such learning maximizes healthy brain development and the cultivation of multiple intelligences (Cassidy, Mims, Rucker, & Boone, 2003).

© Cengage Learning

The presence of an intrinsic dynamic for learning is a given in the guidance approach.

In this regard, an argument of Jean Piaget's has stood the test of time. Elkind (1993) echoes Piaget's case that the early years are "critical for determining whether the child would become a passive learner, mastering everything by rote, or become an active learner who gains new information by discovery and invention" (p. 81). If we want children who are active learners, who construct significant learning, who are intrinsically motivated to learn, and who see themselves as capable learners, we must approach the teaching of young children in developmentally appropriate ways, a central component of which is play (Butzin, 2004).

Classroom Anecdote	*Three kindergarten children are working hard at playing house. The children are Rachel, Mia, and Sarah. Rachel is preparing a meal in the kitchen. She is wearing an apron and cooking on the stove with a frying pan.*
	"Good morning, Honey," said Rachel as she smiled at Miles and continued to cook.
	"Good morning to you, Cupcake," said Miles as he walked up to Sarah. Miles asked, "How is our big girl doing today?"
	"Fine, Daddy," said Sarah as she held her baby doll.
	"Breakfast is ready; have Sarah sit down and it is time to eat," said Rachel. Rachel made a motion to have them sit and they did. I noticed that Sarah dropped her baby doll and
	(continued)

<table>
<tr><td>

Classroom
Anecdote

</td><td>

started drinking from a glass instead of the sipper cup that was on the table. Both Miles and Sarah were sitting at the kitchen table being served by Mom. Then they all said a prayer and began to eat.

"I'm filled," said Miles. "I am late for work." Miles grabbed a hard hat out of the toy box and he also gave Rachel a kiss good-bye (which was promptly wiped off!). When Miles was gone, Rachel started to clear the table, putting the dishes in the sink. Sarah walked over to the baby doll she had dropped and picked it up. She began holding the doll in her arms and wanted Mommy (Rachel) to play with her.

"I have to finish the dishes before I can go out and play," said Rachel. "I want to play with you now," demanded Sarah. "Barney is on now; go and watch him," said Rachel. Rachel continued to wash the dishes, and Sarah went over to the "TV" and watched Barney. Miles also headed into the kitchen area; he had been just wandering around and fixing things in the playroom.

"Honey, I'm home," said Miles. "You're home too early," said Rachel. "Go back to work, I'm not done yet." "I'm bored. I'm going to play with something different now," said Miles. All three children then left and found something else to do. (Gartrell, 2000, p. 30)

</td></tr>
</table>

Despite the "family stereotypes," this anecdote is notable for the detail these kindergartners brought to the family situation. Amazing is that, according to Arlene, the observing student teacher, *all three of the children came from single-parent families.* Through play children expand their understanding about the world, sometimes imagining roles and situations that they may have little direct experience with. This cooperative visioning enhances the perspective, confidence, and world knowledge of young learners.

So much cognitive, language, social, emotional, and even physical learning comes from dramatic play like this. In terms of Gardner's multiple intelligences, in this one example of cooperative dramatic play the children were practicing the use of intrapersonal, interpersonal, linguistic, logical-mathematical, spatial, and bodily–kinesthetic intelligences (six of Gardner's eight established intelligences).

A standard of developmentally appropriate early childhood programs is the scheduled inclusion of play (Bredekamp & Copple, 2009). Teachers and administrators who see the learning benefits of this activity reject the argument that play may not benefit children as to specific answers on performance measures. They look to broader learning outcomes for children and trust the gains in brain development that result from happy, fully engaged experiences—an opening of receptors and brain functioning that allow further learning (Gallagher, 2005).

Stegelin's "Making the Case for Play Policy: Research-Based Reasons to Support Play-Based Environments" (2005) provides a rationale for preschool to primary-grade teachers to include play in their classrooms. (See the Recommended Readings at the end of this chapter.) Certainly, the integrative learning values of play present a strong argument for this activity. An expression among progressive educators is, "Through play children learn what cannot be taught."

"Whoa!" said the teacher who went down a slide for the first time in years! Children appreciate playfulness in teachers, second only to friendliness. Teachers who make playfulness a part of their teaching role are confident in their knowledge and application of DAP.

DAP in the Primary Grades

In many elementary schools, teachers use DAP to *supplement and modify* the traditional academic program. Such practices as integrated curriculum, use of learning centers, informal learning groups, teaching teams, and authentic assessment allow teachers to be fully professional, and classroom practices to become developmentally appropriate. In many schools, however, these changes have taken courage and ingenuity on the part of individual teachers (Burchfield, 1996; Brewer, 2007).

Classroom Illustration	*Kindergarten. Despite a teacher's contention that it was not developmentally appropriate, a work sheet–based arithmetic system had been standard in her school's kindergartens. Being tenured and known as an individual, Ms. Cortez decided she would use the work sheets but in her own way. On the last Friday of each month, the class had a work sheet party. The teacher made plenty of popcorn, and everyone did work sheets. Having used manipulatives to teach the targeted math concepts during the month, Ms. Cortez reported that the children "whipped through the sheets, had fun doing them, and took lots of papers home."*

Classroom Illustration	*First Grade. Mr. Kelly, a first-grade teacher, felt compelled to use the basal series adopted by the school district but found that the reading program did not reinforce the children's excitement about learning to read. Mr. Kelly made a big deal of regular visits to the library and selecting books of real personal interest. He supplemented the reading program with "super silent reading" times when he and the children read their self-selected books. He introduced "just journaling and jotting" times, when he and the children recorded their own thoughts and feelings in journals. He started individual journaling/reading conferences with two or three children each day to assess progress toward standards. When Mr. Kelly discovered children reading and journaling during other parts of the day, he concluded he now had a literacy program that met his expectations.*

For years individual teachers have been "psychologizing" the curriculum, as Dewey termed it (1900/1969). Many teachers have had to do so quietly, behind closed doors. Some—perhaps after receiving tenure—have done their own thing openly and endured the label from colleagues as being that "offbeat one at the

The gains possible through self-directing/open-ended activity (play) help children feel positively about themselves in the classroom situation.

end of the hall." One teacher, known for being creative, commented, "I do as little of what I have to do, and as much as what I want to do, to stay out of serious trouble." The pressures for performance from "No Child Left Behind" have made developmentally responsive teaching more difficult (but not impossible) for many caring teachers (Butzin, 2004).

Working Together for Change. In the drive toward national literacy, some curricula are more developmentally appropriate than others. Often, a committee can make a request for curriculum modification seem more studied and objective than an individual teacher can. For this reason, two or more teachers who attend a workshop, conference, or course together may be successful in introducing developmentally appropriate practices into a school. When all teachers at a grade level, for instance, feel strongly about the need to modify practice, they often succeed by working together.

Classroom Illustration	*Two kindergarten teachers in an urban school became tired of work sheets and drills used to teach phonics and counting skills. They heard from a teacher at another school about alternative approaches using emergent literacy techniques and a manipulatives-based math program. The two teachers began attending workshops, collecting sample materials, and talking with other teachers. The teachers got the principal to agree that the new methods were more responsive to the developmental levels of kindergarten children. With the principal's support, the two teachers convinced the third kindergarten teacher to adopt a manipulatives-based math program to replace the use of work sheets. They currently are reviewing a new program to beginning reading/writing, more child-active and less dependent on a preprimer phonics system. The first-grade teachers are taking notice of what is going on in the kindergarten. The kindergarten teachers plan to involve them further.*

Tact, civility, and communication—starting with the modifications that are most feasible—are the watchwords. As education marketers and inspirational speakers have long known, educators tend to be receptive to changes that are linked to the latest trends. Movement toward DAP is sometimes easier when it is linked with other buzzwords. A noteworthy anecdote about riding the buzzword bandwagon is two first-grade teachers who are alleged to have gotten play into their programs by calling it "self-selected, self-directed autonomous learning periods."

Role of the Principal. The stereotype of the elementary principal is of the middle-aged patriarch, the male secondary teacher who eventually got his administrator's license. A problem some teachers have experienced is that such principals neither have taught at the primary level nor seem to care about the needs of young children.

Contrary to this image, many administrators are open to improvements in programming; they see becoming educated about early childhood education a part of their jobs. They ask only for a clearly spelled-out rationale that the projected program will be cost effective and results oriented.

Now in a new century with a new generation of principals coming to the fore, an increase in administrators with backgrounds in early childhood education can be expected. Nonetheless, knowing the principal well as teachers work to introduce DAP into the school only makes sense. In some situations, she will be the teacher's best ally (Burchfield, 1996). In others, the teacher without tenure should work closely with, but stay in the shadow of, established teachers who know the principal well.

To modify practice in a school or district, teachers and administrators need to plan carefully and organize well. Inviting educators from other areas who are using interesting ideas is a useful technique. Educators need to stay alert for models, methods, and systems that retain developmentally appropriate practice at the heart of the education of young children. The success of innovative programs is sometimes due to the leadership of principals who work on a collegial basis with staff to establish an encouraging environment, and a unifying philosophy throughout the school.

Accommodate the Active Nature of Young Children. As a parent volunteer in an early childhood classroom once commented, "They sure are active little critters, aren't they?" Busyness, not quietness, is the normal sound level in developmentally appropriate classrooms. Part of the natural fit of centers in early childhood classrooms is due to the busy level of child activity that centers accommodate.

Taking a broad health perspective, obesity is a burgeoning problem in our society (Haschke, 2003; Lynn-Garbe & Hoot, 2004/2005; Lumeng, 2005). In a traditional "sedentary" classroom, children may sit at desks or tables for five hours a day. How do most kids travel between home and school? They sit in a bus or car. What do most of these kids do when they get home? The average child watches television from four to six hours a day, and computers used for entertainment may be increasing even further the relative inactivity of children (Lynn-Garbe & Hoot, 2005; Pica, 2000). What do they eat? Too often, high-calorie foods (Lumeng, 2005).

Pica suggests that during early childhood, children begin to set lifelong patterns of activity or inactivity. Moreover, the argument can be made that young children who are physically active accomplish the physiological development that they need in order to be able to sit and concentrate for sustained periods when they are older. An irony of early childhood is that active play, and not sitting and being quiet, may be the best "rehearsal" for this traditional goal of classroom management (Garcia, Garcia, Floyd, & Lawson, 2002).

> *The notion that classrooms are generally quiet places should have been phased out at the end of the 20th century, if not the 19th. Brain development and learning require bodies in motion, and interaction, physical activity, and social activity in the classroom. Individual quiet times are important, but classrooms need to be friendly, busy places.*

Active play encourages perceptual-motor development.

While the recent spotlight on the need for increased physical activity has focused on young boys (Kantrowitz & Kalb, 1998), both girls and boys need opportunities each day to freely exercise their muscles (Pica, 2000). Daily aerobic activity at large-group times assists children (and teachers) to stay in shape. An active-play area, with equipment such as a climber, balance beam, minitrampoline, and hoppity-hops, is ideally located in an adjacent room and, as weather permits, outdoors. But the activity is so important that if necessary, a center is located in the "active end" of even small classrooms.

Classroom Anecdote	*A Head Start program purchased a low mini-trampoline for about thirty dollars. The teacher oriented the preschoolers in its use: Only one child at a time could use it; they could only jump—no tricks—unless an adult held their hands; they could strap wrist weights to their ankles if they wanted to. The trampoline was available during every choice time all year. After a supervised training period, children received "licenses" to use it on their own. Each day, several children bounced on the trampoline, a few very active children for quite long times. Few reminders were needed about its use. No injuries occurred. The mini-tramp proved especially helpful for a few children who were noticeably more mellow after "trampling." The trampoline became an accepted part of the classroom and was quieter than the teachers had expected.*

If the school situation constrains active play, the teacher nonetheless figures out how to provide it each day. One kindergarten teacher led very active large groups and planned playtime with all centers open—including the most active and noisy (music, construction)—when the class next door was out of the room with specialist teachers. She saw her classroom as a place where she, as well as the children, could get, and stay, in shape.

Health studies consistently show the benefits of non-competitive vigorous activity for stress reduction, hormone balance, and healthy development of all of the body's major systems (Pica, 2000). In our high-tech, low-activity, caloric-food society, learning centers can foster and support active lifestyles. (See heading to follow, "Learning Centers and the Encouraging Classroom.")

Classroom Anecdote	*In a mixed prekindergarten–kindergarten class of 14 boys and 4 girls, many of the boys had summer and fall birthdays—and had trouble fitting into the teachers' initial program plans. The teacher and the assistant reduced large groups by substituting small-group activities led by the teacher, the assistant, and an inclusion special education teacher in the room for part of the day. One day, when they saw two of the boys lifting blocks like weights, the teachers decided to set up a physical fitness center. They enlisted the help of some families and came up with a manual treadmill, which they made a makeshift low railing for, a low weight table, some play barbells, and a stationary set of bike pedals that they put under a stool. They included a balance beam and occasionally mats for tumbling activities. They used hollow blocks for step exercises. The children had to take a "course" and pass a "test" before they could use the equipment, and the area was open only when an adult "spotter" could be present. The center was so popular with both boys and girls that it became a permanent center for the rest of the year.*

Active Learning in the Natural World

Contributed by Kathleen Sonsteng, EdD. We know that active learning for young children is a necessity. When that active learning can take place in the natural world, even more benefits will be observed. Research is indicating more and more that a disconnection from nature has enormous implications for human health as well as child development. Studies show what some of these implications might be.

According to the Centers for Disease Control (CDC), two out of ten of America's children are clinically obese, which is four times the percentage of childhood obesity reported in the 1960s (Lumerg, 2005). This study found that the amount of television that children watched had a direct correlation with measures of their body fat. Another study found that the rate at which American children were prescribed antidepressants almost doubled in five years with the steepest increase being among preschool children. (Louv, 2005). The author of *Last Child in the Woods*, Richard Louv (2005) suggests that the need for medications is intensified by children's disconnection from nature. "Although exposure to nature may have no impact on the most severe depressions, we do know that nature experiences can relieve some of the everyday pressures that may lead to childhood depression" (Louv, 2005, p.48).

Dr. Marti Erickson, the founding director of the University of Minnesota's Children, Youth, and Family Consortium, had this to say about the benefits of children being outdoors:

"Children actually pay attention and perform better in school after they've been outside and particularly after they've been outside in natural environments. The kind of activity that being in a natural space triggers for children is really valuable in terms of their ability to settle down and concentrate and learn effectively." (Erickson, 2008, p.4).

Erickson goes on to state that when children are actively involved in natural environments, their creativity, problem-solving, confidence, and independence are all enhanced. These are worthwhile reasons for making sure that we help the children in our care to connect to the natural environment on a regular (daily) basis.

Outdoor Example	*For many years, a child care center in northern Minnesota followed this "outdoor regimen": Except when air temperatures sunk to minus 10 degrees or the wind chill got to minus 20 degrees (!), the preschool class of 18 children and three adults went outside every day. By late morning, the children spent 10 minutes getting on snow suites, boots, and facemasks—they got good at it. The entire group then either played on the playground or took a walk around the block—all adult staff included. When the group took their walks, neighbors would wave and honk at the intrepid preschoolers, including one child in a wheelchair. The teachers pointed out seasonal changes to familiar natural landmarks and features of the daily weather as they walked.*
	From the beginning of the year the teachers went over their outdoor policy with families—which included regular nature walks to a nearby wooded park in warmer weather. No (native Minnesotan) parent every objected. The staff kept extra snow duds for children in need. Annually, they reported ubiquitous rosy cheeks and runny noses, but swore the kids didn't have many colds. (The teachers also reported the class had great appetites at lunch and took sound naps.)

How do we get children to be active outdoor learners? According to author Joseph Cornell (1998) exploring nature with children will help expend children's natural energies. Being active in the natural world can channel children away from boredom and restlessness and toward more constructive and satisfying pursuits. As teachers, we need to be actively involved in nature, right along with our students. Cornell, in his book, *Sharing Nature with Children*, shares five tenets of outdoor teaching.

▶ **Teach less, and share more.** Besides telling children the bare facts of nature, ("This is a red maple tree."), tell them your feelings about being in the presence of that maple tree. By sharing our deeper thoughts and feelings we communicate and inspire in others a love and respect for the Earth. This exercise in "naturalist intelligence" encourages a child to explore, respectfully, his own feelings and perceptions about the "outdoor classroom."

▶ **Be receptive.** Receptivity means listening, and being aware. The outdoors brings out a spontaneous enthusiasm in the child that you can skillfully direct toward learning. Expand your child's interest by teaching along the grain of his own curiosity (like when a child brings you a bouquet of dandelions, a dead insect, or some rabbit droppings). Follow up the interest with resources, activities and themes.

▶ **Focus the child's attention without delay.** Involve everyone as much as you can by asking questions and pointing out interesting sights and sounds. Take the class to visit a bird's nest each day or two. Ask questions about what the children see and hear. Relate the activity to their own experiences. Have them bring personal "science journals" to record their spontaneous observations.

▶ **Observe and experience first; talk later.** At times nature's spectacles will seize the child in rapt attention. Other times, children can have an experience of wonder by just watching ordinary things with close attention. They will gain a far better understanding of things outside themselves by your becoming one with them than from immediate "tour guide" talk. Observe quietly together.

▶ **A sense of joy should permeate the experience.** Children are naturally drawn to learning if you can keep the spirit of the occasion happy and enthusiastic. Remember that your own enthusiasm is contagious (Cornell, 1998, pp. 13–15) including for the dandelions, dead insects, and rabbit droppings. The ideas put forth by Cornell are easy to integrate when working with children of all ages. The focus is to get children active, not just physically but emotionally and socially. Providing outdoor active experiences will address a child's need for active learning while also giving them the added benefits of connecting to nature.

Making the outdoors part of the every day learning experience is perhaps easier in some parts of the country, and in some locations, than others. As the preceding anecdote indicates, even in "hardy" climates, our human ties to our environment are enriched by taking the class outside. When teachers see time outside as vital to the learning experience, they are both touching on the tradition of the *kindergarten* (the German term means "child's garden") and building for the future a citizenry that actively identifies with the outdoors.

Learning Centers in the Encouraging Classroom

In the encouraging classroom, there is no sacrifice of rigorous learning for the sake of healthy personal development. Studies of developmentally appropriate practice show that education can be responsive to the development and experience of individual children and still result in measurable, meaningful educational outcomes (Charlesworth, 1998; Bredekamp & Copple, 2009). Similarly, the use of learning centers in early childhood classrooms is not primarily for the purpose of practicing guidance. Rather, learning centers are the physical embodiment of developmentally appropriate practice as well as the encouraging classroom (Dodge, Colker, & Herdman, 2002). *(Learning centers are distinct areas within the classroom that provide a selection of related materials for children's use. Other commonly used terms are* learning stations, interest centers, *and* learning areas. *The term learning center is used in this text.)*

In the encouraging classroom, learning is not constricted by traditional academic priorities. Early childhood education always has been about educating for the *whole child*, including physical, cognitive, linguistic, social, cultural, and personal domains (Noddings, 2005). In Gardner's terms, learning centers cultivate multiple intelligences.

Learning centers afford the full and positive engagement, through which the child constructs knowledge and undergoes healthy brain development. At the same time, centers encourage social learning. They engender ongoing interactions that allow for the practice and development of democratic life skills. Centers are used because they both assist teachers to guide children in the development of democratic life skills and place children in situations where meaningful cognitive learning can take place (Texas Workforce Commission, 2002).

While still underestimated in traditional public school education, a classroom environment rich in learning centers defines developmentally appropriate practice (Brewer, 2007). Education approaches no less than Creative Curriculum and Reggio Emilia make the learning environment their cornerstones. In the terms of the Creative Curriculum, the classroom environment *is* the curriculum, with learning transactions and assessment criteria built around the use of learning areas (Dodge et al., 2002). In the terms of Reggio, "the environment is the third teacher" (Wurm, 2005). Wurm states:

> *In Reggio it is understood that the environment should support the work and interest of the children without constant adult guidance and intervention. The children work in the spaces, and while the adults are present, the children build their stories there. The environment is set up with enough provocation to fuel the children's worlds and minds. (p. 40)*

Organizing Learning Centers

Teachers have various names for the times children spend at centers: free play, play time, choice time, work time, and center time. The teacher gives thought to the design and management of learning center times in order to fully engage individual learners. The following considerations, discussed by many authors, reduce mistaken behavior in center use and invite learning engagement (Brewer, 2007; Curtis & Carter, 2005; Texas Workforce Commission, 2002).

Consider Traffic Patterns and Noise Levels. Design center locations to prevent "runways." Typically beginning at doors into the room, runways invite the kind of large muscle use that often is not quite what the teacher had in mind. If you are

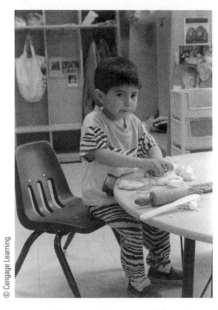

Even toddlers and three-year-olds use learning centers productively.

modifying an existing layout, look for runways. Place centers strategically so that children need to walk around one to get to another. Provide an active-play area that is open for at least some time each day, for "teacher-sanctioned" active play.

As well when locating centers, block or building centers should not be in front of doorways. Active-play areas should not be between library corners and computer centers. Be aware of the "spillover effect" where the natural activity of one center disrupts classroom traffic flow or obstructs the activity of a neighboring center. But design for the "overlap effect," where the activity of one center flows into another—science center into writing center or art, for instance.

Many teachers design classrooms so that centers with typically quiet activity are in one part of the room and centers with louder activity are in another. By using shelving, cupboards, movable bulletin boards, an occasional throw rug, and so on to create centers, noise to some extent can be buffered even in relatively small classrooms. A practical noise-level rating method for centers is the *3B system*:

1. *bucolic* (tranquil, peaceful—smile)
2. *busy*
3. *boisterous*.

Taking into account permanent features such as sinks and carpets, as well as traffic patterns, teachers typically locate the "mostly 1" centers at one end of the classroom, the "mostly 3" centers at the other end, and the "2 to 3" centers in between. If activity levels at bucolic and busy centers grow boisterous, the teacher needs to "check it out."

Build Centers Around the Interests of Children. In many classrooms the dramatic-play center is a home setting with kitchen furnishings, a table, a cabinet or wardrobe, a doll bed, and maybe a doll bathing area. This center invariably is well used, as a previous anecdote illustrated. Increasingly, even in smaller classrooms, teachers are designing theme-based dramatic-play areas, often adjacent

Table 5–2 *Range of Noise Levels in Typical Classroom Centers*	
Center	**Range of Noise Levels (Typical activity level given first)**
Library, science, technology, writing, music (headphone use), art, cooking, sensory table	(1) bucolic to (2) busy
Block-building, carpentry, music (with instruments), housekeeping, theme-based dramatic play	(2) busy to sometimes (3) boisterous
Active play center (climber, mini-trampoline, balance beam, large construction toys, hoppity-hops, indoor swing)	(3) boisterous to (2) busy

to house settings. These centers change with themes, and the themes and centers are determined in line with the interests of the children in the group. Three examples follow:

Classroom Illustrations	1. *Fishing is a big deal in many parts of the country. Near the beginning of fishing season, teachers in a Head Start program do a "fish week." Each center is equipped with fishing-related materials including fish books and computer games, watercolor "underwater" picture making, a rubber raft with actual fishing equipment (minus hooks), and a water table complete with different kinds of minnows!*
	2. *A child's parents operated a shoe store in the neighborhood. The class went to visit, and as a follow-up the teacher designed a shoe store. The two parents provided shoe boxes, a shoe stool, and foot measures. Other parents sent in lots of old shoes. The teachers added a cash register, play money, double-face receipt slips, and pencils.*
	3. *The parents of some children in a kindergarten class were carpenters. A kindergarten teacher persuaded a reluctant principal to let her include a carpentry center in the classroom two afternoons a week. Besides a worktable with a vise, initial materials included soft pinewood scraps, eight former "household hammers," sturdy 2-inch nails, and 12-inch "backsaws." Worried about accidents, the principal visited to view the center for himself. The principal arrived just in time to see Anita hit herself on the thumb with a hammer. Anita was about to cry. She noticed though that if she left the table to go to an adult, another child would take her place. With her thumb in her mouth, Anita continued to pound on the nail. The assistant supervising the table and the principal exchanged smiles. The principal occasionally returned to the classroom to visit the carpentry center, but out of interest, not concern.*

Establish Routines for Center Selection. A traditional center arrangement, used in some kindergarten classrooms, is for more quiet, "academic" centers to be open in the morning "when children are fresh" and all centers—including music, active play, blocks, construction—to be open during afternoon choice times. This arrangement fails to fully recognize the active nature of learning for the young child, but does allow children personal initiative among the centers that are open.

At the preprimary level, the rotation of groups through centers is not developmentally appropriate. The practice deprives children of the benefits of self-selection and self-direction in learning activities. As Montessori discovered at the beginning of the 20th century, no one knows their level of learning better than the children themselves. For models like Montessori, High/Scope, Reggio Emilia, and Creative Curriculum, opportunity for child choice in centers extends throughout childhood, a view still outside the mainstream in American education.

Common methods for determining occupancy of centers include hanging name tags on hooks or having a set number of chairs at the center. These methods limit "real-life" negotiation in the process, but perhaps encourage self-regulation and adaptability—important for educational success. Another method, turns lists, give children the benefits of functional literacy (making and reading names) and active practice in planning, managing time, and transitioning into and out of the center.

The High/Scope Model epitomizes the "metacognitive" view, maintaining that learning occurs in the selection and transition processes—and the child's reflection about them—as well as activity in the center itself. In the famous *Plan, Do, and Review* procedure, children bring reflection, intentionality, and negotiation to the center learning experience (Hohmann, Banet, & Weikart, 1995). Usually in small groups, children plan what they would like to do during work time, with the adult and/or child "noting" the choices on paper. Children then do independent work times of about an hour, perhaps staying with their choices, perhaps not. Following work time, often during snack, children review what they did, sometimes sharing samples of work completed.

Plan, do, and review is just one part of the High/Scope Model. Because of its implementation of Piagetian theory, a solid research base, and close ties to families, High/Scope has been a giant in documenting the lasting benefits of child-initiated activity in early childhood education (High/Scope, 2005).

Provide Ample Time and Activity Choices. As to time, at least 45 minutes—once during a half-day program, twice during a full-day program—is often recommended. Shorter periods prevent children from becoming fully involved. Unfortunately, some teachers use brief play times as *buffer activities* (in between structured lessons), a practice that shows misunderstanding of the importance of the center experience (Brewer, 2007).

Children also need *meaningful choices* in center activities. Where materials are *self-correcting,* such as puzzles, a variety of difficulty levels and puzzle types is important. Where materials are *open-ended,* like Legos and art, patterns and models should not be available. In Erikson's theory, young children are engaged in the life challenges of initiative versus guilt and industry versus inferiority (see Chapter Two).

Young children know how things are supposed to look before they can make them look that way. They are very aware of patterns and models. Unless their products match, they feel frustrated and their motivation for continued creation diminishes (Bredekamp & Copple, 2009). As the child progresses from preconventional to conventional creation, teachers sustain confidence (and persistence) if they affirm the child's unique creations in the here and now.

Likewise, teachers support children's creative dynamic *by not making things for the child.* Process modeling, how to use a tool or material, is sometimes needed to get a child started. Product modeling, like how to make a "bird," is *not* developmentally appropriate (Bredekamp & Copple, 2009). Instead, the teacher is "unrelentingly encouraging" of the child's open-ended creative process. Future musicians, business people, writers, doctors, teachers, and first responders are empowered this way.

Giving enough time for the child to create is crucial for brain development endeavors (Gallagher, 2005). When a child's attention span for an activity is longer than what the schedule typically allows, the author echoes Montessori's thought that such times are sacred, *peak learning experiences*. If teachers prolong an activity for a child, at the occasional expense of the schedule or taking turns, they enhance the brain's creative dynamic—which increases in sophistication as the child grows.

On the matter of "practice," when is it drill for its own sake and when does it have meaning for the child? In practical terms, the issue comes down to whether the teacher needs to enforce it with gentle reminders or with constant monitoring. Reineke, Sonsteng, and Gartrell say this:

> *Practice is developmentally appropriate when teachers offer activities that fully engage children's minds and bodies; children's intrigue-driven experiences stimulate mastery motivation. The elements of intrigue (kindled intellectual interest), activity, experience, and optimum brain development are all aligned (and the child's attention span for the activity often becomes longer than the teacher's). (2008, p. 93)*

Mastery motivation is the brain dynamic children are born with to find out about the world and themselves in it. The balance that the teacher maintains between supporting mastery motivation within the individual and the scheduling needs of the group is sometimes fluid. The teacher acts as a professional when she becomes "intentionally time flexible" during the day on behalf of a thoroughly engaged child.

Centers at the Primary Level

Full use of learning centers in elementary schools remains a progressive idea (Brewer, 2007). Reading centers are fixtures, but less common are music, art, and writing centers. More classrooms do have a computer or two, but in most settings well-stocked computer or technology centers are a need that is still just beginning to be met—a common substitute is a shared computer room. Although many classrooms do have informal science areas, centers that encourage three-dimensional activity—blocks and other building materials, dramatic play, carpentry, a variety of manipulatives, abundant "sciencing" materials—are too seldom seen.

In the 20th century, Dewey, Montessori, Piaget, and Elkind all debunked the philosophical separation of mind and body within our schools. With current pressures toward academic performance, educators appear to be telling children that upon entering elementary school, they must forsake their bodies for long periods of the day and use only their minds. With today's political accountability, educators abandon the natural and essential integration of movement and thought that are so important for healthy development (Garcia et al., 2002).

In an interview with Marilyn Hughes, an elementary teacher with years of Grades K–3 teaching experience from Aspen, Colorado, Willis (1993) depicted well the "active learning" that occurs at learning centers during the primary grades. While the times have changed since 1993, the ways in which primary grade children learn most effectively have not.

© Cengage Learning

The center most commonly found in primary classrooms is the reading or language arts center.

Learning centers "allow for the broadest range of interactions," says Hughes. Her own classroom featured 20 hands-on learning centers, which were run on student contracts. Some of the centers were set up for independent work; others, for pairs or small groups. Students could respond to the centers in a variety of ways: linguistic, visual, or kinesthetic. Hughes taught her pupils how to move independently through the centers, giving them a chance to pace themselves. The centers placed "hundreds of materials within the reach of the children." (p. 90)

Independent Activity at the Primary Level

The values of self-directing/open-ended activity (play) for primary-grade children are clearly discussed by Bredekamp and Copple (2009) and Stegelin (2005). Daily child choice manipulative activity is arguably necessary for children through the primary years (Brewer, 2007)—though teachers feel hard pressed to find this time in their schedules.

The thought, interaction, and expression that occur during self-directing/open-ended activity improves the satisfaction level of children in the primary classroom. Free for a time from external standards of evaluation, children can experience the gratification of learning for its own sake. With happier children, mistaken behavior decreases. For the professional teacher, the regular open-ended use of learning centers should outweigh any criticism that self-directed center activity is time spent "off task." Ongoing justification for the rationale of self-directing/open-ended activity at centers is perhaps the price of teaching progressively in the 21st century.

Learning Centers and Integrated Curriculum

Learning centers lend themselves to *integrated curriculum* in many of its forms, perhaps most commonly in thematic instruction. In the thematic approach the teacher, with direct or indirect input from the children, selects a topic. Often using webbing (the visual "picture" of a theme or unit), the teacher (again with input from the class) plans a variety of activities, some large-group, but most involving the use of centers.

Bredekamp and Copple (2009) argue that DAP means shifting away from the study of isolated academic subjects during defined periods and toward the study of integrated curriculum in broad time blocks. Termed *the project method* by Dewey in laboratory schools at the beginning of the 20th century, integrated curriculum has been a part of progressive education, including the nursery school movement, ever since. Various approaches to integrated curriculum are offered in many educational models ranging from Montessori to High/Scope to Creative Curriculum to Reggio Emilia. Terms like "project method," "thematic instruction," and "the inquiry method" describe different takes on integrating curriculum.

Still, the changeover has yet to occur in most elementary schools, as Brewer (2007) points out:

> The most common approach to curriculum organization in schools in the United States, however, continues to be a subject-matter organization in which learning is segmented into math or science or language arts. You probably remember that in elementary school you had reading first thing in the morning, math right before lunch, and science in the afternoon. (p. 114)

Brewer states that in contrast to this fragmentation of the curriculum, a child's learning outside the school is whole and built around personally relevant experiences. She argues that integrating subject matter, as in themes, enables the child to find meaning in learning: "He recognizes that this information is personally useful, not something learned to please an adult, which has no other utility for him" (p. 114). This commonality in the use of integrated curriculum takes in the differing points of emphasis in the various models and is the fundamental point.

Three Modes of Center-Based Instruction. In a venerable *Young Children* article Myers and Maurer (1987) proposed a model for learning centers that permits their use in structured instruction as well as open-ended activity. The Myers and

Maurer model pertains across the range of the integrated-curriculum models of today. The authors assign three different functions to centers depending on instructional intent. The three functions are:

▶ Self-directing/open-ended: At each learning center, children select and use materials according to their own interests and abilities (the traditional use of centers in early childhood classrooms).

▶ Teacher-instructed/exploratory: The teacher motivates and models exploration of tools and materials at the center according to a preset theme or concept. Children then investigate materials on their own. (For instance, the teacher models pattern making using different sets of materials. Children then make their own unique patterns from the materials selection.)

▶ Self-directing/self-correcting: Children use materials at the center that "have obvious and prescribed uses; the material tells the learner whether a given action is correct or incorrect" (Myers & Maurer, 1987, p. 24), that is, puzzles or object-to-numeral correspondence materials. (One use is homemade puzzles that relate to different themes—culturally diverse fishing scenes, for instance, to go with a theme on fishing.)

The continuing strength of the Myers and Maurer model is that it expands the use of learning centers, as a comprehensive instructional strategy, within the integrated-curriculum approach. By encouraging the distinct learning processes of creativity, discovery, and analysis, the model allows the range of educational inquiry that is developmentally appropriate for elementary school. Through students' using the distinct learning center functions cooperatively, the range of collaborative learning opportunities is enhanced. The model allows for learning in relation to a full range of standards, substandards, which teachers, using authentic, observation-based assessment, can assess.

The model also gives direction to the use of centers for teacher-led small-group activities, applicable throughout the age span. From cooking activities to reading stories to science discovery, when teachers work with co-teachers, assistants, and volunteers to break down the "mass class" factor of large groups, children engage in learning more readily (Curtis & Carter, 2005). The flexible use of learning centers along the lines of the Myers and Maurer model diversifies learning opportunities to better accommodate individual children in the class.

Note to Reader: In the companion website, readers can locate the case study, A Second Grade Theme (in These Academic Times). The case study shows how a teacher used small groups in the three center types to have her class engage in active learning in relation to birds in their area. The case study examines the activity of the teacher and class from the initial webbing of the theme to how the teacher assessed children's progress in relation to state academic standards. The theme, an important part of which occurs outdoors, illustrates integrated curriculum by bringing together the areas of biology, environmental awareness, math, social studies, literacy (reading and writing), and the creative arts.

Building the Classroom for Prosocial Development

Prosocial development means gaining the social–emotional knowledge and skills that young children need to interrelate with others (Preusse, 2005). Abilities attributed to prosocial development typically include:

Caring

Sharing

Cooperating

Helping

In traditional classrooms, discipline methods are largely reactive systems to children's *failure* to show these abilities, rather than proactive (guidance) methods designed to teach them (Mindess, Chen, & Brenner, 2009).

Caring is the foundational element in prosocial development. A child's ability to care directly reflects the relationships with significant others in the child's life. Caring is a product of healthy attachments with adults and of positive relationships with the teacher (Preusse, 2005). The teacher models and teaches caring through the communications and relationships of the encouraging classroom. Daily class meetings designed to build mutual esteem and empathy (discussed in Chapter Seven) are central to communal discussion and reflection about caring.

As young children interact with mutual success in the classroom, and feel fundamentally cared for and included, the transition from developmental egocentrism toward autonomy begins to happen. The interactions around tools and materials in learning centers, sometimes with a theme-related focus, provide children with ongoing opportunities for *sharing*. With daily use of communal materials in individual endeavors and cooperative efforts, children gain sharing experience aplenty. Teachers mediate to facilitate the developing ability of children to care enough about each other to share, as this classroom anecdote shows.

Classroom Anecdote	At center time Cheyenne decided to play in the block area. Rosa decided she would play in the kitchen area. Cheyenne took out the unit blocks. He started to build with them. Rosa began to play with the dishes in the kitchen area. After about ten minutes, Rosa put away all the dishes and went over to the block area. Rosa approached Cheyenne.
	Rosa: Can I play with you?
	Cheyenne: No.
	Rosa immediately ran over to Lori (assistant teacher). Lori was working on a puzzle with another child.
	Rosa: Cheyenne won't let me play with the blocks.
	Lori: Let's go over and talk to him. Lori took Rosa's hand and they walked over to the block area where Cheyenne was playing.
	Lori (to Rosa): Please ask Cheyenne if you can play with him again.
	Rosa (shrugged her shoulders): Can I play here?
	(continued)

> *Cheyenne: No.*
> *Lori (bent down): Could Rosa take some of the blocks (by Cheyenne) and play over there? (Lori points to a spot about five feet away from Cheyenne.)*
> *Cheyenne: Yes.*
> *So Rosa picked up some of the blocks and took them to the spot Lori had pointed to. Both children played in the block area until cleanup time, sharing the blocks (and the space) after a short amount of time.*
> *The teacher knew that Cheyenne liked to "protect his territory" when he used the blocks. The teacher wasn't sure Rosa could persuade him on her own to let her play in the area. With the teacher's assistance Rosa began to learn she had a right to express her needs and Cheyenne began to learn he could share the space and blocks—and still have a good time.*

Sharing is an effort that allows children to work in close proximity. Sharing leads to *cooperation*. Cooperation involves the *ongoing* sharing of ideas and materials, often leading to joint products distinctly different from what a child might do on one's own. Even if the products of the cooperation are separate, vital social/emotional experience is being gained. Successful experience at cooperation builds knowledge and abilities in children that will last them longer than the immediate social experience. Success in cooperation builds empathy.

Through mutual assistance in a common endeavor (cooperation), a child shows the cognitive, emotional, and social foundations of empathy. When teachers see altruism in the actions of one child who helps another, they often simply stop and smile. Freely helping means the child has gained the ability to give of oneself to the group, the gift of friendliness. Teachers set the scene for the learning of prosocial knowledge and skills, including empathy, and they can model and guide for it. But only children who succeed in the social tasks of the daily program show these qualities on their own.

Classroom Anecdote	*At lunch five-year-old Nedra, as always, ate slowly, enjoying her food and the company at the table. Wendell, aged three, would not eat his peas. Rather than eat his one "taster pea" so he could have his peach with syrup in a cup, Wendell swung up his hand to cover his mouth. His other hand went in a different direction, and knocked the peach cup and peach on the floor. Wendell crumpled out of his chair crying, and teacher Alyssa had to work to help him calm down (difficult because there were no more peaches). As he got back in his chair, Wendell and teacher saw a new peach in a new cup sitting in front of him. Nedra smiled at the teacher and said, "He needs it more than me, Alyssa." Alyssa agreed and thanked Nedra. Without prompting, so did Wendell.*

Prosocial Development through Learning Centers. Teachers are sometimes reluctant to "open their classes" through the use of centers. The image of many busy bodies actively encountering the materials of the classroom seems to invite mistaken behavior. The truth is that if carefully planned, even toddlers engage productively in center activities—and certainly second and third graders can (Brewer, 2007). The small group interaction at centers promotes caring, cooperation, and empathy even among quite diverse learners, including those who may be culturally linguistically different. When organization is present and guidelines are known to all, center times are busy, positive, and educational (Brewer, 2007; Texas Workforce Commission, 2002).

Still, even when centers are being effectively used, there will be mistaken behavior. But most of it will be Level One conflicts resulting from full involvement in the center activity. Because children are motivated by their engagement to resolve such conflicts, the teacher can use conflict management to turn mistaken behavior into opportunities for prosocial development.

In fact, teachers know that they are using guidance effectively when they see the mistaken behavior that occurs at centers as opportunities to teach life skills. For most children, Level One conflicts diminish as they learn the routines of center use. When conflicts do occur, they become part of the curriculum between teacher and child, and not a distraction from it. The interactions resulting from learning centers are fundamental for a classroom geared to prosocial development (Preusse, 2005).

Encouraging Classroom Volunteers

Depending on the school or program, there are at least fifteen different ways that teachers work with family members to gain their involvement. The fifteen are listed here.

Ways Parents Can Be Involved in the Preschool or Primary-Grade Program

1. Assist children with home assignments
2. Attend parent-teacher conferences
3. Attend parent meetings
4. Participate in home visits by staff
5. Contribute materials
6. Follow through with staff recommendations
7. Participate in "family journals"
8. Chaperone special events
9. Visit for observation purposes
10. Make presentations to the class
11. Volunteer to help on a regular basis
12. Help to organize special events
13. Assist other parents to volunteer
14. Sit on policy boards
15. Further their own development and education

While programs that offer a full range of services, such as Head Start, might focus on all fifteen, other programs and schools typically address at least a few. One method of gauging effective involvement is to assess success differently for each family, on a family-by-family basis (Rosenthal & Sawyers, 1996). Referring to the list, for some families, participation in the form of items 1–3 might constitute successful participation. For another family, items 1–7 might be used.

The number of parents working outside the home would seem to limit parent availability for in-class involvement (items 8–13). Nonetheless, with pleasant persistence, teachers can often prevail upon parents to find times when they can come into the classroom.

The present section focuses on those levels of involvement that pertain to the classroom, items 8–13. Specifically, the concern is how to help parents feel comfortable enough to volunteer on a regular basis. Previous chapters began the discussion about the importance of parent-teacher partnerships in the guidance approach. Gestwicki (2007) presents the following advantages of extending partnerships into the classroom, with family members being classroom volunteers:

▸ Parents gain not only firsthand experience of a program and of their child's reactions in a classroom, but also feelings of satisfaction from making a contribution.

▸ Children feel special when their parents are involved, feel secure with the tangible evidence of parents and teachers cooperating, and gain directly as parental understanding and skills increase.

▸ Teachers benefit because they gain resources to extend learning opportunities to the class; learn about individual parent-child interactions, and build support systems as parents participate and empathize with them.

Roadblocks to Involving Parents

Despite these advantages, teachers sometimes encounter two roadblocks: (a) Other staff are dubious about the merits of using parent volunteers, and (b) parents cannot find the time or they are not sure they can contribute (Gestwicki, 2007).

In regard to the first situation, few programs and schools have policies forbidding the use of parent volunteers; such a practice is ill-advised. As mentioned in Chapter One, programs such as Head Start, cooperative nursery schools, and preschool/parent education programs have a rich tradition of including parents in the classroom. In a growing number of school districts, as well, parent volunteers are seen as important and are encouraged.

The teacher interested in including parents needs to determine what is policy and what simply has never been done. Talking with sympathetic teachers and speaking with an administrator are important first steps. The teacher is more

© Cengage Learning

*Parents volunteer in the classroom (and outside) in
many ways.* (Courtesy, The Bemidji Pioneer)

likely to experience success by starting on a small scale and keeping a low profile, so that the effort does not become a "burning teacher's lounge issue." As
Gestwicki (2007) suggests, determination on the teacher's part is likely to be the
main ingredient for success.

Helping Volunteers Feel Comfortable

In regard to the second situation, Rockwell, Andre, and Hawley (1996) suggest
that teachers work carefully with parents and not push them to levels of participation beyond their comfort levels. The following suggestions help parents feel more
comfortable about volunteering in the classroom. Note that as a result of social
and cultural differences, some families will respond to some of these suggestions,
other families to others. When teachers work to get to know families at the beginning of the year, they then can tailor ideas to particular families' situations.

1. Hold "Greeting Meetings" for families. One in late afternoon and one in the evening gives parents choices. Distribute flyers or brochures that: (a) tell about your program, and (b) give suggestions and guidelines for parent volunteers. (See samples in Appendix C.) Discuss the flyers at the meetings. Stress that you encourage family members to visit and volunteer. Have a parent who volunteered the previous year share what he did. Mention that you know many parents work outside the home and that finding time to get away is difficult State that you are open to visits on the parents' time schedules.

2. At or after the Greeting Meetings, ask parents to complete a questionnaire (samples are provided in Appendix B). On the questionnaire, ask parents to check different ways they would be willing to participate. Include choices pertaining to the classroom. Don't ask *if* they would like to volunteer. Provide choices of ways that previous parents volunteered and ask them to check as many as they would like.

3. If the teacher makes home visits, mention volunteering at the home visit. During the first parent-teacher conference, at home or school, refer to the questionnaire and discuss volunteering in the classroom.

4. Establish with parents when they are welcome. If you choose not to have a general "open house" policy, specify in the flyer and at the meeting when parents can visit. Be flexible: Parents working outside the home have limited available time.

5. Let parents know that they have three ways to volunteer: (a) Parents can participate on a regular basis; (b) parents can informally visit or initiate a special event, such as a family sharing activity; and (c) parents can help with special events. Let the families know you will help them set up whichever option they choose. Remember that "regulars" often start out as "one-timers."

6. A brother or sister brought with a parent probably will not be as disruptive as a teacher might think. For some parents, permission to bring a younger sibling is necessary for them to visit at all. Make clear your policy about siblings accompanying the parent.

7. Some parents might like to volunteer but don't have transportation. Help parents work this out, such as by having two parents "buddy up." With staff encouragement, parents in some Head Start programs are able to ride the buses with their children.

8. When parents visit your classroom, treat them as you would like to be treated if you were visiting a class. Stop what you are doing and privately greet the parent. If parents seem comfortable with the idea, introduce them to the children. Have a place (such as a "parent corner") where the parent can store coats and belongings. Talk with the parent about what he would be comfortable doing, and help the parent get started. Observe how things are going and provide assistance if needed.

© Cengage Learning

Because this first grader's class is used to visitors, his younger sister does not disrupt the daily program.

9. How first visits end is important. When parents are about to leave, thank them for visiting; let parents know that they are welcome back. Have the children say good-bye. Ask the children to compose thank-you notes or pictures. Send them to the parent with your own thank-you note and an open invitation for a return visit.

The teacher assumes responsibility for relationships with parent volunteers. Teachers who view parent volunteers as a natural extension of the parent-teacher partnership will actively invite parents into the classroom. Everyone stands to gain when parents become members of the teaching team.

Summary

1. *What is an encouraging classroom and how does it prevent school anxiety?*

School anxiety occurs when children experience unmet needs for safety and acceptance in the school situation. The encouraging classroom begins within the minds of teachers who wish to reduce and prevent the effects of school anxiety for every child. The encouraging classroom is defined as the physical surroundings of a school, center, or family child care program in which adults provide ongoing guidance in order to maintain an equilibrium between the needs of each developing member and the right for mutual appreciation by the group. It involves the creation and sustenance of a caring community among children and adults for the purpose of furthering the learning and development of each member.

2. What is the relationship of developmentally appropriate practice and the encouraging classroom?

Developmentally *in*appropriate practice—which tends to be teacher centered, restrictively academic, and overly focused on standardized assessment and student compliance—leads to school anxiety in many young children. Developmentally appropriate practice engages each child in an interactive learning process geared to multiple learning domains and intelligences. Such instructional strategies as learning centers, integrated curriculum, thematic instruction, authentic (observation-based) assessment, child-directed activity (play), and guidance are indicators that teaching practices are developmentally appropriate. Children in DAP classrooms become fully engaged in learning activities. The active nature of young children, within the classroom and outdoors, is fully accommodated; the outdoors is seen as an extension of the learning environment. The inclusive nature of instruction and group processes leads to affirmation of the worth and potential of each child.

3. What is the place of learning centers in the encouraging classroom?

The use of learning centers marks a classroom environment that is developmentally appropriate. To reduce classroom-caused mistaken behavior, consider traffic patterns and noise levels in organizing centers. Build centers around the interests of children. Develop daily routines in center selection and use that involve student choice, enough materials, and sufficient time for center activity. Learning centers make elementary education classrooms into learning laboratories in which thematic instruction can be effectively used. Theme-based instruction constitutes developmentally appropriate primary-grade curriculum because it integrates academic subjects in topics of interest to the child, promotes active learning, allows for individual and small-group experiences, and lends itself to observation-based assessment.

4. How does the teacher organize the classroom for prosocial development?

Teachers build classrooms that encourage prosocial development, the knowledge and skills children need to interrelate. A child's ability to *care* reflects the attachments and relationships with significant family members and teachers.

Children get everyday practice in *sharing*, made easier by the guidance of the teacher. *Cooperation* indicates progress in prosocial development because it is an ongoing ability that arises from sharing. A child who shows the empathy implicit in freely *helping* is the goal for prosocial development. Children learn prosocial skills especially through interactions in learning centers. Teachers use the high engagement in center activities to turn conflicts into social–emotional learning experiences.

5. How does the teacher encourage classroom volunteers?

Family members can be involved in their children's education in 15 or more different ways. Teachers do well to measure success of the parent involvement program by looking at what is possible for each individual family. Parents, children, and teachers all gain when family members volunteer in the classroom. With a positive attitude and friendly persistence, teachers can overcome most roadblocks to involving families. Nine suggestions were provided for encouraging parents to visit classrooms and become regular volunteers.

FOLLOW-UP ACTIVITIES

Note: *An element of being a professional teacher is to respect the children, parents, and educators you are working with by maintaining confidentiality, that is, keeping identities private. In completing follow-up activities, please respect the privacy of all concerned.*

Discussion Activity

The discussion activity encourages students to interrelate their own thoughts and experiences with specific ideas from the chapter.

Recall from your experience as a student a theme or project that you participated in and that means something to you in relation to your professional development. Did you have learning center activities? Was there an outdoor component that you recall? Compare or contrast your experience with relevant ideas from the chapter.

Application Activities

Application activities allow students to interrelate material from the text with real-life situations. The observations imply access to practicum experiences; the interviews, access to teachers or parents. Students compare or contrast observations and interviews with referenced ideas from the chapter.

1. School anxiety and the encouraging classroom.

   a. Observe in a classroom that you believe to be encouraging. Select a child who you perceive to be vulnerable for school anxiety. Observe a situation where the teacher worked directly with the child. Record the observation as objectively as you can. Compare the responses of the teacher, the child, and/or other children in the class to what the book says should happen in the encouraging classroom.

b. Interview a teacher about the following: (1) what some characteristics are of one or two children in the class who may be susceptible to school anxiety; (2) how the teacher works with the group to be inclusive of these children; and (3) how the teacher monitors responses with the identified children to make the classroom encouraging. How does what the teacher says go along with text material about the encouraging classroom?

2. Developmentally appropriate practice today and the encouraging classroom.

a. Observe a small-group/learning center activity that you believe to be developmentally appropriate. Record as objectively as possible verbal and nonverbal responses that characterize one child's responses. Hypothesize what that child may be gaining from the activity in each of these developmental domains: physical, cognitive, language, social/cultural, and emotional. Through comparing your observations with the text, discuss your learning about developmentally appropriate practice.

b. Interview a teacher who uses developmentally appropriate practice. Ask how the teacher engages reluctant children in learning activities so that they can experience success. How does the teacher assess the child's progress in relation to outcomes or standards that might be required in the program or school. What difficulties and successes has the teacher experienced in using DAP? Compare your findings to text material on developmentally appropriate practice.

3. Learning centers in the encouraging classroom.

a. Observe carefully the classroom of a teacher who uses learning centers. Diagram the classroom using as much detail as possible. Compare the pattern of center placement with considerations in the text for planning and using centers.

b. Observe a preprimary or primary class that is completing a theme. Note whether or how the teacher uses: webbing, learning centers, integrated curriculum. Note the children's level of engagement in the center activities. Compare the observations with what the text says about learning centers in the classroom.

c. Interview a teacher who uses learning centers. Discuss advantages and disadvantages of center use as the teacher sees them. How does the teacher work learning centers into the daily schedule? Into the educational program? How does the teacher see learning centers contributing to the atmosphere of an encouraging classroom? Compare your findings with what the text says about learning centers.

4. Building the classroom for prosocial development.

   a. Observe two children in a class, what who is at a beginning point in prosocial development and one who is making clear progress. Watch for each child's use of caring, sharing, cooperating, or helping behaviors. Record one typical situation for each. Without comparing the children, hypothesize about each child's progress with each of the four prosocial skills. Compare and contrast your findings with ideas from the text.

   b. Interview a teacher about how she structures her classroom to encourage proactive development. What are the teacher's priorities for individual children in her class who are at different points in prosocial development? How do the teacher's comments compare with ideas from text?

5. Encouraging classroom volunteers.

   a. Observe a classroom where one or more family members volunteer. Note what the teacher is doing to help the volunteer(s) feel welcome, get involved, and comfortably leave. Compare or contrast your observations with ideas from the chapter about encouraging parents to volunteer.

   b. Interview a family member who has volunteered in a classroom. What went into the member's decision to volunteer in the classroom? How long did the volunteering continue? What part did the teacher play in the decision of the family member to volunteer? Compare what the person said with ideas from the chapter about encouraging family members to be classroom volunteers.

Recommended Readings

Black, S. (2003, January). Too soon to test. *American School Board Journal*.

Cassidy, D. J., Mims, S., Rucker, L., & Boone, S. (2003, Summer). Emergent curriculum and kindergarten readiness. *Childhood Education*, pp. 194–199.

Cornell, J. (1998). *Sharing nature with children*. Nevada City, CA: DAWN publications.

Curtis, D., & Carter, M. (2005). Rethinking early childhood environments to enhance learning. *Young Children, 60*(3), 34–38.

Erickson, M. (2008). Indoors and out-of-touch: A conversation with Dr. Marti Erickson. *Conservation Minnesota Magazine*, Fall, 4–7.

Gallagher, K. C. (2005). Brain research and early childhood development: A primer for developmentally appropriate practice. *Young Children, 60*(4), 22–20.

Haschke, B. (2003, Summer). Childhood obesity. The caregiver's role. *Texas Child Care*, pp. 28–36.

Hatch, J. A. (2002, February). Accountability shovedown: Resisting the standards movement in early childhood education. *Phi Delta Kappan*, 457–462.

Louv, R. (2005). *Last child in the woods*. Chapel Hill, NC: Algonquin Books.

Lumeng, J. (2005, January). What can we do to prevent childhood obesity? *Zero to Three*, National Center for Infants, Toddlers and Families, pp. 13–19.

National Association for the Education of Young Children. (2005). Resources on environments that support exploring, learning, and living. *Young Children, 60* (3), 56–58.

Reineke, J., Sonsteng, K., & Gartrell, D. (2008). Nurturing mastery motivation: No need for rewards. *Young Children, 63*(6), 89–97.

Stegelin, D. A. (2005). Making the case for play policy: Research-based reasons to support play-based environments. *Young Children, 60*(2), 76–85.

Guidance Matters

Dan Gartrell and Kathleen Sonsteng

Promote Physical Activity—It's Proactive Guidance

March, 2008

Five-year-old Jacob attends the preschool where I (Jackie) am student teaching. Jacob often instigates rough-and-tumble play, which sometimes gets him in trouble. One day during outdoor time, Jacob wanted to play catch with a foam football. Even though I am not athletic, I took the opportunity, hoping for a one-on-one conversation.

Jacob: Jackie, do you want to play catch with me?

Jackie: Sure, I would love to play catch with you. (We start tossing the ball.)

Jackie: You like to play catch.

Jacob: I play with my dad all the time. He is really good. (Jacob throws a really nice spiral.)

Jackie: Wow! That was a nice throw. How did you do that?

Jacob: You put your fingers across the laces. (Jacob comes over and shows me where to place my fingers on the ball.)

Jacob: You do it like this. Then you throw the ball. My dad taught me how to throw like that. That is how the quarterbacks throw the ball. (Jacob tosses the ball really hard at me.)

Jackie: Hey, you threw that really hard!

Jacob: Yeah, I did. I work out my muscles. I do push-ups like this (shows me the arm movements) and I do these things (does an impression of a sit-up). My dad does them too. He does them all the time.

Jackie: So, Jacob, what else do you like to play?

Jacob: I play football, baseball, soccer, and basketball. (I wait for him to talk again.)

Jacob: I like to play games. I like to play checkers. It's a game where you have little round disks, and they are red and black. You go and jump over other people and take their pieces away from them. (He jumps.) (We continue playing catch for a while.)

Jacob: Do you want to sit down and play catch?

Jackie: Sure, if you want to. (I sit on the bench and Jacob sits on the play picnic table and we start to play catch again.)

Teacher Emily: Okay, everyone, come in and wash your hands!

Jackie understood here what early childhood educators increasingly recognize: Healthy child development relies on physical activity. From enjoyment in using movement skills to blood circulation that builds brains and bodies, to obesity prevention, to concept formation, the benefits of physical activity make it a must in the schedule every day. In one interaction, when Jacob describes playing checkers and suggests sitting down, he showed cognitive, linguistic, and even social–emotional learning—complete with a physical demonstration.

Because Jackie ventured outside her comfort zone in joining Jacob in physical activity, she made this situation richly educational—for herself and for Jacob. Through their shared experience, Jackie got to know Jacob better. In the future, she can use games and increased physical activity to help him and his buddies become more consistently engaged in the center program.

Rough-and-Tumble Play

Some teachers worry that vigorous activity, if permitted, will degenerate into rough-and-tumble play and someone will be hurt. Many teachers have witnessed the superhero phenomenon in which children assume the role of make-believe heroes and become overly aggressive. Problems can be reduced, however, by using class meetings to set limits for rough-and-tumble play:

> After a class meeting about "friendly touches only," a teacher found this reference point helpful when he came upon a "World Wrestling Federation match" of four boys, one being sat on and yelling! The teacher discussed with them what friendly touches meant, and he got the boys to wrestle instead some "invisible space invaders." The four got bored with the make-believe wrestling and soon became firefighters—still rough-and-tumble play, but without the aggressive undertones (Gartrell, 2000, p. 98).

Two practices can assist teachers in maintaining a balance between addressing children's need for rough-and-tumble play and limiting aggression during this play. First, have guidelines that clearly ensure children's safety. Second, promote imaginative and creative play to move beyond "narrowly scripted play that focuses on violent actions" (Levin, 2003, p. 62). The teacher in the above example used both of these practices.

Melding Movement and Learning

If teachers see the need, they can progress beyond the informal inclusion of vigorous play in the schedule. New curriculum models are effectively integrating physical activity in the educational program. Such models ensure that movement will have diverse expression in the daily schedule—a growing essential in this sit-down world. Overviews of three models follow.

S.M.A.R.T. (Stimulating Maturity through Accelerated Readiness Training) combines physical and learning activities to stimulate high levels of pre-academic and early academic development among children (Farnham, 2007). In the S.M.A.R.T. program, children complete 8 to 10 repetitions of an obstacle course, followed by 10 to 12 activity stations. The 30-minute sessions are done every day and consist of activities designed to improve hand/eye coordination, distance acuity, fine motor skills, sequencing, left/right awareness, and spatial relations.

Spinning is an example of a S.M.A.R.T. activity that encourages body awareness. While it provides focused body movement, which often helps young children sit still for longer periods of time, spinning also has been shown to stimulate the same part of the brain stimulated by prescribed impulse-control medications. Daily spinning activity may lead to doctors rethinking medication dosages for some children (Farnham 2007).

Kids in Action is based on the premise that children love to move. Helping children to be active in appropriate ways can have a tremendous impact on their physical, intellectual, and emotional development. Kids in Action incorporates cardiovascular endurance, muscular strength and endurance, flexibility, and body composition into activities for children in three age groups: infants (birth to 18 months), toddlers (18 to 36 months), and preschoolers (3 to 5 years) (President's Council on Physical Fitness and Sports, 2003). An example of an activity recommended for preschoolers that helps to teach cooperation is the mirror game. While facing the child, ask her to do exactly as you do, as if she were looking in a mirror. This game supports children's social–emotional development when they take turns being the leader. It also means that children have to do with their bodies what their eyes are seeing, enhancing sensory integration that will help with the development of reading and writing skills.

I Am Moving, I Am Learning is a proactive approach for addressing childhood obesity in Head Start children. This approach reinforces the mind–body connection and the relationship between physical fitness and early learning. One of the goals of I Am Moving, I Am Learning is to increase the amount of time spent in moderate to vigorous physical activity during daily routines. The model encourages participating centers to include at least 30 minutes daily of structured physical activity as well as 30 minutes daily of unstructured physical activity. Some of the activities in I Am Moving, I Am Learning are rhythm stick dancing, hoop maze, dancing scarves, balance board, and scooter weaving. One outcome of this model is individual children experiencing moderate improvements on the body mass index for age. In another outcome, teachers found that children who previously needed considerable redirection required less redirection as music and movement increased in the daily routine (Region III ACF, 2006). Centuries of cultural traditions pressure teachers to think that classrooms must be quiet places that socialize rambunctious children into sedate students. The new learning about child development means that guiding children's energy, rather than fighting it, is at the core of developmentally appropriate practice. In workshops, we often say that the daily schedule should keep teachers in shape! We figure then the children will also be getting the movement program they need—one that respects and responds to the naturally active nature of the young child.

To Increase Your Knowledge

Learn more about the three models:

Stimulating Maturity through Accelerated Readiness Training (S.M.A.R.T.) is being used in 235 elementary schools in 12 states. S.M.A.R.T. is also being field-tested in two Head Start settings in Minnesota, with expected availability for preschool use in May 2009. Visit www.themlrc.org.

Kids in Action: Fitness for Children is a joint venture of the President's Council on Physical Fitness and Sports, the National Association for Sport and Physical Education, and the Kellogg Company. For more information, visit www.fitness.gov.

I Am Moving, I Am Learning is easily integrated into other community initiatives designed to address childhood obesity and family wellness. For further information, contact Amy Requa, Region III Administration for Children and Families, at (215) 592-1684, ext. 225.

Learn more about developmentally appropriate movement activities:

Healthy Young Children: Encouraging Good Nutrition and Physical Fitness, the cluster focus in *Young Children*, May 2006, presents a number of articles and a list of resources on movement and nutrition.

Further resources appear in Beyond the Journal, May 2006, at http://journal.naeyc.org/btj/200605.

Active for Life: Developmentally Appropriate Movement Programs for Young Children, by S. W. Sanders, and *Follow Me Too: A Handbook of Movement Activities for Three- to Five-Year-Olds*, by M. Torbert and L. Schneider, are books on exercise and movement from NAEYC.

Steps You Can Take

1. Plan a change to your program that promotes physical activity. Most specialists feel that structured physical activity is just as important as vigorous free play, so together with your colleagues, plan how to enhance both.

2. Research and decide on a program of indoor and outdoor activities that are developmentally appropriate for your group of children. (Remember, the object is participation, not competition nor immediate skill mastery.)

3. Model and participate enthusiastically in the vigorous activities you have implemented. Involve other staff and classroom volunteers.

4. Review the nutrition aspects of your program together with your colleagues. Brainstorm refinements so that nutritious meals and snacks complement your new "mind and body" program.

Column References

Farnham, N. (2007). S.M.A.R.T. principal's packet. Minneapolis: Minnesota Learning Resource Center, http://www.themlrc.org

Gartrell, D. (2000). *What the kids said today: Using classroom conversations to become a better teacher*. St. Paul, MN: Redleaf.

Levin, D. E. (2003). Beyond banning war and superhero play: Meeting children's needs in violent times. *Young Children, 58*(3), 60–63.

President's Council on Physical Fitness and Sports, National Association for Sport and Physical Education, & Kellogg Company. (2003). *Kids in Action: Fitness for children birth to age five.* Booklet, http://www.fitness.gov/funfit/kidsinaction.html

Region III Administration for Children and Families (ACF). (2006). *I Am Moving, I Am Learning: A proactive approach for addressing childhood obesity in Head Start children. Summary report, the first two years.* http://www.acf.hhs.gov/programs/region3/docs/Fatherhood/i_am_moving_summary_report.pdf

For additional website and information on using the guidance approach in the encouraging classroom, visit our companion website at www.cengage.com/education/gartrell.

Chapter 6

Managing the Encouraging Classroom

Guiding Questions

▶ How does the teacher balance reliability and novelty in the daily program?

▶ How does managing transitions reduce mistaken behavior?

▶ How do routines help to build an encouraging classroom?

▶ What part do large-group activities play in the encouraging classroom?

▶ Why is the teaching team important in managing the encouraging classroom?

▶ How can the encouraging classroom benefit from family members and other classroom volunteers?

© Cengage Learning

Key Concepts

▶ Anticipatory set

▶ Buffer activity

▶ Collaboration

▶ Day chart/Day clock

▶ Discussing inclusively

▶ Inclusion

▶ Multidimensional classroom

▶ Passivity

▶ Rough-and-tumble play

▶ Routines

▶ Teaching team

▶ Team-teaching

▶ Time confusion

▶ Transitions

Part Two addresses creating the encouraging classroom through strategies that reduce classroom-caused mistaken behavior. Chapter Five discussed organization of the physical space and the curriculum to engage children in the learning process. Chapter Six examines the:

▶ daily program

▶ limits of large groups

▶ management of transitions

▶ place of routines

▶ benefits of the teaching team

▶ use of family members and other volunteers.

The Daily Program

In the daily program, children need both a sense of reliability and the promise of novelty. Too little reliability results in anxiety and stress. Too little novelty results in tedium. A set schedule that children are familiar with makes these early days away from home predictable and friendly. The schedule provides a baseline for the day that nonetheless allows for both the spontaneous *teachable moment*, the gerbil having babies, and the planned special event, a visit from Smokey the Bear.

More than 100 years ago, Montessori (1912/1964) recognized that young children need a sense of order and continuity. A predictable schedule provides security. Much of life is beyond young children's control, from the time they get up in the morning to the time they go to bed. Some choices, like which of two kinds of cereal to eat, are good for children to make and add to their self-esteem. Other choices, such as whether to go to school or not, children should not make for themselves. When they cannot decide a matter for themselves, children benefit from understanding about a decision that is made for them. During the school day, understanding reasons helps children build trust in the teacher and in the classroom environment—a basic need for personal growth.

The daily schedule is one of those matters that young children don't make direct decisions about, but need to rely on. When unscheduled events enable positive results—celebration, delight, wonderment, enlightenment—they add greatly to the everyday program. An unpredictable program, however—whether it is just inconsistent or an unending series of spontaneous "teachable moments" (basically unplanned)—makes children feel anxious and insecure. The teacher maintains a healthy balance in the schedule by monitoring feeling levels in the class—anxious, bored, interested, or engaged—and responding accordingly. By reading children's feelings and discussing reasons with them, the teacher may vary from the schedule productively. Returning to it allows children the security of knowing what is expected of them. When a time block during the day produces a noticeable amount of boredom or mistaken behavior, the teacher takes these cues from the children and modifies strategies concerning the time block.

When unscheduled events enable positive results, they add to the everyday program.

Three Sample Schedules

The sample schedules shown in Tables 6–1, 6–2, and 6–3 model developmentally appropriate programming, make full use of the classroom, and provide a daily program through which interesting experiences can happen. These schedules balance the novel and the predictable so that children are involved but not overloaded—making mistaken behavior less likely. Again, flexibility in the schedule is a prerequisite for a developmentally appropriate program. The schedules are for prekindergarten, kindergarten, and primary-grade programs.

Tracking the Daily Schedule

To maximize the meaning of the schedule for children, the teacher can use a visual tracking method. Two such tools are the horizontal **day chart** and the circular **day clock**, each with a movable marker or hand that serves as a tracking device (especially in preprimary classrooms).

These visualizations serve multiple functions. One function is to acquaint adults new to the classroom with the daily program. A second function is assisting young children to understand the sequence of events through the day.

Time	Activity
Table 6–1 *Prekindergarten Schedule*	
8:00–8:30	Arrival. Teacher greets each child. Informal child-choice activity until all children arrive. Brief greeting large group.
8:30–9:00	Breakfast in family groups of six to eight, each with a caregiver/teacher. At tables, the caregiver/teacher previews events; **Plan, do, and review** sequence used.
9:00–10:15	Center time. Three uses of centers (from previous chapter). All centers open. Cleanup.
10:15–10:35	Snack in family groups. Review of "special things" done during center time.
10:35–11:00	Active play, inside or out.
11:00–11:15	Large group: music, interactive story, movement activity, or occasional guest. (Sometimes replaced by longer small-group activity that follows.)
11:15–11:45	Small-group activities—literacy, art, cooking, creative drama, or active play, depending on group.
11:45–1:00	Lunch in family groups. Rest.
1:00–2:10	Center time. Three uses of centers (from previous chapter). All centers open. Cleanup.
2:10–2:30	Class meeting, song, and review of day. Get ready to go home.
Note: Six-hour schedule, as in some Head Start programs. Half-day and full-day programs can be adapted.	

A third is to acquaint children with the idea of "telling time." Until they are seven or eight, children have difficulty understanding basic time concepts and frequently show **time confusion** (Elkind, 1976). Van Scoy and Fairchild (1993) point out that in contrast to persons who are older:

> *Young children's reasoning is tied to what they are seeing and experiencing; that is, young children are dependent on concrete, observable events ... to help them "figure things out." Given this need for concreteness, it is understandable that time concepts— which cannot be seen, heard or felt—are difficult for young children to construct.... To help children understand the passage of time, we must relate time to physical objects and/or events that are meaningful to the children. (p. 21)*

When used with a movable marker, the chart or clock helps children to track events that are real to them—snack, center time, rest, active-play time. When each time block is displayed by an illustration along with a name, children

Table 6–2 *Kindergarten Schedule*	
Time	**Activity**
8:30–9:00	Arrival. Teacher greets each child. Breakfast available for all children. Informal child-choice activity as children arrive.
9:00–9:15	Morning class meeting. Quick preview of day.
9:15–9:30	Large-group lead-in to center theme activities through use of discussion, story, song, object, or picture.
9:30–10:10	Small-group activities using learning centers. Focus on learning skills.
10:10–11:00	Snack time. Active play outside or inside.
11:00–11:45	Center time. Three uses of centers (from previous chapter). Cleanup.
11:45–12:30	Lunch and child-choice activity inside or active play outside, depending on the weather.
12:30–1:00	Story. Reading, relaxing, resting.
1:00–1:45	Special activity—gym, art, music, library, or computer. (Specialists lead these activities.)
1:45–2:30	Center activities—theme based or self-selected. Cleanup. Occasional special event during part of this time.
2:30–3:00	Afternoon circle time—songs, movement activities, finger plays, and review of day. Get ready to go home.
Note: Full-day schedule. Half-day schedule can be adapted.	

have contextual clues for building functional literacy. The use of a marker helps children to begin telling time in the natural way that time passes—without the complexity of the two-handed clock (more appropriate for children during the primary grades) or the abstraction of a digital one. (As a kindergartener told his teacher once, 1:23 meant "One, two, three o'clock.")

If the chart or clock has a marker, a daily "time-keeper" can move it. The teacher can use it during the morning meeting to introduce events of the day, including any "special events." He can refer to it during the day to remind children about the order in which events will happen: "Remember? Snack time comes after what?" By constructing time concepts that have personal meaning for them, children gain building blocks for the gradual mastery of chronology.

Table 6–3 *Primary Schedule*

Time	Activity
8:00–8:45	Arrival. Teacher greets each child. Breakfast available for all children. Informal child-choice activity as children arrive.
8:45–9:00	Morning class meeting: business, discussion of important events and issues—brought up by children or teacher. Preview of **language arts focus** (time block). Assignment of small groups to centers.
9:00–10:00	Integrated language arts time block in small groups: book read and share; journaling; language skills instruction; language skills follow-up; language arts choice—reading, journaling, or creative drama. (Groups rotate each day.)
10:00–10:30	Restroom, snack, and break/recess.
10:30–10:45	Transition large group—active to quiet; review of language focus; preview of math focus.
10:45–11:30	Math skill activities—manipulatives based, in small groups; one small group each day has supervised computer use; every Wednesday, art specialist.
11:30–11:45	Review of math focus, story, and transition to lunch.
11:45–12:30	Lunch and recess.
12:30–1:00	Relaxation—relaxation activity or another story, quiet music, and reading; sometimes option of educational video.
1:00–2:05	Large and small groups work on integrative themes having a social studies/science emphasis. (See Mrs. Ryan case study in Supplement for Chapter Five.)
2:05–2:15	Break, restroom, movement activity, and review of theme activities.
2:15–3:00	Monday: Continue work on themes; learning center activities. Tuesday: Alternating music and physical education specialist. Wednesday: Continue work on themes; learning center activities. Thursday: Continue work on themes; learning center activities. Friday: Theme presentations by small groups to class; learning center activities.
3:00–3:15	Afternoon class meeting. Happenings of the day—problems and accomplishments, brought up by children or teacher; future events introduced; preparations to go home.

Classroom Anecdote	*A teacher introduced a one-handed day clock to her class of four-year-olds. Gradually, during the day, children began to ask her, "What comes next again?" Her standard response was, "Go read the day clock." She knew the day clock idea was registering when Sam, an "experienced" four, told her, "Teacher, I know what comes next. Snack. So we gotta go wash our hands." A few days later, a naturalist spoke during large group about protecting the environment. After about 15 minutes of his overly technical talk, Sam, who was sitting by the teacher, whispered, "Teacher, the clock says it's time for centers."*

Mixing Active and Quiet Times

Many teachers believe that their job is to socialize young children to the quiet protocol of traditional classrooms. As discussed in Chapter Five, it is easier to operate a "developmentally appropriate" classroom for children who are more sedentary than active. Many children with active learning styles, often boys, feel constrained by the limits put on them—even in classrooms that their teachers may consider to be "developmentally appropriate." Conflicts, mistaken behavior, and lowered self-esteem result—patterns that can continue during later years at school. A balance of active and quiet times across the day is needed. Still, teachers might consider striking a balance that leans less toward "library quiet" and more toward "summer day camp."

The Need for Physical Activity. In stressing the quiet and orderly classroom, some teachers sacrifice programming that leads to healthy, "whole child" development and the emergence of active lifestyles. Each day, especially in the primary grades, their children sit for hours in school—and also sit for hours on buses and/or at home in front of television, video game players, and computer screens. These teachers unintentionally contribute to the obesity epidemic so prevalent in our society, which typically begins during childhood (*Texas Child Care Quarterly*, 2002). Moreover, hours of seatwork at school contributes to **passivity** (loss of the ability to focus) in learning styles (Elkind, 2003). Being naturally active, young children need movement in their education to make learning come alive.

Articles by Gabbard (1998) and Garcia, Garcia, Floyd, and Lawson (2002) bring a timely viewpoint to this issue. Gabbard examined the relationship between early brain development and motor development. Gabbard's findings are that the "window of opportunity" for the development of basic motor patterns begins to close by age five, and close for fine motor movements by about age nine (Gabbard, 2002). Garcia et al. argue that movement programs in early childhood help children establish physical competence in gross and fine motor skills and a foundation for healthy, active lifestyles. They argue that through everyday movement activities, children also progress in emotional, social, and cognitive development. Gabbard found that fine motor skills too come more easily for children who have daily patterns of active body movement. But developmentally, vigorous total body activity, on a regular basis, must happen first (Gabbard, 2002).

In my lectures, I often say (half seriously) that teachers would do well to consider each day in the classroom as their own physical development program. As mentioned, perhaps the early childhood classroom (for much of the day) should resemble summer camp—or in Dewey's terms "an active learning laboratory." Young children need the benefits of their bodies being in motion through much of the day. Teachers whose goal is to make their classrooms developmentally appropriate for *all* children almost always increase the amount of daily physical activity—and in turn may make themselves more physically active.

When individual young children experience difficulty in classrooms, some adults resort to common labels to describe their behavior: *immature, hyper, antsy, ADHD (attention-deficit hyperactivity disorder), oppositional, and challenging*. For some individual children, these patterns of behavior do have a physiological or psychological basis that needs to be diagnosed and treated. But often such labels result from the mismatch between the program and the child—the teacher striving for a "bucolic" classroom and the children needing to be actively engaged, "busy," and sometimes "boisterous."

Rather than attempt to suppress active learning styles, teachers would do better to use that energy and empower learning through it. Over time students who see themselves as capable, active learners are likely to have fewer conflicts than students who see themselves as failures at fitting the mold of "passive learners" (Elkind, 2003). As their bodies and brains continue to mature in middle childhood, most active learners will figure out how to tone down their enthusiasm—if they must.

Active Play. For teachers to use boisterous activity productively, these ideas are important.

1. **Throughout the age range, moving to music activities refreshes participants and renews their ability to concentrate.** Long a common practice in Asian programs, some American schools now begin the day with movement to music. Pieces by current "aerobics for kids" artists are piped into classrooms over the loudspeakers. Teachers as well as the children move to the music. Because enjoyment and not skill is the purpose, each person moves in her own way. Movement to music is key.

2. **The teacher should not rely only on scheduled active play times or physical education periods to meet children's need for vigorous activity.** Include an active-play center—a climber, mini-tramp, adapted exercise equipment, and so on—that is open each day. Use fun, vigorous play activities in the classroom and outside. Movement using large and fine muscle groups can be integrated into much learning activity. Centers and small-group activities in particular lend themselves movement for learning.

3. **Effective vigorous play activities involve children without the need to compete and take turns.** Young children run for the sake of running, skip for the sake of skipping, and climb for the sake of climbing. The rules

and complexities of competitive games tend to confuse young children and, in determining winners and losers, cause hurt feelings (Honig & Wittmer, 1996). (See "Guidance Matters" column, end of Chapter Two.) As well, wait times between turns are often frustrating and limit the opportunity for physical activity, which is the main reason for the activity. When all participate enjoyably, everybody wins.

Classroom Anecdote	*An early childhood teacher became tired of the usual active game in her class, Duck, Duck, Grey Duck. A large portion of the game was spent in squatting down. Once the children began running, the teacher noticed most did not want to stop. The inability of some children to catch the others also detracted from the fun. The teacher ended the game. Instead, she adapted Red Light, Green Light for her group by requiring different ways to move each time the "green light" showed and declaring the whole class winners as soon as the last child crossed the finish line. The game became the new favorite of the children, especially when the teacher taped a red light to her front and a green light to her back, jumped around, and enthusiastically called out directions.*

4. **Proactively manage rough-and-tumble play.** Use general guidelines set in class meetings outside of the play to manage rough-and-tumble play. Examples are: "Friendly touches only." "Active play yes, weapons play no." In class meetings, teach what these guidelines mean and enforce them during active play. Steer children away from focused superhero play and toward "category" play, such as "firefighters" and "first responders" (Levin, 2003). Be imaginative: Perhaps the first responders can drive the bench with a steering wheel from their station on the climber to where the fire is, in the dramatic-play area. Each teacher's limits will guide the scope of their creativity. Finally, rough-and-tumble play tends to be less aggressive when children have sufficient outlets for their energy. When an administrator removed a climber from an active playroom, thinking it was too dangerous, weapons play increased. When a teacher convinced the administrator to put the climber back, with mats underneath, weapons play decreased.

Rest and Relaxation. Although busy (and sometimes boisterous) sets the tone of the developmentally appropriate classroom (Brewer, 2006), neither children nor teachers can function all day at an active level. Over many years, books by such authors as Clare Cherry (*Think of Something Quiet*, 1981) and albums by such musicians as Hap Palmer (*Sea Gulls*, 1978) and Greg and Steve (*Quiet Moments*, 1983) have been helpful in promoting relaxation in the classroom. With modern family lifestyles and the pressures of school and community, children, like adults, become tense, angry, and anxious. Watson (2003) and Kalb (2003) have pointed out that children do not always have the ability to relax on their own. Marion (2002) discusses teaching children specific relaxation techniques to help them calm down and become more receptive to guidance from adults.

© Cengage Learning

In the encouraging classroom, the normal activity level is busy, not bucolic.

The traditional naps in preschool, the rest periods (more than naps) in kindergarten, and quiet periods in elementary grades—when done positively—all serve to restore a sense of equilibrium for children and teachers. Stories read on a daily basis in a relaxed atmosphere, have regenerating values.

In full-day preschool programs for young children, naptimes can be challenging. Children have different rest needs and show differing behaviors when adjusting to naptime (Saifer, 2004). When children of different ages share the same room for rest, problems can be compounded. The "fingertip guide" shown in Table 6–4 provides suggestions for helping staff meet nap challenges.

Adults help children to nap when they create a relaxing mood and setting. For instance, they may find and repeat a piece of quiet music that children find calming. Maintaining a firm, friendly, and quiet response style is important. Staff who take a problem-solving approach can most often improve the situation (Saifer, 2004), often within a week or two.

Classroom Anecdote	*One group in a child care center had preschoolers along with part-time kindergarten children who arrived from school each day at noon. The kindergarten kids felt they were "too old" for naps, and the younger children were affected each day by their arrival. "Rest" was proving difficult.* *One day an assistant teacher asked a kindergarten child to rub the back of his younger brother to help the three-year-old get settled. It worked. The preschool staff got to talking about this and decided to try something new. They had each kindergarten child rub the back of a selected preschooler. After the preschooler fell asleep, the kindergartners lay down on their mats behind a long bookshelf. On their mats the "k" kids looked at books or listened to relaxing music. In just a few days, rest time at the center changed completely.*

Table 6–4 *Fingertip Guide to Happy Napping*	
Challenge	**Suggestion**
Many children have trouble settling down.	Review: (a) Activity level prior to nap—relaxing, quiet? (b) Method of creating mood—story, music, relaxation activity used? (c) Environment—comfortable temperature, low lighting, enough space? (d) Role of adults—present, speaking quietly, lying with children, rubbing backs?
Children rest, but many are ready to rise too early.	Assess length of naptime. Consider shortening. Start early risers doing quiet activities.
Older children don't sleep; ready to rise before others.	Move older children to different room or separate area. Allow to read books on mats. Allow to rise early and do quiet activities.
Individual child doesn't sleep; ready to rise. Doesn't seem tired.	Check with family member about child's sleep schedule and habits. Some children need less sleep than others. If willing, try solution above for older children; note how child responds.
Individual child doesn't sleep; ready to rise. Does seem tired.	Separate from others. Primary caregiver rubs back, lies by child. At another time talk with child about problem. Talk with family member about child's sleeping habits.
Individual child is not ready to rise with others.	Let child sleep. Monitor health of child. If pattern continues, talk with family member about possible reasons.
Early risers in buffer activity get too active.	Review selection of activities. Allow to read books or make pictures, but *not* watch videos. Young children watch hours of video each day at home as it is. Review placement of children: too near sleepers? too close together?

Two considerations conclude this discussion of "happy napping." First, most children need to be physically tired, and not just mentally drained, in order to nap easily. If your program tires them physically by providing an active program, you will not only help with whole-child development, but also assist them to make the most of their periods of rest and relaxation.

Second, changing family dynamics now mean that more children are coming to classrooms with occasional or chronic sleep deprivation. A health-related condition, sleep disruptions can result in classic Level Three mistaken behaviors that hinder individual development and community building. Once in a while, any child can arrive at school overtired, for any number of reasons. Sometimes, the best thing that teachers can do is help a child leave the group and get some rest. If the teacher detects signs of illness along with the child being tired, they should, of course, contact the family member. If signs of sleep deprivation continue over time, the teacher should work actively with the family to address the situation.

Teachers who take the guidance approach need to consider the balance of active and quiet times in the daily program. Distinct from traditional practices, the general noise level of classrooms should be *busy*, with planned periods that are *boisterous* and *bucolic*. When teachers see most children needing to rest because they are physically tired, and not mentally drained, their balance is on the mark.

The Limits of Large Groups

A hallmark of encouraging classrooms is that they accommodate the entire range of developmental responses that any group of children will show. A productive learning *center* such as a reading center accommodates developmental diversity by providing a variety of materials from picture books to "early readers" to (perhaps) elementary science tests. Productive *materials* such as blocks and clay accommodate developmental diversity by allowing children to construct whatever they will, from a simple stack to a castle, from a simple clay ball to a bird sitting on its nest of eggs. Productive *activities* also are developmentally inclusive. In art, for instance, the teacher avoids predrawn forms and craft projects but instead motivates children to work creatively with the materials provided so that each child can succeed at her level (Bredekamp & Copple, 2009).

Likewise, small groups and individual activities encourage children to function effectively at their various levels of development. A problem with overreliance on teacher-directed large groups is that they easily exceed children's developmental levels and attention spans (Brewer, 2006). Very few preschoolers, and only some kindergarteners and primary-grade children are capable of sitting, listening, and following directions for any length of time (Bredekamp & Copple, 2009).

An argument for large groups is that young children need to get used to sitting and listening to succeed at school. However, the physiology of children prevents them from sitting comfortably for long periods. To the comment that they must learn to sit and listen, the response is that young children are not developmentally ready (Brewer, 2006). In fact, even though the development of primary-grade children means that most can attend longer, the DAP research indicates that even primary-grade children learn more effectively when they are actively doing and interacting (Bredekamp & Copple, 2009; Brewer, 2006; Dunn & Kontos, 1997). The reality is that for some teachers, large groups offer a sense of predictability and control. As the following anecdote indicates, the opposite can be the case.

© Cengage Learning

Children play actively without the need for adult direction, even under less than ideal conditions. (Courtesy Michael Crowly, Family Service Center, Kootasca Head Start, Grand Rapids, Minnesota)

Classroom Anecdote

On a sunny spring afternoon, a first-grade class went to the library. While there, they silently read/looked at books, then heard the librarian read quite a long story. When they arrived back at the classroom, a parent who was scheduled to read a book that morning arrived and asked if he could read then. The teacher felt this was important and agreed. She and the student teacher sat with the children and worked hard to keep them focused on the story.

The next scheduled activity was another large group; the student teacher was to do a lesson on friendship with a puppet named Charlie. After three tries at starting the lesson, the student teacher whispered to the teacher. Then, the Puppet announced, "Boys and girls, Charlie thinks that listening is hard to do right now because you have had to sit so long. When I call a color you are wearing, line up to go outside." Charlie called out the colors very rapidly. After 40 minutes outdoors, the teacher and student teacher again had "happy campers." The class came in and worked industriously on their daily journals.

Throughout the age range, children learn best when they engage in many independent activities, frequent small groups, and *limited* large groups that are friendly, participatory, relevant to the children's experiences, and concise. Brewer (2006) and Loomis and Wagner (2005) recommend that teachers review standard large-group practices for such criteria. From the perspective of the encouraging classroom, this section examines traditional large-group practices—taking attendance, calendar and the weather, show-and-tell, large-group instruction—and presents suggestions for making them more effective in engaging young learners.

Taking Attendance

Attendance can be done efficiently if teachers greet children individually when they arrive and ask them to "register" right away. One way of registering is to have them log in on a computer program. A lower-tech method is to laminate "mushrooms" that display each child's name, a child-made picture, and the child's photo. After learning their names, the children take their own mushrooms from slots in one tag-board sheet and put them in the slots by their names on a second sheet. At a morning class meeting, the teacher quickly reviews the charts with the class, and those absent and present are noted. Even three-year-olds quickly recognize their names—and in time to recognize others'.

An alternative, which many teachers enjoy, is to sing an attendance song that mentions each present child by name. The songs may have made-up words to familiar tunes and sometimes use name cards, such as the "mushrooms," to encourage functional literacy. Songs make taking attendance more participatory, an objective for successful large groups. Teachers who use greeting songs seem to overcome two minor difficulties with them: (a) With a large class, long verses take a lot of time; (b) some children get embarrassed and may not want their names sung. Short verses, perhaps identifying two children at once, and a matter-of-fact approach with individual children are ideas for making this method of greeting successful.

Calendar and the Weather

Many teachers like calendar and weather activities because of the concepts they seemingly reinforce and the social tradition they continue. But for young children, these activities too easily become rituals rather than conceptual learning experiences. As mentioned, until middle childhood children experience *time confusion*, which means they have difficulty understanding conventional time concepts (Elkind, 1976; Van Scoy & Fairchild, 1993). A kindergarten teacher was amused to discover time confusion when she asked her students two questions: What month comes after October? How old did they think she was? She got answers that included "Noctober," 18 *(smile)*, and 62 *(different smile)*!

In their article about time, Van Scoy and Fairchild (1993) say this about activities such as the daily calendar:

> *Time is often taught to children by having them recite social labels such as the days of the week or months of the year. Children who recite labels in this way are being*

Primary grade children, like younger children, learn more effectively when they are doing and interacting.

given an opportunity to construct social knowledge about time. . . . Social knowledge is knowledge of an arbitrary set of symbols and behaviors common to a society. Children who recite labels are not having experiences that will help them develop an understanding of the passage of time. (p. 21)

A common practice at calendar time is for children to sing a song identifying days or months. While the activity hopefully is enjoyable, teachers need to recognize that mainly rote knowledge is being gained. The kindergarten child who contributed "Noctober" (above) had been doing calendar activities in various classrooms just about every day since he was three.

Weather concepts also are more abstract to children than adults may realize. Two partly cloudy days following two cloudy days simply is not an everyday topic of conversation for five-year-olds—though they will show the effects of weather in their behavior! When the selected "weatherperson" goes to the window and looks hard at what's going on outside, she may notice one small cloud and announce that the day is cloudy, or see snow on the ground and declare it snowy. If the child gives a "wrong" report, the teacher has to engage in "damage control," especially with the two others who thought they should have been picked to be the weatherperson to begin with.

Make Sharing Real. Teachers can use alternatives to the ritualized treatment of the calendar and the weather. In a morning class meeting, an alternative is to ask four or five questions that encourage children to think about time and weather concepts in ways that have personal meaning for them. Sample questions are:

▶ Who can recall what you had for supper last night?

▶ Who can share what you will do after school today?

▶ Who can remember three things you saw on the way to school this morning?

▶ Was it hot or cold outside this morning? How could you tell?

▶ It is windy today. Who saw the wind push something?

▶ It is raining this morning. Who hopes it is still raining after school this afternoon? Why? Why not?

These questions relate directly to the children's experience. If children know that all interpretations of questions are welcome and not just one answer that the teacher may have in mind, they will participate readily. Through engagement in meaningful discussion, children gain in observation powers, thinking skills, and communication abilities. They are building a foundation of personal experience that will help them master "conventional" weather and time concepts as they develop.

Despite the criticism that conventional calendar and weather activities mean more to teachers than children, many teachers would rather not give them up. They value the social learning that occurs through a positive group experience, and maintain that the exposure to weather, day, and date vocabulary has its own value. I remember visiting a classroom of three-year-olds in a child care center where the children clearly enjoyed singing a "days of the week" song, and the weatherperson's report was appreciated whatever it turned out to be. These activities helped the children feel a sense of belonging, reliability, and accomplishment—important for young ones away from home.

The suggestion here is that young children may not understand as much from conventional calendar and weather activities as the teacher may think. A compromise is to do calendar and the weather in a way that is concise, positive, and as relevant as possible to the children's own experience. Then move on to activities that have more intrinsic interest for the audience.

Show-and-Tell

Show-and-tell often is criticized as "bring and brag" (Brewer, 2006). The thought behind show-and-tell seems to be that if children bring in familiar objects, they will feel comfortable showing them in group situations and so use communication skills. One problem with show-and-tell is that it is materialistic. Focusing on object possession, children expect one another to bring in interesting items. They fall easily into judging each child on the basis of the items shown. A second problem is that the child may not have a lot to say about the item.

The teacher then has to become an interviewer, and the rest of the group may tune out. Boredom is likely to increase if all in the group are expected to share (Saifer, 2004), and after a few months of following the same show-and-tell ritual.

Teachers handle problems with show-and-tell in various ways. Most directly, some teachers have ended the practice. They spark discussions in the circle time instead that lead to a fuller sharing of thoughts and feelings. Divergent questions that children can personally relate to are a superior medium for developing communications skills. The kinds of questions mentioned under the calendar and weather heading are examples. A few others include:

▶ Who can tell us about a time when you went swimming?

▶ Who can share about when you were in a snowball fight?

▶ Who knows about an interesting pet that someone owns?

Such questions lead well into themes and learning center activities that may follow the large group. They arouse interest and focus on *ideas* rather than *things*.

For teachers who do not wish to end show-and-tell altogether, Saifer (2004) provides ideas for dealing with "bored children during show-and-tell." Useful ideas include:

▶ Do show-and-tell in small groups (such as during center time, for those who are interested).

▶ Schedule show-and-tell on a rotating basis with only some children sharing each day.

▶ Directly encourage other children to ask questions; stand behind the child to direct the group's attention.

Saifer suggests that children share family experiences, a picture they made, or what they did earlier at school. He indicates that sharing themselves rather than things helps children who have no item to share; develops the children's ability to review; and makes for more personal, meaningful sharing (Saifer, 2004).

Some teachers have successfully linked show-and-tell to ongoing themes. The main idea is to replace a competitive materialistic focus (on things) with a spirit of community that the sharing of thoughts, feelings, and experiences can inspire.

Using Stories with Children

The traditional method of delivering stories is in the large group. When doing stories in a large group, to preserve lines of sight teachers frequently sit on low chairs. Children sit on rug samples or other markers, which reduces crowding and the frequent complaint that "I can't see." The technique can be efficient but results in a separation between adult and children. An alternative in story delivery is the small group. With children on the adult's lap or all lying on stomachs around a book, an important closeness results, which is sometimes called "the lap technique."

Ideally, the lap technique begins early in the child's life at home. To encourage an appreciation of books and reading (especially with children who were not read to at home), the lap technique is an important method. (One teaching team does large group activities first, then introduces three books to the children, each read by a different adult in a different part of the room. Children choose the book they want to read and go to that adult.)

Of course, a role remains for stories in large-group settings. There are two different purposes for using stories in large groups that are helpful to note: first, to encourage appreciation; second, to encourage personal expression. By focusing on the particular intention of the story experience, the teacher can reduce mistaken behavior.

Reading to Encourage Appreciation. The long-standing goal of reading for appreciation is to teach children to enjoy the flow of language and pictures, the interesting characters, and the developing plot. Teachers who wish to encourage appreciation of books and stories want the experience to be relaxing and engaging for the children. Usual times when the teacher reads to foster enjoyment are after sustained activity for a calming effect, and to set a relaxed mood for an activity to come such as lunch, naptime, or going home. Adults can use various methods to establish an engaging story setting. The techniques listed in Table 6-5 are the author's top ten suggestions.

Reading to Encourage Personal Expression. Although reading to encourage children's appreciation of stories is common in early childhood, there is a second function, *the encouragement of personal expression.* Some teachers are able to integrate the two functions seamlessly in the large-group setting. Other teachers work better on the second function in small groups, where they may be able to get quieter children to share.

Reading for personal expression means encouraging discussion after the story—but also at times during it as well. At key points while he is reading, the teacher asks open-ended questions and welcomes children's responses. When the teacher thinks it is appropriate, he steers attention back to the book and continues to read—often sooner in large groups and later in small ones.

Discussing Inclusively. Sharing about ideas from books calls for discussing inclusively. Discussing inclusively means that when a child makes a comment that doesn't seem to relate to the discussion, the teacher realizes that the comment *does relate for the child.* The teacher responds in a friendly way and tries to include the comment in the conversation. When discussing inclusively, he does not focus on *correct* or *incorrect* answers but allows the discussion to build, based on a sharing of the unique perspectives of the children.

Though the technique of discussing inclusively, the teacher fosters a number of learner outcomes for children, including integration of listening and speaking skills, comprehension abilities, accommodation of different ideas, engagement

Table 6–5 *Top Ten Techniques for Encouraging Appreciation of Books and Stories ("Tonight Show" style)*

10. **Choose books avidly but carefully.**	Be active in circulating new books and recirculating favorites—few tasks you do are as important. Select books appropriate for the age and backgrounds of the children and that will engage and hold their interest. Think about the children's attention spans and interests when previewing books you will read. Consider whether stories reinforce or go beyond stereotypes pertaining to culture, gender, and disability. Balance books that might appeal to boys and girls (remember that boys these days lag girls in literacy levels and book enjoyment).
9. **Select books that match themes and special events.**	Teachers often have favorites that they get out or feature during "homemade" themes. Often curriculum-based themes have bibliographies that may provide new books for reading aloud and children's independent perusal. Preread such books for appropriateness to ages and interests of the group.
8. **Allow children to read their own books while you read.**	The practice sounds unorthodox, but it is in line with the outcome of appreciation for reading and books. Typically, only some children choose to read their own books. These readers typically stay with their books until the teacher gets to a "good part." Then they look up and follow the teacher's story. These children are often the ones who have trouble attending in the large group. A variation is to make available multiple copies of the book you are reading—they follow along in their own copy.
7. **Tell stories as well as read them.**	Some current stories or historic folktales of relevance to your group may not be accessible in written form. Telling stories takes fortitude the first few times, but children adjust quickly to this "radio way of learning." Ask children to close their eyes and see the pictures in their heads. Having children spread out and lie down adds to the success of this experience and makes the technique useful at rest time.
6. **Feature "big," oversize picture books.**	so that children in large groups can see the important details. Often children "in the back" or with vision difficulties cannot make out the details in pictures when books are "standard" size. Big books in big groups help children engage with stories. They reduce restlessness and the common complaint of "I can't see!"
5. **Do a brief finger play, movement activity, or engaging introduction (perhaps with a prop like a Dr. Seuss hat) to get children ready for the story.**	If an anticipatory set is not established, some children cannot focus enough to pick up the story line. Avoid simply starting the book without first gaining the children's attention; otherwise, you may never have it. Suggestion one: Dramatically point to and read each work in the title and the author's first and last name. Suggestion two: Lead a simple attention grabber such as, "Hands up high. Hands down low. Hands in your laps. Now we're ready to go."
4. **Read with expression.**	If you are not familiar with the story, read it aloud to yourself first. Practice how you want each character to sound. (You don't have to do this perfectly.) Use dramatic tones when you read; animate your usual speaking voice. When you are "into" the story, the children will be too.
3. **Frequently use books with repetitions that children can help read.**	Enjoyment and learning are enhanced when children can actively repeat words and phrases from the book. Many books allow for group participation if we look for and highlight this feature in them. (Say the line the first few times, then leave out words and cue group.)
2. **Place books you have read in a special "Featured Book" section of your library corner where children can easily locate them.**	Go beyond onetime book exposures. Children like to return to featured books and read them (sometimes over and over) on their own. The long-term benefits of a child's follow-up and mastery of a book cannot be underestimated.
1. **Proactively manage your groups.**	Station co-teachers and volunteers near certain children who may need extra support to stay engaged. Establish that all children can see and that children need to stay where they are so that they can continue to see. Remember that using the lap technique in small groups almost always eliminates "restless child syndrome." Find a balance of large- and small-group reading experiences that matches your group's activity levels and attention spans.

with the literature, and comfort with speaking in front of others. A fear of speaking in public is widespread and too often gets its start during classroom discussions that are handled insensitively. Teachers need not, and should not, restrict inclusive discussions to children's books, but reading for personal expression provides an excellent opportunity to build a classroom where all feel their ideas are welcome.

Classroom Anecdote	*After a snowfall, a kindergarten teacher was reading the classic* A Snowy Day *when Clarisse raised her hand: "Teacher, me and Cleo went sliding and she got snow down her pants!" (General laughter.)*
	Teacher: That must have been cold. What did she do?
	Clarisse: She went inside but Paul and me kept sliding. It was fun.
	Teacher: Thanks for sharing, Clarisse; did anyone else go sliding last weekend?
	After several children shared, the teacher commented, "You had lots of good times playing in the snow. Now let's see what's going to happen to Peter."
	At the end of the book, the teacher announced: "It sounds us if you like to do lots of fun things in the snow just like Peter. Right now, when I call your name, you are going to tell me which 'snowy day' center you are going to today, and I will note your choice. Remember that when one center is full, you can pick another. Either today or tomorrow, everyone will get to go to the centers they want." The teacher then quickly had the children choose between five "snowy day" learning centers, including a story picture activity at the writing center where they created stories about what they like to do outside in the snow.

Stories Integrate Curriculum. Often, teachers use reading for personal expression as a lead-in for related expressive activity such as creative drama, journaling, story pictures, or more free-flowing discussion. Effective follow-up depends on the teacher finding topics to which the children can relate. Often the most effective follow-up is in center activities. *Emergent curriculum* in the form of projects, inquiry topics, themes, or mini-themes often starts with an engaging story read to the group. The teacher builds from the plot, characters, and/or artwork in stories to create comprehensive learning opportunities for the class. As children explore learning opportunities that might include music, art, math science, social studies, and often technology, they engage in *integrated curriculum*—meaningful educational interaction with the teacher.

When they use stories to integrate curriculum, teachers encourage a fuller appreciation of the literature they have shared. They encourage personal exploration and the brain development that comes with it. They kindle developing literacy in relation to the written word and beyond.

A Place for Large Groups

Teaching in large groups may seem normal because it is the way most teachers themselves were educated, kindergarten through college. In traditional large-group instruction, the teacher transmits information and then solicits repetition

© Cengage Learning

Large groups work well to orient children to interactive follow-up center activities on an individual basis or in small groups.

or application of the information from "volunteers" who give an indication of group understanding (which can differ markedly from child to child).

The basic criticism of this *direct instruction* is that children are "overtaught and underpracticed." They absorb the information but don't have the opportunity to construct their own knowledge from it. They are not fully able to "own" the learning, make sense of it, and value it (Elkind, 2003). Common signs that children are unable to engage in the learning process include glassy eyes, inattentiveness, and restlessness. With prolonged passivity in large groups, feelings of inadequacy build, and tuning out as well as acting out tend to result (Loomis & Wagner, 2005).

Contrasted with the direct-instruction approach, the DAP position is that learning is *interactive*. The teacher provides opportunities for the child to integrate learning through expression in creative endeavor—art, music, play, creative drama, construction, and discussion (Bredekamp & Copple, 2009). If carefully planned, large groups work well for orienting children to an interactive learning experience called establishing an **anticipatory set**. The child then moves to a follow-up activity, either individually or in a small group. Using large groups to establish an anticipatory set *is* developmentally appropriate.

Classroom Illustration	*A first-year kindergarten teacher returned from fall break and a quick trip to Hawaii (which she had won in a raffle). The kindergarten program at the school had an "A" group that attended on Monday, Wednesday, and Friday of this first week back. That week the "B" group attended on Tuesday and Thursday. (Next year there would be full-time, everyday kindergarten, which the teacher was looking forward to.)*
	On Monday at circle time, the teacher shared items she had brought back from her trip with the "A" group. She told the children about her trip and passed around a coconut, a pineapple, a conch shell, and a quickly drying lei. Some children got impatient for their turns and tried to tug away the items before the children holding them were ready to give them up. After they looked at the items, some children got restless and "bothered their neighbors." A chunk of the petals on the lei got torn off. All, including the teacher, were quite ready for the children to go to center activities after the group.
	The teacher replanned the activity for Tuesday's group. She told the children about her trip, including the hula dance she saw at a luau. She mentioned that both boys and girls danced the hula in Hawaii, put on the lei, started a hula song on a CD, and taught the boys and girls to dance.
	After several minutes, due to requests for "again," the teacher told the children what they were going to do in centers. In the science center, the educational assistant was going to work with the children at opening and tasting a coconut and pineapple. In the sand table, the children would look for and sort buried seashells. In the writing center, they would write and draw stories about what they would like to do on an island that was always warm. In the art center, the children were going to make their own leis, which they would wear tomorrow when they again danced the hula.
	The children went to the centers with an entirely different mind-set from the Monday group. The teacher was already thinking about how she would modify the continuing study of Hawaii for her "A" group on Wednesday.

Whenever a teacher intends a large group to be the main vehicle for instruction, he needs to proceed with caution (Bredekamp & Copple, 2009; Loomis & Wagner, 2005). Successful large-group experiences tend to include a series of short activities—a very concise presentation or orientation, a brief story, a movement activity or song, class business. A quick pace to the large group followed by a crisp transition reduces the mistaken behavior that grows from passivity. To reiterate an earlier statement, for large groups to be a part of an interactive learning program, they should be friendly, participatory, relevant to children's experiences, and concise.

Classroom Illustration	*A teaching team in a preschool class held three 20-minute large groups each day—as soon as all the children arrived, before lunch, and before time to go home. The team, frankly, was having problems with the large groups. The teachers tried preventive methods such as placing themselves strategically in the circle to help children stay focused. Still, many of the children grew restless, and the teachers found themselves calling for attention as much as conducting activities.*
	(continued)

Classroom Illustration	*The lead teacher met with the team, and they reorganized the day. The teachers continued the morning large group but reduced it to singing a single attendance song and doing a "slow transition" game while children washed hands for break-fast. They dispensed with the large group just before lunch; instead, staff read stories to the children in three family groups. The groups also ate lunch together. Brief singing and a transition activity comprised the large group in the afternoon. The class went from one hour of large group each day to about 15 minutes.* *With the change the teachers found that mistaken behavior decreased, and more children seemed engaged in productive activity. Though they had to "sell" the new program to a supervisor, the team was pleased with the results.*

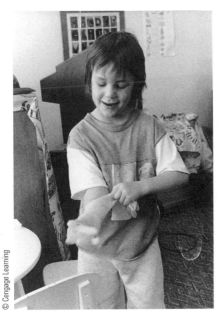
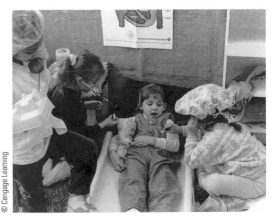

Stimulated by a teacher in surgical garb, children follow up large-group discussion with hospital play, complete with doctors, patients, and even a "new baby."

Managing Transitions

Transitions, changes from one activity to the next, often can be disruptive. One classic transition dilemma occurs at cleanup between individual activity and large group. A conventional approach is to get most of the children into the circle and then call out, "We're waiting for Ryan and Sonya." This approach often embarrasses the targeted children and may make others wonder who is going to get "nagged" next.

Instead, the professional teacher uses alternative strategies that get children to the group on time but do not undercut self-esteem. Here are six basic guidance strategies for transitions. Some are more appropriate for preprimary classrooms; others pertain throughout the age range.

1. Give a notice five minutes before the transition. Some children—like adults— get so involved that they may need additional notices. One student teacher, Amy, made dramatic use of an underused, oversize timer that displayed a decreasing red zone with every tick. Reinforced by Amy's "excited" reminders, the children all clearly knew when the five minutes was up.

2. Model enthusiasm for the cleanup process. Make the process a game with comments like, "I need some strong kids over here who can carry lots of blocks." Model for the children by participating in the cleanup. Remind children of the "cool stuff" the class will do as soon as the room is picked up (the "grandma principle").

3. Give generous encouragement to the group who are conscientious about cleaning up (Saifer, 2004). Ignore or use private matter-of-fact comments to children who are slow to participate. Avoid accusations and debates at the time, but follow up quietly later with the individuals.

© Cengage Learning

For large groups to be developmentally appropriate, they are friendly, participatory, relevant, and concise.

4. Sing a cleanup song with the children. Make up words and put them to a familiar tune. Children capture moods more easily than adults. Songs, or even popular pieces of recorded music, identify the transition and get children into the mood. A classic recorded tune that makes clean-up fun is Gregg and Steve's "The Freeze."

5. Make up and sing a song in the large group that names children as they arrive—for example (to any familiar tune you think of), "We're happy to see you, see you, see you. We're happy to see Cathy, at circle time today." Include latecomers when they arrive so that no one feels left out. The song is likely to speed up the transition and serves as a **buffer activity**, an activity that uses time productively while waiting.

6. With enthusiasm start the large group before all have arrived. The magnetism of an exciting large group will attract the rest of the children. No comment about anyone who is late is needed.

Waiting

A primary consideration in managing transitions is reducing the time that children spend waiting. Young children live in the here and now. Although most will do it better as they get older, children under seven or eight years just do not wait well. Strategies that the teacher uses to manage wait times prevent many problems.

Classroom Anecdote	*Natasha, a kindergarten student teacher, was in charge of "art time," scheduled right after the children came in from active play. She ran into problems with the wait time before the children could do the projects. First, she had the children sit at the tables while she gave directions. Then she handed out the materials to each table. The children grabbed for the materials at the same time and mini-chaos resulted.*
	After talking with her cooperating teacher, Natasha made some changes for "next time." She had all materials out on the tables when the children came in. This time they began using the materials before she could introduce the project, so the idea of the theme was lost.
	Finally, she used a two-step approach. She set the materials out on the tables but had the children sit at the large-group circle when they came in. She discussed the project with them at the circle. Then she dismissed them to their tables a few at a time by the color of clothing they wore: "All wearing purple or yellow may get up and slowly walk to their tables." The student teacher did not interrupt the flow by challenging children who had interesting interpretations of purple or yellow; the purpose was to get them to the tables efficiently without a stampede or hurt feelings.

Pre-primary Buffer Activities. A buffer activity ("buffer") keeps children occupied during wait times. A song in a large group before everyone arrives is an example. Another example is the buffer designed to move children *from* a group into another activity—snack, lunch, or going outside. Teachers use *slower buffers*

© Cengage Learning

Recognize that even after a five-minute notice, children sometimes will need a bit longer to finish. Some activities can be returned to later in the day.

when children have to wash hands, for instance, and only a few can do so at once. Here is a typical song or chant:

> *I roll the ball to Caroline. She rolls it back to me. Oh so slowly, oh so slowly, she rolls it back to me. (The child leaves the group after rolling ball.)*

Suggestion: Get the restless ones going first, then do the kids who tend to be patient or are sitting with an adult. However, don't wait until each child is "sitting straight and tall" before you call on them. "Behavior-based" selection systems are arbitrary—some children sit "straight and tall" all the time, for instance, and may be selected after a child who "never does" gets selected first. As well, the opposite may happen—a teacher may call last on a child who often is often restless but is now sitting "straight and tall." Make your selection process matter-of-fact. Use *fast buffers* when congestion in the transition area is not a problem: "All wearing, blue, pink, red, yellow, orange, green, purple or black can get their coats on to go outside."

Primary Level Buffer Activities. At the primary level, a teacher often has alternative buffer activities for children who finish first. Such activities range from "reading your favorite book" to "working quietly at your desk" to using selected learning centers. Although these types of buffer activities are useful, they should not be so attractive that they encourage hurried completion of the main lesson. Such a pattern discourages thorough work habits and discriminates against children who work methodically or find the task difficult. Popular activities used as buffers should be available at another time of day for all to enjoy. With thought, the teacher can use buffer activities to reduce significant amounts of impatience-related mistaken behavior without hurrying some children through their work.

Waiting during transitions is not a natural activity even for primary grade children. Buffer activities, sometimes planned and sometimes spontaneous, help fill empty times and prevent mistaken behavior.

Classroom Anecdote	Children at a Head Start center were having problems each day just before lunch. The schedule called for them to come in from outdoor play, line up to use the restroom, and wash hands. During this time, the lead teacher prepared the tables for lunch, and the assistant teacher monitored the lines. Waiting in line with nothing to do was difficult for many of the children. Pushing and fights were becoming more frequent.
	The teaching team reviewed the situation and tried a new arrangement. The teacher brought in a few children early. They washed their hands first and helped the teacher set the tables and bring in the food on carts. When the rest of the children came in, they sat at the reading center near the restroom and sink where they looked at books together. During this buffer, the assistant teacher had small clusters of children use the facilities and rotate back to their books until lunch. The waiting in line was eliminated and with it the mistaken behavior.

Learning to Live with Lines

Young children and lines—like with large groups and waiting—are not a natural match. Moving big groups of little people is always a tricky business. In many preschools, formal lines are not used. Out-of-building excursions are safest when the ratio of adults to children is at most 1:4 and lines are not needed. Adult-child ratios are so important, especially on busy streets, that staff should do their utmost to recruit additional volunteers for these occasions. An unsafe alternative is the old-time use of ropes with loops that each child holds. Besides the "chain gang" appearance, anyone who has seen one child stumble and all lose their balance knows this is one piece of equipment that should be retired.

Preschools located in public school buildings sometimes experience difficulty with movement of the group through halls. The concept of two-by-two lines is not a natural one for three- and four-year-olds. School administrators should not

© Cengage Learning

Buffer activities, sometimes planned and sometimes spontaneous, reduce the mistaken behavior caused by waiting. (Courtesy, The Bemidji Pioneer)

expect the same "hall expertise" of preschoolers that they expect of third grad-ers. Discussions with administrators about mutual expectations are important before preschools locate in school buildings or the school year starts.

When having children line up, teachers learn quickly that more is needed than simply stating, "Everyone line up at the door." Instead, teachers often use "creative alternatives," methods for transitioning into lines in a quick but orderly fashion. The methods should *not* violate the principle of unconditional posi-tive regard—"Millie, you've been quiet; you can line up first today." This prac-tice results in hurt feelings among the others who have been quiet and weren't selected. "Chance-based" quick transitions, such as "Everyone whose first name begins with a C or *K* may quietly line up," are more appropriate. Chance-based criteria lessen the appearance of favoritism from the lineup procedure and get the job done efficiently.

Some teachers who designate line leaders and "backups" use strategies that do not seem arbitrary. One method is to have a posted list of the class with a marker to designate the current leader. A teacher can use the chart as a func-tional literacy and counting activity to help children figure out how long before their turn. Some teachers use charts for many classroom tasks, using differ-ent listing criteria—alphabet both ways, age, height, and so on—to vary turn rotations. Here are two considerations about line procedures—the first a tad controversial, the second "commonsense." In accordance with the ideas of antibias curriculum, Phillips and Derman-Sparks (1997) recommend lines that do not pair girls with girls and boys with boys. This practice needlessly exaggerates differences between the sexes in an era when cross-gender cooperation needs to be encouraged. Healthy cross-gender interactions become more difficult in programs that institutionalize gender differences (Phillips & Derman-Sparks, 1997). Instead, the teacher should work to create an atmosphere in which gender is accepted as just another element in who each child is. Comfortable cross-gender relations are in keeping with the encouraging classroom and should be reflected in lineup procedures as well as in all other parts of the program.

The commonsense suggestion is this: Whenever a teacher can bring an element of enjoyment to the experience, he is showing skill at preventing mistaken behavior. Having finger plays and songs ready for when children must wait in line is sound preventive practice. Simple songs that use the children's names are effective buffer activities. Similarly, when children walk in lines, stimulating their imaginations can work wonders.

Classroom Anecdote	A particular kindergarten teacher used the children's imaginations to move her class efficiently. On one day she whispered: "Today, we are colorful birds in the jungle. We have to fly very quietly down the trail through the trees. Please flap your hands like this, not arms, so you don't hit any trees. When we get to the grassland [outside], then we can sing and call and make all the bird sounds we want. Ready?" The children flapped their hands quietly until they hit the playground, then hooted and soared in different directions. Ina, the teacher, smiled.

Routines in the Encouraging Classroom: A Teacher's Perspective

Familiarity with the classroom and its many resources helps children to become confident, productive learners. Pat Sanford, an experienced kindergarten and primary teacher in northern Minnesota, offers these thoughts about organizing the program around **routines**.

Pat says that the secret to classroom management lies in getting children used to routines. She begins on the first day with a tour of the classroom. Right away she makes sure they know where the restroom is and how to use it. She goes over clearly and often how to find her classroom and the right bus at the end of the day.

Later in the year, she shows them how to store their boots, under their coats with the heels to the wall. This way, the boots won't get knocked over and mixed up with someone else's. Mittens go inside one sleeve. Then children can keep them together and know where they are.

Materials go back in boxes and on shelves just where they were. Labels clearly marked with pictures and words help the children accomplish this. Books are to be read and valued; they go back in the bookcase right side up, facing out.

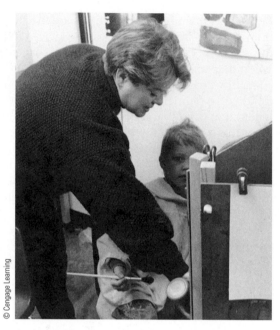

Pat lets children know that asking for assistance is all right.

She dislikes the word *cubby*, so each child has a storage bin and knows how to keep papers and belongings there. The children understand that messes during activities are perfectly okay. They also know that cleaning up afterward is not an optional chore; it is a part of kindergarten life. After commenting about her management style, Pat adds, "Now, if my home only looked like my classroom. . . ."

As a professional, Pat does some things differently than other teachers. For most activities during the day, children sit at tables wherever they wish. She comments:

Adults like to sit wherever they want; kids should be able to also. Like adults, kids settle in next to someone they're comfortable by. Usually, this is not a problem. If it looks like it might be, I just talk with them privately.

Pat believes that not "institutionalizing" a seating order encourages a more comfortable atmosphere. The same goes for the name the children use with their teacher. She makes it clear to the children that she does not want to be called "Teacher" ("Because I am a person"). Some call her "Ms. Sanford," but most call her "Pat." (When she later went to a new school, Pat had to follow a "last names only" policy—the principal also decided against "Ms. Pat.") Pat was saddened, but made the adjustment.

Although she believes that helping children get used to routines is important to future school success, she brings a sense of humor to her managerial style. For Pat, the mixture of elementary school rituals and early childhood innocence often brings a smile.

Pat sees her role not as preparing children for first grade but as providing the best possible kindergarten experience for each child.

Classroom Anecdote	*Pat waits to teach the Pledge of Allegiance until the spring, because of all the "hard" words. One sunny day I was supervising a student teacher in Pat's classroom. With a grin, Pat sent me over to stand by a boy for the Pledge. With a hand on his heart he said loudly and with total confidence, "I pledge Norwegians to the flag...."*

Finally, Pat is definite about her role as a teacher. "My job is not to prepare children for first grade. My job is to help them have the best kindergarten experience it is possible for them to have." Pat attributes the absence of discipline problems in her classroom to helping the children get used to kindergarten routines, "but in a way respectful to each child."

Whether readers agree with all of her ideas about managing the classroom, Pat offers thoughtful suggestions that teachers of children aged three to eight might do well to consider. Enjoyment at being with the children, each and every day, is at the top of her list.

Guidance Means Teamwork with Other Adults

A myth that still afflicts education is that the teacher handles all situations alone. Perhaps the myth goes back to the one-room schools of rural America's past and the expectations upon the teachers who taught in them. Most adults wanted no part of the job of being a teacher, which was seen as making unruly, undisciplined youth sit obediently and master the three Rs. A remnant of the myth of the self-sufficiency still can be seen in the lack of collaboration on the part of some teachers and the almost competitive expectations of some administrators.

Happily, this trend is changing. General acceptance is now given to the importance of new teachers working with mentors. Early childhood educators have led in their understanding of the importance both of cooperative relations among staff and of family and community involvement in education. The myth of teacher as "supermarm" is being replaced by the image of the teacher as a professional who leads but also collaborates.

Team-Teaching

There is **team-teaching**, and then there is the **teaching team**. The two concepts are different. Team-teaching is the practice, mainly at the K–12 level, of having two similarly licensed teachers working together with the same group of children. Thornton (1990) provided an account of the problems and promise when two teachers work together. For Thornton, mutual trust is a prime ingredient, and this quality takes relationship building—hard work, communication, and time.

By virtue of their differing personalities, two teachers can respond more effectively to the wide array of learning and behavioral styles represented in any group of young children. When team-teaching is working, each member has a built-in support system.

The Teaching Team

The technical name for the teaching team is *differentiated staffing*, or the use of adults with differing credentials and experience bases who serve the same group

© Cengage Learning

When a teaching team concept is used, children and adults benefit.

Pats work with an interpreter illustrates how the growing practice of inclusion is advancing the teaching team concept.

of children. The traditional teaching team consists of a lead teacher (sometimes called the "classroom manager"), an assistant teacher, and/or a teacher aide. In actuality, regular classroom volunteers and other staff can also comprise the team. In elementary education settings, a teacher may work with volunteers, teaching assistants ("paraprofessionals"), Title I teachers, special education teachers, and other specialists, all in the same class—a comprehensive staffing arrangement to be sure.

When the adults work together as a team, the teacher provides supervision for the learning environment, but the assistant regularly works with small groups, individual children, and on special occasions (under the supervision of a teacher) with the full group. In other words, assistants co-teach. Conversely, if the situation warrants, the teacher may wipe up a spill or help a child change clothes—typical "paraprofessional" duties.

In classrooms where a strict separation of professional and assistant roles is maintained, the general assumption is that only the teacher does the teaching. Despite appearances, this view is incorrect. In reality, all adults in a classroom serve as models for young children, and so all are teachers. (To young children, anyone bigger than they are is a teacher.) The adult who accepts this premise understands the concept of the teaching team.

Strengths of the Teaching Team Model. In some ways similar to team-teaching, the teaching team goes further in its model of democracy. When children see adults in differing roles converse and work together, they learn that social and cultural differences need not be threatening. When a teacher and assistant work together amicably, the child's expanding social world becomes that much more reliable and friendly. The children are likely to follow the lead of the teacher and feel respect for all the adults in the classroom.

When their co-teaching is appreciated, the assistant feels affirmed. Negative feelings that result from being "trivialized" (limited by role to only menial duties) do not arise. Disagreements do not become conflicts, but get resolved. Like children, assistants who feel accepted participate fully.

Of course, not all assistants are prepared to function as "associate teachers" on the team. Using the criteria of state regulations, program policy, contract language, and personal readiness, the teacher, as team leader, determines how much responsibility other team members are to be given. To make teaming work, unpressured discussion about roles, along with ongoing communication about duties and the goals of the program, are important.

The Teaching Team in the Primary Grades. On the surface, the teaching team concept seems to have less relevance to K–3 classrooms. In most schools the system is set: one teacher, 17 to 35 children. When a teaching assistant is present, it is often for a small part of the day. The assistant typically has "paraprofessional" duties with limitations specified in the "master contract."

Primary-grade teachers who wish to incorporate a team concept into their classrooms have to work hard, but it is happening. The growing practice of inclusion, or broad-scale integration of children with disabilities in the "regular" classroom, is advancing the teaching team concept by bringing special education teachers and assistants into the classroom. Some teachers recruit parents, college students, or senior citizens to come into classrooms on a regular basis. These volunteers read to children, supervise learning situations, work with small groups, or otherwise lend their experience. In a growing number of schools, students from the upper grades assist in prekindergarten, kindergarten, and primary classrooms. Where such efforts are organized and supervised, programs run smoothly, and both older and younger children benefit.

Teacher as Team Leader. With the use of a teaching team, the teacher's role changes. He no longer undertakes all teaching transactions. Instead, he manages an active learning laboratory, teaching and modeling continuously, but also supervising others who are helping. The complexity of the classroom manager or lead teacher role may make it an uncomfortable one for many new teachers just entering the profession and for others steeped in the traditional notion of what a teacher does.

We are still learning about the teacher's role in the differentiated-staffing situation, and about the effects of the teaching team for the classroom and children's behavior. In some ways the role poses additional new tasks for teachers. In others it offers new freedoms and possibilities—in particular the ability to reach children who in the old system might have passed through unassisted. Here is the connection with guidance. With more adults in the classroom on a regular basis, the chances for positive relationships with adults increase, and the need for mistaken behavior diminishes.

Working with Other Professionals. Besides team members in the classroom, the teacher communicates with other professionals: administrators and specialists in the program or school; professionals from other agencies. The buzzword for such communication is collaboration. The term is a useful one if it has the meaning that many educators intend:

> *We have defined collaborations as those efforts that unite and empower individuals and organizations to accomplish collectively what they could not accomplish independently. (Kagan & Rivera, 1991, p. 52)*

In early childhood settings, collaborations typically revolve around two criteria: (a) specifics of the program itself—resources, scheduling, content, methods; and (b) matters pertaining to the children in the class. When children show serious mistaken behavior over time, collaboration is required. Information exchanges within the school or center, professionally done, assist the teacher to better understand the child and the situation. Professional ethics, and often statute and policy, warrant the involvement of parents when assessments and meetings become formal. (See the NAEYC Code of Ethical Conduct in Appendix A.)

As parents, the teacher, and other professionals meet for a possible referral or special services, the teacher assists the collaboration by remaining sensitive to the discomfort that parents often feel in the presence of professionals. The promise of collaboration is that the process allows for a coordinated plan that can assist a troubled child. The use of the teaching team makes many of the ideas in this book work more easily for the teacher who chooses guidance.

Encouraging Family Members and Other Classroom Volunteers

A premise of this chapter is that the shift away from large groups toward small-group and individual activities promotes an encouraging classroom. Moving to a multidimensional classroom, though, does pose challenges for the teacher. In the multidimensional classroom, the teacher is a classroom manager as well as a teacher. The teaching team concept is not an absolute requirement in this classroom environment, but it does make the teacher's tasks easier.

Teaching team members, including volunteers, perform a variety of functions in the classroom. Depending on the circumstances, the teacher's goal is to have volunteers work with individual children, read stories, lead small groups, be in charge of centers, and even share on occasion with the full group. Children gain from the role modeling, encouragement, support, and teaching that team members can provide.

Classroom Anecdote	In a kindergarten with an effective volunteer program, five family members visit the class once a week at center time. (One attends each day.) They usually help with the same center each week, where an index card ("work card") provides them with instructions. Occasionally, Mona (the teacher) will ask a family member to go to a different center or help with a particular project, like making cookies with a small group. Several other family members have visited to share a hobby, interest, or item of family heritage with the class. Many family members have come in on their child's birthday and on monthly class field trips. Family members know they are welcome, and some have brought younger sons or daughters when they have visited.
	Mona is an exception in her school, and developing the program has taken a few years. Not all the teachers approve, though a few more include are including family members than in prior years. It has taken extra work, but Mona believes firmly that involving family members in the classroom is worthwhile for the increased individual attention the children receive, and for what it does for the parents.

A note from Gestwicki (2007) provides a helpful reminder here:

As teachers invite parents to participate in classroom learning activities, they need to concentrate on their skills for working with adults. Teachers need to be able to relax and enjoy the contribution of others to their classrooms and not feel threatened by any attention transferred from themselves to a visiting adult. It is important to remember that as more specific information is given to parents, parents will feel more comfortable knowing what is expected of them. (p. 395)

Helping Family Member Volunteers Feel Welcome

The key to working successfully with family volunteers is to help them feel welcome (Peterson, 2002). At whatever point a family member enters, she or he should be greeted by the teacher and usually introduced to the children. Taking time to orient the family member briefly is important. A "family corner," though not possible in every classroom, provides a place for the volunteer to "hang a coat." The teacher might provide a bulletin board, checkout library, pamphlets and flyers, a collection of newsletters, and perhaps a place where the family member can sit down. One teacher set up a corner behind a tall book stand in the reading center. When not used by the teacher at story time, a rocking chair was kept in the "corner."

First Visits. On the first visit for a family member, the teacher encourages the guest to walk around, interact, and observe but not take on undue responsibility (Gestwicki, 2007). The teacher is aware that the busyness of the developmentally appropriate classroom will draw in the family member. Sitting and talking with

"Oh, yes, Joanie's parents—I recognized you from her drawings!"

Joanie's parents. (Courtesy of Mrs. Ray Morin)

a group as they work, reading a book to children, and helping a child get a coat closely resemble parenting tasks—tasks that family members generally find non-threatening in a home or classroom.

The teacher keeps in mind that a first time visitor might always become a regular, or more involved in their child's education, as a result of a happy visit. Gestwicki offers important ideas for encouraging occasional family volunteers to become regulars:

> *Parents like feeling that they're making a valuable contribution to a classroom. Many parents will try to find the time for a visit if they feel truly needed and wanted. A note of appreciation from the teacher and children afterwards, pictures of the event displayed on a bulletin board, a mention of the event as a classroom highlight in the next newsletter—all these convey to parents that their time was well spent. (Gestwicki, 2007, p. 398)*

Special Events Volunteers. In addition to helping with parties and field trips, family members who share knowledge or skills with a class are important "special events" volunteers. One teacher asked three families per month to share a favorite dish, the vocation of a family member, a family interest (including the interest of a student's older brother or sister), and/or a bit of family heritage. This approach took care of the social studies program for the year, as the class sometimes did follow-up study on topic of a family share. Family members working in nontraditional gender roles are a particularly important resource. An older sister demonstrated her ability to play on the drums, for instance. An aunt who was a police officer talked about her job with the class. Children's consciousness levels and horizons rise with such guests, as well as they would with a visit from a male nurse, a female fire-fighter, or an in-home dad.

When a Family Member Stirs a Child's Emotions. Some children feel strong emotions when family members enter the room or leave for the day. Teachers often cite this as a reason for not encouraging family member involvement (Gestwicki, 2007). The teacher addresses this possibility beforehand by providing reassurance that she will work with the family member to handle any problems that arise (Gestwicki, 2007). Allowing the child to sit with the family member shows sensitivity to the child's feelings. Reassurance and diverting the child to activities are standard at the time of separation. As children adjust to frequent visitations

Family members (including grandparents) who share knowledge or skills with a class are important "special events" volunteers. Here, John helps two children make pinecone bird feeders.

Classroom volunteers often include foster parents, grandparents, college interns, students from older grades, and family members. (Top left photo courtesy, The Bemidji Pioneer)

by family members, their own included, the need for their family members' undivided attention subsides.

Regular Volunteers. When a few family members have begun to volunteer regularly, the teacher may want to meet with them as a group. Such meetings can be useful in further acquainting the family members with the education program or with observation techniques to better understand children's needs (Kasting, 1994). "Old hands" might be invited to attend to share suggestions and sometimes, along with the teacher, to educate about DAP. (An important example is educating family members to let children do their own artwork.)

If a family member needs extra guidance about, for instance, letting the children do things for themselves, the teacher needs to find a way to provide it (Gestwicki, 2007). Open and timely communication can prevent the problem of having to ask a family member to come in less often. A brief guidebook for volunteers often proves useful—a guidebook done for a whole school or program saves work for the individual teacher.

The teacher will know that a volunteer is a true "regular" when ongoing communication becomes unnecessary. Teachers then can begin to rely on the skills of the volunteer by assigning them a center and providing a work card for them, as Mona did in the previous anecdote. Gestwicki (2007) sums up the process of helping parents become productive in the classroom by stating:

> *Perhaps the most important reason for involving family members in the classroom is that it encourages them to be active in their children's education (Peterson, 2002). Each year as a result of family member involvement, families become more interested in their children's success at school—and the children respond. This reason is enough, but annually as well, many family members become interested in personal and professional advancement as a result of a successful volunteering experience. (p. 397)*

© Cengage Learning

The most important reason for involving family members is that it encourages them to become more active in their children's education.

Summary

1. *How does the teacher balance reliability and novelty in the daily program?*

The schedule provides a baseline of predictability for the children about the program. When unscheduled events enable positive results for children, they add to the everyday program. The teacher maintains the balance between predictability and novelty by reading children's behaviors and discussing reasons for changes with them. While "busy" sets the tone for the classroom, children and teachers also need periods of rest and relaxation. Relaxation activities and a thoughtful approach to rest times rejuvenate spirits in children and adults alike. The teacher provides opportunities for vigorous activity each day. Movement to music during large group activities refreshes children and renews their ability to concentrate. Effective vigorous activities avoid formal rules, competition, and taking turns.

© Cengage Learning

Movement activities fit the criteria for developmentally appropriate large-group experiences.

2. What part do large-group activities play in the encouraging classroom?

A problem with overreliance on large groups is that they easily exceed children's developmental levels and attention spans. For this reason, large groups should be used selectively and not as a matter of institutional routine. Teachers who want to use large groups effectively do well to reassess the effectiveness of traditional large-group practices: taking attendance, calendar and the weather, show-and-tell, reading stories, and large-group instruction. A developmentally appropriate use of large groups is to establish an *anticipatory set* for interactive follow-up activities done either independently or in small groups, usually in centers. For large groups to be a part of an interactive learning program, they should be friendly, participatory, relevant to children's experiences, and concise.

3. How does managing transitions reduce mistaken behavior?

Transitions, changes from one activity to the next, can be disruptive. The professional teacher develops and implements strategies for transitions that get the job done, but do not undercut self-esteem. A primary consideration in managing transitions is the reduction of time that children spend waiting. One strategy to reduce waiting is through creative buffer activities. When lines prove necessary, teachers need to plan strategies for lining up and waiting in lines that support each member of the group and capture children's imaginations.

4. How do routines help to build an encouraging classroom?

Pat Sanford, an experienced kindergarten and primary-grade teacher, believes that the secret to managing the encouraging classroom lies in getting children used to routines. Pat begins teaching routines on the first day of school. She teaches that making a mess during activities is fine, but returning materials and cleaning up are parts of kindergarten life.

Although Pat states that learning about routines is important, she believes in creating a warm classroom atmosphere, with a minimum of institutionalized practices. She argues that her job is not to prepare children for "next year," but to provide the best possible "present year" for the children in her class.

5. Why is the teaching team important in managing the encouraging classroom?

Children benefit from positive relations with all adults who may be in the classroom. Effective communication among adults allows for comprehensive strategies for building relationships and working with mistaken behavior. For these reasons, the myth that the teacher handles all situations alone needs to come to an end. In the guidance approach, the teacher moves toward a teaching team model. Serving as a classroom manager, he involves fellow staff and volunteers of diverse backgrounds to provide responsive programming. The teacher collaborates with other professionals: administrators and specialists in the center or school as well as specialists in other agencies. Through collaboration, adults accomplish together what they cannot do alone.

6. How can the encouraging classroom support family members and other classroom volunteers?

In the multidimensional classroom, the teacher is a manager of the daily program as well as a lead teacher. The use of staff and volunteers as a teaching team contributes to the success of the program. Depending on the skills and comfort level of the team members, staff and volunteers perform a variety of functions in the classroom. A first step in working with volunteers in the classroom is to make them feel welcome. The teacher acknowledges and encourages volunteers, assisting those who wish to become regulars. The most important reason for involving family members in the classroom is that the experience encourages them to become more active in their child's education, although the family member stands to benefit in personal and professional ways as well.

FOLLOW-UP ACTIVITIES

Note: *An element of being a professional teacher is to respect the children, parents, and educators you are working with by maintaining confidentiality, that is, keeping identities private. In completing follow-up activities, please respect the privacy of all concerned.*

Discussion Activity

The discussion activity encourages students to interrelate their own thoughts and experiences with specific ideas from the chapter.

Think about a classroom you have visited as a part of your preparation program. Recollect a regular activity or routine during the day in which more mistaken behavior occurred than at other times. Referring to the chapter for possible ideas, if you were the teacher, how would you change this part of the daily program to reduce the mistaken behavior and make the classroom more encouraging?

Application Activities

Application activities allow students to interrelate material from the text with real-life situations. The observations imply access to practicum experiences; the interviews, access to teachers or parents. Students then compare or contrast observations and interviews with referenced ideas from the chapter.

1. Reliability and novelty in the daily program.
   a. Observe an instance of a "teachable moment" when a teacher deviated from the schedule to provide a special experience. How did the teacher manage the change of routine? What did you notice about the children's behavior before, during, and after the special event? Compare your findings to ideas in the chapter.
   b. Talk with a teacher about the daily schedule he uses. What parts of the schedule is the teacher pleased with? If the teacher could modify the schedule, what parts would he change? Why? Compare your findings to ideas in the chapter.

2. Large-group activities.
   a. Observe children in a large-group activity. If most children are positively involved, what about the large group seems to be holding their attention? If several children look distracted, or are distracting others, what do you think are the reasons? Compare your findings to ideas from the chapter.
   b. Interview a teacher about large-group activities. How does the teacher plan large groups to hold children's attention? While teaching, what techniques does the teacher use to hold children's attention? How has the teacher's thinking about the place of large groups changed in the years he has been teaching? Compare your findings to ideas from the chapter.

3. Managing transitions.
   a. Observe transitions to and from an organized activity. How does the teacher prepare the children? How does the teacher manage the physical movement of the children? How does the teacher get the new activity started? Compare your findings to ideas from the chapter.
   b. Interview a teacher about how he handles transition situations. Ask about what he does when some, but not all, children have finished an old activity and are ready to begin the new activity. What suggestions does the teacher have for when he and the class have to wait for an event; when he and the class have to walk in a line? Compare your findings to ideas from the chapter.

4. Routines in the encouraging classroom.
   a. Observe a classroom where there are definite routines. What are the likely effects of the routines on the children? On the teacher? How do Pat Sanford's comments about routines compare or contrast with your observations? Compare your findings to ideas from the chapter.
   b. Interview a teacher about his use of routines. How does the teacher believe routines assist with classroom management? Ask the teacher how he knows when a routine needs change. How does the teacher work with

a child who may have difficulty transitioning within the routine? How do comments in the chapter match with what the teacher said about routines?

5. The teaching team.

a. Observe what you regard as a successful teaching team in operation. Note the kinds of communication that occur between the team members—verbal and nonverbal. What seems to characterize the communication you have observed? What seem to be the benefits for the children and the adults of the teaching team? Compare your findings to ideas from the chapter.

b. Interview a lead teacher and another member of a teaching team. Ask what is important to each in: maintaining positive relations between the adults; a positive atmosphere in the classroom. Compare your findings with what the text says about the benefits of teaching teams.

6. Supporting family members and other classroom volunteers.

a. Observe a teacher working with volunteers in the classroom. What do you notice about how the teacher communicates with the volunteers? What do you notice about how any other team members work with the volunteers? Would you say these is a beginning or regular volunteer? What did their comfort level seem to be about volunteering? Compare your findings to ideas from the chapter.

b. Interview a teacher about having volunteers in the classroom. What benefits does the teacher see in the arrangement for the children, for the volunteer's child, for the volunteer, for the teacher? What difficulties are there in having classroom volunteers? How does the teacher address these difficulties? Ask how the teacher works differently with beginning and regular volunteers. Compare your findings to ideas from the chapter.

Recommended Readings

Educational Productions Inc. (1990). *Give yourself a hand: Guidance techniques for successful group times* [Video]. Program 2 in video training series: Super groups: Young children learning together. Portland, OR: Educational Productions Inc.

Elkind, D. (2005). Viewpoint. Early childhood amnesia: Reaffirming children's need for developmentally appropriate Programs. *Young Children, 60*(4), 38–41.

Garcia, C., Garcia, L., Floyd, J., & Lawson, J. (2002, January). Improving the public health through early childhood movement programs. *Journal of Physical Development, 73*(1), 27–31.

Hvettig, C. I., Sanborn, C. E., DiMarco, N., & Rich, S. (2004). The O Generation: Our youngest children are at risk for obesity. *Young Children, 59*(2), 50–55.

Levin, D. E. (2003). Beyond banning war and superhero play: Meeting children's needs in violent times. *Young Children, 58*(3), 60–63.

Loomis, C., & Wagner, J. (2005). A different look at challenging behavior. *Young Children, 60*(2), 94–99.

Peterson, K. (2002, January/February). Creating home-school partnerships. *Early Childhood News,* pp. 39–45.

Watson, M. (2003). Attachment theory and challenging behaviors: Reconstructing the nature of relationships. *Young Children, 58*(4), 12–20.

Guidance Matters

A Concerned Director Writes:

November, 2005

I recently gave a tour of our center to the mother of a young child. I explained that our program is both play based and developmentally appropriate. The mother asked if academics were included or if the children just played all day. I explained that the academic standards are embedded in the planned activities for the day; therefore, the children are playing and very busy doing the educational work of young children.

The mother then asked a question that caught me completely off guard: "Does anyone ever fail in your three-year-olds' program?"

I am sure the look on my face was complete amazement. "Absolutely not!" I told her. "We strive to develop a love of learning in every child. We want children to feel free to hypothesize, experiment, and reach conclusions. They cannot possibly develop these thinking skills and a love of learning if they are concerned about being right or wrong."

The mother looked relieved. She then told me her son Amos was in a program that would retain him if he were unable to write his name by the end of the year. We talked about what was developmentally appropriate for three-year-olds in the context of name writing. She enrolled Amos on the spot, pulling him out of the other center.

Reprinted with permission from the National Association for the Education of Young Children. All rights reserved.

A Successful Outcome

Since this incident, the director of the preschool who took Amos in reports that Amos has completed a happy and active year in the three-year-olds' class and moved on with his group. Amos prints a pretty clear *A*, and the flourish that is the rest of his name contains an increasing number of recognizable letters.

This director got it right. In a developmentally appropriate setting, we should expect the progress that Amos is making, in his own time. Research on the brain informs us that in any act of learning, there is a thinking component and a feeling component. When a child learns something and feels positive about the learning experience, the brain is developing optimally. Internal development and external teaching are in harmony. The child's engagement in the learning act is total. The child's brain secretes happy hormones (apologies to brain researchers) that make further learning intriguing, not stressful. For this moment and the next, all is well in the child's world. And happy children very much want to get along with each other.

The Heart of Guidance

Developmentally appropriate practice means that within the context of an encouraging community, each individual child is empowered to engage wholeheartedly with all the problems of learning. For this reason, developmentally appropriate practice is at the heart of guidance.

Only in developmentally appropriate practice are chances maximized for healthy development in all the human intelligences. And we must not underestimate the importance of two intelligences in particular: social and emotional—the capacity to feel special "just for who we are" and to treat others kindly because we can accept that they are special too.

The Role of Teachers

Think about your favorite teacher (and I fervently hope you can recall at least one). I'll bet that teacher not only made subjects intriguing but accepted you as a developing person with your own unique approach. You probably accomplished a lot in that class—and still feel warmly about the experience. You may even be a teacher because of that teacher! So, okay, you did have some conflicts, but the teacher helped you understand that you could learn from your mistakes. That teacher knew enough, cognitively and emotionally, to try to make the program developmentally appropriate for you. Am I right? You know, millions of us

▸ can read, but don't much.

▸ would prefer that someone else balance our checkbooks (me for sure).

▸ might never write a letter to a politician or speak up at a hearing—even though we could.

Teaching the Whole Child

In a democracy like ours, these are basic abilities for every adult to have and use. When education is reduced to group-focused instruction of a sequenced curriculum—assessed in standardized ways—much joy goes out of learning (and usually teaching as well).

Too many in our population find little personal meaning in the knowledge and skills they learn at school. Most of these folks just sit there until the time is up, pass their standardized tests—because they have been trained to—and then get out. On the other hand, some young people become stressed, act out, rebel— and are "disciplined." Sometimes these students adjust and become able to sit and listen, but other times they can't change enough for the system and may eventually drop out or be forced out.

Think of the future for a child who must repeat the three-year-olds' class because he cannot write his name. At age three, he may already be regarded as a failure by his family and teachers. Think of an adolescent who drops out because she cannot hide the fact that she hates school and believes she cannot pass state-required examinations. Losing faith in one's ability to learn is a long-term, psychologically jarring life experience.

From my viewpoint, a major task is teaching adults and children the vital role of healthy personal development in education. One could say (without blame to many early childhood educators) that this task should have been accomplished in the last century. It has become our challenge to accomplish the task during this one. Social and emotional intelligences (above all others) will bring our world successfully into the twenty-first century.

To Increase Your Knowledge

Visit the website of The Center on the Social and Emotional Foundations for Early Learning (http://csefel.uiuc.edu). This national center, funded by Head Start and the Child Care Bureau in the U.S. Department of Health and Human Services, is a multi-university, multi-organization collaboration focused on strengthening the capacity of child care and Head Start programs to improve the social and emotional outcomes of young children. A series of "What Works" briefs describe practical strategies, provide references to more information, and include a one-page handout highlighting major points. The website also offers English and Spanish versions of trainer and participant materials for four training modules on social and emotional development.

A Step You Can Take

Think what you can do to help others understand that development and learning must be in harmony for a child's education to be of lasting value.

For additional information on using the guidance approach in the encouraging classroom, visit our website at www.cengage.com/education/gartrell.

Chapter 7

Leadership Communication with the Group

Guiding Questions

▶ *How does the teacher establish leadership in the encouraging classroom?*

▶ *Why are guidelines, not rules, important in the encouraging classroom?*

▶ *How is encouragement more appropriate than praise?*

▶ *Why is discussing inclusively important?*

▶ *How do class meetings build the encouraging classroom?*

▶ *How does the adult teach friendliness in the encouraging classroom?*

▶ *How does leadership communication with parents build and maintain partnerships?*

© Cengage Learning

Key Concepts

▶ *Class meetings*

▶ *Discussing inclusively*

▶ *Dual language learner (DLL)*

▶ *Guidelines*

▶ *I-messages*

▶ *Leadership communication*

▶ *Logical consequences*

▶ *Parent meetings*

▶ *Private encouragement*

▶ *Public encouragement*

▶ *Reflective listening*

▶ *Self-report*

▶ *Starter statement*

Mistaken behavior often results from a mismatch between the child and the education program. Previous chapters discussed reducing this institution-caused mistaken behavior by building a developmentally appropriate educational program. Continuing with the main idea of Part Two that "prevention is the best medicine," Chapters Seven and Eight shift focus to the communication skills of the teacher.

In the guidance approach, leadership communication defines the techniques used by the teacher to positively manage the group and build positive relationships with each child. Teachers who use leadership communication assist children to become active learners and successful group members (Gallagher & Mayer, 2008), so reducing mistaken behavior.

Chapter Seven examines leadership communication that is *group focused*. Elements of group-focused leadership communication include:

- Establishing leadership by being firm and friendly
- Creating guidelines instead of rules
- Using encouragement instead of praise
- Discussing inclusively
- Holding regular class meetings
- Teaching friendliness.

The chapter concludes with a discussion of communication methods teachers use to sustain partnerships with parents.

Establishing Leadership

Building an encouraging classroom environment begins the first day that the teacher is together with the class. The teacher establishes leadership by acquainting the class with routines and guidelines. Children benefit from knowing what is expected of them and what the limits of acceptable behavior are (DeVries & Zan, 2004). The teacher is clear, firm, and friendly in this communication effort. When teachers blur the distinction between *firm* and *strict,* friendliness drops out of the formula. In this matter, the guidance approach differs from conventional discipline.

Conventional thought about discipline holds that the teacher is *strict* at the beginning of the school year, in order to "take charge of the classroom" (Gartrell, 2004). Then, with the teacher's "right to teach" established, she eases up in demeanor. From the guidance perspective, this position has pitfalls. The teacher may fixate on the assertion of will and lose faith in more positive teaching practices. Children and teacher alike get used to the teacher in the role of disciplinarian. She may find it difficult to shed being disciplinarian as part of a permanent teaching style. This unfortunate situation is epitomized by the proverbial teacher who meant only "not to smile until Christmas"—and didn't smile for 40 years!

Through the communication skills used, the teacher reduces mistaken behavior.

Even if the strict teacher gradually does "lighten up," children suffer from negative encounters in the interim. Working with limited experience and brain development, children not helped to problem solve their conflicts early in their school careers may never learn this essential democratic life skill (Gartrell, 2004). Furthermore, a "law and order" environment in the classroom affects even model children who do not normally "get into trouble":

Classroom Anecdote	*Early in September, a parent who was also a health professional noticed that her first grader seemed bothered by something. Shirley asked her daughter what was the matter. The first grader, an early reader, had seen a word on the chalkboard and asked what it was: "D-E-T-E-N-T-I-O-N." Shirley explained, and her daughter then asked several other questions:*
	"Where is detention?"
	"Do the children get to go home?"
	(continued)

Classroom Anecdote	*"Why do Jarrod and Paula go there?"* *"Are they bad children?"* *"Will the teacher put me there?"* *Shirley commented that she saw concern in her daughter's face that she had not seen during kindergarten. Shirley went in and talked with the teacher, who said, "The children need to know that I am here to teach, and they are here to learn. I will not let individual children keep this from happening."* *Shirley wondered about a classroom where some of the first words children learned to read were the names of friends being punished. She monitored her daughter's feelings closely and talked with the teacher several more times that year. Shirley felt her work with the teacher did make the year go a bit better for her daughter. The following spring she worked with the principal to place her daughter with a second-grade teacher whom Shirley knew to be more positive.*

Using Guidance to Teach Routines

No matter how anxious a teacher is about beginning the school year, most children are more anxious. In the first days, the teacher sets a precedent for children's education that makes it either a welcome event, or an event arousing ambivalence and negative feelings. The following illustration contrasts this difference.

Classroom Illustration	*During the first week of kindergarten, teachers responded to a similar situation differently. Trying to acquaint their groups with desired routines, each teacher instructed children to put away the materials they were using and come to the circle for large-group instruction.* *Teacher One reminded Juan, who was building a road, to put away the blocks; she then directed the group into a circle. She was set to begin when she noticed that Juan was still quietly building. From her place at the head of the group, the teacher said loudly, "Get over here, young man. In this classroom, children listen to the teacher." After waiting for Juan to join the group, she explained the daily schedule to the children.* *When Teacher Two was about to begin large group, she noticed that Lumey—whom she had asked to clean up—was still playing with blocks. The teacher walked to Lumey, smiled, and held out her hand. She began speaking in English, but when he looked confused, she tried her beginning Spanish. "You can come back here soon. We need you to join us now." They walked to circle, and the teacher introduced the children to the daily schedule, sprinkling her speech with Spanish phrases.*

Teacher Two was showing leadership no less than Teacher One. She reacted differently, though, to the notion that the teacher must "be tough from the beginning." Teacher Two recognized that children in the first days of school can become overloaded and that they readily identify with materials that seem "safe."

She also recognized that children who are dual language learners (DLLs) may need extra assistance (Macrina, Hoover, & Becker, 2009). Teacher Two did not compromise her leadership, but took a guidance approach by educating the children to the schedule. She used guidance leadership so that Lumey (and the rest of the class) would not develop doubts about themselves and fears about school. She helped them understand that they could learn the classroom routines.

Guidelines, Not Rules

A point of agreement among teachers is the importance of establishing clear expectations with children. Standards for behavior, understood by all, are important in any educational setting. Insufficient attention has been given, however, to differences between rules and guidelines. In making the case for guidelines as a part of the guidance approach, this section looks anew at the conventional use of rules.

Rules tend to be stated in negative terms: "No running in the classroom"; "No gum chewing in school." Frequently, punishments are predetermined for "breaking" a rule:

▶ No bothering others or you flip you card

▶ No hurting others or you sit in the time-out chair

▶ No homework; then you stay in at recess to do it.

The conventional thinking about rules with known consequences is that they convey clear expectations and teach children about governance by law in adult society. There are two problems with this view.

First, rules with defined consequences institutionalize the use of punishment in the school or center. The negative phrasing of rules suggests that teachers expect children to break them. Spelled-out consequences underscore this perception (Wien, 2004). Reason, cooperation, and caring become secondary when educators enforce preset standards that may or may not fit actual situations (DeVries & Zan, 2004). Teachers who react with a strict response often show less than a full understanding of the event. If teachers choose "to make an exception" and not enforce a predetermined punishment, their leadership comes into question. In either case, the teacher is functioning as a technician and not as a guidance professional (as discussed in Chapter Four).

A second problem lies in the effects of punishment itself. Punishment tends to reduce human interaction from the educational to the moralistic. The factor of developmental egocentrism in young children makes this issue critical (DeVries & Zan, 2004). Developmental egocentrism means the younger the age, the less the child understands about social expectations (Elkind, 1987). Because of lack of experience and development, young children have difficulty understanding that when they are punished for breaking a rule, the punishment *is the result of their actions.* They tend instead to internalize the shame associated with the punishment and to feel that they are being punished because they are "bad children."

In the first days of school, children identify with materials that are familiar and seem safe.

Diminished self-esteem results (Gartrell, 2004; Kohn, 1999; Readdick and Chapman, 2000). The child has been influenced away from feelings of initiative, belonging, and industry, and toward shame and self-doubt (Elkind, 1987).

Logical Consequences

More than many others, Theodore Dreikurs raised discipline practice to a level above the traditional reliance on punishment (Dreikurs & Cassel, 1972). Dreikurs suggested that causing conflicts has **logical consequences**, responses taken by adults that "fit" a child's mistaken act. Logical consequences differ from punishment because the redress is a logical extension of the misbehavior itself. For example, if a kindergarten child marks on a table, he cleans it off. If a second grader hurts another's feelings, he figures out how to make amends. These consequences contrast with a punishment like cleaning off several tables, or a time-out or detention.

The use of logical consequences fits the guidance approach if two conditions are met: (a) The consequence is logical to the child as well as the adult; and (b) the consequence is *not* preset and rigidly enforced (DeVries & Zan, 2004).

(a) In reference to the first condition, note the difference between these statements:

"You get a sponge and wipe the marks off these tables right now, young man."

"It's okay; your marker just went off the paper. Let's get a sponge and clean it off."

© Cengage Learning

A logical consequence of climbing on a divider is to choose between staying on the floor in the same area or moving to the "real climber," which is safe.

An adult may have thought the first statement was a "logical consequence," but it was most likely perceived as punishment to the child. The second response both reaffirms the child's worth and teaches that actions have logical consequences, logical to the child as well as the adult.

(b) In reference to the second condition—enforcement of preset consequences—a primary-grade child may have acted out as a result of stress in his or her life. In a guidance approach, a teacher uses professional judgment to evaluate an event before coming to a consequence. The teacher acting as a professional recognizes that every situation is different and scaffolds the particular child's thinking as far as possible at that particular time.

For example, a teacher may help a child who lashes out to calm down, then later has a talk with the child. This guidance response is entirely different than forcing "Ashley" to flip a card from green to red for "showing disrespect." There is still a consequence for the mistaken behavior, but the consequence is for Ashley to learn a new behavior, not to endure humiliation for expressing strong unmet needs.

In a current interpretation of Dreikurs' theories, Linda Albert (2003) handles with care the use of logical consequences. The method is included more as a last resort than the "first line of defense," as it was treated in the past (Charles, 2005). Dreikurs maintained that his approach to discipline was a democratic one, but in fact the teacher often ends up imposing the consequence. In new interpretation of his work, writers place emphasis on communication *before* problems arise (Albert, 2003; Gartrell, 2004), such as by reaching consensus on guidelines and how to maintain them—effective use of leadership in an encouraging classroom.

The Benefits of Guidelines

For children in the classroom, standards are necessary for building understanding about the requirements of social living. Like rules, guidelines set those standards. Unlike rules, guidelines accomplish this understanding in a positive way. An admonishment such as "Don't bother others" is likely to make a "transgressing" child feel that he is "bad." Moreover, enforcement of the rule does not result in the young child learning what the teacher is really asking him to do: A child on a time-out chair is likely to be feeling "Something bad is happening" rather than figuring out how he can improve his behavior (Readdick and Chapman, 2000).

By using guidelines, adults teach children how to act productively. Because their message is positive and instructive, guidelines are more developmentally appropriate in educational settings than are rules. Guidelines contribute to the encouraging classroom. Consider the climate of a primary-grade classroom where the following guidelines are taught and reinforced:

▶ We use words to solve problems

▶ Sometimes we need to stop, look, and listen

▶ We all help to take care of *our* room

▶ We appreciate each other and ourselves

▶ Making mistakes is okay—we just try to learn from them.

Guidelines at Different Age Levels. Teachers working with different age groups use guidelines differently. The NAEYC document on developmentally appropriate practice maintains that standards (guidelines) should not be used formally with children under four (Bredekamp & Copple, 2009). The document points out that children aged three and younger do not easily understand or remember rules. Instead, teachers should use "guidance reasons (guidelines) that are specific to a situation and repeated with consistency in similar circumstances." Examples are: "Friendly touches only" and "Use your words to tell him."

A difference at the preschool, kindergarten, and primary levels is the number of guidelines used. Experts comment that there should not be too many. The exact number of guidelines depends on the teacher and the group, but usual practice is two to three guidelines in prekindergarten classes, three to four in kindergarten, and four to six in the primary grades. These numbers are arbitrary, however. A well-known trio of guidelines, often used at the kindergarten level, is "Be kind," "Be safe," and "Be smart."

As to when to introduce guidelines, some teachers choose not to "present" them as a set procedure at the beginning of the year. Instead, these teachers construct guidelines with children as situations arise, usually through the mechanism of class meetings (DeVries & Zan, 2004). This constructivist approach serves to personalize and maximize the meaning of guidelines for children, a practice in keeping with the developmental nature of the encouraging classroom. Other teachers use guidelines as part of the beginning orientation for the children in order to establish routines. This is a matter of professional preference.

Creating Guidelines

Wien (2004) and DeVries and Zan (2004) present many benefits of having children create guidelines in a democratic classroom atmosphere. These authors point out that children usually make the same rules that adults would, but respect the rules more because they feel ownership of them. They comment that involving children in classroom discussions on creating rules leads to: active involvement, reflection, meaningful connections, respect for rules, sense of community, problem solving through negotiation, cooperation, inductive thinking, and ownership—certainly all attributes of the encouraging-classroom community.

Although these authors do not distinguish between rules and guidelines, the same benefits of guideline formulation certainly apply. With very young children, the teacher may need to take more of a lead in the discussion process. Even if very young children do not actually formulate the guidelines, they develop ownership of a guideline like "Friendly touches only" by having the teacher discuss it with them—why the guideline is important; why we might not always remember to follow it; what we can do if we forget and make a mistake (Vance & Weaver, 2002).

Certainly children aged four and up can significantly participate in the formulation process. The idea is that by replacing external control with democratic leadership, children are likely to take more responsibility for their behavior (DeVries & Zan, 2003). (Remember that in a democratic classroom, there is still one firm and friendly leader, the teacher. The term *democratic classroom* does not mean that each child has an equal "vote" with the teacher—but that all in the classroom are worthy citizens who can participate equally in creating and maintaining guidelines.)

As we have discussed, *a first reason* for using guidelines is that they supportively educate children to standards of behavior. *A second reason* is that guidelines allow teachers a range of choices in conflict situations and so empower them to be professionals (Wien, 2004. In contrast to rules, guidelines create neither hierarchies of authority that young children feel compelled to challenge nor lines of morality that children feel pressed to cross (DeVries & Zan, 2003). Guidelines contribute to an environment where mistaken behavior is seen by the leader as a problem to solve. Note the difference in the teachers' roles in the following illustrations:

Classroom Illustration

Teacher working with rules. *At recess on a rainy day, second graders Clarence and Ruby first argued, then physically fought over a "friendship bracelet." Mrs. Cleary came into the room, separated the children, and declared, "You know the rule about fighting. I am taking you both to the principal's office."*

The principal asked Mrs. Cleary what the punishment was for fighting. Mrs. Cleary stated that it was detention. When the two children returned, others in the class made fun of them. The two looked miserable as they sat in detention. Ruby did not attend school the next day.

Teacher working with guidelines. *At recess on a rainy day, a second-grade teacher, Mrs. Drewry, entered her room to find two children fighting. She separated the children and had them each cool down at their desks. She then asked Richard and Marla each to talk about the problem. Marla said she brought some cookies to eat at recess, and Richard tried to take them. Richard said he didn't either. The teacher acknowledged what each child said and felt. She then requested to hear how they could solve this problem. Marla told Richard he should bring his own stuff to eat. Richard said his mom wouldn't let him. Marla relented and gave him a cookie. Richard said thanks.*

The teacher paused and said, "Our guideline says 'We use words to solve problems.' If you want Marla to share, Richard, you need to ask with words." Richard nodded and Marla looked relieved. The teacher ended the meeting by stating, "Richard, I will talk to the kitchen staff and see tomorrow if you can save something from breakfast for recess, okay?" Richard nodded and told Marla he was sorry.

When young children have disputes, a teacher using guidelines can help to work through the difficulty. To the complaint that she should not be a "referee," the response is that the teacher is a *leader*, teaching conflict management skills, the ability to solve problems with words. Guidelines enable the teacher to act as a democratic leader. For children, learning how to manage conflicts may be the most important life skill of the twenty-first century.

Encouragement

Perhaps the most basic guidance technique is that of *encouragement*. It bridges two dimensions of the teacher's communications in the classroom—with the class and with the individual child. How the teacher uses encouragement in the one dimension influences the other. For this reason, both dimensions of encouragement, group focused and individually directed, are discussed here.

Encouragement More than Praise

A basic difference between encouragement and praise is that encouragement empowers the efforts of the child; praise gives approval to the achievements (Kohn, 1999). With the process orientation young children bring to activities, encouragement is important if only for this reason. Encouragement is preferable to praise for other reasons as well.

A typical example of praise is, "Children, see what a good worker Joshua is." Writers such as Dreikurs and Cassel (1972), Ginott (1972), Hitz and Driscoll (1988), and Kohn (1999) believe that a comment like this creates several problems:

▶ The statement is made more to elicit conformity from the group than to recognize the individual child.

▶ Others in the class feel slighted because they were not praised for working hard.

▶ Class members feel resentment toward Joshua for being praised.

▶ All children in the class are reinforced toward dependency on the teacher for evaluation of their efforts rather than being taught to evaluate efforts for themselves.

▶ The class is uneasy about whom the teacher will single out next and what she will say.

▶ Joshua experiences mixed emotions: pride at being praised, embarrassment at being publicly recognized, worry about how others will react, uncertainty about exactly what he did that was *right,* and concern about what the teacher will say to him next time if he is not "a good worker."

Praise stresses the traditional definition of successful achievement—"winning," "doing the best." When this emphasis is strong, children become anxious about the possibility of not living up to the adult's expectations   of becoming "losers" or "failures" (Reineke, Sonsteng, & Gartrell, 2008). The frequent use of praise leads to a classroom with an environment of conditional acceptance: Children who meet the teacher's criteria for success feel like winners and enjoy the social trappings of winning; other students feel the humiliation and resentment that accompanies their more marginal social status.

Teachers who use encouragement have learned that support is usually needed more during a task than at its completion—the accomplishment frequently being its own reward. They have learned that all children in a class deserve full acceptance and support, and work for a community in which every child feels like a winner. (Gartrell, 2004).

Public Encouragement/Private Encouragement

Encouragement happens in two primary ways, publicly directed to the entire group or privately directed to the individual. A teacher says to her kindergarten class, "You are working very hard on your journals today. Many special story pictures are being made. I am proud of you all." Strengths of this public encouragement include:

▶ The teacher has not made a value judgment, but has given a self-report: She has described the event being recognized and given an I-message or personal response to it.

© Cengage Learning

The child knows that encouragement given privately is truly meant for her.

> ▶ No children feel the ambivalence of being singled out.

> ▶ The teacher has avoided institutionalizing "winners" and "losers" (in-groups and out-groups). She has eliminated the negative social dynamic of differential treatment.

> ▶ The group feels a positive *group spirit*, a sense that "we are doing together and we are succeeding."

> ▶ The teacher has allowed room for children to evaluate their efforts for themselves (Ginott, 1972). She is empowering a sense of competence in the members of the class.

Many of the same benefits apply to **private encouragement** given to an individual child. Note this teacher's response to Julia when the four-year-old tells the teacher she is building a castle:

> *You* are *building a castle, Julia. It has walls and a roof and a tower and a doorway. I am impressed.*

From this one comment, Julia knows what the teacher has paid attention to in her work. Julia sees that the encouragement really was meant for her. Julia was allowed to draw her own conclusions about her building ability, without undue expectations on her for the next time. Julia feels that she and her work are appreciated by the teacher. She feels positively about building again.

Classroom Anecdote	*(From the journal of a student teacher in a kindergarten classroom.) I decided to use both types of encouragement, publicly directed to the entire group and privately directed to the individual. In the second observation, I use (C) for the specific child, and (S) for me.*

Public Encouragement, Directed to the Entire Group

Students were working on story pictures to send to a sister kindergarten class in an Native American community. I made a point of going around to look at each child's creation, not making any specific comments; then I stood in front of the class and said, "You are all working very hard on your story pictures. I'll bet that you are proud of your work." Some children smiled, and they all seemed pleased with this comment. They worked very hard. I noticed a few children even made comments to other children on how nice their story pictures were. By saying something positive to the group, they all wanted to share in that feeling; it was like the domino effect.

Private Encouragement, Directed to the Individual

In the afternoon, the children were involved in center activities around our theme of "waste and recycling," One child in particular was drawing. I went over to him and looked at his creation.

S: *You are really working hard on that picture.*

C: *Yeah, I'm using brown, 'cause that's the main color of it. Can you smell it? (giggle)*

S: *(Smile) No, does it smell?*

C: *No, not for real. It's a piece of garbage under a microscope. I'm gonna color it lots of colors 'cause that's how it looks.*

S: *Wow! You have drawn an enlarged piece of garbage. I see that it has many points, curves, and corners. It really looks like it would look under a microscope.*

After this last comment, the child gave me a very large smile and continued to draw using lots of colors all mixed together. Later I learned the child had been exposed to a microscope by an older sibling, but he applied the idea of garbage under the microscope by himself. I was impressed.

Encouragement—What to Say

In contrast to encouragement, statements of praise like "good job" neither give specific feedback nor invite interaction (Bredekamp & Copple, 2009). Such statements are mental shortcuts; they are quick and easy "fixes" for the teacher (Kohn, 1999). Mastering specific encouragement requires conscious practice over time. The boost in student self-confidence, persistence on-task, and even acceptance of others' efforts make the effort worthwhile. A teacher who uses encouragement will not hear this complaint, when a teacher told a child she did a good job: "Teacher, you say that to everybody."

When teachers begin to use encouragement, it is hard to know what to say. If a child's work is pre-representational or is not what was expected, they often fall back on "almost" encouraging statements.

Trying not to use praise, the author remembers when he used this common alternative comment with Joey who was busy drawing: "Joey, can you tell me about your picture?" Slightly irritated, Joey replied, "This is not a story to tell, Dan. It is a picture to look at." To which Dan replied, "Yes, of course."

Frankly a more productive strategy is to use a **starter statement** that acknowledges features or details in the child's effort. *Acknowledgment* works better than the commonly asked question above for eliciting a response from the child. (The encouragement comes with the recognition *and* the interaction that follows.) An effective starter statement used by the student teacher in the previous anecdote was: "You are really working hard on that picture."

The idea is to begin a starter statement with *you* and describe what the teacher sees that indicates effort or progress. Then give a few moments of "wait time" while the child switches focus.

Classroom Anecdote	*Melissa, a four-year-old, was drawing what she and her family did over the summer. Her paper was completely covered with brown paint. Watching her work, the teacher said, "You are really using that brown paint."* *Melissa put the brush down, and explained to the teacher, "This is my daddy swimming in the lake. You can't see him because the water is dirty." The teacher smiled and nodded. The child said, "Can I do another one?"*

An effective starter sentence tells a child that the teacher is interested, is paying attention, is willing to help. This acknowledgment is a big part of the act of encouragement. Frequently, the child's response will be a smile, discussion of the activity, or, as in Melissa's case, resolve to continue.

The teacher is gaining skill in the use of encouragement when she can pick out details in the child's or group's efforts and positively acknowledge them. *In fact, the ability to acknowledge effort and progress usually ends the "loss for words"—problem.*

Stickers and Smiley Faces: Basically Bribes

Some teachers still use stickers and stamped smiley faces in early childhood education. The following comments are intended to encourage thought about the use and misuse of these token rewards.

Stickers in most uses are praise rather than encouragement (Kohn, 1999). They reward achievement rather than acknowledge effort. They fail to tell the child exactly what the teacher likes about the achievement. Keeping the use of stickers private is difficult. If they are given to some but not all, children make mental comparisons about who gets how many, how often, and even which ones. When used in evaluation of behavior or achievement, stickers reinforce an impression of differential treatment by the teacher—"who the teacher likes."

Table 7–1 *Encouragement Acknowledges Effort and Progress*

- You have made a real start on that puzzle.
- You have printed your whole name.
- Everyone is working so hard to clean the room today.
- We're almost ready for the story. (Just need to scoot back.)
- You got eight of the ten problems correct.
- You have all the letters right in that word but one.
- You really slid down the slide all by yourself.
- You stayed calm all day and didn't get upset once.
- You are really using your words. Do you want my help or can you solve this yourself?

Because they are extrinsic rewards, stickers build dependency upon the teacher. They cause children to lose sight of the intrinsic worth of the learning activity (Reineke, Sonsteng, & Gartrell, 2008). If it is developmentally appropriate, no external reward should be necessary. If the activity is not developmentally appropriate, the teacher should change it (Bredekamp & Copple, 2009).

Personal encouragement instead, either spoken or written privately, is more appropriate for young children. To a first grader, the teacher could either whisper or write, "You got all of your *M*s on the line." If written, the teacher might read the notation to the child; *that* will be a paper likely to be taken home. Written encouragement, even to kindergartners, is a sure inducement to functional literacy.

To some, stickers and smiley faces remain a popular tradition. For those insistent on the use of these "token rewards" here are two suggestions:

1. **Save the use of stickers for children with pronounced needs** (who are perhaps showing Level Three mistaken behaviors). Use the stickers only in defined situations to help the child master a specific behavior (Reineke, Sonsteng, & Gartrell, 2008) such as not taking home small figures from play sets. Give the stickers as privately as possible and each time explain to the child why you are giving them. (Give a general reason as well to children who notice; they can understand more than teachers may think.) Phase out sticker use as soon as the child is making noticeable progress, but keep giving encouragement.

2. **Use stickers to celebrate not evaluate.** Give everyone in the class a sticker. Celebratory use should not be every day, just on special occasions. Older kids will compare stickers, so make them as equivalent as possible—not smelly stickers to some and not to others. Another practice is to have an accessible-to-all sticker box so that children can use stickers as they choose. Use stickers that do not glorify violent "superheroes," but convey friendly and happy themes. (Teachers sometimes can do #1 and #2 together without diminishing the effects of #1.)

In the course of a day there are many opportunities
to offer encouragement.

*Cartoon courtesy of American Guidance Service, p. 8 of
"Teaching and Leading Children" by Dinkmeyer, KcKay,
et al. © 1992.*

When Praise Is Appropriate

Praise is not *always* inappropriate, though it does need to be given with care.
On occasion a solid rationale exists for having the class recognize an individual
child. One reason is to acknowledge achievement after a child has struggled
publicly and persevered. The class can appreciate a hard-fought victory for any
child.

A second example is the practice in some classrooms of recognizing a "Star
of the Week" or "Very Important Kid." If using this practice, the teacher needs
to ensure that children know they will all have a turn (maybe by a list of names
and a marker). When praise is done carefully in select situations, both the individual and the group benefit. The child receives a boost in self-esteem, and the
class a boost in empathy levels toward individual members. Appropriate praise
and encouragement both take conscious thought and decision making by the
teacher. It should be noted that one teacher-acquaintance scoffs at the Star of the
Week practice. She says, "In my class every kid is important every day."

Discussing Inclusively

When doing stories, Chapter Six introduced the idea of discussing *inclusively*
with children. In discussions of all kinds, of course, the teacher listens. She does
not discard comments that seem out of context. On the surface, what sounds

like inattentiveness may indeed be careful listening and hard thought—but from a perspective different from the teacher's.

Classroom Anecdote	*With the coming of spring, a kindergarten class had finished a dinosaur unit and was well into hatching chicken eggs. In a discussion the class talked about how baby chickens right away know to peck for food. The teacher asked if anyone knew what the word* instinct *meant. CeeGee raised her hand and announced, "That's like dinosaurs 'cause they're not alive anymore." The teacher started to call on another child, then turned to CeeGee and thanked her for the comment. With an impressed smile, the teacher explained to the class the difference between* instinct *and* extinct. *In an instant CeeGee changed her expression from concern to a smile.*

The teacher in this anecdote knew that the kindergarten class would not gain a full understanding of *extinct* (*eggstinct?*) and *instinct* from her brief explanation. However, she never could have anticipated the association made by the child. The teacher might have passed over the remark as having no connection to the present discussion—in fact she almost did. Instead, the teacher's open-ended listening was rewarded. CeeGee was saved from feeling not embarrassment but pride. The teacher was discussing inclusively.

When Children Don't Listen. What can the teacher do, however, when children really do not listen? A longtime elementary school practice has been to call on a child who is "chatting" or daydreaming to force renewed focus—often with a difficult question. An emotional memory of embarrassment too often is the result. (Can the reader relate?) When discussions repeatedly require "right" answers that children may not know, many develop defensive strategies—keeping a low profile, playing "dumb," making jokes, acting belligerent—to escape the embarrassment of public correction (Holt, 1964).

Most children do not come from the authoritarian "think before you speak" family structures common in the past. On average, by the time children begin kindergarten, they have watched nine months to a year of television, including perhaps a month of public television (Levin, 2003). From television and media games—as well as from family life—children acquire a host of ongoing experiences to work through and share. They have also refined their "mental off-switches" if things get boring. When teachers overly control discussions and become the center of instruction, children simply tune out (Vance & Weaver, 2002).

Teachers who practice the guidance approach *need to make discussion intriguing so that children will want to participate.* Children learn willingly when ideas are interesting to them. Discussions that are inclusive of a diversity of ideas and opinions mean that the teacher has mastered the skill of discussing inclusively. The atmosphere in such classrooms is likely to be both encouraging and intellectually stimulating. The two go together.

Classroom Anecdote	*A teacher was reading the classic* Harry the Dirty Dog *to her class. A new girl the teacher hadn't gotten to know yet raised her hand and said, "Teacher, we got a canary at our house."*
	The teacher decided to use reflective listening and repeated the girl's comment, "Rita, you have a canary?"
	"Yes," said Rita. "And last night it was dirty so me and my dad gave it a bath, and then it was cold, so we put new newspapers in its cage and put it by the radiator, and this morning its feathers was soft and warm and fluffy."
	The teacher commented, "You gave your canary a bath just like Harry," and thanked her.
	Another child then chipped in, "Guess what, Teacher. We have two canaries!"
	The teacher, who knew this, said, "Yes, Ramon, you do." She then added, "You know what, everybody? Let's see what's going to happen to Harry, because he needs a bath just like Rita's canary did. As soon as we finish the book, we'll talk more about pets and whether you give them baths."
	She finished the book, and resumed the discussion, beginning with Ramon. She then had the class write and/or draw in their journals about when they gave or might give a pet a bath. The children worked hard on their journals, and shared them at language arts focus time the next day.

In reflecting about the activity, the teacher was pleased with Rita's comment. The impromptu discussion gave Rita a chance to successfully share an experience in front of the class. Rita had to use comprehension, sequencing, syntax, and vocabulary skills (canary, cage, newspapers, feathers, fluffy) in telling her story. Rita's grammar wasn't perfect, but grammar is best learned gradually, through "on-the-job training." At a receptive level, the rest of the class similarly gained. In addition, a teachable moment occurred that made the book come alive for the children in a way that the teacher had not anticipated. What was to be a simple story about a dog that needed a bath became a multidimensional language arts experience.

Mattie, the teacher, modified a traditional practice when reading books to children: The teacher reads and the children listen. She commented that if less time was available or the story had been more compelling, she might have reacted to Rita the way she did to Ramon, accepting the comment and gently steering attention back to the book. She would have made a point, though, to return to Rita, either in the large group or later individually. Not all teachers would react as this one did, of course, but Mattie showed that she knew the importance of discussing inclusively.

Class Meetings: Sustaining the Encouraging Classroom

Class meetings are different from circle times. Most often circle times emphasize the routines of the early childhood classroom: opening activity, weather, calendar, lunch count, finger plays, songs, stories, and lead-in for the day's

> ### *Inclusive Discussion Management Hint*
>
> *When a child chimes in and time is short,*
> *You have only so long to get it done.*
> *Agree with whatever the child has to say,*
> *Nod, smile and whisper: make it fun.*
> *Then go back to the task at hand.*
> *But follow up with the child;*
> *He'll still think it's grand.*
>
> *Example: Teacher is reading story to class. Steffan says, "Teacher, I have that book at my house." Teacher whispers while nodding emphatically and smiling: "Yes, I know, Steffan. Thank you." Returns to reading. (The whisper is the secret ingredient. Steffan, and the other children, somehow accept the comment as private.) The nod-whisper-agree-and smile technique takes a bit of practice, but it almost always works, and it is "embarrassment free."*

academic program. As Harris and Fuqua (2000) suggest, when teachers keep circle times concise and engaging, children are more likely to be attentive participants.

Circle gatherings have long been used by Native Americans and other cultural groups for matters of public deliberation in a spirit of equality. Circle times in the classroom go back to Froebel's first kindergartens in Germany. The circle suggests the equality and worth of each individual and lends itself to the community spirit that is the objective of the class meeting.

On occasion circle times flow into class meetings and vice versa. But class meetings (sometimes called *community meetings*) have a different focus, transcending daily routines to deal with life in the classroom. The class meeting is expressly designed for the active involvement of each child. Its purpose is to encourage reflection and sharing by children and teachers about their experiences, needs, concerns, and triumphs (Vance & Weaver, 2002). About the meeting— McClurg (1998) says:

> The purpose of the community meeting is to create an intentional community devoted to a common project: learning to live with and take in the realities and perspectives of others. Here young children encounter and learn to acknowledge multiple realities, discover that they have choices, and realize that they are responsible for their decisions. (p. 30)

Teachers choose to hold class meetings in order to establish a sense of belonging within the group, conduct class business, and solve problems that arise. Whatever the immediate purpose, guidelines such as these apply:

▶ Anyone can talk

▶ Take turns and listen carefully

© Cengage Learning

In an encouraging classroom, children come to value class meetings.

▶ Be honest

▶ Be kind.

Developing these guidelines, and the reasons for them, may well be the subject of one or more early class meetings. Teachers use the creation of guidelines—through consensus rather than "voting"—to engender a spirit of community within the class (Vance & Weaver, 2002).

In addition to class guidelines, the teacher might have personal guidelines for class meetings:

▶ Support each child in the expression of his or her views

▶ Maintain a positive, caring focus

▶ Personal situations may require private remedies

▶ Meetings are to solve problems, not create them

▶ Build an encouraging community that includes everyone.

Teachers use class meetings to establish a sense of belonging, conduct class business, and solve problems that arise.

McClurg (1998) points out that meetings help teach the skills of group living that adults generally want all children to learn:

> *Some children may be too self-conscious; others may need to become more self-aware. Some may need to take control, while others are learning how to give. It is good news that, with a little leadership from an understanding adult, young children can learn these and many other things from each other. (p. 30)*

Class meetings, then, become a primary method for teaching democratic life skills. Each time a meeting occurs, children are reminded the classroom is a community that includes each one of them as well as each adult (Vance & Weaver, 2002). As learning centers do for developmentally appropriate practice, class meetings help to define the encouraging classroom.

Classroom Anecdote	*A prekindergarten teacher held an afternoon class meeting before going home. Marcie explained to the class that there were some problems happening on the climber during activity time and asked if some children could share about them.* *One child said, "I got bumped on the top and I nearly falled off."* *Another child said, "Somebody stepped on my fingers when I was climbing up."* *A third child stated, "I was going down the slide and someone was coming up and I bumped him."* *(continued)*

Classroom Anecdote	Marcie helped the children discuss the problem a bit more. Then (rather than threaten to take the climber down) she asked, "How can we solve this problem so no one gets hurt and we can all use the climber safely?" She wrote down the children's ideas, stating them positively, as guidelines: 1. We sit or crawl on the top and don't stand. 2. We give other people room when they are climbing up. 3. We go down the slide, except on Fridays. (Marcie really liked this last suggestion because she was wanting them to get more upper-body exercise. Also, the practice increased the children's calendar awareness about Fridays.) Marcie slowly read the guidelines back to the children. The children agreed that they would follow them. She "ceremoniously" posted them by the climber. For a few days, she or another adult stayed close to the climber and provided reminders about the guidelines. The children soon had memorized them and reminded each other.

Class Meetings/Magic Circles

William Glasser is credited with popularizing the use of class meetings (1969), which he called "magic circles." In Glasser's model, class meetings are held to identify problems and work toward solutions. The meetings center around behavior issues, curriculum matters, or student concerns. Glasser is adamant that the class meeting occurs without blame or fault finding by participants. Honest opinions stated and respected are the keys that make the method work. When children know they have a say in how the program can be made better, they feel like they belong and want to contribute.

In an account of the writing of Glasser on building "a sense of togetherness" within the class, Charles (2005) states:

> To foster a sense of togetherness, the teacher should continually talk with the class about what they will accomplish as a group, how they will deal with the problems they encounter as a group, how they will work together to get the best achievement possible for every individual in the group. In order to bring this about, responsibilities are given and shared, students are encouraged to speak of their concerns while the class attempts to find remedies, and the teacher takes special steps, when necessary, to incorporate every student into the ongoing work of the class. (p. 142)

Wolfgang (1999) points out that in Glasser's classroom meetings, there are no wrong answers; every child can successfully participate without fear of correction. The teacher works for this goal with direct teaching about the meeting process, but also with ongoing verbal and nonverbal support. To reduce her own personal judgments during meetings, the teacher might use reflective statements that affirm what a child has said or meant:

Child: *It made me mad that someone took my pencil. Chaz thought it was his, but gave it back.*

| Teacher: | *You were upset that your pencil was gone. How did you feel when he gave it back to you?* |

The teacher also may use nondirective statements:

| Child: | *I could write in a story about when I was sad, but I don't know how to.* |
| Teacher: | *Well, you think about how to draw or write it and do it any way you want. Do other children have suggestions?* |

As much as verbal support, the teacher relies on the staple nonverbal responses of *nods and smiles,* allowing the children as much as possible to guide the discussion's flow (Wolfgang, 1999).

Three Types of Class Meetings. For Glasser, there were three types of classroom meetings: open-ended, educational/diagnostic, and problem solving (Wolfgang, 1999). The first type, the *open-ended meeting,* discusses hypothetical or real life problems—"What if you saw a child drop a quarter. What would you do?" (When young children share personal experiences with the group, teachers can sometimes guide discussions into common sharing experiences.)

The second type, the *educational/diagnostic meeting,* is for the purpose of addressing educational ideas—such coming up with a list of questions for when a dentist is coming to visit the class. (The subject of losing teeth is always popular.) Vance and Weaver (2002) emphasize the compatibility of class meetings with the project method, for planning, sharing, evaluating, and celebrating project activities. The authors state:

> Project work is a beneficial but challenging teaching strategy, and class meetings can address these challenges through increased communication. When teachers share the planning of project work with the class, children feel ownership in the way projects develop. (p. 56)

The third type, the *problem-solving meeting,* is for the purpose of discussing "public" conflicts when or shortly after they occur. The anecdote of Marcie meeting with her prekindergarten children to resolve a problem with the climber is an example. Discussion about this third type of class meeting, integral to the guidance approach, continues under another heading.

Holding Class Meetings

Writers have different ideas about how often to hold class meetings and how long they should be. McClurg (1998) suggests a weekly meeting of at least a half-hour for a first-grade class. In contrast, at a kindergarten/first-grade level, Harris and Fuqua (2000) recommend three meetings a day. Harris and Fuqua state: "Twenty minutes, three times a day spent in building a sense of community, we predict, will have an impact on all aspects of the day and make all other times more productive with less time spent in overt management" (p. 46).

Because they are central to the encouraging classroom, I recommend two 5- to 15-minute meetings a day at both the prekindergarten and primary-grade level—after arrival (and breakfast when possible) and just before going home. The teacher can also call a special meeting if something eventful happens that needs immediate discussion.

Morning Meetings. The commonly held morning meeting is a staple of the Responsive Classroom model (Kriete, 2002). The morning meeting often follows and flows from a concise, interactive circle time. A segue might be special events, reported by any child, such as a new pet or a visit to the doctor. The teacher too might contribute a topic at this time, perhaps one that ties in with a theme, project, or topic of the day. She must take care, however, to share the discussion with the children, for the essence of the class meeting is a sharing of authority with the class (Vance & Jimenez, 2002). With knowledge of the group, such discussions are not difficult to spark. At a morning class meeting, before a child's visit to the dentist, a first-grade teacher asked: "I wonder. Have you or someone that you know ever lost a tooth?"

Personal sharing discussions should be handled with sensitivity. Experiences, such as a hospital stay or death of someone close to a child, may be painful for a child to discuss. The teacher needs to know the children and their families well enough to discuss such matters privately first. Discussions involving personal loss are sometimes best kept private, or made general and hypothetical.

Sharing personal experiences at morning meetings sometimes make for an adventure for the teacher as well as the child. Young children do share the darndest things; this comes with the territory:

Classroom Anecdote	*In my kindergarten I had a little boy named Dean who was very shy. One day in group he raised his hand and quietly mumbled, "I had to wear these shoes today because I got b'ture on my good ones."* *I asked him what he had said. He again mumbled it. I said, "You got what?" He looked with frustration at me and said loud and clear, "Cow shit!"*

(Sometimes a teacher has to accentuate the positive, especially when you've put your foot in it yourself.) "Oh, Dean, now I know what you said! You got cow manure on your shoe. That's not much fun, is it?"

A widespread phobia in the United States is a fear of public speaking. When a child speaks up in a class meeting, as in any group situation, we need to be inclusive of his comments—even when they could be embarrassing—so he still feels part of the group and comfortable about sharing in the future.

Anyway, who has not gotten manure of one kind or another on his shoe? (Gartrell, 2000).

Going Home Meetings. A second time for holding scheduled class meetings is just before going home. The purposes of the meeting are to review the day and discuss coming events. Children might share something they learned or enjoyed doing, or something that did not go well. When children or the teacher experience a problem, the end-of-the-day meeting is often a time to discuss it (Harris & Fuqua, 2000; Vance & Jimenez, 2002). For instance, the teacher or a child might bring up a learning center that was left messy or a situation when children excluded others from play. If an afternoon meeting becomes too involved, the teacher asks the class to think about the issue overnight so that "we can discuss it in the morning when we are fresh." The teacher works to end the meeting on a positive note.

Also at the afternoon meeting, the teacher might acknowledge a student who worked hard in a notable way, sing a song with the children, or ask a few students to share how they solved a problem on their own (Vance & Weaver, 2002).

Meeting to Solve Problems

As Glasser (1969) wrote, a key use of the class meeting is to resolve conflicts that affect the group (public, often Level Two, mistaken behaviors). We saw how a teacher used a class meeting to remind her preschoolers about safety on a climber. Other examples include when a daily routine repeatedly gets out of hand, or a word like *butthead* is catching on and driving others in the room "bananas." Class meetings to solve problems may occur during regular morning or afternoon time slots. But sometimes, as mentioned, the teacher calls unscheduled class meetings if a problem becomes urgent—a pressing teachable moment.

According to Glasser (1969), the teacher models the following discussion skills in all class meetings, but especially those called to solve problems:

1. The dignity of individuals is protected.

2. Situations are described, not judged.

3. Feelings are stated as I-messages.

4. All suggestions for solutions are appreciated.

5. A course of action is decided, tried, and reviewed.

This list of guidelines supplements one given earlier and seems particularly relevant to the age groups Glasser primarily addressed, elementary grades and up.

Class meetings that focus on problems provide an excellent opportunity for learning human relations, communications skills, and conflict management abilities. Some of the most important learning that the class and teacher will do occurs during class meetings:

Classroom Anecdote	*In Vicki's kindergarten class, Gary wet his pants. A volunteer took Gary to the nurse's office where extra clothes were kept. Vicki overheard some of the children joking about Gary and decided it was time for a class meeting. She explained to them what had happened. She then told a story about when she was a little girl, she wet her pants too and felt very embarrassed. She said people sometimes have accidents, even adults, and it's important that we be friendly so they don't feel badly. Vicki then paused and waited for a response.*
	The children shared similar experiences they remembered. When Gary came back to the room, another child smiled at him and said, "It's okay, Gary; last time I wet my pants too."
	Other children said, "Me too." Looking greatly relieved, Gary took his seat. The class got back to business.

Class Meetings and Level Three Mistaken Behaviors

A particularly difficult problem that every teacher faces is how to explain to the rest of the class serious mistaken behaviors that one child shows. The teacher must balance the right of the child for the dignity of privacy with the need for other children to express their concerns about the behavior and to try to understand. There is no magic answer to this dilemma. In a course journal, a teacher once shared that she felt she had no alternative but to "go public" when a child over time had many and violent conflicts in her first-grade class. Here is her account, slightly adapted:

Classroom Anecdote	*One day, after Jon calmed down from a tantrum, I told him that we had to have a class meeting and called the children together. After seating Jon beside me with my arm around him, I explained to him and the class that he had been hurting others and himself for days, and he needed to hear from the children how that made them feel. With the mutual respect I had been stressing with the children, each child told Jon how his actions made them feel sad, mad, or scared. When one child said, "I want to be your friend, but I'm scared 'cause you hit me," Jon hung his head and whispered he was sorry.*
	I thanked the class and told them that Jon was trying hard to use his words and be friendly and that maybe the other boys and girls could help him. I stayed close to Jon the rest of the day, and helped him into class activities. Outside of class I worked with the parents and the special education teacher to get Jon additional assistance. Whereas before, most class members were actively avoiding Jon, some now sought to include him—warily to be sure, but they tried. Jon's struggles became less, but I am still not completely sure I did the right thing.

"Going public" about conflicts concerning an individual child is a difficult choice, though Glasser (1969) and Vance and Weaver (2002) make the case that this is a valid use of class meetings. Teachers who do so open themselves and their children to fairly complex social dynamics. At any point the teacher must be prepared to step in to retain a spirit of mutual respect. The following anecdote was recorded by a student teacher in a rural, multicultural primary-grade classroom. Upon graduation, the student received a contract from the school, where she is still teaching:

Classroom Anecdote	*One of the children that we'll call Chris exhibited mistaken behavior on a regular basis. He did things like tipping over his desk, laying on the floor, getting up from his desk on impulse, and other types of mistaken behavior. On this day, Chris started out on the wrong foot, and things grew progressively worse as the day wore on. Right before lunch, after a series of crises, I ended up having the special education teacher physically remove Chris from the classroom.*

I knew the children were bothered by what they had seen. After lunch when we returned to the classroom, I held an unscheduled class meeting. I started out by saying "Sometimes when we come to school, we don't feel good about something that is going on at our home or with our friends. Many of us go to our parents or to someone we trust and talk about how we feel. Sometimes when we haven't been able to let our feelings come out, they start to sneak out in ways that maybe we don't want them to. I think that is how Chris is feeling today. I think he has some feelings that he needs to get out because they are starting to sneak out in ways he can't help. Before lunch today, Mrs. O. helped Chris down to her office so that she could maybe help him get rid of some of those scary feelings."

One child raised a hand and said, "Yeah, one time I was so mad at Joe I could have hit him, but I went home and talked to my mom and that helped."

Another child says, "So you mean that Chris doesn't tip his desk over on purpose?"
I said, "Yes, that is what I mean."

Another student raised her hand and said, "But sometimes I get mad and I don't tip my desk."
Her neighbor said, "Maybe you aren't mad like Chris."

We had just finished an Ojibwe story about a boy and a butterfly. The story was an analogy about people and their feelings. The last comment made was by one of the girls, and she said, "Chris is like the butterfly with the broken wing."

It was so sweet I could have cried. I said, "Yes, Chris is like the butterfly." We ended the class meeting and I felt like the children had a better understanding of their classmate.

I think the biggest thing I learned here was how effective a class meeting can be at helping children understand their classmates. The class meeting allowed them to really think about how Chris felt. I saw this when the one child related his story of being so angry at Joe that he wanted to hit him. By discussing this they had a better understanding of Chris. I also felt they needed to know that Chris was not out there tipping his desk over for the fun of it. Deep down inside, Chris is a hurt little boy trying to cope with a problem that is bigger than he is. I wanted the class to try to see that in him. When the one girl made that reference to the butterfly, I knew I had succeeded in that area.

Another thing that I learned was how effective a class meeting can be at solving a class problem that could have gotten worse. If we didn't have that talk, maybe some of the kids would have teased Chris when he came back into the room. Instead they treated him with respect. I was very pleased to see this response when he did return. Chris did continue with his mistaken behavior during the remainder of the day, but the kids ignored it. They seemed to understand that Chris was having a bad day and needed his space (Gartrell, 2000). |

A basic guidance principle is that to avoid embarrassment, a teacher tries to keep her interventions with a child private. Real life, however, means the teacher must balance this principle with the right of the class to a sense of well-being. In this anecdote, and the previous journal entry as well, the teachers worked hard to preserve the dignity of the child, in his own eyes and in the eyes of the group. Notice that when involved in such a situation, children accustomed to the class meetings do respond. Through these meetings, the community of the encouraging classroom is sustained, and the learning of democratic life skills occurs (Wohlwend, 2004/05).

Meetings with Toddlers—The Biting Issue

Authors are in agreement that class meetings work with preschoolers. Erin, an experienced family child care provider in northern Minnesota, insists conflicts have decreased in her group of infants and toddlers through daily "family meetings." Class meetings—though not necessarily formally held—can indeed happen with toddlers. One of my favorite anecdotes is about a toddler room in a Minneapolis child care center where biting had become a serious problem.

Classroom Illustration	*When biting incidents occurred in a toddler room over a few days, the staff decided to try a toddler group meeting. In simple terms, the teachers first explained the problem. The teachers then taught these very young children this strategy: When a child approached in a menacing manner, they were to hold out their arm with hand up, and state firmly "Stop!" The teachers and children practiced together, that day and the next a few children began to use it.*
	The teachers found that this response broke the impulse of the approaching child, alerted the teachers to get over to the situation for some quick problem solving, and helped children who might otherwise be victims to be rightfully assertive. With this strategy and accompanying guidance for all parties concerned (especially the children doing the biting), the problem lessened, to the relief of all. (One child who had been doing biting began to mock-threaten. When another toddler said "Stop," the first one would run away with a big grin. Compared to the biting, the teachers considered this teasing as an improvement.) The progress was acknowledged in later toddler group meetings.

Getting Class Meetings Started

Vance and Weaver (2002) offer helpful advice for teachers ready to try class meetings with their children:

> *If you are just beginning to use class meetings and are weighing the benefits, make a commitment to hold them for at least three months before judging the results. It may take that long for children to incorporate their new social skills, begin to use them regularly, and learn to trust one another. The change in the classroom's social climate will be noticeable. (pp. 24–25)*

As class meetings become established in the encouraging classroom, children value them. The teacher will know that community meetings are having an impact when children take more responsibility for running them, and the teacher is (sometimes) able to sit back and watch (McClurg, 1998).

> *Over time, children will begin to care for one another, solve their own problems, feel more empowered and more in control of their learning, and come to view all in the community as their "teachers." It will be time well spent when the teacher sees what happens during [class meetings] coming around again and again. (Harris & Fuqua, 2000, p. 47)*

Encouraging Friendliness

The encouraging classroom fosters friendliness, or an *ethic of caring* among all members of the classroom community. An ethic of caring means that members are open to forming relationships with other community members (Harris, Pretti-Frontczak, & Brown, 2009). The process that drives the ethic of caring is effective communication as individuals work and play together (Mecca, 1996). Lawhon (1997) and Watson (2003) point to studies that show children who lack the opportunity to have close personal relationships are more likely to experience long-term mental and physical health problems. Unhealthy social development can begin in infancy if parents and children fail to build positive attachments (Lawhon, 1997; Watson, 2003). By their behavior in the classroom, such children are vulnerable for stigma—further social separation. Because the window of opportunity for social development extends through early childhood, however, teachers can make a significant difference in children's lives by encouraging friendliness among all in the class (Scharmann, 1998).

Friendships and Friendliness

Lawhon (1997) says this about friendship:

> *Friendship is a mutual involvement between two people that is characterized by affection, satisfaction, enjoyment, openness, respect, and a sense of feeling important to the other . . . While most of these alliances are healthy, some are not. Negative associations are restrictive, while healthy relationships allow for freedom. Each pair determines what is acceptable for the relationship. The most healthy relationships will inspire feelings of autonomy, initiative, and industry. (p. 228)*

Most teachers have seen friendships between children of both kinds. For this reason the teacher works to encourage friendliness among everyone in the class (Wohlwend, 2004/2005). Lawhon (1997, p. 230) suggests that the following questions help a teacher decide whether a friendship is healthful or harmful:

▶ Is each child being treated fairly in the relationship?

▶ Does this friend get the other child into trouble?

© Cengage Learning

© Cengage Learning

© Cengage Learning

Teachers encourage friendliness toward all. Children decide for themselves who are their friends.

▸ Is the relationship healthful for both children?

▸ Will others be excluded as a result of this new friendship?

▸ Does this friendship endanger either child?

These questions are important. At the same time, teachers need to recognize that children are just learning how to be friends. In this endeavor, like others, they make mistakes. For instance, the offer, "I'll be your friend if you let me have the truck," may not be an ideal opening line, but it probably represents the child's developmental understanding "of the sharing that is involved in friendship" (Burk, 1996, p. 284). Though not as common as same-gender relationships (Lawhon, 1997), boy-girl friendships are important in encouraging classrooms and may need special support. The expectation that "in our class, girls and boys can be friends and work and play together" reflects a goal for our society no less than the classroom.

Addressing Cliques and Squabbling. Friends who frequently squabble or exclude others from their play present problems for many teachers (Barkley, 1998). Three quick strategies follow:

1. Use class meetings and your curriculum to teach friendliness. Discuss real situations. Dramatize, for example, with puppets, hypothetical situations that the children can then discuss. Many great books—including the classic *Swimmy*—can anchor projects and themes that teach social cooperation (Mecca, 1996).

2. Establish a guideline of *friendliness* such as, "We cooperate with others in our work and play"; "We all play and work together in our class" (Paley, 1992). Actively teach the word *cooperate*; it will become a useful tool for you: "You s'posed to 'coperate'!"

3. Use your leadership to structure small-group experiences that transcend the usual social circles. (We are not talking "ability groups," of course; it is long past time to retire "the bluebirds, robins, and turkey vultures.") Instead, use grouping strategies that show your awareness of existing social dynamics. One way to overcome prejudice toward others is do something successfully with them. Led by members of the teaching team, diverse small groups can experience the ethic of caring.

Being Friends and Being Friendly. When teachers make responsiveness to social dynamics a part of their teaching, things can get complicated. One result is that we occasionally confuse the need for children to be friendly with the need for children to be friends. "We are all friends in this classroom." Question: Is friendship something adults have a right to define for children?

Classroom Anecdote	*One day Roan's teacher thought he needed a reminder and said, "You need to be nice to your friends."* *Roan replied, "But Chip's not my friend."* *The teacher said, "We're all friends in this class."* *Exasperated, Roan stated, "Chip's not my friend. Forrest is." "Chip's my mate!" With that Roan and Chip resumed playing as though nothing had happened. The teacher was about to continue the discussion, then stopped and thought about how children—and, adults— distinguish between friends and classmates.*

In a Chapter Six case study concerning how Pat introduced routines to her kindergarten class, she expressed concern about not "overinstitutionalizing." Pat let children hang their coats where they wanted and sit next to whomever they chose. Pat understood a basic point about human nature: Children, like all of us, need to choose their own friends. The issue of inclusion is a hot one right now, due to the society's awareness of the extremes that can happen when some children at school become chronically stigmatized (Wohlwend, 2004/2005). Yet

Table 7–2 *The Developmental Issue in Preprimary Friend Conflicts*

Developmental understanding helps the teacher resolve young children's "confusion" about being friends (which Roan showed, but handled creatively). Piaget (1971) documented that young children in the preoperational stage experience:

- *developmental egocentrism*—difficulty in seeing situations (and relationships) as others do.
- *centering*—difficulty in comprehending the complexities of situations.
- *exclusivity*—difficulty in understanding that if something belongs to one grouping, it can also belong to another.

These developmental factors are frequently seen in the conflicts of children who frequently play together. Typically, "Abel" decides that because "Bettina" is his friend, then "Carlos" cannot be. Abel and Bettina tell Carlos he cannot play with them. Carlos gets upset.

Robin, an experienced preschool teacher, responds this way (after calming the children down): "People can have lots of friends. I have friends at day care and at home and at church. Children in our classroom can have lots of friends, way more than one. And remember, in our classroom we are friendly to everyone and we play together." Robin comments that on more than one occasion, the children have accepted this direct statement and decided the conflict wasn't worth it. In this case, as the children went off to play, Robin heard Bettina say, "You are both my friends." (Note that this was Bettina's decision, not Robin's.)

at the same time, Roan had an important point. We can and should encourage friendliness among all classmates ("mates" or "neighbors"), but perhaps we need to allow children the right to choose their own friends.

Burk (1996) concludes an important article with this thought about encouraging friendliness:

> We are finding more evidence to support Piaget's position that children are social beings and they do not develop in cognitive isolation from others. If we focus our attention on cognitive development without consideration for the social realm, we may inhibit development in both realms. . . . By recognizing and appreciating children's relationships, teachers show respect for children as members of the social world. (p. 285)

The dynamics are reciprocal: Teaching friendliness is really teaching language arts, social studies, and (sometimes) mathematics skills. Teaching for friendly relationships is essential curriculum in the encouraging classroom.

How One Teacher Brought Friendliness to Her Classroom

In 1998 Tessa Logan set a clear direction for how to bring friendliness to the classroom:

> I had always felt uneasy about small groups of children purposely excluding other children from their play. Exclusions, I had observed, are often motivated by assumptions about particular students, not by anything related to the specific requirements of the play or project.

[In class meetings] I explored with the children how they felt when they were left out and whether or not they thought it was fair for children to be told no and others yes in answer to their request to play. We decided that telling someone she could not play was a type of put down. We agreed that anyone who wanted to play at school would be allowed to do so, unless that child was treating people or materials badly and would not stop when asked. (pp. 22–26)

Logan (1998) was able to introduce and sustain these ideas in class meetings, also discussing such topics as how to express strong emotions and still be friendly. As well, she used community-building activities, teacher-assigned grouping, and conflict management to further the theme of inclusiveness in her kindergarten classroom. She encouraged children to realize that reporting a concern about being exclusive was not tattling, but a learning opportunity in creating a kindergarten community.

After nearly a year of everyday effort, Logan (1998) commented:

In summary, the issues of sexism and exclusion are still with us. That cannot change until the society at large changes. But the practice of divisive behaviors has lessened a great deal in my classroom. The atmosphere of the group is one of caring attachments. The children send out letters when people are sick. They ask after absent children. They raise a cheer when their classmates return. Their arms go around people who are hurt. Our classroom is a nice place to be. (p. 96)

Leadership Communication with Parents

The responsibility for communication with parents lies with the teacher (Sturm, 1997). Parents depend on teachers, even those younger than themselves, to initiate contacts and maintain relations. Most parents respect and appreciate even beginning teachers who enjoy working with young children and take pride in their programs. This section discusses leadership communication with parents to keep communications open and solve problems before they become serious.

Previous chapters discussed the importance of building partnerships with parents to encourage greater involvement in the education of their own children and increased participation in the educational program of the class. Specific activities toward these goals included the following:

1. Send welcome letters (see samples in Appendix B) to children and parents before the start of school. When possible, make home visits. When a visit is not possible, make introductory telephone calls to the home.

2. (When applicable) begin the program on a staggered schedule with half the parents and children attending each of the first two days or on alternating days for the first week. Give a special invitation to parents to attend on these days.

3. Telephone each family on the first night of school. Check with the family about any problems the child had that the teacher might help resolve.

4. Hold an orientation meeting (greeting meeting) on two occasions during the first week or two—ideally on a late afternoon and evening. Invite parents to attend either meeting. Go over a brochure about your education program (see example in Appendix C) at the meeting; discuss policies and highlight opportunities for parent involvement. Ask parents to complete optional surveys during or after the meeting to provide information about the child and family and their preferences for how to be involved (see Appendix B for examples).

5. Have parent conferences during the first month. Use the conferences to get to know each parent, referring to the survey if appropriate.

6. Invite parents to be involved in the program. Make sure parents know they are welcome to volunteer in the classroom. Help them feel welcome and useful when they visit (for suggestions on how to best do this, see Appendix C).

7. Assist parents to find tasks in the classroom that they are comfortable doing.

8. Send thank-you notes—from the class if possible—affirming the value of the visit for the parent.

For parents to feel comfortable with any of these activities, they must feel comfortable in their relationship with the teacher (Sturm, 1997). Leadership communication is the tool of the teacher in building partnerships. Discussion now focuses on five basic types of leadership communication helpful in maintaining positive parent-teacher partnerships and preventing serious problems:

▶ written notes

▶ electronic communication

▶ telephone contacts

▶ parent meetings

▶ parent-teacher conferences.

Written Notes

Many parents associate notes home with criticisms of their children's behavior. In the guidance approach, notes home are not for the purpose of correcting children's behavior. The reason is straightforward: Notes do not allow for discussion. The written message is, as it were, cast in stone. When a critical note arrives, the parent has a limited range of responses, which frequently come down to becoming upset with the child, and/or feeling "dumped on" by the school.

When sending personal notes that discuss a child, the teacher uses *encouragement*. The note is either an occasional, unsolicited "happygram" or a statement of progress, perhaps as follow-up to a conference. Because children wonder about the content of personal notes from the teacher, she does well to read them to the child beforehand. If the tone of the note is encouraging, most children will take pride in seeing that it is delivered. If the matter is serious, it probably is best handled not by a note but by a conference.

During the first few weeks, to alleviate anxiety about notes home, the teacher might send a happygram or two with each child, reading the note to the child beforehand. Such notes give the child an idea about what the teacher thinks, lets the parent know that the teacher is "on the child's side," and helps children feel positively about carrying notes home in general. Those early happygrams actually may improve the rate of note delivery for the rest of the year.

Regarding routine notes that provide information about events, the teacher needs to be aware of three factors:

1. Delivery rates by children are seldom 100%

2. Some parents will forget or misplace the note

3. Some parents are nonreaders.

Regarding the third point, when she knows that a parent is a nonreader, the teacher can either telephone or deliver the message personally. For cultural reasons, some nonreading parents take offense if notes are sent home with an older child to be read to them. Others find the insinuation that they are "illiterate" derogatory. Being identified as a nonreader in modern society often leads to stigma. When parents confide in a teacher that they are non-readers, it is important to appreciate and respect the trust they are showing in the relationship.

Digital Communication

More and more families with young children are accustomed to using e-mail and the Web. In virtually any class, some parents will be regular e-mail/Web site users. In greeting meetings at the beginning of the year, and in informal parent survey letters (see samples in Appendix B), teachers can discover which parents are and are not comfortable with this technology. Fairness suggests that in mixed "yes-no" groups, the teacher needs to make sure technology users will not be "advantaged" in teacher-parent communication. One idea is to ask parents if they would prefer hard-copy notes sent home or e-mails; hard-copy newsletters or a regularly updated Web site. Then be a split-medium teacher—though if all parents and the teacher are "techies," the sky is the limit.

E-mail and Text Messaging. Electronic communication (EC)—meaning e-mails and text messaging—is the digital equivalent of the note home. Yes, EC is more interactive, but it is also potentially more powerful in causing miscommunication. Probably everyone who uses EC has had at least one conversation go in an unanticipated, even bothersome, direction. Parents have high emotional investment in their children, and a blithe comment by a teacher easily can be "overinterpreted." It is difficult to take back a message that either should not have been sent, or should have been sent with different wording—just as can happen with a note. The difference is that with EC the teacher is more likely to write impulsively and receive directly the parent's negative reaction. Until a teacher has an ongoing relationship with a parent, similar precautions pertain to EC as to notes home: Send happygrams; send routine kinds of information, but hold off on serious communication until you can meet face-to-face.

The upside of EC is that due to the possibility of dialogue, teachers can get to know parents through its use. It is unusual for a parent to respond with a thank-you note to a hard-copy happygram. With EC, it is much more common that a parent might reply, so beginning a relationship. *In fact, e-mail relationships blossom so easily that the teacher may need to monitor EC use to make sure she is not conversing too much with only some parents. (The goal is to decrease, rather than widen, the digital divide.)*

Web Sites. The hard-copy equivalent of the web site (or e-mail attachment) is the newsletter. Both inform families what is going on in the class, what projects children are doing, what themes, projects, and events are coming up, and what parents can do to help out. Web sites perform these tasks with flare—such as by including digital video from the *Three Little Pigs* play. Web sites can also provide in-depth information about the educational program, and because it is electronic, more parents might read the information. Undoubtedly, web sites will continue to flower as a medium in teacher-parent-child communication. Many articles—hard-copy and electronic—are being written on this topic even now. (See the web sites listed for each chapter in the Book Companion Web site.)

A consideration for teachers about web sites, again, is that not all parents may be able to access them. Training sessions for interested family members who are novice computer users might really be appreciated. But other parents will not have web capabilities. A new generation of newsletters is appearing that uses such electronic assists as digital photographs of children doing activities. Technology can make hard-copy newsletters more attractive and readable in many ways. The really resourceful teacher will figure out how to coordinate hard-copy materials and electronic communication in ways that cut down effort and expense, and still reach all parents.

Telephone Contacts

Telephone calls allow for personal conversation but not for physical proximity and face-to-face contact. For this reason, unless the teacher knows the parent, telephone calls should be used in a similar fashion as notes home. In other words, under normal circumstances a teacher should not attempt a serious conference on the telephone. Telephone conversations are helpful in underscoring the need for special conferences. They are helpful for personally delivering happygrams, following up after conferences, and inviting parent participation in special events.

When requesting a conference regarding a child's behavior over the telephone, the use of a *compliment sandwich* is important. (See Chapter Eight for more on compliment sandwiches.) The compliments help the teacher put the behavior in perspective. For the parent, they convey the message that "my child is not a total problem because the teacher sees at least some 'good' in him." Note the difference between these two "calls home" regarding Jeremy, a four-and-a-half-year-old.

> *Call One: "Jeremy was a total monster today. He hit two children, bit one, and threw a book at me. We will have to talk about his behavior tomorrow because I've had it. How is eight o'clock?"*

> *Call Two: "Jeremy has been working hard on his behavior, but he had a rough morning. He had conflicts with two children that I had to help him resolve. After that he settled down, and the rest of the day went better. He's making progress, but I think we need to talk. What are some times that would be good for you tomorrow?"*

Telephone calls also are well suited to giving positive feedback after a conference. If the teacher wants to communicate more directly than with a note or e-mail, a call like the following would mean a lot:

> *I just wanted to let you know how Jeremy did this week. No hitting or kicking at all. He only got upset once, but he used his words. He was also playing more with the other children. I'm really pleased. How are things going for him at home?*

Phone calls to families are more direct than either notes or e-mails. Many teachers use them regularly with parents. Especially with parents who are non-readers, phone calls make for an important connection. These days, few families do not have either landline or cell phones.

Answering Machines. Some teachers use classroom telephones with answering machines as "sound bulletin boards." Each night they record assignments, up-coming events, and "do-together" ideas, which parents can access at their leisure. Parents who want regular updates to track and assist with class activities often appreciate teacher-recorded messages. Teachers who use them like them too, except that the messages need to be updated regularly. Sustained teacher initiative keeps the partnerships going.

Family Meetings

Regular meetings offer an important vehicle for parent involvement, but they can be difficult to accomplish with complete success. Foster (1994) provides several ideas for successful parent meetings, incorporated into the six suggestions shown in Figure 7–3.

As Figure 7–3 illustrates, meetings add to the time demands on busy staff as well as busy families. The meetings should be held for a reason, not just because they *should* be held. Once the purpose for the meeting is clear, the work in planning and carrying it out becomes worthwhile. With successful meetings, the classroom community is expanding to include home and school together.

Phone calls and conferences are two important ways to communicate with parents.

© Cengage Learning

Parent-Teacher Conferences

Conferences provide the most direct link between teacher and parent, and much has been written in recent years about them. Gestwicki (2007) suggests that successful conferences consist of three phases: *preparation, conduct,* and *evaluation*. In preparing, the teacher needs to make sure the parent knows the reasons for the conference. A statement about conferences might be included in a booklet about the program (see example in Appendix C) and repeated in a note

Table 7–3 *Suggestions for Successful Meetings*

1. **Consider convening a parent committee to help plan meetings.** Teachers might ask parents who are familiar with the program to serve on the committee. This step is not an automatic guarantee of success, but it shows respect for parent involvement and helps build parent ownership of the meetings (Foster, 1994). Some teachers prefer to plan the topic and have the committee help to make the logistical arrangements. Others prefer to make the arrangements themselves.

2. **Assess parents' interests and needs.** Asking parents to complete an optional questionnaire, contacting parents at the beginning of the school year, and polling the parent committee can all help with this determination. Topics selected should be high priorities for the parents.

3. **Make planned preparations for the meetings** by considering the following:

   a. Date, time of day, and length of the meeting; plan for when most parents can attend. Specify both a starting and ending time so that parents know when the meeting will be over. Keep the meeting concise; under an hour and a half.

   b. Meeting location; an informal location comfortable to the parents is best.

   c. Transportation options; bus line availability; ride-share possibilities.

   d. Free on-site child care; takes work to arrange, but it makes a difference. As Foster (1994) points out, "Babies should be welcomed and allowed to stay with their parents if need be" (p. 79).

   e. Refreshments; good food brings people together and helps bring them back (Foster, 1994).

4. **Get the word out about the meeting.** A useful advertising strategy is to have a "hook" that will draw in people. Teachers need to use their imaginations to attract parents. One center borrowed a camcorder, videotaped the children in activities, and sent home notices saying, "See your kids on TV." Other ideas often used are potluck meal meetings held early in the evening, and activity nights where parents, or parents and children together, do typical class activities or make-and-take projects.

5. **Follow guidelines for the meeting:**

   a. A short greeting is given that includes thanks to presenters, meeting organizers, and parents in attendance. Include a concise overview of the program.

   b. An icebreaker activity—perhaps parents telling (happy) stories about their children—helps participants relax.

   c. Whether it is a lecture, panel discussion, open discussion, or video, the presentation needs to be interesting and keep in mind fatigue levels. A useful technique is to follow a concise presentation with small-group discussions. The large group then reconvenes for small-group sharing, questions of the presenter, and a summary statement. Refreshments and informal conversation follow.

   d. Parents go out the door with make-and-take projects or handouts, fliers about the next meeting, and many thanks for attending.

6. **Include the parent committee and/or all involved to assess how the meeting went** and decide any changes for future meetings.

home. Time options are helpful for the parent, including both nighttime and daytime slots if possible. An informal private setting, in which parent and teacher can sit side by side at a table, is preferable to conversing over a desk. Likewise, adequate time is preferable to the "get them in; get them out" atmosphere common in some schools.

The teacher should have a folder for each child with samples of the child's work over time. Dated observational notes are helpful. Some teachers may include video clips of the child. A form to record notes from the conference, in preparation for a later written summary, rounds out preparation (Gestwicki, 2007).

There is considerable agreement about the *conduct* of the conference (Gestwicki, 2007; Rockwell & Hawley, 1996; Sturn, 1997). The teacher begins with

Serious discussions occur best in the face-to-face setting for the conference.

a positive I statement? about the child, such as: "I really enjoy having Maybelle in class. She works hard and has such a sense of humor." The teacher goes over materials she has prepared, and invites parent discussion about them. She asks about items the parent would like to discuss. The teacher paraphrases comments the parent makes and uses **reflective listening**, which means repeating back the thoughts and feelings the parent is expressing (Gestwicki, 2007). The compliment sandwich is another useful communication technique. If a follow-up plan comes out of the conference, the teacher writes it out and sends it to the parent for approval. The teacher ends the conference on a positive note (Gestwicki, 2007).

Gestwicki (2007) includes a list of pitfalls to avoid during conferences:

▶ Technical terms and jargon. Use terms parents can understand.

▶ The "expert" role. Describe events and trends rather than make broad judgments.

▶ Negative evaluations of a child's capabilities. (Use compliment sandwiches.)

▶ Unprofessional comments: talking about others, becoming too personal, or taking sides. Respect the principle of confidentiality.

▶ Direct advice. Offer alternative suggestions "that have worked for other parents," for the parent to consider.

▶ Instant problem solving. Decide instead on a cooperative plan of action that will be reviewed.

Gestwicki concludes her discussion of conferences with this important paragraph:

> *It should be remembered that nonattendance at a conference does not necessarily indicate disinterest in the child or the school. Instead, it may be a reflection of different cultural or socioeconomic values, of extreme pressures or stress [on the] family or work demands. A teacher's response to nonattendance is to review the possible explanations . . . see if different scheduling or educational action will help, persist in invitations and efforts, and understand that other methods of reaching a parent will have to be used in the meantime. (2004, p. 341)*

Following the conference, the teacher reviews notes and completes a brief summary, perhaps on a prepared form. She files the original form, and when a cooperative plan has been decided upon, sends a copy to the parent. The teacher also reflects in personal terms about the success of the conference, takes agreed upon follow-up actions, and notes possible changes in approach for conferences to come (Gestwicki, 2007).

Summary

1. How does the teacher establish leadership in the encouraging classroom?

An encouraging classroom is one in which the teacher sets and maintains clear limits at the same time as reinforcing a sense of belonging and self-esteem in each child. As soon as the teacher and class come together, the teacher establishes leadership, but in a way that values children and teaches them to value each other. In such an environment, much mistaken behavior becomes unnecessary.

2. Why are guidelines, not rules, important in the encouraging classroom?

Rules tend to be stated in negative terms and have preset consequences. Rules institutionalize the use of punishments, fail to respond adequately to the complexities of situations, and reduce the role of the teacher to a technician. Guidelines educate children toward productive behavior. Helping to formulate guidelines increases children's ownership of the them and their sense of belonging in the class. Guidelines allow the teacher the range of choices needed by a guidance professional.

3. How is encouragement more appropriate than praise?

Praise rewards achievements, often is used to manipulate the group, and fails to distinguish between personalities and deeds. Encouragement empowers effort; does not single out or evaluate personalities; gives specific, positive feedback; and builds an encouraging environment. Public encouragement is directed to the group, private encouragement to the individual. Teachers are mastering the technique of encouragement when they can acknowledge specifics in children's efforts in ways that empower the child.

4. Why is discussing inclusively important?

In group situations, as well as with individuals, the teacher listens. She goes beyond a preoccupation with right or wrong answers and who is and is not listening. Instead, the teacher works to make class discussions opportunities for engagement by children through welcoming all perspectives in a mutually respectful atmosphere. By discussing inclusively with children, the teacher is building an encouraging learning environment in the classroom.

5. How do class meetings build the encouraging classroom?

Class meetings are held to maintain a sense of community, carry on the business of the class, and solve classroom problems. Scheduled class meetings occur most often at the beginning and end of the day. The teacher calls unscheduled meetings when events cannot wait. Guidelines such as the need to be respectful of others make class meetings positive and productive experiences. Even with young preschoolers, class meetings build the encouraging classroom and teach vital democratic life skills.

6. How does the adult teach friendliness in the encouraging classroom?

Beginning with class meetings, the teacher acquaints children with the pain of being stigmatized by others. She models and encourages friendly inclusion in all classroom activities. The teacher uses active leadership, especially during conflicts, to teach children that while they can choose their own friends, they need to be friendly to all.

7. How does leadership communication with parents build and maintain partnerships?

Leadership in communication with parents lies with the teacher. Five types of leadership communication with parents are: notes home, electronic communication, telephone contacts, parent meetings, and parent-teacher conferences. Notes, e-mails, text messages, and telephone calls are best used to deliver happygrams that recognize children's progress and to provide necessary information to the parent. Telephone calls provide direct communication, but should not substitute for face-to-face conferences. Family meetings take planning and should be held for definite purposes. Parent conferences have three phases: preparation, conduct, and evaluation. They are central to parent-teacher partnerships.

FOLLOW-UP ACTIVITIES

Note: *An element of being a professional teacher is to respect the children, parents, and educators you are working with by maintaining confidentiality, that is, keeping identities private. In completing follow-up activities, please respect the privacy of all concerned.*

Discussion Activity

The discussion activity encourages students to interrelate their own thoughts and experiences with specific ideas from the chapter.

Think of a time when you were embarrassed by praise a teacher gave you, or when used praise and received an unexpected reaction from a child. Compare or contrast that experience with what the chapter says about praise. How might the teacher, or you, have given encouragement in that situation instead? What difference do you think giving encouragement might have made?

Application Activities

Application activities allow students to interrelate material from the text with real-life situations. The observations imply access to practicum experiences; the interviews, access to teachers or parents. Students compare or contrast observations and interviews with referenced ideas from the chapter.

1. Leadership in the encouraging classroom.

   a. Observe an example of what you believe to be positive leadership shown by a teacher. What was the situation? What did the teacher say and do? What did the children say and do in response? Using ideas from the chapter, why do you believe this was an example of leadership communication?

   b. Interview a teacher who shows what you believe to be positive leadership in the classroom. Ask the teacher to share how she goes about establishing leadership at the beginning of the school year. How do the methods of the teacher agree or disagree with what the chapter says about leadership communication?

2. Guidelines in the encouraging classroom.

   a. Whether she uses the term *rules* or *guidelines,* observe how a teacher uses these standards in the classroom. Is the use of standards closer to that of *rules* or *guidelines?* Document your conclusion. Compare your findings with ideas from the chapter.

b. Interview a teacher about how she uses standards with young children. (The use of the term *guidelines* is new, so she may use the term *rules*.) What developmental considerations does the teacher make in creating and using the standards? How is the class involved? Is the use of standards closer to that of rules or guidelines? Explain why you think so. Compare your findings with ideas from the chapter.

3. Encouragement more than praise.

a. Observe a teacher giving feedback to a child or to the class. What did the teacher say and do? How did the child or children respond? Was what you observed more like praise or encouragement? Why do you think so? Compare your findings with ideas from the chapter.

b. Interview a teacher about her priorities when giving positive feedback to an individual child and to the class. Write down what the teacher said. How do her ideas correspond to the text ideas about encouragement and praise?

4. Discussing inclusively.

a. Observe a teacher in a discussion or activity with the class. How does the teacher respond to questions or comments that do not seem to "fit"? How has your understanding about discussing inclusively changed by what you observed and read in the text?

b. Interview a teacher about her priorities in discussions with the class. Ask how the teacher responds to comments that do not seem to "fit" the topic or activity. How do the teacher's comments correspond to the text ideas about discussing inclusively?

5. Class meetings.

a. Observe a class meeting as distinct from a circle time. Decide whether the meeting was scheduled or unscheduled and the purpose of the meeting. How do the purpose and conduct of the meeting correspond with ideas from the chapter?

b. Interview a teacher who uses class meetings as distinct from circle times. Does the teacher use scheduled class meetings, unscheduled, or both? What does the teacher believe to be the reasons for holding class meetings? How do the reasons identified by the teacher correspond with ideas from the chapter?

6. Friendliness in the encouraging classroom.

a. Observe a classroom that encourages friendliness. Record an instance of teacher-child interaction and of child–child interaction that you believe to be typical. Compare your findings from the observation(s) with what the text says about teaching friendliness.

b. Interview a teacher about the efforts she makes to encourage friendliness in the classroom. Ask the teacher to give you an informal "case study" based on recent experience. Compare your findings from the interview with what the text says about teaching friendliness.

7. Leadership communication with parents.

a. Observe how a teacher uses notes, e-mails, text messages, web sites or newsletters, telephone calls, meetings, and/or conferences with parents. How does the teacher's use of these communication methods correspond with ideas from the chapter?

b. Interview a teacher about using notes, e-mails, text messages, web sites or newsletters, telephone calls, meetings, and/or conferences as communication techniques with parents. Which communication methods does the teacher use more? How do the teacher's comments correspond with ideas from the chapter?

Recommended Readings

DeVries, R., & Zan, B. (2004, September). When children make rules. *Educational Leadership,* pp. 64–67.

Gallahger, K., & Mayer, K. (2008). Enhancing development and learning through teacher-child relationships. *Young Children, 63*(6), 80–87.

Harris, K. I., Pretti-Frontczak, K., & Brown, T. (2009). Peer-mediated intervention: An effective, inclusive strategy for all children. *Young Children, 64*(2), 43–49.

Harris, T. T., & Fuqua, J. D. (2000). What goes around comes around: Building a community of learners through circle times. *Young Children, 55*(1), 44–47.

Kriete, R. (2002). *The morning meeting book.* Turner's Falls, MA: Northeast Foundation for Children.

Macrina, M., Hoover, D., & Becker, C. (2009). The challenge of working with dual language Learners. *Young Children, 64*(2), 27–34.

Vance, E., Weaver, P. (2002). *Class meetings: Young children solving problems together.* Washington, DC: NAEYC.

Wien, C. A. (2004). From policy to participation: Overturning the rules and creating amiable classrooms. *Young Children, 59*(1), 34–40.

Wohlwend, K. E. (2004/2005). Chasing friendship: Acceptance, rejection, and recess play. *Childhood Education, 81*(2), 77–82.

Guidance Matters

Class Meetings

November, 2006

When student teaching in a second-grade classroom last spring, Julie noticed that the children were having problems during bathroom breaks. Some students crawled under stalls and locked the doors, stood on top of sinks, threw water, and took too long to return to class.

My first response was to give consequences to the children who I thought were doing these things, but this led to finger-pointing because there were always children involved who didn't get caught. On a particularly rough day, we held a class meeting to discuss the problem and come up with a solution. Everyone sat in a circle, since the children were used to sharing in this way in morning meeting.

Me: I want to talk about our bathroom breaks. I'll pass around the talking stick, and you'll have a chance to share. On this round of sharing, I want you to say in one or two sentences how you think bathroom breaks have been going.

Maria: Bad, because we're all goofing around.

Justin: I don't like it when we all get in trouble, because not all of us are being bad.

Brad: I think other teachers are getting mad because we're always loud.

Torii: It makes me mad when I have to go to the bathroom and the doors are locked, and I have to crawl on the gross floor [to unlock a door].

Me (after the class shared): Now I'm going to give everyone a chance to say one thing they think they could do to make bathroom breaks go better (passing the talking stick around again).

Trevor: Not stand on the toilets.

Brad: Pick up the paper towels.

Me: I know Patty [our janitor] would really appreciate that. She already does so much to help us keep our building clean.

Maria: I think we should all try to use quiet voices. We should just do our business and get out.

Jinada: If there are three people in there, we should come out.

Me: I think it would help a lot if people would remember our rule about only having three students in the bathroom at a time. Thanks for reminding us about that, Jinada.

Justin: Maybe we should have a quiet contest in the halls!

Me: These are all really good ideas! I'm going to write them down on a poster, and tomorrow before our bathroom break we'll go over them to make sure we remember our plan.

The children had as much time as they needed to express their feelings and suggest solutions. I offered brief

reminders of our plan over the next few days. The bathroom breaks became much less stressful for all of us!

Encouraging classrooms are classroom communities in which all children are valued members and learn to solve their problems. Teachers who make their classrooms encouraging rely on social problem solving: guidance talks with individual children, conflict mediation with children in small groups, and class meetings if many are involved. When situations include many children, teachers, like Julie in the anecdote above, often do not know exactly who was involved. Group punishments—typically used when a teacher doesn't know who is to blame—demean the group and create negative dynamics among the children. Class meetings, as Julie's anecdote shows, allow all children (including those involved) to become participating citizens who together can solve the problem.

For class meetings to be successful, teachers need to be proactive leaders. As Julie did, it is important for teachers to put aside personal feelings about blame (and work privately with the individuals involved). Teachers should hold class meetings regularly before problems develop. With the children, teachers can create and reinforce a few guidelines for meeting etiquette, such as these:

- Everyone has a chance to speak.
- We listen to each other.
- We treat all with respect.

Sometimes, using a revered prop such as a talking stick to signify who is speaking reminds all others to listen.

To actually solve problems through the meetings, I suggest that teachers follow a five-step procedure: (1) Calm everyone, including themselves if necessary, and orient the children to the process; (2) define the problem cooperatively; (3) brainstorm possible solutions together; (4) decide together on a plan using the solutions suggested; (5) take an active role in guiding the plan's implementation. Julie clearly followed all five steps and turned a budding crisis into a class accomplishment.

Class meetings are a regular activity in many preschool and primary classrooms and are vital components of such education models as the Responsive Classroom (Kriete & Bechtel, 2002). Meetings may occur once or twice a day (opening and ending) for group conversations and discussions of routines and events; or they may take place less frequently, like once a week. Teachers most fully realize the worth of class meetings when they use them to resolve public problems and conflicts that affect the whole group. Sometimes teachers hold class meetings beyond those regularly scheduled to address such issues.

For children, the values of class meetings are many. A common phobia in our society is a fear of public speaking. Class meetings encourage not just the development of a wide range of language skills, but confidence in using them. Because topics discussed are of high interest, speaking and listening skills develop through the meetings.

Another vital contribution is that class meetings, when led with sensitivity by the teacher, build empathy in children. A favorite anecdote of mine indicates this ability. In a Head Start class, a four-year-old who had needed crutches progressed to using a leg brace. On the first day that Charlie wore the leg brace, it squeaked. Children began calling him "Squeaky Leg Charlie." The teacher talked with Charlie, and the next day he willingly gave the class a demonstration. The children listened and looked at and touched his new brace. They and the teacher talked about how fine it was that Charlie no longer needed crutches. The name-calling stopped. On a day thereafter, the children's teacher was out of town at a workshop.

The assistant later told the teacher that two children had approached the substitute and explained, "Charlie's got a new leg brace. It squeaks, but he gets around on it really good."

Meetings to solve common problems have a rich history in the United States, going back to township meetings in colonial times and Native American gatherings before that. No other educational practice prepares children for citizenship in a democracy like class meetings. If done well, they tell children "My ideas matter" and "I'm glad I belong to this group." What a positive message to give to a child! What a positive way for educators to affirm the democratic ideal that our society is still striving to attain.

Class meetings model and teach democratic citizenship. Like nothing else, class meetings sustain encouraging classrooms. They are vital to developmentally appropriate early childhood education, and the references suggest we cannot start them too early.

To Increase Your Knowledge

All of the books cited in the Column References offer useful ideas. The Gartrell and Vance and Weaver books address preschool as well as primary-grade levels. These *Young Children* articles also provide useful ideas:

Harris, T. T., & Fuqua, J. D. (2000). What goes around comes around: Building a community of learners through circle times. *Young Children, 55*(1), 44–47.

McClurg, L. G. 1998. Building an ethical community in the classroom: Community meeting. *Young Children, 53*(2), 30–35.

A Step You Can Take

While reading about class meetings, note ideas you think might work with the children in your group. Discuss them with fellow staff. Try holding class meetings for a few weeks. Review what is working and what you would like to change, and try them again. Think about what you learned from the experience, about the children and about yourself.

Column References

Gartrell, D. (2004). Sustaining the encouraging classroom: Class meetings. In D. Gartrell, *The power of guidance: Teaching social-emotional skills in early childhood classrooms* (pp. 93–105). Washington, DC: NAEYC.

Kriete, R., & Bechtel, L. (2002). *The morning meeting book. Strategies for Teachers series.* Turners Falls, MA: Northeast Foundation for Children.

Vance, E., & Weaver, P. J. (2002). *Class meetings: Young children solving problems together.* Washington, DC: NAEYC.

For additional information on using the guidance approach in the encouraging classroom, visit our website at www.cengage.com/education/gartrell.

Chapter  8   *Leadership Communication with the Individual*

Guiding Questions

▶ *How do teachers' listening skills build relationships?*

▶ *How do contact talks encourage young learners?*

▶ *What is a compliment sandwich and how does it work?*

▶ *Why is friendly humor an important guidance strategy?*

▶ *Is friendly touch still a viable guidance technique?*

▶ *How can teachers care for themselves so they can care for the children?*

▶ *How do teachers use leadership communication in the parent-teacher conference?*

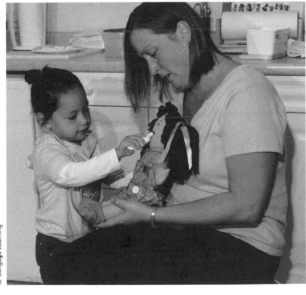

© Cengage Learning

Key Concepts

▶ *Acknowledgment*

▶ *Childism*

▶ *Compliment sandwich*

▶ *Contact talk*

▶ *Friendly humor*

▶ *Friendly touch*

▶ *Listening techniques*

▶ *Listening to life experiences*

▶ *Mandated reporter*

▶ *Overfunctioning*

Children show mistaken behavior because they do not know how else to act; others have influenced them to act in a particular way; or they are driven to act out because of strong unmet needs. When adults get beyond childism, the naive belief that childhood is a rosy time without stress and hardship, they realize that sometimes the opposite is the case (Chenfield, 1997). All children come to school with some unmet needs, and they are unsure how to cope with this new classroom life. When children understand that the teacher will listen to their needs and cares about them, they feel that they belong in the class. They want to be there, fit in, and do well (Ostrosky & Jung, 2003). Almeida phrased the idea this way in 1995. In this age of "No Child Left Untested," it still pertains today:

> *Teachers need to care more about their students as the focal point of the classroom, and less about the curriculum. Without question, the curriculum is important, but if students sense that you're more concerned about [their performance] than you are about them, they'll be less likely to behave the way you'd like them too. . . . Teachers must care about their students as children. (p. 89)*

Guidance teachers have always known what Almeida reminds us of: Relationships come first. To restate Ginott's famous comment: "To reach a child's mind a teacher must capture his heart. Only if a child feels right can he think right" (1972, p. 69). Chapter Seven focused on leadership communication with the class, guidance management techniques to use with the group. Chapter Eight addresses leadership communication with individual children, using "unrelenting encouragement" with the individual child.

The chapter explores five leadership communication skills that assist the teacher to build positive relationships with individual children—even children that teachers find challenging. The five skills are:

▹ listening techniques

▹ contact talks

▹ the compliment sandwich

▹ friendly humor

▹ the use of friendly touch

The chapter concludes with discussions of how teachers can care for themselves and how teachers can use leadership communication with family members in the setting of the family-teacher conference.

Listening Techniques

Throughout the chapter, the reader will notice teachers using particular listening techniques that support the five broad leadership skills listed above. We use the following exchange between a teacher and child to highlight the following listening techniques:

▹ attending

▹ acknowledgment

- wait time
- reflective listening
- expansion
- open-ended questions
- I-messages.

Classroom Illustration	
Jacque:	*Vrmmm. Look, Teacher!*
Rosalee:	*(Sits on floor by Jacque.) You are really loading lots of cubes in that dump truck, Jacque. (Teacher waits about 20 seconds for Jacque to respond; just watches.)*
Jacque:	*Rocks, Teacher, not cubes. Yep, me gonna haul 'em in this 'ruck.*
Rosalee:	*You really like to haul rocks in that dump truck!*
Jacque:	*Yep! I haulin' the rocks to the 'struction place 'cause they are building.*
Rosalee:	*Oh, you are hauling the rocks to the construction zone. I wonder what they are building?*
Jacque:	*They are buildin' the parkin' lot where the cars park, and even the dump truck parks there. Even you can park there, Teacher.*
Rosalee:	*Thank you, Jacque, but I don't need a car. I like just visiting with you while you haul those rocks.*
Jacque:	*Yep, and I gonna get more rocks. (Jacque drives truck over, dumps the "rocks," and returns for another load. Rosalee watches, smiling.)*

These techniques, as Rosalee used them, encourage the child to process and express thoughts and feelings, and to build a positive relationship with the teacher. *Instructional note:* Teachers need not pause in the middle of conversations to figure out which techniques to use (smile). When listening successfully, the techniques tend to blend together—most have "conceptual overlap." But it is important to monitor use of techniques. When a teacher has trouble conversing with a child, he might consciously try a small number of the techniques that feel right at the time. Afterward, reflect how each worked. Start with *attending* and *acknowledgment* and build from there. Seek out children who seem to have few conversations—they often benefit a great deal from personal conversations. If it helps, think of such talks as building language arts skills, which of course they also do.

Listening to Life Experiences

A teacher practicing the guidance approach recognizes that young children who are unhappy cannot easily express their anxieties in words (Graham, 2004). Unless teachers are able to show they care by listening to life experiences, children's pent up feelings tend to show as mistaken behaviors, sometimes serious. The coexisting environments of the child—the school, the home, the transition, and the neighborhood—can all be sources of childhood stress. In listening to children, the teacher must be attuned to problems emanating from each source.

Table 8–1 *Analysis: Listening Techniques That Build Relationships*
Attending. Rosalee sits on the floor next to Jacque to show her *interest* in having the conversation. Teachers need to show children they are listening in order for children to share. (Rosalee will figure out how to get back up later.)
Acknowledgment. Rosalee uses words to "play back" and enhance the actions and brief comments of Jacque. Acknowledgment tells children the teacher is really listening to them. (For less verbal children, acknowledging what they say and do really helps to keep talks going.)
Wait time. Rosalee attentively waits for Jacque to focus, think how to reply, put the reply into words, and speak the words. By doing so, she affirms the child's growing ability to communicate. *Wait time,* especially for some teachers, takes conscious effort. (Silently counting to 20 or 30 can help.)
Expansion. Rosalee rephrased Jacque's wording: "'ruck" as "dump truck" and "'struction place," as "construction zone." She modeled the conventional usage in a sentence without making a big deal of the corrections, which might cause the child to end the conversation. She is giving Jacque new, alternative terms that he can store away in his brain for future use (called *receptive language*).
Reflective listening. Rosalee is actively listening for Jacque's emotions as well as his thoughts. Using descriptive words, she reflects back his feelings, showing she understands and accepts him: "You really like to haul . . ." Reflective listening takes acknowledgment a step further, and is an affirming technique even with adults.
Open-ended question. Having established that they are in a conversation, Rosalee asks an open-minded question that extends Jacque's thinking and encourages further conversation. (Open-ended questions are important, but often work best *after* a conversation is going.)
I-message (or self-report). By disclosing her positive feelings to the child, Rosalee is showing that they are sharing a quality moment together. The underlying message to the child is "Teacher likes me." (Frequent I-messages put undue focus on the teacher. Use them selectively.)

Listening for School-Related Stress. In many children, the symptoms of school-related stress manifest themselves in feelings of ill-health (Novick, 1998). Symptoms range from the twice-a-year stomachache to actual ulcers, from occasional headaches to hypertension and depressive reactions. The causes of school anxiety can be related to specific situations, such as the morning bus ride or the afternoon "power test," or be more pervasive—a child's general feeling of being a failure or being disliked. At an interpersonal level, as Almeida (1995) suggests, the teacher who understands school-related stress through acknowledgment of their experience is alert to the individual support that children sometimes need.

Classroom Anecdote	*(From the journal of a student teacher.) We were getting the room ready for the morning when Raul walked into the room. He stood over by his cubby with his head down. Tami [the teacher] went over, knelt down beside him, and said, "It looks like you might be a little tired this morning." Raul shook his head no. She asked him if anything was wrong. He told her that someone on his bus hit him with a backpack and he felt really bad. Tami affirmed that wasn't a good way to start the day and asked if they could do something together. She suggested a book (The Grouchy Ladybug) and he agreed. They sat down on the beanbag chair and read. She encouraged him to say the words from the book with her. He smiled as he helped her read the book. Later that day the teacher talked with the bus driver about the incident.*

Listening for Stress Related to the Home and Neighborhood. From an early childhood perspective, several writers have discussed the increasing complexities of family life (Bullock, 1993; Furman, 1995; Rich, 1993; Sang, 1994). The rising numbers of dual-working-parent families, single-parent families, blended families, and families in various states of transition and crisis are by now well known. In previous times, grandparents, aunts, uncles, and other family members were available to lend support in times of need. Now, such relatives may not be available to aid the parent—or they may serve as custodial care givers *in place* of the parent. Some children experience the trauma of unsafe and violent conditions outside in their neighborhood, as well as within their home. Children can be *resilient,* but they need, at minimum, at least one significant adult who cares about them (Breslin, 2005). That caring adult sometimes is the teacher.

Classroom Anecdote	*(Student teacher observation.) Marsha was sitting at the breakfast table and tapped Lois [the teacher] on the arm. Lois turned to her and said, "Yes?"* *Marsha said, "My privates hurt." Lois asked her if she had to go potty. Marsha said, "No, they always hurt when Mommy gotta work." Lois thanked Marsha, but did not pursue the conversation any further at that point. Later, alone with Marsha, Lois talked with her and did a report on possible child abuse. I was glad Marsha said it to Lois and not to me. I'm glad Lois stopped the conversation at the table because all the other children were listening, and that she took Marsha aside later.*

The key to helping any child faced with difficult circumstances is to develop a trust relationship before a crisis arises. Marsha went to Lois because Lois was her dear teacher. Every school and center should have a well-understood working policy in regard to suspected abuse, because teachers are **mandated reporters**. The teacher in this classroom followed the program's established policy for reporting. Extreme family situations require a planned response by educators working together, sometimes including or requiring outside social service professionals. Teachers do not intervene by themselves in such situations, but work as part of the team (Seitz, 2008). The individual teacher plays an essential role, though, by maintaining the helping relationship—one that begins and ends with listening.

Various authors, mentioned in the following paragraphs, discuss the effects of unsafe home and neighborhood situations on children, and supportive steps teachers can take in the classroom. Bullock (1993) discusses factors that lead to children being lonely and rejected. She says that "observing is the key to detecting feelings of loneliness in children" (p. 56). Assisting children to express their feelings through open-ended activities and helping them to build social skills can make a lasting difference in their lives. Documentation of children's patterns of behavior, discussed with fellow staff, can assist in helping the child learn to cope (Seitz, 2008).

Furman (1995) suggests that stresses are unavoidable and may offer opportunities for education. He states that, in turning the challenge into an opportunity, teachers can help children deal with their feelings and develop cooperative working relations with family members.

Sang (1994) describes her mental health consultation role in a kindergarten class as the "worry teacher." She recounts how working with children who need help immediately relieves behavioral demands on the teachers, gives the children in need the opportunity to express and work through their feelings, and models for the teacher therapeutic teaching techniques. Today, the values of ongoing mental health consultation in a classroom cannot be underestimated.

Rich (1993) discusses how she worked with "Harry," who showed ongoing disruptive behavior in her kindergarten classroom. Rich was able to get a teaching team member to cover her class for the first ten minutes of each day, and spent the time "for more than a month" talking with Harry in a quiet corner of the hall. They sat in two chairs, and as time went on, Harry began "thinking of things that he wanted to talk about" (p. 52). As a result of this "talking time," the relationship grew, and Harry's impulsive talking and acting out in the class diminished. Rich concludes that "talking time" might not work for every child like Harry, but for him, "talking time was the simple, positive nudge into a calmer, more richly communicative life" (p. 52).

Following a similar strategy, Bowling and Rogers (2001) state that:

The most powerful way we have found to help children heal emotionally is to give them complete focused attention with no interruptions. This works especially well one-on-one. We call this special time and talk about when it will be and for how long.... If there is one thing we really want to share with children, it is this: It's OK to be angry. It's OK to be sad. It's OK to cry. You are loved and are lovable, no matter how you are feeling. (pp. 79–81)

Novick (1998) provides a structure for "fostering resiliency and emotional intelligence, by way of a *comfort corner.* The comfort corner is available to children who are referred for its use by staff and/or parents. Staffed by a child development associate, the comfort corner provides open-ended activities and one-on-one attention, whenever a child feels the need. Capitalizing on the research that for children to be resilient, they need a positive attachment with at least one person, time in the comfort corner affords this special relationship with the teacher (Breslin, 2005).

Listening Beyond the Behavior

The teacher cannot always rely on other adults or a scheduled time or place to give a child the support she needs. On occasion, the teacher must simply make the time—change focus from the program to the child. In the following anecdote, notice how Kaye, a Head Start teacher, really listened.

Classroom Anecdote	*Observation: I heard the words, "Shut up," and walked around the corner to the bathroom to find out what was happening.*

Shayna was sitting in the corner crying. I said, "Shayna, why are you crying?"

Shayna said, "Amanda and Christina said they aren't my friends anymore."

I asked her if she told them to shut up. Shayna said yes. I told her I was sorry that what they had said made her feel sad and angry, but we don't use those words in our center. (Amanda and Christina had been watching and listening to us talk.) I explained to Shayna that maybe next time she could tell the girls it made her sad to hear they didn't want to be her friends. I told Amanda and Christina that Shayna was feeling sad. They came over to Shayna and gave her a hug and said they were sorry.

A little later, Shayna walked over to the breakfast table. She started crying again. I asked, "Is something making you feel sad, Shayna?"

She said, "I miss my daddy." Her father was killed in a car accident a few months before.

I sat down on a chair, hugging and holding her. I said, "Shayna, my daddy died when I was a little girl and it made me very sad, too. I am so glad you told me why you were crying." We sat by each other and ate breakfast.

Shayna went to the housekeeping area for choice time. Later in the day she came up to me and said, "I'm over my daddy now."

I said, "Oh Shayna, it's okay to feel sad about missing your daddy. I still miss my dad. If you need a hug or want to talk, you come and tell me."

Reflection: This incident gave me the "chills." I felt sad for Shayna, but I also felt good that she was able to verbally express her feelings about her father's death. This experience reinforced the importance of listening to young children. As a teacher I need to take the time to listen and "open the door" for the opportunities to be a listener. Shayna had a need to talk about her father's death. Hopefully Shayna can talk more about her feelings, and she knows that I care about her.

Later I talked with Shayna's mother about the incident and Shayna's behavior at home. With Shayna's mother's approval, we asked our Head Start mental health counselor to observe and talk with Shayna the next time he came to our center. I also gave Shayna more personal attention and made other staff aware of the incident. The next day Shayna sat on my lap at the play dough table. We made cookies together.

By sharing her own personal experience, Kaye was able to help Shayna understand that grieving does not just end. With time it sometimes fades, but can last years or even a lifetime. Listening and giving credence to the grieving can assist children to understand and cope. The connection they are able to make with the teacher helps children feel that they have a place within the classroom community (Breslin, 2005). It starts with a teacher who decides to take the time and listen beyond the behavior.

Many teachers believe that consistent on-task behavior is a reasonable and normal classroom expectation, even in early childhood. Unfortunately, some children bring life experiences into the classroom that sometimes makes this expectation a denial of their personal truth. Small teacher-child disagreements can then become major crises. In the following anecdote, a student teacher (a graduate student) recognized what the teacher did not.

Classroom Anecdote	*Monday morning in a kindergarten classroom, the teacher has children working on their journals. The assigned topic is "What did you do over the weekend?" Raymond is staring at his journal and has not picked up his writing tool. The teacher comes over and asks about his weekend to help him narrow down his topic.*

> *Teacher:* So, Raymond, what did you do this weekend?
> *Raymond:* Nothin'.
> *Teacher:* Oh, I bet you can think of something. What did you do on Saturday?
> *Raymond:* I didn't do nothin'. Go away!
> *Teacher:* I just want to help you get started thinking of some ideas. Why don't you pick something to write with, that would be a good place to start.
> *Raymond:* Go away! I'm not doing my f***ing journal and you can't make me.

Raymond goes to another part of the room and gets under a table. The teacher tries to coax him out. Raymond runs out from the other side, goes into the hall, and climbs into his cubby. The teacher approaches him.

> *Teacher:* Raymond, what you said was inappropriate. You need to look at me when I am talking to you. Do you understand? (No response.) I am going to count to 5 and you will need to look at me or you will go to the principal's office until after recess. You don't want to miss recess do you? (No response.) 1...2...3...4...5. I see you have made your choice. You will follow me to the principal's office.

Raymond follows the teacher to the principal's office without looking up or saying a word. The teacher has me bring his lunch to him in the office. The teacher told me the principal spoke to Raymond about using inappropriate language and running away from a teacher. He was returned to class without the teacher speaking with him more about the incident. Later that day I was able to talk with Raymond as we built a Lego house. He told me his mom and dad had fought over the weekend, and his dad was arrested and put in a cop car, with Raymond watching.

> *Reflection:* Raymond walked into school that day with many issues to deal with and was not able or ready to write about them in a journal. Allowing Raymond time under the table to calm himself and then encouraging him to talk about what happened may have stopped Raymond from running from the room. His teacher could have guided him into sharing what made him angry and suggested other ways to express how he was feeling. Listening and guiding Raymond through his mistaken behavior would have helped him learn coping methods for very difficult personal issues. Instead, the teacher punished him for his feelings of loss and distrust of authority.

I spoke with Kim, the graduate student, after she submitted a paper based on this experience. Kim was glad that she was able to give some positive listening time to Raymond right after the incident. The teacher knew that Kim had a positive relationship with the boy and was probably glad as well. Student teachers and other support staff usually do not have the authority to directly address a lead teacher's actions. However, they often can give quiet support to children who have not been fully understood and are hurting. As the anecdote illustrated, teachers would do well to "read" children's feelings when they first enter the classroom, a priority this author suggests for all early childhood teachers.

Using Greetings to Read Children's Feelings

No question, the beginning of the day is a busy time. But if teachers can arrive early or otherwise prepare for the day ahead of time, they are able to listen to as well as greet their individual students. Self-selected activity until all children arrive aids in this effort. When the teacher is able to read children's emotions through an individual greeting, he may be able to reduce or avoid serious conflicts later on. Consider this "pro-action" an investment in a smoother-running day.

Classroom Anecdote	*In a second-grade class, the children each drew in their own way three faces—happy, sad, and angry—on large paper plates. With help, they labeled each face and attached dials to their "face plates." When children came in each morning, they set the dials according to their moods. The teacher and an assistant made a point of noticing each child's setting and attended to those children who might need an adult to listen. In a class meeting, the children talked about how sometimes they felt more than one mood. They decided they could put their dials in between faces on these days. (One said that between sad and angry, though, "was the worse test.")*

Classroom Anecdote	*When a first-grade teacher witnessed Jordan tear up his arithmetic paper and say, "I hate this damn stuff," he reacted with a friendly hand on the shoulder and some kind words. The teacher might have reacted differently except for a talk he had with Jordan earlier that morning:*
	"Hi, Jordan, you're not smiling today." When the boy looked down and shook his head, the teacher asked, "Something you'd like to talk about?"
	Jordan said no, then fighting back tears shared, "Last night a guy hit Bumpers with his truck. We thought he was gonna be okay, but we took him to the vet. The vet took X rays and said his whole back end was broken. We had to put him to sleep. That guy did it on purpose too."
	The teacher said, "Oh, Jordan, I'm so sorry. I know what Bumpers meant to you. Do you want to talk more about it?" Jordan said no, but the teacher knew that for this child it would be a long day.
	The following morning at class meeting Jordan shared about his dog. The other children listened carefully, and during the day some seemed to go out of their way to show Jordan they cared.

An apparent challenge to our schools is the pressure on personnel to be "social workers" as well as educators. Individual support for personal development has become a central part of the modern teacher's role (Loomis & Wagner, 2005). While the early childhood teacher is not licensed to be a psychologist

© Cengage Learning

The teacher uses a listening ear to assist children to work through anxieties, build social skills, and gain self-esteem.

or a social worker, every day he does perform some of these functions. In the presence of Level Three mistaken behaviors caused by stress within or without the school setting, the teacher collaborates with family members, colleagues, and other professionals to help the child solve the problem. Whether a comprehensive approach is needed or not, the teacher uses a listening ear to assist children to work through anxieties, build social skills, and gain self-esteem. Beginning when they arrive, the teacher makes time for listening to individual children each day. Who knows what he will learn!

Contact Talk

Contact talk is the practice of "quality time," adapted for the classroom. Teachers continually must battle the clock to make personal contacts. The point is that even a very short time matters to children; it tells them they are valued so much that their busy teacher finds time to talk with them.

On the surface, contact talk may sound similar to the tactic of "catch them being good," but the two are different. The "catch them" practice involves (an often superficial) one-way conversation with the teacher giving praise. Specific recognition of productive behavior (using encouragement) *is essential* with children, but it is not the main reason for contact talk.

With contact talk, the teacher has the motive of getting to know a child. The teacher initiates, or allows the child to initiate, a conversation. As the child defines the course of the conversation, he responds. For the time that the teacher can give, he is a good listener. Children are generally eager to have contact talks with adults. The teacher's role is pivotal in deciding that a contact talk will happen. He does so by putting aside other work, moving to the child's level, and conversing openly with the child.

Examples of contact talks were given in the previous section. At the preschool level, Rosalee shared quality time with truck-loading Jacque, and Kaye shared in Shayna's grief over the loss of her dad. At the primary level the teacher gave Jordan permission to express his feelings about his dog. Contact talks do not have to be long. They do not even have to be serious nature in nature, but they do need to happen with each child in the class on a regular basis.

Classroom Anecdote	*The sun was shining warmly, and the children could play inside or out until everyone arrived. Mavis bounded in the door of Head Start, ran a circle around the teacher, and announced, "Me gots new shoes, Teacher!"*
	Looking down at Mavis' pulled-up pants, the teacher exclaimed, "Mavis, those are sure some colorful sneakers."
	Indignant, Mavis replied, "Not sneakers. 'Letic shoes!" Grinning broadly, the teacher corrected herself, "I'll bet you can sure run fast in those athletic shoes." With a nod over her shoulder, Mavis skipped out the door to the playground.

© Cengage Learning

The teacher decides that a contact talk will happen by putting aside other work, moving to the child's level, and conversing openly.

Because time is precious during the day, the teacher must look for opportunities for contact talks to occur. Some likely moments in the daily program include:

▶ before other children arrive

▶ during a choice time

▶ during unstructured active playtimes (inside or out)

▶ at lunch

▶ during a break in the day

▶ after a self-directing activity has begun

▶ after school.

Contact Talks at the Preschool Level

The following anecdotes, from the journals of student teachers, illustrate contact talks at lunch and during choice time in two separate Head Start centers. Notice that each contact talk took only a minute or two.

Classroom Anecdote	*(Lunchtime) Karly and I were eating at the lunch table. Some children at the table were talking about what they had done on Easter, where they had gone, and so on. Karly quietly said, "I didn't see my daddy at Easter."* *I said, "Oh?"* *She then said, "He isn't good with kids. He doesn't like them either. My grandma and grandpa don't like kids either."* *I said, "I'm sorry, Karly. I'll bet you have other grown-ups who like kids."* *She smiled and said, "Yes, I do! My other grandma and grandpa love me. And Uncle Tim and Aunt Judy like to play with me. And my mom really loves me."* *I said, "It's okay to still miss your dad, but you are a very lucky girl to have so many people who love and care for you." She nodded seriously, and that ended the conversation.*

Classroom Anecdote	*Matthew and I were about to read a book when our contact talk began:* *Matt: I know where paper comes from.* *Chloe: You do? Where?* *Matt: From trees!* *Chloe: You are right. Do you know how they get paper from trees?* *Matt: Yep! It's inside.* *Chloe: So, if I go out to a tree out there and peel off the bark, there will be a piece of white paper inside?* *Matt: Yep! (Holding his hands about one foot apart.) But you gotta go in about this far.* *Chloe: Oh! So let me see if I got this right. If I go peel bark off a tree and go in about this far, there will be a bunch of white paper inside?* *(continued)*

<table>
<tr><td>Classroom
Anecdote</td><td>Matt: Yeah! But you gotta go way to the top! That's a very dangerous job, you know.
Chloe: I bet it is. Well, what about this purple paper? Where does purple paper come
          from?
Matt: Oh, that comes from apple trees!
Chloe: What about red paper?
Matt: Lava. That comes from lava.

    A volcano with lava was on the book cover, along with a brontosaurus. Our conversation
faded here and we read the book.</td></tr>
</table>

A traditional concern of teachers is passing incorrect information on to students. When children seem to have their facts mixed up, we often feel the need to correct. Important to remember, though, is that through conversation young children get a chance not only to express ideas, but even more important, to get feedback from the adult about the worthiness of their conversing. We need to remember that with development, what seems true to a child today will not seem true next year. In the encouraging classroom, our goal in the contact talks we have with children is neither to impart truth nor to correct what is "made up." Our goal is to encourage confidence and competence in conversation as a lifelong means we humans have for acquiring, sharing, and evaluating information.

To state this another way, we are less concerned about the correctness of the information, than with children's ability to improve on their own sense of correctness as their brains develop and they grow and learn over time. Through acknowledgment of the current insights of children, even if their information base is limited, children gain the confidence to continue in the lifelong process of making meaning.

The Challenge of Finding the Time. The advantage in staffing arrangements of preschools is that contact talks can occur easily. In the supportive prekindergarten classroom, a reasonable goal is *at least* one contact talk with each child every day. Teachers of preschoolers can hardly escape contact talks, and of course shouldn't. Likewise, family child care providers, with their small group numbers, can figure out how to have daily contact talks with each child, sometimes even while daily tasks are getting done. (One caregiver makes a point of having contact talks with infants while changing diapers. The eye contact, facial expressions and vocalizations made the talks two-way.)

Contact Talks in the Primary Grades

Because of typical staff-to-child ratios in the primary grades, teachers must work to find time for contact talks. A system that allows every child to be "contacted" regularly is important. Here is where use of the teaching team can help. If the teacher can bring other adults into the classroom, more contact talks can occur. With only one adult in the room, a teacher can still find time for several/or a few

© Cengage Learning

The value of contact talk is that as teachers and children get to know each other, trust builds, and mistaken behavior lessens.

conversations a day—better than none at all. Elementary teachers who increase the number of contact talks tend to be rewarded.

Classroom Anecdote	*I was reading to my group of first and second graders when one of the boys, I'll call him Pedro, interrupted me. Pedro suddenly said, "My grandma died, will she be up in heaven?"*
	I replied, "Of course she will, Pedro."

I was reading to my group of first and second graders when one of the boys, I'll call him Pedro, interrupted me. Pedro suddenly said, "My grandma died, will she be up in heaven?"

I replied, "Of course she will, Pedro."

Pedro went on, "I wasn't in school because I was at her funeral."

I made a decision to continue the conversation. "Was it sad?"

Pedro said, "Yes, it was sad, but you know what? They said that now my grandma can rest and be comfortable. When she was alive, she just laid in bed always in pain. She cried a lot, and she didn't even know who I was. But she looked so young and happy at the funeral. She didn't even look the way she did when she died. She looked all old and wrinkled when she was alive."

When Pedro was through, I went on to finish the book. After the book, more of the children had experiences to tell the rest of us about relatives, cats, and dogs that have died. These children wanted to say something because Pedro's sharing got them thinking about similar experiences. (Gartrell, 2000, pp. 138–139)

The value of contact talks is that as teachers and children get to know each other, trust builds, and the need for mistaken behavior lessens (Ostrosky & Jung,

2003). Teachers sometimes tend to talk more with children who are talkative and from backgrounds similar to their own. A check-off chart with each child's name may seem mechanical, but it ensures that all children (and the teacher) receive the benefits of contact talks.

Classroom Anecdote	*For a workshop assignment, Gayle, a kindergarten teacher, made a chart of the children's names set against a four-week calendar. Daily, the teacher made a point of having two-minute personal conversations with at least five children and noted these conversations on the chart. Gayle was able to have at least one contact talk with each child every week—and with most children more than one.*
	After the month, Gayle decided to continue the practice. The teacher discovered she was becoming more familiar with the children, especially those who were less outgoing. She found she was not only getting to know the children better, but they were also getting to know her. (They started asking about her dog and cat and how her toddler was doing.) Gayle felt there was a change of atmosphere in the classroom.

The Compliment Sandwich

At a workshop, Dr. Julie Jochum came across the idea of the compliment sandwich. Jochum developed the concept as a feedback technique for teacher education majors when journaling with children (Jochum, 1991). As adapted from Jochum's usage, the spoken or written compliment sandwich provides a focused way of giving encouragement. The technique is useful with children or adults for preventing and resolving problems. (The technique even works with family members, though sometimes a "triple-decker" is needed.)

The compliment sandwich has these parts: at least *one* statement of encouragement; *one* suggestion, recommendation, request, or question; and a second compliment or two. The encouragements recognize effort, progress, or interim achievement. (They are the pieces of "bread.") The peanut butter in the middle guides the child toward further progress. The ratio is important as some research has shown that two positives per negative is the barest minimum for a child to feel supported (Kirkhart & Kirkhart, 1967). In other words, three pieces of bread ("triple-decker encouragement") is desirable. If the teacher considers adding a second request or recommendation, she makes a new sandwich.

What do compliment sandwiches sound like? The reader can tell very quickly what is and is not a compliment sandwich. Let us "overhear" two second-grade teachers, one during language arts, the other during math time.

Language arts: You are being careless again. Look at how those sentences wander over the page. You forgot your period. This is messy work. You will need to do it again.

Math: You have seven of the problems exactly right. This assignment is hard, and you are really staying with it. Use your counters again and see if you can get different answers for the other three. You can do it.

The first teacher probably was *not* causing this student to enjoy writing. On the other hand, by using the compliment sandwich—as opposed to "character assassination"—the second teacher was probably was preventing math anxiety. The compliment sandwich is straightforward—for whatever change the teacher requests, he acknowledges two or more indicators of progress or effort, at least one before and at least one after. The math teacher's use of the technique was in an academic situation. The compliment sandwich also applies in other classroom circumstances. Table 8–2 gives examples of sandwiches, first with a group and then with an individual child, at the preprimary and primary levels:

Table 8–2 *Compliment Sandwiches at Preprimary and Primary Levels*

Preprimary

Group: Holy Hippopotamus! You have put away all the blocks and the books. We just have the table toys to finish and then we can go outside. You guys are going to be out there in no time!

Individual: Jamie, you have your coat hung up, your mittens in your sleeves, and your boots off; just need to wash your hands and you are ready for snack. You sure know how to stow your gear.

Primary

Group: Class, you read lots of books in the library today, and you sat very quietly for the story. Coming back through the hall, though, was a little noisy. Who has ideas for how to make walking back quieter next time because I know you can do it?

Individual: Sondra, you stayed in your seat, worked really hard, and didn't have any problems with your neighbors. That's real progress! Now, how can you remind yourself to use that "inside voice"? I am so happy you had really smooth morning.

The encouragement that is a part of the compliment sandwich reassures children that the teacher is on their side. (It is always easier to improve when the coach is pulling for you.) With serious mistaken behavior, the compliment sandwich also helps to remind the *teacher* of this fact. With family members, the compliment sandwich helps establish a spirit of cooperation that the family member and teacher are working together for the benefit of the child. The technique is an important one, an essential ingredient of leadership communication with children and adults in the encouraging classroom.

Friendly Humor

Friendly humor affirms positive relations with children and supports a friendly atmosphere in the classroom. An attraction of teaching young children is the delightful unpredictability in their responses. Teachers who find themselves refreshed by the reactions of young learners know why they are working at this age level. In light of the challenges that classroom teachers face every day, the ability to find humor in situations adds to the positives of the profession.

Classroom Anecdote	A student kept a journal of her practicum experiences throughout her teacher education program. A few of the enjoyable experiences she recorded:
	When I was helping a boy in kindergarten fold his paper in half, Cody said, "I can't fold very good because I'm from Tenstrike, and people in Tenstrike don't know how to fold."
	While I was helping a four-year-old button her coat, Ashley said, "My grandpa can't snap the buttons very good because his hands are old."
	During a practicum at St. Philip's Preschool, while five of us education majors were doing a theme project with the children, the teacher asked the three- to five-year-olds if they could do anything to help us. One little boy piped up and asked, "Should we pray?" We smiled at each other because it wasn't such a bad idea.
	At a day care center, a little girl arrived late, just in time to pass the "Easter Bunny" on the sidewalk. The Bunny, who had just visited our center, was in a hurry to get to his next visit. The little girl watched wide-eyed as the Bunny got in his car and drove off. She walked into the center shaking her head and muttering, "I didn't know the Easter Bunny could drive a car!"

If they look for it, teachers find humor in many situations. One such occasion is when teachers hear their own words echoed by children.

Classroom Anecdote	A teacher was at first amazed, then amused when a four-year-old made the following request: "I am having a difficult morning, so I need kindness." The teacher remembered making a similar comment in jest earlier in the week.

© Cengage Learning

The ability to find humor in situations adds much joy for a teacher.

The fact that children interpret words quite literally can be a source of enjoyment for adults and children alike.

Classroom Anecdote	*It began raining heavily outside the windows of a kindergarten class. The teacher exclaimed, "Why, it's raining cats and dogs out there."* *The children looked out of the windows intently. Then one child turned to the teacher and said with a smile, "Teacher, it's raining elephants even."*

A classroom atmosphere in which humorous moments are enjoyed by all is a positive atmosphere. Teachers who see humor even in trying moments can defuse problems effectively. Curwin and Mendler suggest the use of mildly self-effacing humor as a remedy for power struggles (1988). This use of humor can be challenging for a teacher, but it has its rewards.

Classroom Anecdote	*On a Monday morning in front of the class, a fearless third grader said to his male teacher, "Boy, Mr. D., you sure are hairy."* *The teacher, who had forgotten to shave, said, "You're right, Willie. I couldn't find my razor today, so I hit my whiskers in with a hammer and bit them off inside. Guess I missed some." The class, including Willie, shook their heads and laughed. The moment was quickly forgotten as Mr. D. started a project.*

Finally, we teachers are often amused, sometimes delighted, by the creative imagination any child might show at any time in an encouraging classroom.

Classroom Anecdote	*The theme this week in our school-age care classroom was "animals in our backyards." As part of the theme, we asked the children who came to the dramatic-play center to dress up like animals and we would guess which ones they were. Shasta, a quiet and studious first grader, found an old brown coat and a floppy brown hat. She also put on some enormous sunglasses. After no one guessed what animal she was, I asked Shasta if she would tell us. With a big grin she said, "Sam, don't you know? I am an owl out in the daytime!" (Another child rolled into a ball. When no one could guess what Louis was, he declared, "I am a rabbit dropping.")*

Humor helps in sustaining positive teacher-child relations. However, humor can also be used against children. Dr. John Halcrow (1988), a professor emeritus in human relations, says this about the use of humor:

We need humor in the classroom but let's be careful about it. Humor can be a two-edged sword. Some rules for humor: Never use it as a weapon, nor to chastise or correct. Never make a student the butt of a joke, and remember not to take yourself too seriously.

We need fun, hope, even frivolity in the classroom. If we put too much focus on the mechanics of what we're teaching, we kill the joy. Work students hard, then let them play with what they've learned. Let them talk to each other, try out their ideas and correct their own errors [and laugh] along the way. (p. 1)

A sense of humor in teachers is much appreciated by learners of all ages. Humor lightens the teaching role because (at least for that moment) it makes it fun (Gartrell, 2006). After I spoke at a conference for Northern Michigan University, teacher Kevin Helgrin e-mailed me:

> *Today after the children gave the babies a bath at the sensory table, I began to take the heads off so that they wouldn't get moldy on the inside. As I was doing that, one of the little girls said, "Mr. Kevin what are you doing?"*
>
> *I said, "I'm taking the babies' heads off so they can dry."*
>
> *She looked at me, shook her head, and said, "Mr. Kevin, that is scusting."*

Kevin, like early childhood teachers everywhere, wouldn't laugh out loud at a remark like this, but probably would grin and agree.

Friendly Touch

Along with humor, a vital practice that conveys warmth in relations is the use of **friendly touch**. Unfortunately, the use of warm physical contact (hugs, sitting on laps, and friendly touches) by teachers, accepted in times past, has become controversial today (Carlson, 2006). Now in some school districts, teachers ask permission of a child before giving a pat on a shoulder or a hug. In many situations, teachers must communicate with administrators and family members before doing what in prior times came so naturally. Every teacher must make personal decisions regarding touch. This section supports the use of friendly physical contact within the guidelines of reasonable policy. To most early childhood teachers, the idea of teaching *without* touch is itself unreasonable.

Classroom Anecdote	*We were just sitting down for circle time when another boy and Erin were trying to take the same place around the circle; there was pushing, something that happens with these two a lot.*
	Erin began to cry, as he was getting frustrated and having trouble expressing his feelings with words. I said, "Erin, would you like to sit on my lap?"
	"Nooo," he wailed, going over and standing in the corner. He didn't budge. I got up and walked over to him, touched him gently on the shoulders, and gave him a tiny squeeze. "Erin, when you calm your body, would you like to come sit on my lap?" I asked again. He nodded and came with me.
	Once circle time got started, he was responding to the teacher's questions from the book she was reading, and each time he did, I "responded" to him by lightly tapping a beat on his leg. I felt like this kind of "affirmed" to him that I was there, and was rooting for him.
	At the same time, one of the other teachers had Evie trying to sit on her lap. Yet, the teacher was trying to get another child to sit on her lap because he had just had a conflict. Evie walked over and sat by me. She looked hurt, so I started rubbing her shoulder and she leaned into my shoulder and stayed there for the rest of circle time along with Erin.

A practice that conveys warmth in relations is the use of touch.

Curwin and Mendler (1988) recommend the use of hugs and touching in communicating with children. They decry the fallacy of prohibition against touch because of sexual misunderstanding, but they seem to assume that this proscription pertains only to teachers of older students (p. 16). Yet, Hendrick (2001) points out that sensationalized court cases have made early childhood teachers as well "uneasy about touching or cuddling youngsters lest they, too, be accused" (p. 107). Nelson (2002) in his study of male teachers in early childhood education stresses that men as well as women still need to use friendly touch. Administrators and colleagues need to support the use of touch as a vital teaching technique for men and women early childhood teachers.

Given the value of nurturing touches for children, physical closeness should not be deleted from the teacher's repertoire (Carlson, 2006). Rather, as Hendrick (2001) points out, educators need to maintain written policies that allow classroom visitation by family members, require clear understanding among all staff regarding physical closeness, and conduct criminal background checks for prospective employees. Rationale for the guideline "friendly touches only" needs to be fully communicated to children, family members, and staff. Such practices are becoming necessary for the continuation of this important teaching technique as a legitimate expression of human caring.

Classroom Anecdote	*A teacher worked to develop a sense of belonging with her class. In her own words, she was "a hugger," and talked with a new principal early in the year about his policy regarding physical closeness. The principal commented that his policy was, "Friendly physical contact is acceptable in the public confines of the classroom with the written permission of the parents and the verbal permission of the child." Bothered but undeterred by the policy, the teacher explained the situation to parents at the September orientation meeting. Almost all the parents signed the written permission slips allowing the teacher to use "friendly touches, hugs, and sitting on my lap."*
	With her kindergartners, the teacher held a class meeting. The class decided that at arrivals and departures if children wanted a hug, they would give two thumbs up; if they wanted a friendly wave or comment only, they would put up one thumb. The teacher also made sure that they knew they could ask for a hug during other times of day, if they needed to.
	Stationing herself by the door each morning, she greeted each child with a one thumb or two thumb hello. She noticed that some children were "everyday huggers," and some children wanted a hug seldom or once in a while. All the children, though, responded warmly to her daily greeting. The teacher believed that putting her preparations aside for the greetings helped the day go better.
	The teacher also gave a one- or two-thumb farewell at the end of the day. She noticed that more children elected a hug at the end of the day than at the beginning. She talked with the two children whose parents had not signed the slips, and gave these children special smiles and verbal comments. Though she saw the policy as a bother, she concluded that it was worth it to make her classroom a friendly place.

Physical closeness accomplishes what words cannot in forming healthy attachments with children (Carlson, 2006). Boys as well as girls have a high need for friendly touch (King, 2003). As Hendrick (2001) points out, children "require the reassurance and comfort of being patted, rocked, held, and hugged from time to time" (p. 107). Hendrick states:

> *Research as well as experience supports the value of close physical contact. Montagu (1986) has reviewed numerous studies illustrating the beneficial effect of being touched and the relationship of tactile experience to healthy physical and emotional development. Investigations documenting the link between touching and the development of attachment confirm those findings. (p. 107)*

Brain research suggested by Wolfe and Brandt (1998), Diamond and Hopson (1998), and LeDoux (1996) provides the psychological link to explain the beneficial nature of friendly touch. Tactile calming promotes helpful hormone secretion and harmonious brain functioning, which enables children to feel acceptance and trust in the encouraging classroom. Considering the benefits of touch for children, teachers should never dismiss this technique. They should use touch carefully but fully and with open communication to the full extent that program policies allow.

Be There for the Children, Be There for Yourself

Gruenberg (1998) mentions that "stress is widely acknowledged to be a problem of our times and early childhood caregiving, while joyful and satisfying is one of the most stressful types of work" (p. 39). To open yourself to the experiences and needs of children (required for leadership communication) the teacher must be attuned to his own needs and circumstances. Gruenberg mentions that a common pattern among early childhood professionals is **overfunctioning**: feeling one must be all things to all people. She comments that it is important to be cognizant about one's situation and to recognize that "a disproportionate workload does not have to occur."

Honestly confronting within oneself the cause of the stress is a first step to making life more manageable. Gruenberg (1998) explains that without this reflection, the symptoms of stress gradually overtake us and show in one or more reaction pattern such as:

- Body: headaches, body aches, fatigue, illness, weight gain or loss, sleeping problems
- Emotions: anger, frustration, fear, anxiety, depression, overreaction
- Actions/behavior: withdrawal, sudden aggression, impulsivity, feeling victimized, casting blame, stigmatizing others
- Mind: disorganization, distraction, rigid thought patterns, compulsiveness, need to control

While anyone can have a day or two with these symptoms, a pattern over time indicates a problem that the teacher needs to address. The adult may turn to family and friends, fellow staff, counselors, and other helping professionals to understand and address the source(s) of the stress. Either with help or on one's own, Gruenberg (1998) suggests options for reducing stress that include purposeful behaviors such as:

- exercising, relaxing strategies
- setting reasonable limits
- taking a break
- practicing flexibility
- prioritizing tasks
- breaking big tasks down into little ones
- letting oneself be silly
- actively collaborating/working with/playing with others
- venting to trusted others
- creatively solving problems

Gruenberg (1998) maintains that regular practice of these actions really helps and often can be done in an enjoyable way. For teachers who can accept the challenge, reducing sources of stress for the classroom community lessens stress for the teacher. Fewer conflicts and conflicts of reduced intensity heighten satisfaction levels for children and adults alike. Consider the suggestions outlined in Table 8–3.

Table 8–3 *Suggestions for Reducing Stress in the Classroom Community*

1. Recognize that the natural state of young bodies is to be in motion. Make the day mostly active. Use intentional quiet periods to recharge bodies and minds and to orient community members to additional activity to come.

2. Recognize that young children must learn to move. Design the environment and plan the program to include movement in teaching-learning activities. Use movement to make learning fun. Building active life and learning styles trumps showy academic performance.

3. Participate with the children in physical activity. See the day as your way to stay in shape.

4. Realize that young children and large groups are not a natural match. Instead, maximize small, family group activities that have assigned primary caregivers. Relationships then trump teacher-child conflicts and build lasting social–emotional skills. Use your smarts to group certain children with certain adults.

5. Recognize that you yourself are the leader in charge. A kindergarten teacher colleague lets the children know that there is only one queen in the classroom, her. But as queen (or king) she can be and is benevolent. (The children work very hard for their dear teacher.)

6. Reach out to the other adults in your classroom community. Figure out how to plan, teach, and evaluate cooperatively, as a team. Look for commonalities of interest in and out of the work setting. Enjoy teaching in a team. Enjoy the children together.

As Gruenberg (1998) states, a personal support system is vital in the positive management of stress:

> *Belief in one's own ability to cope with the situation makes all the difference in taking charge and making healthy choices. . . . Whatever we do to support our own health contributes to the well-being of our relationships, including our relation-ships with children, parents, and colleagues in our early childhood communities. (pp. 41–42)*

To be healthy, teachers need support systems, both on the job and in personal life.

Leadership Communication in the Parent-Teacher Conference

Chapter Seven emphasized five basic teacher-parent communication techniques useful in creating positive relationships: notes home, telephone calls, electronic communication, parent meetings, and parent-teacher conferences. Chapter Eight focuses specifically on the parent-teacher conference and what Rosenthal and Sawyers (1996) argue is the overriding goal of conferences, the accomplishment of *joining,* or helping parents understand that the teacher accepts them and wants to work with them on behalf of the child.

The Setting

The traditional setting for the conference is the classroom, though sometimes family members feel more comfortable in a setting outside the school—the home, a community center, a restaurant. (One of my favorite anecdotes is of the teacher who, after several attempts to reach a single mom, finally located her at a lounge where she worked as a cocktail waitress. The two had a conference in a booth during the mom's coffee break. This parent later became a classroom volunteer.) The teacher needs to give consideration to the site of the conference and its likely meaning for family members.

Classroom Illustration	*In her second year of teaching first grade, a teacher created a "parent corner" in her class-room by placing a cardboard divider, decorated by the children, between her desk and a corner of the room. The corner was small, but it had enough room to squeeze in two chairs, a small table and coffee pot, a bulletin board, a fledgling resource library, and a coat hook with a plastic carton below where parents could stow their belongings. After getting the idea from a parent volunteer, the teacher decided to have her conferences in the parent corner. She noticed that the parents felt quite comfortable having conferences in "their" area. Unlike the previous year, many of the conferences proved downright fun, and holding the conferences in the corner seemed to increase the number of parents who came into the classroom to volunteer. Two other teachers set up parent corners the next year and con-ducted their conferences in them.*

A main purpose of the conference is to help family members understand that the teacher accepts them and wants to work with them on behalf of the child.

Wherever the setting for the conference, Rosenthal and Sawyers (1996) offer a list of suggestions important for the process of building partnerships with families:

1. Speak the language of the family; use their words and definitions. If the family's home language is not English, consider using an interpreter.

2. Work to understand the family's rules, principles, and beliefs.

3. Except with very well educated parents, keep jargon to a minimum—not "He is making impressive cognitive gains," but "He is learning a lot."

4. Monitor your own level of discomfort; do you resort to becoming the "expert" when you become uncomfortable?

5. Try to build a collaborative, rather than an adversarial, system.

6. Ask the family to be partners—notice behaviors, suggest solutions, and contribute ideas.

7. Recognize signs of a power struggle and reinforce you are on the same team (p. 197).

Listening to Parents

As emphasized throughout the chapter, an essential part of communication is listening. Studer points out four reasons for why teachers may not listen to family members as effectively as they might (1993).

First, *the teacher may have negative attitudes about the parent. For instance, if the teacher believes that parents do not care about their child's education, he may not even attempt communication intended to build partnerships.*

Second, *when persons such as teachers are in "power" positions during conversations, they tend to think ahead to the next point they want to make. Instead, the teacher needs to listen to what the other is saying.*

Third, *in a similar fashion, the teacher may finish the comments of parents, or other-wise "politely" interrupt, rather than give the respect of fully listening.*

Fourth, *prejudging a person and anticipating what that person is going to say may keep the teacher from listening openly. (p. 74)*

Real listening for Studer involves both body placement and the honest effort to understand. The teacher sits side by side with the parent or in chairs across from one another; faces and even leans toward the parent in an open posture; and when culturally appropriate, makes eye contact and uses light touch.

While listening, the teacher respectfully acknowledges what the parent says, avoids giving quick advice, and involves the parent as a full partner in the discussion. Notice the difference in the following dramatized reactions of two teachers when Mrs. Dilworth comments to "the teacher" that her son, Cory, has complained about two children picking on him.

Classroom Illustration	Teacher One *sits behind a desk with arms folded, leans away, and looks out the window. Interrupts when he has heard "enough." Speaks in a "lecture" voice: "You know, Mrs. Dilworth, when I was a kid, I had that problem and what I did was join a karate club. Get Cory enrolled in a karate club, Mrs. Dilworth. Your kid has to learn to take care of himself."* Teacher Two *sits next to Mrs. Dilworth, faces her, and lets her fully express what is on her mind. He reflects back what he has heard, how Mrs. Dilworth must be feeling, and what she probably would like to see happen. "Cory has shared that two boys in the class have been picking on him? You must be bothered by that idea, and you'd like this problem addressed. Tell me more about what Cory has said, and then we'll figure out what we can do about this problem."*

In the first scenario, a parent would probably conclude she wasn't going to get anywhere, thank the teacher for the time (maybe), and leave still feeling upset. In the second, the teacher has listened to what the parent has said and joined with the parent as a team. By doing so, he has improved the chances that a positive action will result from the conference and the problem can be resolved. The parent is likely to feel much more satisfied.

One reaction by teachers to situations like the one in the illustration is defensive: "Doesn't happen in my classroom." These thoughts, the result of feeling threatened, may not be directly expressed, but they come through indirectly in defensive communication styles. By staying calm and remembering that the parent, child, and teacher are all on the same team, the teacher is in a better position to work with the parent and prevent problems in parent-teacher relations (Gestwicki, 2007). Studer (1993) concludes her article in this way:

> *Teachers must remember that parents have special needs and special concerns. Conferences need to be approached with an attitude of sharing and learning, as well as a willingness to consider parents' observations. Such a cooperative attitude between home and school can be paramount to a child's achievement. (p. 76)*

The matter is not as simple as starting and ending conference with positive notes about the child. But this "extended" compliment sandwich cannot hurt. Keeping a positive attitude, even when families are socially, religiously, and culturally quite different than the teacher, will result in parents who are not adversaries but allies, because the conference has enabled *joining* (team building) to occur.

Summary

1. How do teachers' listening skills build relationships?

With the complexities of modern life, young children sometimes come into classrooms feeling stress. These feelings may be school related or related to experiences in the home or neighborhood. Unless these children are able to get assistance with their unmet needs, they will show mistaken behavior, sometimes serious. To assist with relationship building and guiding children in social-emotional development, the teacher uses listening techniques to help them make sense of life experiences. In many cases by listening and helping children to cope with stresses, the teacher builds relationships that bolster self-esteem, boost feelings of safety and belonging, and promote healing and the development of life skills.

2. How do contact talks encourage young learners?

Contact talk is the concept of quality time adapted to the classroom. The purpose of contact talks is *not* to "catch the student being good." Rather, contact talks are for the purpose of the teacher and the child getting to know each other. Contact talks need not be long nor especially serious, but the teacher needs to find the time and make sure that they happen regularly. In the process of the contact talk, the teacher learns more about the child and how to work with the child more effectively. The child learns that the teacher cares and that the classroom is an encouraging place to be.

3. What is a compliment sandwich and how does it work?

The compliment sandwich allows a teacher to make a request for change or further progress while conveying to the child that he is on the child's side. By coupling the request with at least two or (even better) more statements of encouragement the teacher communicates that he is working with and not against the child. When a teacher is bothered by a child's behavior, the compliment sandwich assists the teacher to phrase the concern positively. Adults as well as children respond more readily to requests for change when the listener concludes that both individuals are on the same side. For this reason, the compliment sandwich has uses with colleagues and parents as well as with children.

4. Why is friendly humor an important guidance strategy?

One important benefit of being a teacher of young children is the delightful things that they say and do. For children and teachers alike, friendly humor eases tense situations and makes being in the classroom more enjoyable. When laughter is not used against children but with them to create a feeling of community, humor becomes an important guidance strategy. Learners of all ages appreciate teachers who use friendly humor. The ability to enjoy the freshness and unpredictability of children adds much to the profession.

5. Is friendly touch still a viable guidance technique?

Some educators reject using touch because they fear the innuendo of sexual abuse. Such attitudes are unfortunate. Young children experience the world through touch even more than other senses, and brain development is fundamentally enhanced by frequent friendly touch. For younger children and older ones alike, appropriate touch by men and women teachers is fundamentally reassuring. Touch tells children in ways that words cannot that the teacher cares. Programs need to be clear about their guidelines for touch and when and what kind of touch is appropriate; and they need to establish these guidelines with families. Within the accepted guidelines, touch tells children that they are cared for, they are worthy individuals, and they belong.

6. How can teachers care for themselves so they can care for the children?

Stress is an unavoidable part of the early childhood teacher's life. Unless teachers are active in confronting sources of stress, over time they are likely to experience its effects in impaired mental and physical health. Having a support system is important, as is following through on strategies that may include counseling, exercising, setting personal limits, letting oneself be silly, bonding more closely with others, and creatively addressing problems. A challenge for teachers is to recognize that when they lower stress levels for the children in their groups, they reduce stress for themselves. When we keep ourselves healthy, we can be there effectively for the children. Personal and professional support systems are vital in this effort.

7. How do teachers use leadership communication in the parent-teacher conference?

The main purpose of communicating with parents is *joining*, or helping parents understand that you are working with them on behalf of the child. A main vehicle in building partnerships is the parent-teacher conference. The teacher endeavors to make the conference setting comfortable for the parent. In the conference, the teacher must be sensitive to any prejudices toward the family and listen openly without giving quick advice. Listening to parents is crucial in the communication process of the conference. To listen effectively, the teacher takes an open body position and uses eye contact and light touch as culturally appropriate. In a supportive tone, the teacher reflects on what the parent says and states what he thinks the parent is getting at. With personal affirmation, and by making sure conferences start and end positively, the parent become more willing to work with the teacher and share in resolution of the issues at hand.

FOLLOW-UP ACTIVITIES

Note: *An element of being a professional teacher is to respect the children, parents, and educators you are working with by maintaining confidentiality, that is, keeping identities private. In completing follow-up activities, please respect the privacy of all concerned.*

Discussion Activity

The discussion activity encourages students to interrelate their own thoughts and experiences with specific ideas from the chapter.

Think about a time when a child needed to say something to you and you listened. Compare the dynamics of this experience with what the chapter says about listening skills and contact talks. What did you learn about working with this child, and young children in general, by making the decision to listen?

Application Activities

Application activities allow students to interrelate material from the text with real-life situations. The observations imply access to practicum experiences; the interviews, access to teachers or parents. To inter-relate theory and experience, students compare or contrast observations and interviews with referenced ideas from the chapter.

1. Listening Techniques.

   a. Observe an adult in the classroom who is sympathetically listening to a nonacademic experience a child is sharing. What do you notice about how the adult is using listening techniques? What seems to be the child's demeanor at the start of the conversation, at the end? Relate your findings to specific listening techniques mentioned in the chapter.

   b. Interview a teacher about the priority he gives to listening to individual children's personal experiences. Ask the teacher if he can remember an experience when he helped a child by listening. How does the teacher cope with the "time problem" that listening to individual children entails? Compare your findings to ideas from the text.

2. Contact talks.

   a. Observe a teacher having what appears to be a contact talk with a child. What did the teacher do to be available for the talk? Who is doing more talking? What does the child's demeanor seem to be before and after the talk? How is what you observe similar to or different from what the text says about contact talks?

   b. Interview a teacher about contact talks. Explain the term if necessary. What does the teacher believe the place of contact talks should be in the daily program? How and when does the teacher find time for contact talks? How does the teacher's position agree or disagree with the discussion of contact talks in the text?

3. The compliment sandwich.

   a. Observe a teacher talking with a child about a behavior that the teacher would like the child to improve. Watch for whether the teacher used a compliment sandwich? Why or why not? Compare your findings to ideas from the text.

   b. Interview a teacher about the compliment sandwich. Explain the term if necessary. What value does the teacher see in using compliment sandwiches? What importance does the teacher give to the positive feedback part of the "sandwich"? How do the teacher's ideas compare with the text?

4. Friendly humor.

   a. Observe an instance of humor used by a child in a classroom. How did the other children respond? The teacher respond? Observe a second instance of humor, this time used by the teacher. How did the child or children respond? Comparing your observations to the text, what is similar and different from what the book says about friendly humor ? What have you learned about humor in the classroom?

   b. Interview a teacher whom you believe to have a friendly sense of humor. What is important to the teacher about using humor in the classroom? Ask for an example or two of events that the teacher found humorous. Compare what the teacher says about humor with text ideas.

5. Friendly touch.

   a. Observe two instances when a teacher used touch with children in the classroom. What was the situation? What seemed to be the effect on the child in each case? How does each child's reaction correspond to what the text says about touch?

   b. Interview a teacher who you know uses friendly touch. Ask how the teacher deals with concerns that some adults have about touch. Ask if the program has any policies or guidelines regarding touch. Ask what the teacher believes to be important about the use of touch with young children. Compare the teacher's ideas with the ideas from text.

6. Teachers caring for themselves.

   a. Select a teacher who seems to you to cope well with stress. Observe that teacher's interactions with others in a potential "high stress" situation. Decide particular strengths the teacher shows. Which of the options for alleviating stress reactions listed in the text does the teacher seem to use in the classroom?

   b. Interview a teacher about how he deals with job-related stress in order to remain positive. If you and the teacher are both comfortable, ask also how the teacher deals with job-related stress and with life-related stress outside of the classroom. Compare your findings with what the text says about stress, its symptoms, and options for alleviation.

7. The parent-teacher conference.

   a. Observe a parent-teacher conference. Identify some listening behaviors used by the teacher. Notice the comfort level of the parent during the conference. Did the teacher make use of the compliment sandwich? How do the behaviors used by the teacher correspond to the recommendation for effective listening in the text?

   b. Interview a teacher experienced in parent-teacher conferences. Ask how the teacher communicates to make the conference productive for both the parent and the teacher. Ask about how the teacher has addressed challenges experienced in past conferences. How do the communication ideas mentioned by the teacher correspond to the recommendations for effective conferencing in the text?

Recommended Readings

Bowling, H. J., & Rogers, S. (2001). The value of healing in education. *Young Children, 56*(2), 79–81.

Breslin, D. (2005). Children's capacity to develop resiliency: How to nurture it. *Young Children, 60*(1), 47–51.

Carlson, F. M. (2006). Essential touch: Meeting the needs of young children. Washington, DC: NAEYC.

Gable, S. (2002). Teacher-child relationships throughout the day. *Young Children, 57*(4), 42–47.

Gartrell, D. (2006). A spoonful of laughter. *Young Children, 61*(5), 108–109.

King, M. (2003). Building an encouraging classroom with boys in mind. *Young Children, 58*(4), 33–35.

Loomis, C., & Wagner, J. (2005). A different look at challenging behavior. *Young Children, 60*(2), 94–99.

Nelson, B. G. (2002). *The importance of men teachers and why there are so few.* Minneapolis, MN: Men in Child Care and Elementary Education Project. http://www.menteach.org

Ostrosky, M. M., & Jung, E. Y. (2003). *Building positive teacher-child relationships.* What Works Briefs, no. 12. Nashville, TN: Center on the Social and Emotional Foundations for Early Learning.

Seitz, H. (2008). The power of documentation in the early childhood classroom. *Young Children, 63*(3), 88–92.

Sturm, C. (1997). Creating parent-teacher dialogue: Intercultural communication in child care. *Young Children, 52*(5), 34–38.

Guidance Matters

Build Relationships through Talk

September, 2006

Kim, a graduate student doing a practicum in a kindergarten classroom, shared this story.

It's Monday morning and the children are working on their journals. The assigned topic is "What did you do over the weekend?" Raymond is staring at his journal and has not picked up a writing instrument. The teacher comes over and asks about his weekend to help him narrow down the topic.

Teacher: So, Raymond, what did you do this weekend?

Raymond: Nothin'.

Teacher: Oh, I bet you can think of something. What did you do on Saturday?

Raymond: I didn't do nothin'. Go away!

Teacher: I just want to help you get started thinking of some ideas. Why don't you pick something to write with? That would be a good place to start.

Raymond: Go away! I'm not doing my !@#$%^~ journal and you can't make me. (Raymond goes to another part of the room and gets under a table. The teacher tries to coax him out. Raymond runs out from the other side, goes into the hall, and climbs into his cubby. His teacher approaches him.)

Teacher: Raymond, what you said was inappropriate. You need to look at me when I am talking to you. Do you understand? (Raymond doesn't respond.) I am going to count to five and you will look at me or you will go to the principal's office until after recess. You don't want to miss recess, do you? (Still no response.) One . . . two . . . three . . . four . . . five. I see you have made your choice. You will go with me to the principal's office."

Raymond follows the teacher to the principal's office without looking up or saying a word. When he returns to class, the teacher does not speak with him about the incident.

Later in the day I talk with Raymond as we build a Lego house. He tells me his mom and dad fought over the weekend, and his dad was arrested and put in a police car while Raymond watched.

Writing about what children know best—their lives—is a developmentally appropriate learning activity for most children, most days. On this Monday, for Raymond, it wasn't. Kim wrote that she was frustrated about the whole situation. Although she told the teacher what had happened to Raymond, Kim felt she couldn't talk much about it with her. Kim decided she could comfort Raymond, though, and sought out the opportunity. With all that happened to him, Raymond needed a friend in the classroom that day. It is good that Kim was there.

The transition from the familiarity of home to this new place—school—with its many strangers, young and old, must be odd for young children. If a child's perception of the world is that it is tumultuous—due to environmental, neurological, or combined factors—the challenges of entering the classroom become magnified. Incidents at home, ranging from an argument about which cereal to eat for breakfast to experiencing family violence, will definitely have an effect—perhaps numbness at arrival giving way to graphic frustration at "simple" challenges later on. In addition to conflict, a fear of abandonment—provoked by the kind of experience Raymond had—can exacerbate children's anxious feelings.

Quality moments between teachers and children are vital, especially upon the children's arrival to school each day. Rich (1993) reports that in his kindergarten class, spending five to ten minutes each morning with a child who was experiencing multiple conflicts proved to be a worthy investment of his time. (An assistant supervised the other children during this time.) The gift of time conveys to a child, "My teacher cares," making at least part of the day seem less challenging for the child—and perhaps for the teacher too.

LYNN, A KINDERGARTEN TEACHER I KNOW, isn't a morning person. Over time, though, she began arriving at her classroom far earlier than she would have liked. Getting things ready by the time the first child arrived allowed her to give each child the "Lynn greeting": a hug, high five, or handshake, and an eye-to-eye "Good morning, darling, how are you feeling today?"

Lynn used her daily greetings to find out who got new sneakers at the mall, whose dog got hit by a car, and who saw Dad get arrested for fighting with Mom. She used the information to influence her actions, as a caring professional should—being more gentle than usual with one child at transition times, showing understanding if another child swept the glue off the table in frustration when it spilled, celebrating with a

third about going with her long-absent older sister to buy ice cream.

In the years I knew Lynn, I never remember her sending a child to the principal. Over the years students occasionally would visit their former teacher for a Lynn greeting and a hug—including, one day, a fifth grader Lynn had never had as a student!

In her classes of 20 to 30 children, Lynn (by herself) worked hard to overcome the "mass class phenomenon," which still plagues much of public education. In settings with two or more adults, such as many preschools, it is definitely more possible to give the gift of time. Whether it happens at start-up or later in the day, when a teacher and a child talk together I call these times *contact talks*. There are always tasks to do in any classroom—hence there is a lot of *task talk* in schools. Contact talks are open conversations between an adult and child, with the child usually taking the lead.

Important to note is that the adult must decide that a contact talk will happen. The teacher uses wait times (for the child to put thoughts into words), reflective listening, and open-ended questions to get to know the child better, which is the purpose of the talk.

IN A HEAD START CLASSROOM, a student teacher and a child were about to read a book about the first snow. For a paper, Sharon recorded her contact talk with Linnea:

Linnea: My grandma lives in Arizona, and she said they don't ever get snow there.

Sharon: Why do you think they don't get snow in Arizona?

Linnea: It's too far for Santa to drive 'cause he brings the snow. My mom says it's too far for us to drive. I wanted to go last night. We went one time on a big airplane. It was scary, but only a little.

Sharon: It is a long way to Arizona. Your grandma must be a pretty important person to you, and I bet you miss her.

Linnea: She's my favorite.

Sharon: What is your favorite thing about your grandma?

Linnea: But . . . I think there might be another way it snows.

Sharon: I'd like to hear about it. Could you tell me about the other way it snows?

Linnea: Maybe the clouds just melt 'cause they move in front of the sun, and the sun is hot and then they melt.

Sharon: That's neat. Maybe the sun does melt the clouds. It's pretty sunny in Arizona. Do you think that if it got cloudy there that it might snow?

Linnea (laughing): No! There's too much cactuses. Didn't you know there are cactus everywhere there? We saw big ones that were bigger than my dad, and they had really sharp prickles on 'em.

Sharon (pauses): How do the cactus keep it from snowing?

Linnea: Because, silly, snow doesn't like the prickles on the cactuses! When the snow gets on a prickle, it hurts 'em and they don't like that. So that's why. (The conversation ends. The two begin to read the book.)

The whole contact talk took about three minutes. Contact talks don't have to be long, but they do need to happen. Student teacher Sharon had not talked with this child before. Later that day at circle time, Linnea sat on Sharon's lap.

At the NAEYC National Institute for Early Childhood Professional Development in June 2006, a participant shared that the students in her teacher education program often ask how to build relationships with children. "Use lots of contact talks," I said. That is what Kim did with Raymond. That is what Sharon did with Linnea. And, with hugs and affirming greetings, that is what Lynn did with the children in her classes.

As young children and teachers get to know each other, classroom life becomes more encouraging for the children, and the children (along with their families) become more understandable to their teachers. Teachers are then in a better position to work *with* children on their behaviors, rather than just reacting to specific incidents and perhaps regretting their reactions later. They are more able to use guidance rather than traditional discipline, and to build a relationship with each child.

To Increase Your Knowledge

The following resources highlight the importance of building relationships with children, one child at a time, to assist with social–emotional development:

Gable, S. (2002). Teacher-child relationships throughout the day. *Young Children, 57*(4), 42–47.

Loomis, C., & Wagner, J. (2005). A different look at challenging behaviors. *Young Children, 60*(2), 94–99.

Watson, M. (2003). Attachment theory and challenging behaviors: Reconstructing the nature of relationships. *Young Children, 58*(4), 12–20.

A Step You Can Take

Implement a planned approach to contact talks. Before you begin, make a chart including each child in your group and covering a four-week period.

Week 1: Note each contact talk with a child (in which you took the time to listen and follow a child's conversation) in that child's box on the chart.

Week 2: Fill in the blanks on your chart from the first week by talking with children with whom you had few (or no) contact talks.

Weeks 3 and 4: Select different children each day, have contact talks with them, and note the talks on your chart. Have talks with each child in your class.

Week 4: Reflect on what you learned about each child from having had the contact talks. Think what the children may have learned from talking with you.

For extra measure: Initiate contact talks with fellow staff and parents.

Column References

Rich, B. A. (1993). Listening to Harry (and solving a problem) in my kindergarten classroom. *Young Children, 48*(6), 52.

For additional information on using the guidance approach in the encouraging classroom, visit our website at www.cengage.com/education/gartrell.

Part 3

Solving Problems in the Encouraging Classroom

Preview

Nine—Conflict Management

Chapter Nine explores how the adult models and teaches conflict mediation and negotiation skills so that children learn to solve social problems. Discussion is given to: conflict management basics; understanding children's development to assist in conflict management; the five-finger formula for using and teaching conflict management; and the process of teaching conflict management skills to children. The final section examines the growing diversity in family structures, in particular families led by single fathers and families led by grandparents.

Ten—Problem-Solving Mistaken Behavior

Chapter Ten provides strategies for the teacher to resolve mistaken behavior. Strategies include making the decision to intervene, responding to behaviors reported by children, using quick intervention techniques, and intervening when follow-up is necessary. A question addressed is, "Why take the time to find solutions?" The final section discusses building cooperation with today's diversity in families through nonbiased communication.

Eleven—Guidance Through Intervention

Chapter Eleven offers information to help prospective and practicing teachers cope with and remediate strong needs mistaken behavior. The chapter begins by providing considerations for when intervening with boys. The next section addresses conditions that make intervention necessary. Then, methods for managing crises and handling feelings of anger are studied. Comprehensive guidance strategies and a case study for working with Level Three strong needs mistaken behavior are examined. The chapter concludes with techniques to use when teachers and parents disagree.

Twelve—Liberation Teaching: A Guidance Response to Violence in Society

Chapter Twelve develops the concept of liberation teaching as a guidance response to violence in society. The chapter begins with a look at societal violence and its effects on children in the classroom. The discussion then turns to defining liberation teaching and discussing how liberation teaching responds to classroom violence. A section investigates recent research on bullying, and the liberating teacher's response to bullying. The relation of liberation teaching to anti-bias education, guidance, and peace education is explored. The chapter ends with application of the concept of liberation teaching to relations with families.

Chapter 9

Conflict Management

Guiding Questions

▶ *What are the basics of conflict management?*

▶ *How does understanding young children's development assist in conflict management?*

▶ *What is the five-finger formula for conflict mediation?*

▶ *How does the adult teach conflict management skills to children?*

▶ *What do teachers need to understand about the increasing diversity in modern family life?*

Key Concepts

▶ *Child negotiation*

▶ *Conflict management*

▶ *Conflict resolution*

▶ *Five-finger formula*

▶ *High-level mediation*

▶ *Impulse control*

▶ *Low-level mediation*

▶ *Peace props*

▶ *Social competence*

▶ *Social problem solving*

Chapter Nine discusses how adults in the encouraging classroom model and teach conflict management.

First, the chapter reviews basics of conflict management.

Second, the chapter illustrates how understanding children's development assists the teacher in using conflict management.

Third, in a key section, the chapter demonstrates the five-finger formula for conflict mediation, including potholes to avoid.

Fourth, the chapter provides a strategy for teaching conflict management skills to young children.

Finally, the chapter provides information about the increase in single-father families and grandparent-led families and the effects of increasing family diversity on young children in the classroom.

Basics of Conflict Management

Conflicts are expressed disagreements between individuals. Conflicts happen in all human communities. In early childhood classrooms, where many little beings spend long hours of the day with one or a few big beings, conflicts are going to happen. They happen between two children, among more than two children, between children and the teacher.

Contrary to traditional educational thought, conflicts become negative only when they degenerate into violence (Carlsson-Paige & Levin, 2000). By *violence*, I mean words and actions that cause harm, psychologically and/or physically. During conflicts, even teachers can cause harm, by doing too little or by imposing moralistic "solutions" that result in punishment to one or more of the children. Reactions by teachers that punish rather than teach happen for a variety of reasons:

- emotional discomfort caused by the conflict
- need to "remind" certain children who is in charge
- need for a child to "learn the consequences" of his actions
- frustration at being distracted from "time on task"
- not knowing what else to do (Carlsson-Paige & Levin, 2000; Dinwiddie, 1994; Evans, 2002).

Teachers who understand that children are in the conflict because they have not yet learned to manage it tend not to lose patience and resort to punishment (Weber, 2000). In the encouraging classroom, teachers work hard to make conflicts into practical, real-life learning opportunities. When parties use words to resolve problems peaceably, conflicts become effective learning experiences that impact virtually all learning domains (Evans, 2002). (Children are practicing skills in the domains of cognitive processing, language development, social competence, and emotional intelligence—and even physical posturing and restraint.)

These teachers recognize that conflict management is fundamental to developmentally appropriate practice (Copple & Bredekamp, 2009). They understand that taking time to mediate is not time "off task." Teachers in the encouraging classroom know that as children learn democratic life skills, conflicts will take up less classroom time. As the year progresses, the classroom community becomes a more productive learning environment for all (Evans, 2002).

Basic Terms and Guidelines

For teachers who recognize that conflict management is the "gold standard" of guidance, several terms and guidelines are useful to know. Terms we consider are: conflict management, conflict mediation, conflict resolution, social problem solving, social competence, and impulse control. The following anecdote illustrates the discussion:

Classroom Anecdote	*(Contributed by a student teacher.) This is at the art center during choice time. Four students are playing with play dough and Will comes to the table and wants to play with the play dough also.*

Will: *(Walks to the table looks at Jerrod's play dough for a second and proceeds to grab a chunk from Jerrod without asking.)*

Jerrod: *Hey, that's mine! (Jerrod tries to grab the play dough back.)*

Will: *(Pulls away and screams) NO, I want to play too.*

Me: *(I am sitting at the table when this starts.) Okay boys, hang on a second. I see that you are a little upset so could you both take some good deep breaths for me. (They look at me, both really unhappy; so I start by taking a deep breath myself and they follow my example.) Okay, let's talk about this. Will, can you tell me what happened and then Jerrod can tell me what happened?*

Will: *I want to play play dough but there is none in the box.*

Me: *So you wanted to play with some play dough but there was no more left in the play dough box.*

Will: *(Nods head)*

Me: *Okay Jerrod, can you tell me what happened?*

Jerrod: *I was playing with the play dough and then Will came and took my play dough and I said it was mine.*

Me: *So you were playing with the play dough and Will came up and took some of your play dough.*

Jerrod: *Yeah.*

Me: *So the problem is that Will wants to play with play dough also but there is no more left?*

Both: *(Nod heads)*

Me: *Okay, lets think for a second. How can we solve this? (The boys sit for a few seconds and then Will says . . .)*

Will: *I could ask.*

Jerrod: *Yeah! And I can share because you are my best buddy.*

Me: *So Will should ask if he can have some play dough and Jerrod, you are going to share some. Is that right?*

(continued)

Classroom Anecdote		
	Both:	Yeah!
	Me:	(Will sits down and Jerrod shares some of his play dough. A few seconds later one of the other children comes over with a piece of play dough and gives it to Will. Seems like the children were listening closely and wanted to make sure Will got enough play dough.)
	Merilee:	You can have some of mine. (Gives play dough to Will.)
	Will:	Thanks! (I smile at Merilee and nod my head.)
	Me:	(The rest of the play dough goes well. When the students are putting it away, I go to Will.) Thanks for asking if Jerrod could share his play dough. Using words helps kids stay friends. It works better than grabbing, right?
	Will:	Yeah, Jerrod would share if I asked!
	Me:	(I also take a second to walk to Jerrod.) Thanks for sharing your play dough with Will; that helped you two to be friends again.
	Jerrod:	Yeah, we are going to play outside too.

Evans (2002), similarly to Gartrell (2004), considers **conflict management** as the ability to handle "brewing" as well as actual conflicts in peaceable ways. Sometimes, as in five-year-old Merilee's case, conflict management means taking steps on your own to help a solution along. Not all young children are at this point, of course. Due to developmental egocentrism and still developing impulse control, young children tend to react to the immediacy of a situation and show fairly dramatic mistaken behaviors (usually at Level One, experimentation that gets out of control). Teachers serve as vital leaders when they step in and provide *mediation* for conflicts—as Ben did, modeling and reinforcing positive verbal skills as a replacement for acting out (Evans, 2002). A similar term to **conflict mediation** is **conflict resolution**, which often refers to a formal, institutionalized program for resolving conflicts—but does not usually connote the prevention dimension that *conflict management* does.

In Ben's Head Start class, the adults had been teaching conflict management, through mediation and guidance talks, all year. Ben's successful mediation helped Will and Jerrod move past the conflict to a solution that allowed them to again be friendly. When they are not experiencing strong unmet needs, children (with adult guidance) readily learn **social problem solving**—a similar term but even more inclusive than conflict management; it means solving social/cognitive problems together.

Unlike Will and Jerrod, children may not be "best buddies" before or after a conflict. Still, after calming down, they generally appreciate being shown how to resolve the matter so that they can get along. When teachers see children going with the agreed-to solution, and then often playing together, they should smile. At this point in time, they have successfully modeled and reinforced the skills of conflict management. Ben guided Will and Jerrod in progress toward **social competence** (the ability to use social problem solving/conflict management with consistency—a high level democratic life skill).

Managing Feelings. Some writers emphasize "self-regulation"—children's ability to control their emotions and behaviors—as the major factor in social competence (Bronson, 2000). For me, the term *self-regulation* has a puritanical connotation—"just say no" to feelings. In young children, *impulsiveness* during conflicts (shown first by Will, then Jerrod) is a common problem. I prefer the terms of teaching for impulse control and the *managing of feelings.* More so than self-regulation, these latter terms seem more developmentally attuned to the social–emotional learning that young children are actually engaged in.

In the long view, several terms—emotional intelligence, intra- and interpersonal intelligence, social competence, democratic life skills, social problem solving, and conflict management—all refer to about the same set of human abilities. Whatever terms we use, the brain research indicates that social–emotional decision making happens as the executive function develops in the frontal cortex region of the brain (Shonkoff & Phillips, 2000).

The executive function develops rapidly during the early years largely in response to the social–emotional experiences of the child. In turn, the developing executive function governs the social–emotional decisions that the child makes. This is why this many-ingredient stew of terms is important to be familiar with how teachers react to children's conflicts affects how each child's executive function develops, and the child's ability to learn democratic life skills. In my view, the matter comes down to what Ben did in the anecdote: used conflict mediation to teach the children to manage their conflicts.

Did you notice Ben's comment that it "seems like the children were listening closely and wanted to make sure Will got enough play dough"? Spectators as well as participants learn when teachers mediate conflicts. There is a broad social reason for why conflict management skills are important for children to learn. When we teach young children, older children, young adolescents, and older adolescents to solve their real-life problems in a peaceable manner, we reduce violence in society (Carlsson-Paige & Levin, 2000). By reducing violence, we further society's democratic ideals (Evans, 2002). Idealistic? Accepted. To bring us back to the classroom, it all starts with how we teach children to share the play dough.

Conflict Management Guidelines

As mentioned, the children in the previous anecdote had been coached in conflict management over several months. As well, none of these children was dealing with serious personal issues that affected their ability to reach resolution. For the staff in this classroom, the time spent at conflict management was an investment in a shared quality of life. Given the different degrees of verbal ability, development, and social–emotional competence the children showed, the play dough scenario is how conflict management works in many classrooms. (See Guideline Six in following section.) Let us continue using Student Teacher Ben's anecdote to set some guidelines for conflict management.

Guideline One: The teacher calms down all parties before starting. It is difficult for anyone to use civil words when they are upset. Ben assisted the children to *de-escalate* their emotional involvement in two ways. First, he requested the children to take deep breaths. (Sympathetically acknowledging feelings is another method.) Second, he asked each child to explain the situation as each saw it. When children can express their feelings and perceptions, they feel affirmed and are more likely to "buy into" in the mediation.

After witnessing harm, the teacher must sometimes also calm himself. The mediator provides the even keel necessary for conflict management—and must have composure to mediate effectively (Evans, 2002).

Guideline Two: The teacher intervenes fair-mindedly, not as a moral authority but as a democratic leader. Notice that Ben did not make judgments about Will's grabbing and Jerrod's yelling that resulted in punishment. Ben intervened with authority, but put aside who was right and wrong. Instead, he used his leadership to solve the problem in a way beneficial for all (Dinwiddie, 1994). After the conflict was resolved, Ben did reinforce (briefly) alternatives to the mistaken behaviors. Children are more able to face up to and learn from their mistakes *after* mediation has occurred.

Guideline Three: As mediator, the teacher shares power. The process of mediation involves an outside party assisting two or more persons to resolve a conflict they cannot solve on their own (Porro, 1996). In the anecdote Ben involved each child, clearly establishing that each child would have a turn to talk. Being "mediator in charge," the teacher manages power sharing with and among the children. It is the power sharing that enables all to feel ownership of the

Conflicts provide opportunities for teachers to help children learn important life skills.

solution. Power sharing also boosts self-perceptions in the children, making successful outcomes and long-term guidance lessons more possible.

Guideline Four: The teacher supports the right of personal expression and the skill of effective communication. A trade-off for not imposing "retribution" on a child who did harm is offering the child who suffered the injustice the right of *protected response*. Will listened when Jerrod said that Will grabbed some of his play dough. Young children are helped to build empathy when they understand how the other child feels (Evans, 2002; Wittmer & Honig, 1994). The teacher ensures mutual respect throughout the conflict management process. He does so to reinforce that all children are worthy members of the classroom community—regardless where fault might lies in the conflict (Carlsson-Paige & Levin, 2000). By doing so, the teacher helps prevent the bully-victim syndrome.

From a more academic perspective, supported personal expression flows into effective communication (language arts skills). Children make substantial cognitive and linguistic gains when they put feelings into words, analyze social problems, cooperatively generate solutions, and verbalize acceptable alternatives for the future (Dinwiddie, 1994). Ben's brief follow-up guidance talk with each child reinforced the importance of using words.

Guideline Five: The teacher does not impose "solutions." Even when children are "too bummed out" to come up with ideas, the teacher still mediates rather than dictates the conflict's resolution. He may make suggestions, but asks if each child is all right with the suggestions until an agreement is reached. With their experience at mediation and their friendship, Will and Jerrod came up with a solution that they agreed to and followed.

If children come up with a solution and they both are satisfied, try to go with it even if it does not match your adult view of what is logical. An example is two three-year-olds fighting over a chair. As the teacher was mediating (and pulling up a second chair), the two decided they could both sit on the first chair—and did, amicably completing the activity. If the children decide on it, they will make it work.

Guideline Six: The teacher need not mediate perfectly for children to learn conflict management skills. Conflicts can be matters of high emotion, including for the adults concerned. Because of this fact, along with the unpredictability of young children in novel situations, adults need not expect to resolve conflicts "perfectly." Even imperfect mediation, done in a positive manner, teaches children about social problem solving. Especially when children get back together after mediation as though nothing had happened—which is surprisingly often—the adult knows that "imperfect has been good enough." The adult needs to be firm and friendly in enforcing the mediation process, but the outcome is never preordained.

Undergraduate students in my classes almost always have successful (not necessarily perfect) conflict management experiences with young children. In fact, students from my undergraduate relations and management class, like Ben, have contributed most of the anecdotes in this chapter.

Developmental Considerations in Conflict Management

Teachers need to understand developmental characteristics of young children that lead to conflicts—and to possible resolutions (Evans, 2002). Dinwiddie (1994) points out that:

> Children have conflicts over property, territory, or privilege. The younger the child, the more likely the conflict is to concern property: toys, [materials], even people can be viewed by young children as their own personal property. (p. 15)

Property tends to be the most frequent source of conflict in the preprimary years, and the kind of dispute adults most often have to mediate. As teachers know, the concepts of sharing materials and taking turns are not natural ones for preprimary children. These (basically mathematical) concepts take time to teach and learn.

When children begin to play in groups, problems of *territory* arise (Dinwiddie, 1994). These problems typically come down to whether a child gets to join others in the dramatic-play area or where a child can play when joining another in the block area. In some ways, territorial disputes seem easier to mediate than property disputes because "negotiable" space rather than a single object is the issue. However, a child already in an area often defines space needs differently than the other child *or* the adult. In territorial mediation, the adult frequently has to work hard to see the issue as the child does and sometimes *literally* to give a bit of ground.

Problems of *privilege* emerge as children's awareness of social subtleties continues to grow. Privilege conflicts such as who gets to line up first or who gets to play with whom are often seen in sophisticated preschoolers as well as in primary-grade children. Children's increased awareness of "social status" can make mediation of privilege-based conflicts difficult. Guidelines set in class meetings beforehand can help as mediation points in all three types of mediation, but especially in conflicts of privilege: "In our class we work and play together"—the positive wording of the classic rule, "You can't say you can't play."

Dinwiddie (1994) points out that conflicts can be over a combination of the three types of disputes, such as sitting on teacher's lap for reading books. The challenge for the teacher is to understand the issue for each child and mediate a successful resolution—a child on each leg, (the "clump technique") or taking turns. To do so, the teacher uses reading together not as a threat if no solution is found, but as an incentive to reach a solution.

Carlsson-Paige and Levin (1992) frame the developmental factor in teaching social problem solving as follows:

> [Young children] tend to see problems in the immediate moment and in physical terms. They also see problems from their own point of view. Only with age and experience do children slowly learn to see problems in a larger context; in more abstract terms that involve underlying motives, feelings, and intentions; and from more than their own point of view. Until they are able to do this on their own, therefore, the teacher needs to help. (p. 7)

The younger the children, the more likely their conflicts will be over property.

Carlsson-Paige and Levin suggested guidelines for teaching social problem solving to young learners that are still relevant today. The object of such mediation is to explain problems and possible solutions in terms that make sense to each child. The following is an adaptation of their suggestions, combined with those of Evans (2002) and Wichert (1989):

- Empathetically acknowledge feelings as a way to de-escalate emotions and gain trust for the process. Cooperative problem solving requires all to be calm.
- Help children define problems in simple terms: physical objects and specific actions.
- Use the concrete situation to reinforce that their problems have two sides.
- Encourage children to see the whole problem and, in a factual way, how their behavior contributed to it.
- Encourage children to find solutions by themselves. The teacher provides only as much mediation as the children need to negotiate the rest for themselves.
- Reinforce the importance of the process and the solution for the next time a conflict occurs.

If children cannot solve the problem, the teacher helps them find, try, and evaluate a solution.

Peace Props

To make life concrete for young children, some conflict mediation models use **peace props**. An established peace prop is the use of *talk-and-listen chairs*. Other common props are the *peace table*, the *talking stick*, and special *sock puppets* (Janke & Penshorn Peterson, 1995; Kreidler, 1984).

Talk-and-listen chairs and the peace table are both designated places in the classroom where children and adults go to resolve disputes. Children follow established guidelines such as: *respectful words only; explain, don't attack; take turns talking*. The talk-and-listen chairs assist in the "taking turns" guideline by having the children actually switch chairs to talk and listen.

A prop popularized by Janke and Penshorn Peterson (1995) is the talking stick. Teachers introduce the talking stick as a "sacred tool" for helping children talk and listen with one another. One person holds the stick with a hand on each end and takes a turn to talk. Others listen, until the stick is passed to them. Children (and sometimes the teacher) exchange the talking stick until the problem is resolved.

Talking sticks are sometimes used in class meetings. (One Head Start class had the children make their own sticks and take them home to their families.) Another use is in an exchange between individual children when there is a conflict. The teacher calms and mediates, explaining that this "peace prop" can help them resolve the problem. With modeling and practice, even preschoolers will get the talking stick and use child negotiation to resolve problems on their own.

Classroom Anecdote	*Student teacher observation: Charissa and Carlos were building with blocks. Charissa reached for a block, and Carlos decided he wanted the same one. They both tugged on the block and then Carlos hit Charissa on the back. As I hurried over, Charissa fought back tears and said, "Carlos, you're not s'posed to hit, you're s'posed to use the talking stick."* *Carlos said "Yeah" and got the stick. I couldn't hear what they said, but they sat down and took turns holding the stick, one talking while the other one listened. After only a minute, the two were playing again, and Charissa was using the block. Later I asked her what the talking stick helped them decide. The five-year-old smiled and said, "That I use the block this time. Carlos uses it next time."*

Charissa and Carlos illustrated *child negotiation* using a peace prop. Child negotiation is the goal of teachers when teaching conflict management. Another prop that facilitates child negotiation is the sock puppet. Sock puppets are a conflict management prop that Kreidler (1984) popularized and are still in use today. Whether they are called *peace puppets, power puppets,* or *problem puppets* (Janke & Penshorn Peterson, 1995; Kreidler, 1984), hand puppets have almost magical properties that can draw children into communication in ways that other props may not. An anecdote that illustrates how a sock puppet "empowered" two children to negotiate a conflict is found later in the chapter under the section, Child Negotiation.

The Five-Finger Formula

When emotions are high and teachers want to manage the situation effectively, a specific model is useful to follow. Many conflict management models are out there (see Recommended Readings), each having its own steps for teachers to follow. A classic is Kreidler's ABCD procedure (1994): Ask what's the problem. Brainstorm solutions. Choose the best. Do it.

Many variations exist, though, including among others a three-step model (Guth, 1995), a six-step model (Evans, 2002), a seven-step model (Janke & Penshorn Peterson, 1995), and a model that includes 16 "substeps" (Pirtle, 1995). This text features a five-step "formula" that is a composite of several models. Because most people have at least five fingers to count on—and an additional cool-down step makes Kreidler's model more complete—this author is suggesting the following five steps when using conflict management with children, the *five-finger formula.*

To remember the five steps for social problem solving, some adults post them on the wall. Some actually do count them off on their fingers. In using the five-finger formula, note that:

▶ At Step One, after everyone is calm, briefly preview the process.

▶ In Step Two stress not who is right and wrong in their accounts, but how each child sees the situation. Get each child to agree on your restatement of their versions, even if they are quite different.

Table 9–1 *The Five-Finger Formula for Conflict Management*

1. Thumb: Cool down (all of you).

2. Pointer: Discuss and all agree what the problem is.

3. Tall Guy: Brainstorm solutions (with teacher's help if needed).

4. Ringer: All agree on a solution, discuss a bit, and try it.

5. Pinky: Monitor and follow up. (Thank the children for mediating. Have individual guidance talks to teach for "next time.")

▸ In some mediation situations, you may find that Steps Three and Four may blend. Often this happens when the children "take charge" in the process, which is a positive.

▸ If children cannot think of a solution, make suggestions until they both agree on one. Stay firm in the process but flexible in the solution—as long as they both agree to it.

▸ If one or both children need guidance talks because of harm done, hold off until after the mediation is successfully completed.

▸ Often the five-finger formula does not take as long as it would seem. Still, if a teacher cannot take the time at that moment, calm everyone and lead the mediation later. (You may find the children have resolved the conflict in the meantime.)

▸ Stay fair-minded during the mediation. Treat each child positively and non-judgmentally. If you believe the model will work, it will.

Mediate "every time?" A teacher who comes upon a conflict need not intervene in every instance and start mediating. Watch for a minute. A child like Charissa in the previous anecdote may be able to lead child negotiation. A teacher who knows the children may ask, "Do you need my help to solve this problem or can you try it yourselves?" If the children decide to negotiate, stay to see what happens and to reinforce their efforts. But always when harm is happening, the teacher intervenes.

Mediating by the Five-Finger Formula

The following use of conflict management by a student teacher in a kindergarten class is typical of many mediation situations. The anecdote provides the information for an analysis of the five-finger formula and how it is used in early childhood classrooms. (My thanks to "Jenner," who was trying the strategy for the first time.)

Classroom Anecdote	One morning two boys were arguing over some Lego wheels. Their faces were getting really intense and their voices were getting louder.

> Dylan: Hey, those are my wheels. You took my wheels (whining loudly).
> Austin: (Yells) No, I had them first.
>   (Dylan grabs at the wheels. Austin pulls them away.)
> Jenner: Boys, I can see you are upset. Please come sit with me for a minute. I will hold the wheels just for now.

The boys say okay and come over. (It helped that I was holding the wheels.)

> Jenner: Thank you. First, let's all take a couple of deep breaths and then we will see what's going on. Ready, 1 ... 2 ... 3 ... Okay, now let's talk about what happened. Dylan, you can start and then we will ask Austin next.
> Dylan: He took my wheels that I was using yesterday and was gonna use today.
> Jenner: Done? Okay, Austin now you tell me what happened.
> Austin: He wasn't here yet so I thought I could use the wheels.
> Jenner: It sounds to me like we are having trouble figuring out who should get the wheels, huh?
> Boys: Yeah.
> Jenner: Okay, let's see if we can't come up with a way that you will both get a chance with the wheels. Do either of you have an idea?
> Dylan: He should give them back to me.
> Jenner: Austin, do you think that is a fair idea?
> Austin: No, then when do I get to play with them?
> Jenner: Can you think of another idea, so you both will have a chance to use the wheels?
> Dylan: He can keep using them today and then tomorrow I will get to use them.
> Jenner: Austin, what do you think of that idea?
> Austin: Okay.
> Jenner: Great, but next time something like this happens we need to use our words and not get mad right away. Then if it is still a problem come and get me or another adult in the class. Does that sound all right to you?
> Boys: Yes.
> Jenner: Okay, go play!

The boys go over and play together with the Legos. Austin uses the wheels. Dylan finds an older broken-down set but makes them work. There are not any more problems.

Analysis of the Formula

1. **Cool down (all of you).** Jenner got the boys to sit by her, held the property in dispute, and had each take breaths. She also briefly explained what they were going to do. This combination of actions worked for Dylan and Austin.

Sometimes teachers also need to give focused acknowledgment of hurt feelings or separate for a "cooling-down time" before the mediation. (Note that a cooling-down time is *not* a time-out *because* of something a child has done. It is a calming time to help the child regain composure for the purpose of talking the problem through.)

2. **Discuss and all agree what the problem is.** Jenner avoided "loaded" language that found fault and assigned blame. In the words of one student teacher, getting moralistic about the conflict, especially at this point, "bums the kids out." By asking a simple question, and assuring each that he would have a turn, Jenner got each child to share their version of what happened. If children feel respected enough to give their side of the story, they will and so move the mediation process along. Jenner also summarized what they said in an objective way they could each accept.

3. **Brainstorm solutions (with the teacher's help if needed).** An adult often "knows" the "right" solution and tries to steer the children into it. It took Jenner four exchanges, but she stayed focused on getting the boys to come up with possibilities. When Dylan pitched a solution that was in his own interest, Jenner simply asked Austin, "Do you think that is a fair idea?" With a follow-up question that took both boys' interests into account, Dylan came around.

4. **All agree on a solution, discuss a bit, and try it.** In this case Jenner did not suggest a solution, let alone impose one. Dylan suggested a resolution and when Jenner asked Austin what he thought about it, he agreed to it. After the boys experienced the success of an agreement, Jenner discussed with the boys a more productive way to handle this kind of situation in the future. The boys listened and agreed. A guidance talk at Step Four or Step Five of the process, *after the solution is agreed to*, is an important part of the five-finger formula.

5. **Monitor and follow up. Thank the children for mediating. Have individual guidance talks to teach for "next time."** In a surprisingly high number of mediations, the young children involved not only comply with the agreement reached, but actually (then or in a while) end up playing together. That was the case here. Because Jenner had an informal guidance talk with the two boys at the end of Step Four, no further follow-up was needed. If one or both children need extra teaching about "next time," the teacher would follow up as a part of Step Five.

Two Potholes

Teachers do not need to use conflict mediation perfectly to be successful at it. Still, there are two common potholes that adults want to steer clear of. *The first pothole is to blame the children for the conflict, rather than to focus on the mediating*. This reaction is understandable especially when one child is hurting another. In this situation teachers often aren't sure what else to say.

The problem is that blaming one child causes negative self-labeling in that child. She feels ashamed, unworthy, and likely stays angry. If the teacher at the same time comforts the other child, that child may feel better for the moment, but may begin to see herself as a victim—another type of negative self-labeling. The teacher unintentionally may reinforce a bully-victim "syndrome" in the two children, which is not what conflict management is about!

If instead the teacher blames both children "equally," he still defeats the purpose of the mediation. The children feel unworthy for not behaving more to the teacher's liking. They probably feel they are not capable of resolving the conflict, even with the teacher's help. To them at this point, the mediation seems like punishment. The teacher may have to direct the process so much from this point that it is not mediation at all.

Until a resolution is agreed to, the adult needs to work hard to be neutral. The objective is to first resolve the problem in a way all can accept, and only then teach the more positive alternative. Attend to the present and then the future. "Get past the past."

When conflicts are escalating, the teacher does intervene firmly. But, for the sake of the positive mediation, he withholds judgments about the children. The teacher firmly but fairly leads the children through the five-step process. After resolution he can talk with the children about the conflict and alternative behaviors for next time. At this end point, feelings have cooled, the children have experienced the success of the mediation, and they are more ready to listen.

The second pothole on Mediation Road is when a teacher determines the "solution" for the children. This mistake too is understandable. We teachers are usually with-it people. We figure out quickly what a logical resolution of a conflict should be. The problem is that for conflict management to be successful, we need to engage the children fully right through Step Five. This means sharing power and arriving at solutions with the assistance of, or at least the consent of, the children in conflict.

Table 9–2 Communication Techniques That Avoid the "Blaming" Pothole	
Not this:	**But this:**
I saw you hit Larry! What did you do that for?	I think there is a problem here. Let's get calm and we will talk about it.
You two are not playing nice. You need to learn to share.	I hear angry voices here. Let's use our quiet voices and work this out.

Classroom Anecdote (Synopsis)	*A new student teacher, Kelly, came across two veteran preschoolers fighting over a swing. Kelly talked with the children and they agreed that Morgan had gotten off the swing "for a second" and Reia had gotten on. Not getting the preschoolers to compromise, Kelly decided that Morgan could finish her turn "for five minutes" and then Reia would have a turn.*
	Kelly later commented, "Reia threw a fit near the swing. I tried to comfort her, but she told me to leave her alone. She sat and sulked the rest of the five minutes. Then Morgan would not stop swinging, so I felt I had to take her off. She fought me the whole way and was screaming, kicking, and hitting."
	Another teacher stepped in and assisted Kelly, who nonetheless continued working with the girls for the rest of the day. She was determined to get to know these children and figure out how to work with them.

Upon reflection, Kelly recognized an important lesson when doing conflict management: *Children need to actively help decide, or at least consent to, the resolution to be tried.* In this particular conflict, Kelly needed to be more persistent than the two veteran preschoolers in getting them to agree on a resolution. At Step Three, Kelly's "tougher than the kids" strategy might be to say:

> *I suggested one idea. We will sit until we agree on a plan. Or, one of you can find something else to do until another swing is open. What do you want to do?*

This strategy puts the responsibility for acting directly onto the children. Most young children are not patient in situations like this. One child may very well decide to leave. The teacher should thank that child, and help her get a turn later on a swing. However the three decide to resolve the conflict, the teacher might have a guidance talk later with each child.

Kelly learned a lot from this experience. In another conflict management write-up that same week (presented in the next section) Kelly skillfully steers around both of the two potholes.

Teaching Conflict Management Skills

The goal in social problem solving is to move children from dependency on the teacher to reliance on themselves. Although Wichert's *Keeping the Peace* (1989) is not the most recent work, the text pioneered a clear introduction to three levels of conflict management designed to achieve this objective. In an adaptation of Wichert's terminology, the teacher guides children to progress from high-level mediation to low-level mediation to child negotiation.

High-level mediation involves direct, guiding intervention by the adult including, if necessary, explaining the problem, suggesting possible solutions, and reaching a solution—agreed to by the children. At the high mediation level, the adult actively interprets, offers suggestions and works for agreement by the children. The adult provides active leadership in the resolution process, performing a role similar to that of a coach. Typically, the teacher uses high-level mediation when a child is very young, has strong unmet needs, or is new to the mediation process.

Because Jenner needed to prod Dylan and Austin to agree to a solution, this mediation was high level. When children need high level mediation, the teacher should feel confident in using it. For this child, or these children, low level mediation will come later.

In ***low-level mediation***, the adult suggests that children negotiate the conflict, but stands by to offer assistance as needed. Low-level mediation has been achieved when the children in dispute are able to generate a solution and implement it with a minimum of adult assistance. The adult is on hand to provide verbal and nonverbal encouragement, but moves from being a coach to a facilitator. Ben's mediation with Will and Jerrod, because they decided to share the play dough on their own, was low level.

Child negotiation occurs when children take charge of resolving a conflict by themselves. An illustration of negotiation was the anecdote about Charissa and Carlos and the talking stick. An irony of social problem solving is that many

© Cengage Learning

A teacher can act as a coach to assist children in finding solutions.

young children, guided in the conflict management process, can negotiate conflicts successfully, while many older students, who have not been so guided, cannot.

Three Conflict Management Cases

Three case studies follow, taken from the journal entries of student teachers in two kindergarten classrooms and one prekindergarten classroom. The cases illustrate *high level* and *low level* mediation and *child negotiation*. Analysis of each anecdote follows, including these parts:

Defining the Problem
Reaching the Solution
Bringing Successful Closure

Together, the case studies illustrate the progress teachers work for, moving children to take on larger and more active roles until they are able to resolve the problem on their own.

Classroom Anecdote (High Level Mediation)	*At the child care center on April 1 (and it was no April Fool's joke!), I had just finished reading a book to Allie. She had set it aside to hear me read another book. Charmaine came up and took the book from the table that Allie and I had just finished.*
	Allie: *Charmaine, NO! Give me that back. (Allie takes the book from Charmaine's hands and pushes Charmaine down.)*
	Charmaine: *(Screaming and crying) I wanted to look at that!*
	Kelly: *Hey girls, I think we need to work this out, but first we need to cool down a bit. (Taking both girls on either side of me, with my arms around both of them.) Can you each take three big breaths? (Allie shakes her head and turns her back to me.) Okay Allie, you can cool down on your own however you want. (Charmaine and I count out three big breaths.) Are you ready to talk yet, Allie?*
	Allie: *Yes. (She turns back toward us.)*
	Kelly: *Allie, what happened?*
	Allie: *I was reading that book and . . .*
	Charmaine: *You were not. I got it from the table.*
	Kelly: *Charmaine, you will have your turn too, but right now we are listening to Allie.*
	Allie: *Yeah, so I was reading the book and Charmaine came over and took it from me.*
	Kelly: *Okay, are you done now?*
	Allie: *Yes.*
	Kelly: *Charmaine, what do you think happened?*
	Charmaine: *Allie was done with the book. I was going to read it.*
	Kelly: *So Allie thought she was still using the book, and Charmaine thought she was done. Is that right? (Both girls nod.) How do you think we can solve this problem?*
	(continued)

Classroom Anecdote (High Level Mediation)	Charmaine:	Maybe Allie can just give me the book.
	Kelly:	Would that work for both of you?
	Allie:	No, I am not done with it yet. Let me read it one more time.
	Kelly:	One more time and then you will give it to Charmaine? Charmaine, what do you think of that?
	Charmaine:	Okay.
	Kelly:	Thank you, Charmaine. I like how you both solved the problem together. (Charmaine got up to play with other toys and Allie returned to my lap with the book.) Allie, you made me sad when you took the book away from Charmaine like that. What else could you have done instead of pulling and pushing?
	Allie:	Asked her for it?
	Kelly:	I think that sounds like a good idea. How could you have asked?
	Allie:	Charmaine, I am not done yet. Give it back to me now!
	Kelly:	Could you add a friendly word on the end?
	Allie:	(Grins) Please.
	Kelly:	You got it! (I got up to check on another group and I saw Allie look at the book cover and then get up and give it to Charmaine.)
	Allie:	Here.
	Charmaine:	Thanks. (Allie then went to a different center and continued playing.)

Defining the Problem. Kelly recognized that the conflict was over property and privilege. She approached the situation neutrally even though she had seen what had happened. She calmed the children—allowing Allie to calm down in her own way. (Why start a second conflict?) She gave each child a chance to speak, firmly reinforcing this idea with Charmaine. Without any judgment, she interpreted the problem combining each child's input in a way they could both accept: "So Allie thought she was still using the book, and Charmaine thought she was done. Is that right?" (Both girls nod.) Kelly coached the children through this part of the conflict management in an fair-minded, competent way.

Reaching a Solution. Kelly moved the children smoothly from agreeing about the problem to brainstorming possible solutions. She mediated between the children's ideas, moving them from a suggestion that was acceptable to only one child, to a solution that both children participated in making and so found acceptable. Many times, when both children feel they are heard and their ideas for resolving the issue are respected, one child will make the "mature choice." In this case, Charmaine decided she could wait to read the book, assured by the process that she would get a turn. Kelly thanked her for making the solution possible. Kelly again provided helpful coaching.

Bringing Successful Closure. Kelly confirmed the cooperative nature of the resolution by saying, "I like how you both solved the problem together." Kelly had

Guided in the conflict management process, many young children can negotiate their conflicts.

less opportunity to follow up with Charmaine, but did get a chance to thank her. After Charmaine left, Kelly had a guidance talk with Allie, discussing the grabbing of the book and walking Allie through words that she could use instead. The fact that Allie grinned and knew to add "please" indicates she got the message. It was interesting that when Kelly left, all Allie did was look at the cover of the book and give it to Charmaine. This suggests that for Allie the dispute may not have been so much about property as privilege—the privilege of controlling an object in close proximity. Kelly's subtle teaching paid off: Allie did give the book to Charmaine, as they agreed during the mediation. Charmaine thanked her.

Classroom Anecdote (Low Level Mediation)	Dakota and Chante were in the classroom store. Dakota was using the cash register, and Chante was "talking to a customer" on the telephone. Dakota picked up another telephone and started talking to her. Chante turned to him and yelled, "Shut up!"
	Dakota looked very sad. I knelt down and asked if he could tell Chante how that made him feel. He turned to her and said, "I felt really, really sad and bad when you yelled at me."
	Chante responded, "I'm sorry, Dakota. I didn't mean that, I guess. I was talking to a 'custmer.'"
	I asked, "Chante, I think Dakota wants to talk on the telephone with you."
	Chante said, "Yeah, but he's not a 'custmer.'"
	I suggested, "I wonder if Dakota could take the telephone to the house and be a customer?"
	"I could call you from the house," Dakota said.
	"Yeah, you need lots of stuff," said Chante (getting into it). "Go over and tell me what you need."
	Dakota, smiling, "phoned" from the house. Chante had the "stuff" ready for him when he came to pick it up. He gave her some make-believe money, and she even gave him change!

Defining the Problem. Camille (the student teacher) approached the situation calmly and had a calming effect on Dakota by kneeling down and speaking directly to him. She acknowledged his feelings, then encouraged him to tell Chante how what she said made him feel.

The student teacher did not begin a formal conflict resolution procedure that involved acknowledging Chante's feelings and asking each child to describe what happened. Instead, Camille made the decision that encouraging Dakota to express himself was timely and that the chances were good that a satisfactory resolution would occur if he did. (The steps often blend in low level mediation.)

Reaching a Solution. Again, the student teacher did not follow the formal steps of gathering information, restating the problem, and asking for possible solutions. Both children understood the situation. When Dakota let Chante know how he felt, Chante offered a first solution: Apologize. When Camille helped Chante understand that Dakota could be a "customer," Dakota and Chante rolled right into the second solution without further help from the student teacher. Camille observed the children as they negotiated and made two comments, but she let them reach the solutions by themselves.

Bringing Successful Closure. Typical of a successful low-level mediation, the children basically solved the problem themselves and went back to playing as if nothing had happened. The reflection portion of Camille's journal indicated how pleased she was that they solved the problem. Camille stated, "These kinds of examples just prove to me that these children will solve their own problems. Sometimes all they need is a little guidance."

Classroom Anecdote (Child Negotiation)	Nakisha and Suel Lin were caring for a variety of dolls in the kindergarten housekeeping area. They both reached for the last doll that had to be fed, bathed, and put to bed. They started yelling that they each had it first, and Suel Lin took Nakisha's arm and started squeezing it. "Stop, that hurts," exclaimed Nakisha. "Use your words!" "I can't find any," yelled Suel Lin. "Then get Power Sock," Nakisha demanded. Both girls, still holding part of the doll, walked over and got Power Sock. "I will wear him, Suel Lin, and you tell Sock." Suel Lin said to Sock, "Baby needs a bath, but we both want to do it." "Both do it," said Sock. The two girls put back Power Sock and returned to the housekeeping area, still both holding the doll. One girl washed the top half, the other the bottom half. Then Suel Lin held the doll and fed it while Nakisha read a story to the other dolls already in bed. Suel Lin said, "Here's baby; do you want to read another story?" "Yeah," said Nakisha, who read another story while Suel Lin rubbed the babies' backs as they lay in their beds. (In her journal, the student teacher reflected, "I couldn't believe how Nakisha and Suel Lin solved the problem! I didn't have to do anything!")

Defining the Problem. Nakisha acknowledged her feelings calmly enough that Suel Lin let go and agreed to negotiate with her by using the Power Sock. Suel Lin forgot a guideline when she squeezing Nakisha's arm. Conventional discipline would call for a punishment such as a scolding or even sitting on a time-out chair. The result probably would have been Suel Lin feeling upset and Nakisha feeling victimized. The student teacher refrained from intervening long enough to see what would happen. By doing so, she opened the door for negotiation and the opportunity for the children to find a mutually satisfactory solution.

Reaching a Solution. Nakisha and Suel Lin used a sock puppet prop introduced by the teachers to reach a solution. Nakisha was more experienced with Power Sock than Suel Lin and took the initiative to request Sock to help in the negotiation. The discussion did not involve a large amount of verbal articulation. Nonetheless, their negotiation was creative and peaceable and would have made many teachers smile. The self-esteem of each child seems to have been sustained.

Very often in successful child negotiation, one child (usually the older) is able to control the impulse to "hurt back," manage emotions that sometimes include being hurt, and problem solve in the midst of a stressful situation. Charissa showed this social competence in an earlier anecdote; Nakisha did here. Yes, both are girls. We discuss boys and conflicts in a special section of Chapter Eleven.

Bringing Successful Closure. The two children continued to play together and did so with a high level of cooperation. In contrast to conventional discipline, successful mediation and child negotiation reduce residual resentment and

The results of child negotiation are often surprising and sometimes make us smile.

continued conflicts into the future. The ability of children to negotiate conflicts indicates that important goals of an encouraging classroom are being attained. The children are gaining social–emotional competence and are learning democratic life skills. They are also learning important lessons about friendship.

Understanding Diversity in Family Structures

The statistic is now well known that fewer than 20% of families in the United States are "typical" with a married mother and father and a couple of kids. The percentage is lower when the dad is sole wage earner and the mother is at home full-time. Gadsden and Ray (2002) lay out the increasing diversity in modern family life in these stark terms:

One-half of all U.S. children will experience the marital breakup of their parents; of those children, nearly one-half will experience the dissolution of their parents' second marriages. Further, of American children living with a single parent in 1997, 38 percent lived with a divorced parent, 35 percent with a never-married parent, and 19 percent with a separated parent. These statistics strongly suggest that most early childhood practitioners are likely to have considerable [family] diversity in their programs. (p. 34)

We know well that positive attachments between children and family members are essential for healthy social and emotional development in young children (Department of Health and Human Services, 2001). We also recognize the importance, in this day and age, of going beyond the stereotype that nontraditional families are "broken families." Parenting is more challenging in non-traditional families, but wherever healthy adult-child attachments are present, these families—whatever their structure—are intact (Gestwicki, 2009). Still, in the winding river of modern family life, early childhood teachers themselves swim the waters of family diversity, and they help parents—both biological and "acquired"—teach their children to swim.

An essential role of teachers in the encouraging classroom is to work proactively with children from *all* families, including those whose life experiences, lifestyles, and ethnic backgrounds may be different from the mainstream. This section provides an overview of two increasing (but still below the radar screen) nontraditional family structures, both of which virtually all teachers will experience:

▶ single father families

▶ grandparents-as-caregiver families.

Because teachers typically have "less practice" in working with these "trending" family structures, the section offers suggestions for working productively with each.

Single Father Families

The first type of family is where Dad is the primary parent due to divorce, the mother's death, or the mother living away from the home (Gadsden & Ray, 2002; Kim & Yary, 2008). When fathers become primary parents, they call upon the fathering roles they grew up with or experienced vicariously (Frieman & Berkeley, 2002). The traditional male role of father as wage earner, somewhat removed from everyday parenting, has well known deficiencies as a nurturing model. If other complexities were present as well, Dad may be going about his role with limited positive fathering experience to fall back on. Add to these dynamics the common strictures in the rearing of boys relative to emotional responsiveness, and many dad-caregivers may be "up the river" in terms of family leadership.

For teachers, the obvious theme of building a positive relationship with the dad is important. The teacher shares with the father the interests and successes of the child. She is encouraging of the father's efforts at parenting and respectful toward the father. Frieman and Berkeley (2002)—two fathers themselves— remind teachers that many fathers have a hard time accepting criticism and

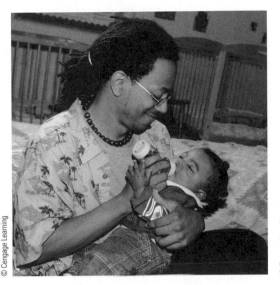

Teachers encourage and support single-parent dads.

unsolicited advice about their parenting. Discussions about parenting need to come out of—and not overshoot—the developing parent-teacher relationship. The teacher might take the preliminary steps of having "routine" information kits available for fathers, and locating father education groups (not "support" groups) where dads might get together.

Involvement of fathers is key, as a high level of father involvement in children's daily activities is associated with healthy social and emotional development, effective cognitive processing, and early literacy (Gadsden & Ray, 2002). Children's books about dads and children, read regularly by teachers (and made available to fathers in the information kits), should be one objective of any teacher. The teacher who models respect for fathers makes it easier for children to appreciative their fathers' efforts.

> *If teachers, especially female teachers, understand the uniqueness of fathers, they will be better able to increase father involvement in their child's educational experience. By understanding the unique paths to fatherhood that many men take, teachers will be better able to engage fathers as allies in educational experiences of their children. (Frieman & Berkeley, 2002, p. 213)*

Fathers are Fathers

With separated and divorced fathers, teachers need to first obtain an understanding of the legal baseline relating to the family's situation. If there are not legal barriers, "by understanding that one's pride might get in the way of involvement, teachers need to treat divorced fathers as if they were single parents, providing them with all information about their child independent of that given to mothers" (Frieman & Berkeley, 2002, p. 212). Teachers are supportive of all fathers as much for their sons and daughters as for the fathers themselves. Strengthened attachments help young children be successful in their future lives.

Grandparents Raising Grandchildren

Over 2.4 million grandparents are raising more than 4.4 million grandchildren without the presence of a biological parent in the home. This number continues to grow (Brickmayer, Cohen, Jensen & Variano, 2005). In addition, high numbers of grandparents in homes with their children provide full-time or part-time care for their grandchildren and are the primary contacts for the family with early childhood teachers.

Brickmayer et al. (2005) point out that the circumstances under which grandparents become the caregivers of their grandchildren are usually unfortunate and even tragic.

> *The reasons include parental drug and/or alcohol use, divorce, mental and physical illness (including AIDS), child abuse and neglect, incarceration, even death. Some skipped generation families (grandparents raising grandchildren) are temporary arrangements while parents are completing their education, on military or business assignment, recovering from illness or serving a jail term. Whether brief or permanent, almost all skipped generation families begin with trauma for children, parents, and grandparents. (p. 101)*

Grandparent caregivers are beset by difficulties that may be beyond the ordinary professional experience of teachers. Few of these grandparents are wealthy, some having to work two jobs to support their unanticipated families—with the added burden then of child care. Many grandparents have concerns about health insurance and health care, for both themselves and the children (Glass & Huneycutt, 2002). Often they do not have full legal custody of the grandchildren (DeToledo & Brown, 1995), which makes for legal hassles and bureaucratic complexities relative to their benefits, rights, and obligations (Williams, 2005). Their child-rearing styles may be rooted in cultural and family traditions that some today might conclude are inappropriate or even abusive. On the other hand, some grandparent-caregivers are too worn out and psychologically stressed to learn or relearn positive parenting skills. Grandparents may encounter conflicts with biological parents on any number of parenting issues, big or small, that can challenge family relationships and in the extreme traumatize the grandparent and the children.

What Teachers Can Do. Teachers first of all need to recognize that grandparent-caregivers can feel overwhelmed with their "lot" and isolated from others in the early childhood community. These grandparents, as well, may have difficulty understanding the "modern" practices of early childhood education (Williamson, Softas-Nell & Miller, 2003). Teachers must begin by being empathetic to grandparents.

Brickmayer et al. (2005) provide a useful list for working with custodial grandparents, adapted as follows:

▶ Build your relationship with the grandparent around your respect for the task they are undertaking and your "precious mutual commodity," the child.

▶ Modify your family communication methods to reach grandparents—perhaps make regular phone calls (or regular e-mails); with printed materials use large-print fonts and simple wording; actively seek out translators for other-language speakers.

▶ Provide information about your program in "grandparent-friendly" ways. Also provide basic materials and information about accessing other materials on parenting and grandparenting.

▶ Introduce grandparents to others in similar circumstances.

▶ Organize or locate workshops and support groups for grandparents.

▶ Collaborate with other staff/agencies to line up services and service advocacy for grandparents.

▶ Assist with referral services and support if children have special needs.

▶ Help grandparents feel welcome in the classroom by talking with them about what they would be comfortable with while there. Find out if they have particular expertise or interests that they might share. Send thank-you notes after they have volunteered.

▶ Teach children about grandparents raising grandchildren with picture books, discussions, and even introductions to assistive devices. Prepare the children for a visit from a child's grandparent and acknowledge the grandparent-visitor in front of the group—at both arrival and departure.

▶ Help grandparents locate children's books about family relationships for them to share with their grandchildren—including, of course grandparent-caregivers. Also encourage and show the grandparents other simple activities they can do with their grandchildren in the home and while traveling.

Many teachers and administrators are unprepared to deal with grandparent-caregivers. For children to be successful, schools need to develop strategies to address the emotional, psychological, and educational needs of children and their grandparent-caregivers (Rogers & Henkin, 2000). Brickmayer et al. (2005) conclude their helpful article this way: "By developing partnerships with grandparents raising grandchildren, early childhood educators can support the growth of stronger families" (p. 104).

With the growing diversity in families, each year more teachers realize that the time is past for "donuts for dads" and "muffins for moms" events and for Mother's Day and Father's Day activities. Instead, they may offer *Special Family Member* events. In their communications, teachers may refer less to "the parents of" and more to "the families of." From the beginning of the year, they celebrate the diversity of the families of the children through activities and home–school events. They do this so that their participating families do not feel they are different and don't belong. They do this as well so that all children know that they and their families are welcome in the encouraging classroom—and that their "natural and acquired" parents are important.

Summary

1. What are the basics of conflict management?

The differences and similarities in such terms as conflict mediation, conflict management, conflict resolution, problem solving, and social competence were discussed. Six guidelines for using conflict management are: (a) The teacher calms down all parties before starting; (b) the teacher intervenes fair-mindedly, not as a moral authority but as a democratic leader; (c) as mediator, the teacher shares power; (d) the teacher supports the right of personal expression and the skill of effective communication; (e) the teacher does not impose "solutions"; (f) the teacher need not mediate perfectly for children to learn conflict management skills.

2. How does understanding young children's development assist in conflict management?

Three common sources of conflict in young children are issues dealing with property, territory, and privilege. The younger the child, the more likely the dispute is to be over property. Young children tend to see problems in immediate and physical terms, and from their own point of view. Children learn to see problems in a broader, more socially responsive context only over time, with development, experience, and guidance. Teaching children conflict management skills at a level they can understand, such as by the use of peace props, helps them to progress with an important life-long skill.

3. What is the five-finger formula for conflict mediation?

A model is a practical, consistent method of practice. By providing specific steps in high-emotion situations, models of conflict management can help the teacher know what to say. The five-finger formula includes the essential steps addressed by many models:

Step One. Cool down (all of you).

Step Two. Discuss and all agree what the problem is.

Step Three. Brainstorm solutions.

Step Four. All agree on a solution and try it.

Step Five. Monitor and follow-up.

Two potholes in using the formula are blaming children instead of objectively mediating and "solving" the conflict without including the children.

4. How does the adult teach conflict management skills to children?

Through modeling and encouragement, the teacher moves children from high-level mediation, with children dependent on the teacher as a coach, to low-level mediation, with the teacher providing support as a facilitator, to child negotiation where children resolve problems for themselves with the adult as onlooker. A "developmental timetable" does not exist for learning social problem-solving skills. With guidance four-year-olds negotiate many conflicts themselves; without guidance many eight-year-olds do not.

5. What do teachers need to know about the diversity in modern family life?

With the increasing complexities of family life, new diversity in family structures is emerging. Two trends in the new diversity are families led by fathers and families led by grandparents. Teachers need to understand the particular ways that fathers see parenting and themselves as parents. From positive relations built with fathers, teachers can provide useful information and resources that respect the father's efforts and reinforce pride in fathering. Grandparents raising children encounter difficulties that may be hard for teachers to understand. Teachers can assist by being empathetic to caregiving grandparents, learning about their situations, and assisting them with support and collaborative referrals. Respect for the reality of each family, whatever the structure, is vital to the guidance approach.

FOLLOW-UP ACTIVITIES

Note: *An element of being a professional teacher is to respect the children, parents, and educators you are working with by maintaining confidentiality, that is, keeping identities private. In completing follow-up activities, please respect the privacy of all concerned.*

Discussion Activity

The discussion activity encourages students to interrelate their own thoughts and experiences with specific ideas from the chapter.

Recall a conflict situation in a classroom resolved by the use of conflict management. Referring to the chapter, was the process used high-level teacher mediation, low-level teacher mediation, or child negotiation? Analyze the possible effects for each individual involved (including the teacher if present, and classmate-onlookers) in relation to self-esteem and life skills.

Application Activities

Application activities allow students to interrelate material from the text with real-life situations. The observations imply access to practicum experiences; the interviews, access to teachers or parents. To interrelate theory and experience, students compare or contrast observations and interviews with referenced ideas from the chapter.

1. Basics of conflict management.

   a. Observe and record an instance of conflict management that you believe to be handled effectively by the teacher. Referring to the text, which of the guidelines for conflict management did you see the teacher using during the mediation? Which did you not see?

   b. Interview a teacher who uses conflict management regularly in the classroom. Ask the teacher to discuss the guidelines. What are her thoughts about the importance of each in the mediation process? Compare the teacher's comments with what the text says about the guidelines.

2. Conflict management and young children's development.

   a. Observe a typical conflict in a classroom and record it. Using the text as a reference, document whether the primary cause of the dispute was property, territory, privilege, or a combination. What did you learn about young children and their conflicts from your observation and analysis?

   b. Interview a teacher who uses a peace prop to aid in conflict management. Find out as much as you can about how the teacher uses the prop. Using the text to compare to the teacher's ideas, what did you learn about the use of peace props in conflict management with young children?

3. The five-finger formula.

   a. Conduct the mediation of a conflict using the five-finger formula. Record what you and the children said and did, including the follow-up. Referring to the text, write a brief reflection about how each step went and which steps, if any, you skipped or merged. When you mediate a conflict in the future, what did you learn from this instance of conflict mediation that may help you? Discuss why. Tie your discussion to ideas from the text.

   b. Interview the teacher about the steps she follows when she uses conflict mediation. Ask the teacher about the two potential potholes? Record the main points from the interview. Which of the five steps did the teacher mention? What did the teacher say about the potholes? Compare your findings with what the book says about conflict mediation.

4. Teaching problem-solving skills to children.

   a. Observe an instance of high-level mediation, low-level mediation, or child negotiation. Which do you believe it is? Referring to the text, discuss why. How effective was the process of social problem solving that you observed? How successful was the solution reached? Compare your findings to ideas from the chapter.

   b. Interview a teacher about her views on the relative importance of teacher-led mediation versus teaching children to negotiate. What surprised you about the teacher's comments? Which of her comments were what you expected? How do the teacher's comments compare or contrast with the text?

5. Family diversity: father- and grandparent-led families.

   a. Interview a father in a single-parent family. Ask about his priorities for the education and upbringing of his child(ren). Ask about the difficulties and benefits of being a single dad. Ask what teachers can do to be supportive of single fathers. Compare your findings to ideas from the chapter.

   b. Interview a grandparent in a grandparent-led family. Ask about her or his priorities for the education of the child(ren). Ask about the difficulties and benefits of being a grandparent raising grandchildren. Ask what teachers can do to be supportive of grandparents who are raising their grandchildren. Compare your findings to ideas in the chapter.

Recommended Readings

Brickmayer, J., Cohen, J., Jensen, I. D., & Variano, D. A. (2005). Supporting grandparents who raise grandchildren. *Young Children, 60*(3), 100–109.

Carlsson-Paige, N., & Levin, D. E. (2000). *Before push comes to shove: Building conflict resolution skills with children*. St. Paul, MN: Redleaf Press.

Evans, B. (2002). *You can't come to my birthday party: Conflict resolution with young children*. Ypsilanti, MI: High/Scope Press.

Frieman, B. B., & Berkeley, T. R. (2002). Encouraging fathers to participate in the school experiences of young children: The teacher's role. *Early Childhood Education Journal, 29*(3), 209–213.

Gadsden, V., & Ray, A. (2002) Engaging fathers: Issues and considerations for early childhood educators. *Young Children, 57*(6), 32–42.

Janke, R. A., & Penshorn Peterson, J. (1995). *Peacemaker's A, B, Cs for young children*. Marine on St. Croix, MN: Growing Communities for Peace.

Kim, A. M., & Yary, J. (2008). Making long-term separations easier for children and families. *Young Children, 63*(6), 32–36.

Mahoney, S. (2004, May). The friendly divorce. *Parents*, pp. 119–120, 122 (copyrighted by author).

Williams, T. (2005, May 21). A place for grandparents who are parents again. *New York Times*, pp. B1, B6.

Guidance Matters

Conflict Mediation

March, 2006

Kelly, a new student teacher, describes a conflict that occurred in a class of three- to five-year-olds: I had just finished reading a book to Allie. She set it on the table to hear me read another book. Charmaine came up and took the book that Allie and I had just put down.

Allie: Charmaine, NO! Give me that back. (Allie takes the book from Charmaine's hands.)

Charmaine (screaming and crying): I wanted to look at that! (Allie holds the book tight, glares at the smaller girl, and with her other arm pushes Charmaine away.)

Kelly (taking one girl on either side of me, with my arms around both of them): Hey, girls, I think we need to work this out, but first we need to cool down a bit. Can you each take three big breaths? (Allie shakes her head and turns her back to me.) Okay, Allie, you can cool down on your own however you want. (Charmaine and I count out three big breaths.) Are you ready to talk yet, Allie?

Allie: Yes. (She turns back toward us.)

Kelly: Allie, what happened?

Allie: I was reading that book and . . .

Charmaine: You were not. I got it from the table.

Kelly: Charmaine, you will have your turn too, but right now we are listening to Allie.

Allie: Yeah, so I was reading the book, and Charmaine came over and took it from me.

Kelly: Okay, are you done now?

Allie: Yes.

Kelly: Charmaine, what do you think happened?

Charmaine: Allie was done with the book. I was going to read it.

Kelly: So Allie thought she was still using the book, and Charmaine thought she was done. Is that right?

(Both girls nod.) How do you think we can solve this problem?

Charmaine: Maybe Allie can just give me the book.

Kelly: Would that work for both of you?

Allie: No, I am not done with it yet. Let me read it one more time.

Kelly: One more time and then you will give it to Charmaine? Charmaine, what do you think of that?

Charmaine (shrugs shoulders): Okay.

Kelly: Thank you, Charmaine. I like how you both solved the problem together. (Charmaine gets up to play with other toys, and Allie returns to my lap with the book.) Allie, you made me sad when you took the book away from Charmaine like that. What else could you have done instead of pulling and pushing?

Allie: Asked her for it?

Kelly: I think that sounds like a good idea. How could you have asked?

Allie: Charmaine, I am not done yet. Give it back to me now!

Kelly: Could you add a friendly word on the end?

Allie (grins): Please.

Kelly: You got it! (I leave to check on another group, and I see Allie briefly look at the book cover, then get up and give it to Charmaine.)

Allie: Here.

Charmaine: Thanks.

Allie then went to a different center and continued playing.

CONFLICTS ARE EXPRESSED DISAGREEMENTS BETWEEN PEOPLE. Conflicts happen all the time in early childhood classrooms—and just about everywhere else in life! In my view, *conflict management* includes the ability to:

▹ prevent conflicts from becoming too serious to resolve easily and

▹ resolve conflicts peaceably no matter how serious they get.

When a third person assists others in resolving a conflict, this is *conflict mediation*, and it is the gold standard of guidance interventions.

Teaching through conflict mediation takes time and effort. If teachers commit to this intervention, they are saying children's social–emotional learning needs to be part of the curriculum. In this sense, conflict mediation is central to developmentally appropriate practice: You can't have one without the other. The real-life benefit of using conflict mediation is that children learn to manage conflicts by talking things through themselves.

In one of her first efforts at conflict mediation, Kelly used a five-step process I call the "five-finger formula." She used it well. Let's look at how:

1. **Thumb:** Cool everyone down.

   Kelly suggested each child take three deep breaths. Allie said no, and Kelly perceptively accepted this decision in order to keep the cool-down process going (Why start a second conflict?). No one can negotiate when they are upset. Calming all parties is essential.

2. **Pointer:** Agree about what the problem is.

   Significantly, Kelly stayed neutral during this step. Without taking sides or moralizing, she got the children to take turns talking and to agree: "Allie, you thought . . . and Charmaine, you thought . . . Is that right?" (Both girls nod.)

3. **Tall Guy:** Brainstorm possible solutions.

   Kelly got the children to make suggestions, cross-checking with each child. She did not side with either or impose a solution on both. She quietly facilitated. This is called *low-level mediation*. With children who are younger or who have strong unmet needs, the teacher becomes a more active "word

coach." This is called *high-level mediation*. Always, our goal is to move the children toward negotiating for themselves.

4. **Ringer:** Agree on a solution.

   In conflict mediation, the teacher never knows what the outcome will be and does not impose one. This lack of control over the outcome makes conflict mediation difficult for some teachers. What Kelly did was control the *process*. This is where the real leadership comes in.

5. **Pinky:** Facilitate the solution.

   Notice two things about the resolution. First, after each child had her say, each compromised a little. Charmaine let Allie have "one more time." Allie gave the book to Charmaine without rereading it. Charmaine said, "Thanks."

   Second, it was after the conflict was resolved and Charmaine walked away, and not during the mediation, that Kelly had a *guidance talk* with Allie. A guidance talk is a conversation about what a child could do differently next time to manage a conflict more peaceably. After Allie felt success through the mediation, she was willing to have the guidance talk. (Sometimes the teacher uses a guidance talk with *both children*, together or separately, but always at the end of the mediation.)

   The students in Kelly's college class all do papers on conflict mediation. Some may blend the steps and not use them perfectly, but almost all get mediation to work—even on the first try or two, even when the students themselves are second-language learners. An academic degree is not necessary to use this guidance tool. How do teachers know when mediation works? The children at least go along with the solution—as in the anecdote—and very often end up playing together as though a conflict never occurred. (I'll bet you've seen this happen.)

   When adults use conflict mediation successfully, they avoid reinforcing in children the roles of bully and victim; these roles perpetuate unhealthy self-images, additional conflicts, and negative classroom dynamics. Instead, the adults sustain an encouraging classroom in which *all* children are helped to feel they are worthy, contributing members. Children learn to negotiate their conflicts peaceably, and social–emotional intelligences develop and thrive.

To Increase Your Knowledge

Look up these two books.

Evans, B. (2002). *You Can't Come to My Birthday Party: Conflict Resolution with Young Children.* Ypsilanti, MI: High/Scope.

Wichert, S. (1989). *Keeping the Peace: Practicing Cooperation and Conflict Resolution with Preschoolers.* Philadelphia: New Society.

Many other fine books and articles on conflict management and peace education are out there. Locate one you like and share it with others.

A Step You Can Take

Get together with other teachers or caregivers, post the five steps as a reminder, and go for it! Mediation does not have to be perfect to work, but it must be used consistently to make a difference in how the children in your group relate to others.

Avoiding Potholes on the Way to Successful Mediation

1. Calm everyone first, including yourself. One legitimate use of "separation" (not time-out) is to help children cool down so you can use guidance with them.

2. Prevent yourself from siding with either child or telling them what they "did wrong." Moralizing during mediation kills the willingness to negotiate. Delay your own interpretations until a guidance talk at Step Five, even though this is hard.

3. Wait for the children to suggest solutions. If your patience wears out, suggest but do not impose. Asking "Will this work for both of you?" allows children to be the participants they have to be if they are going to learn to negotiate. Remember, when the children agree, go with their solution even if it doesn't fully meet your own interpretation of justice.

4. Help children learn how to reconcile after successful mediation. Forced apologies are not appropriate because they leave children (like all of us) with unresolved conflicted emotions. Instead, ask "How can you help [the other child] to feel better?" If the child is not ready, suggest "That's okay, maybe you can think of something later." (Most children forgive more easily than many of us adults.)

5. Monitor activity after the mediation. So children know the process matters, acknowledge their accomplishment and compliment reconciling behaviors.

For additional information on using the guidance approach in the encouraging classroom, visit our website at www.cengage.com/education/gartrell.

Chapter 10

Problem Solving
Mistaken Behavior

Guiding Questions

▶ *What goes into the decision to intervene?*

▶ *What are four quick intervention strategies?*

▶ *What about mistaken behaviors reported by children?*

▶ *What are four strategies when interventions require follow-up?*

▶ *Why take the time to problem solve mistaken behavior?*

▶ *How does the teacher build cooperation with today's diverse families?*

© Cengage Learning

Key Concepts

▶ *Child-report*

▶ *Code of Ethical Conduct*

▶ *Commanding choices*

▶ *In Choice/Out Choice*

▶ *Inviting choices*

▶ *Marginal mistaken behaviors*

▶ *Negotiation reminders*

▶ *Nonverbal intervention techniques*

▶ *Positive consistency*

▶ *Reconciliation*

▶ *Requesting choices*

▶ *Sentence frame*

▶ *Teachable moment*

▶ *With-it-ness*

When conflicts occur, the teacher has a number of decisions to make, beginning with whether she should intervene at all. Chapter Ten considers the range of decisions teachers make when they encounter conflicts in the classroom.

We begin with a note about vocabulary. From earlier chapters, a *conflict* is an expressed disagreement between individuals (Girard & Koch, 1996). In the case of children, the expressed disagreement is typically over property, location, and/or privilege (Dinwiddie, 1994). We also learned in Chapter Nine that conflicts need not be negative. If through mediation or negotiation children come to a solution peacefully, the conflict actually has a positive result. (Children are learning how to problem solve, a democratic life skill.)

A *mistaken behavior* is a conflict that typically happens when a child takes a verbal or physical action, and an adult disagrees with the action. The adult may react with punishment, in which case the mistaken behavior has a negative outcome, or with guidance, in which case the mistaken behavior more likely has a positive outcome. (The child is learning how to problem solve.)

Another possibility, of course, is that the teacher may initiate a conflict and the child may object to the *teacher's* mistaken behavior. This possibility (remote for readers of this book ☺) is also addressed in Chapter Ten.

The Decision to Intervene

When they perceive mistaken behavior, beginning teachers often feel concern about intervention: They fear alienating the children in their charge. In response to a basic question about the role of the early childhood teacher, she *is* a friend to children—but as an adult and a child must be friends, with the adult friend as a mentor and guide.

In intervention situations, the adult retains the element of friendliness, even if circumstances call for responses that are firm and that children may not like. Feelings change, and there will be time after the intervention for the adult and child to "make things right." Writers about child behavior from Glasser (1969) to Kaiser and Sklar-Rasminsky (2006) share the view that children need to know the limits of acceptable behavior.

The teacher acts with firmness if safety or well-being are endangered. Guidance rests upon the authority of the teacher to protect the learning community for all. Children feel secure when clear limits are consistently reinforced. Note, however, that punitive discipline practiced with consistency is still punitive discipline. With guidance, the teacher is firm when necessary but also friendly; she practices **positive consistency**.

Guidance teachers are firm when they have to be firm, but they are not one-dimensional. Firmness as an *overriding* personal characteristic limits other

Teaching children to identify their feelings helps them learn to negotiate their conflicts.

important personality dimensions, such as flexibility and a friendly sense of humor. The professional teacher is sometimes permissive and sometimes firm, depending on the judgments she makes about each situation. As long as children know when the teacher will smile and when she will be firm, *positive consistency* has been achieved. In this sense, establishing predictability in your response tendencies at the beginning of the year is more helpful than being "consistently" firm.

With-it-ness

Kounin's (1977) concept of **with-it-ness** (synonymous with "having eyes in the back of the head") is an important teaching skill. Yet, because we can't always know what exactly happened, teachers recognize that the "judgments" they make are better thought of as *hypotheses*. Teachers must act quickly and firmly in some situations, but they do not hold their judgments as infallible. Instead, they stay flexible, able to learn even while working to resolve a conflict.

Classroom Anecdote	*In an early childhood classroom, a four-year-old named Sharisse was playing with Kiko, also four, at the water table. After a few minutes, Sharisse stormed over to the teacher and said, "Kiko spilt water on me." She had a water spot on her overalls. Bothered, the teacher walked over to the water table. Kiko turned around. His shirt and pants were soaked and he was crying silently. The teacher got down to Kiko's level and asked what happened. After listening to him and talking with Sharisse, she figured out that Kiko had dropped a bottle and it splashed up on Sharisse. Sharisse then dumped a bowl of water on his front.*
	The teacher helped Kiko get a change of clothes. She then talked with Sharisse and Kiko together. Kiko had been having a rough week with frequent displays of mistaken behavior, and the teacher was pleased when Sharisse decided to tell him she was sorry. The teacher felt fortunate that she had gotten the additional facts.

In this situation Brittney, the teacher, was able to collect information that helped her modify her original hypothesis. Anytime a teacher can act less like a police officer on the street and more like a mediator (in the classroom), she is better able to make informed decisions.

Another important part of *with-it-ness decision making* is determining the number of children involved. With one child, the teacher uses *guidance talks*. With two or a small group of children, conflict mediation (perhaps with a follow-up guidance talk) is the intervention of choice. If several children in the group are experiencing a conflict—or if a conflict is affecting the entire group—the teacher frequently holds a class meeting. Discussed in this chapter and Chapter Eleven, other firm but friendly intervention techniques serve as handy backups for the "guidance three." But, a first, essential decision the teacher makes is whether one, a few, or several children are experiencing the conflict.

Two other determinations then follow:

1. Whether to intervene at all
2. The degree of firmness to use in the intervention

Discussion of these determinations follows in the following two sections.

When to Intervene

The key decision is whether to intervene. In cases of serious mistaken behavior, the teacher has no choice; she must enter the situation. In other cases, the decision is not so clear. Three situations that require thought about whether to intervene are **marginal mistaken behaviors**, "bossy" behaviors, and arguments.

Marginal Mistaken Behaviors. Teachers have different comfort levels regarding minor mistaken behaviors. One teacher intervenes; another does not. Because no one way is the only way to use guidance, this human difference is to be expected.

An important determination is if the behavior is bothersome only to the teacher and not particularly to the group. A certain child who "pushes the teacher's buttons" may show a behavior like restlessness in a large group. The other children long ago may have gotten used to this child's behavior and basically tune it out. The teacher may feel a need to "correct" the child. Unless the teacher mediates the impulse, his intervention may embarrass the child, put the rest of the children on edge, change the mood of the activity, and may actually frustrate the teacher further.

With marginal mistaken behavior, the teacher needs to take care in the intervention decision. Sometimes, the most productive course of action is to hold back on the "impulse," but continue to observe and see how the situation plays out. The time can allow the teacher to think of unobtrusive interventions such as altering the activity to increase the child's engagement, having another adult sit by the child, or whispering a refocusing reminder to the child. (As mentioned in Chapter Seven, whispers are surprisingly effective with young children in groups.)

A second important determination is whether the teacher's intervention may be more disruptive than the child's "precipitating" behavior. The following anecdote illustrates this situation.

Classroom Anecdote	*During rest time in a child care center, a teacher witnessed the following event. Five-year-old Missy, who "never misbehaved," reached out and tugged a neighbor's hair. Then, she rolled over and pretended that she was asleep. The neighbor, a three-year-old, sat up, rubbed his head, and complained. He then lay back down and again closed his eyes. The teacher did not wade through the sleeping bodies and scold Missy. Instead, she smiled quizzically at this unusual event and commented later to a colleague that she thought Missy was finally feeling comfortable at the center.*

The teacher decided that Missy's Level One mistaken behavior did not warrant intervention. To do so would have embarrassed a child with high personal standards and perhaps aroused a group of sleeping preschoolers. The teacher did make a point of watching Missy's behaviors more closely, having Missy help lead in some activities, and working on her positive relationship with the child.

Marginal mistaken behaviors are the sort that some teachers may react to one day but not the next. In deciding whether to intervene, the teacher does well to reference mistaken behavior to guidelines that have been established, the specifics of the situation, the personalities of the children, and her own mind-set on this particular day. Ultimately, the teacher makes intervention decisions by relying on professional judgment. Reflection after the event helps the teacher decide whether adjustments are necessary for the future. In relation to marginal mistaken behaviors, the individual child and the group need *positive consistency* in teacher response—the guiding idea regarding marginal mistaken behaviors.

Table 10–1 *The Decision to Intervene: Two Quick Reality Checks*
1. Is this behavior bothering only me, only another staff person, or the whole group?
Children adapt to an individual child who frequently gets restless or expresses frustrations dramatically. Sometimes, the tolerance level of the teacher may be lower than that of the group. Sometimes, the tolerance level of another staff person may be lower still. The teacher needs to do a "reality check" on this question before jumping in. Similarly, the teacher may need to talk with another staff member who intervenes when the behavior seems to be a bother only to that one person.
2. Will my intervention reduce or add to the disruption in this situation?
The teacher does intervene if a situation is seriously disruptive or harmful to one or more children in the group. Regarding "the disruption factor," the reality check is this: If the teacher thinks that her intervention will de-escalate tensions and restore group productivity, she intervenes. If the teacher judges that her intervention will be a bigger disruption to the group than the child's mistaken behavior, she holds back or modifies her response.

Bossiness. Many teachers experience negative feelings about the marginal mistaken behavior of bossiness. A democratic society depends on citizens with leadership abilities. When young children show beginning leadership behaviors, they do so with the developmental egocentrism that they show in all behaviors. Because a sense of fair play is strong in most teachers, they need to check tendencies to come down quickly on "bossy" behavior.

Classroom Anecdote	At choice time four young girls were playing cards. The game went like this: Lisa, who frequently organized play situations, stacked and dealt the cards. All four children picked up their cards, put them face up on the table, and giggled. Lisa stacked the cards again and redealt.
	The teacher, who was watching, fought a tendency first to teach the children a "real game" and second to have each girl get a turn stacking and dealing. As it was, none of the other children pressed to have a turn, and the game went on as it was several minutes!

The anecdote provides a clear illustration of what might be considered a marginal mistaken behavior. (Lisa was not giving anyone else a turn to deal.) A teacher could easily have disrupted this smoothly running (preconventional) card game by well-meaning intervention. Yet, children learn about leadership *and* group membership through experiences such as this. (I'll bet many readers can remember playing "school," with themselves as the teacher, in their younger days.)

Teachers may need to remind a child to give others a chance; this is understandable. At the same time, they should positively acknowledge "beginning leadership." The children themselves provide an indication of how leadership is showing itself. If others willingly associate with the leading child, as in the

Teachers positively acknowledge and encourage beginning leadership.

anecdote, intervention should be minimal. Children will learn to play conventional card games later, especially if they are not discouraged in their initial attempts.

Sometimes, however, a child will show extreme bossiness that drives others away. Teachers frequently can help a child feel less need to dominate by building a personal relationship and helping the child feel more secure and accepted by the group. Teachers also model and teach cooperation over competition through general teaching practices, specific curriculum activities (often small-group), and games (Evans, 2002). Children are able to view competition as less threatening when they are older (Pirtle, 1995). If a child has strong unmet needs, he tend to cross the line between bossiness and **instrumental aggression** (bullying to achieve a specific objective). In these cases, harm happens, and the teacher intervenes. Conflict mediation allows the child who has been harmed, as well as the other, to reestablish their rights as full classroom citizens and to learn to solve problems together.

Table 10–2 Problem Solving Classroom Arguments with Children Aged Three to Eight	
Situation	**Teacher Response**
1. Reasonable chance children can work out difficulty.	Monitors, but may not intervene. If needed, encourages the children to negotiate.
2. Argument proving disruptive to a focused group activity.	Teacher intervenes. Redirects parties to class activity. States that he will help them solve problem later. Teacher follows up.
3. Argument becoming heated. Children don't seem able to resolve on own. Perhaps one child dominating.	Teacher mediates. May use props like talking sticks or puppets. Follows five-finger formula starting with cool-down to assist children to resolve problem.
4. One child reports argument to teacher; wants assistance.	Teacher avoids taking sides. Determines whether #1, #2, or #3 above applies. Responds accordingly.
5. One or both have lost control; children are yelling or fighting.	Teacher intervenes. Separates children for cool-down time. Uses five-finger formula at high-level mediation and follows up with guidance talks when tempers have cooled.

Arguments. Teachers generally feel a need to intervene when children quarrel. In the guidance approach, the teacher uses with-it-ness skills to analyze the situation and takes any of several possible courses of action, as Table 10–2 suggests.

As presented in Chapter Nine, children who learn to solve problems with words are gaining skills in the language arts, social sciences, and often even math. Beyond school they are gaining a democratic life skill of lasting value (Evans, 2002; Gartrell, 2004). Using words to solve problems can be learned by prekindergarten children no less than by third graders.

Classroom Anecdote	Team teachers Tammy and Connie had a stock phrase whenever children had a disagreement: "We have a problem here. How can we solve this problem?" At the beginning of the year, they helped children settle arguments on a daily basis with the phrase. As the year went on, the two needed to use it less and less. The reason was that other staff (including a teenage assistant) and even the children themselves began to say: "We have a problem here. How can we solve this problem?"

Degree of Firmness of the Intervention

Besides deciding whether to intervene, the teacher must determine *the degree of firmness to use*. Matching firmness to the seriousness of the mistaken behavior is often taken for granted. After deciding whether to intervene, the teacher should be thinking about the degree of firmness to use.

Giving Choices. Giving choices to children illustrates how to use degrees of firmness in teacher responses. As Ginott (1972) points out, "Children are dependent on their teachers, and dependency breeds hostility. To reduce hostility a teacher deliberately provides children with opportunities to experience independence" (p. 76). The teacher avoids communication that pits her authority against children. Instead, she *invites*, *requests*, or *commands* choices. The teacher does so in factual, nondemeaning ways, because children "resist a teacher less when his communications convey respect and safeguard self-esteem" (Ginott, 1972, p. 77).

A first degree is **inviting choices**:

I need some strong helpers to help move the tumbling mat.

For some teachers, a mild invitation in situations like this is all children need. For others (and in other situations for all teachers), increased firmness is needed.

A second degree is **requesting choices**:

As soon as some strong helpers move the tumbling mat, we can go outside.

Or

Suggesting a reward after a task is known as the Premack Principle or the "grandma principle" (Jones, 1993). (As Grandma says, "Eat your peas, and then we can have dessert.") When requesting cooperation, the tone of voice as well as the words convey a confident determination that the task be done.

A third degree of firmness is **commanding choices**. We use a different example to illustrate:

Children, you are pushing near the computer. Sit in your chairs and we will discuss this, or move apart and work on something else. You choose.

There is a clear expression of disapproval in these words, but the teacher is addressing the situation, not attacking the personalities of the children involved. Some teachers are uncomfortable with the particular choice given: Stay here and discuss this or do something else. For some children, the decision to leave an argument may be a positive choice in this situation. The teacher uses her judgment about whether or not to offer an "out-choice" from mediation. This old teacher thinks that the mediation itself gives choices to children. In my view a kindly insistence that the mediation occur, when children are calm, is almost always justified: "We can calm down and talk about this now, or we can do other things now and talk about it later; which will it be?"

In-Choice/Out-Choice. When putting choices to children at any degree of firmness, an objective is to make the *in-choice* attractive. The **in-choice** is the one the teacher hopes the child will make. The teacher must be prepared, though, for the occasional *out-choice*. The **out-choice** is the less preferred option for the teacher, but one she can still live with. Children may select the out-choice because they need to feel significant in the situation. Or, the out-choice just sounds better to them. The teacher accepts either choice the child makes. Life is choice making, and choices have consequences—sometimes not what one wants, but always to learn from.

Classroom Anecdote	*(From a student teacher journal) Observation: Eric [a new child at Head Start] was climbing over the playground fence by a street. By the time the teacher realized what he was doing, she had time only to reach up and hold him until I went around to bring Eric back. Eric didn't want to go back. He said, "Teachers don't make the rules. Kids do." I explained to him sometimes to keep kids safe, the adults do make rules.* *Meanwhile, the teacher had come around the fence and took over. She said, "Kids go home later, Eric, not now. You have two choices: You can walk with me back to the playground by yourself or you can be carried back."* *I could tell the teacher expected Eric to say walk, but he replied, "Carried."* *The teacher didn't miss a beat. She said. "You want me to carry you over my shoulder like a sack of potatoes?" Eric said yes, so the teacher picked him up and carried him over her shoulder. She made jokes about him being a heavy sack of potatoes and then said she thought she could beat the sack of potatoes in a race to the playground. Eric won. The teacher talked with him about the incident. When it was time to go in, they walked in together.* *Reflection: I wouldn't have thought to give Eric this choice. Since he picked a way that might have caused him embarrassment, the teacher decided to make carrying him funny and non-threatening. I think this was a respectful and appropriate way to handle this situation, but the teacher got quite a workout!*

Giving choices is a basic in the guidance approach, but the skill takes practice. Beginning teachers sometimes offer choices that are too open-ended, or where choosing really is not warranted, for example: "Do you want to wash your hands for lunch?" Children need to know what the teacher wants them to do in order to cooperate. So, the teacher might rephrase the request: "Use this sink or that one to wash hands. Soon as we do, we get Cook Marie's delicious spaghetti!"

Four Quick Intervention Strategies

Unlike marginal mistaken behaviors, teachers agree that serious conflicts require intervention. When teacher time is limited, the resolution of problems becomes more difficult. With very serious conflicts, the teacher always "triages" for physical and emotional injury, provides any first aid, and calms everyone down. If necessary, the mediation can happen later. In most classrooms, very serious conflicts (hopefully) are not that common.

With more common, run-of-the-mill conflicts, the teacher is still challenged to give them as much time she would like. Techniques for resolving everyday problems quickly are important for teachers to learn. With quick and effective intervention, little problems tend not to become big ones, and the spread of mistaken behavior to other children—socially influenced mistaken behavior—is prevented. The quick intervention strategies discussed here are:

▷ Negotiation reminders

▷ Humor

▷ Nonverbal techniques

▷ Explain briefly

Negotiation Reminders

When a child reports a conflict, common responses by teachers who use guidance are:

"I understand that bothers you; can you use your words to tell him?"

"I hear what you are saying. You need to tell him how you feel so he knows."

When conflict management is a part of the everyday program, friendly negotiation reminders are often enough to stimulate child negotiation. Though it might not seem so, the message to a child in these statements is "I had a complaint, and the teacher listened." Having told the teacher and been heard, children often feel less need to force the issue with the other child. If a child does approach the other, it is often with righteous indignation rather than belligerence. The other child (usually aware that the teacher has been consulted) tends to respond in interesting ways.

With quick intervention, little problems tend not to become big ones.

Classroom Anecdote	*Observation: First graders Aureole, Amber, and Kendra were decorating doilies with sequins and other materials. After a couple of minutes, Amber came up to me and said, "Teacher, Aureole keeps telling me what to do. She's bossy."*
	I bent down, looked her in the eye, and said, "Can you tell her how that makes you feel?" Amber nodded her head, returned to Aureole, and said, "I don't like when you tell me what to do. That makes me sad."
	"Sorry," replied Aureole. "I won't be bossy, okay?"
	Amber smiled and said, "Okay."
	Student Teacher's Reflection: These children are used to using their words and are comfortable with it. It was effective for Amber to explain how she felt after telling me about it. Aureole knew she had told me, and listened to Amber's feelings. They were able to continue working together just like nothing had happened.

A stock phrase like the student teacher used is not a panacea, but it does tend to remind children that they can handle many issues for themselves: "Can you tell her how that makes you feel?"

Sentence Frames. Sue Liedl has reframed a classic negotiation reminder attributed to Marshall Rosenburg (Pirtle, 1995). Probably most useful at the primary grade level, Liedl's *sentence frame* is as follows:

I feel _____

when _____.

Next time please _____.

Many accidental or mostly accidental things happen when groups of children are in confined spaces for long periods of the day. Children can use **sentence frames** as recognized cues to prevent conflicts from getting more serious. This way of framing the statement opens the door to solving the problem in a relatively nonconfrontational way; for example:

Sentence frame: "I feel really sad when you bumped my arm 'cause I'm writing. Next time, please try to be more careful, okay?"

Response: "Well, I didn't mean to, but okay."

Sometimes, children (like adults) just do not know how to respond in a conflict situation. Taking the time to teach a sentence frame like this as a part of lesson or class meetings provides a helpful reminder: "Did you use your sentence frame?" A teacher is rewarded for repeated modeling of the frame when she hears children begin to use it on their own.

Humor as Tension Reliever

Just as good-natured humor prevents mistaken behavior (discussed in Chapter Eight), it also can defuse problems that do occur. The ability to see humor in a difficult situation relieves tension. When not at the expense of a child, a sense of humor complements the firmness that teachers sometimes must show, and helps children and teachers alike put mistaken behavior in perspective. The following anecdote and discussion are excerpted from the July 2006 "Guidance Matters" column that appeared in *Young Children* (Gartrell, 2006).

Classroom Anecdote	*Student teacher Jessica has had a conflict with Ryan over getting him to come in from the snow-covered playground. He is sitting in his cubby.*

Jessica:	*I need you to start taking off your stuff now, Ryan.*
Ryan:	*NO!! I don't want to.*
Jessica:	*We can't go to the multipurpose room with all of your snow clothes still on.*
Ryan:	*I don't care.*
Jessica:	*Please, Ryan. It's going to be a lot of fun. Don't you want to go and play with your friends?*
Ryan:	*NO!! (He crosses his arms in front of him.) I'm going to keep all my stuff on.*
Jessica:	*Are you going to keep them on all day? Even when you go to bed?*
Ryan:	*Yep, all day. (He nods his head and smiles.) I'm even going to wear them around my house.*
Jessica:	*Oh, really? Are you going to wear them in the bathtub too?*
Ryan:	*No, that's silly. I'd sink like a stone. (He laughs and takes off his outside clothes.)*
Jessica (smiles):	*Thank you for taking your stuff off, Ryan. (He smiles back at Jessica.) The two go into the room.*

Discussion: A (seemingly eternal) classroom challenge occurs whenever a teacher asks a child to do something and the child says no. Ryan felt upset because Jessica had made him come in from the playground. He said no to taking off his snowsuit. Rather than prolong the struggle, with some thought Jessica decided to try a different approach. She picked up on a comment Ryan made and used humor. And her friendly humor, a quality that learners of all ages appreciate in teachers, worked.

When Ryan pictured what it would be like to take a bath wearing snow duds, he laughed. The tension was broken. Jessica found a response that redeemed Ryan's dignity *and* their relationship. Not even experienced teachers can always recover as Jessica did. Forgiveness (including of one's self) and a bit of creative thinking are wonderful qualities for all teachers to practice—even if it is on the second try.

Friendly humor shows children that adults can be understanding and gracious; that the teacher is working with them not against them; and that the child as well as the teacher has a valued place in the classroom community. In a broader sense, a shared humorous moment removes the dilemma faced by every person in a less-powerful position: What do I do when this more powerful person and I disagree? Humor can change the perception of "you are against me" to "you and I can work this out together"—essentially the difference between making war and building peace. (This learning is good preparation for life in a democratic society.)

Please note that the person in charge has to decide to let humor into the situation and determine how to go about doing so. These are high-level skills. It is my own experience that the person we are "in charge of" is usually so relieved we are using friendly humor—rather than an alternative—that the jokes don't even have to be good ones. If we don't use force, the person is more likely to want to get along!

Alice Honig (1989) has studied humor as a developing attribute in young children. Honig concludes that older preschoolers delight in their newfound conceptual understanding of wordplay, which is the basis of much of our humor. To take a bath with your clothing on is silly. Just ask children's authors, such as Laura Joffe Numeroff (*If You Give a Mouse a Cookie*), who have perfected wordplay techniques in their books (Gartrell, 2006, pp. 108–109).

Classroom Anecdote	*Some years ago a teacher in an elementary school classroom was also the part-time principal. The children knew that when she was out of the room, silence was to reign. On one occasion when Mrs. Kling returned, she was dissatisfied with the noise level and demanded, "Order, please!"*
	From the back of the room came the "order," "Ham and eggs!" The young man (whose voice sounded a lot like the author's) was greatly relieved at the teacher's response: She laughed with gusto.

Using humor in a difficult situation is the teacher's choice. For some teachers, humor comes easily and helps everyone to function comfortably in the classroom. For others, humor takes work; it requires that the teacher look freshly at events when "the pressure is on." Because young children look freshly at all situations, young children make friendly humor a developmentally responsive technique to use. The challenge is for teachers not to take themselves too seriously and to remember that shared laughter can both prevent conflicts and also help to resolve them.

Nonverbal Techniques

The advantage of **nonverbal intervention** (also called body language) is that they can remind children about guidelines without causing undue embarrassment. Charles (2004) comments that nonverbal techniques typically include: eye contact, physical proximity, body carriage, gestures, and facial expression. In an encouraging classroom, smiles and a friendly facial expression are, of course, fundamental nonverbal techniques. A key nonverbal technique, physical proximity is useful in both prevention and intervention with young children. In the active, developmentally appropriate classroom, the teacher is constantly moving about and establishing physical proximity.

The skillful teacher does so without disrupting the flow of the activity or lesson.

Fredric Jones (1993) has long been known for his writing about body language as a method in positive classroom discipline. For purposes of intervention, Jones' nonverbal techniques apply mainly to children in the *primary grades and up*. Preprimary children get so involved in situations that they tend to be oblivious to all but the most direct nonverbal techniques—physical proximity with a whisper or friendly physical contact. A proviso about nonverbal techniques is that sustained eye contact and some touches, such as a pat on the head, may be appropriate with European American children, but not with some children of other cultural backgrounds. Knowledge of the cultural expectations of the individual families one works with is important.

As they progress through the primary grades, children become attuned to the teachers' use of body language. A strategy for addressing mistaken behavior follows, building from the work of Jones (1993). Although the final steps involve words, the words are private, carefully chosen, and follow from the nonverbal foundation.

Step One: *Eye contact*
The power of eye contact, the age-old stare, is remembered by most adults from their own school days. Generally, making eye contact involves less embarrassment than if the teacher calls out a child's name, writes it on the board, or flips a card. A slight smile lessens the intensity of Step One.

Step Two: *Eye contact with gestures*
A slow shake of the head with a gesture such as the palm up or an index finger pointed up at about shoulder height reinforces the message of the eye contact. Jones (1993) maintains that holding eye contact until the child resumes attention is important.

Step Three: *Physical proximity*
Mistaken behavior occurs most often away from the teacher. An important finding of Jones (1993) was that nearness of the teacher to children is effective at reestablishing limits. In early childhood classrooms, getting near to conflicts is a given. Jones emphasizes movement by the teacher, a necessity for teachers who are encouraging active learning in their classrooms.

Step Four: *Proximity with general reminder*
Having moved close to children, the teacher makes a general reminder such as "I need everyone's attention for this." (A quick glance at the children makes this step more emphatic.)

Step Five: *Proximity with direct comment*
After establishing proximity, the teacher makes eye contact and privately requests the behavior expected. (The teacher protects self-esteem by speaking in a low but determined tone.) The teacher may follow up with a guidance talk.

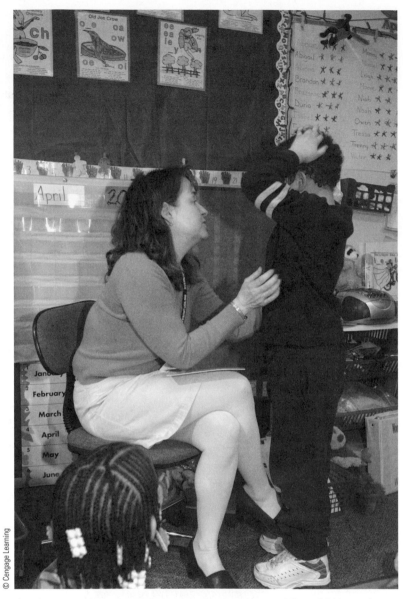

A caring expression communicates acceptance and support for a child in need.

According to Jones (1993), body carriage even more than spoken words tells children about the sureness of the teacher and her comfort level with the group. The basic element of body language, of course, is facial expression. About facial expression, important for all teachers of young children, Charles (1996) says the following:

Like body carriage, facial expressions communicate much. Facial expressions can show enthusiasm, seriousness, enjoyment, and appreciation, all of which tend to encourage good behavior; or they can reveal boredom, annoyance, and resignation, which may encourage misbehavior. Perhaps more than anything else, facial expressions such as winks and smiles demonstrate a sense of humor, the trait students most enjoy in teachers. (p. 133)

Friendly facial expressions, along with the most fundamental form of non-verbal expression, touch, together can calm children in ways that words alone cannot (Carlson, 2006). Teachers use touch when they sense that the physical contact will calm and refocus children, so that problems can be cooperatively solved. Children, with whom teachers have taken the time to build relationships, accept touch as a part of the teacher's calming efforts and afterwards as an indicator of renewed relations. Teachers have a sense of how to use touch and when, based on their knowledge of the child. Used with intentionality, friendly touch guides children through tough times even while it helps to build relationship.

Explain Briefly

Among writers about teacher-child relations, none discusses the use of language more constructively (or eloquently) than Ginott (1972). Ginott states:

Teachers like parents, need a high degree of competence in communication. An enlightened teacher shows sensitivity to semantics. He knows that the substance learned by a child often depends on the style used by the teacher. (p. 98)

About the use of language during intervention, Ginott speaks of the importance of *brevity*. Young children have difficulty understanding lengthy explanations. Concise explanations that address the situation and motivate toward change are the objective.

Classroom Illustration	*When Justin spoke to a neighbor for the third time during a class discussion, the teacher <u>did</u> <u>not</u> state: "Justin, you certainly have a lot to say today. Your mouth and your ears can't work at the same time. When you're talking, others can't hear either, and the class can't have important discussions. Do you think you could sit quietly for the rest of the group? You can talk all you want to the other children when you're out on the playground. Now, let's see you use your listening ears. Do you have them on? I am certainly glad that you do."*
	Establishing eye-level proximity, the teacher did *say (quietly but firmly), "Justin, only one person talks at a time. You have good ideas to share, but you need to raise your hand and wait for a turn."*

The brief use of encouragement along with reinforcing a guideline captures well Ginott's (1972) sense of the positive power of words To defuse conflicts, these examples show "open-faced" compliment sandwiches. For Ginott, "correction is direction," as Table 10–3 illustrates:

Table 10–3 *Examples of Encouragement with Direction to Briefly Reinforce Guidelines*	
Toddlers:	Yay! You used your words! Let's calm down with some deep breaths. (as the teacher reacts to a toddler who—this time—didn't bite, but did yell at another child)
Preschoolers:	You two are holding tightly onto the tray. Just keep it steady while you walk. (as the teacher gently steadies the tray of milk containers that the children—grinning—were starting to rock)
Primary-grade children:	You are so eager to get started, you are arguing over a pencil! Decide at break whose pencil it is. Darrin, use my really cool "loaner" pencil for now. (as the teacher approaches two children arguing over a pencil at start of assignment)

Behaviors Reported By Other Children

"Tattling" bothers most teachers. They would prefer that children "attend to their own affairs" and solve their own problems. In some classrooms, children are punished for tattling. In others, a child who chronically tattles acquires a label in the teacher's mind such as "busybody" or "whiny butt." (See Recommended Reading, "Tattling: It Drives Teachers Bonkers!" [Gartrell, 2007].)

Child-report (an alternate term for *tattling*) is difficult to deal with because the motives of children are not always what they seem. The reasons for child-report range from a legitimate concern to a need for attention to a desire to manipulate the teacher. From a guidance perspective, sometimes a teacher wants a child to report, for instance, when:

▶ a child has wandered from the playground

▶ children are fighting, and one has been seriously hurt

▶ a child has been injured in an accident

▶ a child is having a seizure or is otherwise ill

▶ others are acting inappropriately toward a child.

Children should be encouraged to report such incidents. In a class meeting, the teacher may discuss with children what such an emergency is and what children should do in the event of an emergency. The well-being of children and the professional integrity of the teacher are supported by children acting as "concerned citizens."

On the other hand, the teacher might discuss with the class how reports that are "not emergencies" should be handled. One technique that attempts to balance the priorities of teachers and the needs of children is a "report box" (Gartrell, 2007). Children who have concerns can write or draw out the problem

Child-report can be for many reasons—including a legitimate request for assistance.

on prepared "report forms" and put them into the box. The teacher consults the box daily, reads the name the child has put on the "name line," and asks if the child still wants to talk about the concern. Follow-up actions to address the concern, such as a class meeting, may result, though often a little individual attention is enough to resolve the situation.

Other teachers have used "Big Mouth Billy Bass" (with the batteries out), or a large audiologist ear (both bought at garage sales) for children to express their concerns to (Gartrell, 2007). Lots of times these props take care of the child's concerns just by "listening." The teacher is there only for backup. One fifth-grade student remarked to her former kindergarten teacher that she still remembered talking to "the ear" and feeling better! (Expressing concerns to an inanimate prop and then feeling better is the kind of reason so many of us care so much about this age group.)

Motives for Child Reports. When children report, the teacher does well to take a moment and consider which of several possible motives may be operating. As Table 10–4 indicates, teachers respond differently depending on the suspected motive of the child.

Why Bother. Why should teachers bother with the complex, sometimes bothersome interactions that come with child-report? By listening, the adult affirms the budding citizenship of the young child. By using guidance the adult teaches

Table 10–4 *Teacher Responses to Child Report*

Suspected Motive of the Child	Suggested Response of Teacher
Child has legitimate difficulty in relations with another child.	Teacher encourages children to solve on their own— "tell him how you feel about that"—or mediates to the extent necessary.
Child honestly reports problem situation involving other children.	Teacher thanks the child for being a "caring citizen." Monitors situation. If necessary, intervenes taking a guidance approach.
Child reports only once or twice to get the teacher's attention or to see what the teacher will do (Level One mistaken behavior).	Teacher reassures child that things are under control. Monitors situation in low-profile manner "just in case." Notices whether the reporting child seeks attention in other ways. Works on building relationship with the child. Gives attention in other ways.
Child reports minimal problems on a regular basis (Level Two mistaken behavior).	Teacher thanks the child for concern but explains that the teacher is watching and other children can take care of themselves. Tells the child what the serious problems are that the child can report. Builds relationship. Gives attention in other ways.
Child reports to either manipulate the teacher or get another child into "trouble." Does so on a regular basis (Level Three mistaken behavior).	As in all cases, the teacher avoids "charging into the situation." Keeps open mind about the children involved. Monitors "reporter" for other Level Three mistaken behavior. If necessary, follows procedures for working with this level.

children to resolve their own conflicts, to respect others' efforts at problem solving, and to come to the aid of peers who are genuinely in need. These capabilities are desirable in citizens of any age in the 21st century. From this perspective, "tattling" too becomes an opportunity to teach democratic life skills.

Intervention Strategies When Follow-Up Is Needed

When adults disagree, the immediate resolution of differences is not assured. Yet, with children who lack personal resources and experience, adults seem to frequently expect "instant resolution." In academic settings that emphasize decorum and academic achievement, many view teachers who mediate conflicts as using time unproductively.

Time is required if serious differences are to be settled in ways from which all can benefit. In the mutually satisfactory resolution of problems, everyone learns (Evans, 2002; Wichert, 1991). In the peaceful resolution of difficulties, teachers actively support children's self-esteem and children's faith in the institution of the school.

Ginott (1972) recognized that whereas brevity works in mild conflict situations, in more serious conflicts there should be "no hurried help." He wrote that when the teacher quickly "solves" problems for children, they feel inadequate. In anticipation of the conflict management movement to come, Ginott stated:

> *The teacher listens to the problem, rephrases it, clarifies it, gives the child credit for formulating it, and then asks, "What options are open to you?" "What are your choices in this situation?" Often the child himself comes up with a solution. Thus, he learns that he can rely on his own judgment. When a teacher hastily offers solutions, children miss the opportunity to acquire competence in problem-solving and confidence in themselves. (p. 92)*

The guidance teacher can address some situations quickly with nonverbal or verbal responses that sustain self-esteem and increase understanding. In these cases, follow-up is not necessary. In other cases, speedy resolution is not possible. When the teacher must give time to a situation, she does so either at the moment of the occurrence or later in the day. (Response at a later time is due to conflicting demands on the teacher at the moment, the need for a cooling-down time if emotions are high, or the need for privacy.)

Chapter Nine explored conflict mediation, the gold-standard intervention when teachers need to take time to fully resolve a conflict. This section addresses five related problem-solving techniques when follow-up is needed:

- Reflective listening
- Guidance talks
- Teacher-child negotiation
- Including children's ideas
- Reconciliation.

Reflective Listening

Reflective listening is a key tool in problem solving conflicts. Teachers use reflective listening to model and teach self-calming and impulse management. Other names for this technique are "active listening" and "acknowledging feelings." When using reflective listening, the teacher articulates or rephrases the child's feelings and perceptions. The teacher does so to show the child she understands, and to model the use of helpful language in stressful situations. By having feelings and perceptions articulated and affirmed by the teacher, the child calms and is more open to discussion. This *release function* is the common use of reflective listening.

A second function of reflective listening is *impulse management*. Many times young children show mistaken behavior because their impulse control system is still developing (Preusse, 2005). Because reflective listening allows children to release strong emotion, they have less need to act on the impulse. The teacher can then direct children to nonhurting alternatives, such as a requested choice,

Table 10–5 *Reflective Listening to Teach Self-Calming and Impulse Management*	
Situation	**Reflective Responses**
• Preschooler upset that doll has been taken.	• "You are upset and that is okay. Take five deep breaths, cool down, and we will make this better."
• First grader says another child has stolen his quarter. Is approaching the suspect with an angry expression.	• "Your quarter is gone and you are angry. You have a right to be. Sit down here, chill a bit, and think about some words you can use. I will bring Martin over."

a guidance talk, or conflict mediation. Having regained a measure of calm, the child is more likely to comply. (Reflective listening is central to the first step in mediation, cooling down.)

Over time, the teacher uses this two-part technique—reflectively listening and guiding to alternative selection—to teach the child to self-initiate an impulse management strategy. See Table 10–5 for examples.

Guidance Talks

Guidance talks between a teacher and child occur either during the last steps in conflict management or, when appropriate, instead of conflict management. Teachers usually have guidance talks "after the fact" when emotions have cooled. The guidance talk, held privately to avoid embarrassment, differs from the age-old lecture. Instead of an adult talking *at* a child, the guidance talk is a conversation *with* the child.

The teacher bases guidance talks on the five-finger formula, as used in conflict mediation. The steps may be blended, depending on the situation, but most or all are usually evident. In guidance talks, after everyone is calm, the teacher:

▶ Discusses what happened and helps the child understand why the behavior was mistaken. For example, she explains that it is okay to feel frustrated when the top of the glue bottle comes off with the glue, but it is not all right to throw the bottle and accidentally hit a friend.

▶ Assists the child to understand how all parties in the situation may have felt. (A goal of guidance talks is to build empathy.)

▶ Brainstorms with the child alternative acceptable behaviors to use the next time a similar situation arises. "Next time, you can say, 'That makes me angry!' Or come to me and say, 'Teacher, help!' And I will."

▶ Asks how the child can help the other child feel better or how the situation can be made better. (Note that this is different than forcing an apology. After a guidance talk, the child hopefully feels relieved rather than guilty. Involving him in a choice of how to help the other feel better teaches the importance of reconciliation. If the child is not ready, suggest "maybe later.")

When teachers in encouraging classrooms work with an individual child, they use guidance talks frequently, including in "heavy-duty" circumstances.

Classroom Anecdote	*Les was building a barn with blocks when Craig accidentally knocked it over. Les had fists clenched when the teacher, Jerlean, arrived.*

Jerlean: Craig didn't mean to, Les, but it's too bad about your building, and it's okay to feel upset about it.

Les was too upset to listen and kicked the remaining blocks, a unit smacking the teacher on the ankle. When Les saw what happened, he looked like he was about to cry.

Jerlean grimaced slightly, then said, "Les, take deep breaths please so that you feel better . . . in and out, that's right." She put her arm around Les' shoulder and continued, "It's all right, Les, that only hurt a little, and I'm not upset because I know you didn't mean to. You're not having a very good day, are you?"

Then Les did cry. The teacher held him, and soon the two picked up the blocks together. Later they talked about what happened.

Jerlean: You got very upset today, Les. It is all right to get upset, but besides you, two other people felt sad because of what happened. Instead of doing something that could hurt people, what are some words you could say?

Les: Stop it! Teacher, help!

Jerlean: Those words would do it. Now, I wonder how you could help the two people feel better? You know who I mean.

Les told the teacher he was sorry, then found Craig and told him too. The teacher thanked Les and they again rehearsed what he could do next time.

The teacher used reflective listening with Les during the conflict. The de-escalation did not go perfectly, and of course doesn't always. The teacher still was able to remain calm and continue with reflective listening to help Les defuse his anger. Significantly, Jerlean used *I-messages* (or *self-report*) to reassure the child. Self-report helped Jerlean to use "personalized reflective listening" and assist with her own impulse management. Her ability to remain calm enabled successful social problem solving through the guidance talk. (This teacher was working with Les, who was dealing with some Level Three issues, in other ways as well.)

Teacher-Child Conflicts

Writers about guidance usually focus on conflicts between children that the teacher mediates. With the active learning encouraged by developmentally appropriate practice, child–child conflicts become the natural focus. Yet, a concern among many beginning teachers is the *teacher-child conflict*. When the teacher is directly involved in the conflict, the emotional stakes are higher. While the opportunity for significant learning is high, for both the child and the adult, this outcome is not assured.

Teacher-child conflicts occur more frequently when the education program is less responsive to developmental needs. Unrealistic expectations create a mismatch between children and the program that can lead to defiance, stress, and frustration. The teacher reduces this mistaken behavior when she modifies the program to make it more developmentally appropriate.

Still, even in encouraging classrooms, differences occur between teacher and child. Moreover, children with serious needs will show Level Three mistaken behavior regardless of classroom climate. Intentionally or unintentionally—as shown in the anecdote involving Les—the teacher may become the target.

When two individuals resolve a conflict between themselves, they have *negotiated* a solution. The idea of *teacher-child* negotiation makes some teachers uncomfortable: The term seems to imply "peer-to-peer" communication. The reasoning is that if negotiation can happen only between peers, teachers would have to relinquish their leadership roles and their standards. In fact, it is quite likely that the leaders who people most look up to frequently negotiate.

When a teacher negotiates with a child, she does not give up the mantel of leadership, but just uses it with dignity and mutual respect. In fact, a measure of the teacher's commitment to the civil resolution of conflicts is her growing ability to use teacher-child negotiation. (When she negotiated with Ryan about taking his snowsuit off, Jessica probably helped to *establish* her leadership with the boy.) For many teachers who use guidance, these negotiations become "not a big deal." In fact, every time a teacher holds a *guidance talk* with a child, as in the example of Les and Jerlean, she engages in teacher-child negotiation. Negotiations happen whenever a teacher regards a conflict involving a child as a **teachable moment**.

Including Children's Ideas

A strategy mentioned as helpful in both mediation and negotiation is *involving children in the solution process*. When children contribute to the solution, they feel ownership in the process and capable as problem solvers. Including some suggestions of Ginott (1972), questions like these empower children to "work things out":

▶ Do you think you can solve this problem on your own?

▶ What are your choices in this situation?

▶ How can we solve this problem?

▶ Who has an idea about what we can do?

▶ What can we do to make this work for both of you?

▶ How could you solve this differently?

▶ Maybe the two of you can solve the problem together?

▶ What words could you use next time?

Such questions assist the teacher in conflict mediation, guidance talks, and class meetings. When a teacher asks children for their views, ideas, and assistance, children are encouraged to show initiative and to work for a cooperative solution. The challenge for the teacher is to think of and use these questions during the management experience, as the following example illustrates.

Classroom Anecdote	*Second grader Elaine had a difficult time concentrating during large-group activities. She visited with neighbors and showed inattentiveness to topics being discussed. At a break time, the teacher talked with the child:*

> *Teacher:* *Elaine, we need to talk about a problem we are having during large group. I have to remind you to pay attention too many times.*
>
> *Elaine:* *Well, the other kids are always talking to me.*
>
> *Teacher:* *Yes, I know; it is hard to listen when too many people are talking. What can we do about it?*
>
> *Elaine:* *(long pause) Maybe I could move.*
>
> *Teacher:* *That sounds like an idea. Why don't you choose? Where could you sit where you wouldn't be bothered by other children?*
>
> *Elaine:* *By Renee, (a para) maybe.*
>
> *Teacher:* *All right, let's try it. But remember our guideline, one person talks at a time, okay?*
>
> *Elaine:* *Okay, Teacher.*

The teacher followed through by making sure Elaine sat where they agreed and by using nonverbal techniques, including smiles, to hold her attention. Two days later the teacher complimented the progress that Elaine had shown.

Teachers seek children's input, of course, with groups as well as individuals. In fact, many class meetings are called so that teachers and children can negotiate solutions to problems together. The leader is the teacher, who is perhaps bothered by an event, and calls a class meeting to request the children's input in solving the problem (Vance & Weaver, 2002).

Reconciliation

To reemphasize a key idea concerning *reconciliation*, the teacher does not force apologies. Children no less than adults know when they are ready to apologize and when they are not. (To their credit, children do tend to forgive more easily than most adults, but they still shouldn't be forced to do so.) Instead, the adults ask the child for ideas about "how to help the other child feel better." Children come up with creative solutions when they are encouraged to make amends on their own. Students in my classes tell me they have heard ideas like:

"Tell him I would be his friend again."

"Put a wet towel on it."

"Shake her hand and say I'm sorry."

(When a child offers to say he's sorry, then the apology is more likely authentic.) The teacher then uses the suggestions to help the child to get the relationship

In a group setting, a request to solve a problem becomes part of a class meeting, or a negotiation between the teacher and the class.

back on track. While some children may take a while to come around, they generally are more willing to apologize when their feelings and thoughts have been respected—including about how to reconcile.

In the most serious conflict situations, to prevent harm teachers physically restrain or remove children for cooling down (see Chapter Eleven). In these cases, the primary focus of the child's anger may be the teacher. Wherever the focus of blame in a teacher-child conflict, the teacher is the one who initiates the reconciliation process—even if it takes a while. The principle of unconditional positive regard means that the teacher works for reconciliation as a part of daily practice. In the guidance approach, the teacher recognizes that the act of reconciling comes not from weakness, but from strength. Guidance differs from punitive discipline in this regard.

Why Take the Time?

The criticism has been made that the intervention methods discussed in Part Three take time away from "actual" teaching. The author's response is that teaching children democratic life skills is at the heart of what good education is.

A growing number of studies on the development of young children are coming to a similar conclusion, which the author summarizes here:

Children are at low risk for social problems and school failure if they are accepted as contributing members of the classroom community by peers and adults, and if they see themselves as capable learners and worthy group members. Prime years for developing this social-emotional competence are the early childhood years. (Coie, 1996; Dodge, 1991; Klass, Guskin & Thomas, 1995; Slaby, Roedell, Arezzo, & Hendricks, 1995)

To put this another way, for young children to succeed in their education, they need to be accepted members of the learning community and see themselves as such.

These researchers have verified the finding that children whose behavior has caused them to be stigmatized (disqualified from healthy group membership)

Teachers take the time because though child guidance children learn democratic life skills.

puts them at much higher risks for failure in school and social life. Persistent negative self-perceptions tend to lead to future behaviors that are self-defeating and potentially violent (Surgeon General's Report, 1999).

The encouraging classroom is about helping all children in the class feel they are members in good standing. In line with Katz's recommendation, the encouraging classroom makes relationships *the first R* (Kantrowitz & Wingert, 1989). Through using guidance to solve problems of mistaken behavior, the adult is teaching children the skills they need not just to succeed in school, but also to function as productive citizens and healthy individuals. As a reminder, those democratic life skills include:

1. The ability to see one's self as a worthy individual and a capable member of the group.
2. The ability to express strong emotions in nonhurting ways.
3. The ability to solve problems ethically and intelligently.
4. The ability to work cooperatively in groups, with acceptance of the human differences among members.
5. The ability to be understanding of the feelings and viewpoints of others.

These outcomes of guidance in the encouraging classroom can also be put in terms of educational/developmental outcomes, as follows. The child gains in:

▶ Emotional development through the ability to see situations positively, express feelings acceptably, and resolve problems constructively.

▶ Language development through the vocabulary, phrasing, and functional communication necessary for the resolution of difficulties.

▶ Cognitive development by the information processing and critical thinking inherent in problem solving, including the growing ability to understand the perspectives of others.

▶ Physical development through freedom from the effects of stress, tension, and hostile feelings when problems remain unresolved or become aggravated.

▶ Social development by learning life skills important for productive functioning as a member of the learning community and a democratic society.

A Matter of Ethics

The research-verified connection between social–emotional competence and academic success is the crucial reason for taking the time to assist children to succeed in the social world of the classroom. In fact, the National Association for the Education of Young Children (NAEYC) has made assisting children to solve problems peaceably a matter of *professional ethics*. The entire field should embrace ethical teaching, but in any classroom, program, and school things can become complicated.

Classroom Anecdote	A new teacher in a group of three-year-olds noticed one large boy who showed the following pattern of behavior. When he wanted something or became upset, he would strike out at the nearest child. The new teacher took a problem-solving approach to the boy's behavior that included learning more about him. She discovered that he had limited language development, and could not easily use words to express his needs. She noticed that he seemed to get a "glint in his eye" before he would hit out. She noted that the other teachers would give him a time-out after he hit, talk briefly with him, and get him to say he was sorry. They would then leave him alone until the next episode. The new teacher noticed the pattern repeat itself over several days.

After talking with the other teachers and not getting much response, the teacher took her notes to the director. She suggested to the director that a more comprehensive response was needed, involving the child's parents and perhaps other professionals. The director told her she was new in the center, that this is how the boy was, and that the parents were not to be involved. She was told to let the more experienced staff handle the situation.

The teacher concluded that the director and staff turned a "blind eye" to the situation because they didn't want to do anything that might cause the family (influential in the small community) to drop the program. The teacher continued her observations and noted that the child's behavior, if anything, became more extreme. As a professional, the teacher felt bound to continue pressing the issue. Because of her actions, the director asked her to leave.

The Code of Ethical Conduct. The NAEYC has published a **Code of Ethical Conduct**, included as Appendix A of this text. The Code "provides a shared conception of professional responsibility that affirms our commitment to the core values of our field." One important use of the Code is to provide guidance when practitioners face ethical dilemmas. The new teacher was acting ethically, and the director and other staff unethically, in relation to key statements in the Code, especially principles P-1.1 and P-2.5:

> *P-1.1—Above all, we shall not harm children. We shall not participate in practices that are disrespectful, degrading, dangerous, exploitative, intimidating, psychologically damaging, or physically harmful to children.*

Harm was being done to other children who were victimized by the child, and to the child himself, by not being guided to alternative behaviors and communication skills. The director apparently did not recognize that she was under an ethical mandate. Her duty was to prevent the harm that this child, with Level Three mistaken behavior, was causing and experiencing.

> *P-2.5—We shall inform the family of accidents involving their child, or risks such as exposures to contagious disease that may result in infection, and of events that might result in psychological damage.*

Whatever the staff did or did not say to parents of the other children, the family in question was denied information about events that were causing psychological harm to their son and to others in the class. In not communicating with the parents about the problem, the director failed to act in the best interests of the family. The director denied the family an opportunity to cooperate in a plan that would have improved prospects for the child's healthy development and for a healthy climate in the class. She acted in a repressive manner as well toward the new teacher.

As an "afterword," the teacher thought about reporting the incident to the state licensing agency, but concluded that nothing would come of it. If the NAEYC had accredited the program—the association responsible for the Code of Ethical Conduct—she could have reported the incident to the NAEYC. In the end, the teacher did what dedicated young teachers sometimes do when encountering frustrations in the field. She returned to a university for more education.

The teacher has now completed a master's program in early childhood education. She is the author of a handbook to educate parents and teachers about ethics in early childhood education and the importance of liberation teaching. She is still a professional in the field, though more on her own terms and with less dependence on administrators and staff who act as technicians rather than guidance professionals.

Building Cooperation with Today's Diverse Families

As a professional, the teacher cooperates with families in the education of the child. Building cooperation is easier when families and teachers have similar backgrounds, but sometimes more difficult when social and cultural characteristics differ. Many factors make cooperation with families a challenge. Parents from any background have distinct roles and perspectives inherently different than the teacher's. Typically, parents (including custodial "acquired" parents):

▶ have a strong emotional investment in their own child

▶ at times question their own effectiveness

▶ have views about acceptable behavior and discipline influenced by their backgrounds more than formal education

▶ may regard the teacher as a "superior" who will be unreceptive to efforts at communication (Gestwicki, 2007).

Unless teachers understand that parents' viewpoints are role based, they may take personally contacts with families who seem defensive or unfriendly. Clearly, social and cultural differences between the teacher and family accentuate the possibility of misunderstandings.

To accommodate role and social–cultural differences, Galinsky (1988) recommends: "Rather than the dispenser of correct information, the professional builds an alliance in which the parent's own expertise is strengthened" (p. 11). More recently, Pappano (2007) makes the same point—see Recommended Readings.

Establishing relationships early on helps family members and children feel supported by your role as the teacher.

Galinsky (1988), Pappano (2007), and Gestwicki (2007) provide useful suggestions for taking this collaborative approach. The following discussion builds upon points made by the authors. These five steps guide the teacher toward achieving cooperation with families who may have values and lifestyles different from their own.

Step One: Monitor Your Feelings Toward the Family

Teachers sometimes feel uncomfortable around some families. One reason for ambivalent feelings is the view that a family has not met implicit "minimum expectations" that the teacher has about parenting or lifestyle (Galinsky, 1988). In this event, the teacher needs to understand circumstances within the family that may make her expectations unrealistic. For instance, a family of a different cultural heritage may seem to the teacher to be "male dominated," with the wife and daughters kept in apparent subservient roles. The teacher who discerns this difference in cultural—rather than moral—terms is in a better position to still accept the common bond she has with the family, work for the well-being of the child, and treat *all* members of the family respectfully in working toward this goal (Gestwicki, 2007).

Cultural, economic, and social factors contribute to family situations and parenting styles sometimes quite different from the teacher's. When the teacher perceives discomfort about a family, her challenge is to increase understanding so that she can engage in team building ("joining") around what she and the families have in common: the child. On occasion, the effort can and does result in heightened cross-cultural understanding for both.

Step Two: Understand Parent Development

About this topic Galinsky (1989) states:

> It is much easier to understand families if you know the normal course of parental growth and development. For example, before decrying the super baby phenomenon, it helps to know that all parents want perfection for their children—that is normal. It is their definition of perfection you want to alter, not their desire for the best for their child. (p. 10)

Single parents in their late teens or early twenties are still growing into adulthood, hopefully with family support (White, Graham, & Bradford, 2005—see Recommended Readings). The needs of young parents are considerably different from parents in their thirties who have achieved relative stability in their professional and/or family lives. Parents in the first category may need a mentor in education and personal development processes—for both their children and themselves. More-established parents may be more interested in the teacher's competence and vision for her educational program.

The task of balancing work or school with parenthood provides challenges for many parents. Teachers might be attuned to expressions of attachment by the child for the family and make a point of relaying these to the family. Families who hear from a teacher how much they mean to the child tend to recognize both that they matter and that the teacher understands. In particular, working families who are just starting out need early childhood teachers to be active in the support role. The teacher avoids the appearance of a "substitute parent" and portrays herself instead as a caring professional who works as a team member with family members (Gestwicki, 2007).

Parents and caregivers who stay at home often feel strongly about their roles and identities. The early childhood teacher shows she accepts stay-at-home family members. If they are willing, the teacher invites them to extend their family interest to the class by becoming volunteers. The development of parents is affected not just by their age, but by the roles they define for themselves in the home, workplace, and community.

Step Three: Choose Words That Avoid Value Judgments

Describing without labeling is a basic of the guidance approach that pertains to family members no less than children. Here is a tongue-in-cheek variation of an example used by Morgan (1989):

Instead of: Karla was a real terror this afternoon. It was "isolation corner" for her today. After that she shaped up, and she is being a good girl now.

Say: Karla's morning went well, but this afternoon she had a conflict with two children. She needed a cool-down time, but we talked about it and she is having an easier time now.

Note the non-judgmental tone and the recognition of progress included in the second statement, which is a compliment sandwich. As a contrast, in the first statement the use of "value-laden" language is clear. The compliment sandwich, I-message, and reflective listening all provide alternatives to value judgments, and are useful in communications with families as well as with children to encourage cooperation.

Step Four: Problem Solve with Families

Teacher-parent negotiation often becomes necessary when a child's mistaken behavior grows serious. Galinsky (1988) suggests a six-point approach to *teacher-parent problem solving*. The goal is to convert disagreements into discussion points. Galinsky's formula is similar to the processes suggested earlier for helping children solve problems in the classroom. The points include:

1. Describe the situation as a problem to be solved. Avoid accusations or the implication that the source of the problem resides in the personality of the parent or the child.

2. Generate multiple solutions. Families and professionals should both do this, and no one's suggestions should be ignored, put down, or denounced.

3. Discuss the pros and cons of each suggestion.

4. Come to a consensus about which solutions to try.

5. Discuss how you will implement these solutions.

6. Agree to meet again to evaluate how these solutions are working so that you can change your approach, if necessary (p. 11).

On occasion, resolving differences proves difficult, and negotiation needs to give way to third-party mediation. As Galinsky (1988) comments, "Having others to turn to when there are tensions is crucial in working effectively with families" (p. 10). Seeking a senior staff member to assist in the problem-solving process is a mark of maturity for the guidance teacher (Koch & McDonough, 1999).

Sources of support for the teacher outside of the immediate situation—fellow staff members and friends or family members—is equally important. The support person should recognize the need for a teacher to privately "vent" with no repercussions. Hopefully, if the person providing support is a colleague, he can also assist the teacher to plan a constructive course of action regarding the situation.

Step Five: Use Support Services

Head Start has led the way in assisting families to access health and social service agencies as well as educational services. Increasingly, schools and other programs are coming to realize that not just the child, but the family is the unit of service. The ability to remove the stigma of special education or social service assistance for families is a goal of the teacher (Coleman, 1997).

Galinsky (1988) identifies a crucial role for the teacher in referring families to other services. She states, "It is just as important to know when to say no and to refer as it is to know when to say yes" (p. 10). The teacher is not a therapist or a social worker, but she can refer a family to a needed service and be supportive through the referral process. Rosenthal and Sawyers (1996) provide a list of steps important in making a referral:

1. Know the agencies in your area.

2. Know competent people with whom you can work at these organizations.

© Cengage Learning

Understanding families is much easier if the teacher understands the normal course of parental growth and development.

3. Refer to specific people, not just an organization.

4. Get an agreement from the family preferably in writing that they will participate.

5. Ask the family to predict what might prevent them from participating and ask for solutions (such as transportation and child care).

6. Check on families' ideas about solutions and arrangements.

7. Make sure you provide for a follow-up meeting (p. 199).

Head Start staff might be comfortable helping with more of these steps; a child care professional or an elementary school teacher might be able to help with a few. The individual teacher usually should not think in terms of taking referral actions on his own. Instead, working with other staff as a team, teachers can and should endeavor to make referrals, including the preliminary step of learning as much as possible about the services available. Families who are helped with successful referrals tend to strengthen their commitment both to their children and to the classroom staff.

The success of the referral process depends on the quality of the teacher-family relationship. The relationship comes first. Teachers always involve families in discussions and decisions about referrals.

The child is an extension of the family. The teacher cannot separate the child's life at school from the child's life at home (Boyd-Zaharias & Pate-Bain, 2008—see Recommended Readings). The teacher knows when she and the family have achieved cooperation in relation to the child. The family speaks openly about their child and home dynamics that may affect the child at school. They take an interest, and may become actively involved in, the child's classroom world (Gestwicki, 2007). The family becomes willing to accept the teacher's support in their leadership with the child. Children's education and development improve when teachers and families work together.

Summary

1. What goes into the decision to intervene?

The teacher is a friend to children, but she is an adult friend who accepts the responsibility of leadership. The adult works to understand situations by practicing "with-it-ness." She determines the level of mistaken behavior, and whether problem situations involve one or two children or a number of children. The teacher decides whether to intervene and the degree of firmness of the intervention. The strategy of inviting, requesting, or commanding choices illustrates the use of different degrees of firmness and at the same time grants children a measure of independence.

2. What are four quick intervention strategies?

Quick intervention strategies resolve little problems before they become big conflicts. These four quick strategies still protect self-esteem, which is important in guidance. A negotiation reminder that cues children to use their own developing social skills is a first strategy. Humor is a second strategy, by which the teacher can relax children in tense situations. A third strategy is nonverbal communication that includes using facial expressions, establishing proximity, and friendly touch. Brevity or "acknowledge and direct" is a fourth strategy, an effective alternative to moralizing and "lectures."

3. How does the teacher respond to mistaken behaviors reported by children?

Child-report (an alternate term to *tattling*) is difficult to deal with because the motives of children are not always what they seem. Teachers should neither ban nor disparage child-report because a teacher wants a child to report when safety is threatened. A useful strategy is to teach children to tell whether a situation is an emergency, and give them ways to express other concerns that do not always involve the teacher. Children need positive contact even if they don't always know how to ask for the contact appropriately. Suggestions were provided to help teachers determine children's motives for child-report and take appropriate actions.

4. What are five strategies when interventions require follow-up?

A first strategy that enables social problem solving is reflective listening. The technique de-escalates tension by acknowledging children's emotions and assists them to manage impulses. A second strategy is the guidance talk. Teachers informally use the five steps of conflict management to teach social lessons to children who have experienced conflicts with either other children or the teacher. A third strategy is teacher-child negotiation, which is "the guidance way" to resolve conflicts that happen directly between a child and teacher. A fourth strategy to include children's ideas in solutions, which assists children to feel ownership in the social problem solving. A fifth strategy is to facilitate reconciliation after conflicts are resolved. Teachers work with the knowledge that most children forgive easily, and the teacher works with all children to 5. Why take the time to problem solve mistaken behavior?

Assisting children to develop democratic life skills is an integral part of the curriculum for the 21st century. Individual children and the society both benefit when teachers take the time to problem solve mistaken behavior. The NAEYC Code of Ethical Conduct specifies that teachers must work to prevent harm to the children in their care. Guidance enables the teacher to reach children who are the victims of their own or others' mistaken behavior and is reflected clearly in the NAEYC Code.

6. How does the teacher build cooperation with today's diverse families?

Collaboration with families is sometimes difficult for teachers because of differences in roles, perspectives, and social–cultural values. To accommodate these differences, teachers foster relationships though which the families' own expertise is strengthened. In this effort, the teacher monitors feelings toward the family, understands about parent development, chooses words that avoid value judgments, and makes referrals for support services. The teacher uses a six-step problem-solving approach in collaboration with families to solve problems that may arise. When communication becomes difficult, the teacher calls upon third-party assistance both to resolve the issues of difficulty and to provide an important support base for the teacher.

FOLLOW-UP ACTIVITIES

Note: *An element of being a professional teacher is to respect the children, parents, and educators you are working with by maintaining confidentiality, that is, keeping identities private. In completing follow-up activities, please respect the privacy of all concerned.*

Discussion Activity

The discussion activity encourages students to interrelate their own thoughts and experiences with specific ideas from the chapter.

Recall an incident when you or a teacher intervened in a situation that required follow-up. What strategies did you or the teacher use that are identified in the chapter? How did one or two principles from the NAEYC Code of Ethical Conduct (see Appendix A) apply to the intervention?

Application Activities

Application activities allow students to interrelate material from the text with real-life situations. The observations imply access to practicum experiences; the interviews, access to teachers or parents. To interrelate theory and experience, students compare or contrast observations and interviews with referenced ideas from the chapter.

1. The decision to intervene.

   a. Observe a situation when a teacher had to decide whether to intervene. Reflect about the teacher's intervention in relation to the issues of with-it-ness, the level of the mistaken behavior, and the degree of firmness of the intervention. Respecting privacy, how did the decisions of the teacher correspond to the discussion in the chapter?

    b. Interview a teacher about how she decides whether to intervene in a situation. Ask how she takes into account the disruption factor regarding both the child's behavior and her potential intervention. How does she determine the level of firmness of the intervention? Compare your findings to ideas in the chapter.

2. Four quick intervention strategies.

    a. Observe a teacher use one or more of the four strategies in an intervention. Which strategy(ies) did she use? How did the teacher use the strategy? How did the child or children respond? Compare your findings to ideas in the chapter about quick intervention.

    b. Interview a teacher about which of the four strategies she regularly uses. What are the teacher's thoughts about each strategy? What does the teacher think are the strengths and weaknesses of each strategy? Why? For the strategy(ies) discussed, compare your findings to ideas in the chapter.

3. Mistaken behavior reported by children.

    a. Observe an instance of child-report. Referring to Table 10–4 as a guide, what seemed to be the motivations of the child in making the report? How did the teacher handle the situation? What seemed to be the effect on the child who reported? Compare your findings to ideas in the chapter.

    b. Interview a teacher about "tattling" or child-report. What practices does the teacher follow with the class regarding child-report? How does the teacher handle incidents of child-report regarding real emergencies versus personal concerns? Compare your findings to ideas in the chapter.

4. Strategies when interventions require follow-up.

    a. Observe an instance of serious mistaken behavior where a teacher intervened using guidance. Which of the follow-up strategies did the teacher use? What seemed to be the effect of the intervention on the child? Compare your findings to ideas in the chapter.

    b. Interview a teacher about his approach when intervening during serious mistaken behavior. What does he try to accomplish at the point of the conflict? After the parties involved have cooled down? Ask the teacher his views on one or more of the intervention strategies? Compare your findings to ideas in the chapter.

5. Why take the time.

    a. Observe an instance when you believe a teacher took a problem-solving approach to mistaken behavior. What seemed to be the immediate and possible long-term outcomes for the children involved? Using your observations as a guide, reflect about the text position that problem solving mistaken behavior is worth the time.

    b. Interview a teacher who takes a problem-solving approach to mistaken behavior. What are the priorities of the teacher when she intervenes? What does the teacher want children to learn from the intervention? How do the teacher's priorities compare with principles from NAEYC's Code of Ethical Conduct in Appendix A?

6. Building cooperation with diverse parents.

   a. Observe, and if possible participate in, an instance of teacher-family communication—a conference, meeting, home visit, or classroom exchange. How many of the five steps for building cooperative relations did you observe the teacher use? What seemed to be the results in terms of teacher-family cooperation? Compare your findings with ideas from the chapter.

   b. Interview a teacher about a family that she was uncomfortable working with or had trouble understanding. How did the teacher communicate with the family to build cooperation? How satisfied was the teacher with the success of the effort? If she would change anything in her approach, what would that be? Compare your findings with ideas from the text.

Recommended Readings

Boyd-Zaharias, J., & Pate-Bain, H. (2008, September). Class matters—in and out of school. *Phi Delta Kappan,* pp. 40–44. (Reprinted in *Annual Editions: Early Childhood 2009–2010.*)

Freeman, N. K., & Feenie, S. (2004). The NAEYC code is a living document. *Young Children,* 59(6), 12–16.

Gartrell, D. J. (2006). Guidance matters: A spoonful of laughter. *Young Children,* 63(4), 108–109.

Gartrell, D. J. (2007). Guidance matters: Tattling: It drives teachers bonkers. *Young Children,* 64(2), 46-48.

Koch, P. K., & McDonough, M. (1999). Improving parent-teacher conferences through collaborative conversations. *Young Children,* 54(2), 11–15.

Pappano, L. (2007, July/August). Meeting of the minds [in conferences with parents]. *Harvard Education Letter,* http://www.edletter. (Reprinted in *Annual Editions: Early Childhood 2009–2010.*)

White, B. A., Graham, M., & Bradford, S. K. (2005, March). Children of teen parents: Challenges and hope. *Zero to Three,* pp. 4–6. (Reprinted in *Annual Editions: Early Childhood 2009–2010.*)

Guidance Matters: Boys and Men Teachers

Teacher Bruce and Darnell—

May, 2006

When Darnell entered our program, he was fairly nonverbal and very big (already 75 pounds as a three-year-old). He lived with his grandparents, and we three teachers guessed they did not hold him in their laps much, let alone pick him up. We could see that Darnell craved physical attention; he tried to climb onto our laps and wanted us to carry him all the time. But it was hard to meet his needs because of his size and the way he had of demanding attention. The other teachers tried to encourage Darnell to talk more and to build relationships that way, but he responded very little. It was like he spaced us out. Something more had to be done.

I am not a particularly large guy, but I knew I had to give comfort to this child, at least hold him on my lap a few times a day and carry him once or twice. After several weeks of this, Darnell began to open up. He talked more and began to try things on his own. On the playground he started to run with the other kids and me and play chase. For the first time, we saw Darnell pleased to be part of the group—and he asked to be carried less. He adjusted, and the other teachers did too. They came to accept Darnell as a typical three-year-old boy who was just learning how to ask for and give affection.

Teacher Jay and Scott—

Scott was a smallish four-year-old. Every day in class he struggled to be accepted and to get attention. Scott was a whiz at building things and with large muscle activities, but he had trouble interacting with others and often resorted to hitting. I worked with him on using words and friendly touches, and the hitting got less. Still, whenever he got upset, he would throw himself backward against a wall and then either totally ignore everyone or storm off in anger.

One day Scott had a struggle with a peer, and I intervened, not letting him hit the other child. Scott started to close down, and I quietly encouraged him to use his words. Just this side of throwing himself against the wall, Scott stopped, clenched his fists, and screamed as loud as he could, "I'm angry at you, Jay!"

I was thrilled, and as I gave him a big hug I told him so: "That's wonderful, Scott!" He stayed for a moment in the hug and visibly relaxed.

That moment marked a sea change for the child. Scott used his words fairly consistently after that. He would often come to me and ask for a hug. He had many engaging conversations with his peers, more fully enjoyed the activities he had done so well before, and was enthusiastic about trying new things.

Reprinted with permission from the National Association for the Education of Young Children. All rights reserved.

SEVERAL YEARS AGO, U.S. EDUCATORS REALIZED that we were not encouraging young girls in math and science. Today girls are catching up, but another void in our classrooms has appeared. Some children, especially high-energy boys, face increasingly inappropriate programs, which offer lots of seatwork and little movement. It is as if some teachers are rehearsing their young students for the sit-down academic world to come. Children who are *kinetic* or total-body learners suffer. They need active classrooms that affirm and accept them. This column is for the guys—for three reasons.

REASON 1. *Many boys are being left by the wayside.* The cover story in the January 30, 2006, issue of *Newsweek* was "The Trouble with Boys" (Tyre, 2006). Conventional wisdom holds that boys develop more slowly than girls, but eventually catch up. The article cites studies indicating that many boys do not catch up, even by college age. They have troubles in school and life that go way beyond the early years. According to the article, "Often boys are treated like defective girls" (p. 46). The implication is that boys' slower developmental rates, physical response styles, and kinetic learning behaviors are seen as deficits. Rather than accepting these characteristics as *who most boys are*, some teachers see them as faults to be firmly and swiftly "corrected" (Viadero, 2006).

When early childhood educators overemphasize "acceptable" behavior (which many adults are still learning) and prescribed programming, we slight children's physical and emotional needs. At first, Darnell's teachers may have thought of him as defective. Bruce accepted Darnell, though, and through simple hugs and friendly touch helped the boy see that in this safe classroom he could learn and grow. The foundation for showing thoughtful, empathetic behaviors is to experience them yourself. Boys in particular need regular physical affection as a part of the nurturing mix (King, 2004).

REASON 2. *Active boys are not finding classrooms encouraging.* Boys are almost five times more likely than girls to be expelled from preschool programs (Gilliam, 2005; see "Guidance Matters" in the January 2006 issue of *Young Children* for discussion about the National Prekindergarten Study). We, as early childhood teachers, tend to give young boys less nurturing (especially physical) than we do young girls, and our classroom discipline for boys tends to be harsher (King, 2004). A reasonable inference is that too few teachers have learned how to positively guide young boys' behavior. Rather than learning and taking an active classroom approach, we often find it more convenient to ease boys out—or medicate them.

In the second anecdote, Jay clearly bucks this trend. He understands Scott's needs and works actively to make the program developmentally appropriate for the boy. Jay builds a relationship with Scott that includes guiding him through his emotional outbursts. Over time Scott learns that he can manage his strong emotions and become a member of the classroom community. The child's learning skills blossom as a result.

Some early childhood teachers find it easier to be "developmentally appropriate" with girls than with boys. In my view this is not developmentally appropriate practice at all. Young girls are often more compliant than boys, who are more likely to chafe under constraints on their behavior and learning styles (King, 2004). Programs are developmentally appropriate only if they support *all* children, not some or even most. When teachers clamp down on—or turn away from—children for being "needy" like Darnell or "aggressive" like Scott, they tell those children that they cannot succeed in the education process.

Other teachers, of both genders, have an amazing knack for reaching boys and girls alike. They enjoy young children who are energetic and just learning how to become members of the group. They like being outside with children and make outdoors part of the classroom. These teachers positively handle boisterous play, restlessness when things get passive, and physicality in communication—and they are to be treasured.

A message of the two anecdotes is that energetic classrooms, rich in nurturing and encouragement, are good for all children. Let's face it: Classrooms in general (particularly in light of the obesity epidemic) need to be less like Sunday school and more like summer camp—which of course would make them more developmentally appropriate and healthier. Teachers can prevent many *institution-caused* conflicts (resulting from a poor match of the children and the program)

when we remember that young children—boys *and* girls—learn through movement.

REASON 3. *Too few men teach in early childhood classrooms.* In a 2002 study, Nelson states that only about 4% of NAEYC members are men working directly with children (98% of Nelson's sample of NAEYC members believed it is important for men to be early childhood teachers). Beyond the chronic issue of low pay in the early childhood workforce, Nelson's study suggests that stereotypes about men teachers have kept male application, hiring, and retention rates all sadly low (Nelson, 2002).

With today's emphasis on sit-down lessons, the kinetic learning needs of boys are the unacknowledged Tigger in the classroom. We need more teachers who know Tigger, who speak *the language of boys*. Teachers Bruce and Jay speak the language. They communicate that nurturing relationships with young children—especially boys—comes first, before traditional behavioral and academic expectations. They model that physical activity is a natural part of a young child's life and that active learning should be a natural part of the daily program. Nurturing men who enter the field are kindling and rekindling an awareness of the language of boys in the rest of us, both women and other men. This is why Nelson (2002) concludes that it is crucial to have these guys in our classrooms, even if they don't know all the ropes when they begin.

For a year or two, Darnell and Scott were in encouraging classrooms. What about now, I wonder. And what of the early years at school for countless children who are expected to succumb to mostly seatwork and paper drill (and go home to watch TV and play computer games)? Boys and girls who are allowed to engage positively in an active education process learn more. A courageous kindergarten teacher points out, "My job is not to prepare children for first grade. It is to provide the best possible kindergarten experience for each child." And the best kindergartens and preschools encourage children to move and learn, in the classroom and out. To the men teachers who naturally speak the language of boys, or have recalled it, and to the women teachers who always have been, or recently have become, "second-language speakers," many thanks. You serve as examples to us all.

To Increase Your Knowledge:

Read the *Newsweek* article "The Trouble with Boys" (see references). Check out William Pollack's *Real Boys: Rescuing Our Sons from the Myths of Boyhood*, Michael Thompson's *Raising Cain: Protecting the Emotional Life of Boys*, and Bryan Nelson's *The Importance of Men Teachers and Why There Are So Few* (see references). Also, read Margaret King's and my collaborative chapter, "Guidance with Boys in Early Childhood Classrooms" (see Column References). Think about how boy-friendly and girl-friendly classrooms for young children are different and/or alike.

A Step You Can Take

Recruit, support, and retain men teachers. Model and practice ideas for building man-friendly and boy-friendly early childhood classrooms. Look into support systems locally and through websites such as www.MenTeach.org and its links. Support children's active learning and the teachers who make it happen!

Column References

Gilliam, W. S. (2005). *Prekindergarteners left behind: Expulsion rates in state prekindergarten systems.* New Haven, CT: Yale University Child Study Center. Available online at http://www.fcd-us.org/PDFs/NationalPreKExpulsionPaper03.02_new.pdf

King, M., with Gartrell, D. (2004). Guidance with boys in early childhood classrooms. In D. Gartrell (Ed.), *The power of guidance: Teaching social-emotional skills in early childhood classrooms* (pp. 106–124). Clifton Park, NY: Delmar/Thomson Learning and NAEYC. Available online at http://www.hcs.ohiou.edu:16080/boys/BOY%20GUIDANCE%20PAPER%20for%20WEB%20PAGE.htm

Nelson, B. G. (2002). *The importance of men teachers and why there are so few.* Minneapolis, MN: Men in Child Care and Elementary Education Project.

Tyre, P. (2006, January 30). The trouble with boys. *Newsweek,* pp. 44–52. Available online at http://www.msnbc.msn.com/id/10965522/site/newsweek/

Viadero, D. (2006, March 15). Concern over gender gaps shifting to boys. *Education Week, 1,* 16–17.

For additional information on using the guidance approach in the encouraging classroom, visit our website at www.cengage.com/education/gartrell.

Chapter 11 Guidance Through Intervention

Guiding Questions

▶ *What considerations are important for when boys have conflicts?*

▶ *What conditions make intervention necessary?*

▶ *What are four methods of crisis management?*

▶ *What are comprehensive guidance strategies for working with Level Three strong needs mistaken behavior?*

▶ *What techniques assist the teacher to manage personal feelings of anger?*

▶ *What helps when teachers and parents disagree?*

Key Concepts

▶ *Boy behavior*

▶ *Cooling-down time*

▶ *Creative conflicts*

▶ *Crisis management*

▶ *Describe-express-direct*

▶ *Individual guidance plan (IGP)*

▶ *Instrumental aggression*

▶ *Labeling versus diagnosis*

▶ *Nonverbal intervention*

▶ *Personal safeguards*

▶ *Physical restraint*

▶ *Post-traumatic Stress Disorder (PTSD)*

▶ *Self-removal*

▶ *Separation*

▶ *Time-out*

From early experiences in baby-sitting or high school child development classes, some young adults gravitate toward early childhood education. After teaching in the upper grades, other adults shift to early age groups, feeling they can relate more naturally with young children.

As well, some classroom volunteers find a calling in early childhood education through gratifying experiences with young children and their teachers. The opportunity to be fully nurturing in the teaching role, and the rewards for being so, motivate many women and a small but select number of men toward early childhood education.

Teachers want to be friendly and supportive toward young children. Aware of the trust that is placed in them, early childhood teachers take seriously the decision to intervene. They worry about hurting feelings, impairing development, and damaging relationships. They wonder how intervention will affect other children and the atmosphere of the class. They may feel anxiety as well about what a child may say to a parent, and what the parent may do in response.

Still, intervention sometimes is necessary, and timely intervention is the measure and foundation of the authenticity of the teacher (Brewer, 2007; Gartrell,

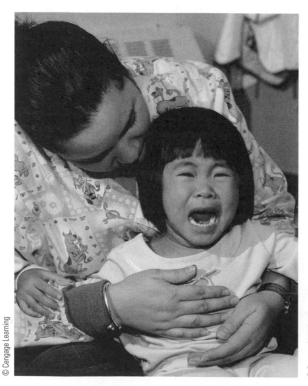

The opportunity to be nurturing within the teaching role motivates many toward early childhood education.

2004). Enforced limits provide security for the child, other children, and the teacher. To paraphrase Dreikurs (1972):

> *Reluctance to intervene in the face of harm or serious disruption marks an unproductive level of teacher permissiveness, as distinct from "democratic discipline" [guidance].*

A premise of Part Three is that even in crisis situations, intervention techniques remain problem solving in nature, intended to guide not punish. The last chapter examined strategies for solving "routine" problems in the classroom. The strategies discussed were for those situations that could be resolved without undue difficulty, either immediately or with simple follow-up. Chapter Eleven gives "featured attention" to serious mistaken behavior, when strong emotions make solving problems difficult. The chapter begins though with discussion of guidance and the gender issue, considerations for teachers when they intervene with boys.

When Boys Have Conflicts

In my writing, I like to take an inclusive viewpoint. For this reason, the text does not offer separate sections on "guidance with children having disabilities" or "guidance with children of color." Hopefully, readers can adapt the philosophy and ideas of the guidance approach to the variety of learning communities which they may join. But, when 80 out of 100 preschoolers who are expelled are boys, and the national rate of preschool expulsions is high (Gilliam, 2005), the matter of how teachers handle conflicts involving young boys needs attention.

Culture Clash

By the early 1990s, studies showed that an education gap existed that disfavored girls (Webb, Metha, & Jordan, 2007). Boys received more attention in classes, had higher scores on college exams, and attended postsecondary programs in higher numbers. Now, with the exception of teacher attention, the gender gap has not just been closed, but reversed (Kohn, 2005).

Perhaps because of the emphasis on test scores, teachers even in prekindergarten have tended to bring more structure to their classes. To an extent, the traditional classroom culture, one of decorum with controlled transactions between teacher and students, has again become the rule. Students able to succeed in this culture have been those who could hold focus on sit-down, paper-and-pencil, teacher-directed lessons for many hours each day. For developmental and behavioral reasons, more girls and fewer boys fit the profile of learners who are successful in traditional classroom culture (Kindlon & Thompson, 1999).

In the last ten years, it has become evident that boys even more than girls face challenges to their schooling, ranging from preschool expulsions to severe discipline practices, low test scores, summer school classes, grade retentions, and special education placements (Kohn, 2005). Mounting research is showing that a lag in educational achievement begins for boys in preschool (Webb,

Metha, & Jordan, 2007) and continues into adulthood (Kohn, 2005). More female than male students now graduate from high school, college, and many graduate programs. The inability of educators to adjust classroom culture to fit many boys, and the inability of many boys to adapt to traditional classroom culture, are key reasons for both high preschool expulsion rates and the new education gender gap (King, 2004).

Gap Affects Teachers. This culture clash apparently is resulting in a gender gap for teachers as well. Nelson's (2002) study of a large population of NAEYC members showed that most teachers of young children are female; few are male. Increasingly, this trend is holding true for teachers at the K–12 level as well (Scelfo, 2007).

One possible explanation is that because more females than males succeed in the traditional classroom culture, more women than men are comfortable becoming teachers. The few men early childhood teachers can and do greatly benefit both young boys and girls, of course (King, 2004). Male teachers have developed survival skills relative to traditional schooling. Many are likely, at an intuitive level, to accept the high activity of most young boys and to make the classroom flexible enough to accommodate active learning styles (Nelson, 2002). (See the "Boys and Men Teachers" column at end of Chapter Ten.)

Since they have "been there and done that," men teachers also may be intuitively responsive to the needs of young boys when they experience conflicts—whatever the classroom culture (Nelson, 2002). This is not to say that many women teachers do not relish having a goodly number of young boys in their classes; they do, and adjust their classrooms accordingly (King, 2004). That is the point: To help more children succeed in school (particularly many boys), educators need to tweak classroom cultures "into the 21st century."

Boy-Friendly Classrooms

Two dynamics help women and men early childhood teachers make their classrooms boy-friendly. *The first dynamic* has been developed in previous chapters: developmentally appropriate practice (DAP) for *all* children.

One challenge to DAP is the misconception that if a program is developmentally appropriate for most, that is sufficient. This misconception often results when a teacher shrug offs limited engagement by boys with such reasons as: "They are not ready"; "they have short attention spans"; they "just want to do rough-and-tumble play." An unhelpful term used to explain away this non-engagement is **boy behavior**. Teachers sometimes use the excuse of *boy behavior* to stay in their comfort zones and not revitalize programs to become more developmentally appropriate for all (including active boys).

King provides a case study to show how teachers can move beyond the *boy behavior syndrome*. In "Guidance with Boys in Early Childhood Classrooms," King (2004) illustrates how a teacher changes the curriculum, the schedule, and the environment in ways that increase the engagement of all children, most especially boys. The benefits of making programs developmentally appropriate for all should be clear: "Boy behavior" lessens, productive learning behavior increases, and conflicts involving boys decline (Bredekamp & Copple, 2009). Programs fundamentally become more active, which stimulates physical as well as brain development and contributes to active, healthy lifestyles for all children, girls and boys. (See the column titled "Physical Activity: It's Proactive Guidance" at the end of Chapter Five.)

Intervention Considerations

The second dynamic in a boy-friendly classroom is an intervention approach with conflicts that is responsive to boys. King (2004) also provides guidance considerations for when boys experience conflicts. Adapting that material here, 11 guidance intervention techniques (some familiar to the reader from previous chapters) are listed. Specific suggestions for using the techniques then follow:

- **Diagnose the conflict as best you can.** Honestly determine if you know what happened or if you need more information. (Sometimes accidents happen during active play.) Decide what level of firmness you need to use— and how to show warmth with firmness. Boys—like all of us—do not respond well to coercion (loud scolding, threats, criticism, forced removal). Try to be authoritative rather than authoritarian in responding to the conflict (Pollack, 1998; Kindlon & Thompson, 1999; Newberger, 1999). The teacher will need to decide: Is this a situation that calls for a guidance talk, conflict management, or a requested choice with follow-up? Teachers make these decisions quickly, sometimes too quickly. Remember that the professional teacher learns even while teaching, both in the moment and in later reflection.

- **Defuse the situation.** If emotions haven't hit the boiling point, the teacher works to downplay the conflict. (Using a calm voice is key.) Sometimes the situation is accidental, or at least not totally intentional. The teacher points this out and informally mediates: "Denard, Ephram didn't mean to knock over your tower. He feels badly about it. I wonder how you can fix it. Maybe the two of you?" The teacher identifies and accepts emotions, so the child knows the teacher cares. Example: "Julian, it is all right to cry. That hurt when you fell over Noah's leg. You have a real owie on your knee. Let's get a band-aid for that and see how Noah is doing."

- **Use humor, the great tension reliever.** Humor suggests that the adult is "in charge enough not to get up-tight," and so tells boys they don't have to get "worked up" either. For example, the teacher kneels down to where two boys are quarreling and says with a smile, "You guys sound like gorillas with stomachaches over here. How about taking some tummy medicine and getting your friendly faces back on?" Humor takes thinking on your feet and, for many of us, actual practice. The "joke" doesn't have to be hilarious—just enough to bring smiles—but it does have to be friendly, not laughing "at" but laughing "with."

- **Calm everyone down.** Neither adults nor children can resolve conflicts when emotions are high. A first step is for the teacher to get calm, then help the child or children to cool down. Often in boys, being upset gives way to an unwillingness to talk; time is needed *for them to calm down*. Sometimes the fast pace of the classroom does not allow boys the extra time they need. A "timed silence" (Pollack, 2001; an alternate term is "cooling-down time") provides the boy time so that he can process the upsetting event without adult interaction.

When the teacher feels he is ready, she supports the boy by acknowledging his feelings, which helps him feel accepted and regain composure. Again, remember that a boy may need time to "check in" with his feelings and regulate his response to the situation before resolution can happen.

▶ **Talk in a private manner.** The teacher may want to remove the boy to a private space in the classroom. Private interactions protect the child from critical self-feelings as a result of being shamed (Pollack, 1998). Kindlon and Thompson (1999) point out that boys are likely to respond negatively to adults when they are criticized in front of their peers. For lesser conflicts, the adult might just get down to the child's eye level and speak in low tones. Speaking calmly reinforces the ideas that the child is not being made an example of and the conflict can be worked out cooperatively.

▶ **Stay away from threats.** Threats set up power struggles that negatively affect both the teacher-child relationship and the likelihood of successful (win-win) resolution of the conflict situation. Instead, request choices that the child must make. In requesting choices, the adult poses the more desirable alternative as positively as possible, but accepts the "out-choice" if the boy makes it.

To illustrate, the adult does not say, "Martin, either you share the counting cards or I will move you to another area." Rather, the adult puts a choice to the child: "Martin, you choose, share the counting cards, or find an activity in another area. Which will it be?" Remember that if the boy is upset about the choice, or if the boy thinks that the choice is unfair, he may leave the area. The teacher needs to be ready to accept the decision that the boy makes, and follow up with a guidance talk.

▶ **Follow through.** It is important for teachers to follow through when responding to a boy's mistaken behavior. Boys seem to be sensitive to whether or not adults do what they say they will do. When adults do not follow through, they lose boys' respect (Kindlon & Thompson, 1999). Boys may feel that they do not have to listen because the adult appears powerless or doesn't really care. As an example, don't shout across the room for Mitchell to behave and then go on to something else. Walk over, establish your presence, diagnose, and interact. Give Mitchell choices. Correct by direction. Stay with it.

▶ **Use guidance talks, mediation, and class meetings.** After emotions have cooled, the adult implements guidance talks, conflict mediation, or class meetings depending on the situation. In any of these interventions, the adult practices the five steps of social problem solving: Calm everyone down, agree what the problem is, brainstorm solutions, agree on one and try it. Follow up with guidance and reinforcement—informally is fine.

▶ **Teach boys to manage their impulses.** Many young boys are impulsive. When faced with a difficult situation or a conflict, a boy might react by acting out. Build your relationship with the boy so he will be more apt to listen in conflict situations. A helpful method is to teach the child exactly what he can say and do instead of acting out. With coaching, one child might say loudly, "I am angry!" (The teacher is then over there quickly.) Another child might leave the conflict and report his feelings to the teacher ("He is making me mad") or go to a "peace island" (an area of the room set up for when a child—or adult—needs a self-selected break.) Self-removal is not a cure-all, but can help in teaching individual children to manage strong feelings. (The Responsive Classroom model uses self-removal as an impulse control technique.)

▶ **Talk with boys about their emotions.** It is important for adults to talk with boys about their emotions (Pollack, 1998; Kindlon & Thompson, 1999; Polce-Lynch, 2002). Sometimes when boys appear to be angry, they are masking feelings of pain, embarrassment, or fear. Encourage boys to develop a large repertoire of labels for the emotions they are feeling (Newberger, 1999). Clearly, teaching about emotions and their expression goes beyond conflict interventions by teachers. The curriculum needs to have social–emotional intelligence as an educational priority—basic to learning democratic life skills.

▶ **Nurture boys.** Boys want and need emotional connectiveness (Pollack, 1998; Kindlon & Thompson, 1999; Newberger, 1999). Boys need to be cuddled, held, and responded to with kind words. They need unconditional personal regard from their teachers. When they fall or when a friend uses unkind words when talking to them, boys need the teacher to respond in a warm, caring, and nurturing manner. Even when a boy is defiant or has hurt another child, we need to let that child know he is still a fully accepted and valued member of our class. He just needs to work to on a few things, and it is our job to help.

Teachers who make it a priority can mold their programs and their interpersonal relationships to be boy-friendly. In classrooms where teachers make these changes, girls as well as boys respond to the active programming and the consistently positive leadership. With encouragement and education, parents, as well, stand to increase their appreciation of what teachers are doing for their boys. Families that understand all that their boys can accomplish in the classroom are in a good place to help equalize the education gender gap (King, 2004, pp. 117–122).

Conditions that Make Intervention Necessary

Varying tolerance levels toward mild mistaken behaviors mean that teachers differ in responses to these situations. To maintain consistency in response to mild mistaken behaviors, teachers do well to link interventions to established guidelines, work to understand the child and the situation, and self-monitor moods and response tendencies. In contrast to mild mistaken behaviors, a large majority teachers choose to intervene when:

1. children cannot resolve a situation themselves, and the situation is deteriorating.
2. one or more children cause serious disruption to the education process.
3. the danger of harm exists.

In the event of serious mistaken behavior, two or all three of these conditions are present; all teachers should then intervene.

Whenever possible, if the teacher can control the situation with quick interventions discussed in the previous chapter—negotiation reminders, body language including friendly touch, humor, brief comments, and requesting choices—such strategies are desirable. They minimize classroom disruption, cause minimum upset to children, and restore equilibrium effectively. When mistaken behaviors become serious, however, the nature of the intervention becomes more involved. The teacher then uses *combination strategies* for the purpose of resolving the conflict.

Classroom Anecdote	1. *Deteriorating situation: Nigel was in the space under a four-sided climber playing by himself. Dinee opened the door and started to come in. Nigel pushed against the door and said, "You can't come in here." Dinee pushed her way in, and the two were yelling at each other when the teacher arrived.*
	With firmness she said to both: "You are having a problem, so let's see if we can solve this problem, or you can play somewhere else." Nigel made a fist at Dinee, who hit his fist and then pushed him back. The loud voices got louder. The teacher, halfway in the door, put a hand on each child's shoulder and stated: "You have decided. Please separate, and we will talk about this later."
	Dinee left, but Nigel lay down and began to cry. Outside the climber, the teacher sat by him for a bit and got him started on a favorite puzzle. Later, the teacher talked with the children about how they felt they might handle the problem "next time," and how they could be friends again.

Classroom Anecdote	2. *Serious disruption: Although the teacher had given a "five-minute warning," Randy was not ready to stop using the Legos as cleanup began. The teacher asked him to help put the Legos away, but Randy instead grabbed several loose ones and brought them to where he was building. The teacher went over to Randy and told him he could leave his structure for later, but he would have to put the new Legos away. Randy became upset and began to throw them. After ducking and bobbing, the teacher approached Randy, looked him in the eye, and stated firmly, "Randy, I know you are angry, but Legos are not for throwing. Let's go sit so that you can cool down." She looked at the assistant teacher, who nodded and took over supervising cleanup. The teacher took Randy's hand, and the two sat down. After he calmed down, the two talked about what happened and what he could do differently next time. At the end of cleanup, the teacher made sure that Randy successfully joined the next activity.*

Classroom Anecdote	*3. Danger of harm: Darwin and Rita were painting on opposite sides of an easel. Darwin peeked around the side and painted some red on Rita's blue sky. Rita painted blue on Darwin's bare arm. Darwin dropped his brush and pushed Rita down. Rita yelled and while sitting began to kick Darwin's ankles. Looking furious, Darwin was in the act of pouncing when the teacher arrived and restrained him.* *Darwin struggled with the teacher to get loose until he realized that he couldn't. After a few minutes in the teacher's "bear hug," with the teacher speaking soothingly to him, Darwin quieted down. When she felt she could leave him, the teacher tended to Rita, who was still sitting on the floor. She followed up later with the children together. She asked each to explain what happened and how they felt. She let them know how she felt about the conflict, and got them to agree on a nonviolent course of action they could take next time.*

In these three situations the teachers chose to resolve conflicts by combining intervention strategies. In each case, the teacher worked with the children to calm everyone down, restore boundaries, gain reconciliation, and teach acceptable behavior alternatives for the future. During a conflict, everyone involved is at risk for psychological and sometimes physical harm. For this reason, *combination intervention* is neither easy nor pleasant. Still, firm, friendly nonpunitive intervention is the measure of the value the teacher places in the guidance approach: Combination strategies are important to use.

Teaching Emotions Management. In a published research summary, Bronson (2000) points out that during the early years, the *executive function* in the brain is quickly developing. Preprimary children make great strides in learning to manage emotional responses, comply with external requests, control impulses, and engage in self-directed thinking and problem solving. She cites studies to show, however, that the capacity to develop these abilities is affected by innate factors such as neurological and health factors and by the child's environment (Bronson, 2000). As every teacher knows, due to the combination of these factors, some children have considerable difficulty managing their emotions.

A child who "loses it" and acts out is upsetting for everyone in the encouraging classroom. When repeated over time, the raw expression of emotions is a classic Level Three mistaken behavior that most adults would find "challenging." As such, the child needs the comprehensive approach to strong needs mistaken behavior described later in the chapter. Essential components—though sometimes not enough by themselves—are the immediate steps of **crisis management**: halting the impulse, calming the child, and then *after the child is calm*, engaging in a guidance talk.

For teaching self-management of emotions, the *guidance talk* is key. When the child has cooled down, the primary caregiver discusses the problem and teaches alternatives to the emotional outburst that the child can use next time. The adult then works with the child to implement the emotions management strategy and enlists the team to provide encouragement. As strong as the child's emotions are, the teacher needs to be stronger in firm but friendly persistence that the child learn alternative behaviors.

The process of teaching and learning emotions management is interactive. As long as the child trusts the teacher, he can make progress. A primary challenge for the teacher in maintaining the relationship is when a child is losing control and the teacher must intervene. At this point, guidance-oriented *crisis management techniques* are key.

Crisis Management

Conflict management gives way to *crisis management* when the conflict is getting out of hand, emotions are running high, and the communication process is breaking down. (The conflict may not have completely deteriorated, but the teacher feels it is about to happen.) In crisis management, the teacher makes a final effort to restore communication so that mediation can take place.

If civil communication proves impossible, the teacher works to calm the child or children and restore boundaries, so that the basic conflict management techniques can be used when emotions have cooled. In other words, *the goal of crisis management* is to restore the situation to where communication can occur, in order to solve the problem. Four basic crisis management techniques appear in Table 11–1 and are discussed in the following sections.

The four techniques appear roughly in the order of use by a teacher as a conflict escalates into a crisis. Note that *redirection* and *separation* are included as options under broader headings, a reminder that these two techniques tend to lapse into punishment when teachers use them as automatic responses.

When conflicts cause emotions to intensify, crisis management techniques steer the teacher away from a common misimpression: that children "know better" and just need moralistic reminding in order to behave better. In fact, due to developmental immaturity, young children are just beginning the lifelong learning process of "knowing better." They may have rote knowledge of "right and wrong" and can perhaps even tell you in a particular situation if they "were bad." But, young children have not yet mastered—as some adults never do—the management of their perceptions and feelings in ways that result in productive decision making (Gartrell, 2004).

Table 11–1 Four Crisis Management Techniques

- Being direct (describing-expressing-directing)

- Commanding a choice (including redirection)

- Calming everyone involved (sometimes by separation)

- Using physical restraint (the passive bear hug)

During crises, children do need friendly, firm, and clear direction, but not punishment. The crisis management techniques that follow assist teachers to manage their own emotions and to use guidance effectively when emotions are running high.

1. Being Direct

Crises require direct teacher intervention. Yet confrontation as an intervention technique must be used with care. Especially when a teacher's emotions are rising, it is important to focus on the need to be firm *but not harsh*.

Being direct is actually a collection of three techniques that constitute the *crisis response of first resort*. The teacher uses first-resort responses when the situation is deteriorating, mediation for the moment looks doubtful, and the teacher wants to keep a crisis from becoming full-blown. Three ideas from Ginott (1972) provide a useful set of tools when harm or serious disruption is imminent and the teacher needs to be direct:

▶ Describe without labeling.

▶ Express displeasure without insult.

▶ Correct by direction.

Describe without Labeling. A first step in confronting a crisis is to describe to the children what you see. Describing events lets children know why you are intervening—and helps the teacher pull thoughts together for what to do next.

In guidance, the teacher accepts the individual but not individuals' serious mistaken behavior. To paraphrase Ginott (1972): address the situation; do not attack personality. The teacher *describes what he sees* that is unacceptable (the line in italics below), but does so without labeling personalities: "Labeling is disabling."

> *Example: "I hear loud words over here and see hitting.* We need to stop right now and sit down. Then we can figure how to fix this problem."

Express Displeasure without Insult. Anger leads to mistaken behavior, in children and in adults. For this reason, even obedience-based discipline models maintain that teachers should not act out of anger. As Ginott (1972) points out, anger is an emotion that all teachers feel; they either manage it or are controlled by it. Because they are in the business of guiding children to express emotions in acceptable ways, professional teachers need to model the management of anger themselves. The careful expression of displeasure, to show that you mean business but will not harm, is a necessary guidance skill. Ginott advocates the use of *I-messages* to report personal feelings without condemnation (The line in italics below).

> *Example: "You forgot our guideline about wrestling and Lionel got hurt. This bothers me.* You need to take deep breaths and calm down so we can think of a way to help him feel better."

Correct by Direction. *Correct by direction* echoes a guidance basic: "Don't just tell children what not to do; teach them what to do" (Ginott, 1972). Direct children to alternative acceptable behaviors. Young children are still learning "what to do instead" and have a need for and a right to this guidance. (If you won't tell them, you cannot expect them to know.) *Correct by direction* (indicated in italics below) can be the difference between intervention that is punitive and intervention that is educational.

> *Example:* "Ronson, I cannot let you hit anyone, and I will not let anyone hit you. *You need to take three deep breaths so we can talk about this."*

Using the Ideas Together. When teachers enter a situation, they inevitably add a new layer of complexity to the conflict. For this reason, the teacher uses the **describe-express-direct** sequence carefully. These techniques are guidance only when they reestablish boundaries and at the same time support self-esteem.

Often in crisis situations, the *describe-direct* techniques, without the *express*, are enough. Expressing personal feelings, even when done professionally, tends to "up the emotional ante." For this reason, the teacher does not make expressing feelings (I-messages) an *automatic* part of the intervention sequence, but intentionally chooses when to express feelings.

> *Example of describe-direct alone:* "You are hitting. You need to stop and sit down. Let's get calm so we can talk."

The teacher expresses displeasure only when he feels bothered enough by events that he needs to get personal feelings "on the table." Sometimes the teacher decides that children need to know how their teacher feels—adults have feelings too. When conflicts have escalated to crises, the teacher states personal feelings as a way of insisting that established classroom limits need to be respected.

The purpose of being direct is to restore order so that problems can be solved, reconciliation achieved, and the safety of the classroom community reaffirmed. As with all crisis management techniques, the teacher describes, sometimes expresses, and directs in order to make conflicts manageable—not simply to bring a swift end to the crisis. The teacher who firmly intervenes—such as by redirecting a child to another area—*but provides no follow-up*, needs to be aware of "the negative power of silence." Failing to guide children to learn from a conflict means that children's feelings of hurt and anger may well continue. In this situation the intervention has failed to rise above punishment.

Emotional outbursts warrant follow-up discussion. Even two-year-olds benefit from talking about it. True, knowing what to say and how to say it (guidance talks) takes practice. Calming first, listening carefully, and responding with friendly respect help prevent the hands-on-ears reaction—a sign that to the child this is not a talk but a "lecture." The long-term effectiveness of guidance depends on talk:

> *Example: After calming a child, "Are you feeling better now? (pause) That was quite a fracas (intentionally teaching a word). Tell me what you think happened. (wait time for child to respond)."*

2. Commanding a Choice

Under a guidance approach, the teacher matches the firmness of the intervention to the seriousness of the mistaken behavior. *Giving choices* (discussed in Chapter Ten) illustrates this idea. At a prevention level, the teacher *invites* choice making: "I need some super strong helpers to move these chairs." At a problem-solving level, the teacher *requests* choice making. "We have almost finished picking up. As soon as the books are on the shelves and the blocks are in the box, we can go outside."

At a looming-crisis level, the teacher *commands* a choice: "Brett, you choose: Use words to tell us your feelings, or sit for a bit to cool down and then we will talk." *Commanding a choice* is a form of correction by direction. Teachers use this technique when emotions are rising and they feel they must "cut to the chase." Because of the power of commanding a child to choose, it is the crisis management method of second resort.

When commanding a choice, the teacher is not forcing a "me against you" ultimatum—"Either you play nice or I will give you a 'red light.'" Such ultimatums set up adversarial relationships between teachers and children and undermine mutual trust and respect (Greenberg, 1988). Instead the adult has children choose a personal course of action, teaching them that they can share power

A teacher may request children to choose whether they can solve a problem on their own or with the teacher's help.

© Cengage Learning

in the situation. The child may not like the options, but the choice allows some dignity—in contrast to the "do it or else" alternative imposed by a threat.

As discussed in Chapter Ten, when commanding choices there is an *in-choice* (the choice that the adult hopes the child will make) and an *out-choice* (the choice the adult prefers less, but still can live with). Typically, the in-choice is for the child to participate in a process that works the problem through. The out-choice is to cool down so the conflict can be resolved later. The teacher avoids out-choices that impose a predetermined "solution" for the child's mistaken behavior. In the midst of a crisis, what seems a logical consequence may really be punishment—so the teacher always gives thought to the "out" alternative.

For example, an in-choice for continued reckless play on the climber would be to leave it for a talk with the teacher now. An out-choice would be to go to a different activity and discuss the situation later; it would not be to stay off the climber for a week. A guidance talk that teaches safer behaviors is a key part of the procedure in either case. The out-choice gives the child a choice of self removal. Commanding a child to choose remains nonpunitive only if the out-choice is a logical consequence to the child as well as the teacher, and if guidance is later offered.

Some authors criticize the command of a choice, as by itself the technique does not help children realize the immediate and long-term benefits of mediation (Carlsson-Paige & Levin, 1992). The follow-up is what keeps commanding choices in the "guidance camp": "We can talk about this now or you can choose to talk about it later when you are more calm," rather than "We can talk about this or you can sit by yourselves and think about how to use your words." The second out-choice is not one a young child can really accomplish on his own and is punishment (Katz, 1984).

Because of its power, commanding a child to choose is a crisis management method of second resort. But the technique does hold out the possibility of mediation to resolve the difficulty and so has its place for teachers when emotions are starting to run high.

3. Calm First, Teach Later

Teachers intervene in crises first by being direct and second by commanding a choice. They use these techniques as first and second resorts when they perceive that children may still be calm enough to mediate the conflict. When children are "too upset to talk about it," the teacher uses calming techniques, with or without commanding choices or separation, the crisis management of third resort.

Getting calm during conflicts is a high-level democratic life skill. Many *adults* have trouble talking to resolve conflicts when their emotions are running high. We cannot expect young children, with months rather than years to build on, to have mastered this ability—though most young children do progress in this skill over time.

The teacher knows that conflict management must be delayed and crisis management used when children are too upset to talk. (This is why *calming everyone* is the first step in the five-finger formula.) Children who are totally upset give the adult no choice but to help them calm down first and talk later. At the moment, feelings are all that is real for the child. Anything else, such as explaining the reasons for behaviors, will just add to the child's frustration. So, in using this method of third resort, the question becomes how to help the child calm down.

Calming Techniques. There are different terms for the most basic technique the adult uses: *reflective listening, active listening,* and *acknowledgment of feelings.* Whichever term is preferred, the technique calls for the adult to give words to the emotions the child is showing, letting the child know that the adult cares.

> *Example: "Cheryl, the tears are flowing down your cheeks and you look very sad. Would you like to sit on my lap?"*

> *Example: "You hurt your foot when you kicked his shoe, and it hurt you again when he kicked you back. Let's just stay here for a few minutes so you can feel better. Then we'll talk about how to solve this problem."*

One calming technique that can be used with, after, or instead of reflective listening is to have children take deep breaths, counting or breathing with them as they breathe. A teacher who taught this technique reported seeing a child breathing deeply on his own. The child commented to the teacher that if he didn't he "would really get mad!"

Counting to 10 without deep breaths is another common technique, often used with older children. A teacher once relayed that she heard a six-year-old speed through the counting. She suggested he still seemed upset and suggested he count more slowly up to 30.

If a child declines the deep breathing or counting suggestions, don't fight it. Suggest the child think of his own way to calm down. Remember that some children, particularly some boys, require more than a few moments to process events and settle their emotions. Separation in this case may be a helpful technique for crisis management.

Separating to Cool Down. Sometimes the only way that teachers can help a child to calm down is by **separation** from the situation. This **cooling-down time** is different from a time-out. In the traditional time-out, a teacher isolates the child in a quiet place in the room *as a consequence* of being in the conflict. The teacher typically asks the child to "think about" what has happened. Katz (1984) and Preuesse (2002) point out that this request is developmentally inappropriate. Children can begin to understand what happened only if they are guided to do so by an adult. Without this assistance, children are likely to experience stress reactions, internalize anger and hurt feelings, and engage in a negative self-labeling process (Readdick & Chapman, 2000).

When making the decision to remove a child from a group, the guidance professional asks and answers two difficult questions.

The first question is: Am I removing this child to cool down so we can talk later, or am I removing this child because of what he did (Gartrell, 2004)? The

Separations as a consequence of something a child has done is punishment. The child is likely to internalize negative feelings rather than "think about" how to behave "better."

truth is that sometimes teachers separate a child as a way of expressing their own anger. Although there are worse things a teacher could do as a result of feeling angry, there are better responses to feeling anger than separating a child from the group and putting him on a chair.

Instead of separation, if the child is not upset, a more fitting consequence is to count to 10 yourself and mediate the conflict. A child who has hurt another child typically does not want to hear from the other child or the teacher about the hurt he has caused. But, within the framework of protected dialogue, empathy building is exactly the consequence that the child needs. The adult who can manage personal anger and actively resolve the conflict through mediation or a guidance talk has mastered a high-level guidance skill.

The second question is: Will the child calm down more easily if I am near; or will my proximity complicate the situation? The adult stays near a child to reassure against the punishing effect of separation, and to calm so that remediation can occur. A child who knows that he is sitting out to be able to feel better is not likely to find the teacher's presence reinforcing for the mistaken behavior, but may find it comforting.

Sometimes, however, teachers know a child well enough to recognize a definite need for personal space as part of the calming process. Many boys, and some girls, need "time and space" (Pollack, 2001). In this case, teachers get the child settled, give the child alone-time, and then facilitate the transition into resolution.

Replacing Time-Outs. In-room isolation—commonly known as the **time-out**—occurs when a child is removed from a situation and placed alone in a separate part of the room, usually with no alternative activity. (Isolation in either a closed-off portion of the room or outside the room, unless in the company of an adult, is an inappropriate and harmful intervention practice.) The time-out has received criticism for overuse in early childhood classrooms (Betz, 1994; Clewett, 1988; Gartrell, 2004; Marion, 1999; Preuesse, 2002).

In sports, a time-out is a break from the game for the purpose of substitution and strategy. For young children the time-out should be a break from a tense situation for the purpose of regaining composure. In his clinical studies, Piaget (1960) documented that young children—due to developmental egocentrism—have difficulty conceptualizing the intricacies of social situations. The ability of young children to "think about what happened" is limited, especially when put on a chair by themselves. During the time-out, young children do not logically "analyze the consequences of their actions," even if directed to do so (Katz, 1984; Schreiber, 1999). Instead, they are likely to internalize the shame of being separated, while sometimes simultaneously relishing the negative attention received from the teacher. This developmental reality means that periods of isolation fail to teach children "how to get along better." Even when considered a "logical consequence" by the teacher, the effect on the child is not logical; it invariably is punishment (Readdick & Chapman, 2000).

Two common practices for ending the time-out period have long been the timer and the child's own judgment about when to rejoin the group. Clewett (1988), Gartrell (2004), and Marion (1999) agree that the cooling-down separation is serious enough that direct teacher assistance is needed to transition the child into mediation or a guidance talk. As Clewett maintains, isolation reinforces a teacher's sense of power by forcing conformity to his expectations. Isolation also pressures the child toward diminished self-esteem and negative feelings toward the teacher and the education environment (Marion, 1999; Readdick & Chapman, 2000).

The following anecdote illustrates an appropriate use of separation to cool down—as distinct from the punishment of a time-out.

Classroom Anecdote	*Four kindergarten children were sitting down to "supper" in a housekeeping center. The pretend food was a large quantity of Styrofoam "peanuts" used in packing. Mark, a developmentally delayed five-year-old, arrived to join the group. The table was too small, and before Ina, the teacher, could arrive to mediate the problem, the children told Mark he couldn't play. Irate, Mark swept the bowl of "peanuts" on the floor and began to scream. He*
	(continued)

Classroom Anecdote	*was in the act of dumping the four plates upside down when Ina arrived. She stooped, put her arm around Mark (still highly agitated), and guided him to an unoccupied beanbag chair. Sitting by him, Ina stayed near until he quieted down.*
	The teacher reminded Mark to come to her when he had a problem, and told him the children felt sad about what had happened. She asked Mark what he could do to make things better. Mark said, "Pick up."
	Mark and the teacher went over and helped the children who were already picking up the Styrofoam. When they were done, Ina asked the children if Mark could join them for supper. "Okay," said Shelley, "Mark can be the little kid." Shelley then measured carefully the "peanuts" they put onto his plate. Mark smiled at being included.

Self-Removal. A strategy that teachers work out with individual children to help them manage their emotions is **self-removal**. Self-removal is an intermediate objective in the long-term goal of teaching children to use nonhurting words to solve their problems. Self-removal is an important accomplishment for some children. Teachers know when a child is using self-removal effectively, and mark it as progress with a child facing strong unmet needs.

Classroom Anecdote	*Observation: We were making a video for the parents. Nick was getting restless, and during one of the songs he chose to take himself out of the singing. He said, "I don't want to sing this song."*
	I asked, "What are you going to do, Nick?"
	His comment, "I'll sit on a chair."
	I followed with, "That would be fine. We want to finish singing for the movie, though. Come back as soon as you are ready."
	Nick sat out for two songs and then when we started with the instruments he said, "I want to play."
	I remarked, "If you are ready to come back, that is fine." He came back and picked out some rhythm sticks.
	Reflection: Nick has had a lot of difficulty this year controlling his impulses and participating in activities planned for the group. We teachers have been working with both him and his parents to help him increase his impulse control. Choosing to sit out for a few minutes has helped him so that he didn't get into trouble with other students and to get his composure back. We often told him that when he was ready to return to what the other students were doing, he could. He was given the opportunity to monitor himself, and now in April he has made a giant step when we were making the video—to sit down and not interrupt the other children. I hope he is in Head Start again and that we can continue to help him with his social development.

Over time teachers may notice a child beginning to use self-removal less as impulse control and more as a learned behavior to get out of everyday activities.

If so, they should smile. The child is progressing from Level Three mistaken behavior to Level Two. Guidance talks should continue, but in addition the staff works to make involvement in activities more meaningful for the child.

Finally, one now-established approach to the whole matter of self-removal—available to staff as well as children—is the following. A class makes one small corner of their classroom into "Australia." The corner is equipped with a ring of "ocean" and "sand" on the floor, a palm tree, stuffed koala bear, music, sitting pillows, and a beach towel. When adults or children are having a "Level Three day," and need to relax, they go to Australia! (The author wonders if classrooms in Australia have a "Florida" or a "Canada" corner.) The teachers watch for "visitors" and provide assistance to them in quiet but friendly ways.

4. Physical Restraint

Some children experience violence in their lives and as a result use it against others. The emotional payoffs from aggression can be reinforcing for a child, and teachers must use firm but friendly words and actions to halt "an upward spiral of violence" (Slaby et al., 1995). The foundations of guidance are undermined if teachers allow children to hurt themselves or others. At the same time, the encouraging classroom promotes nonviolence in adults as well as children. The adult intervenes firmly but nonpunitively. "Grownups as well as children are *never* allowed to hurt anyone in the classroom" (Slaby et al., 1995, p. 93).

The Crisis Prevention Institute (CPI, 1994) offers training "on how to use minimal-force restraint techniques that are appropriate, effective, and safe in given situations" (Slaby et al., 1995, p. 93). More so with older children, CPI training is helping teachers learn to cope in potentially violent situations. The following discussion of **physical restraint**, *the passive bear hug*, has been used by teachers of young children for many years.

The Passive Bear Hug. Physical restraint is the crisis management technique of *last resort*. It is *not* any of the notorious methods of subtle or not so subtle corporal punishment used on children over time. Physical restraint is *not* paddling, spanking, slapping, ear pulling, hair yanking, back-of-the-neck squeezing, knuckle whacking, retribution child biting, mouth taping, or binding to a chair. Neither is it pushing or pulling a child, nor holding a child upside down(!).

Physical restraint means holding a child, so that his arms, legs, and head cannot harm you or himself. Teachers use physical restraint when a child has lost control, physically and emotionally. A child in need of restraint may be attacking another child, the teachers, or another adult. The child may also show such behaviors as hitting body parts against a floor or wall.

Once the teacher decides that physical restraint is necessary, the commitment is total. Sitting down and clamping arms around arms and legs around legs is what physical restraint is about. The teacher often holds the child facing away and at an angle to prevent rear head butts. Children generally react strongly and negatively to being restrained. The teacher stays with it and often speaks soothingly to the child. With many children, calm words, quiet singing, or rocking helps; other children calm down more easily with stillness. The *passive bear hug* provides limits that the child, for the moment, cannot provide for himself. As the child comes to realize that the teacher is not hurting her, but providing needed behavioral and emotional controls, the child calms down.

Gradually, the child finds the closeness comforting and, strange as it might seem, the passive restraint often ends with the child snuggling against the teacher. (Who needs a hug more at this point is an open question.) If the child becomes able to talk about the event at the time, the teacher provides guidance. But usually, a guidance talk happens at a later time. After physical restraint, children (and adults) are drained. Helping the child into a quiet activity, like reading a book, promotes reconciliation.

Whenever possible the teacher relies on the teaching team during crisis management, and certainly when passive restraint is used. One adult works with the group, keeping them as busy as possible. Another adult uses the procedure. In this day and age, staff witnesses of the restraining are important. For teachers who are alone with a group, this is one important reason for nearby telephones and a preplanned contact system.

A follow-up self-check by the teacher later in the day is needed: Did the teacher use a level of force necessary to prevent further harm and not cause more? Was either the child or teacher injured? Most programs have a written report system for when a crisis intervention technique such as passive restraint is used. Class meetings to allay concerns in classmates sometimes are a good idea—teachers work hard to restore a sense of safety in the classroom. The adult who models and teaches democratic life skills as a part of the curriculum makes guidance more effective when conflicts become crises.

Any young child is entitled to "lose it" at least once during the program year. When serious mistaken behavior continues over time, however, crisis management techniques in themselves are not enough. A comprehensive strategy for addressing Level Three mistaken behavior—behavior that most teachers find *challenging*—follows.

Comprehensive Guidance/The Individual Guidance Plan

There is no such thing as a bad kid, only kids with bad problems that they need your help to resolve. The challenge is that their behavior is challenging. These kids are often the hardest to like, even though they need a caring relationship with us the most.

Serious (Level Three) mistaken behavior is due to strong needs that a child feels, cannot meet, and acts out in relation to. The strong needs arise from *biological or emotional factors*, or a combination of the two. Often, the causes of strong needs mistaken behavior lie outside the classroom.

Untreated physical, neurological, and health conditions that bother a child are one source. To the list of long-standing health conditions, such as physical disabilities, illness, hunger, and lack of sleep, teachers are seeing less

© Cengage Learning

Nonpunitive physical restraint provides a child who has lost control with the limits needed to regain composure.

"traditional" (but now common) conditions: attention-deficit/hyperactivity disorder, fetal alcohol syndrome, autism disorder spectrum, chronic allergies, and environmental illnesses, among others. Most of these physical conditions, undiagnosed and untreated, can cause the persistent "challenging" behaviors, ranging from withdrawal to aggression, that constitute Level Three.

In recent years teachers have gone beyond the stereotype of "a bad home life" to address more specifically the *emotional sources of strong needs mistaken behavior* of children. Due to life circumstances, for instance, some children show a fear of abandonment more severe than that commonly felt by many young children. Other children may show the psychological effects of abuse: both victimization by the act and internalization of aggression as a relational style due to modeling of the act (Slaby et al., 1995).

Teachers are seeing an increase of *posttraumatic stress disorder,* due to violence perpetrated on children themselves or others in their presence. Once thought to affect mainly soldiers in war, experts now recognize that violence in families and neighborhoods can impact severely the sensibilities of direct and indirect victims, including young children (Rogers, Andre, & Hawley, 1996).

Whether biological, environmental, or both, these traumatic conditions cause chronic stress, undermine healthy brain development, and generate the extreme behavior that is characteristic of Level Three. The similarities in behavior of a child suffering the effects of trauma and a child "being antisocial" are becoming better known (Lowenthal, 1999). The difficulty these children sometimes experience in developing a conscience and empathy for others is a particular challenge for educators.

A Comprehensive Guidance

Though it may not seem so, children who show chronic Level Three mistaken behavior are making a request for help. Gootman (1993), Heath (1994), and the Surgeon General's Report (1999) point out that using a *comprehensive intervention strategy* with a child who has strong unmet needs is likely to be more effective than traditional discipline practices. Teachers may have to remind themselves more than once that the time and energy the child requires is an investment in the future. On the "upside," teachers do not need specialized licenses or advanced degrees to use comprehensive guidance successfully. Sometimes, though not always, the investment of time and effort pays back quickly.

Comprehensive guidance includes components most of which have been introduced in previous chapters. Of necessity, the strategy begins before patterns of conflict arise with the relationships teachers build with children and their families. With each act of serious mistaken behavior, the teacher intervenes to prevent harm and disruption—using the crisis management techniques discussed earlier. Adapting from the sources above as well as Rogers, Andre, and Hawley (1996) and Slaby et al (1995), the steps commonly included in comprehensive guidance follow in Table 10–2.

Classroom Anecdote	*I remember a resourceful teacher named Nellie who was guiding a child to manage his anger. One day when I arrived at the classroom, Jackson was standing with the teacher outside a closed side door yelling into the wind. Another day, Jackson walked over to the teacher and said, "Teacher, I am so mad!"*
	Nellie responded, "I can see you are, Jackson. Thank you for coming and telling me. How about if you go into the restroom, close the door, and spit in the sink as long as you want." Two minutes later, emotions calmed, Jackson walked out of the restroom and headed right for the water fountain. He was a dry little kid! After quickly cleaning the sink, the teacher complimented Jackson for removing himself from the situation and handling his anger. She had a quiet guidance talk with him and helped him rejoin the group.
	Crisis intervention was not all the teacher and staff did to help Jackson with his problems. From her relationship with the mother, Nellie knew that she and her husband were fighting. Jackson and his younger sister had witnessed violence in the family, but her father had begun going to AA. The teacher worked hard to maintain relations with the mom and also communicate with the father (whom Nellie also knew). In the classroom, staff members spent quality time with Jackson that included contact talks each day, to build his trust and their relations with him. Over time, Jackson progressed in his ability to manage his emotions.

Comprehensive Guidance at Work. In some situations not all of the steps of comprehensive guidance are necessary. Teachers can achieve results with Steps One through Five. Nellie, the primary teacher working with

Table 10-2 *Steps in Comprehensive Guidance*
1. Work to develop relationships with families when the child first begins, before conflicts start.
2. Use crisis management techniques to prevent harm to the child and others.
3. Learn more about the child at home and at school.
4. Implement what you have learned in programming for the child
5. Improve the quality of the teacher-child relationship.
6. Hold an individual guidance plan (IGP) meeting and develop a written IGP if necessary.
7. Utilize specific support, prevention, and intervention techniques designed for the child.
8. Review and modify the IGP if necessary.

Jackson, was able to build a relationship with Jackson's mom. Learning about the mother's difficulties, the teacher got the staff to have daily contact talks with the boy. The teacher not only built her relationship with Jackson, but also took the lead in making positive, consistent interventions when he had conflicts. With time she succeeded in her goal of winning his trust. The result, over time, was Jackson's learning to leave situations and come to her when his stress levels got high.

In this case a formal meeting with the mother was not needed. Neither was a recorded plan that needed implementation and review. An experienced teacher's dedication to reaching a child with a problem and a cooperative staff were enough. In other situations, when mental health is clearly strained and a child's behaviors remain extreme, a teacher will need to follow all eight steps. The following section provides guidelines helpful in using a formal individual guidance plan (IGP) with children who have strong unmet needs.

The Individual Guidance Plan

For school-age children with severe unmet social–emotional needs, special education screening along with possible assessment, diagnosis, and an *Individual Education Plan* (IEP) can and should happen. K–12 students in the "gray area" who do not qualify for formal special education assistance may still qualify for *RTI* (Response to Intervention) services, which, in many schools, allow them to function as normally as possible in the regular classroom. Preschool children can receive a special education assessment and have a plan developed for them as well, but without the necessity of a categorical diagnosis like "emotionally disturbed."

The IGP procedure provides a model for addressing strong needs mistaken behavior in school-age and preschool children who do not qualify for formal special education. When classroom staff, parents, and sometimes other professionals cooperate in forming and implementing a plan, the groundwork is set for an effective problem-solving strategy to improve the mental health of children who are having ongoing classroom conflicts. There is no getting around it: Serious mistaken behaviors require comprehensive strategies to assist the child in learning necessary personal and interpersonal skills. The following guidelines provide information for the use of the IGP:

1. Work to Build Relationships with the Child and Family Prior to Crises. From the entry of the child and family into the program, the *teaching team* (lead teacher with any other classroom staff) develops relationships with both the child and family. The knowledge gained helps the team understand the needs, interests, learning qualities, and response styles of the child. The relationships and information are invaluable if a child shows eventual strong needs mistaken behavior. There is no substitute for trust levels already developed in the event that comprehensive intervention becomes necessary.

2. Use Crisis/Conflict Management Techniques. In the event of strong unmet needs mistaken behavior, the team uses the crisis intervention techniques previously discussed: being direct, commanding choices, calming methods, and physical restraint, as well as the conflict management techniques of guidance talks, mediation, and class meetings. One teacher, usually the primary caregiver, may take charge in crisis situations, providing consistent limits, interventions, and follow-ups for the child.

3. Obtain Additional Information. The lead teacher and team seek to understand the child's behavior and the child more fully. Staff make extra effort to talk with the child. Designated staff complete two-part anecdotal observations, with Part One objectively describing words and actions and Part Two containing the teacher's reflective attempts to understand what has been observed. Incidents of mistaken behavior are charted against days of the week, times of the day, and the daily schedule.

The teacher contacts the parent and (carefully using compliment sandwiches) explains the pattern of mistaken behavior. The teacher and parent discuss whether similar behaviors are being noted at home and if the parent has noticed any changes in the child's life that might be causing the child some difficulty.

4. Implement Information Gained. The teaching team and staff again meet. (A key ingredient in comprehensive guidance teaching is the inclusion of all staff—including any specialists—to work together as a team.) While one teacher takes the lead in interventions, team members participate and provide support in modifying the program, preventing crises when possible, and resolving conflicts as peacefully as possible. The teaching team incorporates the information gained in their responses to the child. Follow-up contact with the family often happens after the initial "staffing."

5. Improve the Quality of the Teacher-Child Relationship. Improving adult-child relationships is vital in comprehensive guidance. Unless staff consciously sustain positive relationships, they may harbor negative expectations that make it difficult for the child to change. Children who have trouble trusting in adults and the environment to meet their basic needs experience stress and withdraw or act out. A fundamental effort is to assist the child to build basic trust. Even if the "outside world" remains threatening, the trust the child comes to feel in the classroom supports resiliency. The teacher knows she has this trust when the child looks to her for support, not just in the "good times" but also in the conflicts. Knowing that she does not substitute for the family, but is on a team with the family, provides important perspective for the teacher in this task. The professional teacher does not have to "like" every child, but works to build a positive relationship with each child.

6. Hold the Individual Guidance Plan Meeting. If actions to this point do not seem to be resolving the problem, a meeting is held with parents, the teaching team, and other relevant adults to develop an IGP. The teacher calls upon her relationship with the family to convey the importance of the meeting. She explains what will and what will not happen, and decides on a time when one or more family members can attend. The team completes the IGP Worksheet that outlines the process (found in Appendix E and in electronic form on the book companion website). Team members, often with the family, may share the plan with the child.

7. Implement the Guidance Plan. The team works together to put the IGP into operation. (The plan may have both classroom and in-home components.) Consistent, nonpunitive crisis and conflict management intervention is a part of the plan. One component of Individual guidance plans are steps to further improve relationships between the child and adults—perhaps including family members. Another is adaptation of the program to improve developmental appropriateness for the child. Referral for assessment by special education or other professionals may be part of the IGP. Counseling (for the child or child and family) or other support services may be included. If special education services are warranted, an IEP may supersede the IGP.

8. Review and Modify the Plan If Necessary. The staff continues observations, reviews the plan, communicates with parents, and makes modifications as needed. If needed, the staff holds follow-up IGP meetings and acts upon modifications decided. To prevent needless/premature talk of removal of the child from the program, only at Step Eight should such discussion happen. Preferable, of course, is the team's coming up with additional resources that expand the comprehensiveness of services and allow the child to remain in the classroom.

The Case of Geri

A few years ago, I taught a class on the use of comprehensive guidance. Eighteen Head Start and child care staff attended, including four family child care providers. The class met for two days in March for an overview of the comprehensive guidance process. During the next six weeks, the students formed teams and completed IGPs with children in their classes, kept a record of what happened, and wrote a draft report. Over two days in late April, each team shared their drafts, received feedback from class members and instructors, and prepared and submitted final reports.

"Geri's" story is an amalgamation of the IGP studies of these students. Rather than an anecdotal representation of a single case study, this account is a composite illustration, based on what the class members wrote and said. A summary of class findings from using the IGP procedure concludes the section. Geri's case illustrates the eight steps in comprehensive guidance.

1. Work to Build Relationships with the Family When the Child First Begins, Prior to Conflicts. Geri's mom was a single parent with two other children, an older brother and a younger sister. Geri's teacher, Ronnie, met the mom when she enrolled her daughter. The teacher met twice with Raylin after that and found mom a bit quiet and at times close to her limit with managing the family. To keep in touch with Raylin, Ronnie talked with her at pickup and drop-off and phoned her every few weeks to let her know how things were going. Raylin seemed to enjoy the contacts with the teacher. She said more than once she would like to visit Geri's classroom, but had not made it the one time she had agreed to visit. Ronnie noticed that Raylin seemed more distant after this, but she kept working on the relationship. The teacher wondered if something had changed in the home situation.

2. Use Crisis/Guidance Management Techniques. During March, almost daily Geri experienced conflicts involving objecting to directions, showing defiance toward adults, and displaying instrumental aggression toward her classmates. Geri also began to show behaviors that the assistant teacher described as "sneaky aggressive." When she thought she wouldn't be caught, Geri shoved a child down, hit a child, or took something away. When confronted by a teacher, she would angrily deny that she did anything, or try to toss it off with a quick "I'm sorry, I won't do it again."

One day, Ronnie saw Geri hitting a four-year-old in the hallway to the playground. Francisco was trying to push Geri away, but was not hitting back. Ronnie got over there quickly and separated the children. She noted a clenched expression on Geri's face, and as Geri started to strike at her teacher, she held the child firmly: "This is hitting and there is no hitting at school. Both of us will sit down, now!" She sat down using the passive bear hug, to both comfort and restrain. Francisco's teacher arrived and sat down with her arms around Francisco to comfort him.

Geri had been struggling against Ronnie's passive restraint. Her eyes were tightly closed and she was repeating, "You let me go!" Her expression went from angry to miserable, and her body lost its rigidity and became limp. The teachers decided this was not a time for mediation. Ronnie held Geri for a few minutes, and using reflective listening told her, "You were very angry, so angry you hit, and now you look sad."

Geri said, "He bumped me and I hit him."

Ronnie replied, "He bumped you and that made you upset. I wonder what else makes you angry, Geri?" Geri did not respond. After a few minutes, Ronnie said, "Would you like to stay out here by me, or go inside where Sam [assistant teacher] is getting ready for lunch?"

Geri said inside, so they went in, and Ronnie briefly mentioned to Sam that Geri could use a friend. Geri watched Sam for a while, then helped him finish setting the table. Geri ate little and slept a long time at rest. Afterward, she and Ronnie had a guidance talk. They discussed what happened, how everyone felt, how Geri could make things better, and what she could do differently next time so that no one would be hurt. Ronnie kept the tone friendly and her words brief. She helped Geri get started in a quiet activity.

3. Gain Additional Information. In discussing Geri's situation, the staff first reviewed what they knew about this child: Geri had been in the child care program since January, and now in March had just turned five. From the beginning Geri had been active and independent, seldom settling down in activities and often acting on impulses without apparent awareness of consequences. The teaching team (consisting of a teacher, assistant teacher (Sam), and student teacher) enjoyed her enthusiasm and worked hard to help her manage her impulses. They noted that Geri liked dramatic play, could "hold her own with the boys," and enjoyed art and books. She had occasional difficulties settling in and staying with the group during circle times. In the last few weeks, Geri had been experiencing an increasing number of conflicts, including with the staff when they tried to intervene. One staff member said she thought Geri had "oppositional defiant disorder" (a need to constantly challenge authority). Ronnie reminded the staff about Geri's home situation and suggested they try to see Geri "as just a kid who needs our help."

Ronnie wrote up the incident, and shared it and an informal report with administration. That night she called Raylin, Geri's mom, but discussed the incident carefully, aware that Raylin had a lot on her plate already. She asked Raylin if there were any changes at home that would help in understanding why Geri seemed to be having some difficulties lately at school. Raylin paused, then said that the father of the youngest child had moved in, and they all were having some trouble adjusting. Ronnie acknowledged this and told Raylin that if there were anything they could do at school to help, to let her know.

4. Implement Information Gained. Ronnie talked more with her teaching team early the next morning. They agreed that Geri might be showing stress from the transition dynamics in her family.

The team decided to increase daily contact talk time with Ronnie, to let her know they cared and that she belonged (see Step Five below). Sam and the student teacher took turns sitting with Geri during group time, helping her to stay focused. The three informally "shadowed" Geri at "high-risk" times during the day, such as at moments during outdoor play, transitions, and center times. They looked for and acknowledged prosocial actions by Geri, and in general gave her positive attention, hugs, and smiles. The team met informally every day or two and kept Raylin up-to-date.

5. Improve the Quality of the Teacher-Child Relationship. Ronnie decided to use the playtime before breakfast to spend 10–15 minutes of "just Geri time." The assistant teacher and student teacher greeted children and got them into activities while Ronnie worked with Geri. Ronnie explained to Geri that she needed to get to know Geri better and to be a good teacher for her. Each morning she gave Geri a choice of activities to do, and the two moved into some space in the hall to be together. The other members of the teaching team as well found a few quality minutes to spend with Geri. Sam or the student teacher sat with Geri during circle time and helped her focus. Rhonda, the student teacher, made a point of reading books with Geri each day. The team used contact talks during these times to convey their acceptance of Geri as a valuable member of the class.

6. **Hold the Individual Guidance Plan Meeting.** The team did not see crises quite like what had happened on the playground, but Geri kept up her active pace, with the new wrinkle that she became frustrated very easily. The team was contending with daily bouts of dramatic loss of emotional control. They did notice, though, that Geri was showing less aggression toward other children and the adults in the classroom. The team used specific, dated anecdotal observations to document the pattern they were seeing, Ronnie set up an individual guidance plan meeting with Geri's mother. Ronnie asked if Raylin would like to bring her partner, but Raylin said no. The team arranged with the director to have their group covered, and all were waiting at 4:30 P.M. on the day. Raylin showed up at 5:15 and said she couldn't talk because her son was home alone. The next morning Ronnie suggested that Raylin bring her son with her, and the three siblings could play while they met. They set up another meeting.

This time the meeting happened. The team (including the student teacher) started with the interests and achievements of Geri. Raylin knew there was a problem on the agenda, but still appreciated hearing "some good stuff." The team matter-of-factly went over their observations. Raylin commented about Geri's pattern of impulsivity with quick apologies, which she and the team had talked about before. Raylin said the pattern was getting worse, along with "tantrums over little things." Raylin seemed guarded in what she said about the home life. But they all agreed, Raylin too, that Geri needed more positive attention.

Raylin said she might try an idea she had heard about in Head Start. Once each week she would have two of the children stay with Grandma, and then do something special that she would decide with the third child. She said she would start with Geri. She also agreed to allow an early childhood special education teacher to do an observation, relative to Geri possibly receiving special education services. Ronnie asked if the family would like a home visit, but Raylin said probably not at this time. They agreed they would meet again in two weeks.

7. **Implement the Guidance Plan.** Geri was "an angel" during the entire special education observation. The observing teacher remarked that Geri had a high activity level, but not abnormally so. She agreed to come back if the team asked. Ronnie continued with her "just Geri times." One of Geri's favorite activities became writing and drawing "books" of three to five blank pages stapled together. One of her books was of Raylin and Roger (the boyfriend)

fighting and a child looking on. The book ended with Geri "reading," "And he goed away." Ronnie wondered about this, but decided to discuss the matter only if Raylin brought it up. With the increased positive attention from the team, Geri became less agitated and aggressive, but continued to be "her 78-rpm self." The teaching team decided that with reduced amounts of aggression and frustration, they could easily live with Geri's energy level.

8. **Monitor Guidance Plan.** During the next two weeks, Geri had days that went smoothly and days that had conflicts. Overall, the team found that Geri was having an easier time at school. Perhaps as important, all three teaching team members realized that they were feeling more attached to Geri. Sam admitted, "That kid used to bug me to pieces, but I understand her more now." In the follow-up meeting, cut short because the youngest child wasn't feeling well, Raylin said Geri was having fewer tantrums at home. She commented that Roger was out of the house, but was still hassling her. Ronnie and Raylin agreed to weekly phone calls. In the first call, Raylin mentioned that she had gotten a restraining order against Roger and "it would be hard for a while."

The team worked to stay in touch with Raylin and to make Geri a fully accepted member of the class. They recognized that helping Geri make friends and fit in would build the child's sense of self and trust in the world, important for her progress to continue.

Note: Readers can find another case-study illustrating comprehensive guidance at the end of this chapter in the Guidance Matters column titled "Comprehensive Guidance" (Gartrell, 2008).

Class Findings—IGP Projects

This section discusses the findings of the class of 18 early childhood professionals, a majority of whom were from Native American communities in northern Minnesota. Most had childhood development associate (CDA) credentials, while two had four-year degrees. In nine teams, the class completed the IGP procedure for individual children in their classrooms and family child care settings. From their written reports and discussion about them, six trends emerged, reflected in Geri's story.

First, all the participants that taught with other staff reported that the adults came together as a team in using the comprehensive guidance procedure. One teacher who was concerned that her staff were "on different pages about discipline" was surprised at the spirit of cooperation engendered by the project.

Second, two family child care providers who worked on their own became a "phone team," talking often about their "cases." These participants also found themselves talking with other family child care providers as well. Without the benefit of an "in-room" teaching team, support systems for family child care providers around guidance issues are important. (Matters of confidentiality need to be respected, of course, whatever the teaming arrangement.)

Third, a majority of students reported improved communication with the family. About half of these students reported that they had positive relations with

Teachers who use the guidance approach work to accept children and view them nonjudgmentally.

the family already, and the project caused them to join together even more. The other half basically built teacher-family relationships during the project.

Fourth, two teams found families cooperative as long as the intervention strategy did not go beyond classroom staff. In these instances, family members balked at "getting involved" with an early childhood special education teacher or a psychologist. Building on the trust relationship they had previously created, three teams were able to involve other professionals, either to do observations or through referral visits. The other four teams did not see a need to extend services beyond what the program directly could provide.

Fifth, the students felt positively about the experience of implementing a comprehensive guidance plan. All 18 students documented that they had improved their relationships with their selected children and understood more how to work with them. At the same time, however, no student felt that their case study children completely turned their lives around—or that their own efforts at comprehensive guidance went "perfectly."

Sixth, most students were able to document progress in the children by way of gaining democratic life skills. Although they did not find "magic answers," the fact that most reported their children were able "to get along better" is significant.

Recap. The research of Ladd, Price, and Hart (1990) indicates that children not able to fit in and make friends during their early years are statistically vulnerable for recurrent problems in school and life. The action research presented here was meant for illustrative purposes. Still, helped by the teachers completing this class, the nine children in the studies may be increasing their chances for educational success.

Teaching that uses comprehensive guidance can be difficult; it calls for teachers to go beyond their immediate feelings and reaction tendencies and to view children—and their families—supportively. Sometimes, as indicated, an IGP will not work out as completely as a teacher would wish. We may not be able to greatly change life circumstances for every child, but in the time they are with us we can make their lives better. The professional teacher does not win every battle, but learns as she teaches and contributes to the life of the child, and sometimes the family, in the effort. And, working with others, she accomplishes what she cannot on her own.

When Teachers Feel Anger

Because teachers are human and cannot always accomplish what they want, they feel anger. The source of the anger may be the children themselves—a child who manipulates or harms others—or a group that too many times fails to live up to expectations. The source may have to do with communication with adults, such as a parent who does not follow through, a fellow staff member who is erratic, or a friend or family member who lets us down. In 1972, Ginott pointed out that teacher preparation programs rarely educate about anger and how to handle it—a problem still widely true today.

The teacher of young children may feel particularly guilty about anger— because consistent nurturing is such an expected part of the role. Yet, teachers of young children no less than teachers at other levels face anger within themselves. The issue is not feeling guilty about the reality of this emotion; the issue is how we manage the anger we feel (Ginott, 1972).

Teachers practice **personal safeguards** that assist in the management of anger through three guidelines:

1. Monitor feelings and making adjustments.

2. Express anger carefully.

3. Practice reconciliation.

Monitor Feelings; Make Adjustments

An effective anger management strategy begins before a crisis occurs. Teachers need to *self-monitor* moods and predispositions. For physical and emotional reasons, all teachers occasionally function at the "survival" level. Perhaps later in the 21st century, more teaching contracts will include adequate mental health policies to allow for this aspect of the human condition. In the meantime, teachers—both men and women—do well to prepare contingency plans for when they are emotionally or physically "down." Participants in early

© Cengage Learning

Once in a while a strategy for down days is increased playtime for children, outside when possible.

childhood classes and workshops in the upper Midwest suggested the following coping strategies.

1. Aware of DAP guidelines about the use of videos, a kindergarten teacher uses them only for two special purposes: to link curriculum to an outstanding video presentation and to provide very occasional, emergency relief for the teacher. He talks regularly with the children about their favorite videos, and for the second purpose has a few favorites on hand, using them only two or three times a year.

2. A third-grade teacher keeps a list of high-interest, largely self-directed activities to use when she is overtired or has a sinus infection and cannot take sick leave.

3. Three first-grade teachers have an agreement among themselves and with their rotating teacher aide that for "special occurrences," the aide spends more time in a particular classroom.

4. In several preschool programs, teachers and associates work as "teaching teams," rather than in sharply defined professional and paraprofessional roles. As needed, one or the other adult can assume more leadership on a particular day.

5. In both preschool and elementary school classrooms, on Level Three days one member of a teaching team asks another to work with a child who shows frequent mistaken behavior. (One kindergarten teacher stated: "I have a good relationship with the special education teacher who works with three children in my room. Most days, I work fine with a particular 'active-alert' child.

Once in a while, I rely on Jan to help with this child. We have become a real team.")

6. A first-grade teacher, on days when he is overly tired, intentionally soft-pedals expectations for two children in his class, whom he otherwise "might come down hard on." (On these days he also gives in to the weakness of hoping one or both of these children won't be in school that day—and shrugs off the guilty feelings connected to this wish.)

7. A principal has a policy in his school that if any teacher ever needs a break, he will stop what he is doing and take over the teacher's class. He says it took a few months for teachers to ask, but now he gets a request every week or two. The principal states the teachers like this policy—and teachers from other schools have asked to transfer to his.

8. Teachers in a particular school have a buddy system. The system was set up carefully to match teachers who get along. If a teacher feels that a day will be challenging, the two might talk for a while before the children arrive or go for a walk off school grounds during a break.

9. The most frequent comment of workshop participants is that they let children, even preschoolers, know how they are feeling. In classrooms where the teacher models concern for the well-being of all, children respond in kind. Even three-year-olds have been known to tiptoe and whisper, "'cause Teacher's not feeling good today."

Ongoing problems that keep teachers from being at their best need attention. Just as it is important to understand the reasons for the behavior of children, it is also important for adults. Teaching is a difficult occupation. The teacher who seeks a friendly ear, counseling, or therapy to improve her state of mind in the classroom is acting as a true professional.

Use Safeguards

By monitoring feelings and adjusting the program on Level Three days, the teacher reduces the risk of losing emotional control. But on *any* day, a teacher may become justifiably—or at least understandably—angry, even when teaching young children. Ginott (1972) provides guidance on the expression of anger. His contention is that anger cannot always be controlled but that it can be managed. He states:

> *The realities of teaching—the overloaded classes, the endless demands, the sudden crises—make anger inevitable. Teachers need not apologize for their angry feelings. An effective teacher is neither a masochist nor a martyr. He does not play the role of a saint or act the part of an angel. . . . When angry, an enlightened teacher remains real. He describes what he sees, what he feels, what he expects. He attacks the problem, not the person. He knows that when angry, he is dealing with more elements than he can control. He protects himself and safeguards his students by using "I" messages. (pp. 72–73)*

In his discussion, Ginott referred to the communication basic, "describe, express, and direct," introduced earlier in the chapter. This safeguard steers the teacher toward the problem, rather than the child's personality. If two children are fighting, the safeguard might well result in the comment: "I see hitting and children being hurt. I do not like what I see. You will separate and sit down. Then we will talk." The teacher backs up the words by establishing physical proximity and indicating where the children are to sit. As soon as feelings have "cooled"—including the teacher's—she and the children use mediation and/or a guidance talk.

Note that *I-messages* express strong feelings relatively nonpunitively and focus children on the teacher's concerns. Ginott (1972) discusses the use of I-messages this way:

> *"I am annoyed," "I am appalled," "I am furious" are safer statements than "You are a pest," "Look what you have done," "You are so stupid," "Who do you think you are?" (p. 73)*

Nonetheless, I-messages are powerful. They should be used with discretion and routinely.

Directing comments to the situation and not to the personality of the child is an important guidance safeguard. This "cardinal principle" pertains in many situations, but especially in the expression of anger. Ginott's (1972) contention is that when teachers express displeasure but still observe the safeguards that protect self-esteem, children are more likely to listen and more able to respond.

Practice Reconciliation

Classroom Anecdote	*R.J. was holding a door open for his first-grade class while they walked to another room for a special activity. He began swinging the door toward children as they passed, making believe he was closing it. As Kaye walked by, R.J. lost his grip and the door banged into her, knocking her down. After tending to Kaye, the teacher looked for R.J., but he had disappeared. She asked an aide to take the class into the room for the activity and, getting more upset by the minute, went to look for him. She found him in the farthest corner of their classroom, looking anxious.*

> *Teacher:* (Loudly) You banged the door on Kaye, and then you ran away! I am really upset about this.
> *R.J.:* (Crying hard) I didn't mean to.
> *Teacher:* (Surprised at his reaction) What can we do about it?
> *R.J.:* (Still crying, barely gets out) Say I'm sorry.
> *Teacher:* All right. Anything else?

Still crying, R.J. shakes his head no. The teacher decides she has been a little hard on him. After helping R.J. feel better, she suggests that they join the group. When they sit down with the class, R J. leans against the teacher. She puts her arm around his shoulder. They both sit quietly for a short while. After the activity, R.J. apologizes to Kaye.

Readers perhaps can remember a conflict with a teacher when they were students. If on the following day the teacher acted as if nothing had happened, the reader probably recalls a feeling of relief. If from that day on things never seemed the same, the year probably seemed long indeed. Teachers, like all of us, make mistakes. For this reason as the leaders in the classroom, when they overreact, teachers need to practice *reconciliation* (Gartrell, 2004). Under normal circumstances, children are resilient and bounce back. They also forgive easily, more easily than most adults. Because teachers are important in their lives, children want to be on friendly terms with them. This was the case with R.J. and Kaye.

Still, a challenge for any teacher is when she has clearly overreacted and crossed the boundary between firmness and harshness. Because the skill of expressing strong emotions in nonhurting ways takes effort, even for experienced adults, teachers sometimes do cross the line.

Perhaps a first step in learning to recover from a bad episode is to recognize our feelings and forgive *ourselves*. Only then can we figure out how to make the best of the situation and forgive the other. Thoughts in the middle of the night may be part of this healing process, and talks with others important to us certainly are (Jersild, 1985). Children are forgiving and *need* us to be firm. If the undercurrent of our firmness is appreciation of the worth of each individual child, reconciliation offers the possibility of fuller understanding and more productive relationships.

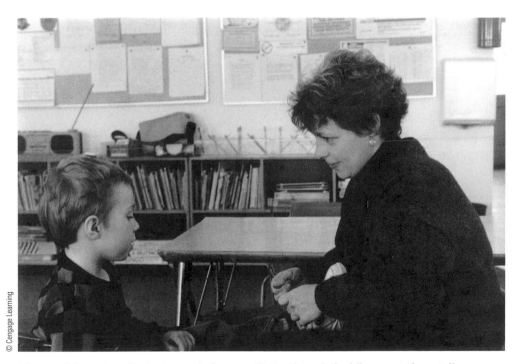

© Cengage Learning

After a cool-down time, the teacher works for reconciliation through the follow-up guidance talk.

A Matter of Timing. Reconciliation is a matter of timing and inviting. Immediately after a confrontation few are ready to apologize and make amends. This is as true for adults as it is for children. Children (especially boys) may not be ready to reconcile with a teacher until they have had time to work through their feelings. (Children are ready to talk when they are not actively resisting the conversation.) After an adequate cool-down time, reconciliation often occurs with the follow-up guidance talk. Sometimes, though, children will take longer. Accept this reluctance and continue to model acceptance of the child.

When the teacher invites reconciliation, children are more apt to oblige. With young children, apologies and the acceptance of apologies are often expressed nonverbally. As in the anecdote, a hug says a lot—"Please forgive me" and "I forgive you" all at once. In the encouraging classroom, teachers need to model that they too can learn from mistakes. True reconciliation means change. For professional teachers who care about young children, change means learning and growing.

When Teachers and Parents Disagree

At one time or another, teachers and parents have differences in viewpoints about program priorities, program content, teaching style, behaviors of the parents' own children, or the actions of other children. Boutte et al. (1992), Lightfoot (1978), Pappano (2007), and Powell (1989) make similar points about such differences: They should not become negative dissonances but can serve as creative conflicts, which retain the possibility of being solved (Lightfoot, 1978).

Negative dissonance is the result of differences that alienate the parent from the teacher. In such cases, the teacher may hold the power of the education institution over the parent, often on the basis of the parent's social or cultural background. Views, values, and communication styles of the parent are considered of lesser importance than those of the teacher, as an "official representative" of the school or center (Powell, 1989).

Creative conflicts arise from the diversity of life in a complex, pluralistic society in which the right of the individual to his own views is accepted (Lightfoot, 1978). The teacher who respects parents, whatever their background, realizes that differences in values or viewpoint need not impede positive teacher-parent relations. The common ground of the child whose life they share makes differences an opportunity for creative communication, and possible resolution, not inevitably a point of division (Jacobs, 1992; Manning & Schindler, 1997; Pappano, 2007).

Yet, the reality remains that some parents are difficult to communicate with, and many teachers feel underprepared for this part of the job (Boutte et al., 1992; Pappano, 2007). Teachers who find that they are in disagreement with parents engage in the basic negotiation process discussed for use with parents in Chapter Ten. Seven guidelines assist in a variety of situations when teachers and parents disagree.

1. **Encourage Mutual Respect.** Warren (1977) makes the case that parents who seem unworthy were once children whose unmet needs are preventing them from a healthy adulthood. The teacher who does not let personal judgments get in the way of involving parents in their children's education understands the importance of Warren's words.

Parents from backgrounds different from the teacher's have legitimate points of pride and values that their family members share. Remaining open to learning about customs and lifestyles new to the teacher conveys respect for the family and the child.

At the same time, the teacher can take pride in being a professional and need not be defensive about educational practice that she knows to be appropriate. Regardless of differences in age or experience, self-respect is a right of the early childhood teacher. As a professional, the teacher uses appropriate practice in relations with parents, no less than with children. Appropriate practice means an invitation to parents to become involved and to collaborate in the education process of the child (Pappano 2007; Rogers et al., 1996).

2. **Model Reflective Listening.** When parents feel strongly to the point of anger or confrontation, the teacher needs to listen, allow them to cool off, and not

At one time or another, teachers and parents will have differences in viewpoints.

dispute or "block out" what they say (Boutte et al., 1992). To ensure the parent that the teacher is listening, she repeats the substance of what the parent has said, the basic element in reflective listening. The teacher uses her judgment in relation to specifics in the argument, but stops personal criticism, redirecting communication to the point of the meeting. Use of parents' ideas when deciding on follow-up shows that listening was at work. As part of the listening process, reiterating that everyone wants what is best for the child is important. Invitation for another contact in the future communicates that the teacher is serious about having parents involved. Parents who know they are being listened to are more likely to listen in return (Rogers et al., 1996).

3. **Talk to Situations.** In conferences the teacher should have specific, objective information on hand about the child and the situation being discussed: observations, samples of the child's work, and written accounts of situations. The teacher describes events and does not judgmentally evaluate the child, the child's behaviors, or the child's family background. Galinsky (1988) notes:

> *Certain statements tend to create distrust and worry rather than an alliance. For example: If a teacher says, "Is something going on at home?" the parent may feel accused. Instead, try, "Did Arthur have a hard time getting up today? He seems tired." (p. 11)*

Basic guidance communication techniques like compliment sandwiches highlight progress and pose problems constructively. Honestly meant, open-ended questions make conversations more friendly. A goal is to generate possible solutions to problems together, discussing the pros and cons of each (Rogers et al., 1996).

4. **Invite Continued Involvement.** For parents who are assertive, the teacher works to increase their involvement. Positive strategies include providing current literature to discuss later, encouraging attendance at parent meetings, and seeking the parent's participation in the classroom. Such measures give the parent a respectful opportunity to learn more about, and contribute to, the program. As Boutte et al. (1992) state:

> *Parents usually will feel less alienated and will be more willing to participate if they are involved more in the decision-making regarding their children. All parents should be allowed to contribute to the program in some significant way. (p. 20)*

In this effort, the teacher makes hypotheses about the level and type of involvement the parent may accept. She adjusts expectations as necessary to keep the communication going. The teacher who works around a point of difference and wins an ally has truly mastered the principle of "creative conflict" (Manning & Schindler, 1997).

5. **Communicate with Staff and Consulting Professionals.** When a teacher suspects that a conflict may arise with a family, and certainly if a conflict continues, she should discuss the situation with other staff (Rogers et al., 1996). The communication may range from asking for information from a colleague who knows a parent to discussing the matter with an administrator.

Venting to trusted others may be important for the teacher's mental health, but communication about families needs to avoid the "teachers' lounge phenomenon" (gossip). Beyond fellow staff, consulting colleagues—such as home visitors or home-school liaisons—can also be valuable resources (Manning & Schindler, 1997). In the complex world of today, teachers need to collaborate to extend their ability to assist children, and their families, to learn and to grow (Pappano, 2007).

6. **Switch to Mediation.** As mentioned in Chapter Ten, in some situations negotiation with parents may not be successful. In the event that productive communication becomes difficult—including in the midst of a meeting—the teacher takes the initiative to reschedule the meeting with a third party. Often this person is a colleague who knows the family, a supervisor, or an administrator. A mediator makes it easier for all parties to understand that the disagreement is not a "personal grudge" or a personality conflict. When emotions are high, the mediator can help teacher and parent focus on the facts and on a strategy for positive resolution (Koch & McDonough, 1999). Teachers sometimes feel that they are "failures" if they have to call on a third party. For the benefit of the child and relations with the family, this decision is among the most professional a teacher can make.

7. **Collaborate for Safety.** When dealing with serious family situations, the teacher needs to collaborate with colleagues for another reason: her own safety. In some circumstances, such as suspected child abuse, the teacher by law must report to authorities. She does this according to the policies of the school or program. On rare occasions a teacher may feel vulnerable because of actions she has taken. The teacher immediately involves other staff.

The teacher is not a social worker, but is a member of a team of professionals helping the child and family. Serious decisions regarding the safety of the child must be made by a team led by a person trained in this area. From this point on, communication with the family usually comes *not* from the teacher, but from the team leader (Manning & Schindler, 1997).

But what if an inebriated adult arrives to pick up a child? Sometimes, in an effort to save a child from imminent harm, a teacher must risk the possible wrath of a family member. From the beginning of the school year, the teacher works with the family to prevent creative conflicts from becoming negative dissonances. In the event of a threatening situation, however, the teacher takes necessary action to preserve the child's safety, immediately informs a supervisor, and works with a team as much as possible.

When a teacher begins in a new school or program, she determines the policy for handling serious situations. The teacher should discuss the policy with families as part of an orientation or "greeting meeting." The teacher then follows the policy, getting the assistance of other staff and administrators whenever necessary. When in doubt about a situation involving family members, working together with other staff is key. Good relationships with other staff are vital for when teachers and parents disagree.

Summary

1. What considerations are important for when boys have conflicts?

Traditional classroom culture works against the behavior patterns and learning styles of many boys. With the emphasis on accountability, even early childhood classrooms are becoming more traditional. An education gender gap that disfavors boys is becoming evident—from preschool age into adulthood. Male teachers may have some "gender advantages" in working with young boys, but male and female teachers alike can make their classrooms more boy-friendly. Two boy-friendly dynamics are programs that are developmentally appropriate for *all* children and guidance intervention techniques that preserve dignity, acknowledge emotions, affirm individual worth, and teach rather than punish.

2. What conditions make intervention necessary?

Three conditions make intervention necessary:

- Children cannot resolve a situation themselves and the situation is deteriorating.
- One or more children cause serious disruption to the education process.
- The danger of harm exists.

In these situations the teacher uses *combination intervention*, a nonpunitive *mix* of crisis management and conflict management techniques that reaffirm guidelines, mediate the conflict, and accomplish reconciliation. A measure of the teacher's authenticity is her willingness to intervene in the event of imminent harm or serious disruption.

3. What are four methods of crisis management?

Being direct is the crisis management method of first resort. The teacher describes the conflict that she sees, chooses whether to express her feelings about it, and directs the children to needed action. The teacher keeps the "express" step optional, and uses the sequence to restore enough balance to resolve the conflict.

Commanding a choice is the crisis intervention method of second resort. Related to the "direct" step above, the teacher puts responsibility on the child to decide between an in-choice and an out-choice—often to discuss the conflict then or after the child has calmed himself. The teacher works with whichever choice the child makes.

Calming techniques comprise the intervention method of third resort. The teacher uses reflective listening to acknowledge the child's feelings and tell the child he is understood. The teacher helps the child to become calm by methods such as taking deep breaths, counting slowly to 10, having a cooling-down time—different from a time-out—or doing self-removal. The purpose of these techniques is to assist the child regain composure so a conflict can be resolved.

Physical restraint is the method of last resort when a child has lost total control. The passive bear hug communicates to the child that the teacher will reestablish limits. Physical restraint is exhausting but important for preventing harm to the child himself or to others. The adult follows guidelines regarding the level of force used in the restraint, files a report, and reviews the event with fellow staff. The event is communicated to families.

4. What are comprehensive guidance strategies for working with Level Three strong needs mistaken behavior?

When working with children who show serious mistaken behavior, the teacher uses comprehensive guidance that often includes an individual guidance plan (IGP). Depending on the frequency and intensity of the child's mistaken behaviors, comprehensive guidance follows some or all of the following steps. The teacher:

- ⟩ Develops relationships with the family
- ⟩ Uses consistent guidance intervention techniques
- ⟩ Obtains additional information about the child
- ⟩ Implements the information gained to assist the child
- ⟩ Improves the teacher-child relationship
- ⟩ Holds an IGP meeting
- ⟩ Implements the guidance plan
- ⟩ Monitors the guidance plan.

The more serious the behavior, the more comprehensive the response, and usually the more persons that need to be involved. Parents are central parties in the use of the IGP.

5. What techniques assist the teacher to manage personal feelings of anger?

An effective anger management strategy begins before a crisis occurs, as the teacher *self-monitors feelings* and *makes adjustments* to the program. Teachers do well to prepare contingency plans for when they are emotionally or physically "down" and are at risk for loss of control.

The teacher practices *safeguards* in the expression of anger. The teacher uses I-messages that express feelings without humiliating others. She uses the describe-express-direct technique to address the problem without disparaging personality.

The teacher *practices reconciliation*. Teachers like all of us make mistakes and will overreact. The first step in reconciliation is that the teacher needs to forgive herself. Reconciliation initiated by the teacher models an important guideline of the encouraging classroom: We all make mistakes; we just need to learn from them.

6. What are considerations when teachers and parents disagree?

At one time or another, teachers and parents will have conflicts. The teacher works to avoid having conflicts become divisive. *Negative dissonances* occur when the teacher asserts the authority of the institution over the parent. Such division happens most often when parents are of differing social or cultural circumstances than the teacher. Instead, the teacher works to have expressed differences become *creative conflicts* that the parties can work out. Seven strategies assist the teacher to sustain positive relations with the parent when disagreements occur. The more serious the conflict, the more the teacher works as a team with colleagues, supervisors, and administrators to cooperatively resolve it.

FOLLOW-UP ACTIVITIES

Note: *An element of being a professional teacher is to respect the children, parents, and educators you are working with by maintaining confidentiality, that is, keeping identities private. In completing follow-up activities, please respect the privacy of all concerned.*

Discussion Activity

The discussion activity encourages students to interrelate their own thoughts and experiences with specific ideas from the chapter.

Identify a situation involving serious mistaken behavior shown by a child in a classroom you are familiar with. Referring to the chapter, what parts of comprehensive guidance did the teacher use in addressing the problem? What parts did the teacher not use? What would you do that is similar to what the teacher did to resolve the problem? What would you do that is different?

Application Activities

Application activities allow students to interrelate material from the text with real-life situations. The observations imply access to practicum experiences; the interviews, access to teachers or parents. To interrelate theory and experience, students compare or contrast observations and interviews with referenced ideas from the chapter.

1. Considerations for when boys have conflicts.

   a. Observe a teacher who intervenes when one or more boys is experiencing a conflict. Which of the guidance intervention guidelines for boys listed in the chapter did the teacher use? Which of the guidelines did the teacher not use? In guidance terms (teaching, not punishing), assess the outcome of the intervention. Compare your findings to ideas from the chapter.

b. Interview a teacher you think has gone beyond the *boy behavior* stereotypes and works well with boys in the classroom. Ask about steps the teacher takes to ensure that the curriculum is developmentally appropriate for all children in the class, including active boys. Ask about steps the teacher takes when intervening with boys to ensure that the outcome "teaches rather than punishes." Compare the teacher's responses to ideas from the chapter.

2. When intervention is necessary.

a. Observe an instance when a teacher used guidance to intervene in a serious conflict. How do the apparent reasons for the intervention correspond to the reasons for intervening presented in the chapter? What combination of crisis management and conflict management techniques did the teacher use? In guidance terms (teaching, not punishing) assess the outcome of the intervention. Compare your findings to ideas from the chapter.

b. Interview a teacher who uses guidance about the reasons she has for when to intervene. Ask about steps the teacher takes to calm everyone down and to resolve the conflict. How does the teacher ensure that guidance and not punishment is being used in the intervention? Compare your findings to ideas from the chapter.

3. Four methods of crisis management.

a. Observe an incident when a teacher intervened in a crisis. What methods did the teacher use to calm the child or children down? Were the methods the teacher used any of the four mentioned in the chapter? Why or why not? In what ways did the intervention help to resolve the crisis?

b. Interview a teacher about how she uses calming techniques during conflicts. Ask about two or three of the crisis management methods discussed in the chapter. What is the teacher's "take" on the methods? Compare your findings to ideas about crisis management stated in the chapter.

4. Comprehensive guidance with Level Three mistaken behavior.

a. Observe over at least a week's worth of classes how a teacher uses comprehensive guidance with a child. (The use of comprehensive guidance may be informal.) Take notes for each class period. Discuss which of the eight steps the teacher did or did not seem to use. Talk with the teacher if possible about the progress the child is making. Compare your findings to ideas from the chapter about comprehensive guidance.

b. Interview a teacher about how she worked with a child, colleagues, and the child's family to help the child overcome Level Three (serious) mistaken behavior. Referring to the chapter, which steps of comprehensive guidance were formally or informally followed? How was the child's family involved?

How did the teacher assess the progress the child made? Compare your findings to ideas from the chapter about comprehensive guidance.

5. Techniques for managing anger.

   a. Talk with a teacher about the following:

   ▶ Adjustments they make on days when they are encountering physical or emotional difficulties.

   ▶ How they manage angry feelings toward a child or a situation.

   ▶ How they work for reconciliation after they have intervened in a crisis situation when feelings are high.

   b. Compare your findings to the three ideas about how teachers manage anger from the chapter.

6. When teachers and parents disagree.

   a. Interview a *teacher* about a time that she and a parent disagreed. Acknowledging the importance of protecting identities, discuss how the teacher tried to resolve the disagreement. Did the teacher feel the effort was successful? Why or why not? What does the teacher generally think is important to successfully resolve a conflict with a parent? Compare your findings to the guidelines from the chapter.

   b. Interview a *parent* you are comfortable with and who will give you open feedback. Acknowledging the importance of protecting identities, talk about a time when the parent disagreed with a teacher. Discuss whether the parent felt the disagreement got resolved successfully. Why or why not? What does the parent think a teacher should do to resolve a difference with a parent successfully? Compare your findings to the guidelines from the chapter.

Recommended Readings

Fox, L. (Ed.). (2003). Responding to behaviors that challenge children and adults. *Young Children, 58*(4), 57.

Gartrell, D. (2007). Guidance matters: He did it on purpose! *Young Children, 62*(6), 62–64.

King, M. (2004) Guidance with boys in early childhood classrooms. In D. Gartrell, *Power of guidance: Teaching social emotional skills in early childhood classrooms*. Clifton Parks, NY: Thomson/Delmar Learning.

Kohn, D. (2003). The gender gap: Boys lagging. Available at http://www.cbasnews.com/stories/2002/10/31/60minutes/main527678.shtml

Preuesse, K. (2002, March/April). Guidance and discipline strategies for young children: Time out is out. *Early Childhood News*, pp. 12–16.

Readdick, C. & Chapman, P. (2000). Young children's perceptions of time out. *Journal of Research in Childhood Education*. October 1, 2000. HighBeam Research (July 14, 2009). http://www.highbeam.com/doc/1P3-63976636.html

Scelfo, J. (2007, September 17). Come back, Mr. Chips. *Newsweek*, p. 44.

Schreiber, M. E. (1999). Time-outs for toddlers: Is our purpose punishment or education? *Young Children, 54*(4), 22–25.

Guidance Matters

Comprehensive Guidance
January, 2008

I met Joe and his mother, Becky, at a Getting to Know You conference before school started. Joe seemed to be a curious, typical two-and-a-half-year-old. His mother was young and a full-time college student. I could tell immediately that Becky truly loved her son, and she appeared to be a good caregiver.

Two weeks into the program, Joe began to have trouble getting along with other children. His anxiety level, beginning at drop-off time, seemed to be high. When his personal space was "invaded," often during group activities, Joe responded by pulling children's hair, kicking, or yelling "Shut up!" When teachers intervened, Joe cried and kicked them. After a few weeks of attempting to guide Joe to use kind words and gentle touches, the director, other staff members, and I decided we needed to pursue a more comprehensive approach.

I began holding short weekly conferences with Becky to get to know her better and to offer her encouragement in her parenting. One day, shortly after our meeting, I happened to look out the window and notice Becky sitting on the steps, crying. I took my break early and went out to talk with her. Becky shared her frustration over Joe's behavior: "Why does he act this way? I am tired and don't understand. He is so naughty!"

I responded, "Joe is a very sweet and special boy, and his behavior is the way he responds to stress. He feels threatened by many things right now, and he reacts in the only way he knows. It is mistaken behavior, and it is our job to guide him. It isn't an easy job." I reached over and gave her a hug.

My friendship with Becky continued to grow and so did her trust in me. Together with other staff members and the director, we developed an Individual Guidance Plan for Joe. At one conference, Becky suggested that we implement a reward system. We tried a sticker chart that recorded and rewarded hourly progress.

Becky and I decided that Joe and I would call her any time three serious conflicts occurred in a day. When we called, I first explained the situation to Becky and then had Joe talk with her. Becky was firm but loving. Joe loved talking with his mother, and we would generally see a more relaxed Joe after these phone calls. (I kept tabs to make sure the calls didn't become a "habit.")

Joe's conflicts with other children continued, and he needed someone nearby at all times to direct him to more appropriate behavior. I would calm Joe by holding and rocking him. Sometimes I sang. After Joe was calm, I used guidance talks, and he talked to me about what happened. These interactions encouraged bonding and a feeling of trust between us.

I also used humor. I gave Joe options of words to use when he was upset. Yelling "Pickle!" became a favorite. I also gave Joe a cushy ball to hold during stressful situations such as circle time, and made sure that a student teacher or I sat next to him. We rubbed Joe's back or arm or held him on our laps. The ball kept his hands busy, and the touch calmed him.

Drop-off time was difficult for Joe and set the mood for the day. With the director's assistance, I arranged to meet him in the office or lounge to spend one-on-one time with him, playing a game or reading. The other staff noticed the difference in Joe—and the entire group—on the days I helped ease him into the class.

Eventually Becky agreed with the staff that an outside mental health assessment was needed for Joe's behavior. Dealing with people outside our center made Becky uncomfortable; to ease her stress, I stayed involved during the assessment process. I worked with the director and others to find resources for Becky; these included a family play therapy program and the school district's Early Childhood Family Education classes for young parents. To keep up communication, the teaching staff who worked the later shift talked daily with Becky, and I left happygrams. Throughout this whole time, the director was a great support to me—and to Becky too.

One day, four months into working with Joe, he was building with Legos when a classmate sat down next to him and took a Lego off Joe's tower. Joe's previous response would have been to pull the child's hair. This time, however, he shouted, "NO, thank you!" We were so proud of Joe for using his words.

Our guidance plan was finally showing success. Joe learned to say what he needed and what he didn't like. Baby steps were all we needed. Joe grew and so did we.

Reprinted with permission from the National Association for the Education of Young Children. All rights reserved.

The experienced professional in this case study (Robin) teaches young preschoolers at a university lab center located, like some university child care centers, in converted dormitory space. Her success with Joe and Becky was due to her belief in them and hard work to provide the leadership that supports comprehensive guidance.

From this column and many other sources, teachers can learn ways to address children's conflicts that build social–emotional skills—through teaching rather than punishment. Teachers use comprehensive guidance when the individual techniques that usually resolve problems don't work by themselves and a child's conflicts continue.

Comprehensive guidance begins with a plan for use with a particular child and family, sometimes (but not always) called an Individual Guidance Plan (Gartrell, 2007). The plan includes a mix of strategies that build relationships (teacher-child and teacher-family), reduce the need for conflicts, guide children to resolve their conflicts, and teach children to get along in groups. (See the To Increase Your Knowledge section.) Comprehensive guidance relies on the teacher working with other staff and the family as closely as possible, so that the child receives a unified message from the important adults in his life. As suggested in the case study, the program administrator must give support for comprehensive guidance to happen.

Relationship with the Family

Teachers often find relationships with families the most challenging part of comprehensive guidance. Robin began building a relationship with Becky even before Joe started his first day. Knowing a custodial adult *before* conflicts (or accidents) happen is important. Notice also that Robin didn't meet with Becky just to deal with Joe's problems. Sometimes teachers see families only as a "cause" of the child's conflicts and a likely obstacle to improving the situation (Manning & Schindler, 1997). The relationship with a child's family members should have a life of its own. The teacher takes an interest in the family because they are members of the classroom community.

Individual Guidance Plans

Individual guidance plans (IGPs) often are the outcome of a formal meeting of all staff who work with the child, family members, and even (with the family's permission) outside professionals. The plans can be written out on forms and periodically reviewed and revised or can be arrived at more informally, through a series of phone calls and on-the-run discussions. In either case, family and teachers must be on the same page. (See the A Step You Can Take section for information on using an IGP.)

Robin got Becky actively involved in writing and using the plan and even facilitated an outside assessment for Joe. The teacher kept the cooperation going, taking suggestions and giving them in a friendly way. Robin also worked out a series of techniques that she consistently used with Joe—and encouraged other staff to use. The approach:

▪ recognized Joe's need not just for attention but for a positive attachment with a teacher who cared about him.

▪ engaged Robin in contact talks (quality time) with Joe outside of conflict situations to build Joe's sense of worth and belonging. Key here were Robin's "good morning" contacts when Joe first arrived.

▶ used crisis management techniques, especially touch, that calmed Joe and helped maintain his relationship with the teachers (Carlson, 2006).

▶ taught Joe coping skills to handle strong feelings through guidance talks.

▶ was "unrelentingly positive" (to borrow a term I once heard Marian Marion use), giving ongoing acknowledgment of Joe's and Becky's efforts, progress, and worth as individuals.

Comprehensive guidance takes teamwork among staff, family members, and sometimes outside professionals. Comprehensive guidance means trying, evaluating, and modifying a mix of guidance techniques that convey to the child this message: "You are special because you are you and are in this class. You can learn to get along with others and have a good time." All staff, beginning with the director, need to work together in this complex effort. Administrative support is essential.

Only after comprehensive guidance has been used to the fullest ability of staff without success should anyone raise the possibility of removing a child from the program. In such a case, the staff should work hard to help the family find a good alternative placement that will address the child's needs.

Comprehensive guidance can and often does succeed. Joe remained in Robin's classroom for the whole program year. He and his mom moved to another community the following summer. Were their lives touched for the better? What do you think?

Column References

Carlson, F. M. (2006). Essential touch: Meeting the needs of young children. Washington, DC: NAEYC.

Gartrell, D. J. (2007). *A guidance approach for the encouraging classroom* (4th ed.). Clifton Park, NY: Delmar Cengage Learning.

Manning, D., & Schindler, P. (1997). Communicating with parents when their children have difficulties. *Young Children, 52*(5), 27–33.

To Increase Your Knowledge

Teachers are rarely taught how to discuss troubling information about their children with parents. This book and article offer some useful ideas:

Gartrell, D. (2004). *The Power of Guidance*. Clifton Park, NY: Delmar Cengage Learning. Chapter Ten of this book discusses comprehensive guidance and includes a case study illustrating the use of an IGP.

Kaufman, H. (2001). Skills for working with all families. *Young Children, 56*(4), 81–83. Kaufman offers strategies for building working relations with families with low incomes and those that speak a home language other than English, a key element in the guidance approach.

A Step You Can Take

Develop and use an individual guidance plan with a child who is having continued conflicts over time. Go to http://danielgartrell1.cfoliomn2.com. Here you can access information on comprehensive guidance and individual guidance plans, including Seven Steps of Comprehensive Guidance and Notes for Conducting IGP Meetings. You can also get an Individual Guidance Plan Worksheet by clicking on Download Versions.

For additional information on using the guidance approach in the encouraging classroom, visit our website at www.cengage.com/education/gartrell.

Chapter 12

Liberation Teaching: A Guidance Response to Violence in Society

Guiding Questions

▶ *How are children in the classroom affected by violence in society?*

▶ *How is liberation teaching a response to societal violence?*

▶ *What is the liberation teaching response to bullying?*

▶ *What is the connection between liberation teaching and other socially responsive education practices?*

▶ *How does liberation teaching apply to relations with parents?*

© Cengage Learning

Key Concepts

▶ *Antibias education*

▶ *Bullying as violence*

▶ *Continuum of violence in children's lives*

▶ *Liberation teaching*

▶ *Multicultural education*

▶ *Peace education*

▶ *Protective buffer*

▶ *Resiliency*

▶ *Resiliency mentoring*

▶ *Socially responsive education*

▶ *Societal violence*

▶ *Stigma*

▶ *Suppressed conscience*

▶ *Tossed salad approach*

▶ *Tourist curriculum*

Chapter Twelve examines at violence in society, its effects on children in the classroom, and the guidance response to violence: liberation teaching. Just as *antibias education* means proactive teaching in the cultural dimension, liberation teaching is proactive education in the social–emotional dimensions. Liberation teaching, which in brief means *not giving up on any child*, is the pivotal concept of the chapter. In a featured section, liberation teaching is discussed as a response to the "hot discipline topic" of bullying. The concept's relationships to other socially responsive education practices—the encouraging classroom, everyday guidance, antibias education, and peace education—are also explored. Liberation teaching, as a guideline for relations with parents, concludes the chapter.

Societal Violence and the Classroom

Compared with the Western European democracies, Canada, and Japan, ours is an exceedingly violent society. According to the Children's Defense Fund (CDF) report for 2008:

Every second a public school student is suspended.

Every 20 seconds a public school student is corporally punished.

Every 35 seconds a child is confirmed as abused or neglected.

Every 7 minutes a child or teen is arrested for a violent crime.

Every 3 hours a child or teen is killed by a firearm.

Every 5 hours a child or teen commits suicide.

Every 6 hours a child or teen is killed by abuse or neglect.

To put these figures in perspective, the U.S. homicide rate for infants to 24-year-olds is higher than the homicide rate of 11 industrial nations combined. The chances of an African American child born in 2001 ending up in prison are one in three; for Hispanic children one in six (CDF, 2008). According to a report titled "A Violent Education: Corporal Punishment of Children in U.S. Public Schools," during the 2006–2007 school year 223,190 students received corporal punishment in American schools (one-quarter of the students from one state, Texas) (Stoddard, 2008). In 2009 the National Institutes of Health received figures that suggested with the "foundering of the economy," the child abuse/neglect rate may be spiking still further (Szep, 2009).

It is hard to overestimate the impact of **societal violence** on the child. The Surgeon General's Report of 1999 states that violence results in debasement of the child's self-concept and impairment of healthy brain development. This graphic statement gains perspective when we define *societal violence* to include acts of neglect and aggression that result in physical and psychological injury with attendant feelings of stress, anxiety, fear, anger, confusion, and abandonment. Implied in the term is the assertion of will by a more powerful individual against a less powerful individual, without regard for physical and psychological well-being.

Ironically, through being victimized by violence, children may experience suppressed conscience, which means having the capacity to empathize with others physically and psychologically "beaten" out of them (Surgeon General's Report, 1999). An individual whose brain development results in *suppressed conscience* is at risk of morphing from a victim to an aggressor, even in early childhood (Levin, 1994). This possibility is heightened by the perceptions the child gains from the modeling of adults that violence is a "normal" part of human relationships. Teachers need to be aware of the significant emotional and cognitive impact on the child of victimization by violence.

The Violence Pyramid

Either through direct or indirect exposure, few children escape societal violence. Most children experience violence vicariously through television, media-based games, and playing with action figures and toy weapons. In 2003, Levin reported that on average, American children view between four and six hours of television, videos, and media games each day. In 2005–2006, Neilsen Media Research reported that television watching by 2- to 11-year-olds was increasing by about 4% annually (Holmes, 2006). Generally accepted figures are that by the age of 18, children on averaged will have watched/experienced the equivalent of five years of video media. By age 12, children will have viewed literally countless acts of violence and perhaps 8,000 television murders (Levin, 2003).

Although parents often believe they are screening what their children watch, a large portion of shows, videotapes, and video games that young children are exposed to are actually designed for older viewers. (Young children often have little choice but to experience the media that older family members select.) Books and toys based on action figures as well as play weapons flood the market for children to read and play with. As they get older, children become aware as well of popular youth culture and the violence that is a part of it (Levin, 2003). Most children in the society experience violence at least indirectly by exposure to these sources.

Through her construct, the continuum of violence in children's lives (Figure 12–1), Levin (2003) points out that smaller numbers of children have more direct and intense exposure to violence. For instance, children from low-income situations may view more television than their middle-income counterparts *and* experience more direct violence in the neighborhood (Levin, 2003). Further, some children at all income levels are exposed to direct violence in their homes. Levin (1994) comments:

> *The more frequent, varied, and extreme the violence children experience, the more likely their ideas and behavior will be affected by that violence, and the more help they will need from adults in working through the harmful effects of that violence in learning how to be nonviolent themselves. (p. 15)*

With a still developing ability to understand, young children face conflicting, even bewildering messages about violence. On television they view both *Sesame Street* and *Transformers*. At home they receive contradictory messages from

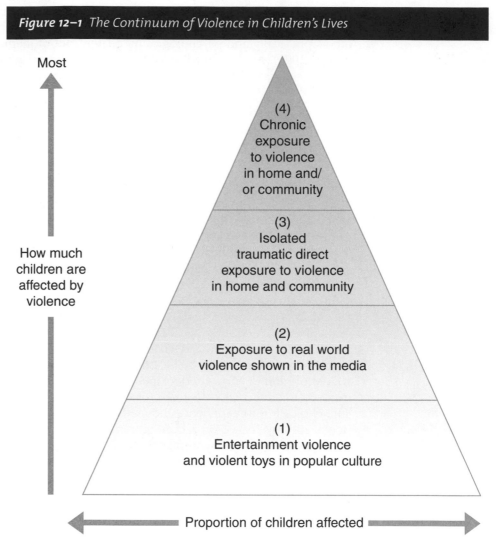

Figure 12–1 *The Continuum of Violence in Children's Lives*

Most

How much children are affected by violence

(4)
Chronic exposure to violence in home and/ or community

(3)
Isolated traumatic direct exposure to violence in home and community

(2)
Exposure to real world violence shown in the media

(1)
Entertainment violence and violent toys in popular culture

Proportion of children affected

Reprinted with permission from Teaching Young Children in Violent Times, by Diane E. Levin © 2003. Published by Educators for Social Responsibility. For more information call 1-800-370-2515.

adults: "Don't hit," "play nice," "stand up for yourself," "fight back" (Levin, 2003). More so in the United States than in many countries, children are spanked if they hurt others. Though linked with aggression and sexual problems as children grow, many parents continue to regard spanking as "a right," and corporal punishment in schools is still allowed in 22 states (Kalb, 2008).

Violence in society is a significant cause of classroom mistaken behavior (Levin, 2003). Its impact on the child depends on the intensity of the violence and on the ability of the individual child to cope. The next section discusses the effects of violence in the classroom.

Assessing the Effects of Violence, by the Levels

Using the three levels of mistaken behavior as guideposts, the following classroom behaviors are typical of children who have been affected by vicarious and/or direct violent experiences. Applying Levin's (2003) pyramid concept, note that mistaken behaviors at Level One are more common in children who have experienced indirect "background violence." Level Two mistaken behaviors are learned behaviors as a result of either indirect violence (watching and then playing "the Incredible Hulk") or "mild" forms of direct violence. Level Three mistaken behaviors are typical of children intensely victimized by violence in the home or community.

Level One: Experimentation Mistaken Behavior. The following mistaken behaviors are typically influenced by indirect societal violence, such as via the media or teasing by family members or peers. The behaviors are level One if a child shows them once in a while, but not on a repeated "emotionally driven" basis. The child:

- makes play-guns and weapons out of "nonviolent" materials such as blocks, Lincoln logs, and Legos
- initiates aggressive play such as wrestling, chase, and "guns"
- "plays rough" with puppets, dolls, and miniature figures
- draws a picture with violent themes
- is surprisingly competitive in play situations.

These behaviors become mistaken, of course, when they cause conflicts between children or with the teacher (Boyatzis, 1997).

Consideration (Reiterated): Most young boys and many young girls have a need to be active through much of their day. Unless classrooms allow for the activity levels of young children, children (often boys) find ways to engage in boisterous, sometimes rough-and-tumble play. Some teachers view such behavior as "rowdy" and overly interpret the effects of violence in this type of play. For programs to be developmentally appropriate, they must be appropriate also for active young children. If teachers keep them active, young children will have less need to engage in boredom-caused aggressive play.

Level Two: Socially Influenced Mistaken Behavior. Indirect societal violence sometimes shows in children who are *influenced by others* to engage in aggressive play. *Superhero play*, in which children identify with action heroes and play roughly illustrates the impact of exposure to media violence. Another example of socially influenced mistaken behavior occurs when an "in" group stigmatizes other children by excluding them from play, calling names, or bullying. Children who oppress others often have learned this behavior from being oppressed themselves. Likewise, children who show purposefully aggressive behaviors toward others, "instrumental aggression" to achieve a goal, may well be imitating behaviors they have learned through being victimized themselves.

Consideration: When oppression occurs, direct violence is happening in the classroom, and the teacher must show clear leadership—often by class meetings, ethics instruction ("you can't say you can't play"), and conflict management (Gootman, 1993). Teachers also need to proactively support children who are particularly vulnerable for stigma, often because of appearances, abilities, or behaviors that differ from others in the class. When there are conflicts, of course, mediation is an important tool for teaching the equality of all class members.

Level Three: Strong Needs Mistaken Behavior. When the emotional motivation for a behavior is intense and continues over time, the child has strong unmet needs and shows the mistaken behavior at Level Three. Signals include violent pictures drawn repeatedly, rough-and-tumble play that *often* becomes aggressive, and bullying that is continuing and severe. Other common indicators are children who repeatedly lose emotional balance, try to harm others, influence others to serious acts or, at the other extreme, psychologically withdraw or show marked anxiety (Gootman, 1993). A major cause of Level Three mistaken behavior is direct violence experienced by a child. Helping professionals now recognize that Level Three mistaken behavior is nothing more or less than *post-traumatic stress disorder (PTSD)* affecting the mind and body of the child.

Consideration: Our goal with children who are the victims of violence is to help them build resiliency. A first step in this process is to create a positive relationship with the child in order to help her find trust in the classroom environment (Alat, 2002). Interventions must be firm but friendly to retain the child's sense of trust. A child who has experienced violence may have lost most ability to define and meet limits. When we enforce limits nonpunitively, the child eventually will appreciate the safety that our limits provide.

Children who show Level Three behaviors require comprehensive guidance strategies (discussed in Chapter Eleven) that involve teachers, family members, and often other professionals (Gootman, 1993). *Liberation teaching* occurs in the active support, encouragement, and guidance of all children showing vulnerabilities in the classroom, but especially children showing Level Three mistaken behavior.

Impact of Direct Violence on the Child

Teachers *misunderstand* Level Three mistaken behavior when they regard it as the child's intentionally "being bad" instead of the child's reaction to having deep unmet needs—for safety, security, and a sense of belonging. At the top of Levin's (2003) continuum of violence, the child is a victim of direct acts of violence—physical and emotional. (Such victimization happens as well by witnessing violence done to others.) In an important article, Lowenthal (1999) develops the case that most children's serious mistaken behavior is in fact **post-traumatic stress disorder (PTSD).**

Just as authorities sometimes have misdiagnosed PTSS in members of the military as willful antisocial behavior, so that same misunderstanding happens with children in classrooms. Lowenthal provides a graphic account of the effects of violence on the behavior of young children adapted here. Note that the overlap of PPST and Level Three Mistaken Behaviors is "total and complete":

▶ **Difficulty in managing emotions.** Past experiences may overwhelm the child's ability to handle emotions, especially those associated with traumatic events. For these children, gaining a measure of self-regulation—learning to manage strong feelings—is an important first step in learning democratic life skills. At times, one-on-one assistance becomes necessary. Such techniques as "worry teachers" and "comfort corners" ("Australia" in one corner of the classroom) attempt to address these situations.

▶ **Avoidance of intimacy.** Loss of trust causes children to view intimate relationships as increasing their vulnerability and lack of control. "To avoid intimacy, children may withdraw, avoid eye contact, be hyperactive, or exhibit inappropriate behaviors" (Lowenthal, 1999, p. 205). A motivation for mistaken behaviors, then, may be to avoid forming close relationships, which in the past the child has found unreliable and profoundly painful.

▶ **Provocative behaviors.** Violent reactions may be the main form of adult attention the child has known. For these kids, provoking negative reactions becomes a learned behavior. It is how they have come to relate to adults. In terms of brain function, a defensive reaction to violence is hormone activity in the brain that numbs the individual to the extreme emotions these experiences arouse. Over time this defensive reaction by the brain wears off, and the emotional pain returns.

Lowenthal suggests that without therapy, children feel a human need to again numb themselves. By acting "provocatively and aggressively," children seek to produce the extreme reactions that cause renewal of the "self-anesthetizing" process. (Later drug or alcohol dependencies may serve the same purpose.) For early childhood teachers who use guidance, these understandings bring new meaning to the need to "keep your cool."

▶ **Disturbances in the attachment process.** The attachment process is the long-term bond that forms between a child and primary caregivers. Abuse and neglect make attachment difficult, due to children's feelings of mistrust, unworthiness, anger, and anxiety. These feelings may cause children to become hostile toward adults who genuinely wish to build positive attachments. Building attachments under such circumstances becomes a challenging but essential task.

▶ **Effects on cognition and learning.** Over time violent experiences cause children's emotion-based brain reactions to overwhelm cognitive processes. Cognitive functions involved in learning become more difficult (LeDoux, 1996).

At the same time, self-perceptions tell the child that she is incapable of learning and unworthy of teacher assistance, lowering motivation levels. "On average, abused, maltreated, or neglected children score lower on cognitive measures and demonstrate poorer school achievement compared to their non-abused peers of similar socioeconomic backgrounds" (Lowenthal, 1999, p. 206).

This list of reactions to violence is daunting indeed. Alat (2002) agrees with Jackson (1997) that teachers must step forward and provide active support for children who have experienced violence. Teachers who are "enlightened witnesses" affirm the goodness within each child and that the child is not to blame for the violence experienced (Gootman, 1993). Such teachers work to build positive attachments and make the classroom a trustworthy place where learning can happen (Alat, 2002). By encouraging **resiliency**—personal strength that promotes self-healing—they practice liberation teaching.

Socially Responsive Education. Writers who believe that our education system must respond proactively to violence generally agree on these findings:

1. Popular culture glorifies violence in ways that make civil problem solving difficult to teach and learn.

2. Family education and support systems are as yet inadequate to reduce family violence and the abuse of children in society. Educators need to emulate family outreach systems practiced by such programs as Head Start.

3. Some children, touched deeply by violence, are affected for years, perhaps their whole lives—unless they experience comprehensive intervention while they are young.

4. If we as a society are to increase our capacity to resolve conflicts peacefully, we need to educate children toward this end, beginning while they are young, in the home and in school (Girard & Koch, 1996; Levin, 2003; Slaby et al., 1995; Surgeon General's Report, 1999; Swick, 2005).

For society to become more peaceful, a paradigm shift is necessary in how we look at education (Levin, 2003). **Socially responsive education**—stressing resiliency, interpersonal and intrapersonal intelligence, social–emotional competence, democratic life skills—whatever terms one is comfortable with—is at least as important as scores on standardized tests. Yet, this change will occur only as educators and families agree to it, and much public education about the effects of violence on children has yet to happen.

Liberation Teaching: The Guidance Response

In the "olden days" of teacher preparation, an instructor sometimes told education majors: "You can divide any class into three groups. The top third will learn even if they are not taught. The middle third will learn if they are well taught.

The bottom third will not learn however they are taught." Today, most educators reject this callous view.

Liberation teaching means that the teacher does not give up on any child. In Ginott's (1972) terms, the teacher who practices liberation teaching sees children beyond the frailties they may show. The methodology of liberating teachers is developmentally appropriate, culturally responsive, and guidance oriented. The teacher realizes that each child is an extension of the family system and works with the family to benefit the child. Much like what antibias teaching is to multicultural education, liberation teaching is the proactive application of guidance principles.

As introduced in Chapter Four, liberation teaching has its roots in the social psychology of the 1960s and 1970s. The term derives from such disparate sources as liberal Catholic theology and the writings of Faber and Mazlich (1974). Maslow (1962) provides a useful dynamic for the concept in his statement that all individuals have two sets of needs, one for safety and one for growth. To the extent that children feel that safety needs—security, belonging, self-esteem—are unmet, they are likely to become preoccupied with meeting these needs at the expense of more productive ("growth") behavior. In Maslow's terms liberation teaching would be assisting the child to meet safety needs and empowering the child toward growth.

The works of other psychologists also apply to the concept. In Piaget's terms liberation teaching would be teaching for autonomy (Kamii, 1984; Piaget, 1960). In Elkind's (1989) refinement of Erikson's work, liberation teaching empowers the child to move away from shame, doubt, and inferiority toward initiative, belonging, and industry. For Harlow (1975), cited in Chapter Three, liberation teaching would be assisting the child to rise from the social relations of the survival level toward encountering.

In the guidance theory of this text, children benefiting from liberation teaching show significant gains in the ability to understand, develop, and use democratic life skills. Liberation teaching means extending the encouraging classroom environment to every child. Specific to the issue of violence, liberation teaching assists children to find the inner resources for resiliency—to begin a healing process. The teacher's challenge in nurturing resilience lies in the harm done to these children by the effects of violence, which may make them fight the teacher's efforts (Lowenthal, 1999).

Stigma Versus Liberation

A form of psychological violence, **stigma** happens when group members or even teachers act in a way that excludes another from full group membership and participation (Goffman, 1963). In the classroom stigma occurs in two ways. *The first is if members of the class fixate on a child's vulnerability* and exclude the child. (There are many names for this event: oppression, rejection, exclusion, stigmatization, and bullying.) In this case the teacher may fail to notice the act of stigma, ignore it, or even contribute to it.

The second is when a teacher fixates on a vulnerability of a child and negatively separates the child from the group. The separation at times may be physical (such as time-outs), but at the source it is psychological, first in the mind of the teacher, and then, by social influence, in the minds of the class. The extreme act of teacher stigmatization is expulsion, covered by commonly heard excuses—"developmentally young for the program," "not emotionally ready," "in need of services that we can't provide."

Either way that stigma happens, psychological violence has found its way into the classroom. The child feels debasement of the self-concept and confusion in relation to social identity (Goffman, 1963). Unless helped by a teacher, the child may experience a life at school that is marked by frustration and failure (Hymel & Ford, 2003). It is from this dynamic that the victim of violence may become violent in later years (Nansel, Overpeck, Pilla, Ruan, Simons-Morton, & Scheidt, 2001).

Preschool Expulsion. Children most at risk for stigma are those who are regarded as challenging, who show frequent mistaken behavior. These are the children who need a positive relationship with the teacher the most, but often are the most difficult for the teacher to like and accept. There is an irony here. Young children at Level Three are already victims of difficult if not violent life circumstances. Through the mistaken behavior they show in the classroom, they are vulnerable for further victimization by the teacher and/or peers' act of stigma.

Perhaps the most obvious example of the "stigma effect" in the early childhood field is documented in the 2005 Gilliam study titled "Prekindergarteners Left Behind: Expulsion Rates in Preschool Programs." This national study found among other things that the expulsion rate of children in preschool is three times that at the K–12 level, about 6.7 cases in 1,000. Trends in the study are:

▶ Boys are 4.5 times more likely to be expelled than girls.

▶ African American children are twice as likely to be expelled as Latino and Caucasian children.

▶ Four-year-olds are 1.5 times more likely to be expelled than threes.

Head Start and public school preschool programs, with more resources for working with children, had lower expulsion rates than religious and for-profit programs. The strong implication from the study is that the main reason that children were expelled is that staff could not cope with the high conflict levels in these children. Further study is needed to determine the effects of the stigma placed on these children (and their families) as they enter public school. The study's call for increased mental health resources for early childhood educators should be heeded.

Vulnerability Factors for Stigma. While mistaken behavior is a primary cause of stigma, children come into the classroom vulnerable for other reasons. (These are noted here because a child who is stigmatized for any reason experiences violence in the classroom.)

1. **Personality qualities.** Children with unique temperaments, learning capacities, learning styles, verbal abilities, and attention needs can be a bother and difficult to accept.

2. **Disabilities.** Children having disabilities still pose challenges for those peers and teachers who find human differences uncomfortable. The kinds of disabilities some children face have grown in recent years. In addition to the "established disabilities" such as cerebral palsy, developmental delays, sensory impairments and the autism spectrum (on the rise), some children suffer from more recently identified disabilities such as attention-deficit/hyperactivity disorder and fetal alcohol syndrome, and less commonly recognized conditions such as allergies and frail health syndrome. If their condition is known, children who are HIV positive or have AIDS are most vulnerable for stigma.

3. **Physical factors.** Children who are of differing racial characteristics, of unusual facial appearance, short or tall, underweight or overweight, unkempt or unclean may cause some to feel a "discomfort of association." Gender differences constitute a source of stigma in some early childhood teachers who noticeably prefer working with either girls or boys.

4. **Social factors.** Children from family backgrounds different from the norm in terms of income, religion, family structure, child-rearing priorities, parent careers, or family lifestyles may make children vulnerable for stigma. Typically in early childhood, adults before children would distance themselves from a child of differing social background. Examples are a family whose religious preferences are markedly different from a teacher's; a family that has a reputation for its "elite" social status; a family of mixed-race parents, same-sex parents, a single parent, or a caregiver who is not a parent (foster parent, grandparent, or other family member).

5. **Cultural factors.** Children are vulnerable for stigma if they are from cultural and ethnic backgrounds that may be emotionally charged for teachers or classmates. Examples would be children of Central American families who work in a meatpacking factory; or of a Muslim or Jewish family from the middle east.

Teachers are apt to show stigmatizing behaviors especially if they feel marginal acceptance in their teaching role. When support is inadequate, teachers are likely to find reasons beyond their control for why children do not "perform." If the reason is "the child's fault" or "the family's fault," then the teacher is "not to blame." Administration- sensitivity to the difficulty of the job is an essential first step in assisting the teacher to overcome tendencies toward stigma. Support systems for teachers are important.

Liberating Teacher Responses. With the practice of liberation teaching, the teacher helps each child to feel accepted as a worthy individual and member of the group. Supported through the encouraging classroom, children come to accept perceived vulnerabilities as a part of but not dominating their identities. With

One way to encourage the acceptance of differing human qualities is through the use of puppets.

acceptance assured through positive teaching, children become more open to the human qualities of others (Alat, 2002; Honig & Wittmer, 1996), the essence of what an encouraging classroom is.

Like teachers' acts of rejection, liberating responses can be unintentional or intentional. Liberating responses:

▸ show clear acceptance of the child as a worthwhile individual and member of the group

▸ empower the child's abilities

▸ educate both the child and the class away from rejecting responses and toward accepting responses

▸ adapt the physical and social environment so that all are included

▸ facilitate cooperative and individual activities so that each child can experience success

▸ appreciate the child's family background

▸ sensitively incorporate elements of the child's family background and language into the program

▸ use forms of discipline that guide rather than punish and that teach democratic life skills

▸ help the class understand and cope with challenging behaviors from the child.

The teacher is effectively using liberation teaching when differing human qualities do not polarize the class, but instead become opportunities for personal affirmation and mutual enrichment. The classrooms of liberating teachers are encouraging, caring communities for every child.

Liberation Teaching and Resiliency

In an important article on **resiliency mentoring**, Weinreb (1997) makes a statement similar to Levin's about the effects of violence:

> *When children are faced with multiple issues such as family violence and substance abuse, compounded by the risks of living in poverty, they are more likely to be adversely affected; these issues intensify each other. (p. 14)*

In such children, factors of PTSD, suppressed conscience, and violence as modeled behavior combine to make the child susceptible to Level Three mistaken behavior and for stigma. In the face of this prospect, Weinreb (1997) reports consistent findings that some children "exposed to various forms of adversity grow up to enjoy productive, normal lives, even though some may suffer silent anguish and emotional wounds in some area of their lives" (p. 15). These children are considered *resilient*, possessing "the capacity to cope effectively with their vulnerabilities" including the effects of violence (Weinreb, 1997, p. 15). Weinreb uses the term resiliency mentoring to indicate teaching practices that empower the ability of the child to be resilient.

Three dynamics that promote resiliency seem to be personality factors in the child, the social environments in which the child finds herself, and characteristics of the child's family. Liberating teachers contribute to resiliency mentoring in relation to all three of these dynamics.

The Child. Major personality traits like temperament, basic brain neurology, intelligences potentials, learning style, and ego strength are within each individual's unique psychology and are not apt to change much with social influences. Teachers do have influence, however, on how these inborn traits *develop and how the developing individual expresses these traits*. By building a positive attachment with her, the child feels affirmed as a person of worth. From a relationship built on trust, the teacher engages in resiliency mentoring. By using the liberation teaching practices listed under the previous heading, the teacher assists the child to make the most of the personality traits that form who that developing person is. The success of these efforts can be seen in the child's self-esteem (Weinreb, 1997) and adaptability to new situations.

The Social Environment. Weinreb (1997) mentions that the ability to find meaning in activities helps children surmount adversity. In the encouraging classroom, the teacher empowers the child at risk for Level Three mistaken behaviors to experience success in classroom transactions. Through observation and intentional contact talks, the teacher picks up on the child's interests and provides materials and activities that she thinks might engage the child.

In the anecdote that follows, student teacher Ben helps Jon—who was showing the effects of family stress and frustration with an activity—calm down after a conflict. Notice how Ben works hard to use reflective listening, has a contact talk with Jon, and helps the boy back into a group activity. Ben told me later that Jon has an interest in art activities "where he can do his own thing" and in media game figures. Liberation teaching comes down to interactions like Ben's with Jon on this day:

Classroom Anecdote	*After an incident Jon was brought to his cubby by one of the teachers to cool off. After a minute I walked over to Jon and had a conversation.*

> *Me:* How are you feeling?
>
> *Jon:* I'm mad.
>
> *Me:* You're mad?
>
> *Jon:* Yeah, I'm mad at you and I hate you.
>
> *Me:* Oh, I am sorry I made you mad.
>
> *Jon:* (Pauses and starts thinking) And I hate this (pulls out a small piece of paper with blue crayon on it, rips and throws it on the floor) and I hate my name.
>
> *Me:* You hate your name?
>
> *Jon:* Yeah, I hate it and I want to make a different one.
>
> *Me:* You want to make a new name?
>
> *Jon:* Yeah, (he stops and thinks for about five seconds and I wait for him to add more) I hate this (points at the paper on the floor). I want to make a new name (stands up and walks over to the paper, picks it up, and rips it again).
>
> *Me:* You want to make a new name?
>
> *Jon:* Yeah,
>
> *Me:* What color do you want to make it?
>
> *Jon:* Blue.
>
> *Me:* You're going to make your name blue? Do you like blue?
>
> *Jon:* Yeah. (stops and thinks) NO! I hate blue.
>
> *Me:* You hate blue?
>
> *Jon:* Yeah, I hate blue.
>
> *Me:* (I thought about asking why he hates blue but decided to ask something else.) What color do you want to make it?
>
> *Jon:* Red.
>
> *Me:* Oh? Do you like red?
>
> *Jon:* Yeah, I like red.
>
> *Me:* Red like your shirt?
>
> *Jon:* Yeah, like my shirt. And like Mario. Mario is red and Luigi is green.
>
> *Me:* Mario is red.
>
> *Jon:* And I am going to make a new name.
>
> *Me:* So you will make your new name red?
>
> *Jon:* Yeah and it will have an "A."
>
> *Me:* An "A"?

(continued)

Classroom Anecdote	Jon:	Yeah, do you know what else starts with "A"?
	Me:	What?
	Jon:	(beckons me closer and whispers in my ear) Aburane.
	Me:	Aburane? You're right. That name does start with an "A."
	Jon:	Yeah. (He starts looking intently at the other children who were in circle dancing to the chicken dance.)
	Me:	Do you want to join in with the other children?
	Jon:	Yeah.
	Me:	Where is your spot?
	Jon:	It's the purple one. I can show you. (Brings me to his spot and joins in the circle activity.)

A Protective Buffer. In a review of research about teachers' interactions with children, Kontos and Wilcox-Herzog (1997) conclude that "children exhibit higher levels of stress when teachers are harsh, critical and detached" (p. 11). In contrast, when teachers develop positive attachments with children, through sensitivity to their needs and positive interaction with them, children's development, including social–emotional development, is enhanced. This finding dovetails with that of Weinreb (1997) and Alat (2002) that the single most important factor in the classroom is the early childhood teacher.

By the practice of liberation teaching, the teacher provides a protective buffer that prevents the vulnerable child from being stigmatized and teaches the democratic life skills that enable the child to overcome vulnerabilities. (To empower resiliency, the teacher must help the child to meet both the need for safety and for growth.) In the anecdote, Ben was able to help Jon meet both of these basic needs.

Weinreb (1997) points out that not all victimized children can show the resiliency teachers hope for. Moreover, the limitations of most classrooms sometimes prevent the full provision of a protective buffer. Still, the practice of liberation teaching, in collaboration with others, increases the possibilities for resiliency. "Few studies have explored the role of teachers as protective buffers; those that do exist concur that teachers of young children can have an enduring and profound effect on the children they teach" (Weinreb, 1997, p. 19).

The Guidance Response to Bullying

Bullying has become a much-studied topic in American education, and for good reason. Bullying is the most common form of violence that children experience. A major report from the National Institutes of Child Health and Human Development ("National Study"; Nansel et al., 2001) gives an often-quoted definition:

Bullying is a specific type of aggression in which (1) the behavior is intended to harm or disturb, (2) the behavior occurs repeatedly over time, and (3) there is an imbalance of power, with a more powerful person or group attacking a less powerful one. (p. 2094)

The definition indicates that bullying happens "over time." However, Nansel et al. and Froschl and Sprung (1999) indicate that even single occurrences of bullying can be harmful to a child. The National Study found that *youth who bully* have more behavior problems, regard school more negatively, and are at greater risk for legal problems as adults. And *children who are bullied* "generally show higher levels of insecurity, anxiety, depression, loneliness, unhappiness, physical and mental symptoms, and low self-esteem. Witnesses to bullying as well are affected." (See the Guidance Matters column, "Understand Bullying," at the end of the chapter.)

While the National Study focused on adolescents rather than young children, Froschl and Sprung (1999) discuss bullying in early childhood education. These authors emphasize the importance of comprehensive prevention and intervention with young children to prevent the onset of the long-term consequences of bullying. The Texas Workforce Commission (2008) makes two related points:

1. Bullying becomes more intense with heightened social awareness as children move from early to middle childhood. Teachers do well to begin preventive education about bullying while children are young.

2. Bullying occurs on a continuum from playful teasing to outright assault. Teachers respond differently to bullying depending on the intensity observed.

Significantly, bullying is a form of violence that happens in the education community itself. Three characteristics of bullying at school are: (a) children already stigmatized tend to be the targets of bullying; (b) bullying further stigmatizes the targeted child; and (c) as children who bully get older, they themselves become

© Cengage Learning

Bullying has detrimental effects on the child who bullies as well as the child who is bullied.

targets of bullying and are at risk both in their own further schooling and when they enter adulthood (Nansel et al., 2001).

Froschl and Sprung (1999) report that in one study 78% of K–3 children who initiated bullying were boys, though girls and boys equally were likely to be the targets. This finding was similar in the National Study, which provided the additional data that bullying by boys was more likely to deteriorate into physical aggression while the bullying of girls was more likely to include taunting, exclusion, and gossip (Nansel et al., 2001). The Texas Workforce Commission (2008) noted similar gender-related bullying patterns.

This discussion of **bullying as violence** has two parts. The first part examines the continuum of bullying from playful to hostile by providing an analysis in relation to the three levels of mistaken behavior. The second part discusses the importance of a comprehensive approach to prevention and intervention rooted in liberation teaching. Attention is given to how the teacher works with the class, child, staff, and family.

Bullying as Levels of Mistaken Behavior

Level One is experimentation level mistaken behavior. A child picks on another child, calls another child a name, or excludes another child from play in order to find out what will happen. From the statistics, children who initiate bullying are likely to be boys. Level One bullying may happen "out of the blue," and in fact may be a first occurrence for the child. Yet, this is not a time for the teacher to conclude, "It is just once and boys will be boys" (Texas Workforce Commission, 2008). According to Froschl and Sprung (1999), a common adult response to bullying is to ignore it. Adults condone bullying when they fail to recognize it or deny the importance of intervention when they do recognize it.

The child who tries out bullying and is not helped to learn from the experience may be reinforced by bullying behavior. For this child, the inaction by the teacher may cause bullying to become a Level Two mistaken behavior. The teacher therefore intervenes gently, but firmly, to reinforce a classroom guideline, such as "We are friendly to our classmates" or "Remember, friendly words spoken here." Without overreacting, reestablishing a limit is often enough.

Level Two is socially influenced mistaken behavior—the child learns a behavior from the actions of others. Bullying becomes Level Two when a child has been reinforced for bullying behavior. Reinforcement happens most frequently when a teacher ignores, and so condones, experimentation bullying. Reinforcement also can happen if a teacher overreacts with punishment to the child doing the bullying. The child then learns that bullying elicits powerful reactions, even if negative, and may repeat its use. (Teachers need to be careful how they implement "zero tolerance" policies—Is the policy intended "to discipline" or to guide?)

Children also show Level Two bullying if they are influenced by peers to join in the stigmatization of a vulnerable child. Group bullying through name-calling, ostracism, or even aggression is common. By identifying with others against an "outsider," children who are the group members feel a sense of belonging and power—which they may be denied during parts of the classroom day.

Conflict management is the intervention of choice in the event of one-on-one bullying. Mediation gives the targeted child a chance for needed self-assertion, reestablishes equality among classmates, and teaches the child doing the bullying that friendly behaviors "only" belong in the classroom (Texas Workforce Commission, 2008). When bullying becomes "public" in a group, class meetings as well are called for. Prevention, by teaching activities that promote the friendliness and inclusiveness of the encouraging classroom, also may be needed. Families might be enlisted to bring the message of friendliness "home" to children as well.

Level Three, strong needs mistaken behavior, is due to trouble in a child's life that is beyond her capacity to cope with and understand. Children at Level Three often show "serious" bullying with the emotional intensity and aggressive persistence that are associated with this act. With more social savvy, some older children at Level Three instigate others to join in the bullying or even coerce others to do the bullying for them, which elevates annoyance bullying to the pernicious. As they move through the elementary grades, children at Level Three may also become the targets of bullying—the group of high concern in the National Study.

With Level Three bullying, the teacher takes the prevention and intervention steps outlined for Level Two. In addition, the teacher uses comprehensive guidance with the child to address the underlying causes of the unmet needs the child is showing through the bullying behaviors. This next section more fully discusses the steps a teacher might take.

Bullying and Liberation Teaching

Liberation teaching is being proactive in the use of guidance principles. Writers agree that the key to solving problems of bullying in the classroom lies with the teacher. They agree that the teacher's responses must show active leadership and be comprehensive (Beane, 2000; Froschl & Sprung, 1999; Hoover & Oliver, 1996; Nansel et al., 2001; Texas Workforce Commission, 2008). The tasks of the liberating teacher concern the class, the child, the staff, and the parents.

With the class, the liberating teacher works on *prevention* by talking and teaching about bullying and the need for friendliness (Bullock, 2002). The teacher uses children's books (see Recommended Readings and the Guidance Matters column at the end of the chapter); puppet and role plays, story pictures, experience charts, journals, and class meetings to teach children the importance of empathy and inclusion (Beane, 2000; Froschl & Sprung, 1999; Hoover & Oliver, 1996). The teacher and children together make a short list of guidelines, as much as possible in the children's words, to define the spirit of encouragement. The teacher forgoes competitive practices in instruction and games that set children against each other and put an artificial premium on performance. He designs activities and encourages cooperation and relationships that go across genders, "because everyone can be friends in our classroom, girls and girls, girls and boys, boys and girls, and boys and boys" (Froschl & Sprung, 1999, p. 72).

The teacher holds class meetings to assess and further the development of a cooperative group spirit. To lessen tension and aid in group problem solving, he may use relaxation activities and soothing sound effects, like flowing water (Froschl & Sprung, 1999). The prevailing intent of the meetings is to accept and celebrate human differences in the class. The adult teaches children that if they negotiate themselves, it is all right to report bullying. In the encouraging class-room, bullying is hurting behavior and does not have a *code of silence*.

The adult may teach the use of de-escalating words or actions—such as the sentence frames in Chapter Ten—for children to use. (When a toddler got into a habit of biting, a teacher taught the other children, if threatened by the child, to hold up their hands and say "Stop!" This defensive action disrupted the impulse of the child who was biting, and alerted the teachers to intervene. The strategy encouraged the children to use their words, a guidance basic.) The adult teaches that children have a right not to be bullied, and at the same time a child who is bullying needs to be accepted as a full member of the class. The child just has a problem that she needs help in solving. This challenging balance is at the heart of liberation teaching, the belief that all children can get along together and learn democratic life skills.

With the child, right from the beginning of the program, the liberating teacher develops positive relationships. In the event of bullying, the teacher uses careful observation to assess whether the bullying is the result of experimenta-tion, social influence, or deep unmet needs. He uses his relationship to help the child find a sense of belonging and self-esteem through creative and cooperative activities in the educational program. He knows that bullying is an expression of a lack of perceived power, and the child has chosen mistaken behavior as a way to gain power and prestige. He helps a child prone to bullying to find other ways to feel capable and productive.

For a child who is bullying at Level Three, teachers use the crisis interven-tion techniques and comprehensive intervention strategies discussed in Chapter Eleven. After the children are calm, the teacher intervenes in firm but friendly ways using conflict management and guidance talks. Outside of immediate con-flicts, the teacher continues working on the relationship with the child, helps the child find success in the program, involves fellow staff and family members, and, if necessary, implements a formal Individual Guidance Plan.

Most of all, the teacher is vigilant, ever aware of the possibility of bullying behavior. In fact, the liberating teacher has a zero tolerance for bullying. But he also has a zero tolerance for disqualifying any child from full participation in the class. When he sees bullying, he acts to make it a teaching opportunity because he knows that all children—including the child doing the bullying—can learn democratic life skills. Some children will just take longer to learn than others.

This balanced concern for the well-being of the child who bullies, as well as children bullied, is an emphasis in the guidance approach and in liberation teaching.

Classroom Anecdote	*I walked out onto the playground and immediately saw that a child from another room was hitting Kevin. Kevin stood against the fence with his arms up over his head. I hurried over and arrived at the same time as the teacher of the other child. She pulled the child off of Kevin, and we both knelt down, holding each child, to talk to them. Before either of us said anything, Kevin looked at the other child and said, "It made me very mad when you hit me." He told the other boy, "You're supposed to use words, not hit." The boy from the other class did not respond in any way during the discussion. I thanked Kevin for using his words and not hitting back. The teacher stayed to talk with the other boy. She later told me that she and her teaching team had scheduled a "staffing" concerning him that day and would meet with the parents soon (Gartrell, 2000). They needed to find out what was bothering him.*

With staff, liberating teachers work for a unified, program wide approach to bullying (Bullock, 2002). If all teachers in a school or program team together to build encouraging classrooms, develop positive relations with families, handle mistaken behavior with guidance, and take a planned approach to bullying that includes both systematic prevention and intervention, stigmatizing behaviors (bullying) will decrease (Beane, 2000; Hoover & Oliver, 1996). General policies addressing bullying/friendliness issues need to be clear to children and adults alike, and enforced in firm but friendly ways (Beane, 2000). Administrators need to be visible leaders regarding guidance policies in relation to bullying. Both students and teachers need to participate in the policy guidelines process. "Cohesiveness among the teaching staff and the principal [or director] relates to less violence" (Beane, 2000, p. 6). (Administration leadership is clearly needed to implement a coordinated program.) Working with fellow staff, the liberating teacher benefits from being on a dedicated team.

With families, the liberating teacher starts from the beginning of the year to build positive relations and makes sure that family members know they and the teacher are on the same team. He makes guidance priorities, including teaching democratic life skills, known to family members right away. He shares guidelines with family members that he and the class have developed. He involves family members in simple activities with their children that encourage empathy building and the acceptance of human differences (Froschl & Sprung, 1999).

When problems involving bullying become serious, the liberating teacher communicates with families. He holds conferences for face-to-face discussion, using reflective listening, compliment sandwiches, and social problem solving. If differing viewpoints about bullying grow evident, the teacher works to make them *creative differences* rather than *negative dissonances*. He works cooperatively with other staff and takes leadership if there is need for an individual guidance plan. A support system with fellow staff, family, and friends allows the teacher to persist in the risks and challenges of liberation teaching. Reaching a child who bullies, is bullied, or both—and helping the child to overcome—is the goal and reward of liberation teaching.

Classroom Anecdote	*Jeremiah was almost three when I started teaching at the center. He was one of those very physical kids, whose feelings and thoughts always moved through his body first. He'd had a turbulent life, and when I came to the center, he was living mostly with his mom and some with his dad. They were separated, and neither made very much money. Jeremiah was a shiningly bright kid, curious about and interested in everything, who loved stories and connected with others with his whole heart. He knew so much about the natural world and was observant and gentle with animals, insects, and plants.*
	When I first started working with Jeremiah, he had a lot of angry outbursts. The center used time-out at that point (the dreaded "green chair"), and Jeremiah spent considerable time there. While I was at the center, we moved away from using time-outs. Instead, we introduced a structured system of problem solving called "peer problem solving" developed by a Montessori teacher in New Hampshire. By the time Jeremiah graduated to kindergarten, we had been using the system for three years, and he was one of the experts.
	One day, I overheard a fracas in the block corner. I stood up to see what was going on, ready to intervene. The youngest child in the room, who was just two and talking only a little bit, and one of the four-year olds were in a dispute over a truck. There was an obvious imbalance of power, and I took a step forward, ready to go to their aid. Then I saw Jeremiah approach them.
	"What's going on?" he asked (my standard opening line). He proceeded to facilitate a discussion between the two children that lasted for five minutes. He made sure both kids got a chance to speak; he interpreted for the little one. "Jordan, what do you think of that idea?" he asked. Jordan shook his head and clutched the truck tighter. "I don't think Jordan's ready to give up the truck yet," he told the four-year-old.
	It was amazing. Jeremiah helped the kids negotiate an agreement, and then he walked away with a cocky tilt to his head I'd never seen before. His competence was without question; his pride was evident (Gartrell, 2000). (Thanks to Beth Wallace for this anecdote.)

Liberation Teaching and Related Educational Practices

Liberation teaching matches philosophically with other education practices, which together might be termed *socially responsive education*. In this day and age, many educators feel the need for socially responsive education as a counterforce to the violence in our society. These educators note the failure of traditional education to muster the coordinated resources to proactively teach cooperative problem solving when conflicts occur. This section explores the relationship of liberation teaching to the socially responsive education methods of:

- the encouraging classroom
- guidance

⯈ anti-bias education

⯈ peace education.

The Encouraging Classroom

Elkind (2007) points out that *along* with the increase in media viewing, parents are having even young children participate in organized activities such as team sports, gymnastics, Scouts, swim classes, and music lessons. Less time is available for the informal, unstructured neighborhood play that in the past has been instrumental in helping children learn social problem solving (Elkind, 2007; Pirtle, 1997). With their lack of experience, children today easily acquire "unrealistic and superficial beliefs" about productive and nonproductive ways to handle conflicts (Slaby et al., 1995).

While this education needs to happen in the home, teachers too have an important role (Swick & Freeman, 2004). Unless teachers intentionally structure programs to do so, classrooms similarly lack opportunities for children to learn social problem solving—the essence of democratic life skills. For children to learn democratic life skills—appreciating one's self and others, expressing strong feelings in non-hurting ways, making decisions intelligently and ethically, cooperating with others to resolve problems--they need encouraging classrooms. Both in the teaching/learning process and in the everyday modeling/practice of the skills, classrooms become encouraging. Educational models such as the well-known Second Step Program (Committee on Children, 2008) assist educators with curriculum and teaching strategies that guide children to develop democratic life skills.

Class Meetings. In the encouraging classroom, children learn to solve social problems on an everyday basis. A standard practice for building and maintaining problem solving skills is the class meeting. From class meetings, children learn that they are not the clients of the teacher but the citizens of a classroom community. They have a say in managing the classroom, with the mentoring of a teacher who is committed to the community concept.

Like no other classroom activity, class meetings, reflecting the democracy shown in centuries-old town meetings, prepare children to be citizens of our complex society. The widely used Responsive Classroom model relies on class meetings, in particular morning meetings, as a bedrock of its approach (Kriete, 2002).

The adult practicing liberation teaching recognizes that the encouraging classroom is sustained by regular, reliable class meetings. As children get more skilled in conducting the meetings themselves, teachers step back when they can and relinquish control. The teacher learns when to share power and when to take leadership (often during discussion of conflicts or to protect the right of civil expression for every child). Successful class meetings indicate the professionalism implicit in liberation teaching.

Developmentally Appropriate for Every Child. A vital dimension of the encouraging classroom is that its programs are developmentally appropriate for every child. As discussed in earlier chapters, some teachers find it convenient to think that their programs are developmentally appropriate when most children, but not necessarily all, are able to engage in activities. Learners who find success difficult to achieve lapse into the typical behaviors of "passivity," including frustration, tuning out, and restlessness. The incomplete use of DAP leads as well to the "boy behavior" syndrome.

In contrast, the teacher who practices liberation teaching is *inclusive*. The teacher monitors and modifies the schedule, program, and environment to make learning transactions encouraging for every child, including the most active and challenging class members.

Guidance

Traditionally, discipline systems have been used to safeguard the curriculum of the classroom. The purpose of discipline was to keep children in line so that the teacher could present lessons, and the children could learn lessons, without distraction. Guidance rises above this obedience emphasis. When teachers use guidance to prevent and resolve conflicts, the social–emotional skills that children learn are basic to social studies and the language arts, and often to literacy, math, and science as well. Essentially, children learn the abilities to think and express thought and to work through complex problems. In this sense, guidance if fundamental to developmentally appropriate practice. Along with the other learning children do, they learn democratic life skills. Through this social learning, they improve the chances of their own academic success (Hymel & Ford, 2003).

Empowers Human Relations. Just as guidance enlightens the encouraging classroom, liberation teaching empowers the teacher to model the human relations—the appreciation of human qualities in the self and the other—fundamental to the use of guidance. By helping everyone in the class to see others as worthy members of a shared community, the teacher models that differing human qualities are not a source of suspicion, but of mutual affirmation.

In the use of guidance imbued with liberation teaching, children learn human relations skills. Liberation teaching brings a proactive appreciation for the humanity of each child to the guidance approach, and for the humanity of the teacher:

Classroom Anecdote	*In a suburban first grade, Tom, a member of an all-European-American class, approached his teacher, an African American. Without looking directly at her, but with some emotion, Tom declared: "Teacher, somebody's different in here."*
	The teacher responded, "Do you mean me, Tom? My skin is a darker color than yours and that's one of the special things that makes me who I am." Tom frowned and shook his head, but the teacher thought that her skin color was probably what Tom had on his mind.
	The next day Tom's mother, an occasional classroom volunteer, called the teacher and said; "Annie, I just have to tell you what happened last night. Tom and I were in the supermarket when an African-American woman went by with a shopping cart. Tom turned to me and said, "Look, Mom, there goes a teacher."

Antibias Education

As the proactive implementation of guidance in the classroom, liberation teaching has much in common with the concept of **anti bias education**. As defined by Louise Derman-Sparks (1989), anti bias education means:

> An active/activist approach to challenging prejudice, stereotyping, bias, and the "isms." In a society in which institutional structures create and maintain sexism, racism, and handicappism, it is not sufficient to be non-biased (and also highly unlikely), nor is it sufficient to be an observer. It is necessary for each individual to actively intervene, to challenge and counter the personal and institutional behaviors that perpetuate oppression. (p. 3)

In antibias education, this disposition is institutionalized in the educational program of the school or center (Levin, 2003). For instance, Derman-Sparks comments that antibias curriculum incorporates the positive intent and awareness of **multicultural education**, but avoids the surface treatment of other cultures—such as making sombreros and serapes and doing the "Mexican Hat Dance" to "learn about" Mexico. She regards such "units" as **tourist curriculum** (p. 7). Teachers who practice antibias education actively involve families in the program and utilize families to individually educate the class about the complexities of modern cultures (Derman-Sparks, 1989; McCracken, 1992; Neuman & Roskos, 1994; Wardle, 1992; York, 2003). (A teacher might invite a Mexican American family to visit the class and share something valued by their family—which in northern Minnesota could be raising sled dogs!)

Liberation teaching is in harmony with the proactive nature of antibias education. The basis of the antibias approach is creation of an affirming environment in the classroom, in which children learn to appreciate others beyond their differences. This too is the goal of liberation teaching. Liberation teaching goes beyond the definition, though not the spirit, of antibias curriculum in one respect. Teachers using antibias education prevent factors of race, gender, and disability from negatively separating members of a class. Liberation teaching focuses on an additional element that leads to stigmatization in the classroom—behavioral and personality characteristics of the individual child.

According to Bullock (2002), aggressive behavior is the most prevalent reason for why a child might be stigmatized by others. Children who are withdrawn and lack social skills also tend to experience the "passive oppression of being ignored" (p. 93). Though Bullock found differences in children "rejected" versus "neglected," her review of the research indicates that "many adolescents who drop out of school experience poor peer adjustments in their earlier years of school" (p. 93).

Oppression (stigma) as a result of cultural, physical, or *behavioral* factors is not acceptable in the encouraging classroom. Liberation teaching seeks to reduce the effects of stigma, both to the child oppressed by others *and* to the child showing the oppression. Teachers who assist both the children to build ties with peers not only lessen the effects of the bully-victim syndrome but enable better school adjustment for each child (Ladd, Kochenderfer, & Coleman, 1996; Hymel & Ford, 2003). These teachers extend the intent of antibias education.

In her discussion of the *power of silence*, Stacy York (1991) criticizes teaching practices that prevent open discussion of tacitly oppressive behavior based on race:

> *Teachers and schools create "no-talk" rules for classrooms. Controversial situations occur, and questionable things are said or done. A Euro-American child calls a Native American child a "dumb Indian." Three boys in the block corner won't let a Laotian boy join them. They chant, "Go away, poopy boy. You talk funny." Everyone in the classroom hears it and sees it. Children may even look at each other as the situation occurs, but nothing is said then or thereafter.*

> *Many times, people feel paralyzed and make no response. [Teachers] have told us that they fail to act because they are uncertain of the right thing to say; or they fear making a mountain out of a molehill; or because they feel they should not be influencing children with their ideas. But the silence only serves to reinforce the hurt, pain, fear, hatred, and distorted thinking. (pp. 197–198)*

York's examples illustrate the overlap of mistaken and racially stigmatizing behavior. In such situations, teachers need to intervene. Using nonpunitive conflict management techniques, they explain the unacceptable behaviors and teach prosocial alternatives. They may follow up as well with a class meeting, a planned activity, or a discussion with a family member to reinforce the message that different human qualities are not to be feared or scorned, but learned from

Oppression as a result of cultural, physical, or behavioral factors is not acceptable in the guidance-oriented classroom.

© Cengage Learning

and accepted. The activist message in antibias education offers much to guidance by empowering teachers to be liberating.

Classroom Anecdote	In a kindergarten classroom some boys were playing "fireman," using the climber for their station and the dramatic-play areas for the "house on fire." Charlene asked to play, but was told, "You can't 'cause you're a girl. Only boys can be firemen." Charlene tried to get on the climber anyway, but the boys pushed at her and began yelling. The teacher intervened: "Hey, guys, do you remember our book about firefighters? Men and women can both be firefighters. That's why we call them firefighters instead of firemen. How can Charlene help you as a firefighter?" The other boys didn't object when Steve said, "Okay, Charlene, you can steer on the back." The teacher watched as the four got on their long wooden "fire truck" and "sped off" to the fire. Charlene turned a make-believe steering wheel in the back, helped to fight the fire, and even found a baby that needed to be saved. After the fire was out, the boys included Charlene on the climber fire station, " 'cause Charlene saved the baby." That Friday a female firefighter, who was a friend of the teacher, visited the class. She arrived in street clothes and with the class's participation discussed, put on, and demonstrated her gear. No one commented the next week when Charlene and Della played firefighter with two boys.

Liberation Teaching and Peace Education

The goal of liberation teaching, to help any child at risk for stigma overcome her vulnerabilities, is the goal for all children in **peace education**. When conflict occurs, teachers traditionally regard children according to their role in it: *aggressor* and *victim*. A child who is treated as an aggressor is at risk for stigma because even if the teacher is able to control personal negative feelings, others in the classroom may come to avoid or reject the child (Bullock, 2002). Significantly, the child who is the victim is also at risk. Some children, perhaps victimized often in early childhood, suffer from low self-esteem and feel incapable in social situations. They may find themselves assuming a generalized "victim role" and continue to be a target of acting-out behaviors by others.

Conflict management enables teachers and children alike to overcome the labeling phenomena and find success in their efforts at peaceable communication (Levin, 2003). It allows children victimized in conflict situations to express their feelings, participate in an equitable resolution process, and achieve vindication. At the same time, the child who has shown aggression is growing in the ability to understand the perspectives of others while still being affirmed as a person of worth in the group. In terms of peace education, this second child is being liberated from the vulnerabilities inherent in the use of violence.

Peace education, like liberation teaching, elevates all members of the encouraging classroom and teaches that mutual respect shows itself most fully in the peaceful resolution of social problems (Levin, 2003). In an adaptation of earlier

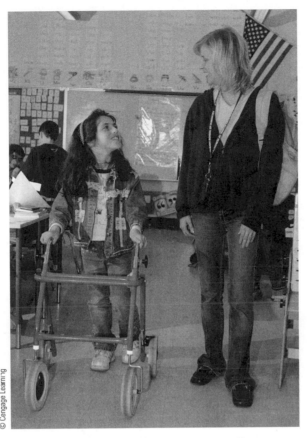

Liberation teaching engenders an appreciation of human qualities in oneself and others.

works on the subject, Janke and Penshorn Peterson (1995) set out eight tasks of peace education:

▶ Bringing out in people their desires to live in peace

▶ Providing awareness of alternatives to violence

▶ Teaching skills, content, and a peaceful pedagogy

▶ Examining the roots and causes of violence

▶ Empowering students to confront their fears of violence

▶ Helping to build a peaceful culture to counteract militarism

▶ Challenging violent ways of thinking and acting

▶ Promoting loving behavior toward oneself, others, and the environment.

Readers may react to some of these issues as being political as much as philo-sophical; such an interpretation is certainly the individual's right. Nonetheless, the philosophy behind democratic life skills has much in common with the priorities of peace education. Given the violence prevalent in modern life, teachers today can hardly engage in liberation teaching without addressing the issues of peace and the need for peace education. Peace education, like guidance in the encouraging classroom, takes liberating teachers. In this effort liberation teaching sustains the democratic ideals of our society.

Liberation Teaching and Parent Involvement

The adult who practices liberation teaching accepts the fundamental connection between the classroom life of the child and the family. The teacher works with and seeks to understand the family in order to benefit the child (Neuman & Roskos, 1994; Pappano, 2007). Liberation teaching with parents means the teacher encourages the maximum involvement in the education of the child that is possible for each family. Over time, as trust builds, the teacher nudges the family toward higher levels.

© Cengage Learning

Liberation teaching with families means that the teacher encourages their maximum participation in the education of the child.

Recapping information from previous chapters, a strategy for increasing parent involvement is suggested, using the following levels:

1. sharing of information
2. active involvement
3. program participation
4. personal/professional development.

Level One—Sharing Information

At the beginning of the school year, the teacher introduces family members as well as children to the program. The teacher becomes acquainted with each family and seeks ways to involve the family in the child's education. Families differ in the level of participation that they are ready to accept (Coleman, 1997). Most families are at least willing to receive information. The teacher makes the most of this willingness, recognizing the two sources of information that families have: the *teacher* and the *child*.

On the teacher's part, he uses the methods of communication discussed in previous chapters—phone calls, happygrams, electronic communication, orientation meetings, home visits, and parent conferences. The teacher works for three outcomes at this first level of involvement:

▶ Understanding by the family member that the teacher accepts and appreciates the child

▶ Comfort felt by the family member in communicating with the teacher about family background, including information about the child

▶ Willingness on the part of the family member for increased involvement.

The child is the second source of information for the family member. If the child wants to come to school even when sick, the foundation is set for further family member involvement. If the child does not want to come to school when well, participation beyond the passive receipt of information may be the best the teacher can expect. Through the foundation provided by a successful program for the child and active inviting by the teacher, family participation is encouraged at additional levels.

Level Two—Active Involvement

The nature of active involvement will differ for each family. Working family members may not be able to come into the classroom, except (perhaps) on a special occasion. They may be able to contribute materials, read or do other enriching activities with children at home, or arrange for a nonworking family member to attend the class. The use of a home-school journal—a running dialogue by hard copy or e-mail between the teacher and family—is a clear indication of active involvement with some families who cannot participate with the

© Cengage Learning

One method of family involvement is to invite families to share with the class something of their heritage and interests. (Courtesy, The Bemidji Pioneer)

group. The teacher works actively to keep communication going with working parents. For instance, if they drop off and pick up their child, the teacher always has words, and perhaps happygrams, to share. Electronic connections such as e-mails or twittering work for some; recorded phone messages on a classroom telephone for others may prove useful.

With families who can come into the classroom, McCracken (1992) suggests a **tossed salad approach** in which families from differing backgrounds add to the program in informal but important ways. Rather than focus on family presentations around holidays or specific customs, family members interact informally with children and other adults—with friendships and discovered family interests providing incidental educational opportunities. As McCracken points out, when the families served are diverse, the tossed salad approach allows for multicultural education in a natural and supportive way. For such a program to work, families must feel welcome and comfortable in the classroom—the job of the teacher, as leader of the teaching team (McCracken, 1992).

Another approach, a bit more formal, is to ask each family to have members come into class and share something about their interests (Gestwicki, 2007).

> **Table 12–1** *Shareable Interests of Family Members in Northern Minnesota (Not Necessarily Tied to Ethnic Roots or Gender Role Stereotypes)*
>
> - Mexican American family that raises sled dogs. Brings in dogs and gives children rides.
> - Scandinavian American family that owns Mexican take-out restaurant. Comes in and makes fried ice cream.
> - Native American couple that wins ballroom dancing contest. Teaches simple waltz steps.
> - African American family member who plays accordion. Plays songs for children.
> - Hmong family that brings in a special food dish to share at pot luck family meeting—hotdog hot dish and white bread.
> - Woman logger mom. Comes in and plants seedlings on school property with children.
> - Teen son of single working mom. Comes in and plays tunes on tuba, accompanied by children's rhythm band.
> - Early-teen twin girls from working family. Brings in soccer balls and gives demonstration.
> - Male nurse dad. Demonstrates different examination tools and explains how they are used.
> - Between-jobs dad. Comes in and reads his family's favorite picture books to class.

Every family would be asked, not just those with an "exotic" heritage, and the members could share anything that was important to their particular family. The teacher might ask families he already knows to share at the beginning of the year. Use of the tossed salad approach would help other families become used to the classroom before being asked to share. As mentioned, working parents might be able to have a nonworking member participate.

With planning and coordination, the teacher can provide follow-up activities for children around the topics of individual family visits. For instance, integrated curriculum activities could be set up around pets if one or more families brought pets to share. One benefit of a family-share program is that it introduces cultural differences in functional ways for the children—two families of the same ethnicity would still have different items and interests to share. A second benefit is that it allows children to bridge the gap between home and school in personally satisfying ways. Some families who came only to share might be encouraged to come back to the class at other times.

Level Three—Program Participation

Level Three is participation in program activities: event committees, advisory councils, policy boards. Some families start at Level One and move to Level Three, but prefer program participation to educational participation. Each family is different, and progress to either Level Two or Three should be supported. The importance of program participation is that it means the family member is taking a leadership role in the education of *all* children in the school or center. If a family member begins at Level One and moves to Level Three, the children, the program, and the family member all stand to benefit.

The model that Head Start has provided for encouraging low-income, often low-esteem families to become active participants in their children's education is one of liberation teaching on a broad scale. A family member who over time comes to a meeting, volunteers in a class, gets elected to a policy council, and positively influences the program is what liberation teaching with families is about. The gain in confidence levels in such family members is impressive. The family member who says, "I sent my child and hoped that she would benefit, but I have benefited as much or more," indicates liberation teaching with families at its best.

Level Four—Personal/Professional Development

Perhaps with families an ultimate goal in liberation teaching is a family member who experiences successful involvement and as a result is motivated to pursue further education or a career. It doesn't matter if the additional schooling is to get a high school diploma, job training, or a bachelor's degree. Whether the family member becomes a paid teacher assistant, family child care provider, a Head Start or elementary grade teacher, or a worker in another field, for this person the success of the family involvement program cannot be denied. They began only as a volunteer whom a teacher took an interest in, and over time improved life circumstances for themselves and their families in substantial ways.

Classroom Anecdote	*(Journal of a graduate student) Margaret was a parent volunteer in the Head Start classroom I observed. She had volunteered in the center previously. A staff member said "Good morning" when Margaret arrived. "We are glad you could come today. How are you feeling?"*

Margaret said, "My mouth is still sore, but it feels better than yesterday." (She was still recovering from a serious dental appointment.)

The teacher said, "If you don't feel well, Margaret, you can come in another day." Margaret indicated that she would stay. She hung up her coat and, without any direction from the teacher, went out to meet the second group of children who arrived on the bus. Margaret waited with the children while they hung up their coats, walked with them to wash their hands, and then sat down to breakfast with them. She reminded them how to open their milk and quietly asked Calvin to keep his feet still.

After breakfast, the teacher asked Margaret if she would like to play the alphabet fishing game that she brought. Margaret played the game with three children and had to ask four others to wait for a turn. The teacher came over to the table and said, "Margaret, the children are enjoying the game so much." Margaret smiled. Margaret then helped the children with brushing their teeth. The teacher asked Margaret if she could sit close to Ray during story time. She said, "He needs some extra attention today." Margaret sat down by Ray, and he crawled onto her lap.

Later, I interviewed Margaret and asked her what went into her decision to volunteer in the classroom. Margaret said, "At first, I volunteered because I wanted to make Alicia

(continued)

Classroom Anecdote	*[her daughter] feel more comfortable. Alicia was with us most of the time and wasn't used to being with groups of children without us. I felt more relaxed if I knew she was happy at school. Then I got used to being with the kids, and it was a lot of fun being with them, so I came back to volunteer. My hours changed, and I got put on part-time, so I could volunteer more easily."*
	I asked Margaret what part the teacher played in her decision to volunteer. Margaret said, "On the first home visit, the teacher encouraged us to volunteer in the center, but she wasn't pushy about it. When I came into the center, I felt welcomed by the teachers. There was always a 'Hi' or 'Good morning.' The kids all said 'Hi' or gave me a hug. I felt like I was really contributing, giving more attention, and sometimes, like on the playground, making it safer for the kids. The teachers always thank me for helping out when I leave. When someone is appreciated, it makes them want to come back. If someone's not appreciated, they're not going to come back. Now, I know this is what I want to do. My family has seen a change in me. I'm starting college this fall to become a teacher. They weren't for it at first, but now they're all for it." Margaret paused, then said, "Just because (the teacher) got me to volunteer."

Many teachers in Head Start programs, as well as child care centers and schools, have success stories like this one. The long-term societal benefits of early childhood education in the area of family involvement have not been fully realized. In fact, measures of the success of early childhood education in general have focused too narrowly on the immediate measurable gains of children. When educators see the classroom more broadly, as an encouraging community involving families no less than children, the full potential of the encouraging classroom is being realized.

Summary

1. How are children in the classroom affected by violence in society?

Virtually all children are touched by societal violence. At the low end of Levin's (2003) continuum of violence, large numbers of children are exposed to many hours of television programming (often meant for adults), computer games, action toys, and play weapons, along with life experiences like teasing. In addition to this indirect violence, smaller numbers of children, at the upper end of the continuum, experience violence directly in their homes and neighborhoods. The more extensive and intensive the exposure to violence, the more direct the effect of violence on children in the classroom. Children directly exposed to violence have unmet needs for safety, security, and a sense of belonging. They may show extreme mistaken behavior as a result, which has much in common with post-traumatic stress disorder.

2. How is liberation teaching a response to societal violence?

Liberation teaching is the proactive application of guidance principles. The concept derives from the work of educators, clerics, and psychologists during the 20th century. Specific to the issue of violence, liberation teaching assists children to find the inner resources they need for resiliency—the child's own healing process. Because of behavior, physical appearance, and sometimes social and cultural factors, some children are vulnerable for stigma—or negative separation from the group. The effects of stigma—which is psychological violence in the education setting—are the effects of violence on the child. Teachers who practice liberation teaching work to eliminate stigma in the classroom and to assist children vulnerable for stigma to find affirmation and a sense of belonging in the class.

3. What is the liberation teaching response to bullying?

Bullying is the most prevalent form of violence that children experience, taking the form of physical or psychological oppression or both. Children vulnerable for stigma tend to be targets of bullying. Bullying stigmatizes both the targeted child and the child who bullies, with possible long-term negative consequences for each. The response of the liberating teacher to bullying is a comprehensive one that involves education, prevention, and guidance intervention. The teacher determines the motivational source of the bullying and intervenes with different levels of bullying in different ways. The comprehensive approach the adult practicing liberation teaching includes the class, the child, fellow staff, and the family. Reaching a child who bullies, is bullied, or both—and helping the child to overcome—is the goal and reward of liberation teaching.

4. What is the connection between liberation teaching and other socially responsive education practices?

Liberation teaching is one of a cluster of socially responsive education methods that teachers use to combat the effects of violence in society: building the encouraging classroom, using guidance, practicing anti-bias education, and espousing peace education The methods have in common the inclusion democratic life skills as a core element in the curriculum. Teaching for social–emotional competence is at least as important in these methods as achieving adequate test scores. Liberation teaching empowers the modeling and teaching of positive human relations in the classroom.

5. How does liberation teaching apply to relations with parents?

The practice of liberation teaching means that the teacher accepts the fundamental connection between the classroom life of the child and the family. The teacher encourages the maximum involvement possible for each family, and over time as trust builds, invites increased involvement. The teacher encourages family members to progress along a continuum that includes four levels: (1) acceptance of information, (2) active involvement, (3) program participation, and (4) personal/professional development. Liberation teaching broadens the encouraging classroom to a community that includes children and adults together.

FOLLOW-UP ACTIVITIES

Note: *An element of being a professional teacher is to respect the children, parents, and educators you are working with by maintaining confidentiality, that is, keeping identities private. In completing follow-up activities, please respect the privacy of all concerned.*

Discussion Activity

The discussion activity encourages students to interrelate their own thoughts and experiences with specific ideas from the chapter.

Referring to the text, identify a guiding principle important to you in relation to each of the following:

▶ guidance response to bullying

▶ liberation teaching

▶ resiliency mentoring

▶ antibias education

▶ peace education

▶ levels of parent involvement

Discuss the importance of these principles to you in your professional development.

Application Activities

Application activities allow students to interrelate material from the text with real-life situations. The observations imply access to practicum experiences; the interviews, access to teachers or parents. To interrelate theory and experience, students compare or contrast observations and interviews with referenced ideas from the chapter.

1. Effects of societal violence on children in the classroom.

   a. Observe a child whose behaviors seem to show the effects of indirect or direct violence. Assuring confidentiality, interview a teacher who knows the child about the child's life outside of school. Record your observation and interview. Compare your findings to what the text says about the effects of societal violence on classroom behavior.

b. Ask an experienced teacher to consider a child or two in the class who show serious mistaken behaviors. Interview the teacher about whether he believes that societal violence is a major factor in the conflicts the child experiences in the classroom. Compare your findings to what the text says about the effects of societal violence on classroom behavior.

2. Liberation teaching: a response to societal violence.

a. Record an observation of what you believe to be liberation teaching with a child who is vulnerable for stigma. Why do you think the child is vulnerable for stigma? How did the teacher respond to this child and any other children? Referring to the text, why do you think the teacher's responses were liberating?

b. Interview a teacher about liberation teaching. Ask the teacher to recall an instance of liberation teaching in his professional career. What was the situation? What was the teacher's approach? What were the outcomes for the child, for the teacher? Compare your findings from the interview with what the chapter says about liberation teaching.

3. The liberation teaching response to bullying.

a. Record an observation of bullying behavior, including the words and actions of all involved. Compare specifics from your observation with what the text says about the reasons for bullying and the levels of mistaken behavior shown in bullying behavior. Discuss intervention in this situation. Did you or another staff person intervene? What happened? If there was no intervention, how would you intervene in a similar situation in the future? Compare your findings and thoughts to ideas in the chapter about the liberation teaching response to bullying.

b. Interview a teacher about bullying and his response to it. Do some children seem to bully more than others? Are some children more likely to be targets? How does the teacher work with the class to prevent bullying? Work with individuals frequently involved? Compare your findings from the interview with what the text says about these questions.

4. The connection between liberation teaching and other socially responsive education practices.

a. Record an observation of when a teacher intervened to halt stigmatizing behavior that seemed to be for reasons of cultural, racial, gender, ability, or behavior differences. Which of these factors seemed to trigger the stigmatizing behavior? How did the teacher respond to each of the children involved? Comparing the teacher's response to the text, what have you learned about liberation teaching? Relate what you learned to one of the other socially responsive education practices.

b. Interview a teacher about an experience of stigmatizing behavior in the class the teacher thought was due to cultural, racial, gender, ability, or behavior differences. What did the teacher do? What was the result? Record the interview and compare your findings with the text regarding the practice of liberation teaching. Also relate what you learned to one of the other socially responsive education practices.

5. Liberation teaching and relations with parents.

a. Discuss with a *teacher* a situation in which he helped a family overcome initial reluctance to be involved and one or more family members ended up growing from the participation. Ask the teacher to reflect about the likely effect of the experience for the family, the child, and the teacher. Compare your findings with ideas from the chapter.

b. Interview a *family member* whom you believe to be participating successfully in a classroom or program. Ask what the family member believes that she is gaining personally from the experience. Ask in what ways, if any, the experience has changed the family member's view of her own personal development, education, or career aspirations. Compare your findings with ideas from the chapter.

Recommended Readings

Agassi, M. (2000). *Hands are not for hitting*. Minneapolis, MN: Free Spirit Publishing.

Alat, K. (2002). Traumatic events and children: How early childhood educators can help. *Childhood Education, 79*(1), 2–7.

Bullock, J. R. (2002). Bullying among children. *Childhood Education, 79*(3), 130–133.

Children's Defense Fund. (2008). *The state of America's children: 2008*. Washington, DC: Author.

Committee on Children, Second Step Program. (2008). Seattle, WA. http://www.cfchildren.org (phone: (800) 634-4449; e-mail: info@cfchildren.org).

Elkind, D. (2007). *The power of play*. New York: Decapo Press.

Kalb, C. (2008). Spare the rod. *Newsweek Web Exclusive. February 28, 2008. http://www.newsweek .com/id/116788*

Stoddard, E. (2008, August 20). Corporal punishment seen rife in U.S. schools. Reuters News Service. http://www.reuters.com/articla/topNews/idUSN1931921320080820?pageNum ber=2&virtualBrandChannel=0&sp=true

Szep, J. (2009). Child abuse spikes as U.S. economy founders. Medline Plus, a service of the U.S. National Library and the National Institutes of Health. http://www.nlm.nih.gov/ medlineplusnews/fullstory_83019.htmlC

Swick, K. (2005). Promoting caring in children and families as prevention of violence strategy. *Early Childhood Education Journal, 32*(5), 341–346.

Guidance Matters

Dan Gartrell with Julie Jochum Gartrell

May, 2008

Understand Bullying

Karen, a Head Start teacher, writes:

I heard the words shut up *and went into the bathroom to find out what was happening. Shayna was sitting in the corner crying. I said, "Shayna, why are you crying?" and she answered, "Amanda and Christina said they aren't my friends anymore."*

I asked Shayna if she had told them to shut up, and she said yes. I told her I was sorry that they made her feel sad and angry, but those words bother people in our classroom. (Amanda and Christina were watching and listening to us talk.) I explained to Shayna that maybe next time she could tell the girls it made her sad to hear they didn't want to be her friends.

I told Amanda and Christina that Shayna was feeling sad because of what happened. They went over to Shayna and gave her a hug and said they were sorry. Later, I saw the three playing together (Gartrell, 2007).

This column explores the longtime hot topic of bullying. In a broad-based study for the *Journal of the American Medical Association,* Nansel and his colleagues (2001) discuss bullying from the viewpoints of young people who bully *and* the victims of bullying, both of whom tend to perceive themselves as being less than fully accepted members of a group. The authors state that bullying often has to do with inflicting aggression on another in order to establish a perceived place of prestige by lowering the social status of the other. Although the Nansel team's study focuses on preteens and teens, the findings generally apply in early childhood as well.

Moving from a place of established social status in the family to the social uncertainty of the early childhood classroom, most young children feel some level of stress. Couple this dynamic with the young child's limited social perspective and ongoing brain development, and the result is the almost daily I'm-your-friend/I'm-not-your-friend phenomenon heard in the comments of Amanda and Christina. And who is likely to be the odd child out? The child who may be moody, sometimes unfriendly, not consistently outgoing—that would be Shayna.

In early childhood classrooms, children are just beginning to learn patterns of social acceptance and rejection. Sprung, Froschl, and Hinitz (2005) emphasize that this is why a teacher's response to early bullying needs to be proactive and preventive. Although it may almost sound like Karen was beating up on the victim, the teacher knew Shayna well and was teaching her an alternative response to *shut up* that the other girls would find less objectionable. At the same time, by including all three children in the mediation, Karen was sensitizing Amanda and Christina to the fact that Shayna has a right to be fully accepted as a classmate.

According to the sound approach recommended by Sprung, Froschl, and Hinitz (2005), mediation is only the immediate follow-up in a broad-based effort. Through ongoing class meetings, the teacher establishes from day one that the classroom is an encouraging place for all. The teacher builds such an environment by modeling inclusive group spirit as well as teaching it. In the clarion call of Vivian Gussin Paley (1992), "You can't say you can't play." Children have the right to choose their own friends, but in the encouraging classroom, they need to be friendly to all their "mates."

Because it is a hot-button issue, some programs advocate zero tolerance for bullying. However, quick fixes lead to automatic reactions that do not encourage teachers to think about the individual situations of the children involved. Let us continue with the anecdote involving Karen and Shayna:

A little later, Shayna walked over to the breakfast table. She started crying again. I asked, "Is something making you feel sad, Shayna?"

She said, "I miss my daddy." Her father had been killed in a car accident a few months earlier.

I sat down on a chair, hugging and holding her. I said, "Shayna, my daddy died when I was a little girl, and it made me very sad too. I am so glad you told me why you were crying." We sat by each other and ate breakfast.

Shayna went to the housekeeping area for choice time and joined Amanda and Christina. Later in the day, she came up to me and said, "I'm over my daddy now."

I said, "Shayna, it's okay to feel sad about missing your daddy. I still miss my dad. If you need a hug or want to talk, you come and tell me."

I made other staff aware of the incident and that night talked with Shayna's mom. The next day, Shayna sat on my lap at the play dough table, and we made cookies together (Gartrell, 2007).

Reprinted with permission from the National Association for the Education of Young Children. All rights reserved.

We do well to remember that children's life stories, although not usually as heartbreakingly sad as Shayna's, lie behind every incident of bullying. Recognizing that certain children may be vulnerable to bullying—due to life experiences, behavior, and/or physical appearance—we befriend these children and guide them toward behaviors that will help them gain the acceptance of their peers. Every child has a story worth knowing, one that hopefully resonates with a caring teacher, as Shayna's did with Karen.

Bullying as Physical Aggression

Nansel and his team (2001) make the case that bullying by girls usually involves taunting, exclusion, and gossip. Bullying by boys can, and sometimes does, degenerate into physical aggression. While (sadly) physical aggression may be on the increase with older girls, the pattern found by Nansel and his team tends to hold true in early childhood.

Liz, a Head Start teacher, writes:

I walked onto the playground and immediately saw that a child from another room, Paul, was hitting Kevin. Kevin stood against the fence with his arms up over his head. I hurried over and arrived at the same time as Paul's teacher. She pulled Paul away from Kevin, and we both knelt down to talk to them, each holding a child.

Before either of us spoke, Kevin looked at Paul and said, "It made me very mad when you hit me." He continued, "You're supposed to use words, not hit." Paul did not respond in any way during the discussion.

I thanked Kevin for using his words and not hitting back. The other teacher stayed to talk with Paul. She later told me that she and her teaching team had scheduled a "staffing" concerning him that day and would meet with Paul's family (They needed to find out what was bothering the child.) (Gartrell, 2007).

For many young children, bullying is a form of instrumental aggression—harming another physically or psychologically in order to obtain a goal. Teachers need to use their leadership skills to guide children to more socially responsible, alternative behaviors. For a few children, bullying is reactive aggression—a child experiences stress, does not know how to ask for help, and acts out against a perceived unjust world as a reaction to the stress. The child attacked may have done little or nothing to provoke the aggression. Teachers sometimes must work hard to figure out what made the child vulnerable.

Not many children would have responded as Kevin did. Support for him in the days following the incident was important. At the same time, Paul had problems in his life that were bigger than he was. The circumstances required staffing, meeting with parents, and a comprehensive guidance strategy. Paul's teacher showed she was committed to that process.

Liberation Teaching

Liberation teaching is a term I use in my writings, part of the meaning of which is to not give up on any child (Gartrell, 2007). Liberation teaching means the teacher realizes that comforting the victim and punishing the bully only further the bully-victim syndrome in the class. Instead, the teacher helps the one child express feelings about being bullied and assists the other child to learn that bullying does not help with finding an identity within the group. With each intervention the teacher responds to the question, What can I teach these children right now so they can learn to get along? This teaching process is interactive, with the teacher learning about the children even while teaching mutual acceptance and negotiation skills.

Liberating teachers work for a unified, program wide approach to bullying. When teachers *and* administrators work together to build encouraging classrooms, develop positive relations with parents, use guidance to handle conflicts, and take a planned approach to bullying that includes both prevention and intervention, bullying behaviors markedly decline (Hoover & Oliver, 1996; Beane, 2005). Working with fellow staff and administrators, liberating teachers can accomplish what they cannot do on their own.

To Increase Your Knowledge

Professional Resources

Beane, A. L. (2005). *The bully free classroom: Over 100 tips and strategies for teachers K–8*. Minneapolis, MN: Free Spirit Publishing.

Positive and practical, reinforced with true stories and enhanced by reproducible forms, checklists, and resources, this solution-filled book can make yours a classroom where all students can learn without fear. Other Bully Free resources include miniguides for educators; a workbook; Bully Free Bulletin Boards, Posters, and Banners; and The Bully Free Classroom CD-ROM.

Jackson, C. (2007). "The ABCs of bullying." Teaching Tolerance, Classroom Activities (January).

Bullying often begins with verbal abuse. In this article, Teaching Tolerance offers resources to help educators, families, and students address bullying in the classroom and beyond. Available at http://www.tolerance.org/teach/activities/activity.jsp?ar=771.

Minnesota Association for Children's Mental Health. (2006). *SuperMe: A campaign to end hurtful teasing*. Saint Paul, MN: Author.

In this packet, short stories, coloring pages, classroom activities, and a bulletin board display get students thinking, drawing, and writing about nonviolent ways to handle teasing and bullying. The packet includes the SuperMe Booklet and the SuperMe Team Materials, with new lesson plans and bulletin board pinups of the SuperMe Team.

Moss, P. (2007). Gender doesn't limit you! *Teaching Tolerance* 32 (Fall).

A prominent researcher and an elementary school team up to identify what works—and what doesn't—when teaching young children about gender bullying. Available at http://www.tolerance.org/teach/activities/activity.jsp?ar=841&pa=3.

Sprung, B., Froschl, M., & Hinitz, B. (2005). *The anti-bullying and teasing book for preschool classrooms*. Beltsville, MD: Gryphon House.

This guide addresses teasing and bullying as a continuum of intentionally hurtful behavior, from making fun of someone to repetitive physical abuse. Creating a caring environment at the beginning of the school year reduces the need for children to assert themselves through negative behavior such as teasing and bullying.

Children's Literature (Preschool to Grade 3)

Bateman, T. (2004). *The bully blockers club*. Morton Grove, IL: Whitman (30 pp., Grades pre-K–3).

On the first day of school, Grant Grizzly, the class bully, taunts and teases Lotty Raccoon. After trying several tactics that do not work, Lotty comes up with a solution: the Bully Blockers Club. A class discussion on bullying ensues, and the teacher and students compose rules to help everyone feel safe and welcome.

Carlson, N. 1990. *Arnie and the new kid*. New York: Viking Press (32 pp., Grades pre-K–3).

Philip uses a wheelchair and is new in school. This combination makes him the target of bullying by Arnie, until Arnie falls, breaks his leg, and finds himself in a similar situation. As Arnie begins to understand Philip's challenges and capabilities, they become friends.

dePaola, T. (1979). *Oliver Button is a sissy*. Orlando, FL: Harcourt, Brace (48 pp., Grades K–3).

This picture book tells the story of a boy who is teased because he likes to dance. He overcomes the bullying not by fighting, but by continuing to do what he likes best in spite of the harassment.

Henkes, K. (1991). *Chrysanthemum*. New York: Morrow (32 pp., Grades K–2).

After being taunted by her peers at school, Chrysanthemum wants to change her name. When the class learns that their popular music teacher has an unusual name—Delphinium—Chrysanthemum feels better and the other children accept her.

Hoffman, G. (1996). *The big bad bully bear*. New York: Reverie (24 pp., Grades K–3).

Arthur and his friend Emmy Bear invite all the teddy bears in the neighborhood for cake. They join together to teach Bully Bear a valuable lesson, and Bully Bear realizes he would rather have friends than be a bully.

Keats, E. J. (1998). *Goggles!* New York: Viking Press (40 pp., Grades pre-K–2).

Archie and Peter find a pair of motorcycle goggles, and the neighborhood bullies try to take them. They use their dog, Willie, to help them outsmart the bullies.

Levy, J. (2005). *Alley oops*. New York: Flashlight Press (32 pp., Grades K–3).

This story relates the aftermath of bullying from the perspective of the bully, J.J. Jax, who has been tormenting an overweight boy, Patrick. After Mr. Jax tells J.J. a story about when he acted as a bully and how sorry he feels now, J.J. talks things over with Patrick. The boys' shared interest in arm-wrestling becomes the conduit for resolution and a budding friendship.

Lovell, P. (2001). *Stand tall, Molly Lou Melon*. New York: Putnam (32 pp., Grades pre-K–2).

When Molly Lou Melon starts at a new school, Ronald, the class bully, teases her for being short, being bucktoothed, and having a voice like "a bullfrog being squeezed by a boa constrictor." Molly remembers what her grandmother told her, and she feels good about herself, which helps her overcome the bully's taunts.

McCain, B. R. (2001). *Nobody knew what to do*. Morton Grove, IL: Whitman (24 pp., Grades K–3).

A boy tries to figure out what to do when he repeatedly witnesses a classmate being bullied. Though frightened, he decides to tell his teacher. When the bullies start up again, the boy and his classmates band together with the student being harassed until adults intervene and help.

Moss, P. (2004). *Say something*. Gardiner, ME: Tilbury House (32 pp., Grades 2–4).

A young narrator describes different examples of bullying that she witnesses at school and on the bus.

One day, she must sit alone in the cafeteria, and several students make jokes at her expense. The girl feels angry and is frustrated with the other kids, who look on sympathetically but say nothing. The next day, she approaches a quiet girl who is often teased and finds a new friend.

O'Neill, A. (2002). *The recess queen*. New York: Scholastic (32 pp., Grades pre-K–2).

All the children fear Mean Jean, the playground bully. Then a new student, Katie Sue, unknowingly does all the things Mean Jean forbids. When Mean Jean attempts to set the record straight, Katie Sue pulls out a jump rope and asks Mean Jean to play with her. She does, and the social environment of the playground improves for everyone.

Thomas, P. (2000). *Stop picking on me* (A First Look At series). Happauge, NY: Barron's (29 pp., Grades pre-K–3).

Written by an experienced psychotherapist and counselor, this picture book examines bullying in simple terms—the fears, worries, and questions and the dynamics in young children's relationships. The book encourages children to understand personal and social problems as a first step toward solving them.

Websites

About Bullying is part of the 15+ Make Time to Listen … Take Time to Talk initiative. It provides information about bullying and methods for communicating with children about the climate of fear created by bullying. The messages exchanged between children and their caregivers in just 15 minutes or more a day can be instrumental in building a healthier, safer environment. http://mentalhealth.samhsa.gov/15plus/aboutbullying.asp

Anti-Defamation League Curriculum Connections focuses on Words That Heal, a tool to help educators find books and other resources to include in the curriculum to teach about bullying, stopping bullying, and so on. http://www.adl.org/education/curriculum_connections/Default.asp

Bullying—No Way! from Australia's educational communities, creates learning environments where every student and school community member is safe, supported, respected, and valued—and free from bullying, violence, harassment, and discrimination. http://www.bullyingnoway.com.au/who/default.shtml

Connect for Kids gives action steps and tips for parents whose children are bullied. It explains cyber bullying, how it affects an individual, and how to prevent it. It also has a place for parents and students alike to share their comments and concerns and support one another. http://www.connectforkids.org/node/3116

PACER Kids Against Bullying, for elementary school children, focuses on children with disabilities. Informative and creative, it educates students about bullying prevention and suggests methods to respond in bullying situations. The site features animated characters, information, celebrity videos, webisodes, interactive games, contests, and other activities. Parents and professionals will find helpful tips, intervention strategies, and resources for use at home or school. http://www.pacerkidsagainstbullying.org

Steps You Can Take

Learn more about bullying and the dynamics that lead to it. Consciously work with colleagues to build a classroom in which every child feels valued and accepted. Notice incidents of bullying that still may occur. Even as you intervene, study the situations. Work to make these conflicts into learning experiences for the children involved, the class, fellow staff, and families.

Column References

Beane, A. L. (2005). *The bully free classroom: Over 100 tips and strategies for teachers K–8*. Minneapolis, MN: Free Spirit Publishing.

Gartrell, D. (2007). *A guidance approach for the encouraging classroom* (4th ed.). Clifton Park, NY: Delmar Cengage Learning.

Hoover, J. H., & Oliver, R. (1996). *The bullying prevention handbook*. Bloomington, IN: National Education Service.

Nansel, T. R., Overpeck, M., Pilla, R. S., Ruan, W. J., Simons-Morton, B., & Scheidt, P. (2001). Bullying behaviors among U.S. youth: Prevalence and association with psychosocial adjustment. *Journal of the American Medical Association* 285(16): 2094–2100.

Paley, V. G. (1992). *You can't say you can't play*. Cambridge, MA: Harvard University Press.

Sprung, B., Froschl, M., & Hinitz, B. (2005). *The anti-bullying and teasing book for preschool classrooms*. Beltsville, MD: Gryphon House.

For additional information on using the guidance approach in the encouraging classroom, visit our website at www.cengage.com/education/gartrell.

Appendix A

The NAEYC*
Code of Ethical Conduct

*National Association for the Education of Young Children

This Code of Ethical Conduct and Statement of Commitment was prepared under the auspices of the Ethics Commission of the National Association for the Education of Young Children. The Commission members were Stephanie Feeney (Chairperson), Bettye Caldwell, Sally Cartwright, Carrie Cheek, Josué Cruz, Jr., Anne G. Dorsey, Dorothy M. Hill, Lilian G. Katz, Pamm Mattick, Shirley A. Norris, and Sue Spayth Riley.

Preamble

NAEYC recognizes that many daily decisions required of those who work with young children are of a moral and ethical nature. The NAEYC Code of Ethical Conduct offers guidelines for responsible behavior and sets forth a common basis for resolving the principal ethical dilemmas encountered in early childhood care and education. The primary focus is on daily practice with children and their families in programs for children from birth to 8 years of age: such as infant/toddler programs, preschools, child care centers, family day care homes, kindergartens, and primary classrooms. Many of the provisions also apply to specialists who do not work directly with children, including program administrators, parent educators, college professors, and child care licensing specialists.

Core Values

Standards of ethical behavior in early childhood care and education are based on commitment to core values that are deeply rooted in the history of our field. We have committed ourselves to:

▶ Appreciating childhood as a unique and valuable stage of the human life cycle

▶ Basing our work with children on knowledge of child development

▶ Appreciating and supporting the close ties between the child and family

▶ Recognizing that children are best understood in the context of family, culture, and society

- ▶ Respecting the dignity, worth, and uniqueness of each individual (child, family member, and colleague)
- ▶ Helping children and adults achieve their full potential in the context of relationships that are based on trust, respect, and positive regard.

Conceptual Framework

The Code sets forth a conception of our professional responsibilities in four sections, each addressing an arena of professional relationships: 1) children, 2) families, 3) colleagues, and 4) community and society. Each section includes an introduction to the primary responsibilities of the early childhood practitioner in that arena, a set of ideals pointing in the direction of exemplary professional practice, and a set of principles defining practices that are required, prohibited, and permitted.

The ideals and principles in this Code present a shared conception of professional responsibility that affirms our commitment to the core values of our field. The Code publicly acknowledges the responsibilities that we in the field have assumed and in so doing supports ethical behavior in our work. Practitioners who face ethical dilemmas are urged to seek guidance in the applicable parts of this Code and in the spirit that informs the whole.

Section I: Ethical Responsibilities to Children

Childhood is a unique and valuable stage in the life cycle. Our paramount responsibility is to provide safe, healthy, nurturing, and responsive settings for children. We are committed to supporting children's development, respecting individual differences, helping children learn to live and work cooperatively, and promoting health, self awareness, competence, self worth and resiliency.

Ideals:

I–1.1   To be familiar with the knowledge base of early childhood care and education and to keep current through continuing education and in-service training.

I–1.2   To base program practices upon current knowledge in the field of child development and related disciplines and upon particular knowledge of each child.

---

*The **ideals** reflect the aspirations of practitioners. The **principles** are intended to guide conduct and assist practitioners in resolving ethical dilemmas encountered in the field. There is not necessarily a corresponding principle for each ideal. Both ideals and principles are intended to direct practitioners to those questions which, when responsibly answered, will provide the basis for conscientious decision making. While the Code provides specific direction for addressing some ethical dilemmas, many others will require the practitioner to combine the guidance of the Code with sound professional judgment.*

I–1.3   To recognize and respect the uniqueness and the potential of each child.

I–1.4   To appreciate the special vulnerability of children.

I–1.5   To create and maintain safe and healthy settings that foster children's social, emotional, intellectual, and physical development and that respect their dignity and their contributions.

I–1.6   To support the right of each child to play and learn in inclusive early childhood programs to the fullest extent consistent with the best interests of all involved. As with adults who are disabled in the larger community, children with disabilities are ideally served in the same settings in which they would participate if they did not have a disability.

I–1.7   To ensure that children with disabilities have access to appropriate and convenient support services and to advocate for the resources necessary to provide the most appropriate settings for all children.

Principles:

P–1.1   Above all, we shall not harm children. We shall not participate in practices that are disrespectful, degrading, dangerous, exploitative, intimidating, psychologically damaging, or physically harmful to children. *This principle has precedence over all others in this Code.*

P–1.2   We shall not participate in practices that discriminate against children by denying benefits, giving special advantages, or excluding them from programs or activities on the basis of their race, religion, sex, national origin, or the status, behavior, or beliefs of their parents. (This principle does not apply to programs that have a lawful mandate to provide services to a particular population of children.)

P–1.3   We shall involve all of those with relevant knowledge (including staff and parents) in decisions concerning a child.

P–1.4   For every child we shall implement adaptations in teaching strategies, learning environment, and curricula, consult with the family, and seek recommendations from appropriate specialists to maximize the potential of the child to benefit from the program. If, after these efforts have been made to work with a child and family, the child does not appear to be benefiting from the program, or the child is seriously jeopardizing the ability of other children to benefit from the program, we shall communicate with the family and appropriate specialists to determine the child's current needs, identify the setting and services most suited to meeting these needs, and assist the family in placing the child in an appropriate setting.

P–1.5   We shall be familiar with the symptoms of child abuse, including physical, sexual, verbal, and emotional abuse, and neglect. We shall know and follow state laws and community procedures that protect children against abuse and neglect.

P–1.6   When we have reasonable cause to suspect child abuse or neglect, we shall report it to the appropriate community agency and follow up to ensure that appropriate action has been taken. When appropriate, parents or guardians will be informed that the referral has been made.

P–1.7   When another person tells us of their suspicion that a child is being abused or neglected but we lack evidence, we shall assist that person in taking appropriate action to protect the child.

P–1.8   When a child protective agency fails to provide adequate protection for abused or neglected children, we acknowledge a collective ethical responsibility to work toward improvement of these services.

P–1.9   When we become aware of a practice or situation that endangers the health or safety of children, but has not been previously known to do so, we have an ethical responsibility to inform those who can remedy the situation and who can protect children from similar danger.

Section II: Ethical Responsibilities to Families*

Ideals:

I–2.1   To develop relationships of mutual trust with the families we serve.

I–2.2   To acknowledge and build upon strengths and competencies as we support families in their task of nurturing children.

I–2.3   To respect the dignity of each family and its culture, customs, and beliefs.

I–2.4   To respect families' childrearing values and their right to make decisions for their children.

I–2.5   To interpret each child's progress to parents within the framework of a developmental perspective and to help families understand and appreciate the value of developmentally appropriate early childhood practices.

Families are of primary importance in children's development. (The term family may include others, besides parents, who are responsibly involved with the child.) Because the family and the early childhood practitioner have a common interest in the child's welfare, we acknowledge a primary responsibility to bring about collaboration between the home and school in ways that enhance the child's development.

I–2.6 To help family members improve their understanding of their children and to enhance their skills as parents.

I–2.7 To participate in building support networks for families by providing them with opportunities to interact with program staff and families, community resources and professional services.

Principles:

P–2.1 We shall not deny family members access to their child's classroom or program setting.

P–2.2 We shall inform families of program philosophy, policies, and personnel qualifications, and explain why we teach as we do.

P–2.3 We shall inform families of and, when appropriate, involve them in policy decisions.

P–2.4 We shall inform families of and, when appropriate, involve them in significant decisions affecting their child.

P–2.5 We shall inform the family of accidents involving their child, of risks such as exposures to contagious disease that may result in infection, and of occurrences that might result in emotional stress.

P–2.6 To improve the quality of early childhood care and education, we shall cooperate with qualified child development researchers. Families shall be fully informed of any proposed research projects involving their children and shall have the opportunity to give or withhold consent without penalty. We shall not permit or participate in research that could in any way hinder the education, development, or well-being of children.

P–2.7 We shall not engage in or support exploitation of families. We shall not use our relationship with a family for private advantage or personal gain, or enter into relationships with family members that might impair our effectiveness in working with children.

P–2.8 We shall develop written policies for the protection of confidentiality and the disclosure of children's records. The policy documents shall be made available to all program personnel and families. Disclosure of children's records beyond family members, program personnel, and consultants having an obligation of confidentiality shall require familial consent (except in cases of abuse or neglect).

P–2.9 We shall maintain confidentiality and shall respect the family's right to privacy, refraining from disclosure of confidential information and intrusion into family life. However, when we have reason to believe a child's welfare is at risk, it is permissible to share confidential information to agencies and individuals who may be able to act in the child's interest.

P–2.10 In cases where family members are in conflict we shall work openly, sharing our observations of the child, to help all parties involved make informed decisions. We shall refrain from becoming an advocate for one party.

P–2.11 We shall be familiar with and appropriately use community resources and professional services that support families. After a referral has been made, we shall follow up to ensure that services have been adequately provided.

Section III: Ethical Responsibilities to Colleagues

In a caring, cooperative work place human dignity is respected, professional satisfaction is promoted, and positive relationships are modeled. Our primary responsibility in this arena is to establish and maintain settings and relationships that support productive work and meet professional needs. The same ideals that apply to children are inherent in our responsibilities to adults.

A—Responsibilities to Co-workers Ideals:

I–3 A.1 To establish and maintain relationships of trust and cooperation with co-workers.

I–3 A.2 To share resources and information with co-workers.

I–3 A.3 To support co-workers in meeting their professional needs and in their professional development.

I–3 A.4 To accord co-workers due recognition of professional achievement.

Principles:

P–3 A.1 When we have a concern about the professional behavior of a coworker, we shall first let that person know of our concern, in a way that shows respect for personal dignity and for the diversity to be found among staff members, and then attempt to resolve the matter collegially.

P–3 A.2 We shall exercise care in expressing views regarding the personal attributes or professional conduct of co-workers. Statements should be based on firsthand knowledge and relevant to the interests of children and programs.

B—Responsibilities to Employers Ideals:

I–3 B.1 To assist the program in providing the highest quality of service.

I–3 B.2 To maintain loyalty to the program and uphold its reputation unless it is violating laws and regulations designed to protect children and the provisions of this Code.

Principles:

P–3 B.1 When we do not agree with program policies, we shall first attempt to effect change through constructive action within the organization.

P–3 B.2 We shall speak or act on behalf of an organization only when authorized. We shall take care to acknowledge when we are speaking for the organization and when we are expressing a personal judgment.

P–3 B.3 We shall not violate laws or regulations designed to protect children and shall take appropriate action consistent with this Code when aware of such violations.

C—Responsibilities to Employees Ideals:

I–3 C.1 To promote policies and working conditions that foster mutual respect competence, well-being, and self-esteem in staff members.

I–3 C.2 To create a climate of trust and candor that will enable staff to speak and act in the best interests of children, families, and the field of early childhood care and education.

I–3 C.3 To strive to secure an equitable compensation for those who work with or on behalf of young children.

Principles:

P–3 C.1 In decisions concerning children and programs, we shall appropriately utilize the training, experience, and expertise of staff members.

P–3 C.2 We shall provide staff members with safe and supportive working conditions that permit them to carry out their responsibilities, timely and nonthreatening evaluation procedures, written grievance procedures, constructive feedback, and opportunities for continuing professional development and advancement.

P–3 C.3 We shall develop and maintain comprehensive written personnel policies that define program standards and, when applicable, that specify the extent to which employees are accountable for their conduct outside the work place. These policies shall be given to new staff members and shall be available for review by all staff members.

P–3 C.4 Employees who do not meet program standards shall be informed of areas of concern and, when possible, assisted in improving their performance.

P–3 C.5 Employees who are dismissed shall be informed of the reasons for their termination. When a dismissal is for cause, justification must be based on evidence of inadequate or inappropriate behavior that is accurately documented, current, and available for the employee to review.

P–3 C.6 In making evaluations and recommendations, judgments shall be based on fact and relevant to the interests of children and programs.

P–3 C.7 Hiring and promotion shall be based solely on a person's record of accomplishment and ability to carry out the responsibilities of the position.

P–3 C.8 In hiring, promotion, and provision of training, we shall not participate in any form of discrimination based on race, religion, sex, national origin, handicap, age, or sexual preference. We shall be familiar with and observe laws and regulations that pertain to employment discrimination.

Section IV: Ethical Responsibilities to Community and Society

Early childhood programs operate within a context of an immediate community made up of families and other institutions concerned with children's welfare. Our responsibilities to the community are to provide programs that meet its needs and to cooperate with agencies and professions that share responsibility for children.

Because the larger society has a measure of responsibility for the welfare and protection of children, and because of our specialized expertise in child development, we acknowledge an obligation to serve as a voice for children everywhere.

Ideals:

I–4.1 To provide the community with high-quality, age and individually appropriate, and culturally and socially sensitive education/care programs and services.

I–4.2 To promote cooperation among agencies and professions concerned with the welfare of young children, their families, and their teachers.

I–4.3 To work, through education, research, and advocacy, toward an environmentally safe world in which all children receive adequate health care, food, shelter are nurtured and live free from violence.

I–4.4 To work, through education, research, and advocacy, toward a society in which all young children have access to quality education/care programs.

I–4.5 To promote knowledge and understanding of young children and their needs. To work toward greater social acknowledgment of children's rights and greater social acceptance of responsibility for their well-being.

I–4.6 To support policies and laws that promote the well-being of children and families. To oppose those that impair their well-being.

To participate in developing policies and laws that are needed and cooperate with other individuals and groups in these efforts.

I–4.7 To further the professional development of the field of early childhood education and to strengthen its commitment to realizing its core values as reflected in this Code.

Principles:

P–4.1 We shall communicate openly and truthfully about the nature and extent of services that we provide.

P–4.2 We shall not accept or continue to work in positions for which we are personally unsuited or professionally unqualified. We shall not offer services that we do not have the competence, qualifications, or resources to provide.

P–4.3 We shall be objective and accurate in reporting the knowledge upon which we base our program practices.

P–4.4 We shall cooperate with other professionals who work with children and their families.

P–4.5 We shall not hire or recommend for employment any person whose competence, qualifications, or character makes him or her unsuited for the position.

P–4.6 We shall report the unethical or incompetent behavior of a colleague to a supervisor when informal resolution is not effective.

P–4.7 We shall be familiar with laws and regulations that serve to protect the children in our programs.

P–4.8 We shall not participate in practices which are in violation of laws and regulations that protect the children in our programs.

P–4.9 When we have evidence that an early childhood program is violating laws or regulations protecting children, we shall report it to persons responsible for the program. If compliance is not accomplished within a reasonable time, we will report the violation to appropriate authorities who can be expected to remedy the situation.

P–4.10 When we have evidence that an agency or a professional charged with providing services to children, families, or teachers is failing to meet its obligations, we acknowledge a collective ethical responsibility to report the problem to appropriate authorities or to the public.

P–4.11 When a program violates or requires its employees to violate this Code, it is permissible, after fair assessment of the evidence, to disclose the identity of that program.

The National Association for the Education of Young Children Statement of Commitment*

As an individual who works with young children, I commit myself to furthering the values of early childhood education as they are reflected in the NAEYC Code of Ethical Conduct. To the best of my ability I will:

▸ *Ensure that programs for young children are based on current knowledge of child development and early childhood education.*

▸ *Respect and support families in their task of nurturing children.*

▸ *Respect colleagues in early childhood education and support them in maintaining the NAEYC Code of Ethical Conduct.*

▸ *Serve as an advocate for children, their families, and their teachers in community and society.*

▸ *Maintain high standards of professional conduct.*

▸ *Recognize how personal values, opinions, and biases can affect professional judgment.*

▸ *Be open to new ideas and be willing to learn from the suggestions of others.*

▸ *Continue to learn, grow, and contribute as a professional.*

▸ *Honor the ideals and principles of the NAEYC Code of Ethical Conduct.*

---

*The Statement of Commitment expresses those basic personal commitments that individuals must make in order to align themselves with the profession's responsibilities as set forth in the NAEYC Code of Ethical Conduct.

Appendix  B

Sample Greeting Letters and Surveys to Children and Their Families

Sample Introductory Letters to Children and Their Families

The following letters were composed by small groups of students in early childhood education classes at Bemidji State University. Many of the groups included experienced teachers. In a few cases the author combined wording from more than one letter. Readers may prefer some letters over others; the samples are intended to provide "starter ideas" for preparing introductory correspondence with families. Some letters were keyed into computers and included computer drawings, such as animals, to give them a friendly appearance. Stickers could also be used for this purpose.

To personalize the letters, the name "Shawn" is used for the child. The name given to the teacher is "Ann Gilbert." The university students recommend that the teacher locate and use the actual name of the parent or caregiver, rather than generic terms like, "Dear Parent(s)," or "To the Parent(s) of_____." In the samples the name of a single parent, "Ms. Reno," appears. The school name, "Central," is used, though the program might be a prekindergarten center as well.

The sample letters are in four types:

1. Greeting letters to children

2. Greeting letters to families

3. Survey letters to help the teacher learn about the child and family

4. Survey letters to obtain information about how parents might be involved.

1. Greeting Letters to Children

These letters are sent together with letters to parents. Usually the correspondence would be mailed a week or two before the start of the program year. A day care program may modify the greeting to send as soon as a child begins attending.

Dear Shawn,

Welcome to our kindergarten class. I am excited about this year and have a lot of fun learning activities planned. I look forward to having you in our classroom and am sure we will have a successful year together.

Your teacher,

Ann Gilbert

(Froggy computer drawing)

Dear Shawn,

Hello, my name is Ann Gilbert. I will be your teacher this fall. I am very pleased to have you in our classroom. We will be doing many fun things this year. On the first day of school, we are going to start talking about elephants. When you come to school the first day, I will have a picture of an elephant on my door so you know where to go. Be sure to let your family know they can visit our classroom any time. See you soon!

Your teacher and friend,

Ann Gilbert

(Elephant computer drawing with the words, "See you at School!")

Dear Shawn,

I was very happy to hear that you will be coming to my class this year. I know starting school can be a little scary, but you will be meeting new friends and doing many fun things.

Your mother told me she would like to come to our class with you. That is just great. If you like, you are also welcome to bring your favorite toy to play with during playtime.

I am really looking forward to seeing you and your mother next week. This year is going to be great fun. I hope you are as excited to come to school as I am. A big welcome, Shawn.

Your teacher,

Ann Gilbert

2. Greeting Letters to Families

Greeting letters to families accompany the letters to children. They should let parents know they are welcome participants in their child's education. Often, the letters invite parents to "greeting meetings," "open house" class days, or introductory conferences—at home or school. Not all parents have an easy time with reading, and teachers need to be alert to this possibility. A transition meeting that includes last year's and this year's teachers or caregivers can often provide helpful information about the child and family. **[Note: In some situations, teachers may not feel comfortable giving out home telephone numbers. Some classrooms have answering machines (with a recorded "message of the day"—or week)—always "on" for parents to call; the teachers then return calls.]**

Dear Ms. Reno,

Welcome to the world of Central School! I am looking forward to having your child in our classroom this year. I am also very happy to welcome you into our classroom.

Room visits will be all of next week, and I would like to invite you to join us and learn about our "developmentally appropriate" classroom. Parents are always welcome in my class, and if next week is inconvenient, or there is anything you would like to talk with me about, my number at school is _____. At home, you can call me anytime before ten at _____.

Again, I am looking forward to working with you and your child throughout the school year.

Sincerely,

Ann Gilbert

Dear Ms. Reno,

Hi, I will be Shawn's teacher this year. I am pleased that Shawn is going to be in my class.

I would like to set up a time when we could meet sometime soon.

Whatever time is available for you, I'll be happy to set up a meeting. I could come to your home if that would be convenient. I would like to get to know the families before the school year starts. I will be getting in touch with you in the next few days to set up a meeting.

I look forward to getting acquainted with both you and Shawn.

Sincerely,

Ann Gilbert

Dear Ms. Reno,

Hello! It is the start of a new year and I'm excited about having Shawn in our classroom. This fall I have many activities planned, and I would like to invite you to come in and join us. Next week I am going to have two "greeting meetings" for parents to learn about our program. They will be in our classroom on Wednesday and Thursday evenings at 7 P.M. and won't go over an hour. Feel free to attend either evening.

At the meetings, we will discuss the activities and projects your child will be doing and also talk about things that you can do to help at home and perhaps at school. I believe that parents are very important in children's education and want parents to feel welcome in our class.

If you cannot make it to either meeting or if there is anything else you would like to talk about, my number at school is _____. At home, you can call me anytime before ten at _____.

Feel free to stop by whenever you have time to visit the classroom.

Thanks,

Ann Gilbert

3. Survey Letters to Help the Teacher Learn about the Child and Family

Survey letters of this type help the teacher to better understand and work with the child and the family. Teachers who use surveys need to be careful not to give the impression of "prying." Instead, they need to convey that the information requested is optional and will help the teacher get acquainted with the child. **[Teachers might wait until after they have met families before asking parents to complete surveys.]** Some teachers prefer not to mail these surveys out at all, but have them completed at orientation meetings or use them to structure the initial parent-teacher conference.

A request for health information is included in some of the letters. This information usually is collected more officially by the school, or program, but sometimes immediate information about health situations can be important.

Dear Shawn and Family,

My name is Ann Gilbert. I am looking forward to this year and what it will bring. I would like to tell you a little about myself. I graduated from Bemidji State University with an Elementary and Early Childhood degree. I have a family of my own, and I am looking forward to sharing things about them with you.

In order for me to get to know you better, will you and someone in your family complete this "open letter"? It will be used to say "hello" to me and your classmates.

If there is anything else you or your family would like to tell me, please feel free to write on the back. You can return it in the addressed envelope.

Your teacher,

Ann Gilbert

Dear Teachers and Friends,

The long official name I was given when I was born is _____. But my favorite name I like to be called is _____. I am _____years old. My birthday is _____.

When I grow up I want to be _____.

My favorite TV show, video, or book is _____.

Some things I like to do are _____.

My favorite food is _____. Something that makes me happy is _____.

Something that makes me sad is _____.

I am excited to see you on the first day of school.

Your Friend,

_____

(Please invite child to write name. Any way she or he wants to is fine.)

(COMPUTER PICTURE LOGO)

School to Home Family News

Issue Number One, September, 20___/20___

To the family of _____

This first issue of our class newsletter is a survey to help me get to know your child and the rest of your family better. It would be helpful if you fill out the information below and bring it to our first conference (already scheduled on _____). The survey is optional, but it will help me to work with your child and also with a lesson we will be doing on "Ourselves and Our Families." We will be talking about the survey at our conference.

The name your child would like to be called at school _____

Your child's age _____ Your child's birth date _____

The people in your family are:

Name _____ *Relation to child* _____

Name _____ *Relation to child* _____

Name _____ *Relation to child* _____

Name _____ *Relation to child* _____

(If others, write on back.)

Home phone _____ *Emergency phone* _____

Name and phone of emergency contact person _____

_____

Any allergies or health concerns you want me to know about _____

_____

_____

Your child's:

Favorite toy _____

Favorite TV show, Video or Book _____

Special Pet(s) _____

Favorite story _____

Favorite things to do/play _____

Names and ages of special friends _____

_____

Holidays your family does/does not celebrate _____

_____

_____

Please share any cultural or religious traditions that are important to your family

_____

_____

Please feel free to share anything else about your family that will help me to work with your child _____

_____

_____

_____

4. Surveys about Family Involvement

Surveys about parent involvement should also be done after the teacher has met the parent. Two ways to distribute the surveys are either at, or by mail after, the greeting meeting. One of the following flyers, "Suggestions for Parent Involvement," might be sent with this survey.

Dear Ms. Reno,

Family involvement is a special part of our program. Here is a menu of ways that parents can be involved, and they are all important. I invite you to participate in as many ways as you can.

I would be willing to:

Read a story to a small group _____ or the class _____

Make materials at home _____

Save materials at home _____

Share about my career with the class _____

Help with special occasions, parties, field trips _____

Share a talent or hobby _____

Share something of our family's cultural background _____

Help with small groups in centers/stations _____

Please comment on the choices you selected _____

_____

_____

Right now, I can help mainly at home _____

I can volunteer in the classroom. The time(s) best for me are _____

Please feel free to visit the class any time you can. You do not need to sign up in advance. I will help you find activities that you are comfortable with. My telephone number at school is _____.

Thank you,

Ann Gilbert

Dear Ms. Reno,

I enjoyed meeting you and Shawn at the Open House last Tuesday. I am happy to have Shawn in my class and am looking forward to an exciting year for all of us.

Children and parents alike really seem to benefit from working together in their children's education. There are many ways that parents and caregivers can be involved, and they are all important. I invite you to participate in any way you can.

Here are a few things that parents have done in the past. Please check any ways in which you would like to help:

_____Share or read a story

_____Help with small-group activities

_____Help with special events (field trips and so on)

_____Donate materials, such as buttons or milk cartons

_____Talk about my job

_____Bring snacks

_____Other: I can help by _____.

I can:

_____come in on a regular basis.

_____come in once in a while.

_____not come in due to my schedule, but can help in other ways.

_____not sure at this time.

Parents are always welcome to come into the classroom to visit or help out. Two great times to come in would be at either 10 A.M. or 2 P.M. when we have learning centers.

Please call me if you have any questions. My school telephone number is _____. Just return this letter in the enclosed envelope. I am looking forward to a fulfilling school year for all of us.

Sincerely,

Ann Gilbert

Appendix C

Sample Guidebook: The Education Program in Our Class

The following brochure was developed with input from undergraduate and graduate students in early childhood education at Bemidji State University. (The brochure needs to be condensed and simplified in order to be used effectively with many parents.)

The students and I invite you to modify the brochure, such as by simplifying it, to make it work for you.

Hi Marie's Family,

I am very happy that Marie will be in our class this year! You are the most important teacher in your child's life, and I am hoping that we can be true partners in your child's education. This guidebook tells you some important things about our program. It also gives you some ideas for activities you can do at home, ways you can help with your child's education. I hope you will find this information interesting and helpful.

You can reach me by phone at school at _____. Better times to call are_____. You can also call the following number, _____, to receive a recorded message of our "class doings," updated regularly. You can reach me by phone at home most nights between 7:30 and 9:30, at _____.* My e-mail address is_____.* The classroom answering machine is always "on" for you at _____. I always try to reply to e-mails and phone messages ASAP.

Your Teacher,

Chris Dorphenheimer

This GUIDEBOOK is for you, the families of our students this year. It has eight parts. Each section tells you about an important part of the program in our classroom. Each part ends with fun activities that you can do with your child at home.

---

*Many opportunities for teacher-family communication are important, but teachers need to decide their own comfort levels with providing home phone numbers and e-mail addresses.

A. Reading and Writing

Learning to read and write are "hot topics" these days. It is important to remember that "regular" reading and writing take time to learn. My job is to make reading and writing *intriguing*. This way the children will find the beginning skills they are learning fun and will want to keep learning these skills.

Daily, the children will do "early" writing so they see themselves as beginning writers. They will have a variety of experiences with books and the sounds and shapes of letters and words. Daily practice along with time is what our class provides, a whole year of time!

Your child will be learning about reading and writing in these ways:

- By having conversations and discussions every day. Learning to read and write is easier if children know and use lots of spoken words in their daily lives.

- By creating stories on paper through art and "early writing." (Writing that doesn't look real to us yet, but has meaning for the children.) Children's own stories have special meaning for them, and this motivates them to keep learning to read and write. They must use reading skills like comprehension and interpreting marks, letters, and words every time they write.

- By understanding letters have certain sounds and shapes that the children can learn and use. We won't "grill and drill" so that children become discouraged, but we will give them real practice with letter sounds every day.

- By reading books and being read to everyday. By having book experiences every day, children learn the wonder of books, a powerful motivation to learn to read. They also learn that books tell stories and contain specific words and letters that they can recognize. Books make children's lives richer.

Activities You Can Do at Home

1. Have frequent conversations with your child to help them practice their spoken language.

2. Encourage your child to explore books by having picture books in your home. (Our community has a library with many great children's books.)

3. Read books to your child and enjoy the books together—bed times are great for this. Keep a goal of reading to your child every day.

4. Encourage your child to put their own stories on paper with beginning writing and art. After they are done, ask if you can write their stories another way, because "not all adults can read children's writing." (If they say yes, write down what they say and read it back to them.)

5. Have a place reserved for your child where they can use paper and pencils, markers and crayons. Staple a few sheets of paper together so the children can be "arthurs" and create their own books.

6. Turn the television off on a regular basis and have the whole family read, write, or play games together. This tells the child that these activities—and not just watching TV—are important.

B. Hands-On Math Skills

Do you remember doing lots of work sheets in school? Did you like it, or were you bored? We now know that young children need to handle and sort real objects in order for their young brains to learn about numbers. In our class we use a hands-on approach. They will learn to count, but so much more! My job is to ask questions and guide your child's thinking so they will learn actual math skills, and actually enjoy doing it.

Your child will learn math skills in these ways:

▶ Your child will begin to think about numbers by grouping and comparing materials like buttons, plastic dinosaurs, animal sets, cubes, dominoes, blocks, and many other things.

▶ Using these hands-on materials every day, your child will be learning about sizes, patterns, and quantities, and, very important, that numerals stand for quantities. (Four means 4.)

▶ Even in their play, they will have math experiences. They will divide play dough, share dolls and trucks, and figure out what to do when there is one thing and two kids who want to use it. Children learn how to solve "real-life" number problems through play experiences, even when they help clean up or set the table.

▶ Your child will also learn math skills by combining mathematical thinking with literature, music, science, movement, and other subjects such as through the themes that we do.

Activities You Can Do at Home

1. Encourage your child to make collections, and to sort and group sets of objects (things like shells, pebbles, buttons, and small play figures).

2. Provide materials like Legos and other building materials. (I have some building materials available for one-week checkout.)

3. Do food preparation activities together. Talk about measurements, amounts, servings, and preparation times. (Preparing food together is a great learning experience.)

4. Have your child help set the table. Encourage them to think about how many plates, eating utensils, and so on are needed.

5. Count things and enjoy numbers together. Remember that an understanding of numbers takes time, so correct very gently (or just enjoy) number mistakes. ("Uncle, you must be one hundred-deleven years old!") They will learn the real number concepts soon enough!

C. Our Science Program

In our classroom, we encourage children to explore and make discoveries about the world around them. Science for young children cannot be taught without touching, tasting, smelling, listening, and observing.

Your child will be learning these science skills in our classroom:

- Sense awareness—learning what the senses are and how they work separately and together.
- Experimentation—seeing what happens when things are mixed, moved, or changed in certain ways.
- Problem solving—figuring out solutions by using the senses and others' ideas to get results.
- Do research—using beginning reading and writing skills to get new information (like finding a bug outside and looking its picture up in a book).
- Use "science" language—hearing and using new words like *ingredients, scent, mixing*, and temperature.
- Cooperation—working with others to explore, discover, and learn together.

Activities You Can Do at Home

1. Model and teach how to recycle things and care for the Earth.
2. Enjoy together the outdoors, the seasons, and local plants and animals.
3. Do gardening and outdoor tasks together.
4. Do cooking and food preparation activities with your child.
5. Read books about nature and people in their natural surroundings.
6. Encourage your child to keep a journal about pets and things you observe.

D. Social Studies: Learning to Get Along

Because children have a natural interest in people and the world, social studies is important. We will use what we teach and how we teach to reinforce social skills that they will use throughout their lives—how to get along in groups and to be an individual in a democracy.

Your child will be learning these social studies ideas and skills:

- How to get along with others who may have different feelings and ideas.
- How to cope with problems in their classroom lives.
- How to work together as a classroom community.
- That each child's family is important to that child.
- That each person is a citizen of a community, state, country, and the world.
- That people have cultural differences and belong to the same human family.
- That people need to be civil with each other whatever the differences in ideas and human qualities.

Activities You Can Do at Home

1. Do activities and play games together.
2. Acquaint children with the life stories of members of your extended family.
3. Talk with your children about our community, state, nation, and the world.
4. Help your children understand human differences when they ask about them.
5. Read books about children from different cultures and countries.
6. Take trips with your children to see and do things together—within or outside of your neighborhood.

E. Creative Arts Activities

Your child expresses what they are learning through the creative arts. We provide many different ways that your child can express their developing thoughts and feelings: *visual arts* using markers, paints, crayons, scissors and glue, and sculpture; *music and dancing* using voices, instruments, and different ways to move to music; *dramatic play* with make believe figures and materials and other children; *creative drama* with puppets, other children, and the teacher.

Because our children are young, we help them feel comfortable expressing themselves rather than evaluate their products and performances. Our hope is that children enjoy expressing themselves through the arts and appreciate others' expressions.

Your child will learn the following through the creative arts:

- That they can express their thoughts and feelings through art, music, dance, and drama and not have to worry about finished products and performances.
- That they can learn to control their large muscles through dance and drama and their small muscles through drawing, painting, cutting, constructing, and early writing.
- That they are supported in their creative expression.

Activities You Can Do at Home

1. Limit TV viewing and provide creative activities on a regular basis.

2. Provide activities that include such materials as markers, crayons, paints, play dough, and lots of blank paper—not coloring books, which discourage young children's artistic thought and expression.

3. Date and save samples of your child's creations and watch for development over time.

4. Sing with your child and provide daily music experiences. (Music helps children's brain development.)

5. Provide materials for dramatic play such as dolls, miniature figures, hand puppets, cars and trucks, capes, adult clothes, and dramatic-play spaces (such as blankets over tables).

6. Encourage your child to participate in the arts without worrying about the final product.

7. Enjoy your child through what they are creating.

F. Play, an Important Part of Our Program

Without the opportunity for physical activity, the education program quickly becomes stressful for most children. When they play, your child is practicing language, social abilities, thinking, and large muscle and small muscle skills, in rich and varied ways. Studies show that children who play well in the early years learn better as they get older. Through play children learn about life and themselves in ways that cannot be taught.

This is what your child will learn through play:

▶ Social and emotional skills through experiencing other children's ideas and managing one's own feelings.

▶ Language skills through discussing things with others.

▶ Confidence to try new experiences, and self-esteem from succeeding and overcoming frustrations.

▶ Thinking skills by solving "real-life" problems such as how to share materials.

▶ Knowledge provided by real-life experiences.

▶ Physical abilities and "body confidence" from total involvement in physical activities. (Fun, vigorous activity is a part of our everyday program.)

▶ Emotional release by being able to express and act out tensions and strong feelings.

Activities You Can Do at Home

1. Provide daily opportunities for physical activity that are fun for you as well as your child—such as playing catch, going for a walk, dancing, and "jazzercising."

2. Decide as a family to have regular playtimes (like playing games) when the television and video games are turned off.

3. Until your child is older, steer away from overly organized and competitive physical activities. If your young child doesn't naturally enjoy it, help your child find another activity that is enjoyable.

4. Encourage vigorous activity for your child, and the whole family. Being fit and active is an important health need for all of us nowadays.

G. Health Education

We teach physical health by following daily hygiene practices, providing happy nutrition experiences, learning about personal safety, and having an active class-room. If young children learn positive health practices now, they will be better able to make smart decisions about their bodies, their safety, and their overall health as they get older.

Your child will learn about personal health by doing these activities:

▶ Through cooking and food preparation, your child will learn healthy nutrition practices and good food choices. They will understand the differences between everyday foods and "special time" treats for meals and snacks.

▶ Through daily practice at washing hands, brushing teeth, using facial tissues, and coughing into sleeves, your child will be reinforced in important personal health habits.

▶ Through lessons about street safety, poison safety, fire safety, and good touch–bad touch safety, your child will be gaining a foundation for making decisions to prevent emergencies and how to react in them.

▶ Through the modeling of healthy physical activity as an integrated part of the day, children will be learning that the development of their minds and bodies are both important.

Activities You Can Do at Home

1. Teach and model personal health practices such as washing hands, taking baths, and brushing teeth.

2. Teach and model healthy nutritional decisions by teaching the difference between "everyday foods" and "special times" foods.

3. Teach and model safety practices at home, in the car, and in public places.

4. Teach and model healthy and fun physical activity (and agree to schedules for "sit-down time" in front of television and computer games).

Parting Wish

It used to be people thought that parents did their job and teachers did their job, and "never the twain should meet." We now know that children learn best when teachers and parents work together. My goal is to be a partner as we work together to help your child have a great learning year. Please feel free to talk with me in person—or by phone, note, or e-mail—about your child whenever you have a concern or question. Remember, you are always welcome to visit or volunteer in our class. We can always use you to read to children, talk with them while they do activities, and help give them "quality time," so important for enriching their young lives.

With Best Wishes for Our Year Together,
Chris Dorphenheimer.

Appendix D

Developmentally Appropriate Guidance of Young Children

Expanded Fifth Edition

A Position Statement of the Minnesota Association for the Education of Young Children

This position statement of the Minnesota Association for the Education of Young Children is the fifth edition of a document first published in 1989. Its intent remains the same: to give direction to the use of developmentally appropriate guidance with young children ages birth to eight. The fifth edition is expanded to include the essential element of family-teacher partnerships in the use of guidance and additional information on guidance intervention techniques for when young children experience conflicts.

The importance of guidance techniques that are based on sound child development principles has been well established, made even more so by events of violence in our schools and society since the initial edition. Now in the 21st Century, our ability to guide children's development in ways that result in what Piaget called "autonomy" (the ability to make decisions intelligently and ethically) has become a paramount education priority. By responding to classroom conflicts in ways that teach rather than punish and include all in the group, rather than exclude some from the group, teachers of young children are contributing to a more peaceful world.

Three Considerations

This document is intended for use by administrators, teachers, and all other caregivers of young children. *A first consideration* for readers is that the DAG Guidebook is written for use in all early childhood settings and not just classroom-oriented preschools. MnAEYC has attempted to make language adapt to the diversity of early childhood settings. But readers will note a compromise or two that we are asking you to make. Perhaps most noteworthy, we use the term "teacher" to refer to any provider, caregiver, classroom assistant or teacher who works with young children. We accept the notion that "to a child anyone bigger than they are is a teacher," but we also maintain that there are "more better teachers" and "less better teachers." The Guidebook is about helping all teachers become the first kind.

A second consideration is that the Guidebook is a bit more oriented to working with older toddlers and up, rather than infants and younger toddlers. The principles of DAG certainly hold for *all* age groups. The methods in the Guidebook, though, clearly have an interactive verbal component. With infants and toddlers, teachers will be adapting the interactive nature of the approach to the more *receptive* language activity of very little ones in their first few months.

This is not to say that DAG is entirely or even mostly verbal. The approach absolutely depends on hugs, laps, and friendly touches. To this end, MnAEYC gives first acknowledgment to its Recommended Readings by referring to the article and text on "Essential Touch" by Frances M. Carlson (2002 & 2006).

The teaching/learning process that results in growing individuals being able to put strong emotions into non-hurting words begins in infancy and never ends. That process is dependent on friendly (though sometimes firm) words and ever-friendly touches.

A third consideration is the special attention that teachers need to give to guidance with the boys in their programs. In a landmark 2005 study in our Recommended Readings (Gilliam, 2005), young boys were nearly five times more likely than girls to be expelled from preschool programs, and preschool expulsion rates general were alarmingly high. The fact is that it is easier for many preschool teachers to have programs that are developmentally appropriate for the more quiet children (mostly girls) than the more active children (mostly boys). Mounting research indicates the importance of active programming for all young children, and MnAEYC now makes its second and third suggestions for Recommended Readings: The Guidance Matters Columns from *Young Children*, "Boys and Men Teachers," and "Promote Physical Activity/It's Proactive Guidance." The need to be responsive to the needs of the active boys in our programs underpins the discussion of DAG.

In this Guidebook, **guidance** is defined as an approach to children's development in which conflicts are viewed as teaching and learning opportunities; the adult helps children learn from their mistakes, rather than punishing them for the mistakes they make, assists children in learning to solve their problems, rather than punishing them for having problems they cannot solve.

Teachers who use guidance are sometimes firm but always friendly, protecting self-concept and respecting feelings so that children do not come to label themselves as behavioral failures. MnAEYC holds that teachers of young children should use guidance, which is educational in tone and responsive to the child's level of development, rather than traditional discipline, which too often lapses into punishment. The definition and discussion of *Ten Principles for Developmentally Appropriate Guidance* follows. We hope readers find this Guidebook helpful in their journeys to be guidance professionals.

Summary of Principles for Developmentally Appropriate Guidance

Principle One: Democratic Life Skills

The teacher uses guidance in order to teach children *democratic life skills.* Democratic life skills are the goals of guidance.

Principle Two: Partnerships with Families

The teacher builds relationships with families as a vital link that impacts the success of *developmentally appropriate guidance.*

Principle Three: An Encouraging Classroom

The teacher builds and maintains *an encouraging classroom* in which all children feel welcome as fully participating members.

Principle Four: Developmentally Appropriate Practice

The teacher implements *developmentally appropriate practice* for each child in the group to prevent classroom-caused mistaken behavior.

Principle Five: Conflicts as Mistaken Behavior

The teacher regards classroom conflicts not as misbehavior but as mistaken behavior and uses conflicts as teaching opportunities.

Principle Six: Seeks to Understand Children's Behavior

The teacher *seeks to understand* the reasons for children's behavior and focuses on the basic motivations for mistaken behavior.

Principle Seven: Crisis Management Techniques

The teacher uses *crisis management techniques* to calm children, restore an encouraging environment, and set the scene for using *guidance intervention techniques.*

Principle Eight: Guidance Intervention Techniques

The teacher relies on *guidance intervention techniques,* regularly using the "guidance three": guidance talks, mediation-to-negotiation, and class meetings.

Principle Nine: Comprehensive Guidance

When children show serious mistaken behavior over time, the teacher practices *comprehensive guidance*, which sometimes includes an Individual Guidance Plan, and is always carried out collaboratively with colleagues and families.

Principle Ten: Teacher as Professional

The teacher functions as a professional and learns even while s/he teaches.

Principle One: Democratic Life Skills

The teacher uses guidance in order to teach children democratic life skills. *Democratic life skills are the goals of guidance.* The usual purpose of traditional discipline has been to keep children "in line." When teachers make this purpose a priority, they tend to use discipline techniques that rely on "blame and shame" and slide into punishment. Embarrassment-based discipline—singling children out; scolding; flipping "green, yellow, red" cards; using time-outs—causes children to feel unwelcome in the group and unworthy as individuals. As a result of these punishments, children may begin to fall into a self-fulfilling prophecy and have more, not fewer, problems in the classroom.

The purpose of guidance is to teach the **democratic life skills** that children need to be healthy individuals and productive citizens. *Democratic life skills* include the ability to:

▶ see one's self as a worthy individual and a capable member of the group

▶ express strong emotions in non-hurting ways

▶ solve problems ethically and intelligently

▶ be understanding of the feelings and viewpoints of others

▶ work cooperatively in groups, with acceptance of the human differences among members.

Democratic life skills are the goals of guidance. As a number of our Recommended Readings indicate helping children progress in learning these skills during the early years improves their chances of success in school and life. The attainment of democratic life skills, perhaps more than scores on standardized tests and other measures of academic achievement, may keep our society strong, just, and free.

Example

Two four-year-olds first argued then hit and kicked at each other over sharing new miniature family figures. The teacher did not take the figures away and give them a time out for fighting. The teacher did separate the children to cool them down and bring them together to resolve the conflict. With the teacher's mediation, the children each said their side of the story. She then asked them "how can we solve this problem?"

To her surprise, one suggested and the other agreed that the first child would have his two adult figures run "the store." The other child would bring in the rest of the family "and buy lots of food and stuff." (This was not the solution the teacher anticipated, but the children decided it so she went along.) At the end of the mediation the children agreed that when they have a conflict, they can use words and perhaps seek the teacher's help, rather than fight to solve the problem.

With developmentally appropriate guidance when children have conflicts, there *are* consequences: The consequence for the teacher is to teach and re-teach democratic life skills. The consequence for the child, made clear by the teacher, is to continue learning the skills. The teacher's *mediation* saved the children from frustration at not being able to solve their problem and embarrassment by a teacher for their failure. Instead, the mediation is teaching the children that they can learn to resolve their problems and that the adult is there to help. Children are only months old. (A four-year-old has only 48–60 months of total life experience.) They are just beginning to learn to get along with others. The teacher's job is to help.

Principle Two: Partnerships with Families

The teacher builds relationships with families as a vital link that impacts success of developmentally appropriate guidance. Five authors listed in the Recommended Readings—Ostrosky & Jung (2003), Pappano (2007), Peterson (2002), and Gartrell (2004)—are in agreement about an accepted research finding over many years. When teachers and families partner in the education of young children, the children become their shared trust and do better. The importance of building early teacher–family member partnerships becomes clear with a "big duh" rhetorical question: You, the teacher, are outside with your group on a "January thaw" warm day. A child slips on ice and breaks an arm. Would you rather have your first meaningful contact with the child's family on this day, or during the start-up week for your class?

The analogy applies to a pattern of severe conflicts that a child may begin to show in your class, say in October. Building relationships with families right from the beginning of their enrollment helps to establish trust-based communication for when safety or behavior issues come up later. With a relationship established, the teacher finds it easier to work through problems on a cooperative basis.

Notice that we interchange the word *family member* with *parent* as a reminder of the complexity in today's family structures. Please also notice that when we use these terms, we really mean the more cumbersome term "parent or custodial adult." Our suggestion is that teachers need to rethink "Donuts for Dads" and "Muffins for Moms" type events to fully respond to the diversity family structures that may be present in the class.

In tying together parent-family partnerships with developmentally appropriate guidance, we now look at two key ideas: 1. Techniques for building partnerships and orienting families to your program; and 2. Reaching hard to reach families.

1. Techniques for building partnerships. When the teacher can establish communication with families right at start-up, s/he can be proactive in many ways. Here are several communication-suggestions based on the input of veteran early childhood teachers. Please note that some apply in some situations, others in other situations:

▶ If families are new to the program, when possible, invite children and family members (preferably in small groups) to visit the program. If possible, arrange for them to arrive and leave by the transportation system the child will use. If families are already in the program and the child is moving to a new classroom, again, if possible, invite the child and family to visit beforehand. Establish contact information with family members around the visits. Determine phone accessibility, home language spoken, etc.

▶ Before children start, or upon startup, send home separate introductory notes to the families and children. Acknowledge visits if they made them. Be sure to say how pleased you are that their child is going to be in your class. Computer process the letters so you can input each child's name and perhaps include a digital photo or two—like of you and your pet.

▶ When possible, a day before the child starts in your class call families and discuss concerns that the child and family might have. Using your judgment, perhaps also speak to the child. If the family speaks a language you don't, try to have a translator with you when you call.

▶ Call each family on the first night. A veteran teacher once told the primary author, "Frankly, Dan, I'd rather drink a beverage and get to bed early, but this is the best investment in parent-family partnerships I make all year.

▶ Hold greeting meetings for families during the first week--offer a choice of late afternoon and evening times to get maximum attendance. Introduce (or re-introduce) families to the room; go over a guidebook that explains the program, routines, procedures (including guidance procedures), and opportunities for family-involvement.

▶ At the meetings go over several ways family members can be involved. Perhaps present opportunities in a continuum from passive recipient, to active with child at home, to special events volunteer, to regular volunteer, to advisory/policy committee participation. Say any level is wonderful, but you hope each family will be as involved as they can. Explain why. Be encouraging and inviting relative to family involvement in your classroom program.

▶ Introduce at the meeting and send home friendly survey letters, so you can better work with each family's child. Include items like a choice of ways parents can begin to volunteer; books and/or activities the child and family enjoy; holidays the family does or does not celebrate. Make sure the family members know only to complete items they are comfortable with.

▶ Send home *happy grams to families,* at least two in the first week so, Compliment interests, activities, and behaviors that the child is showing. Perhaps read the note to the child at the end of the day—this will ensure a high delivery rate!

▶ Hold an early "get better acquainted" conference with each family in a location they are comfortable with—home, local fast food restaurant, park, the classroom. Really listen, and show you are listening, to information the family gives you. Keep the conferences positive. Think in terms of "compliment sandwiches." Start and end every conference with complimentary comments.

▶ Establish and consistently use family-friendly communication systems. There is no substitute for regular "happy grams." If families have access to technology, emails, websites, and blogs may prove popular. Be aware, though, of the *digital divide* and don't exclude families who may not have access to computers and online connections. Hardcopy versions of newsletters (which digital photographs of children can really spice up) and recorded phone messages that parents can access for program updates are two ways to stay in touch. Depending on your program's policy, consider giving families your phone number(s), with clear times for when parents can call. Keep the happy grams going home—on a schedule you can live with.

▶ Welcome volunteers to your setting. Leave what you are doing and privately greet family members. Have a small *parent corner* where parents can stow belongings. Help first-timers find activities they are comfortable with. Always thank the volunteer and have the class say goodbye. A nice touch is to have the class make "story picture" thank-you notes. Remember, "Today's first timer may become tomorrow's regular," and their own child, the class, and you, the teacher, will benefit.

2. Reaching hard to reach families. A challenge for teachers is families that do not respond to contact efforts. When this happens, teachers need to avoid making assumptions and in a friendly way try to find out why. One possible reason is work schedules—in these times parents may be working more than one job. Another is that maybe the parent had an unfortunate experience when they were in school. The thought of talking to any teacher may be "challenging" for them. A third possibility is that maybe life is a bit overwhelming for the family right now—for job, housing, transportation, food, and/or mental health reasons.

This illustration shows a helpful teacher response in such a situation.

Example

Maria, a new preschool teacher had tried the entire list above to try to get to know Raymond's family. No reply to notes home; no answers to phone calls or returns of phone voice-messages; no attendance at either greeting meeting; no show at the get-acquainted conferences. Maria commented to her colleagues that she had run out of ideas and was fighting the notion that the family didn't care. One colleague had worked with the family. She told Maria, "Didn't you know? Raymond's Mom is a single parent. She works as a cocktail waitress and has an afternoon/evening shift. Raymond and his siblings go home to Grandma's every day. Usually Mom just crashes there at night, rather than pick up the kids and take them home. She probably doesn't check her phone messages or mail that often. She is barely keeping her head above water."

With this new information, Maria got pro-active. She called Mom at the lounge. She got Mom to ask her boss' permission to meet with her in a booth on the Mom's break. The two hit it off. They met again. Within the month, Mom stopped by the classroom for a late morning visit to her son's class.

Parents educate children. Teachers only help. An experienced colleague once said, "A teacher needs to give 100% to build a 50-50 relationship with a parent, so the parent can become the 100% co-teacher that they need to be." (The teacher minored in math.) Another experienced teacher commented, "Working with parents is like visiting New York City. You have to be friendly first." The teacher develops relationships with families to reach the child. S/he also builds relationships with the child to reach the family. The teacher does so by having an *encouraging classroom*.

Principle Three: An Encouraging Classroom

The teacher builds and maintains an encouraging classroom *in which all children and families feel welcome as fully participating members.* As suggested in the principle statement above, the teacher builds an encouraging classroom by ensuring that all children and their families feel affirmed and supported in the *classroom community*. Informally defined, an encouraging classroom is a place where children want to be when they are sick as opposed to not wanting to be there when they are well. Trust and acceptance are the foundation of the relationship between an adult and a child. In the encouraging classroom, the teacher is able to build this relationship with every child, even those children who experience frequent conflicts that teachers may find "challenging." Except in rare circumstances, which always involve the family, colleagues, and often other professionals, the child's status as a member of an encouraging classroom is not up for debate.

In the encouraging classroom, the teacher does not need to love each child—teachers are human and not angelic. But as a professional, the teacher does need to build a working relationship of trust and acceptance with each child. The reason is that children who understand that they are valued and belong tend to develop positive self-concepts and have less need to act out against the world.

With all children in the encouraging classroom, the teacher's goal is the same: to assist in making progress toward democratic life skills. Some children just need more time and extra help to learn the skills, because they face difficult biological and/or environmental life circumstances, and their road is longer.

Three practices mark the encouraging classroom:

First, the teacher creates a climate in which every child feels they are a welcome member of the group, and positive group spirit abounds. In this effort, the teacher does not single out children for either praise or criticism. S/he acknowledges individuals privately; then they know the teacher's acknowledgement is really meant for them. S/he addresses public acknowledgement to the group as a whole. In both cases, the teacher understands that acknowledgement is often more needed by learners as encouragement during the learning process than as praise given after the task is completed.

Example

(In a summer prek/k group)

The children were making story pictures of thanks to send to the rescue workers after the Minneapolis bridge collapsed. I was really impressed with their efforts and said, "I like how you are all working so hard on your story pictures. Your work shows such thought about all the rescuers did." After I made this comment, I noticed several children smiling as they worked. Some even complimented their neighbors' pictures.

One child had made a very detailed picture and was printing "Thk u fr hlp." She said, "But I don't think they could read it." I knelt down and put my arm around her shoulder. I told her I could read it, and did. She said "Yeah, maybe they could" and (with a smile) wrote more invented-spelling words that I also read back to her.

Second, the teacher works with other adults, both teaching team members and parents, to form partnerships that anchor the encouraging classroom. To children, anyone bigger than they are is a teacher. "Official" teachers in encouraging classrooms work hard right from the beginning of the year to build partnerships with children and other adults. With parents, the teacher might send notes home, make phone calls, do home visits, set up E-mail systems (minding the "technology divide"). The teacher takes the lead to let parents know what is happening and that their involvement and input are important.

Orienting all staff (and regular volunteers) to guidance ideas through meetings, workshops, and booklets (like this one) is important. Staff together might make a handout of their own guidance ideas and use this as a basis of discussion with parents. Children who see significant adults in their lives modeling democratic life skills with each other will understand more fully that these skills are important to learn.

Family child care providers, of course, often don't have these same staffing possibilities. Close relations with parents are then even more vital. "Telephone colleagues" with other providers also are important. Just remember during work hours to keep calls "profession-related" (though a certain amount of venting is sometimes important for mental health) ☺.

Third, the teacher follows **Principle Four**.

Principle Four: Developmentally Appropriate Practice

The teacher implements developmentally appropriate practice *for each child in the group to prevent classroom-caused mistaken behavior.* Many conflicts children do not cause as much as fall into. "Classroom-caused" mistaken behavior is sometimes the result of pressures teachers feel to "get children ready for the next level." (Examples are an over-reliance on teacher-directed large groups and an over-emphasis on successful completion of skill-based assignments.) We all have a right to expect *educational accountability*—that children learn productively given their age, development, and experience. When children can *engage* fully in *active* learning experiences, activities involving literacy and numeracy concepts often prove successful. But at the same time it is important to note the words of a veteran kindergarten teacher: "My job is not to prepare children for first grade. It is to give them the best possible kindergarten experience they can have." This, of course, is the main idea behind NAEYC's Developmentally Appropriate Practice for Children in Early Childhood Programs (New edition, 2009—See Recommended Readings).

In the interest of genuine educational accountability teachers monitor and modify practices in their classrooms that unintentionally cause mistaken behavior:

▶ Group activities that require too much sitting and listening.

▶ Required projects and lessons that have prescribed results too easy for some and too difficult for others.

▶ Schedules that fail to provide physical activity, balanced routines and efficient transitions

▶ Competitive expectations and evaluation techniques that make some children feel like "winners" and some like "losers."

Young children "are wired" for active, personally relevant learning experiences that fully engage their minds and their bodies. Because of slower overall development and their particular genetic make-up, many young boys in particular need physically active classrooms, with a minimum of traditional seatwork. When teachers recognize that young children will be more able to perform the tasks of traditional classrooms when they older—and benefit from active programming rather than from "rehearsal"—they understand the true connection of developmentally appropriate practice and the encouraging classroom.

Example

In a prekindergarten class of 18 children (14 boys) the teachers had centers set up around the edges of the classroom for reading, "house" and blocks and trucks. Lead teacher, Ted Gonzales, felt pressured to have a lengthy large group, including a "phonics focus," right away in the morning "while the children were fresh." Gradually, he noted boredom, restlessness, and frustration among many children, especially some boys, with this arrangement. Moreover, he noted that the centers seemed too crowded, and some boys used the large open center area of the room as a raceway (with and without cars and trucks).

After attending a workshop on active learning, Ted's teaching team added centers for writing, art, music, science, construction, and technology. They also added a "physical fitness center" (with mini-tramp) where children could channel their classroom energy.

They spaced the centers around the room to eliminate runways, and clustered them by estimated activity/noise levels. Ted shortened the large group and phonics drills, making group-time more active with music and dance. In small groups the children planned the centers they intended to use and recorded in journals (with early writing and art) what they did.

The teaching team still worked on academic skills—just integrated them more into learning centers and themes. Ted realized what many experienced teachers do: that developmentally appropriate programming must include active boys too. In making his classroom developmentally appropriate for every child, the children were happier, and conflicts became fewer and more manageable.

Principle Five: Conflicts as Mistaken Behavior

The teacher regards classroom conflicts not as misbehavior but as mistaken behavior *and uses conflicts as teaching opportunities.* Democratic life skills are a life-long endeavor. Some adults never learn them and most of us have to work hard to use them consistently. Children, with only months of life experience and brain development, are just beginning to learn these complex skills. In the process of learning, they (like all of us) make mistakes. For this reason, a teacher who uses guidance views children's conflicts not as misbehavior, but as **mistaken behavior.** This shift enables the adult to think about what s/he can teach children as a result of the conflict, not what s/he has to "do to" the children for having it. The shift in attitude empowers the adult to be a guidance leader rather than "rule enforcer."

Let's face it. When a large number of small bodies are in a relatively small space with a small number of large bodies, there are going to be conflicts. Conflicts are expressed disagreements between individuals—between and among children and occasionally between a child and a teacher. Through use of the principles in this Guidebook, teachers works to prevent some conflicts and de-escalate and resolve others. A challenge to guidance professionals is to teach short-term and long-term conflict management skills whenever they intervene. A first step is to observe situations as closely as possible before getting involved.

Example A: Conflict of a child with a teacher

Sammie knew that Marsha was in for a hard week. It was the first day back after vacation and Marsha's dad had been deployed to Afghanistan. A new classroom volunteer began scolding Marsha when the girl became upset about having to put some books away. Marsha "lost it." Sammie saw what happened, got down on the floor next to Marsha and said softly, "It's okay to be upset, Marsha, I will help you get calm." Marsha yelled, "I hate you," lay down on the floor, and sobbed.

Sammie gently moved Marsha to her lap and held the child, whispering "It's okay to be sad. It's okay." Gradually, Marsha calmed down. After a while the two read a book together. While they read Sammie talked with Marsha about what she could do when she felt sad and perhaps what she could say to the volunteer "to help her feel better." The teacher later explained the situation to the volunteer.

Example B: Conflict among children

Damon, aged 23 months, didn't make it back from outdoor play in time and wet his pants. Charissa, aged four, saw this and with Bradley began calling Damon "piss pants Damon." Even though she was helping all in from outside, Miss Edie saw enough to know what had happened. While the children were coming in and finding things to do, the provider got Damon dry cloths. She then had a private guidance talk with Charissa and Bradley. She told them she once wet her pants at school and asked them if they had ever had an accident and wet their pants. Charissa said she did once. Bradley said he didn't but his little brother did.

The teacher got the children to say how Damon probably felt and then asked them to think of some ways they could help Damon feel better. Later in the day, the teacher smiled when she saw Charissa talking with Damon. She smiled again when she saw Damon and Bradley playing together.

We all make mistakes. We just need to learn from them. Notice in these examples of *guidance talks*, the teacher did not force the children to say they were sorry. She talked them through what happened and how the other person probably felt. She asked them to think of a way to make amends to the other person. When children are helped to get beyond their mistaken behavior, they want to make things better—but (with the adult's help) they have to do it in their own way.

Principle Six: Seeks to Understand Children's Behavior

The teacher seeks to understand the reasons for children's behavior and focuses on the basic motivations for mistaken behavior. There are always reasons for children's behavior. Working to understand these reasons assists the adult in helping the child. Although we can never know another person fully, we can increase our understanding and that effort in itself can lead to a better relationship and progress in learning democratic life skills. The teacher understands these basic motivations for mistaken behavior.

1. Children do things to see what will happen. Children learn from their actions, and others' reactions. Sometimes "experimentation mistaken behavior," if harmless, should be ignored. If the adult decides to intervene, s/he should do so in a way that teaches the child about consequences and alternatives, but also appreciates the child's vital need to learn. When the two children fought over the miniature figures in an earlier example, that was experimentation mistaken behavior—an experiment that "got out of control." The following is an illustration of "more controlled" experimentation mistaken behavior:

Example

> *With a grin a child is using a marker on a table. Teacher: "Maria, you forgot that we color on paper. Let's get some soapy water and wash the table. Then we'll get some cool paper to use with those markers." The two clean the marker off together. Child chooses some "cool" colored paper cut in various shapes to make pictures.*

2. Children do things because they have been influenced by others to do them, either at home or in the classroom. This "socially influenced" mistaken behavior is learned behavior. The adult firmly but matter-of-factly reinforces a limit, but also teaches an acceptable alternative for next time. When Charissa and Bradley influenced each other to tease Damon, that was socially influenced mistaken behavior. Another example is when teasing, or a similar mistaken behavior, "gets catchy" and "goes public":

Example

> *Toward the end of a long childcare day, a teacher noticed first two boys and then three teasing another child and excluding him. Other children saw the teasing. The next morning she and her assistant held a class meeting that started with a puppet play. After "act one," the children discussed how the frog puppet felt when the two bear puppets wouldn't let the frog play with them. The teachers then did act two with the happy ending suggested by the class. The group discussed the need to be friendly with all our "mates," and the importance of everyone being able to join in play. The teachers monitored for the next few days, intervening if the socially influenced mistaken behavior occurred, to re-teach the "inclusive" guideline.*

Sometimes mistaken behavior is influenced by significant persons outside the classroom. A child with older brothers who is "always" starting rough and tumble play is one example. Here is another:

Example

> *Ryan says, "that damned kid makes me so mad." Teacher (hiding smile) responds: "Peter made you feel upset, and you can tell him that or tell me. But in our classroom we don't need to call names.*

3. Children show serious mistaken behavior (due to strong unmet needs) when they have trouble in their lives that is beyond their ability to understand and manage. Sometimes the trouble can be physical, such as an untreated disability, neurological condition, illness or injury. Other times, the trouble may be caused by a serious situation at home, center, school or in between.

When a child shows extreme mistaken behavior, the first action of the teacher is to improve the relationship with the child. Children whose behavior is "challenging" are often the hardest to like, but need a trust-based relationship with us the most.

The adult should also work to gain more information, especially if the behavior continues for more than a day or two. Observing and talking with the child can often add to an adult's understanding. Protecting privacy, talks with colleagues can be helpful. A phone call or conference with parents may well be essential to better understanding the problem. Occasionally, consulting with an outside professional can help.

When staff fully use their resources to understand what is going on, *comprehensive guidance* is easier to provide.

Example

A teacher notices that a child develops uncharacteristic irritability and shows angry outbursts especially toward the beginning and end of each week. The teacher takes actions to get to know the child better and learn what is going on. Talks with a parent determine that Mom and Dad have separated and the child is living with the mother during the week and the father on the weekends.

The staff works with the two parents to make the transitions more understandable and less traumatic for the child. They extend extra support to the child during this difficult time. When the child has outbursts, they work hard at being friendly even when they need to be firm, supporting the child's self-esteem and maintaining teacher-child trust.

Children with serious problems may act out in the classroom because it is the safest place in their lives. These children are asking for help, inappropriately perhaps, but in the only way they can. With such children MnAEYC cautions against the use of such labels as "challenging" or "difficult"—even if the terms happen to be in vogue. The problem with labels is that they can cause a teacher to become sensitized to only the challenging or difficult behaviors a child may show. S/he may miss productive behaviors and admirable qualities in the child, instead giving feedback that is distancing and negative. The child may feel stigmatized and disqualified from group membership, at a time when a sense of belonging is crucial for healthy development.

To assist children who show strong unmet needs mistaken behavior, the teacher relies on the guidance techniques outlined under Principles Seven through Nine.

Principle Seven: Crisis Management Techniques

The teacher uses crisis management techniques *to calm children, restore an encouraging environment, and set the scene for using* guidance intervention techniques. *Conflicts*—expressed disagreements between individuals—are a part of life. Young children, at an early point in brain development and experience, have frequent conflicts and often show them dramatically (☺). The challenge to the adult is to teach children to work through conflicts using words. It is difficult for anyone to negotiate when emotions are high. In a conflict, then, the first action is to check for physical harm, then calm down all parties (starting with one's self.) Only when all are calm can teaching and learning about the conflict happen.

A crisis management technique of first resort is **describe-express-direct**. *Before* children have lost control of their emotions, the teacher: *describes* what s/he sees; sometimes *expresses* feelings about the situation; and *directs* the children to an action that will help resolve the conflict. For example:

"I see goldfish and water on the floor." (*Describe*)

"I am concerned the goldfish will die." (*Express*—optional)

"You put cups of water in the bowl. I will scoop the fish back in. We will talk about this later." (*Direct*)

The *express* step is optional, because it "ups the emotional ante" of the conflict. Sometimes "expressing" your feelings is not necessary, as in the following example.

"You sound like two angry bears over here." (*Describe—using humor*).

"Can you solve this by yourselves or do you want my help?" (*Direct*)

Often the *direct* step involves giving an in-choice and an out-choice. The teacher hopes the child will select the in-choice but accepts the out-choice. If the out-choice involves a child finding something else to do, and the child decides to do this, the adult later may have a *guidance talk* with the child (when he is calm) to do some strategic teaching.

A crisis management technique of second resort is **calm everyone down**. Children, like adults, have to get their emotions in check before they can resolve a problem using words. The teacher does what teachers have long done to help children calm down: Acknowledge the child's feelings; Take deep breaths with the child; separate the child for *cool-down time*. Notice, *cool down time is not a time out*. Teachers need to self-monitor on this. It is a time-out if a teacher removes a child as a result of something the child has done. It is cool-down time if a teacher removes a child to regain composure so they can talk and resolve the conflict.

Acknowledgement of feelings is an essential calming technique, statements like: "I can see the tears on your cheek." "It is alright to be upset." "That hurt you and made you feel bad." "When he did that, how did it make you feel?" Nonverbal hugs or other gentle touches are key to acknowledgement. For the calming to work, hold off on interpreting, and especially blaming and judging. Acknowledge to calm first, use a *guidance talk* or *mediation later.*

A crisis management technique of last resort is **the passive bear hug**. Teachers use the passive bear hug only when a child has lost total control and is causing real harm to self or others. Policies should always be set and discussed before the bear hug is used. If possible, another adult should be present. A follow-up written report is customary. Talk with a family member is also important.

The *passive bear hug* is not physical punishment. It is arms wrapped around arms; legs around legs in order to prevent harm. The adult and child go into a sitting position with the child on the adult's lap, but held to one side or the other to prevent head butts. The adult may sing or talk softly or rock or just hold until the child calms down. The child will fight for a while, and then gradually realize that the adult is not there to hurt but to help the child regain lost limits. Surprisingly, often a bear hug ends with the child snuggling against the adult.

When the child is calm, the teacher helps the child back into an activity, such as reading a book together. Later the adult and child have a guidance talk. The purpose of crisis management techniques is always to calm everyone down in order to talk about what happened. Whenever teachers must use this most difficult of guidance interventions, they should think in terms of a need for *comprehensive guidance*.

Principle Eight: Guidance Intervention Techniques

The teacher relies on guidance intervention techniques, *regularly using the "guidance three": guidance talks, mediation-to-negotiation, and class meetings.* With developmentally appropriate guidance, any time teachers intervene in a conflict, they do so to teach what they perceive the child can learn at that point in time about social problem solving. The first step with any guidance intervention is to "de-escalate" the conflict and calm everyone down. If the teacher decides the focus of the conflict is an individual child, s/he uses a *guidance talk*. If the teacher decides the focus is two or a few children, s/he uses *conflict mediation*. If the teacher decides a conflict has "gone public" and many children are involved, s/he holds a *class meeting*.

Sometimes a teacher cannot follow-through with any of the "guidance three" at the moment the conflict happens. Calming everyone is the first, essential step. The teacher then uses *describe-express-direct* to explain which of the techniques will happen later.

Guidance talks. The teacher routinely uses a guidance talk when one child is at the center of a conflict, either with other children or with an adult. (Sometimes a teacher holds a guidance talk with two children who are on the same side of a conflict.) To avoid embarrassment, the teacher holds the guidance talk as privately as possible. The talk is a discussion, not a "lecture." The steps the teacher follows are the general steps of social problem solving. In guidance talks the steps are often followed informally.

1. Calm down and help the child calm down.

2. Come to agreement about how the child saw the situation.

3. Brainstorm on a cooperative basis what the child can do to make the situation better (resolve the conflict).

4. Help the child decide on a solution and carry it out. (Negotiate here; don't force—then it may be a "solution" for you, but not the child!)

5. Discuss with the child what s/he should do differently next time. If not addressed earlier, also discuss with the child how to help others involved in the conflict feel better. (Restitution restores harmony.)

A sample guidance talk is found under Principle Five. The teacher held an informal guidance talk with Charissa and Bradley who teased a child about having an accident. This guidance talk illustrates the flexibility possible in talks. The teacher indirectly moved the children to resolve the conflict by building their empathy for Damon. Heightened empathy might also keep the two from teasing in a similar situation in the future. Making amends was the solution.

Conflict Mediation. Under traditional discipline, if a teacher sees one child harm another, s/he "supports the victim and disciplines the perpetrator." The misguided idea here is that the comforted victim will feel better and the punished perpetrator will be "shamed into being good." We know instead that the "victim" is being made dependent on the authority of others for "protection" and the "perpetrator" is likely to internalize angry feelings and feel alienated from the group. This traditional reaction by the teacher may actually reinforce a bully-victim syndrome in the classroom, which is not what any teacher wants.

A primary reason for using conflict mediation is that it supports the right of a hurt child to be rightfully assertive, and it protects the status of a child who has hurt as a full and worthy member of the group. Teachers do not have to use conflict mediation perfectly to have it be successful. Teachers are often surprised by the success of their mediations—which they see when children go along with the solution agreed to, and even more so when the children soon play together as though no conflict has happened.

Beginning teachers do well to formally follow the steps of social problem solving listed above, perhaps even counting them off on their fingers. During the mediation, the teacher is the leader: friendly, but firm in getting the children to follow the process. A suggestion for successful conflict mediation includes five steps:

- *One:* As always calm everyone down first. Delay the mediation until all are calm.

- *Two:* Do not interpret the situation for the children. Remain impartial. Coach them to agree how each child views the conflict—not what happened as you saw it. Tell each child they will have a turn, and prevent disruptions. Rephrase what each child says and see if they agree.

- *Three:* When brainstorming solutions, encourage the children to come up with ideas themselves. With many older preschoolers, the teacher serves as a *facilitator*, with the children actively participating. With toddlers and younger preschoolers, and with children facing difficult circumstances, the teacher provides words and serves as a *friendly coach*.

- *Four:* Hold out until both children agree to a solution. (You may sometimes have to make suggestions.) Remember to ask each child if a solution will work for them.

- *Five:* Either as a part of Step Four or Step Five, tag on a brief guidance talk with one or both children, stressing what they could do differently next time. Monitor the solution as it is being tried, and offer reinforcement.

The process sounds complicated, but Dan Gartrell (principle author) reports that over the years almost all (close to a thousand) of his undergraduate students have had successful (not necessarily perfect) mediations on their first or second try. An example of conflict mediation can be found under Principle One, with the two children fighting over the miniature figures. Another more thorough example is listed in the Recommended Readings, the "Guidance Matters" column titled "Conflict Mediation." Providers who work with toddlers also use mediation—they just supply the words.

Class Meetings. Teachers hold class meetings, even with younger prekindergarten children, when conflicts in the class become public and affect many members. Instead of traditional punishment of the whole group, the teacher meets with the class to resolve the problem together. Guidelines for class meetings typically are that anyone can have a turn to speak; we listen carefully to each other; we tell the truth; we appreciate and respect each other.

Class meetings sustain encouraging classrooms by ensuring that every child has a say and is a worthy member of the group. Class meetings often blend with circle times, but usually are for the purpose of teaching and reinforcing classroom guidelines and routines. The frequency of class meetings varies with the teacher and the classroom situation. A suggestion from the recommended readings is twice a day in the morning and close to leaving time. Teachers can also call special class meetings to discuss serious events. One example of a class meeting was given under Principle Five around "teasing gone public." Another example follows:

Example

An early childhood class had to walk down the hall of a school to reach the gymnasium. A few teachers complained to the principal that the children were being too loud as they walked down the hall. The teacher held a class meeting to solve the problem. After the children discussed the problem, the teacher asked if anyone had ideas about how they could remember to walk down the hall quietly. One child said, "I know, we can be mommy and daddy elephants who have to tiptoe so we don't wake the babies." To the teacher's amazement, the other children liked the idea. As they walked down the hall the next day, the principal loudly complimented the class. "Ssh," said one of the children, "You'll wake the babies!"

Principle Nine: Comprehensive Guidance

When children show serious mistaken behavior over time, the teacher practices comprehensive guidance, which sometimes includes Individual Guidance Plans, and is always done collaboratively with colleagues and families. As discussed in Principle Six, there is no such thing as a bad child, just children with bad problems who don't know how to solve them. When teachers detect that children are showing serious mistaken behaviors on a continuing basis, they identify this pattern as due to strong unmet needs. Serious mistaken behavior requires **a comprehensive approach** that involves working together with other adults on behalf of the child. Comprehensive guidance includes some or all of these steps:

▷ *Use crisis management techniques to prevent harm or serious disruption.*
(Discussed under Principle Seven.)

▷ *Rely on the three basic guidance interventions to resolve the immediate problem and teach democratic life skills.*
(Discussed under Principle Eight.)

▷ *Improve relationships of adults in the classroom with the child.* Children who show frequent conflicts are sometimes difficult for teachers to like and understand. Yet, these children uniquely need a positive relationship with their teachers. In a guidance approach teachers practice *liberation teaching*: They never give up on any child. They figure out ways to build trust with the child so that when conflicts occur, the child knows the teacher will not punish, but help. This means finding regular opportunities for quality time with the child outside of conflict situations, beginning when the child first arrives.

▷ *Works to understand the child and the child's situation.* From the day each child joins the program, the teacher builds relationships with the family so that if conflicts happen, all have a relationship they can work from. In the event of a pattern of conflicts, the teacher observes and talks with the child; talks with fellow staff; and talks with the family. If necessary, the teacher holds a meeting with all concerned to discuss the child and develop an *Individual Guidance Plan*.

▷ *Implement the Individual Guidance Plan (IGP).* The IGP is a coordinated plan to use at school and home that involves parents and staff working together. The plan typically includes strategies for:

　▷ improving adult-child relationships

　▷ making the program less frustrating and more engaging for the child

　▷ teaching the child conflict prevention and coping strategies

　▷ implementing crisis management and guidance intervention techniques

　▷ referring for therapy with other professionals (when appropriate)

　▷ observing and reporting progress

　▷ reviewing and revising the plan.

(A user-friendly version of the IGP can be downloaded at Dan's efolio2 website at end of Recommended Readings.

Teachers report that a common result of IGPs is not the miraculous "cure" of strong needs mistaken behavior, but progress by the child in the management of the behavior. Moreover, there is also frequently progress on the part of the child and family in dealing with the underlying problems. Teachers report that for themselves a welcome gain is a restored sense of professional competence and lowered stress levels both in working with the child and the class. A thorough case study is listed under the Recommended Readings, the Guidance Matters Column titled "Comprehensive Guidance."

Too often, in the view of MnAEYC, programs seek to remove (expel) children who show serious mistaken behavior due to unmet strong needs. We believe commitment to the use of comprehensive guidance can decrease this potentially stigmatizing experience—for child, family, and even the program. Teachers must use their resources fully, however, to make comprehensive guidance work. Almost always, these efforts include collaboration with colleagues and cooperative leadership with the family. By working with others, teachers accomplish what they cannot on their own.

Principle Ten: Teacher as Professional

The teacher functions as a professional and learns even while s/he teaches. Teachers who react to conflicts in the traditional ways of disciplining in their classrooms, frequently slide into the use of punishment. Rather than seek to understand the mistaken behavior and teach alternatives to it, they enforce rules (often on the basis of first impressions) to keep children obedient to the teaching staff. Children who cannot adjust tend to be labeled and isolated from the group.

Teachers who act as professionals respond to behavior based on careful observations and their judgments of the events at the time. They seek to understand situations, not just react to them. They work to build encouraging classrooms in which all children are included. The intent of their interventions Is to teach democratic life skills.

The role of *teacher as profe*ssional takes time to learn. Sometimes even very professional teachers jump in too quickly, over-react, show inconsistency, lose their tempers, or otherwise show human frailties. Just as they encourage children to, teachers who are professionals learn from their own mistakes. They know that their job is challenging because young children are just at the beginning of a complicated, life-long learning process. The one task more difficult than learning democratic life skills is consistently modeling and teaching them.

When upset, teachers use methods to diffuse and express their feelings that do not put down the other person. They may pay attention to the "victim" first and conduct a guidance talk or mediation after they've cooled down. They may use *describe-express-direct* rather than accuse and disparage the "culprits." They may firmly request more information before they make a hasty judgment. They may check themselves before responding to a child who is difficult for them to understand. They may work with others who know a child or family better than they. They monitor their moods and feelings, aware of their impact on teaching effectiveness.

Example

"Skip, I saw what happened. You need to wait here until I find out if Jenny is all right. We'll talk about it in a few minutes when I've calmed down."

Early childhood teachers who are committed to using guidance continue to learn even as they teach.

Examples

▶ Teachers and caregivers participate in peer assessment including observation by and of other professionals in order to get feedback and engage in personal review of teaching practices.

▶ Teachers use collaborations with parents, staff, and outside professionals in order to continue learning about the children they work with.

▶ Teachers read, attend courses, conferences, and workshops in order to update their store of ideas.

▶ Teachers use observation and communication skills to learn from the best of all teachers, the children themselves.

Finally, just as teachers need close collegial relations on the job, they need personal support systems that extend outside of the program. In the taxing role of early childhood professional, people who are there to support the teacher are crucial. In order for teachers not to give up on a child, they need the personal resources to give them the strength not to give up on themselves.

Concluding note, Code of Ethics. A helpful guide for defining professional practice is the National Association for the Education of Young Children Code of Ethical Conduct (listed in Recommended Readings.) The Code outlines core values for the profession and provides guidance about professionals' responsibilities to children, families, colleagues, community, and society. The Code concludes with the NAEYC "Statement of Commitment," important for professional teachers to read, think about, and discuss.

Recommended Readings

Alat, K. (2002). *Traumatic events and children: How early childhood educators can help*. Childhood Education, 79(1), 2–7.

Carlson, F.M. (2005). Significance of touch in children's lives. *Young Children, 60*(4), 79–85.

Carlson, F.M. *Essential touch: Meeting the needs of young children*. Washington, DC: NAEYC.

Copple, C. & Bredekamp, S. (2009). *Developmentally Appropriate Practice in Early Childhood Programs*. Washington, DC: NAEYC.

Corso, R. (2003). The center on the social and emotional foundations for early learning. *Young Children, 58*(4), 46–47.

Curtis, D., & Carter, M. (2005). Rethinking early childhood environments to enhance learning. *Young Children, 60*(3), 34–38.

Da Ros, D.A & Kovach, B.A. (1998). Assisting toddlers & caregivers during conflict resolutions: Interactions that promote socialization, *Childhood Education, 75*(1), 25–30.

Feeney, S.& Lipnes, K. (1990). *NAEYC Code of ethical conduct and statement of Commitment.* Washington, DC: National Association for the Education of Young Children.

Fox, L., Dunlap, G., Hemmeter, M. L., Joseph, G. E., & Strain, P. S. (2003). The teaching pyramid: A model for supportive social competence and preventing challenging behavior in young children. *Young Children, 58*(4), 48–52.

Gallahger, K.. & Mayer, K. (2008). *Enhancing development and learning through teacher-child relationships.* Young Children, *63*(6), 80–87.

Gartrell, D.J. (2004). *The Power of Guidance: Teaching Social-Emotional Skills in Early Childhood Classrooms.* Joint publication of NAEYC, Washington, DC, and Delmar Publishers, Albany, New York.

Gilliam, W.S. 2005. Prekindergarteners left behind: Expulsion rates in state prekindergarten systems. New Haven, CT: Yale University Child Study Center. Online: http://www.fcd-us.org/PDFs/NationalPreKExpulsionPaper03.02_new.pdf

Harris, T.T. & Fuqua, J.D. (2000). What goes around comes around: Building a community of learners through circle times. *Young Children, 55*(1), 44–47.

Kalb, C. (2008). Spare the rod. *Newsweek Web Exclusive.* February 28, 2008. http://www.newsweek.com/id/116788

King, M. (2003). Building an encouraging classroom with boys in mind. *Young Children, 58*(4), 33–37.

Kohn, D. (2003). *The gender gap: Boys lagging.* Available at http://www.cbasnews.com/stories/2002/10/31/ 60minutes/main527678.shtml

Loomis, C., & Wagner, J. (2005). A different look at challenging behavior. *Young Children, 60*(2), 94–99.

Nelson, B. G. (2002). *The importance of men teachers and why there are so few.* Minneapolis, MN: Men in Child Care and Elementary Education Project. http://www.menteach.org

Ostrosky, M. M., & Jung, E. Y. (2003). *Building positive teacher-child relationships.* What Works Briefs, no. 12. Nashville, TN: Center on the Social and Emotional Foundations for Early Learning.

Pappano, L. (2007, July/August). Meeting of the minds [in conferences with parents]. *Harvard Education Letter,* http://www.edletter. (Reprinted in Annual Editions: Early Childhood 2009–2010.)

Peterson, K. (2002, January/February). Creating home-school partnerships. *Early Childhood News,* pp. 39–45.

Preuesse, K. (2002, March/April). Guidance and discipline strategies for young children: Time out is out. *Early Childhood News,* pp. 12–16.

Reineke, J., Sonsteng, K., & Gartrell, D. (2008). Nurturing mastery motivation: No need for rewards. *Young Children, 63*(6), 89–97.

Schiller, P. & Willis, C.A. (2008). Using brain-based teaching strategies to create supportive early childhood environments that address learning standards. *Young Children, 63*(5), 52–55.

Schreiber, M.E. (1999). Time-Outs for Toddlers: Is our goal punishment or education. *Young Children 54*(4), 22–25.

Sprung, B., Froschl, M., & Hinitz, B. (2005). *The anti-bullying and teasing book for preschool classrooms*. Beltsville, MD: Gryphon House.

Vance, E., & Jimenez, P. (2003). Words to describe feelings. *Young Children, 58*(4), 45.

Vance, E. & Jimenez, P. (2002). Class meetings: Young children solving problems together. Washington, DC: NAEYC.

Watson, M. (2003). Attachment theory and challenging behaviors: Reconstructing the nature of relationships. *Young Children, 58*(4), 12–20.

Wien, C. A. (2004). From policy to participation: Overturning the rules and creating amiable classrooms. *Young Children, 59*(1), 34–40.

Guidance Matters Columns from Young Children, Dan Gartrell

Source One: http://www.naeyc.org/yc/columns/guidance (Available for download)

Understand Bullying, May 2008

Promote Physical Activity—It's Proactive Guidance, March 2008

Swearing and Words That Hurt, November 2007

"He Did It on Purpose, September 2007

"You Worked Really Hard on Your Picture!" Guiding with Encouragement, May 2007

Competition: What Place in Our Programs?, March 2007

Tattling—It Drives Teachers Bonkers, January 2007

The Beauty of Class Meetings, November 2006

Build Relationships through Talk, November 2006

A Spoonful of Laughter, July 2006

Boys and Men Teachers, May 2006,

Responding to Challenging Behavior, March 2006

Source Two: http://danielgartrell1.efoliomn2.com (Available for download—click "publications.")

Comprehensive Guidance, January 2008

Conflict Management, March 2006

DAP and Guidance, November 2005

Approved by the MNAEYC BOARD—September 25, 2009

Developmentally Appropriate Guidance Committee

Fifth Edition
Approved by Minnesota Association for the Education of Young Children
September 25, 2009

Author:

Dan Gartrell Ed.D.
Bemidji State University
Bemidji, MN 56601

Review Committee:

Sharon Bergen
Sandra Heidemann
Beth Menninga
Julie Murphy
Gail Roberts
Brian Siverson-Hall
Cory Woosley

MNAEYC
1821 University Avenue West
Suite 324-South
Saint Paul, MN 55104
www.mnaeyc-mnsaca.org
651-646-8689

For copies of the Booklet, Developmentally Appropriate Guidance of Young Children, contact MnAEYC.

Appendix  E

Individual Guidance Plan Worksheet

Individual Guidance Plan Worksheet*

Child's name_____   Initial Write-Up Date_____

1. Noted Behaviors

   Behavior Observed: _____

   _____

   Thoughts about Behavior: _____

   _____

2. Additional Information

   Check procedures used. Then summarize information gained.

   __ Discussion with child.   Date: _____

   __ Discussion with parent.   Date: _____

   __ Discussion with other staff.   Date: _____

   __ Discussion with other professionals.   Date: _____

   Information gained: _____

   _____

3. Cooperative Strategy Meeting   Date: _____

   Persons attending meeting: _____

   _____

   continued

• *An explanation of the Individual Guidance Plan and illustrations for its use were provided in Chapter Eleven. In addition, in both the Instructor's Manual and the Book Companion website to accompany this book, a full-length useable form of the work sheet can be found. Suggested steps for using the IGP accompanies the form in both resources. The work sheet can be used without permission. The author does ask for feedback on its use by e-mail: dgartrell@bemidjistate.edu.*

Strategy to be tried: _____

_____

4. Follow-up Meeting or Review   Date: _____

   Effort/progress shown by child: _____

   _____

   Progress still needed: _____

   _____

   Any change in strategy: _____

   _____

5. Summary of Results/Changes as of   (Date) _____

   _____

6. Summary of Results/Changes as of   (Date) _____

   _____

7. Summary of Results/Changes as of   (Date) _____

   _____

Glossary

A

academic performance—Demonstration by the child of knowledge and or skills within the framework of academic instruction, sometimes under "one-time, high-stakes" circumstances that are not developmentally appropriate.

acknowledgment—The listening technique of verbal reframing of words and actions of a child that communicates that the adult is listening.

aggression—Any direct or indirect action intended to do harm to another; classified as *instrumental* if the purpose is to achieve an objective; classified as *reactive* if there is an encroachment by another or an objective is not being met.

antibias education—An education program designed to prevent the development of bias in relation to racism, sexism, and children with disabilities.

anticipatory set—A feeling of positive anticipation or motivation in children created by the teacher, often in a large-group setting toward a follow-up activity often done individually or in small groups.

attachment theory—A theory addressing the formation of relationships between infants, toddlers, and young children with parents and other custodial adults. The theory holds that behavioral and coping mechanisms that young children develop are a function of the nature of their relationships with others significant to them. When positive, the attachment is likely to result in enhanced self-esteem and social responsiveness in the child.

authentic assesment—observation-based assesment of samples of children's everyday activities usually in relation to progress toward standards.

autonomy—Piaget's term for the ability to make ethical, intelligent decisions that balance others' viewpoints with one's own. Opposite of *heteronomy*.

B

belonging—A basic need of children codefining Erikson's period in early childhood of initiative versus guilt; failure to meet the need for belonging results in alienation (stigma).

body language—Nonverbal language, such as smiles, eye contact, and physical proximity used to support children and remind of guidelines. **boisterous activity level**—The level of play at learning centers that is very active and often loud.

boy behavior—A pejorative term for when teachers complain about behaviors such as short attention spans, aggressiveness, frustration, and anger that boys show in classroom situations. In the guidance approach, teachers see "boy behavior" as a reaction by many boys (and some girls) to classroom programming that is not developmentally appropriate for them.

buffer activity—An activity that uses time productively while waiting.

bullying as violence—Bullying is the assertion of the will of one person upon the other through psychological and physical means. Bullying causes harm to both the victim and the perpetrator and as such is a form of violence.

C

cardinal principle—The intervention strategy attributed to Ginott in which the teacher addresses mistaken behaviors, firmly if needed, but remains respectful of the personality of the child.

challenging behavior—Conflicts that cause harm or serious disruption; the term often connotes a continuing pattern of such conflicts shown by individual children.

childism—The misguided notion of some adults that because of the innocence of children, childhood is a "rosy" period of life.

child negotiation—The process whereby two or more children are able to resolve a conflict peaceably on their own.

child-report—An alternate term for tattling by which children express concerns to teachers about perceived conflicts or urgent situations.

class meetings—Scheduled or unscheduled meetings of the teacher and the class to address business matters and matters of concern to one or more members of the group; other terms sometimes used with specialized meetings include *sharing circles* and *magic circles*.

Code of Ethical Conduct—This position statement of the National Association for the Education of Young Children "offers guidelines for responsible behavior and sets forth a common basis for resolving the principal ethical dilemmas encountered in early childhood care and education" (from the Preamble of the Code).

collaboration—Working in a team with others to solve problems and accomplish tasks that cannot be done on one's own.

commanding choices—Firm direction by the teacher for a child to choose between two alternative appropriate behaviors, one of which may be preferred by the teacher, but either of which is acceptable.

compliment sandwich—An encouragement technique that provides at least two acknowledgments of effort and progress accompanied by one request or suggestion for further progress.

comprehensive guidance—A multifaceted guidance strategy that is used with continuing strong needs mistaken behavior and includes improving the relationship with the child, learning more about the child's situation, nonpunitive crisis intervention, holding one or more meetings with fellow staff and parents, and determination, implementation, and assessment of an Individual Guidance Plan.

conditional acceptance—A classroom atmosphere in which students are aware that they will be accepted or rejected by the teacher on the basis of their performance academically and behaviorally, their backgrounds, or their personalities.

conflict—A conflict is an expressed disagreement between children, usually involving property, territory, or privilege; or a mistaken behavior by a child or children, disagreed with by a teacher.

conflict management—The ability to prevent and resolve disputes in a civil, peaceable manner.

conflict mediation—The process a third party uses to help two or more other parties to resolve a conflict. The term is more specific than conflict management, which refers to an overall ability to prevent and resolve conflicts, and to conflict resolution, which also refers to formal systems of mediation involving a third party.

conflict resolution—The ability to resolve disputes in a peaceable, civil manner.

constructivist education—The concept that the child constructs knowledge through interaction with the social and physical environment, and the educational strategy that enables this learning process to take place.

contact talk—Conversation between an adult and child for the purpose of sharing time together and becoming better acquainted rather than to accomplish an ulterior purpose.

continuum of violence in children's lives—Represented by Levin's pyramid of violence, the concept explains that the more intensive and ongoing the violence that children experience, the more they are affected by that violence.

cooling-down time—A nonpunitive alternative to the time-out chair in which a teacher removes a child from the group and assists the child to regain control of her or his emotions.

creative conflicts—Disagreements with another that the parties resolve by negotiation and cooperative problem solving.

crisis management techniques—Guidance intervention strategies teachers use to de-escalate conflicts that have gotten out of hand so that they can be resolved, including describe-express-direct, commanding choices, calming techniques, and physical restraint.

culturally linguistically different (CLD)—Refers to an individual or group that has a cultural background and a spoken language different from the mainstream. Teachers who respect the differing culture and language of a child, even while they teach about mainstream culture and language, are teaching inclusively for this child in the encouraging classroom.

D

day chart—A visual used to help children understand routine time blocks in the daily schedule.

day clock—A particular kind of period chart that uses a "one-handed clock" to track routine time blocks in the daily schedule.

democratic life skills—The skills children need to be healthy individuals and productive citizens of a democracy, including the acceptance of self, intelligent and ethical decision making, cooperative problem solving, and the acceptance of others regardless of human differences.

describe-express-direct—A crisis management technique that allows the teacher to stop a conflict and restore civility so that the problem can be talked through and resolved. The teacher describes the conflict, has the option of expressing feelings about it; and directs the child or children to a corrective action, often in the form of a stated choice.

developmental egocentrism—The inability of young children to understand the complexity of social factors in situations and to see things from other than one's own perspective.

developmentally appropriate practice (DAP)—Educational practice that accommodates the development and individual needs and learning styles of each child in the class.

differentiated staffing—Adults of differing educational and experience backgrounds working together as a teaching team.

direct intervention—A sequence of responses to serious mistaken behavior that involves the teacher's describing what he or she sees, sometimes reporting feelings, and directing to alternative behaviors.

discipline—Derived from the Latin term *disciplina* meaning teaching, instruction. In this "classical" sense, synonymous with guidance. In its everyday meaning, the use of rewards and punishments to keep children "in line." As a verb, "to discipline" commonly means to punish in order to bring under the teacher's control.

discussing inclusively—During discussions, the ability to respond in an encouraging fashion to unexpected comments so assisting each child to feel part of the group.

disequilibrium—Piaget's term for when the individual experiences contradiction between perceptions and understanding.

displeasure without insult—The use of self-report or I-messages to express, without character attack, strong feelings about a mistaken behavior. "I see hitting and this makes me upset."

dual language learners (DLLs)—Refers to children who speak a native language and are also learning English. The practice indicated is not to replace the native language, but to complement it with knowledge of a second language, English. "Dual language learner" implies acceptance of diversity in society more fully than the term "English language learner."

E

ecological perspective—A comprehensive viewpoint when working with children that encompasses the family's social, cultural, economic, educational, and behavioral dynamics.

educational accountability—The need for educators to validate the effectiveness of the teaching-learning process in order to show that children have achieved educational goals.

emotional intelligence—The capacity to use one's perceptions and understandings of another to work cooperatively with the other in the attainment of mutual goals.

encouraging classroom—A "community" classroom environment in which each child is empowered to feel a sense of belonging, self-worth, and a capacity to learn.

equilibrium—Piaget's term for when the individual experiences harmony between perceptions and understanding.

executive function—The set of cognitive abilities that control and regulate other abilities and behaviors. Located in the prefrontal cortex, the executive function begins to develop during the early years, but is not fully formed until adulthood. Experiences impact how the executive function develops, and the executive function impacts how individuals interpret experiences.

experimentation (Level One) mistaken behavior—Mistaken behavior that occurs as a result of involvement in or curiosity about a situation.

F

family groups—A grouping system long used in early childhood that includes children of diverse ages and developmental characteristics in the same group, under the supervision of a primary caregiver.

five-finger formula—A strategy for mediating conflicts that includes five steps: cool-down; identify the problem; determine possible solutions; try one; monitor and facilitate the effort.

friendly humor—A quality much appreciated by children that can both prevent and reduce the negative effects of mistaken behavior.

friendly touch—The use of touch to calm and affirm children and to assure them of positive relations with the teacher.

G

guidance—A way of teaching that empowers children to make decisions that are ethical, intelligent, and socially responsive; the teaching of democratic life skills.

guidance approach—The use of guidance, distinct from discipline, to reduce the need for and resolve the occurrence of mistaken behavior in ways that are nonpunitive and teach democratic life skills.

guidance intervention practices—Practices used by a teacher who enters conflict situations in order to teach, such as guidance talks, conflict mediation, class meetings, and other crisis management techniques. A common first step in these practices is to calm everyone down so that resolution, reconciliation, and the learning of democratic life skills can begin.

guidance professional—Teachers who are professionals rather than technicians and who consistently use guidance in their classrooms. Instead of reacting to conflicts according to established discipline practices, guidance professionals bring a problem-solving intentionality to conflicts. They use conflicts to guide children in the development of social-emotional skills.

guidance talk—A discussion with a child after an incident that helps the child understand what happened, how the other felt, what he or she might do to bring about reconciliation, and what acceptable alternative behaviors might be.

guidelines—Agreements often made with the class that identify prosocial behavior; distinct from rules that tend to be stated negatively and lack direction relative to the life skills desired by the teacher.

H

high-level mediation—Intervention by an adult at an "active coaching level" to assist children to resolve a conflict that calms children, helps them put the conflict into words, and assists them to reach a mutually acceptable solution.

I

I-message—A communication technique in which one person reports perceptions and feelings to another in a straightforward but respectful manner.

impulse control—The ability to manage one's feelings so as to prevent conflicts with others from escalating, an ability that most young children are just beginning to develop.

In-choice/Out-choice—Choices that teachers give a child as a way of resolving a conflict quickly or keeping a conflict from becoming a crisis. The child makes the choice and so is actively involved in the resolution. The teachers prefer that a child select the in-choice, which typically allows the child to continue in an activity, but they frame the out-choice in a way they can live with if the child chooses this option—often following up with the child later.

inclusion—The educational practice of including learners of diverse abilities and physical and behavioral characteristics in the classroom. Related terms are *inclusiveness* and *inclusivity.*

individual guidance plan (IGP)—A strategy that is collaborative, systematic, and comprehensive to assist a child showing serious mistaken behavior; involvement of parents in the IGP process is a priority.

industry—A basic need in the middle childhood period defined by Erikson, with inferiority resulting if the child is unable to meet the need.

initiative—A basic need in the early childhood period defined by Erikson, with self-doubt resulting if the child is unable to meet the need.

institution-caused mistaken behavior—Mistaken behavior that results from a mismatch of the educational program and a child's level of development learning style, and individual needs. The child reacts to an educational program that he or she finds developmentally inappropriate educational program. A related term is "classroom-caused mistaken behavior."

instrumental aggression—The infliction of harm on another for the purpose of achieving an objective.

integrated curriculum—Instruction that is interdisciplinary, interrelating separate content areas through thematic instruction.

intentionality—When mistaken behaviors are done on purpose due to an error in judgment by the child.

intentional mistaken behavior—Mistaken behavior that is done on purpose. Mistaken behavior can be intentional: at Level One when a child initiates a conflict to see what will happen; at Level Two when a child is influenced by another to initiate or continue a conflict; at Level Three when a child initiates a conflict to act out against the experience of having deep unmet needs.

inviting, requesting, commanding choices—Communication techniques used by a teacher in which she or he uses different degrees of intensity matched to a conflict in order to solicit cooperation.

L

labeling—Stereotyping of a child's character as a result of a pattern of mistaken behavior that the child may show.

labeling versus diagnosis—Labeling is stereotyping of a child's character, sometimes as a result of diagnosis. Diagnosis is formed assessment of perceived atypcial development or behavior that results in a plan for remediation of the condition.

leadership communication—The cluster of communication skills used by a teacher with the group and the individual that encourage life skills and prosocial behavior.

learned behavior—Behavior, including Level Two mistaken behavior, that a child is influenced by significant others to show.

learning centers—Distinct areas within the classroom that provide a variety of related materials for children's use; other similar terms preferred by some professionals include *learning areas, interest areas,* and *interest centers.*

learning community—a classroom, school, and/or home setting in which there is clear commitment to each member being a successful learner and learners together feel part of the group.

liberation teaching—The acceptance, support, and empowerment of every child who might be singled out negatively from the group for physical, cultural, or behavioral reasons.

listening techniques—A cluster of techniques used by the teacher to better understand a child, which include *attending, acknowledgment, wait time, rephrasing, reflective listening, divergent questions,* and *contact talks.*

listening to life experiences—Contact talk that a teacher has with a child, during which the child feels comfortable enough to openly share experiences, thoughts, and feelings.

logical consequences—Responses taken by adults that are a "fitting" reaction to a child's mistaken act.

low-level mediation—The level of conflict resolution in which children need a minimum of adult assistance in calming themselves, defining the problem, and reaching a solution. The adult acts as a facilitator rather than an active coach.

M

mandated reporter—A person in a helping profession required by law to report instances of child abuse and neglect. Teachers, providers, and caregivers, as well as members of the social and medical professions, are mandated reporters. An early task of employees in helping professions is to determine the policies of the program or school in regard to reporting procedures.

marginal mistaken behaviors—Milder mistaken behaviors that different teachers react to differently and that the same teacher might react differently to on different occasions.

mastery motivation—The intrinsic motivational source that empowers individuals to find meaning in life and their place in it. In Piaget's usage, the term refers to the drive within each individual to turn disequilibrium into equilibrium. Significant adults have the power to support mastery motivation in children or to suppress it.

mediation—A conflict management strategy in which a third person, often a teacher, uses high- to low-level intervention to assist others to resolve a conflict.

misbehavior—The conventional term applied to conflicts that the child is involved in, resulting in consequences that often include punishment and the internalization of a negative label such as "naughty."

mistaken behavior—Errors in judgment and action made in the process of learning life skills. Mistaken behaviors occur at three levels: experimentation, socially influenced, and strong needs.

more gifted/less gifted labeling—the informal labeling process that results from institutionalized peer assistance programs where a more able learner assists a less able learner and both learners are of the same age.

multiage classrooms—This approach places children of different ages in the same classroom. The term "multi-aged" indicates the curriculum is personalized for each child, with children of different ages regularly working together in informal mentoring arrangements. "Multiage" is contrasted with "multigrade" which implies set grade-based curricula taught simultaneously to distinct "classes" of children within the same room.

multicultural education—Curriculum and methods that teach children to respect and learn from points of uniqueness and commonality in various cultures; the celebration of cultural diversity for the commonality of human values that the respectful treatment of cultural differences engenders.

multidimensional classroom—A classroom in which a variety of activities and grouping arrangements occur, and where the teacher is a manager of the daily program as well as a lead teacher.

multiple intelligences (MI)—The theory that individuals possess natural intelligence in many dimensions of human behavior, above and beyond the cognitive/analytical abilities usually associated with standardized tests. Most often attributed to Howard Gardner, a distinguishing feature of MI theory is that the various intelligences can be developed through education.

N

negative dissonance—A conflict that has gone past the point where it can be resolved by negotiation with another, and mediation through a third party is necessary if the conflict is to be resolved.

negotiation reminders—Informal or formal forms of encouragement intended to motivate children to engage in peer negotiation (without a third party) to peaceably resolve conflicts. An informal reminder would be a comment like, "Can you work it out by yourselves?" A formal reminder would be the suggestion that a child use a *sentence frame*, a scripted comment that a child learns and uses in a conflict situation.

No Child Left Behind—Law evolved through reauthorizations of the Elementary and Secondary Act of 1968. No Child Left Behind (NCLB) places an emphasis on educational accountability through standardized testing. Published annual yearly progress (AYP) indexes, based heavily on test scores, provide public notice of schools' relative "success" in meeting the standards of NCLB.

nonverbal intervention—The teacher's use of techniques including body language, facial expressions, gestures, or physical proximity to keep learners on task with a minimum of attention being drawn to the situation.

O

obedience-based discipline—Systems and techniques of discipline the intent of which is to subjugate children to the authority of the teacher.

overfunctioning—The stressful and ultimately exhausting situation that results when teachers feel they must meet unrealistic goals, standards, and responsibilities in the performance of their roles.

P

parent meetings—A vital method of furthering teacher-parent communication and building teacher-parent partnerships; these meetings often involve parents in planning and implementation and may be held at different times to accommodate parents' schedules.

parent-teacher partnerships—The state of relations when parents and teachers have joined together on behalf of the child; partnerships result in involvement in the child's education to the fullest extent possible for the parent.

passive restraint—Also known as the passive bear hug, teachers use this technique when children have lost total emotional control and there is an imminent danger of harm to themselves or others. Distinct from corporal punishment, the technique involves wrapping arms around arms, legs around legs and going into a sitting position with the child facing away from you and head out to one side. This crisis management technique of last resort is only to be used as a part of a defined behavior management policy of a school or program.

passivity—The opposite of "activity," the term refers to both experiences that cause children to become passive learners and the passive state of mind caused by these experiences. Boredom, restlessness, frustration, and mistaken behavior are common reactions to passivity.

peace education—The use of curriculum and teaching practice to empower children to learn and advocate peaceful alternatives to violence in daily life and the solving of social and environmental problems.

peace props—Objects such as puppets, the talking stick, talk-and-listen chairs, and the peace table that teachers use to assist young children to manage conflicts.

peer mediation—A system of conflict management in which trained older children in a school mediate conflicts of their peers, frequently used in out-of-classroom situations.

peer scaffolding—Refers to the actions of a peer that help another move from what she can learn on her own to what she can learn with assistance. Traditionally, the peer is thought to be "more capable." A less traditional view is that two "equal" peers who solve a problem or create a product together provide an example of mutual peer scaffolding.

performance assessment—Assessment of children's efforts in selected tasks to determine performance in relation to identified outcomes; measures used in early childhood may include, but are not limited to, teacher interviews, observations, and checklists.

personal development—the development of the person of the child that encompasses self-image, self-concept, self-esteem, and social-emotional intelligence.

personal safeguards—Techniques used by the teacher for managing strong emotions to prevent harm, such as monitoring one's feelings, describing conflicts objectively, expressing feelings nonpunitively (by the use of self-report) and teaming with colleagues.

physical restraint—The passive bear hug that teachers use with children who have totally lost emotional control and an imminent danger of harm exists; the crisis management technique of last resort in the classroom also known as passive restraint.

play—Self-selected, self-directed activity that is inherently pleasurable and through which the child constructs meaning and "learns what cannot be formally taught."

political accountability—Unrealistic expectations of academic performance held by officials and administrators usually for reasons of appearance and often involving single measures of performance, such as scores on standardized tests.

positive consistency—The ability to be positively consistent in teachers' treatment of children and classroom conflicts. "Positive consistency" reminds teachers of the kind of consistency that guides rather than punishes.

post-traumatic stress disorder (PTSD)—The mix of behaviors that individuals, including young children, show as a reaction to experiencing violence. In early childhood classrooms, teachers need to be aware that the onset of anxiety, aggression, extreme frustration, hostility toward authority, and rejection of relationships are possible signs of PTSS. Children who experience PTSS are showing Level Three mistaken behaviors and are in need of comprehensive guidance that includes resiliency mentoring.

private encouragement—Recognition of effort and progress directed by a teacher to an individual in such a way as to avoid singling out the individual in relation to the group.

private speech—The talking that young children do with themselves as they engage in learning activities. Vygotsky theorizes that this speech gives the child skills that enable later conceptual acts of cognitive and social-emotional problem solving.

process modeling—Refers to showing a child how to use a tool, medium, or material without influencing the child toward a specific teacher-defined product.

product modeling—Refers to showing a child how to use a tool, medium, or material in order to achieve a specific teacher-defined product.

professional teacher—A teacher who does not depend on established routines and practices but takes a positive problem-solving approach responsive to the needs of children and the dynamics of the situation.

prosocial development—Development of the collection of skills that show in an individual's ability to be helpful to others. Consistency in showing prosocial skills can be attributed to what some refer to as social-emotional competence, others to intrapersonal and interpersonal intelligence.

protective buffer—Strategies used in liberation teaching to prevent children from being stigmatized by their vulnerabilities and to encourage children toward resilience.

public encouragement—Recognition of effort and progress directed by a teacher to the group without singling out of individual group members.

R

reconciliation—The process of positive resolution of an incident of mistaken behavior that might involve an apology, making amends, and/or reuniting with the group.

reflective listening—A communication technique in which an adult repeats back or supportively acknowledges a remark, action, or implied emotion of a child.

relational patterns—Levels of social relations shown by children; three relational patterns are survival, adjustment, and encountering.

requesting choices—An intervention level of medium intensity in which the teacher communicates a clear expectation that the child will choose from among two or three acceptable options for behavior.

resiliency—The capacity to overcome a vulnerability for stigma by meeting a need for safety, and so being able to engage in learning and personal growth.

resiliency mentoring—The empowering of children to be resilient. In this effort, teachers build a relationship with the child; modify the social environment to make it reliable and engaging; and work with the family to extend the child's ability to cope. In guidance terms, teachers who are resiliency mentors are practicing liberation teaching and are using comprehensive guidance.

rough-and-tumble play—Spontaneous play that is active and involves a level of physical contact and jostling ranging from super hero play to variations of "chase."

routines—Reliable practices happening regularly throughout the day that provide the child with a sense of predictability and order; must be carefully implemented, and occasionally deviated from, in order to sustain the child's full engagement in the program.

S

scaffolding—The teaching-learning process by which another person aids a learner to move from a comfortable level of performance to a higher level possible only with that assistance.

school anxiety—Stress felt by children as a result of routines, activities, or incidents at a school or center that are threatening or harmful.

school readiness—The diverse skills, experiences, and qualities that make initial functioning in the classroom a successful experience for young children.

self-fulfilling prophecy—The phenomenon that persons who become labeled by others for particular behaviors come to see themselves as they are labeled and show an increase in the behaviors that others have come to expect.

self-psychology—A branch of psychology that focuses on the developing self as the primary dynamic in human behavior, with mental health being a function of continuing development and mental ill-health the result of obstacles to that development.

self-removal—The arrangement between a child and teacher whereby the child voluntarily leaves a situation in order to prevent a conflict from becoming mistaken behavior.

self-report—The use of I-messages to express strong feelings to others in a nonpunitive way: "I feel upset when. . . ."

sentence frame—Open-ended statements that children learn for use in conflict situations. Examples are: "It bothers me when . . . , please . . . instead." In class meetings, teachers instruct children in how and when to use sentence frames, and how other children should respond when they are used.

separation—Helping a child to leave a situation in order to calm down so that a conflict can be resolved.

separation anxiety—The stress that children feel upon leaving the familiar world of the family and entering the unfamiliar world of the classroom.

social competence—The consistent ability to use social and emotional skills to act in prosocial ways. Social competence is a work in progress for young children, as their executive functions develop. Positive attachments with significant others are crucial to the development of social competence.

socially influenced (Level Two) mistaken behavior—Mistaken behavior that is learned behavior, a result of the intentional or unintentional influence of a significant other.

socially responsive education—Refers to a number of related educational practices that are responsive to the social-emotional needs of each child in the group. Guidance, liberation teaching, peace education, and antibias instruction are some terms for these practices. Adherents make the case that socially responsive education does not dilute, but rather enhances, the cognitive gains of young children.

social problem solving—The ability to manage and resolve problems and conflicts in peaceable ways.

societal violence—The dynamics and patterns of violence that are widespread in a society. Statistics indicate that societal violence is high in the United States, compared to other developed nations. Children experience societal violence along a continuum of mild and indirect to intense and direct. Direct societal violence shows itself in abuse and neglect of the child that results in physical and/or psychological harm with resulting chronic stress, debasement of the self concept, impairment in healthy brain development, and potential suppression of the conscience.

starter statement—A pre-framed statement that reminds the teacher to acknowledge a child's effort or progress, example: "You are really. . . ."

stigma—The psychological and social process whereby an individual is negatively separated from the group for cultural, physical, or behavioral reasons.

story pictures—Children create story pictures when they use early art with or without early writing to tell a story of personal significance to them. Not being bound by the conventions of writing and reading, story pictures allow children to express a wide range of thoughts and feelings.

strong unmet needs (Level Three) mistaken behavior—Mistaken behavior shows itself in extreme, inappropriate behaviors over time and is the acting out of strong unmet physical and/or psychological needs.

superhero syndrome—The identification of a child with a "heroic figure," either real or media created, the result of which is overly aggressive play.

suppressed conscience—The experience of chronic violence undermines children's ability to develop empathy and prosocial behavior as a part of healthy brain development. Instead, stress hormones sensitize the brain to "fight or flight" reactions that make formation of a healthy conscience difficult.

T

table talk—The naturally occurring conversing that occurs when individuals are seated around a table working on an activity.

teachable moment—An unplanned, unexpected situation that an adult uses as a teaching opportunity to build cognitive, social, emotional, and/or emotional understanding.

teaching team—Adults of differing educational levels and experience backgrounds who work together as a team in the classroom.

team-teaching—Two adults of similar educational backgrounds who share duties and tasks.

Thematic Instruction—An instructional method that integrates traditional curriculum subjects in interest-based topics that provide active learning experiences.

time confusion—The inability to understand time concepts in early childhood due to developmental factors.

time-out—When teachers remove a child from a conflict situation, the common term is to give the child a "time-out." When the purpose is the consequence of an act by the child, with the expectation that the child should "think about" the behavior, the time-out is punishment. When the purpose is to help a child calm down so the conflict can be resolved, the time-out is guidance.

tossed salad approach—An approach to multicultural education in which adults of diverse backgrounds, usually parents, interact informally in the classroom community.

tourist curriculum—The mistaken notion that by studying token facts about a culture, which may or may not be accurate, important instruction about that culture is occurring; for example, "Eskimos live in igloos."

transitions—Events that occur in the process of moving children from one activity to another in the daily program, which the teacher may or may not have planned.

U

unconditional positive regard—Full acceptance of the child as a developing human being and member of the classroom group despite mistaken behaviors that the child may show.

W

webbing—A visual brainstorming activity often done with the group in which content, learning activities, and sometimes teaching methods are generated for thematic instruction.

with-it-ness—The idea that the effective teacher is aware of the important dynamics of behavior in the classroom; that teachers have "eyes in the backs of their heads."

Z

zone of proximal development—The psychological distance at any point of cognitive and social development between what a child can learn on her own and with the assistance of responsive others.

References

Chapter 1

Berger, S. K. (2007, 7e). *The developing person through childhood and adolescence.* New York: Worth Publishers, Inc.

Bredekamp, S., & Copple, C. (Eds.). (1997). *Developmentally appropriate practice in early childhood programs* (3rd ed.). Washington, DC: National Association for the Education of Young Children.

Brewer, J. A. (1995). *Introduction to early childhood education: Primary through the primary grades.* Needham Heights, MA: Allyn & Bacon.

Canter, L. (1988). Assertive discipline and the search for the perfect classroom. *Young Children, 43*(2), 24.

Canter, L. (1989). Let the educator beware: A response to Curwin and Mendler. In J. W. Noll (Ed.), *Taking sides: Clashing views on controversial educational issues.* Guilford, CT: The Dushkin Publishing Group.

Canter, L., & Canter, M. (1976). *Assertive discipline.* Seal Beach, CA: Canter and Associates.

Charles, C. M. (1996). *Building classroom discipline.* White Plains, NY: Longman.

Cherry, C. (1983). *Please don't sit on the kids.* Belmont, CA: Pitman Learning.

Clewett, A. S. (1988). Guidance and discipline: Teaching young children appropriate behavior. *Young Children, 43*(4), 26–36.

Combs, A. W. (Ed.). (1962). *Perceiving, behaving, becoming: A new focus for education.* Washington, DC: Association for Supervision and Curriculum Development.

Copple, C. & Bredekamp, S. (2005). *Basics of developmentally appropriate practice.* Washington, DC: National Association for the Education of Young Children.

Curwin, R. L., & Mendler, A. N. (1988/2000). *Discipline with dignity.* Alexandria, VA. Association for Supervision and Curriculum Development.

Curwin, R. L., & Mendler, A. N. (1989). Packaged discipline programs: Let the buyer beware. In J. W. Noll (Ed.), *Taking sides: Clashing views on controversial educational issues.* Guilford, CT: The Dushkin Publishing Group.

deMause, L. (Ed.). (1974). *The history of childhood.* New York: Peter Bedrick Books.

DeVries, R. (1994). *Moral classrooms, moral children: Creating a constructivist atmosphere in early education.* New York: Teachers College Press.

DeVries, R., & Zan, B. (1995). Creating a constructivist classroom atmosphere. *Young Children, 51*(1), 4–13.

Dewey, J. (1900/1969). *The school and society.* Chicago: The University of Chicago Press.

Dewey, J. (1944/1966). *Democracy and education.* New York: The Free Press.

Dreikurs, R. (1968). *Psychology in the classroom* (2nd ed.). New York: Harper and Row, Publishers.

Dreikurs, R., Grunwald, B. B., & Pepper, F. C. (1982). *Maintaining sanity in the classroom.* New York: Harper and Row, Publishers.

Elkind, D. (1987). *Miseducation: Preschoolers at risk.* New York: Alfred A. Knopf.

Erikson, E. H. (1963). *Childhood and society.* New York: W. W. Norton and Company.

Gage, J., & Workman, S. (1994). Creating family support systems: Head Start and beyond. *Young Children, 50*(1), 74–77.

Gandini, L. (1993). Fundamentals of the Reggio Emilia approach to early childhood education. *Young Children, 49*(1), 4–8.

Gartrell, D. J. (1987). Assertive discipline: Unhealthy for children and other living things. *Young Children, 42*(2), 10–11.

Gartrell, D. J. (1992). Discipline. In L. R. Williams & D. P. Fromberg (Eds.), *Encyclopedia of early childhood education.* New York: Garland Publishing, Inc.

Gartrell, D. J. (2004). *The power of guidance: Teaching social-emotional skills in early childhood classrooms.* Clifton Park, NY: Thomson Delmar Learning.

Ginott, H. (1972). *Teacher and child.* New York: Avon Books.

Gough, P. B. (2002). Interest matters. *Phi Delta Kappan, 83*(8), 566.

Greenberg, P. (1988). Avoiding 'me against you' discipline. *Young Children, 43*(1), 24–25.

Greenberg, P. (1989). Parents as partners in young children's development and education: A new American fad? Why does it matter? *Young Children, 44*(4), 61–75.

Greenberg, P. (1992). Ideas that work with young children. How to institute some simple democratic practices pertaining to respect, rights, responsibilities in any classroom. *Young Children, 47*(5), 10–21.

Hamachek, D. E. (1971). *Encounters with the self.* New York: Holt, Rinehart and Winston.

Hitz, R. (1988). Assertive discipline: A response to Lee Canter. *Young Children, 43*(2), 24.

Jalongo, M. R. (2007). Beyond benchmarks and scores: Reasserting the role of motivation and interest in children's academic achievement: An ACEI Position Paper. *Childhood Education/Infancy through Early Adolescence. 83*(6): 395–407.

Kaiser, B., & Sklar-Rasminsky, J. (2003). *Challenging behavior in young children.* Boston: Allyn & Bacon.

Keating, B., Pickering, M., Slack, B., & White, J. (1990). *A guide to positive discipline.* Boston: Allyn & Bacon.

Kohn, A. (1999). *Punished by rewards.* Bridgewater, NJ: Replica Books.

Lilley, I. M. (Ed.). (1967). *Friedrich Froebel: A selection from his writings.* London: Cambridge University Press.

Locke, B. (1919, July). Manufacturers indorse [sic] the kindergarten. *Kindergarten Circular No. 4.* Washington, DC: Department of the Interior, Bureau of Education.

Marcus, P. & Rosenberg, A. (1998). *Psychoanalytic versions of the human condition: Philosophies of life and their impact on practice.* New York: New York University Press.

Marion, M. (2006). *Guidance of young children* (7th ed.). Upper Saddle River, NJ: Prentice Hall.

Maslow, A. H. (1962). *Toward a psychology of being.* Princeton, NJ: D. Van Nostrand Company.

Montessori, M. (1912/1964). *The Montessori method.* New York: Schocken Books.

National Association of Early Childhood Specialists, State Departments of Education. 2000. *STILL Unacceptable Trends in Kindergarten Entry and Placement.* Position statement adopted by NAEYC in 2001. Washington, DC: NAEYC.

Osborn, D. K. (1991). *Early childhood education in historical perspective* (3rd ed.). Athens, GA: Daye Press.

Owen, R. (1967). *The life of Robert Owen,* AM Kelley Publishers: New York, NY.

Piaget, J. (1932/1960). *The moral judgment of the child.* Glencoe, IL: The Free Press.

Prutzman, P. (Ed.). (1988). *The friendly classroom for a small planet.* Philadelphia: New Society Publishers.

Purkey, W. W. (1970). *Self-concept and school achievement.* Englewood Cliffs, NJ: Prentice-Hall.

Read, K. H. (1997). *The early childhood program: Human relationships and learning* (10th ed.). Fort Worth, TX: Harcourt Brace Jovanovich.

Render, G. F., Padilla, J. E. N. M., & Krank, H. M. (1989). Assertive discipline: A critical review and analysis. *Teachers College Record, 90*(4). New York: Teachers College, Columbia University.

Reynolds, E. (2006). *Guiding young children* (4th ed.). Mountain View, CA: Mayfield Publishing Company.

Rogers, C. R. (1961). *On becoming a person.* Boston: Houghton Mifflin, Co.

Schickedanz, J. A., & Shickedanz, D. I. (1981). *Toward understanding children.* Boston: Little, Brown.

Shonkoff, J. P., & Phillips, D. A. (Eds.). (2000). *From neurons to neighborhoods: The science of childhood development.* Washington, DC: National Academies Press.

Standing, E. M. (1962). *Maria Montessori: Her life and work.* New York: The New American Library.

Stone, J. G. (1978). *A guide to discipline* (Rev. ed.). Washington, DC: National Association for the Education of Young Children.

Swick, R. (2001). Nurturing decency through caring and serving during the early years. *Early Childhood Education Journal, 29*(2): 131–137.

Weber, S. H. (1919, December). The Kindergarten as an Americanizer. *Kindergarten Circular No. 5.* Washington, DC: Department of the Interior, Bureau of Education.

Wichert, S. (1989). *Keeping the peace: Practicing cooperation and conflict resolution with preschoolers.* Philadelphia: New Society Publishers.

Wolfe, J. (2002). *Learning from the past: Voices in early childhood education.* Mayerthorpe, Alberta, Canada: Piney Branch.

Wurm, P. (2005). *Working in the Reggio way: A Beginner's Guide for American Teachers.* St. Paul, MN: Redleaf Press.

Chapter 2

Berk, L. E., & Winsler, A. (1995). *Scaffolding children's learning: Vygotsky and early childhood education.* Washington, DC: National Association for the Education of Young Children.

Brazelton, T. B., & Greenspan, S. (2000). *The irreducible needs of children—what every child must have to grow, learn, and flourish.* Cambridge, MA: Perseus Publishing.

Bredekamp, S., & Copple, C. (Eds.). (1997). *Developmentally appropriate practice in early childhood programs* (rev. ed.). Washington, DC: National Association for the Education of Young Children.

Bukatko, D., & Daehler, M. W. (1992). *Child development: A topical approach.* Boston, MA: Houghton Mifflin Company.

Charlesworth, R. (2007). *Understanding child development* (7th ed.). Clifton Park, NY: Thomson Delmar Learning.

Crain, W. (2005). *Theories of development—concepts and applications* (5th ed.). Upper Saddle River, NJ: Prentice Hall.

DeVries, R., & Zan, B. (1996). Assessing interpersonal understanding in the classroom. *Childhood Education, 72*(5), 268.

Dewey, J. (1900/1969). *The school and society*. Chicago, IL: The University of Chicago Press.

Diamond, M., & Hopson, J. (1998). *Magic trees of the mind: How to nurture your child's intelligence, creativity, and healthy emotions from birth through adolescence*. New York: Dutton.

Elkind, D. (1987). *Miseducation: Preschoolers at risk*. New York: Alfred A. Knopf.

Elkind, D. (1993). *Images of the young child*. Washington, DC: National Association for the Education of Young Children.

Elkind, D. (1997, November). The death of child nature: Education in the postmodern world. *Phi Delta Kappan, 79,* 241–245.

Elkind, D. (2005). Viewpoint. Early childhood amnesia: Reaffirming children's need for developmentally appropriate programs. *Young Children, 60*(4), 38–40.

Erikson, E. H. (1963). *Childhood and society*. New York: W. W. Norton and Company.

Gardner, H. (1993). *Multiple intelligences: The theory in practice*. New York: Perseus Book Group.

Gardner, H. (1995). On multiple intelligences: ECT interview of the month. *Early Childhood Today, 10*(1), 330–332.

Gardner, H. (1999). *Intelligence reframed: Multiple intelligences for the 21st century*. New York: Basic Books.

Gartrell, D. J. (2000). *What the kids said today*. St. Paul, MN: Redleaf Press.

Gartrell, D.J. (2008). Promoting physical activity: It's proactive guidance. "Guidance Matters" column, *Young Children. 63*(2), 51–53.

Gestwicki, C. (2004). *Home school, and community relations: A guide to working with parents* (5th ed.). Clifton Park, NY: Thomson Delmar Learning.

Goleman, D. (1995). *Emotional intelligence*. New York: Bantam Books.

Goleman, D. (1998). *Working with emotional intelligence*. New York: Bantam Books.

Honig, A. S., & Wittmer, D. S. (1996). Helping children become more prosocial: Ideas for classrooms, families, schools & communities, part 2. *Young Children, 51*(2), 62–70.

Kagan, J. (1997, February). Temperament and the reactions to unfamiliarity. *Child Development, 68,* 139–143.

Kaiser, B., & Sklar-Rasminsky, J. S. (2003). *Challenging behavior in young children: Understanding, preventing, and responding effectively*. Boston: Pearson Education.

Kamii, C. (1984). Autonomy: The aim of education envisioned by Piaget. *Phi Delta Kappan, 65*(6), 410–415.

Kohn, A. (1999). *Punished by rewards*. Bridgewater, NJ: Replica Books.

Ladd, G. W., & Price, J. M. (1987). Predicting children's social and emotional adjustment following the transition from preschool to kindergarten. *Child Development, 58,* 986–992.

Ladd, G. W., Kochenderfer, B. J., & Coleman, C. (1997). Classroom peer acceptance, friendship, and victimization: Distinct relational systems that contribute uniquely to children's school adjustment. *Child Development, 68,* 1181–1197.

LeDoux, J. (1996). *The emotional brain*. New York: Simon & Schuster.

Lollis, S. P. (1990). Effects of maternal behavior on toddler behavior during separation. *Child Development, 61,* 99–103.

Mayer, J. D., & Salovey, P. (1997). What is emotional intelligence? In P. Salovey & D. J. Sluyter (Eds.), *Emotional development and emotional intelligence: Educational implications* (pp. 3–31). New York: Basic Books.

Newberger, J. J. (1997, May). New brain development research—A wonderful window of opportunity to build public support for early childhood education. *Young Children,* 4–9.

Novik, R. (1998, Summer). The comfort corner: Fostering resiliency and emotional intelligence. *Childhood Education, 74*(4), 200–205.

O'Neil, J. (1996, September). On emotional intelligence; A conversation with Daniel Goleman. *Educational Leadership, 54*(1), 6–12.

Piaget, J. (1932/1960). *The moral judgment of the child*. Glencoe, IL: The Free Press.

Pica, R. (2006). Physical fitness and the early childhood curriculum. *Young Children, 61*(3), 12–19.

Raver, C. C., & Zigler, E. F. (1997). Social competence: An untapped dimension in evaluation of Head Start's success. *Early Childhood Research Quarterly, 12,* 363–385.

Rolnick, A. & Grunewald, R. (2003). Early childhood development: Economic development with a high public return. *Fedgazette* (Electronic newsletter of the Federal Reserve Bank of Minneapolis). March, 2003, p. 1.

Schickedanz, J. A., Schickedanz, D. I., Forsyth, P. D., & Forsyth, G. A. (2001). *Understanding children and adolescents* (4th ed.). Needham Heights, MA: Allyn & Bacon.

Salovey P., and Grewal D. (2005). The Science of Emotional Intelligence. Current directions in psychological science, 14.6.

Shonkoff, J. P. & Phillips, D.A. (Eds). (2000). *From neurons to Neighborhoods: The science of early childhood development*. Washington, D. C.: National Academy Press.

Shore, R. (1997). *Rethinking the brain*. New York: Families and Work Institute.

Shores, E. F. (1995). Interview with Howard Gardner. *Dimensions of Early Childhood, 23*(4), 5–7.

Shores, R. E., & Wehby, J. H. (1999). Analyzing classroom social behavior of students with EBD. *Journal of Emotional and Behavioral Disorders, 7,* 194–199.

Trawick-Smith, J. (2006). *Early childhood development: A Multicultural Perspective* (4th ed.). Upper Saddle River, NJ: Merrill.

Vygotsky, L. S. (1934/1986). *Thought and language* (A. Kozulin, Trans.). Cambridge, MA: MIT Press.

Vygotsky, L. S. (1930–1935/1978). *Mind in society: The development of higher mental processes* (M. Cole, V. John-Steiner, S. Scribner, & E. Souberman, Eds. and Trans.). Cambridge, MA: Harvard University Press.

Webster-Stratton, C. M., & Reid, M. J. (2004, April–June). Strengthening social and emotional competence in young children—The foundation for early school readiness and success: "Incredible Years" classroom social skills and problem-solving curriculum. *Infants and Young Children, 17*(2), 96–114.

Weinraub, M., & Lewis, M. (1977). The determination of children's responses to separation. *Monographs of the Society for Research in Child Development, 42* (Serial No. 172).

Wolfe, P., & Brandt, R. (1998, November). What do we know from brain research? *Educational Leadership,* 8–13.

Zelazo, P. D. (2008)., Executive Function: A six part Series. Toronto, CA: Hospital for Sick Children, University of Toronto. http://aboutkidshealth.ca/News/SeriesArchive.aspx#ExecutvieFunction

Chapter 3

Corso, R. (2003). The Center on the Social and Emotional Foundations for Early Learning. *Young Children, 58*(4), 46–47.

DeVries, R., & Zan, B. (2003, September). When children make rules. *Educational Leadership.* 22–29.

Erickson, M. F., & Pianta, R. C. (1989). New lunchbox, old feelings: What kids bring to school. *Early Education and Development, 1*(1), 35–49.

Gardner, H. (1999). *Intelligence reframed: Multiple intelligences for the 21st century.* New York: Perseus Books Group.

Gartrell, D. J., & Sonsteng, K. (2008). Promote physical activity—It's Proactive Guidance. *Young Children, 53*(3), 46–49.

Gartrell, D. J. (2004). *The power of guidance: Teaching social-emotional childhood classrooms.* Clifton Park, NY: Thomson Delmar Learning.

Ginott, H. G. (1972). *Teacher and child.* New York: Avon Books.

Goleman, D. (2006). *Social intelligence: The new science of social relationships.* New York: Bantam Books.

Greenberg, P., (1988). Avoiding 'me against you' discipline. *Young Children, 43*(1), 24–31.

Gurham, P. J., & Nason, P. N. (1997). Why make teachers' work more visible to parents. *Young Children, 52*(5), 22–26.

Harlow, S. D. (1975). *Special education: The meeting of differences.* Grand Forks, ND: University of North Dakota.

Honig, A. S. (1986). Research in review. Stress and coping in children. In J. B. McCracken (Ed.). (1986). *Reducing stress in young children's lives.* Washington, DC: National Association for the Education of Young Children.

Kaiser, B., & Sklar-Rasminsky, J. (2003). *Challenging behavior in young children: Understanding, preventing, and responding effectively.* Boston: Pearson Education.

Kamii, C. (1984, February). Autonomy: The aim of education envisioned by Piaget. *Phi Delta Kappan,* 410–415.

Kantrowitz, B., & Kalb, C. (1998, May 11). Boys will be boys. *Newsweek,* 54–60.

Kohn, A. (1999). *Punished by rewards.* Bridgewater, NJ: Replica Books.

LeDoux, J. (1996). *The emotional brain.* New York: Simon and Schuster.

Levin, D. E. (2003). Beyond banning war and superhero play: Meeting children's needs in violent times. *Young Children 58*(3). 60–63.

McCracken, J. B. (Ed.). (1986). *Reducing stress in young children's lives.* Washington, DC: National Association for the Education of Young Children.

Maslow, A. H. (1962). Some basic propositions of a growth and self-actualization psychology. In A. W. Combs (Ed.), *Perceiving, behaving, becoming: A new focus for education.* Washington, DC: Association for Supervision and Curriculum Development.

Piaget, J. (1932/1960). *The moral judgment of the child.* Glencoe, IL: The Free Press.

Slaby, R. G., Roedell, W. C., Arezzo, D., & Hendrix, K. (1995). *Early violence prevention.* Washington, DC: National Association for the Education of Young Children.

Stone, J. G. (1973). *What about discipline?* Cambridge, MA: Education Development Center.

Thomas, A., & Chess, S. (1977). *Temperament and development.* New York: Brunner/Mazel.

Warren, R. (1977). *Caring: Supporting children's growth.* Washington, DC: National Association for the Education of Young Children.

Wichert, S. (1989). *Keeping the peace: Practicing cooperation and conflict resolution with preschoolers.* Philadelphia, PA: New Society Publishers.

Watson, M. (2003). Attachment theory and challenging behaviors: Reconstructing the nature of relationships. *Young Children, 58*(4). 12–20.

Chapter 4

Almy, M. (1975). *The early childhood educator at work.* New York: McGraw Hill Book Company.

Berger, S. K. (1986). *The developing person through childhood and adolescence*. New York: Worth Publishers, Inc.

Brand, S. (1996). Making parent involvement a reality: Helping teachers develop partnerships with parents. *Young Children, 51*(2), 76–81.

Bredekamp, S. & Coople, C. (2008). *Developmentally appropriate practice in early childhood programs* (4th ed.). Washington, DC: National Association for the Education of Young Children.

Charles, C. M. (2007), *Building classroom discipline* (4th ed.). White Plains, NY: Longman.

Clewett, A. S. (1988). Guidance and discipline: Teaching young children appropriate behavior. *Young Children, 43*(4), 26–31.

Crosser, S. (2002, May–June). What's the difference between right and wrong: Understanding how children think. *Early Childhood News,* 12–16.

de Mause, L., ed. (1974). *The history of childhood*. New York: Peter Bedrick Books.

DeVries, R., & Zan, B. (September 2003). When children make rules. *Educational Leadership,* 64–67.

Dreikurs, R. (1972). *Discipline without tears*. New York: Hawthorn Press Books, Inc., Publishers.

Elkind, D. (1993). *Images of the young child*. Washington, DC: NAEYC.

Erickson, M. F., & Pianta, R. C. (1989). New lunch box, old feelings: What kids bring to school. *Early Education and Development, 1*(1), 35–49.

Faber, A., & Mazlich, E. (1974). *Liberated parents, liberated children*. New York: Avon Books.

Gallagher, K. C. & Mayer, K. (2008). Research in Review: Enhancing development and learning through teacher-child relationships. *63*(6), 80–87.

Gartrell, D. J. (2004). *The power of guidance*. Clifton Park, NY: Thomson Delmar Learning.

Gestwicki, C. (2007). *Home, school, and community relations: A guide to working with parents* (6th ed.). Clifton Park, NY: Thomson Delmar Learning.

Gilliam, W. S. 2005. Prekindergarteners left behind: Expulsion rates in state prekindergarten systems. New Haven, CT: Yale University Child Study Center. Online: http://www.fcd-us.org/PDFs/NationalPreKExpulsion-Paper03.02_new.pdf

Ginott, H. G. (1972). *Teacher and child*. New York: Avon Books.

Girard, K., & Koch, S. J. (1996). *Conflict resolution in the schools: A manual for educators*. San Francisco: Jossey-Bass Publishers.

Goffman, E. (1963). *Stigma*. Englewood Cliffs, NJ: Prentice-Hall.

Gottlieb, D. (Ed.). (1973). *Children's liberation*. Englewood Cliffs, NJ: Prentice-Hall.

Greenberg, P. (1989). Parents as partners in young children's development and education: A new American fad? Why does it matter? *Young Children, 44*(4), 61–75.

Grossman, S. (2008). "I just don't like that kid" Confronting and managing personal feelings about children. *Childhood Education, 84*(3), 147–149.

Hardy, L. (2003, April). Overburdened, overwhelmed. *American School Board Journal,* 7–12.

Hatch, J. A. (2002, February). Accountability shovedown: Resisting the standards movement in early childhood education. *Phi Delta Kappan,* 457–462.

Honig, A. S., & Wittmer, D. S. (1996). Helping children become more pro social: Ideas for classrooms, families, schools, and communities, Part 2. *Young Children, 51*(2), 62–70.

Kagan, S. L., & Rivera, A. M. (1991). Collaboration in early care and education: What can and should we expect? *Young Children, 46*(1), 51–56.

Kaiser, B., & Sklar-Rasminsky, J. (2003). *Challenging behavior in young children*. Boston: Allyn & Bacon.

Kohn, A. (1999). *Punished by rewards*. Bridgewaker, NJ: Replica Books.

Kounin, J. (1977). *Discipline and group management in classrooms*. New York: Holt, Rinehart and Winston.

Kreidler, W. J. (1984). *Creative conflict resolution: More than 200 activities for keeping peace in the classroom*. Glencoe, IL: Scott, Foresman.

LeDoux, J. (1996). *The emotional brain*. New York: Simon & Schuster.

Lundgren, D., & Morrison, J. W. (2003). Involving Spanish speaking families in early childhood programs. *Young Children, 58*(3), 88–95.

Maslow, A. H. (1962). *Toward a psychology of being*. Princeton, NJ: Van Nostrand Company.

Merton, R. K. (1949/1968). *Social theory and social structure*. New York: The Free Press.

National Association for the Education of Young Children. (1989). *The National Association for the Education of Young Children code of ethical conduct*. Washington, DC: Author.

Noddings, N. (2005, September). What does it mean to educate the whole child? *Educational Leadership.* 8–13.

Osborn, D. K., & Osborn, J. D. (1989). *Discipline and classroom management*. Athens, GA: Daye Press, Inc.

Ostrosky, M. M. & Jung, EY. (2003). Building Positive Teacher-Child Relationships. *What Works Briefs*. The Center on the Social and Emotional Foundations of Early Learning. Vanderbilt University, Nashville, Tennessee. http://www.vanderbilt.edu/csefel/

Peterson, K. (2002, January/February). Creating home-school partnerships. *Early Childhood News,* 39–45.

Piaget, J. (1932/1960). *The moral judgment of the child*. Glencoe, IL: The Free Press.

Read, K. H., Gardner, P., & Mahler, B. C. (1993). *Early childhood programs: Human relationships and learning*. Fort Worth, TX: Harcourt Brace Jovanovich College Publishers.

Rightmyer, E. C. (2003). Democratic discipline: Children creating solutions. *Young Children, 58*(4), 38–45.

Rogers, C. R. (1961). *On becoming a person*. Boston, MA: Houghton Mifflin, Co.

Slaby, R. G., Roedell, W. C., Arezzo, D., & Hendrix, K. (1995). *Early violence prevention: Tools for teachers of young children*. Washington, DC: National Association for the Education of Young Children.

Warren, R. (1977). *Caring*. Washington, DC: National Association for the Education of Young Children.

Watson, M. (2003). Attachment theory and challenging behaviors: Reconstructing the nature of relationships. *Young Children, 58*(4), 12–20.

Weber-Schwartz, N. (1987). Patience or understanding. *Young Children, 42*(3), 52–54.

Wichert, S. (1989). *Keeping the peace: Practicing cooperation and conflict resolution with preschoolers*. Santa Cruz, CA: New Society Publishers.

Wittmer, D. S., & Honig, A. S. (1994). Encouraging positive social development in young children. *Young Children, 49*(5), 4–12.'

Chapter 5

Abramson, S., Robinson, R., & Anenman, K. (1995). Project work with diverse students: Adapting curriculum based on the Reggio Emilia approach. *Childhood Education, 71*(4), 197–202.

Black, S. (2003, January). Too soon to test. *American School Board Journal*.

Bredekamp, S., & Copple, C. (2009). *Developmentally appropriate practice in early childhood programs* (4th ed.). Washington, DC: National Association for the Education of Young Children.

Brewer, J. A. (2007). *Introduction to early childhood education: Preschool through primary grades* (6th ed.). Boston, MA: Allyn & Bacon.

Burchfield, D. W. (1996). Teaching all children. Four different curricular and instructional strategies in primary grade classrooms. *Young Children, 52* (1), 4–10.

Butzin, S. M. (2004, December). Stop the insanity! It takes a team to leave no child behind. *Phi Delta Kappen*.

Cassidy, D. J., Mims, S., Rucker, L., & Boone, S. (2003, Summer). Emergent curriculum and kindergarten readiness. *Childhood Education*, 194–199.

Charlesworth, R. (1998). Developmentally appropriate practice is for everyone. *Childhood Education, 74*(5), 274–282.

Curtis, D., & Carter, M. (2005). Rethinking early childhood environments to enhance learning. *Young Children, 60* (3), 34–38.

Dewey, J. (1900/1969). *The child and curriculum*. Chicago, IL: The University of Chicago Press.

Deyell-Gingold, P. (2006, May/June) Successful transition to kindergarten: The role of teachers and parents. *Early Childhood News*, 14–19.

Dodge, D. T., Colker, L., & Herdman, C. (2002). *Creative curriculum for preschool* (4th ed.). Washington, DC: Teaching Strategies Inc.

Elkind, D. (1993). *Images of the young child*. Washington, DC: National Association for the Education of Young Children.

Elkind, D. (1997, November). The death of child nature; Education in the postmodern world. *Phi Delta Kappan, 97,* 241–245.

Feeney, S., & Freeman, N. (2002). *Ethics and the early childhood educator using the NAEYC code*. Washington, DC: National Association for the Education of Young Children.

Gallagher, K. C. (2005). Brain research and early childhood development: A primer for developmentally appropriate practice. *Young Children, 60*(4), 22–20.

Garcia, C., Garcia, L., Floyd, J., & Lawson, J. (2002). Improving public health through early childhood movement programs. *Journal of Physical Education, Recreation, and Dance, 73,* 27–32.

Gartrell, D. (2004). *The power of guidance: Teaching social-emotional skills in early childhood classrooms*. Clifton Park, NY: Thomson Delmar Learning and Washington, DC: National Association for the Education of Young Children.

Gestwicki, C. (2007). *Home, school, and community relations: A guide to working with parents* (6th ed.). Clifton Park, NY: Thomson Delmar Learning.

Greenberg, P. (1989). Parents as partners in young children's development and education. *Young Children, 44*(4), 61–75.

Haschke, B. (2003, Summer). Childhood obesity. The caregiver's role. *Texas Child Care*, 28–36.

Heidemann, S., Chang, C. J., & Menninga, B. (2005). When teachers are learning, Children are too: Teaching teachers about assessment. *Young Children, 60* (3), 86–92.

High/Scope. (2005, Spring). The High/Scope Perry Preschool Study and the man who began it. *High/Scope Resource: A Magazine for Educators, 5–10.*

Hohmann, M., Banet, B., & Weikart, D. P. (1995). *Educating young children: Active learning practices in preschool and child care programs*. Ypsilanti, MI: The High/Scope Press.

Kantrowitz, B., & Kalb, C. (1998, May 11). Boys will be boys. *Newsweek, 54–60.*

Lumeng, J. (2005, January). What can we do to prevent childhood obesity? *Zero to Three,* National Center for Infants, Toddlers and Families. 13–19.

Lynn-Garber, C., & Hoot, J. (2004–2005). Weighing in on the issue of childhood obesity. *Childhood Education, 81*(2), 70–76.

Mindess, M., Chen, M, Brenner, R. (2008). Social-emotional learning in the primary curriculum. *Young Children, 63*(6), 56–60.

Myers, B. K., & Maurer, K. (1987). Teaching with less talking: Learning centers in the kindergarten. *Young Children, 42* (5), 20–27.

National Association for the Education of Young Children. (1995). Position statement on school readiness. Washington, DC: NAEYC.

Noddings, N. (2005, September). What does it mean to educate the whole child? *Educational Leadership,* 8–13.

Pica, R. (2000). *Experiences in movement with music, activities, and theory.* Clifton Park, NY: Thomson Delmar Learning.

Preusse, K. (2005). Fostering prosocial behavior in young children. *Early Childhood News.* March/April, 2005. Excellence Learning Corporation.

Reincke, J., Sonsteng, K, Gartrell, D. (2008). Nurturing mastery motivation: No need for rewards. *Young Children, 63*(6), 89–97.

Rockwell, R. E., Andre, L. C., & Hawley, M. K. (1996). *Parents and teachers as partners: Issues and challenges.* Fort Worth, TX: Harcourt Brace College Publishers.

Rosenthal, D. M., & Sawyers, J. Y. (1996). Building successful home/school partnerships: Strategies for parent support and involvement. *Childhood Education, 72*(4), 194 200.

Stegelin, D. A. (2005). Making the case for play policy: Research based reasons to support play-Based Environments. *Young Children. 60*(2).

Texas Workforce Commission. (2002, Spring). Learning centers: Why and how. *Texas Child Care,* 30–42.

Wardle, F. ((1999). In praise of developmentally appropriate practice. *Young Children, 54*(6), 4–12.

Willis, S. (1993, November). Teaching young children: Educators seek "developmental appropriateness." *Curriculum Update,* 1–8.

Wien, C. A. (2004). From policing to participation: Overturning the rules and creating amiable classrooms. *Young Children, 59* (1), 34–41.

Workman, S., & Anziano, M. C. (1993). Curriculum webs: Weaving connections from children to teachers. *Young Children, 48* (2), 4–9.

Wurm, P. (2005). *Working in the Reggio way: A beginner's guide for American teachers.* St. Paul, MN: Redleaf Press.

Chapter 6

Bredekamp, S., & Copple, C. (1997). *Developmentally appropriate practice in early childhood programs* (3rd ed.). Washington, DC: National Association for the Education of Young Children.

Brewer, J. A. (2004). *Introduction to early childhood education: Preschool through primary grades.* Boston, MA: Allyn & Bacon.

Cherry, C. (1981). *Think of something quiet.* Belmont, CA: David S. Lake Publisher.

Dunn, L., & Kontos, S. (1997). What have we learned about developmentally appropriate practice? *Young Children, 52* (5), 4–13.

Elkind, D. (1976). *Child development and early childhood education: A Piagetian perspective.* New York: Oxford University Press.

Elkind, D. (2003). Thanks for the memory: The lasting value of true play. *Young Children, 58* (3), 46–51.

Gabbard, C. (1998). Windows of opportunity for early brain and motor development. *Journal of Health, Physical Education, Recreation, and Dance, 69*(8), 54–60.

Garcia, C., Garcia, L., Floyd, J., & Lawson, J. (2002, January). Improving the public health through early childhood movement programs. *Journal of Physical Development,* 27–31.

Gestwicki, C. (2004). *Home, school, and community relations: A guide to working with parents* (5th ed.). Clifton Park, NY: Thomson Delmar Learning.

Honig, A. S., & Wittmer, D. S. (1996). Helping children become more prosocial: Ideas for classrooms, schools, and communities. *Young Children, 51*(2), 62–70.

Kagan, S. L., & Rivera, A. M. (1991). Collaboration in early care and education: What can and should we expect? *Young Children 46*(1), 51–56.

Kalb, C. (2003, September 22). Troubled souls. *Newsweek,* 68–70.

Kasting, A. (1994). Respect, responsibility, and reciprocity: The 3Rs of parent involvement. *Young Children, 70* (3), 146–150.

Loomis, C., & Wagner, J. (2005). A different look at challenging behavior. *Young Children, 60*(2), 94–99.

Marion, M. (2002). *Guidance of young children.* Columbus, OH: Merrill Publishing Company.

Montessori, M. (1912/1964). *The Montessori method.* New York: Schocken Books.

Palmer, H. (1978). *Sea gulls.* Topanga, CA: Hap-Pal Music.

Peterson, K. (2002, January/February). Creating home-school partnerships. *Early Childhood News,* 39–45.

Phillips, C., & Derman-Sparks, L. (1997). *Teaching/learning anti-racism: A developmental approach.* New York: Teachers College Press.

Saifer, S. (2004). *Practical solutions to practically every problem: The early childhood teacher's manual.* St. Paul, MN: Redleaf Press.

Scelsa, G., & Millang, S. (1983). *Quiet moments with Steve and Greg.* Los Angeles, CA: Young-heart Records.

Thorton, J. R. (1990). Team teaching: A relationship based on trust and communication. *Young Children 45*(5), 40–42.

Van Scoy, I. J., & Fairchild, S. H. (1993). It's about time! Helping preschool and primary children understand time concepts. *Young Children, 48* (2), 21–24.

Watson, M. (2003). Attachment theory and challenging behaviors: Reconstructing the nature of relationships. *Young Children, 58* (4), 12–20.

Chapter 7

Albert, L. (2003). *A teacher's guide to cooperative discipline*. Circle Pines, MN: American Guidance Service.

Barkley, S. (1998). On teasing, taunting, and "I can do it myself." *Young Children, 53*(2), 42.

Bredekamp, S., & Copple, C. (2009). *Developmentally appropriate practice in early childhood programs* (3rd ed.). Washington, DC: National Association for the Education of Young Children (NAEYC).

Burk, D. I. (1996). Understanding friendship and social interaction. *Childhood Education, 72*(5), 282–285.

Castle, K., & Rogers, K. (1993). Rule-creating in a constructivist classroom community. *Childhood Education, 70*(2), 74–80.

Charles, C. M. (1996, 2005). *Building classroom discipline*. New York: Longman.

DeVries, R., & Zan, B. (2004, September). When children make rules. *Educational Leadership*.

Dreikurs, R., & Cassel, P. (1972). *Discipline without tears*. New York: Hawthorn Books.

Elkind, D. (1987). *Miseducation: Preschoolers at risk*. New York: Alfred A. Knopf.

Foster, S. M. (1994). Planning successful parent meetings. *Young Children, 50*(1), 78–81.

Gallahger, K., & Mayer, K. (2008). Enhancing development and learning through teacher-child relationships. *Young Children, 63(6), 80–87*.

Gartrell, D. J. (2004). *The power of guidance: Teaching social-emotional skills in early childhood classrooms*. Clifton Park, NY: Thomson Delmar Learning and Washington, DC: NAEYC.

Gartrell, D. J. (2000). *What the kids said today: Using classroom discussions to become a better teacher*. St. Paul, MN: Redleaf Press.

Gestwicki, C. (2004/2007). *Home, school and community relations: A guide to working with parents*. (5th & 6th eds.). Clifton Park, NY: Thomson Delmar Learning.

Ginott, H. (1972). *Teacher and child*. New York: Avon Books.

Glasser, W. (1969). *Schools without failure*. New York: Harper and Row.

Harris, K. I., Pretti-Frontczak, K., & Brown, T. (2009). Peer-mediated intervention: An effective, inclusive strategy for all children. *Young Children, 64*(2), 43–49.

Harris, T. T., & Fuqua, J. D. (2000). What goes around comes around: Building a community of learners through circle times. *Young Children, 55*(1), 44–47.

Hitz, R., & Driscoll, A. (1988). Praise or encouragement? New insights into praise: Implications for early childhood teachers. *Young Children, 43*(4), 6–13.

Holt, J. (1964). *How children fail*. New York: Pitman.

Kohn, A. (1999). *Punished by rewards: The trouble with gold stars, incentive plans, A's, praise, and other bribes*. Somerville: Replica Books.

Kriete, R. (2002). *The Morning Meeting Book*. Turner's Falls, MA: Northeast Foundation for Children, Inc.

Lawhon, T. (1997). Encouraging friendships among children. *Childhood Education, 73*(4), 228–231.

Levin, D. (2003). Teaching young children in violent times: Building a peaceable classroom. Boston, MA Educators for Social Change.

Logan, T. (1998). Creating a kindergarten community. *Young Children, 53*(2), 22–26.

McClurg, L. G. (1998). Building an ethical community in the classroom: Community meeting. *Young Children, 53*(2), 30–35.

Macrina, M., Hoover, D. & Becker, C. (2009). The challenge of working with dual language learners. *Young Children, 64*(2), 27–34.

Mecca, M. E. (1996). Classrooms where children learn to care. *Childhood Education, 72*(2), 72–74.

Piaget, J. (1971). *Science of education and the education of the child*. New York: Viking Press.

Paley, V. (1992). *You can't say you can't play*. Cambridge, MA: Harvard University Press.

Rockwell, R. E., Andre, L. C., & Hawley, M. K. (1996). *Parents and teachers as partners: Issues and challenges*. Fort Worth, TX: Houghton Mifflin Company.

Rosenthal, D. M., & Sawyers, J. Y. (1996). Building successful home/school partnerships: Strategies for parent support and involvement. *Childhood Education, 72*(4), 194–200.

Scharmann, M. W. (1998). We are friends when we have memories together. *Young Children, 53*(2), 27–29.

Sturm, C. (1997). Creating parent-teacher dialogue: Intercultural communication in child care. *Young Children, 52*(5), 34–38.

Vance, E., & Weaver, P. J. (2002). *Class meetings; Young children solving problems together*. Washington, DC: NAEYC.

Watson, M. (2003). Attachment theory and challenging behaviors: Reconstructing the nature of relationships. *Young Children, 58*(4), 12–20.

Wien, C. A. (2004). From policy to participation: Overturning the rules and creating amiable classrooms. *Young Children, 59*(1), 34–40.

Wohlwend, K. E. (2004/05). Chasing friendship: Acceptance, rejection, and recess play. *Childhood Education, 81*(2), 77–82.

Wolfgang, C. H. (1999). *Solving discipline problems*. New York: John Wiley & Sons.

Chapter 8

Almeida, D. A. (1995, September). Behavior management and "the five C's." *Teaching Prek–8, 88–89.*

Bowling, H. J., & Rogers, S. (2001). The value of healing in education. *Young Children, 56*(2), 79–81.

Breslin, D. (2005). Children's capacity to develop resiliency: How to nurture it. *Young Children, 60*(1), 47–51.

Bullock, J. R. (1993). Lonely children. *Young Children, 48*(6), 53–57.

Carlson, F. M. (2006). *Essential touch: Meeting the needs of young children.* Washington, DC: NAEYC.

Chenfield, M. (1997). *Creative experiences for young children.* San Diego, CA: Harcourt Trade Publishers.

Curwin, R. L., & Mendler, A. N. (1988). *Discipline with dignity.* Alexandria, VA: Association for Supervision and Curriculum Development.

Diamond, M., & Hopson, J. (1998). *Magic trees of the mind: How to nurture your child's intelligence, creativity, and healthy emotions from birth through adolescence.* New York: Dutton.

Furman, R. A. (1995). Helping children cope with stress and deal with feelings. *Young Children, 50*(2), 33–41.

Gartrell, D. J. (2000). *What the kids said today: Using classroom conversations to become a better teacher.* St. Paul, MN: Redleaf Press.

Gartrell, D. (2006). A spoonful of laughter. *Young Children, 61*(5), 108–109.

Gestwicki, C. (2007). *Home, School, Community Relations* (6th ed.). Clifton Park, NY: Cengage Learning.

Graham, A. (2004). Life is like the seasons: Responding to change, loss, and grief through a peer-based education program. *Childhood Education, 80*(6), 317–321.

Gruenberg, A. (1998). Creative stress management: Put your own oxygen mask on first. *Young Children, 53*(1), 38–42.

Halcrow, J. (1988). *Laughter in the classroom.* (Professional education document). Bemidji, MN: Bemidji State University.

Hendrick, J. (2001). *The whole child.* Englewood Cliffs, NJ: Merrill/Prentice Hall.

Jochum, J. (1991). Responding to writing and to the writer. *Intervention, 26*(3), 152–157.

King, M. (2003). Building an encouraging classroom with boys in mind. *Young Children, 58*(4), 33–35.

Kirkhart, R., & Kirkhart, E. (1967). The bruised self: Mending in the early years. In K. Yamamoto (Ed.), *The child and his image: Self concept in the early years.* Boston: Houghton Mifflin Company.

LeDoux, J. (1996). *The emotional brain.* New York: Simon & Schuster.

Loomis, C., & Wagner, J. (2005). A different look at challenging behavior. *Young Children, 60*(2), 94–99.

Nelson, B. G. (2002). *The importance of men teachers and why there are so few.* Minneapolis, MN: Men in Child Care and Elementary Education Project. http://www.menteach.org

Novick, R. (1998). The comfort corner; Fostering resiliency and emotional intelligence. *Childhood Education, 74*(4), 200–204.

Ostrosky, M.M. & Jung, E.Y. (2003, December). Building positive teacher-child relationships. *What Works Briefs.* Center on the Social and Emotional Foundations for Early Learning. 1–3.

Rich, B. A. (1993). Listening to Harry (and solving a problem) in my kindergarten classroom. *Young Children, 48*(6), 52.

Robinson, B. E. (1988). Vanishing breed: Men in child care programs. *Young Children, 43*(6), 54–57.

Rosenthal, D. M., & Sawyers, J. Y. (1996). Building successful home/school partnerships: Strategies for parent support and involvement. *Childhood Education, 72*(4), 194–200.

Sang, D. (1994). The worry teacher comes on Thursdays. *Young Children, 49*(2), 24–31.

Seitz, H. (2008). The power of documentation in the early childhood classroom. *Young Children, 63*(3), 88–92.

Studer, J. R. (1993). Listen so that parents will speak. *Childhood Education, 70*(2), 74–77.

Wolfe, P., & Brandt, R. (1998, November). What do we know from brain research? *Educational Leadership, 56,* 8–13.

Chapter 9

Brickmayer, J., Cohen, J., Jensen, I. D., Variano, D. A. (2005). Supporting grandparents who raise grandchildren. *Young Children, 60* (3), 100–109.

Bronson, M. B. (2000). Research in review: Recognizing and supporting the development of self-regulation in young children. *Young Children, 55* (2), 32–37.

Carlsson-Paige, N., & Levin, D. E. (1992). Making peace in violent times: A constructivist approach to conflict resolution. *Young Children, 48* (1), 4–13.

Carlsson-Paige, N., & Levin, D. E. (2000). *Before push comes to shove: Building conflict resolution skills with children:* St. Paul, MN: Redleaf Press.

Copple, C. & Bredekamp, S. (2009). *Developmentally appropriate practice In early childhood programs.* Washington, DC: National Association for the Education of Young Children.

Department of Health and Human Services. (2001). Report of the Surgeon General's Conference on Children's Mental Health: A National Action Agenda. http://www.surgeongeneral.gov/cmh/childreport.htm

DeToledo, S., & Brown, D. (1995). *Grandparents as parents: A survival guide for raising a second family*. New York: Guilford.

Dinwiddie, S. A. (1994). The saga of Sally, Sammy, and the red pen: Facilitating children's social problem solving. *Young Children, 49* (5), 13–19.

Educational Productions. (1997). *Doing the groundwork: From stopping misbehavior to teaching skills* [video]. Beaverton, OR: Educational Productions.

Evans, B. (2002). *You can't come to my birthday party! Conflict resolution with young children*. Ypsilanti, MI: High/Scope Press.

Frieman, B. B., & Berkeley, T. R. (2002, Spring). Encouraging fathers to participate in the school experiences of young children: The teacher's role. *Early Childhood Education Journal*, 209–213.

Gadsden, V., & Ray, A. (2002) Engaging fathers: Issues and considerations for early childhood educators. *Young Children, 57*(6), 32–42.

Gartrell, D. J. (2004). *The power of Guidance: Teaching Social-emotional Skills in early childhood classrooms*. Clifton Woods, NY: Cengage Learning/NAEYC

Gestwicki, C. (2009). *Home, school, community relations* (7th ed.). Clifton Woods, NY: Cengage Learning.

Glass, C. J., & Huneycutt, T. L. (2002). Grandparents parenting grandchildren: Extent of situation, issues, involved, and educational implications. *Educational Gerontology, 28,* 139–161.

Janke, R. A., & Penshorn Peterson, J. (1995). *Peacemaker's A, B, Cs for young children: A guide for teaching conflict resolution with a peace table*. Marine on St. Croix, MN: Growing Communities for Peace.

Kim, A. M. & Yary, J. (2008). Making long-term separations easier for children and families. *Young Children, 63* (6), 32–36.

Kreidler, W. (1984). *Creative conflict resolution: More than 200 activities for keeping peace in the classroom*. Glenview, IL: Scott, Foresman.

Kreidler, W. J. (1994). *Teaching conflict resolution through children's literature*. New York: Scholastic Professional Books.

Pirtle, S. (1995). *Conflict management workshop guide*. Shelburne Falls, MA: The Discovery Center.

Porro, B. (1996). *Talk it out: Conflict resolution in the elementary classroom*. Association for Supervision and Curriculum Development.

Roger, A. & Henkin, N. (2000). School-based interventions for children in kinship care. In B. Hayslip, Jr. & R. Goldberg-Glen (Eds.), *Grandparents Raising Grandchildren: Theoretical, Empirical, and Clinical Perspectives*. (pp. 221–238). New York: Springer Publishing.

Shonkoff, J. P. & Phillips, D. A. (Eds.) (2000). *From neurons to neighborhoods: The science of early childhood development*. Washington, D. C.: National Academy Press.

Wichert, S. (1989). *Keeping the peace*. Philadelphia: New Society Publishers.

Williams, T. (2005, May 21). A place for grandparents who are parents again. *New York Times,* pp. B1, B6.

Williamson, J., Softas-Nell, B., Miller, J. (2003). Grandmothers raising grandchildren: An exploration of their experiences and emotions. *The Family Journal: Counseling and Therapy for Couples and Families, 11*(1), 23–32.

Wittmer, D. S., & Honig, A. S. (1994). Encouraging positive social development in young children. *Young Children, 49*(5), 4–12.

Chapter 10

Boyd-Zaharias, J. & Pate-Bain, H. (2008, September). Class matters—In and out of school. *Phi Delta Kappan*, 40–44.

Carlson, F. M. (2006). Essential touch: Meeting the needs of young children. Washington, DC: National Association for the Education of Young Children.

Charles, C. M., & Seuter, G. W. (1996, 2004). *Building classroom discipline* (8th ed.). White Plains, NY: Longman.

Clewett, A. S. (1988). Guidance and discipline: Teaching young children appropriate behavior. *Young Children, 43*(4), 26–36.

Coie, J. D. (1996). Prevention of violence and antisocial behavior. In R. DeVries, Peters & R. J. McMahon (Eds.), *Preventing childhood disorders, substance abuse, and delinquency* (pp. 1–18). Thousand Oaks, CA: Sage.

Coleman, M. (1997). Families and schools: In search of common ground. *Young Children, 52*(5), 14–21.

Dinwiddie, S. A. (1994). The saga of Sally, Sammy, and the red pen: Facilitating children's social problem-solving. *Young Children, 49*(5), 13–19.

Dodge, K. A. (1991). The structure and function of reactive and proactive aggression. In D. J. Pepler & K. H. Rubin (Eds.), *The development and treatment of childhood aggression* (pp. 201–218). Hillsdale, NJ: Erlbaum.

Evans, B. (2002). *You can't come to my birthday party! Conflict resolution with young children*. Ypsilanti, MI: High/Scope Educational Research Foundation.

Feeney, S., & Freeman, N. (2002). *Ethics and the early childhood educator using the NAEYC code*. Washington, DC: National Association for the Education of Young Children.

Galinsky, E. (1988). Parents and teacher-caregivers: Sources of tension, sources of support. *Young Children, 43*(3), 4–12.

Gartrell, D. J. (2004). *The power of guidance: Teaching social-emotional skills in early childhood classrooms*. Clifton Park, NY: Thomson Delmar Learning.

Gartrell, D. J. (2006). Guidance Matters: A spoonful of Laughter. *Young Children, 63*(4), 108–109.

Gestwicki, C. (2007). *Home, school and community relations. A guide to working with parents* (6th ed.). Clifton Park, NY: Thomson Delmar Learning.

Ginott, H. (1972). *Teacher and child.* New York: Macmillan Publishing Company.

Girard, K., & Koch, S. J. (1996). *Conflict resolution in the schools.* San Francisco: Jossey-Bass.

Glasser, W. (1969). *Schools without failure.* New York: Harper and Row.

Honig, A. S., 1989. Talk, read, joke, make friends: Language power for children. *Early Childhood Education Journal 6*(4), 14–17.

Jones, F. H. (1993). *Instructor's guide: Positive classroom discipline.* Santa Cruz, CA: Fredric H. Jones & Associates.

Kaiser, B. & Rasminsky, J. S. (2006). *Challenging behavior in young children: Understanding, preventing, and responding effectively* (2nd ed.). Pearson Education, Inc.: Boston, MA.

Kantrowitz, B., & Wingert, P. (1989, 17 April) How kids learn. *Newsweek,* 50–56. New York: Newsweek, Inc.

Klass, C. S., Guskin, K. A., & Thomas, M. (1995). The early childhood program: Promoting children's development through and within relationships. *Zero to Three, 16,* 9–17.

Koch, P. K., & McDonough, M. (1999). Improving parent-teacher conferences through collaborative conversations. *Young Children, 54*(2), 11–15.

Kounin, J. (1977). *Discipline and group management in classrooms.* (p. 259). New York: Holt, Rinehart and Winston.

Morgan, E. L. (1989). Talking with parents when concerns come up. *Young Children, 44*(2), 52–56.

Pappano, L. (2007). Meeting of the Minds. *Harvard Education Letter.* July/August 2007. www.edletter. (Reprinted in *Annual Editions: Early Childhood Education 09/10.*)

Pirtle, S. (1995). *Conflict management workshop guide.* Shelburne Falls, MA: The Discovery Center.

Preusse, K. (2005, March/April). Fostering prosocial behavior in young children. *Earlychildhood NEWS.* (Reprinted in *Annual Editions: Early Childhood Education 09/10.*)

Rosenthal, D. M., & Sawyers, J. Y. (1996). Building successful home/school partnerships: Strategies for parent support and involvement. *Childhood Education, 72*(4), 194–199.

Slaby, R. G., Roedell, W. C., Arezzo, D., & Hendrix, K. (1995). *Early violence prevention: Tools for teachers of young children.* Washington, DC: National Association for the Education of Young Children.

Surgeon General. (1999). *Surgeon General's report on mental health.* Washington, DC: Department of Health and Human Services.

Vance, E., & Weaver, P. (2002). *Class meetings: Young children solving problems together.* Washington, DC: NAEYC.

White, B. A., Graham, M., Bradford, S. K. (2005, March). Children of Teen Parents: Challenges and Hope. Zero to Three. 4–6.

Wichert, S. (1991, March). Solving problems together. *Scholastic Prekindergarten Today,* 46–52.

Chapter 11

Betz, C. (1994). Beyond time out: Tips from a teacher. *Young Children, 49*(3), 10–14.

Boutte, G. S., Keepler, D. L., Tyler, V. S., & Terry, B. Z. (1992). Effective techniques for involving 'difficult' parents. *Young Children, 47*(3), 19–24.

Bredekamp, S. & Copple, C. (2009) *Developmentally appropriate practice in early childhood programs.* Washington, DC: National Association for the Education of Young Children.

Brewer, J. A. (2007 6e). *Introduction to early childhood education: Preschool through primary years.* Boston: Allyn & Bacon.

Bronson, M. B. (2000). Recognizing and supporting the development of self-regulation in young children. *Young Children, 55*(2), 32–37.

Carlsson-Paige, N., & Levin, D. E. (1992). Making peace in violent times: A constructivist approach to conflict resolution. *Young Children, 48*(1), 4–13.

Clewett, A. S. (1988). Guidance and discipline: Teaching young children appropriate behavior. *Young Children, 43*(4), 25–36.

CPI (Crisis Prevention Institute). (1994). *Managing the crisis moment* (catalog). Brookfield, WI: National Crisis Prevention Institute.

Dreikurs, T. (1972). *Discipline without tears.* New York: Hawthorn Books, Inc.

Galinsky, E. (1988). Parents and teacher-caregivers: Sources of tension, sources of support. *Young Children, 43*(3), 4–12.

Gartrell, D. J. (2004). *The power of guidance: Teaching social-emotional skills in early childhood classrooms.* Clifton Park, NY: Thomson Delmar Learning and Washington, DC: NAEYC.

Ginott, H. (1972). *Teacher and child.* New York: Avon Books.

Gootman, M. (1993). Reaching and teaching abused children. *Childhood Education, 70*(1), 15–19.

Greenberg, P. O. (1988). Ideas that work with young children: Avoiding 'me against you' discipline. *Young Children, 44*(1), 24–29.

Heath, H. E. (1994). Dealing with difficult behaviors—Teachers plan with parents. *Young Children, 49*(5), 20–24.

Hendrick, J. (2001). *The whole child.* Columbus, OH: Merrill Publishing Company.

Jacobs, N. L. (1992). Unhappy endings. *Young Children, 47*(3), 23–27.

Jersild, A. S. (1985). *When teachers face themselves.* New York: Columbia University Press.

Katz, L. (1984). The professional early childhood teacher. *Young Children, 39*(5), 3–10.

King, M. (2004) Guidance with boys in early childhood classrooms. In Gartrell, *Power of Guidance: Teaching social emotional skills in early childhood classrooms.* Clifton Parks, NY: Thomson/Delmar Learning.

Koch, P. K., & McDonough, M. (1999). Improving parent-teacher conferences through collaborative conversations. *Young Children, 54*(2), 11–15.

Kindlon, D and Thompson, M. (1999) *Raising Cain: Protecting the emotional lives of boys,* New York: Ballantine Books.

Ladd, G. W., Price, J. M., & Hart, C. H. (1990). Preschoolers' behavioral orientations and patterns of peer contact: Predictive of peer status? In S. R. Asher & J. D. Coi (Eds.), *Peer rejection in childhood* (pp. 90–115). New York: Cambridge University Press.

Ligh, G (2002) *Traditional gender role behaviors in kindergartner's choices of play activities.* ERIC Document Reproduction Service No. ED448918.

Lightfoot, S. L. (1978). *Worlds apart: Relationships between families and schools.* New York: Basic.

Manning, D., & Schindler, P. J. (1997). Communicating with parents when their children have difficulties. *Young Children, 52*(5), 27–33.

Marion, M. (1999). *Guidance of young children.* Columbus, OH: Merrill Publishing.

McCormick L., & Feeney, S. (1995). Modifying and expanding activities for children with disabilities. *Young Children, 50*(4), 10–17.

Newberger, E. H. (1999). *The men they will become: The nature and nurture of male character.* Cambridge, MA: Perseus Publishing.

Nelson, B. G. (2002). *The importance of men teachers and reasons why there are so few. Washington, DC: NAEYC. www.MenTeach.org.*

Pappano, L. (2007). Meeting of the Minds [in conferences with parents]. *Harvard Education Letter.* July/August 2007. www.edletter. (Reprinted in *Annual Editions: Early Childhood 2009–2010.)*

Piaget, J. (1960). *The moral judgment of the child.* Glencoe, IL: The Free Press.

Polce-Lynch, M. (2002). *Boy talk: How you can help your son express his emotions,* Oakland, CA: New Harbinger Publications.

Pollack, W. (2001) *Real boys workbook: The definitive guide to understanding and interacting with boys of all ages.* New York: Villard Books.

Pollack, W. (1998). *Real boys: Rescuing our sons from the myths of boyhood,* New York: Henry Holt and Company.

Powell, D. R. (1989). *Families and early childhood programs.* Washington, DC: National Association for the Education of Young Children.

Preuesse, K. (2002, March/April). Guidance and discipline strategies for young children: Time out is out. *Early Childhood News,* 12–16.

Rogers, R. E., Andre, L. C., & Hawley, M. K. (1996). *Parents and teachers as partners: Issues and challenges.* Fort Worth, TX: Houghton Mifflin.

Scelfo, J. (2007, September). Come back, Mr. Chips. *Newsweek.* 44.

Schreiber, M. E. (1999). Time-outs for toddlers: Is our goal punishment or education? *Young Children, 54*(4), 22–25.

Slaby, R. G., Roedell, W. C., Arezzo, D., & Hendrix, K. (1995). *Early violence prevention.* Washington, DC: National Association for the Education of Young Children.

Surgeon General. (1999). *Surgeon General's report on mental health.* Washington, DC: Department of Health and Human Services.

Warren, R. M. (1977). *Caring.* Washington, DC: National Association for the Education of Young Children.

Webb, L. D., Metha, A., Jordan, K. F. *Foundations of American education.* Upper Saddle River, NJ: Merrill.

Wittmer, D. S., & Honig, A. S. (1994). Encouraging positive social development in young children. *Young Children, 49*(5), 4–12.

Chapter 12

Alat, K. (2002). Traumatic events and children: How early childhood educators can help. *Childhood Education, 79*(1), 2–7.

Beane, A. L. (2000). *Bully free classroom.* Minneapolis, MN: Free Spirit Publishing.

Boyatzis, C. (1997). Of Power Rangers and v-chips. *Young Children, 52*(7), 74–79.

Bullock, J. R. (2002). Bullying among children. *Childhood Education, 79* (3), 130–133.

Children's Defense Fund. (2008). *The state of America's children: 2008.* Washington, DC: Children's Defense Fund.

Coleman, M. (1997). Families & schools: In search of common ground. *Young Children, 52*(5), 14–21.

Committee on Children, Second Step Program. Seattle, WA. Phone: (800) 634-4449 E-mail: info@cfchildren.org Web site: http://www.cfchildren.org

Derman-Sparks, L. (1989). *Anti-bias curriculum: Tools for empowering young children.* Washington, DC:

National Association for the Education of Young Children.

Elkind, D. (2007). *The power of play*. New York, NY: Decapo Press.

Elkind, D. (1989). *Miseducation: Preschoolers at risk*. New York: Alfred A. Knopf.

Faber, A., & Mazlich, E. (1974). *Liberated parents, liberated children*. New York: Avon Books.

Froschl, M., & Sprung, B. (1999). On purpose: Addressing teasing and bullying in early childhood. *Young Children, 54*(2), 70–72.

Gartrell, D. J. (2000). *What the kids said today: Using classroom conversations to become a better teacher*. St. Paul, MN: Redleaf Press.

Gestwicki, C. (2004). *Home, school and community relations: A guide to working with parents* (5th ed.). Clifton Park, NY: Thomson Delmar Learning.

Gilliam, W. (May, 2005). *Prekindergarteners left behind: Expulsion rates in preschool programs*. Yale University Child Study Center.

Ginott, H. (1972). *Teacher and child*. New York: Avon Books.

Girard, K., & Koch, S. J. (1996). *Conflict resolution in the schools*. San Francisco: Jossey-Bass Publishers.

Goffman, E. (1963). *Stigma: Notes on the management of spoiled identity*. Englewood Cliffs, NJ: Prentice-Hall.

Gootman, M. E. (1993). Reaching and teaching abused children. *Childhood Education, 70*(1), 15–19.

Harlow, S. D. (1975). *Special Education: The meeting of differences*. Grand Forks, ND: University of North Dakota.

Holmes, G. (2006). Nielsen Media Research reports television's popularity still growing. Nielsen Media Research. http://www.nielsenmedia.com/nc/portal/site/Public/menuitem.55dc65b4a7d5adff3f65936147a062a0/?vgnextoid=4156527aacccd010VgnVCM100000ac0a260aRCRD

Honig, A. S., & Wittmer, D. S. (1996). Helping children become more prosocial: Ideas for classrooms, families, schools, and communities. *Young Children, 51*(2), 62–70.

Hoover, J. H., & Oliver, R. (1996). *The bullying prevention handbook*. Bloomington, IN: National Education Service.

Hymel, S. & Ford, L. (2003). School completion and Academic Success: The impact of early social-emotional competence. *Encyclopedia for Early Childhood Development. June 6, 2003*. http://www.child-encyclopedia.com/documents/Hymel-FordANGxp.pdf.

Jackson, B. R. (1997). Creating a climate for healing in a violent society. *Young Children, 52*(7), 68–70.

Janke, R. A., & Penshorn Peterson, J. (1995). *Peacemaker's ABCs for young children*. Marine on St. Croix, MN: Growing Communities for Peace.

Kaiser, B., & Sklar-Rasminsky, J. (2003). *Challenging behavior in young children: Understanding, preventing, and responding effectively*. Boston, MA: Allyn & Bacon.

Kamii, C., (1984). Autonomy: The aim of education envisioned by Piaget. *Phi Delta Kappan, 65*(6), 410–415.

Kontos, S., & Wilcox-Herzog, A. (1997). Teachers' interactions with children: Why are they so important? *Young Children, 52*(2), 4–12.

Ladd, G. W., Kochenderfer, B. J., Coleman, C. (1996). Friendship quality as a predictor of young children's early school adjustment. *Child Development, 67*, 1103–1118.

Kriete, R. (2002). *The Morning Meeting Book*. Turner's Falls, MA: Northeast Foundation for Children, Inc.

LeDoux, J. (1996). *The emotional brain*. New York: Simon & Schuster.

Levin, D. L. (1994/2003). *Teaching young children in violent times: Building a peaceable classroom*. Cambridge, MA: Educators for Social Responsibility.

Lowenthal, B. (1999). Effects of maltreatment and ways to promote children's resiliency. *Childhood Education, 75*(4), 204–209.

Maslow, A. H. (1962). *Toward a psychology of being*. Princeton, NJ: D. Van Nostrand Company.

McCracken, J. B. (1992). Tossed salad is terrific: Values of multicultural programs for children and families. In *Alike and different: Exploring our humanity with young children*. Washington, DC: National Association for the Education of Young Children.

Nansel, T. R., Overpeck, M., Pilla, R. S., Ruan, W. J., Simons-Morton, B., & Scheidt, P. (2001). Bullying behaviors among U.S. youth: Prevalence and association with psychosocial adjustment. *Journal of the American Medical Association, 285*(16), 2094–2100.

Neuman, S. B., & Roskos, K. (1994). Bridging home and school with a culturally responsive approach. *Childhood Education, 70*(4), 210–214.

Pappano, L. (2007, July/August). Meeting of the Minds [in conferences with parents]. *Harvard Education Letter*. www.edletter. (Reprinted in *Annual Editions: Early Childhood 2009–2010.)*

Piaget, J. (1932/1960). *The moral judgment of the child*. Glencoe, IL: The Free Press.

Pirtle, S. (1997). *Linking up: Building the peaceable classroom with music and movement*. Boston: Educators for Social Responsibility.

Stoddard, E. (2008). Corporal punishment seen rife in U.S. schools. August 20, 2008. Reuters News Service. http://www.reuters.com/article/topNews/idUSN1931921320080820? pageNumber=2&virtualBrandChannel=0&sp=true

Slaby, R. G., Roedell, W. C., Arezzo, D., & Hendrix, K. (1995). *Early violence prevention*. Washington, DC: National Association for the Education of Young Children.

Surgeon General. (1999). *Surgeon General's report on violence*. Washington, DC: Department of Health and Human Services.

Szep, J. (2009). Child abuse spikes as U.S. Economy Founders. Medlline Plus, A Service of the U.S. National Library and the National Institutes of Health. http://www.nlm.nih.gov/medlineplus/news/fullstory_83019.htmlC

Swick, K. (2005). Promoting caring in children and families as prevention of violence strategy. *Early Childhood Education Journal, 32*(5), 341–346.

Swick, K. J. & Freeman, N. K. (2004). Nurturing peaceful children to create a caring world: The role of families and communities. *Childhood Education, 81*(1), 2–8.

Wardle, F. (1992). Building positive images: Interracial children and their families. In *Alike and different: Exploring our humanity with young children*. Washington, DC: National Association for the Education of Young Children.

Weinreb, M. L. (1997). Be a resiliency mentor: You may be a lifesaver for a high-risk child. *Young Children, 52*(2), 14–19.

York, S. (1991/2003). *Roots and wings: Affirming culture in early childhood programs*. St. Paul, MN: Redleaf Press.

Index

A

Ability tracking, 63
Academic performance, 141
Academic, losers and winners, 51
Academics, 20, 175, 252–253
Acceptance
   and behavior, *172*, 400, 474
   conditional, 60–61
   social, 16–19
Accountability,
   educational, 142, 170
   political, 170
*Accountability Shove-down: Resisting
   the Standards Movement in Early
   Childhood Education*, 142
Acknowledgment, and listening, 268, 306
Active play, 105
Activities. *See also* Encouraging classroom;
      Groups; Learning centers; Schedules;
      Transition time
   active and quiet times, 187–188, 213–
      218
   active play, 105, 214–215
   boisterous level, 185, 214–215,
      218, 413
   bucolic level, 185, 214, 218
   buffer, 231–233
   busy level, 178
   calendar, 220–222
   handout for parents, 524–530
   music, 7–8, 45, 65, 67, 86, 525,
      527, 528
   and large groups, 220
   physical, 203–206
   productive, 218
   and productive materials, 218
   self-directed, 58, 191
   show and tell, 222–223
   transition time, *212*, 228, 229, 230–235
   vigorous play, 214–215
   weather, 221–222
Adjustment, and social development, 60,
      71, 94, 132
Adjustor level, 96, *99*
Adler, Alfred, 14–15
Adult intervention, 428, 453
Adults, and child interaction

guidelines and, 262
inebriated, 453
and teacher teamwork, 55–56, 237–241
Aggression, 115–117
   bullying as, 477, 480, 500, 501
   defined, 115, 464
   direct, 115, 116
   indirect, 467
   instrumental, 115-116, 379, 468
   and levels of mistaken behavior,
      116–117
   mental, 501
   and mistaken behavior, 92, 115–117
   physical, 115, 479, 501
   psychological, 115
   and spanking, 466
   reactive, 115–116, 117, 501
   uses of, 115
Aggressor, in conflicts, 488
Amygdala, 74. *See also* Brain development;
      Brain research
Anger, 445–450, 455–456
   coping strategies, 451–453
   and creative conflicts, 450
   developmentally appropriate practice,
      24–25, 31
   and negative dissonances, 450, 482
   personal safeguards, 445
   reconciliation, 448–450
   safeguards, 447–448
   self-monitoring of, 445–447
   and teaching, 445–450, 455–456
Answering machines, 291
Antibias education/curriculum, 484,
486–488, 496
Anticipatory set, 227
Anxiety. *See also* Attachment
   and culturally linguistically different
      (CLD), 168
   and Encouraging classroom, 168-170
   and mistaken behavior, 168
   peak of, 55
   reduction of school, 168–170
   separation, 54–56
Arguments, *380*. *See also* Intervention
Art activities guidebook sample, for parent
      handout, 527–528

Assertive discipline, 20–22
   effects on children, 21
   effects on parents, 22
   effects on teachers, 21
Assessment, 66
   authentic, 66
   and multiple intelligences, 66
   performance, 66
Associates, and teaching team, 446
Assumptions, and intelligence, 63
Attachment
   healthy, 71, 76
   outside immediate family, 56
   process, and violence, 469
   at risk children and, 71
   separation anxiety and, 54
   stress and, 72
   theory, 54
   in toddlers, 57
Attendance,
   laws, 30
   taking of, 220
Attending, as listening technique, *306*
Attention deficit disorder (ADD), 106
Attention deficit/hyperactivity disorder
      (ADHD), 106, 214
Authentic assessment, 66
Autonomy, 45–47, 56–57
   defined, 4, 46
   educational practices that encourage,
      51, *67*
   heteronomy, 46, 98
   intellectual, 97
   moral, 46, 47
   parents and, 57
   and Piaget, 45–47
   versus shame and doubt, 56–57
Autonomy versus shame and doubt,
   56–57

B

Back to the basics, 20
Behavior. *See also* Boys; Mistaken
      behavior; Strong unmet needs
   challenging, 117–118
   and experimentation, 538
   goal-directed, 16

Behavior (continued)
  influence by others, 538
  and name calling, 279
  primary goal of, 17
  proactive, 469
  prosocial, 45, 192–194
  purpose of, 16–17
  selfish, 44
  and social acceptance, 17
  principles for understanding, 532,
    537–539
  and violence, 115–117, 123, 217,
    467–468, 477–483
Behavior management
  and boys, 418–419
  and clergy, 5
  and guidance tradition, 4, 37
  listening beyond, 308–311
Belonging, 60
  versus alienation, 60
  and initiative, 60
Bodily-kinesthetic intelligence, 60. See also
    Multiple intelligences
Boisterous activity level, 185, 214–215,
    218, 413
Books, 225
Bossiness, 15, 377, 378–380
Boys, 417–421
  behavior syndrome, 418
  combination strategies for, 422
  culture clashes, 417–418
  and friendly classrooms,
    418–419
  intervention considerations,
    419–421, 454
  and physical activity, 419
Boys Will Be Boys (Kantrowitz and
    Kalb), 105
Brain development, 72–75. See also Brain
    research
  at birth, 73
  and emotions, 74–75
  enriched environments, 73–74
  and personal development, 81
  research trends and, 72
  three and eight years of age, 16
  windows of opportunity, 74
Brain research, 72, 75–76. See also Brain
    development
  appropriate child care
    characteristics, 75
  contributions of, 72
  and early childhood education, 75–76
  infants, 76
  intelligence theories, 64, 74
  partnerships with parents, 75–76
  toddlers, 75–76
Bredekamp, Sue, 19
Brevity, and intervention, 389–390
Bribes versus encouragement,
    268–270
Bucolic activity level, 185, 214, 218

Buffer activities, 231–233. See also
    Transition time
  fast, 232
  primary level, 233
  slow, 231
Building Classroom Discipline
    (Charles), 16
Bullying
  case study, 500–504
  child approach, 481–482
  and children, 478
  communication with parents, 482–483
  in early education, 478
  family approach, 482–483
  guidance response to, 477–479
  level one, 479
  level three, 480
  level two, 479–480
  and liberation teaching, 480–483,
    501 502
  as physical aggression, 501
  preschool to grade 3 literature, 502–503
  staff approach, 482
  steps for, 504
  teacher-child relationship, 481–482
  as violence, 479
  websites for, 503–504
Bureau of Education in the Department of
    the Interior, 30
Busy activity level, 178

C
Calendar, activities for, 220–222
Calming, in interventions, 428–429,
    454–455
Canter, Lee, assertive discipline, 29–30
Cardinal principle (Ginott), 137
Caring, 192
Carlsson-Paige and Levin guidelines,
    346–348
Case study
  play dough conflict, 146, 309, 341–342
  theme-based instruction, 186
The Centers for Disease Control
    (CDC), 180
The Center on the Social and Emotional
    Foundations for Early Learning, 253
Challenging behavior, 117–118
  and emotional intelligence, 70–71
  and mistaken behavior, 92,
    117–118, 128
Challenging Behavior in Young Children
    (Kaiser and Sklar-Rasminsky), 23
Charlesworth, Rosalind, 41
Cherry, Clare, 215
Child care
  appropriateness of, 75–76
  matching with child, 139, 141–145
  and partnerships with parents, 156–157
  and separation anxiety, 54–56
Child-centered approach, 10
Child development. See Development

Childhood and Society (Erikson), 53
Childism, 304
Child negotiation. See Conflict
    management
Children. See also Early childhood; Strong
    unmet needs
  active nature of, 178–180
  and adult interaction, 420
  appropriate care, 75–76
  focus attention of, 182
  behavioral principles, 537–539
  and brain research, 72–76
  bullied, 478
  challenges faced by, 15, 140–141
  and concentration, 214
  ethical responsibilities toward,
    506–508
  and experimentation, 538
  growth and metamorphosis, 9
  and health issues, 70, 178–180, 213–214
  ideas, in the solution process, 396–397
  influenced behavior, 538
  and joy, 182
  labeling, 21, 51, 135-136
  need for novelty, 208
  need for reliability, 208
  observe, 182
  be receptive to, 182
  sedentary lifestyle of, 178, 213
  teach less, share more, 181–182
  and the whole child, 183
Children's Creative Response to Conflict
    Program, 26
Children's Defense Fund, 133, 464
Child-report, 390–392, 408. See also
    Intervention
Child study movement, 204–205
Circle gatherings, 276–277
Circle time, 272–273
Class meetings, 272–283. See also
    Encouraging classroom; Leadership
  case study, 299–301
  versus circle time, 272–273
  and democratic life skills, 275–276, 400
  educational/diagnostic, 277
  and encouraging classroom, 296, 300
  going home, 279
  guidelines for, 273–274
  holding of, 277–279
  and interventions, 420
  and liberation teaching, 153, 155
  and magic circles, 276–277
  and mistaken behavior, 148–149,
    280–282
  morning, 278–279
  open-ended, 191, 277
  in preschool, 30, 262, 279, 296, 286
  to solve problems, 277, 279–280,
    300–301
  starting, 282–283
  successful, 293, 300
  and toddlers, 282

types of, 277
workshops, 10
value of, 301
Classroom, 53–62, 94–97
and boys, 418–419
bullying, 478–479
disruptions, 134
model for social development in, 94–97,
192–194
multiage, 51
and personal development, 53–62
and positive teacher-child relationships,
132–133
responsive, 149, 151, 278, 421, 484
and stress, 325
Classroom, encouraging. See Encouraging
classroom
Clergy
and behavior management,
and guidance tradition, 4–7
Clinical approach, 11
Cliques, 285. See also Friendliness;
Leadership
Code of silence, and bullying, 481
Cognition, and violence, 469–470
Cognitive skills,
Collaboration, 241. See also Family;
Partnerships with parents; Teaching
team; Teamwork
Combs, Arthur, 19
Comenius, John, 6
Comfort corner, 308
Commanding choices, 427–428. See also
Crisis management; Intervention
Communication; Leadership;
Leadership communication; Listening
and children's feelings, 427
conflict management, 381,
427–428, 454
and contact talk, 37, 312–317
crisis management technique, 438,
424, 454
described, 381
e-mail, 289–291
and follow up, 428
and friendly humor, 318–321, 419
and friendly touch, 321–324
and follow up, 428
in-choice, 428
mediation, 381, 428
out-choice, 381, 428
and overfunctioning, 324
parent and teacher disagreements,
450–453
parental meetings, 291
parent-teacher conferences, 326–329
at prevention level, 427
and school-related stress, 306, 325
and ultimatums, 427
Community Board Program, 26
Community meetings. See
Class meetings

Competition, in child development, 85–86
Compliment sandwich, 37, 120–121,
317–318
Comprehensive guidance, 109–110,
434–437, 544–545. See also Guidance;
Mistaken behavior; Strong unmet
needs
applications, 436–437
case study, 439–443, 459–461
engagement and, 37–38
findings, 443–444
Individual Guidance Plan (IGP),
437–439, 443–445, 544–545
intervention strategy, 436, 544
and mistaken behavior, 109–110,
434–435
overview, 436
principles for, 532, 544–545
and special education, 437
steps in, 437
Compulsory attendance laws, 30
Concrete operations. See Development
Conditional acceptance, 60
Conferences, 292–295, 326–329
listening to parents, 328–329
parent-teacher, 292, 326–329
phases, 292–294
pitfalls to avoid in, 294–295
and reflective listening, 294, 306,
451–452
setting for, 326–327
suggestions for successful, 293, 327
Conflict management, 4, 26–27, 87,
145–146, 162–164, 340–372
basics, 340–341, 366
blame and, 352–353
and boys, 417–421
brainstorm solutions, 352
Carlsson-Paige and Levin guidelines,
346–348
case studies, 356–361, 459–461
child mediation, 146, 345, 453
child negotiation, 146, 348 –349,
355–356
closure, 357–358, 359, 360–361
cool down period, 351–352,
429–431
defining the problem, 357, 359, 360
democratic leadership, 263
described, 342
and developmental considerations,
346–349
and discussions, 352
executive function, 343
family structures and diversity,
361–366, 367
and feelings, 343
five-finger formula, 112, 147,
349–354, 366–367, 371
and guidance approach, 27, 61, 145–146
guidelines for, 341, 343–345
high adult intervention, 146

high-level mediation, 354–355
use of humor for, 419
impulse control, 343, 393
institution-caused, 413
low-level mediation, 355
mediation, 112, 342, 350–354,
370–372, 453
mediator, 341, 344
minimal adult intervention, 146
and mistaken behavior, 26–27, 91,
145–146, 148–149, 532, 537
monitoring, 352
negotiation, children take charge,
355–356
and parent involvement, 452
peace props, 348–349
peer mediation, 36
and potholes, 352–354
principles for, 27
protected response, 345
responsive leadership,
social competence, 342
social problem solving, 342, 347
solutions, reaching, 345, 357, 359–360
steps for, 461
talk and listen chairs, 348
teaching skills, 340–341,
354–361, 367
terms, 341–343
and unconditional positive regard,
138–139, 398, 421
and violence, 340, 343
Conflict resolution, 26–27, 342. See also
Conflict management
Conflict resolution movement, and
guidance tradition, 26–27
Conflicts, 145–146. See also Conflict
management
and boys, 417–421
case study, 370–372
creative,
defined, 91, 340, 371
life, 54
mediation procedure, 145–146, 112,
349–354, 440, 453
as mistaken behavior, 537
punishment and, 340
teacher-child, 395–396
Confrontation, and intervention, 425
Consistency, 262, 342, 374–374, 377
Constructive process, 47
Constructivist education, 13–14
Contact talk, 312–317
case study, 334–335
and early childhood, 37, 313,
314–315, 329–330
finding time for, 315
opportunities for, 314
planned approach to, 336
preschool level, 314–315
and primary grades, 37, 313,
315–317

Continuum of violence. *See* Violence
Cooling-down time,
Cooperation, 192, 193, 285
Cooperation with parents, 28, 318,
402–407. *See also* Family; Parents
Coping strategies, 451–453
Copple, Carol, *19*
Cornell, Joseph, 181
Corporal punishment. *See* Guidance
tradition
Correction, versus criticism, 92,
120–121, 389
Creative conflicts, 450, 452, 453, 456
Creative dissonances, 482
Crisis. *See* Conflict management; Crisis
intervention; Crisis management;
Intervention
Crisis intervention, 398, 436, 438, 454. *See
also* Commanding choices; Guidance;
Intervention
Crisis management, 149–153, 424–434
calming, 150–151, 419–420,
428–433, 540
commanding choices, 381, 427–428
cooling-down time, 151,
429–431, 540
correct by direction, 425–426
crisis intervention, 436, 438, 454
describe-express-direct, 426, 540
describe without labeling, 425
and being direct, 425–426, 454
displeasure, expression of, 425
and emotions management, 423
five-step process, 300, 371–372
goal of, 424
and guidelines and rules,
259–260, 295
overview, 424
passive restraint, 151–153, 433
physical restraint, 398,
433–434, 455
principles for, 532, 540–541
purpose of, 149
redirection, 424
request a choice, 149–150
and self-management, 423
self-removal, 432–433
separation, 424, 429
techniques, 424–434, 440–441,
454–455
time-out, 431–432
Criticism, versus correction, 92,
120–121, 389
Cross-age groupings, 51
Cross-grade groupings, 51
Cueing, 148, 208, 384, 408
Culprits, 21
Culturally linguistically different CLD)
in, 168
Curiosity, and mistaken behavior,
99–100

D
Daily program/schedule, 208–218. *See also*
Schedules
active and quiet times, 187–188,
213–218
and contact talk, 314
happy napping guide, 217
need for novelty, 208
predictability of, 218, 247
need for reliability, 208
sample, 209
teachable moments, 208
tracking, 209
DAP. *See* Developmentally appropriate
practice
Day chart, 209
Day clock, 209
Democratic life skills, 532, 533–534
and class meetings, 275–276
and encouraging classroom, 263
and guidance approach, 67, 400
and intervention, 400
principles for, 532, 533–534
Dendrites, 73, 74
Describe-express-direct, and mistaken
behavior, 426
Development, 41–44. *See also*
Developmental egocentrism; Social
development
actions to take, 88
and art, 59
and brain research, 16–17
concrete operations, 41–42, 50
and conflict management, 145–146,
162–164
and emotional intelligence, 68–71
Erikson's theory of, 53–62
foundation for, 41–44
Gardner's theory of, 62–68
inappropriate practices, 24
parent, 404
Piaget's stages of, 41
and play, 7–8, *67*, 79
preconcepts, 58
Vygotsky, 47–53
zone of proximal, 48
Developmental and self psychologists,
11–14. *See also* Developmental
psychology; Self psychology
Developmental egocentrism,
44–47, *286*
Developmentally appropriate practice
(DAP), 24–31, 170–182, 531–549
and accountability, 170
and active learning, 180–182
and anger, 24–25, 31
anticipatory set, 227
case study, 252–253
curriculum, 171, 175
and encouraging classroom,
170–182, 199

and guidelines/rules, 181–182,
259–260, 295
and interaction, 227
and large group instruction, 171-*172*
and learning centers, fo171, 175
Minnesota Association for the Education
of Young Children, 531
and mistaken behaviors, *172*
and primary grades, 175–180
principles for, 532, 535–537
role of principal, 177-178
and school anxiety, 168-169, 198
and school readiness, 172–175
and self psychologists, 15
successful outcomes, 252
techniques, 24
and volunteers, 245
working for change, 177
*Developmentally Appropriate Practice
in Early Childhood Programs*
(Bredekamp & Copple), 58
Developmentally Appropriate Practice in
Early Childhood Programs Serving
Children From Birth Through Age 8,
(NAEYC), 24
Developmentally inappropriate
practices, 24
and encouraging classroom,
improvement of, 144–145
Developmental psychology, 11
DeVries, R., *19*, 44–45
Dewey, John, 9, 10–*11*
Diagnosis, and special education, 64
Didactic method, 7
Differentiated staffing, 238–239. *See also*
Teaching team; Teamwork
Digital communication, 289–290
Direct aggression, 115, 116
Direct instruction, 227
Directresses, 9, 28
Discipline, 20–22. *See also* Guidance
tradition
assertive, 20–22
defined, 4
effects on children, 21
effects on teachers, 21
effects on parents, 22
guidance-based, 22–23
obedience-based, 20–21, 97
positive, 15
problems with, 20
versus punishment, 4, 340
transition to guidance, 22–27
Discipline with dignity, 61, 279, 428
Discussing inclusively, 224, 226, 270–273,
295. *See also* Leadership
Discussions. *See* Discussing inclusively;
Leadership
Disequilibrium, 43
Displeasure, expressing, 425
Diversity in families, 361–366

Dorphenheimer, Chris, 530
Dreikurs, Rudolph, 15–18, 163, 260, 261
  acceptance, child's need to have, 16
  conflicts, as social goal, 17–18
  goals of misbehavior, 16
  and positive discipline, 15
  praise as a final judgment, 15
  teachers as leaders, 15–16
Dual language learners (DLLs), 259

E
Early childhood. *See also* Brain research; Children
  and brain research, 75–76
  bullying and, 478
  calendar and weather activities, 220–222
  challenges of, 140–141
  and collaboration, 241
  and conflict management, 145–146, 162–164
  and contact talk, 37, 313, 314–315
  guidebook sample for families, 523–530
  and industry versus inferiority, 14, 60–62
  and large groups, 138–139, 144
  and lines, 233–235
  and multiple intelligences, 66–67
  partnerships with parents, 76–80, 156–157
  show and tell, 222–223
  and stories, 223–226
  unconditional positive regard, 136–139, 234
Early Childhood Education in Historical Perspective (Osborn), 5
Early Head Start, 29
Educational accountability, 170
Educators for Social Responsibility, 26
Egocentric speech, 50
Egocentrism. *See* Developmental egocentrism
Eight stage-based crisis. *See* Erikson, Erik
Elkind, David, *19*, 60–61, 87, 188
E-mail, and parental communication, 289–290
Emergent curriculum, 171, 177, 226
Emilia, Reggio, 13, 183, 186, 190. *See also* Reggio Emilia schools
Emotional Brain, The (Ledoux), 74
Emotional intelligence, 68–71
  and challenging behaviors, 70–71
  components of, 68–70
  defined, 68–70
  and emotional literacy, 69
  and personal development, 81
Emotional literacy, 69
Emotional readiness, 86–87
Emotions. *See also* Mistaken behavior; Strong unmet needs
  and brain development, 16
  management of, 53, 70, 421,

423–424, 469
  private speech and, 53
  and self-management, 423
  and strong unmet needs mistaken behavior, 98, *99*, 105–110, 122
  trivialized, 240
  and violence, 108, 468
Encounterer
  and mistaken behavior, *99*
  and social development, 92
Encountering level, 97, *99*
Encouragement, 264–270
  and effort, *269*
  and guidelines reinforcement, 262
  and praise, 15–16, 264–265, 295
  private, 266–267
  and progress, *269*
  public, 265–267
  Rudolph Dreikurs, 15–16, 163, 265
  starter statement, 268
  stickers and smiley faces, 268–270
  what to say, 267–268
Encouraging classroom, 165–198, 484–, 532, 534–535. *See also* Activities; Developmentally appropriate practice; Guidance; Learning centers; Schedules; Teamwork
  accountability in, 170
  active and quiet times, 213–218
  and active nature of children, 178–180
  active learning, 180–182
  activities, 187–190
  and attendance, 30, 220
  calendar and weather, 220–221
  class meetings, 272–283, 484
  culturally linguistically different CLD) in, 168
  curriculum, 171, 190–191, 226
  and daily schedule/program, 208–218, 247
  described, 4
  and developmentally appropriate practice, 24–25, 31, 170–182, 484–485
  and developmentally inappropriate 24, 188
  educational/developmental outcomes, 400
  and friendliness, 283–287
  and intervention, 374–409
  and large groups, 218–220, 226–229, 248
  and learning centers, 182–191
  and liberation teaching, 153–156, 484–485
  and life skills, 170, 172, 183
  management of, 207
  and mistaken behavior, *172*
  and outdoor teaching, 181–182
  overview, 169–170
  and parents, roadblocks to involvement of, 195–196

personalization of programs, 52
physical activities, 213–214
and play, 172–175, 214–215
primary grades, 175–177, 188–190
principal, role of in, 177–178
principles for, 532, 534–535
and prosocial development, 192–194
and reading encouragement, 224
and responsive leader, 177
rest and relaxation, 215–218
and routines, 186–187, 235–237, 248, 258–259
sharing in, 222
and school anxiety, 168–169
and school readiness, 172–175
show and tell, 222–223
and stories, 223–226
and teaching, 4
and teaching team, 241–242
and transitions, 230–235, 248, 230–235
unconditional positive regard, 136–139, 234
volunteers, 194–198, 241–246, 249
and zone of proximal development, 48
Enriched environment. *See also* Brain development; Encouraging classroom; Environment
  and brain development, 63, 73, 81
  enriched, 76
Equilibrium, 43
Erickson, Erik, 53–62
  autonomy versus shame and doubt, 56–57
  classrooms and development, 53–62
  four childhood stages, *54*
  eight stage-based crisis, 53
  industry versus inferiority, 14, 60–62
  initiative and belonging, 60
  initiative versus guilt, 57–60
  life conflicts, 87
  link between child development and guidance, 80–81
  self psychologists, *19*
  separation anxiety, 54–55
  trust versus mistrust, 53–56
Erickson, Marti, 181
Ethic of caring, 283. *See also* Friendliness
Ethics, 40, 400–402. *See also* National Association for the Education of Young Children (NAEYC)
  code of, 400–402, 505–514
  children and, 40
  and intervention, 400–402
  responsibilities toward children, 506–508
  responsibilities toward colleagues, 510–512
  responsibilities toward community and society, 512–514
  responsibilities toward families, 508–510

Eugenics, 63
Executive function, 46, 71, 343
Expansion, as listening technique, *306*
Experimentation. *See also* Mistaken
  behavior
  and learning centers, 342, 467, 479, 526
  and mistaken behavior, 98–100, 122
Exploratory activities, 191
Expulsion, 133
Eye contact, for conflict management, 387

F
Family. *See also* Parents
  and conflict management, 460
  cultural factors, 168
  diversity in, 361–366
  economic factors,
  ethical responsibilities toward, 508–510
  fathers, 363–364
  feelings toward, 403–404
  grandparents, 364–366
  parent development, 404
  problem solve with, 405
  single father, 362–363
  social factors, 102
  stereotypes, 174
  structures, 361–366
  and support services, 406–407
  and teacher meetings, 291
  and teacher partnerships, 156–157, 159
  and teacher relationship, 438, 440
  and team concept, 438
  toddler conflicts, 57
  as volunteers, 194–198, 242–243, 248
Fellowship or Reconciliation in Nyack, 26
Firmness. *See* Intervention
Five-finger formula, 147, 349–354. *See also*
  Conflict management
Fixed intelligence. *See* Intelligence
Formal operations stage, 41
Friendliness, 283–287. *See also* Leadership
  cliques and squabbling, addressing, 285
  defining, 285–286
  example of, 286–287
  friendships and friendliness,
  283–284, 296
  in preprimary conflicts, *286*
Friendly Classroom for a Small Planet,
  The, 27
Friendly Classrooms, for boys, 418–419
Friendly humor, 294, 318–321, 330, 419
Friendly touch, 321–324, 330
Friends, and preschoolers, *286. See also*
  Friendliness
Friendship, 283–286 Froebel, Friedrich, 7–8
  and kindergarten, 28

G
Galinsky, E., 405–406
̇andini, *19*
̇ner, Howard, 62–68. *See also* Multiple
  ̇telligences

Ginott, Haim, 18–20
Glasser, William, 276–277, 279–280
Goal-directed behavior, 16
Godly Form of Household Government,
  A (1621), 5
Goleman, Daniel, 69–70. *See also*
  Emotional intelligence
Grace Contrino Abrams,
  Foundation, 26
Grandparents, support for, 364–366
Great Didactic, The (Comenius), 6
Greenberg, Polly, 162
Greetings, 311–312
Groups. *See also* Encouraging classroom
  assessment of, 50
  attendance taking, 220
  calendar and weather, 220–222
  and early childhood, 66–68
  and group spirit, 266
  inclusive, 134
  instruction of large, 171-*172*
  limits of large, 218–229
  our-groups become in-groups, 134
  show and tell, 222–223
  stories with children, 223–226
Growth, and safety, 154, 159
Growth needs, 48, 69, 153, 365, 404
Guidance. *See also* Comprehensive
  guidance; Guidance tradition;
  Mistaken behavior; Strong unmet
  needs
  childhood challenges, 140–141
  childhood educators, 22
  comprehensive and strong unmet
  needs, 37, 109–110
  and conflict resolution management,
  26–27
  crisis intervention, 436, 438, 454
  defined, 25–26, 531
  discipline and, 22
  and IEP (Individual Education
  Plan), 437
  and IGP (Individual Guidance Plan),
  437–445,
  and labeling, 51, 135–136, 425
  learning while teaching, 130–132
  and liberation teaching, 153–156,
  470–477, 485
  and misbehavior, 91, 112, 158
  mistaken behavior reduction, 91,
  112–114, 158
  and multiple intelligences, 67–68
  NAEYC definition of, 531
  and physical restraint, 398,
  433–434, 455
  positive, 137
  problem-solving approach, 23
  protecting personality, 136–139
  responsive classroom, 278, 300, 421
  routines and, 258–259
  six principles of, 37–38
  solution-orientation, 145–153, 158

and special education, 437
  successful outcomes, 252
  teacher-child relations, 132–139, 438
  and teaching, 37–38
  and teaching routines, 186–187,
  235–237, 248, 258–259
  and teamwork, 237–241
  tips, 120–122
  unconditional positive regard,
  136–139, 234
  with-it-ness, 375–376
Guidance approach. *See also* Guidance;
  Guidance tradition; Piaget, Jean
  and autonomy, 45–47, 56–57
  and conflict resolution management,
  26–27
  and developmentally appropriate
  practices, 252
  and democratic life skills, 275–276
  and discipline versus punishment,
  4, 340
  educational/developmental
  outcomes, 400
  firm and friendly, 4
  and Friedrich Froebel, 7–8, *11*
  and Johann Pestalozzi, 7, *11*
  and John Comenius, 6, *11*
  and John Dewey, 10–*11*
  and Maria Montessori, 8–10, *11*
  and Robert Owen, 7, *11*
  roots of, 4
  and teaching approach, 186–187,
  235–237, 248, 258–259
Guidance-based discipline, 22–23
  and teacher-directed
  education, 24–25
Guidance talks, 112-114, 147–148, 394–395
  conflict mediation, 112, 147–148
  and intervention, 163, 112–114,
  394–395, 420
  and mistaken behavior, 112–114
  and teachers, 114
Guidance tradition, 4–11
  child-centered, 10
  and clergy, 5, 6
  and conflict resolution movement,
  26–27
  and corporal punishment, 5–6
  developmental and self
  psychologists, 11
  and developmentally appropriate,
  24–25, 13
  discipline and, 22–23
  practice, 188
  early childhood educators, 22–23
  Froebel's kindergartens, 7–8
  goals of, 4
  Head Start, 29, 76, 138
  Jeremiah case study, 35–38
  and management of behavior, 4–5
  mid-20th-century influences,
  11–20, 32

Montessori's children houses, 9
and multiple intelligences, 62–68
in the 1980s, 20–22, 32
nursery school, 29
and partnerships with parents, 27–31, 33, 76– 80, 156–157
pioneers of, 4–11, *19*, 32
practices, 8
prepared environment for, 9
principles, 7
public schools, 29–30
state of today, 33
techniques for, 37
three-way relationships, 4–5
transition from discipline, 22–27
views of human nature, 5
Guidance with Boys in Early Childhood Classrooms, King (2004), 418
Guidelines, 259–264
age levels for, 262–263
benefits of, 262–263
class meetings, 273–274
for conflict management, 343–345
creation of, 263–264
and democratic classroom, 263
at different age levels, 262–263
and encouragement, 265–267, *269*, *390*
for Individual Guidance Plan (IGP), 438–439
and logical consequences, 23, 260–262
and peace props, 348
reasons for, 262–264
and rules, 259–260, 295
parent and teacher disagreements, 450–453
and punishment, 5–6, 259–260
and teacher's role, 264
and transitions, 230–231
Guiding Young Children (Reynolds), 23

H
Happygram, 288
Harlow, Steven D., 94–95, 98, 108. *See also* Social development
Hatch, J.A., 142
Head Start, 27, 30, 335–336
Health, and strong unmet needs, 105, 106. *See also* Mistaken behavior; Strong unmet needs
Health education guidebook, handout for parents, 529–530
Healthy, personal development, 17
Helping, 192
Heteronomy, 46, 98. *See also* Autonomy and scaffolding,
High adult intervention, 146
High level mediation. *See* Conflict management
High/Scope Model, 187
High-stakes testing, 61

school anxiety and, 168
Hippocampus, 74. *See also* Brain development; Brain research
Home visits, 28–30
Hughes, Marilyn, 188–189
Humor, and intervention, 384–386, 419. *See also* Friendly humor

I
I Am Moving, I Am Learning, 204–205
IGP (Individual Guidance Plan), 437–445
case study, 439–443, 460–461
findings, 443–445
guidelines, 438–439
implementation, 439, 442–443
Individual Education Plan (IEP), 437
and comprehensive guidance, 37, 437–439, 443–445, 455
meetings, 439, 442
and mistaken behavior, 437–439
review and modify, 439, 443
and special education, 437
trends in, 443–444
worksheet, 551–552
I-messages, 265, *306*, 395, 448, 455
Immigrants and education, historical, 28, 30
Impulse control, 343
Impulse management, 393, 421. *See also* Intervention
Impulsiveness, 343
In-choice. *See* Intervention
Inclusion, 60
Inclusive solutions, 224, 226, 485
Independent activity, 189–190
Indirect aggression, 467
Individual Education Plan (IEP), 437
Individual Guidance Plan (IGP). *See* IGP
Industry versus inferiority, 60–62.
See also Erickson, Erik
feelings of inferiority, 14
and industry promotion, 14, 61–62
and low self-esteem, 14
Infants
autonomy versus shame and doubt, 56–57
and brain research, 76
separation anxiety, 54
and trust versus mistrust, 53–56
Inferiority, feelings of, 14
Information, application, 438, 441, 491
Insults, 425
Intelligence, and ethics, 40
Initiative
and belonging, 60. *See also* Initiative versus guilt and friends, 57–60. *See also* Erickson, Erik
and play, 57–60
In-room isolation. *See* Time-out
Institution-caused mistaken behavior, 133–134

and learning centers, 142–142
Instruction, large group, 171–*172*. *See also* Groups
Instrumental aggression, 115–116
Integrated curriculum, 171, 226
and learning centers, 190–191
Intellectual autonomy. *See* Autonomy
Intelligence, 63–64, 74. *See also* Emotional intelligence; Multiple intelligences
brain research, 64, 74
emotional, 69–70
environmental factors, 71
fixed, 63, 73
physiological factors, 70
psychological factors, 70–71
quotients, 69
Intentionality, and mistaken behavior, 92, 100, 111–115, 162–164. *See also* Mistaken behavior
Interaction, adult-child, 55–56, 237–241, 262
Interpersonal intelligence, *65*, 67–68, 81. *See also* Multiple intelligences
Intervention, 374–409. *See also* Conflict management; Crisis management; Mistaken behavior
and arguments, *380*
and bossiness, 378–380
and boys, 411–414, 417–421
and brevity, 389–*390*
calming in, 419–420
children's ideas, 396–397
and child-report, 390–392, 408
choices, 376–380
combination, 423
commanding choices, 381, 427–428
conditions necessitating, 421–424
and consistency, 374, 375, 377
correct by direction, 389–*390*
degrees of firmness, 380–382
as democratic leader, 344
and democratic life skills, 400
and describe-express-direct, 426
diagnose the conflict, 419
diffusion, of the situation, 419
direct, 387
and ethics, 400–402
and family diversity, 402–407, 409
fair-mindedness, 344
and feelings toward the family, 403–404
firmness of, 374–375, 380–382
and follow-up, 392–398, 408, 420
guidance practices, 145, 420, 436
guidance talk, 112–114, 394–395, 420, 421
and humor, 384–386, 419
impulse management, 393, 421
in-choice, 381–382
instrumental aggression, 379
intentional mistaken behavior, 112–115, 162–164
inviting choices, 381

Intervention (*continued*)
  labeling, 136, 425
  marginal mistaken behaviors, 376–378
  and moral authorities, 344
  necessity for, 421–424
  and negotiation reminders, 383–384
  non-punitive, 57, 109–*110*, 423, 433
  and non-verbal techniques, 386–389
  and nurturing, 421
  out-choice, 382
  overview, 374, 407
  and parents, 402–403, 404
  parents and teachers, 450–453, 456
  positive consistency, 374, 377
  principles for, 532, 541–543
  private, 37
  private talks, 420
  problem solving, with families, 405
  quick strategies, 382–392, 408
  reality checks for, *378*
  reasons for, 412–413
  and reconciliation, 394, 397–398
  reflective listening, 393–*394*, 451–452
  respectfulness, 37
  requesting choices, 381
  sentence frames, 384
  strategies, 382–390
  for stress in children, 76
  and support services, 406–407
  and tattling, 390, 408
  teachable moment, 396
  teacher-child conflict, 395–396
  techniques, 417–421
  threats and, 420
  time considerations, 398–400
  with-it-ness, 375–376
  words, and value judgments, 404–405
Intimacy, and violence, 469
Intrapersonal intelligence, *67*, 68.
    See also Multiple intelligences
Inviting choices. *See* Intervention
Involvement, and mistaken behavior, 99
Isolation. *See* Time-out

J
Jones, Fredric, 387-389
Jochum, Julie, 317
Journal of the American Medical
    Association, 500

K
Kaiser, Barbara, 117-118
*Keeping the Peace: Practicing Cooperation
    and Conflict Resolution with
    Preschoolers* (Wichert), 146
Kids in Action, 204, 205
Kindergarten
  academic programming, 20, 141
  and Friedrich Froebel, 28
  idelines for, 262
  erships with parents, 77

  and play, 173–174
  sample schedule for, *211*
Kreidler's ABCD procedure, 349

L
Labeling, 135–136
  behavior, 214
  describe without, 425
  in encouraging classrooms, 51
  and special education, 64
Language,
  and brain development, 74
  and dual learners, 259
  value-laden, 404–405
Large groups, 218–229. *See* Groups
  activities, 248
  arguments for, 218–220, 226–229
  attendance, 220
  calendar and the weather, 220–222
  class meetings, 148–149, 220, 222,
    287, *293*
  communication, 222–223
  discussing inclusively, 224, 226, 295
  and encouragement, 224
  encouraging friendliness, 219, 283–284
  establishment of, 227, 248
  limited, 220
  prolonged sitting and listening in, *172*
  sharing in, 222
  show-and-tell in, 222–223
  using songs, 220
  using stories, 223–226
Last Child in the Woods, (Richard
    Louv), 202
Leadership, 256–259, 287–295
  addressing cliques and squabbling, 285
  and answering machines, 291
  class meeting guidelines, *293*
  class meetings, 287
  communication, 256
  discussing inclusively, 270–273, 295
  and e-mail, 289–290
  and encouragement, 264–270
  encouraging friendliness, 283–284
  establishment of, 256–259, 295
  group focused, 256
  guidelines and rules, 259–260, 295
  line leaders, 234
  parental communication, 287–295
  parental meetings, 291
  parent-teacher conference, 292–295,
    326–329
  reflective listening and, 294, *306*,
    451–452
  successful meetings, *293*
  and teamwork, 240–241
  and telephone calls, 290–291
  and text messaging, 289–290
  and websites, 290
  and written notes, 288–289
Leadership communication, 287–295,
    301–336. *See also* Communication;

    Compliment sandwich; Contact talks;
    Friendly humor; Friendly touch;
    Listening
  activities toward, 287–288
  and compliment sandwich, 37, 290, 294,
    317–318
  and contact talk, 37, 312–317
  described, 256
  five skills for, 304. *See also* individual
    terms
  and friendly humor, 294, 318–321
  and friendly touch, 321–324
  grouped focused, 256
  joining with parents, 287–295
  and life experiences, 305–308
  and listening techniques, 271–272,
    304–312
  and overfunctioning, 324
  with parents, 287
  in parent-teacher conferences,
    326–329, 331
  teachers as leaders, 15–16
Learning centers, 183–191. *See also*
    Developmentally appropriate practice;
    Encouraging classroom
  active nature of, 178–180
  active play, 105, 214–215
  described, 183
  and encouraging classroom,
    183–191, 199
  and guidance, 183
  and integrated curriculum, 190–191
  interests of children, 185–186
  models for, 190–191
  noise levels, 183–185
  organizing, 183–188
  primary level, 188–190
  routine use of, 186–187, 235–237, 248,
    258–259
  and theme-based instruction,
    185–186, 190, 199
  time and choices for, 187–188
  3B system, 185
  traffic patterns, 183–185
*Learning from the Past: Historical Voices
    in Early Childhood Education*
    (2002), 6
LeDoux, Joseph, 74–75
Letters, introductory. *See also* Surveys
  to families, 515, 517–518
  to children, 515–516
Liberation
  defined, 154
  versus stigma, 153, 471–472
Liberation teaching, 153–156, 470–477
  antibias curriculum, 484,
    486–488, 496
  and bullying, 496, 501–502
  bullying prevention, 478, 480–482,
    502, 504
  child's needs and, 154, 475
  and class meetings, 153, 155, 484

defined, 464
developmentally appropriate practices, 484–485
and encouraging classroom, 158–159, 484–485
and educational practices, 153–156, 483–490, 496
and guidance, 485
guidance response, 470–477
human relations empowerment, 485
level four, personal development, 494–495
level one, sharing information with parents, 491
level three, program participation, 493–494
level two, active parent involvement, 491–493
multicultural education, 486
parent involvement, 452, 490–495, 496–497
peace education, 488–490
personal/professional development, 494–495
policy, 479, 482, 493–494
preschool expulsion, 472
professional development, 494–495
program participation, 493–494
protective buffer, 477
and resiliency, 475–477
responses, 473–475
self-acceptance and, 155–156
sharing with parents, 491–493
and societal violence, 464, 496
social environment, 475–477
staff, 482
stigma versus liberation, 153, 471–473
tossed salad approach, 492
tourist curriculum, 486
and vulnerability factors, 472–473
Lines, 233–235. See also Transition time
Linguistic intelligence, 64–65. See also Multiple intelligences
Listening, 271–272, 304–312
and acknowledgment of feelings, 268, 306
active, 306,
beyond the behavior, 308–311
children who aren't, 271–272
discussions and, 271–272
fully, 311
and greetings, 311–312
home-related stress, 307–308
and parents, 308
reflective, 294, 306, 451–452
for relationship building, 306
school-related stress, 306, 325
techniques, 304–312
to life experiences, 305–308
Literacy, national drive toward, 177
Logan, Tessa, 286–287

Logical consequences, 23, 260–262. See also Guidelines
Logical-mathematical intelligence, 64–65, 67, 174. See also Multiple intelligences
Low-level mediation. See Conflict management

M
Making the Case for Play Policy: Research-Based Reasons to Support Play-Based Environments (Setgelin), 174
Mandated reporters, 307
Microcosmography (Earle), 5
Magic circles. See Class meetings
Management of behavior, and guidance approach, 4–6
Maslow, Abraham, 14, 19, 154
Mastery motivation, 188
Mathematics guidebook sample, for parent handout, 525–526
Mediation, 48, 349–354, 453
case study, 370–372
and the five-finger formula, 147, 349–354
and intervention, 420
and personal grudge, 453
Meetings. See Class meetings; Communication; Leadership
Melting pot, 30
Metacognitive view, 187
Minimal adult intervention, 146
Minnesota
Association for the Education of Young Children, 531
Early Childhood Family Education, 30
Misbehavior, 90–92. See also Experimentation; Guidelines; Harlow, Steven, D.; Social development; Socially influenced misbehavior; Strong unmet needs
Miseducation: Preschoolers at Risk (Elkind), 88
Mistaken behavior, 90–128. See also Experimentation; Guidelines; Harlow, Steven, D.; Social development; Socially influenced misbehavior; Strong unmet needs; Violence
and adults, 102, 108, 120
and aggression, 115–117
appropriate practice to reduce, 24–25, 172
and bullying, 115, 116, 123, 479–480
buttons relating to, 92
and challenging behavior, 117–118, 128
childhood challenges and, 140–141
and class meetings, 102, 103, 104, 117, 127
conflict as, principles for, 532, 537

and conflict management, 26–27, 91, 145–146, 148–149, 162–164, 280–282
concept of, 92–93, 121
consequences for, 91
considerations in, 122–123
described, 90–91
and describe-express-direct, 426
and developmentally appropriate practice, 24–25, 31
and developmentally inappropriate practices, 24
and directness, 24
emotional causes of, 423–424
and emotional intelligence, 70–71
environmental causes of, 71
experimentation, 98, 99–100
factors involved in, 139
and going public with, 280–282
and guidance, 91, 158
and guidance talks, 112–114
goals for, 16
and health problems, 70, 106–108
as inappropriate term, 121
institution-caused, 133–134, 142–143
and intentionality, 92, 111–115, 162–164
and intervention, 102, 112–115, 376–378
Level One, 98–100, 467, 468
Level Three, 98, 99, 105–110, 217, 280–282
Level Two, 98, 99, 100–105, 479–480
levels of, 110–111
and logical consequences, 23, 260–262
marginal, 376–378
matching problems with the program, 141–145
and misbehavior, 90–92
and parent communication, 118–121
physiological causes of, 70, 106–108
psychological causes of, 71, 108
reduction of, 139–145
and relational patterns, 94–97, 122
research conclusions, 71
and school anxiety, 168
socially influenced, 98, 99, 100–105
sources of motivation, 98–99, 111
strong unmet needs, 98, 99, 105–110, 122
swearing, 126–127
and transition time, 109, 110, 248
vicious cycle of, 134
and violence, 115, 116, 117
and words that hurt, 127–128, 481
Montessori Children's Houses, 28–29
early centers, 9
and parents, 27
and the daily program, 208
Montessori, Maria, 8–10, 32
and Children's Houses, 28–29
Montessori Method, The, 9

Moral autonomy. *See Autonomy Moral Judgment of the Child, The* (Piaget),
The Moral Judgment of the Child (1932/1960), 13
Multiage classrooms, 51
Multicultural education, 486
Multidimensional classroom, 241–242
Multiple intelligences, 62–68
  and ability tracks, 63
  and assessment, 66
  assumptions for, 63
  bodily-kinesthetic, 67
  compatible principals, 65–67
  defined, 62, 64
  and early childhood, 66–67
  emotional, 68–71
  fostering, 67
  and guidance, 67–68, 81
  identification of, 65
  implications of, 64–66
  as an integrative theory, 64
  interpersonal, 67
  intrapersonal, 67, 68
  linguistic, 67
  logical-mathematical, 67
  overview, 62–64
  musical, 67
  naturalist, 67
  social policy and, 63
  spatial, 67
  and special education, 64
  and standardized tests, 63, 65–66
Musical intelligence, 65. *See also* Multiple intelligences
Mutual respect, 452

N
NAEYC. *See* National Association for the Education of Young Children
Naps
  guide to, 217
  purpose of, 217–218. *See also* Schedules
National Association for the Education of Young Children (NAEYC),
  code of ethics, 400–402, 505–514, 546
  conceptual framework, 506
  core values, 505–506
  and developmentally appropriate practice (DAP), 22, 170
  guidance defined, 25
  and guidelines, 262–263
  inappropriate discipline, 24
  preamble, 505
  responsibilities toward children, 506–508
  responsibilities toward colleagues, 510–512
  responsibilities toward community and society, 512–514
  responsibilities toward families, 508–510
  school readiness, 172
  statement of commitment, 514

National Association for Mediation in Education, 27
National Institute for Dispute Resolution, 27
National Institutes of Child Health and Human Development, 477
National Prekindergarten Study, 36
Naturalist intelligence, 65, 67, 182. *See also* Multiple intelligences
Negative dissonances, 482
Negotiating. *See* Intervention; Teacher-child negotiating
Negotiation,
  children take charge, 355–356
  reminders, and intervention, 383–384
Neo-Piagetian, 13
Neurons to Neighborhood: The Science of Early Childhood Development, 72
No Child Left Behind Act, 24–25, 177
Noise levels, and learning centers, 183–185
Nonstratified sharing, 51
Non-verbal intervention techniques, 386–389
Nursery school, 29

O
Obedience-based discipline, 20–22. *See also* Assertive discipline
  and teacher-directed education, 21, 97
Obesity, and physical activity, 71, 180–181
Open-ended activity, primary level, 191
Open-ended question, as listening technique, 306
Out-choice. *See* Intervention
Out-door teaching, 181–182
Out-groups, 21
Overfunctioning, 324
Overgeneralizations, 41
Overspecializations, 41–42
Owen, Robert, 7, 11

P
PACER Kids Against Bullying, 504
Paley, Vivian Gussin, 500
Palmer, Hap, 215
Paraprofessionals, 239
Parental development, 404
Parents. *See also* Conferences; Family; Leadership; Partnership with parents
  accepted beliefs about, 157
  and bullying, 482–483
  and conflict management, 26–27
  continued involvement, 452
  and cooperation with teachers, 28, 402–403
  custodial grandparents, 365
  and developmentally appropriate practice, 24–25, 31
  and e-mail, 289–290
  five-step approach, 403–407
  and guidance tradition, 33
  guidebook sample for, 523–552

  and Head Start, 29, 76
  and industry, 61-62
  Juanita case study, 77–79
  and kindergarten, 28
  and leadership communication, 287–295, 535
  and liberation teaching, 490–495
  listening to, 328–329
  and meetings, 78–79
  and mistaken behavior, 118–121
  and Montessori Children's Houses, 28–29
  and nursery school, 29
  and partnership with teachers, 77–80, 156–157
  and problem solving, 405
  and public schools, 29–30
  roadblocks to involving, 195–196
  surveys, 79
  and teacher conferences, 292–295, 326–329
  and teacher disagreements, 22, 450–453, 456
  and teacher meetings, 291
  and telephone calls, 78, 290–291
  team concept, 241–246
  and websites, 290
  and written notes, 288–289
  as volunteers, 194–198
Parent-teacher conferences. *See* Parents
Partnerships with parents, 27–31, 76– 80, 156–157. *See also* Leadership; Parents; Volunteers
  climate for, 76–77
  collaboration for safety, 453
  consult with staff and professionals, 452–453
  first day of school, 78
  first-night phone call, 78
  Froebel's, kindergartens, 28
  greeting meetings, 78–79
  and Head Start, 29
  invite involvement, 452
  mediation, when to use, 453
  Montessori's children's houses, 28–29
  and mutual respect, 451
  and nursery schools, 29
  preschool, 77–78, 194
  and public schools, 29–30
  and reflective listening, 451–452
  roadblocks to involving, 195–196
  settling in, 78
  use specific situations, 452
  surveys, 79–80
  teachers and, 156–157
Passive restraint, 151–153, 433–434
  bear hug, 152, 433–434, 541
Passivity, 141, 213
Peace education, 488–490
Peace props, and conflict management, 146, 348–349
Peace puppets. *See* Puppets
Peace table, 348

Peak learning experiences, 188. *See also* Windows of opportunity
Peer
    assisted learning, 51
    influence, and socially influenced mistaken behavior, 103
    mediation, 483. *See also* Conflict management
    scaffolding, 51
Perceptual field theory, 14
Performance assessment, 66
Personal development, 17
Personal feelings, and teaching, 224
Personality, protecting, 136–139
Personal safeguards, 445
Personal support system, for stress management, 326
Pestalozzi, Johann, 7, *11*
Peterson, Janke, 157, 242, 246, 348–349, 489
Peterson, Penshorn, 348–349, 489
Physical activity, 203–206
Physical intervention, 387
Physical restraint, 398, 433–434, 455
Piaget, Jean, 12–14, 41–47. *See also* Autonomy; Development; Developmental egocentrism
    and autonomy, 45–47
    and developmental egocentrism, 12–14, 44–47
    foundation for development and guidance, 80
    and liberation teaching, 154-155
    and school readiness, 51, 173
    stages of development, 41
    and Vygotsky, 47, 48, 50, 51
Play, 172–175, 204, 214–215, 528–529. *See also* Activities; Boys
    academics, 252–253
    active, 214–215
    in child development, 58
    as guidance, 203–206
    guidebook handout for parents, 528–529
    and initiative versus guilt stage, 57–60
    and learning centers, 180–192
    physical activity, 213–214
    and problem solving, 50
    rough-and-tumble, 204, 215
    and school readiness, 172–175
Political accountability, 170
Positive consistency, 374, 377
Posttraumatic stress syndrome, 435
Power puppets. *See* Puppets
Praise. *See also* Encouragement
    appropriate use of, 24–25
    and encouragement, 264–265, 295
    creating problems, 265
    and Rudolph Dreikurs, 15–16
Preconcepts. *See* Development
Prekindergarteners Left Behind: Expulsion Rates in State Prekindergarten Systems (Gilliam, 2005), 133

Preoperational stage, 41–43, 45, 50, 57–58, *286*
Preschoolers
    belonging, and initiative, 60
    and class meetings, 148
    and compliment sandwiches, *318*
    and contact talks, 37, 314–315
    encouragement with direction, *390*
    and friends, *286*
    guidelines for, 262
    and initiative versus guilt, 57–60. *See also* Erickson, Erik
    Head Start and, 30
    and parental involvement, *194*
    and play, 58
    programs, 30
    prosocial, 45
    sample daily schedule for, *210*
Primary grades
    and compliment sandwiches, *318*
    and conflict management, *380*
    and contact talk, 37, 315–317
    and developmentally appropriate practice, 24–25, 31, 175–180
    exploratory activity, 191
    guidelines for, 262
    and industry versus inferiority, 14, 60–62
    and learning centers, 188–189
    and non-verbal techniques, 386–389
    open-ended activity, 191
    parental involvement, *194*–195
    problem solving arguments, *380*
    sample daily schedule for, *212*
    self-correcting activity, 191
    self-directing activity, 58, 191
    and teaching team, 240
Principal, role of in developmentally appropriate practice, 24–25, 177–178
Private encouragement 265–267. *See also* Encouragement
Private speech, 49–50
    emotions management and, 50, 53
    problem solving, 50
    and scaffolding, 49
Privilege, and conflict management, 346
Problem puppets. *See* Puppets
Problem solving. *See also* Conflict management; Intervention
    and arguments, *380*
    and class meetings, 277
    cooperative, 347
    and family, 405
    and guidance, 23, 347
    independent, 48
    instant, 295
    logical-mathematical, *67*
    and mistaken behavior, 373–414
    and parents, 405
    personal, *67*
    and play, 50
    social, 53, 342

steps for, 403–407
strategies, 23
techniques for, 393–398
and violence, 464–470
Process modeling, 187
Product modeling, 187
Professionals, 130, 494–495, 452, 533, 545–546
Project Head Start. *See* Head Start
Property, and conflict management, 346
Prosocial behavior, 45, 192–194
Protective buffer, 477
Provocative behaviors, and violence, 469
Proximity, for conflict management, 387
Psychological "distance", 48
Psychology in the Classroom (Driekurs), 16
Public encouragement, 265–267. *See also* Encouragement
Public schools, 29–30
Punishment, 5–6, *172*, 259–260, 340
Puppets, and conflict management, 146, 348
Purkey, William, *19*

Q

Quality time. *See* Contact talk
Quiet Moments, 215
Quiet periods, purpose of, 213

R

Reactive aggression, 115–116, 117
Reading
    appreciation of, 224–*225*
    and discussing inclusively, 224, 226, 273
    encouragement of, 224
    guidebook sample, for parent handout, 524–525
    for personal expression, 224
    techniques to encourage, *225*
Reading center, 188, 218, 233, 242
Reconciliation, 394, 397–398, 448–450
    and anger, 398, 394, 395
Redirection, 424
Referrals. *See* Support services
Reflective listening, 294, *306*, 393–394, 451–452
Reflective statements, 276–277
Reggio Emilia schools, 13
    and learning centers, 183, 186, 190
Relational patterns. *See* Social development
Relaxation, schedule, *212, 217. See also* Schedules
Release function, 393
Requesting choices. *See* Intervention
Resiliency, 475–477
    child, 475
    and liberation teaching, 475–477
    mentoring, 475
    as protective buffer, 477
    and social environment, 475–477
Resilient, 475

Responsive leader, 26. *See also* Conflict
　management; Teaching
Response to Intervention. *See* (RTI)
Rest, 215–218. *See also* Schedules
　napping guide, *217*
　purpose of, 215
　schedule, 216–218
Rethinking the Brain (Shore), 75
RTI (Response to Intervention), 437
Rogers, Carl, *19*
Rough-and-tumble play, 204, 215
Routines, 186–187, 235–237, 248
　and teacher's perspective,
　　235–237, 248
　teaching through guidance, 258–259
Rules. *See* Guidelines

s

Safeguards, for emotions, 447–448
Safety
　and growth, 154, 155
　needs, 154, 471
　parent and teacher disagreements, 453
Salovey, Peter, 69
Sandford, Pat, 41–42, 235–236
Scaffolding, 48–49
　defined, 48
　and liberation teaching, 155
　with peers, 48, 51
　and private speech, 49
　teacher and child collaboration, 49, 51,
　　241
　and teacher-directed instruction, 50
　zone of proximal and, 49
Schedules. *See also* Activities;
　　Encouraging classroom; Groups;
　　Transition time
　active times, 187–188, 213
　day chart, 209
　day clock, 209, 213
　and encouraging classroom, 209–218
　kindergarten sample, *211*
　naps, *217*
　physical activity and, 71, 213–214
　pre-kindergarten sample, *210*
　primary sample, *212*
　quiet time, 213
　relaxation, 215–218
　rest, 215–218
　rest periods, 216
　samples of, 209
　time confusion prevention, 210–213
Schemata, 41
Science guidebook sample, for parent
　　handout, 526
School and Society, The (Dewey), 10
School anxiety, 168–169, 198–199
School democracy, 263. *See also*
　　Democratic life skills
School Mediation Associates, 26
School readiness, 172-175
Schools

American, 27, 214, 464
　failure and frustration in, 15
　and multiage classrooms, 51
　preschools, 233–235
　public, 29–30
　and violence, 464
Second language, and brain
　　development, 74
Self-calming, *394*
Self-concept, 11, 14
Self-concept psychology. *See* Self
　　psychology
Self-correcting activities, 191
Self-directing activities, primary level, 58,
　　189–190, 191
Self-discipline, 10
Self-esteem, low, 14, 136–139
Self-fulfilling prophecy, 134–135
Self-image, 14
Self-labels, 51
Self-management, 69, 81, 423
Self-monitoring, and teaching,
　　445–447
Self psychologists, 11–15
Self psychology, 11
Self-regulation, 343
Self-removal, 432–433
Self-report, 265, *306*, 395
Self talk, 48, 50
Sensorimotor stage, 41
Separation, and crisis management,
　　424, 429
Separation anxiety, 54–56. *See also*
　　Erickson, Erik; Infancy
Sharing, 192–193, 222
Sharing Nature with Children
　　(Cornell), 181
Shore, Rima, 75
Show-and-tell, 222–223
Significant learning, 172
Silence, power of, 487
Sklar-Rasminsky, Judy, 117–118
Small-group
　activities, 67, 164, 180, 214
　discussions, *293*
　nonstratified sharing, 51, *293*
　and reading, *225*
　schedules, *210–211*
　and social circles, 285
Social acceptance
　and behavior, 17, 163
　goals of, 17
Social competence, 342
Social development. *See also* Mistaken
　　behavior
　adjustment, 60, 71, 94, 132, 155, 445–447
　encounterer, 92
　mistaken behavior relationship, 98, *99*,
　　100–105
　prosocial preschoolers, 45, 192–193
　and relational patterns, 94–97, 122
　survival, 94, 98, 108, 122

Socially influenced mistaken behavior,
　　100–105
　intentional, 100
　family influences, 102
　learned behavior, 101–102
　and liberation teaching, 102–105
　and mistaken behavior, 98, *99*,
　　100–105, 122. *See also* Mistaken
　　behavior
　overview, 100–101
　and peer influence, 51, 103
　private speech and, 53
　sources of, 101
　and superheroes, 104–105, 467
　unintentional, 100, 101
　and violence, 467–468
Socially responsive education. *See*
　　Liberation teaching
Social policy, and intelligence, 63
Social problem solving, 342. *See also*
　　Conflict management
Social Studies guidebook sample, for
　　parent handout, 526–527
Sock puppets. *See* Puppets
Socrates, 68
Solution-orientation, 145–153, 158
Songs
　and calendars, 221, 222
　in class meetings, 272
　and large groups, 228, 231–232
　musical intelligences, *67*,
　in prekindergarten schedules, *210–211*
　and standing in lines, 235
　and taking attendance, 220, 229
　and transitions, 231
Spatial intelligence, 65, *67*, 174, 204.
　　See also Multiple intelligences
Special education. *See* Guidance;
　　Intervention; Mistaken behavior;
　　Strong unmet needs
Staff, communication, 452–453
Standardized tests, and multiple
　　intelligences, 63, 65–66. *See also*
　　High-stakes testing
Starter statement, 268. *See also*
　　Encouragement
Stickers and smiley faces, 268–270.
　　See also Encouragement
　appropriate use of, 269
Stigma, 471–475
　and bullying, 471
　cultural factors, 168, 472
　disabilities, 472
　and liberation teaching, 153,
　　471–472
　personality qualities, 134–136, 472
　physical factors, 472
　preschool expulsion, 472
　responses to, 473–475
　social factors, 471, 472
　teacher behaviors that cause, 472
　versus liberation, 153

Stimulating Maturity through Accelerated Readiness Training (S.M.A.R.T.), 204, 205
Stone, Jeanette, 108
Stories, 223–226. *See also* Reading encourage appreciation of, *225*
Stress, 324–326
  home and neighborhood related, 307–308
  and overfunctioning, 324
  personal support system and, 326
  poverty, 71
  reaction patterns, 324
  reduction of, 325
  school related, 306, 325
  symptoms, 325
  and talking time, 308
Strong unmet needs, 105–110. *See also* Mistaken behavior
  causes for, 434–435
  and comprehensive guidance, 37, 109–110, 455
  crisis/conflict management techniques, 438, 440–441
  and emotional factors, 105, 106, 108
  and environmental factors, 106
  and guidance, 109–*110*
  and health factors, *99*, 105, 106
  and Individual Guidance Plan (IGP), 438
  and mistaken behavior, 98, *99*, 105–110, 122
  physical discomfort, 106
  physiological factors, 106
  posttraumatic stress syndrome, 435
  principles for, 539
  responding to, 108–110
  and school anxiety, 168
  sources of motivation for, 98–*99*
  and special education, 437
  stickers for, 269
  and Surgeon General's Report, 436
  survivor pattern, 105
  and teaching, 106
  and violence, 108
Superhero
  and socially influenced mistaken behavior, 104-105, 467
  syndrome, 104, 467
Support services, 406–407
Support system, building, 37
Surgeon General's Report, 26, 400, 436, 464, 465
Surveys, 79–80, 518–522
  for child and family information, 518–520
  digital communication, 289
  about family involvement, 515, 521–522
  leadership communication, 288
Survival
  and liberation teaching, 155, 418, 471
  and mistaken behavior, 99, 105

  and social development, 94, 98, 108, 122
Survivor level, 99, 105

T
Table talk, 51,
Talk-and-listen chairs, 348
Talking stick, and conflict management, 146, 348
Talking time, and school-related stress, 308
Talk to situations, 452
Tattling, 390–392, 408. *See also* Intervention
Teachable moment, 396
Teacher and Child (Ginott), 18, 91
Teacher-child negotiating, 146, 395–396
Teacher-directed instruction
  and scaffolding, 50
  and zone of proximal development, 48
Teachers. *See also* Teaching
  and accepting humanness, 47
  achieving higher levels in children, 49
  and anger, 445–450, 455–456
  bossiness and, 15, 378–380
  and child conflicts, 43
  and child relations, positive, 132–139, 158, 438–439
  and child-reports, 390–392, 408
  classroom conflicts, 93
  conflict management, 343–345
  discipline, effects on, 21
  exploratory activities, 191
  guidance tradition, 33
  losing one's temper, 93
  and loss for words problem, 268
  as mandated reporters, 307
  as mediator, 344
  men teachers and boys, 411–414
  and obedience, 97
  and parent communication, 118–121
  and parent conferences, 292–295, 326–329, 331
  and parent disagreements, 450–453, 456
  teacher-parent problem solving, 405
  partnerships with parents, 27–31, 76–80, 156–157
  and positive relationships, 237
  and prosocial development, 192–194, 199–200
  as professionals versus technicians, 130–132, 157–158, 533, 545–546
  punishing misbehavior, 92, 340
  as responsive leaders, 5–16, 26
  role of, 42, 253
  and personal stress, 324–326, 330–331
  and separation anxiety, 56

  as social workers, 311–312
  encouraging successful participation, 45
  as team leaders, 240–241. *See also* Leadership communication
  welcoming children and families, 37
  with-it-ness ability, 130–131, 375–376
  and volunteers, 194-198, 200, 241–246
Teaching. *See also* Brain development; Brain research; Conferences; Encouraging classroom; Guidance; Liberation teaching; Teachers; Teamwork
  and anger, 445–450
  appropriate child care characteristics, 53–54, 57, 74, 76
  behaviors that stigmatize, 283, 285, 289, 467, 471–473
  calendar and weather, 220–222
  and calming, 344, 419–420
  child relationships, 441–442
  cliques and squabbling, 285
  communication with parents, 123
  and competition, 45, 60, 85–88, 379
  compliment sandwich, 109, 120–121, 317–318
  conflict management skills, 146, 162–164, 343–345, 354–361
  consultations with staff and professionals, 452–453
  and crisis intervention, 424–434, 440–441, 454–455
  and culture clashes, 417–418
  and developmental egocentrism, 45–47, *286*
  and developmentally inappropriate practices, 24
  direct instruction, 227
  discussing inclusively, 270–273, 295
  emotions management, 423–424
  and encouragement, 265
  and family feelings, 403–404
  and guidance, 37–38
  and industry promotion, 61–62
  infants, 29, 76, 139, 282, 315
  and inferiority, 61
  and labeling, 51, 135–136, 425
  and leaders, 240–241, 264
  learning while, 130–132
  liberation, 153-156
  and low self-esteem, 14, 61
  and multiple intelligences,
  and parent disagreements, 450–453
  partnerships with parents, 77–80, 82, 156–157
  and personal expression, 224, 345
  and personal feelings, 36, 138, 300, 426, 455–456
  and play, 172–175, 204, 214–215, 528–529

Teaching (*continued*)
professional, 130–132
responding to strong unmet needs, 108–110, 122
and scaffolding, 48–49
and separation anxiety, 54, 56
show and tell, 222–223
and social development, 53
and socially influenced mistaken behavior, 102–104
and stress, 306, 324–326
and superhero syndrome, 104–105, 467
test preparation and, 25
toddlers, 29, 139, 193–194, 204, 282, *390*
and unconditional positive regard, 136–139, 234
the whole child, 253
with-it-ness, 130–131, 375–376
young children, *19*, 23, 37, 44–45, 71, 86, 108, 127–128, 178–180, 187, 190–191, 205, 210, 336
and zone of proximal development, 48
Teaching team, 238–241. *See also* Teamwork
Teamwork, 237–241. *See also* Teaching team
other adults, 237–241
advantages of, 195
and associates, 461
leader of, 240–241
other professionals, 241
and primary grades, 240
strengths of, 239–240
teaching, 238–240
Team-teaching, 238–240, 248–249
and volunteers, 198, 241
Technicians, 130
Territory, and conflict management, 346
Thematic approach, 190. *See also* Learning center
Thematic instruction
case study of, 185–186
described, 190
3B system, 185. *See also* Learning center
time confusion, 210–213
and weather, 222
Think of Something Quiet, 215
Threats, use of, 420
Time confusion, 210–213
Time-out, 431–432. *See also* Crisis management
Toddlers
and biting issues, 282
and brain development, 16–17
and brain research, 75–76
and class meetings, 282
family challenges, 57
sample daily schedule for, *210*

Tossed salad approach, 492–493
Total development process, 17
Touch. *See* Communication; Friendly touch; Leadership communication
Tourist curriculum, 486
Traffic pattern, and learning centers, 183–185
Transition time, 230–235. *See also* Activities; Encouraging classroom; Groups
buffer activities, 187–188, 231–233
guidance strategies for, 230–231
lincs, 233–235
management of, 230–235, 248
and mistaken behavior, 233
waiting, 231–233
Trust versus mistrust, 53–56. *See also* Erikson, Erik
TV, and children, 174, 413, 525, 528. *See also* Violence

U

Unconditional positive regard, 136–139, 234
Universal education, 30

V

Value judgments, avoiding, 404–405
Victim, in conflict, 488
Violence, 464–470. *See also* Liberation teaching; Mistaken behavior
and aggression, 115
and attachment process, 118, 468
and bullying, 123, 477–483
versus conflicts, 340
cognition and learning, effects on, 469–470
continuum of, 465–466
defined, 340
direct acts of, 468–470
direct effects of, 468–470
effects by level, 467–468
effects in classroom, 464–470
and emotions, 108, 468
experimentation mistaken behavior, 467
guidance response to, 470–477
and intimacy, 469
Level One, 467
Level Three, 117, 217, 468
Level Two, 116, 467–468
and media, 465, *466*, 467
physical, *115*
and post-traumatic stress syndrome, 468
and provocative behaviors, 468
and punishment, 340
pyramid, 465–467
resiliency and, 470, 475

socially influenced mistaken behavior, 108, 467–468
socially responsive education and, 470
societal, 464, 495
and stigma, 467, 468
and strong unmet needs, 108, 468
and Surgeon General's Report, 26, 400, 464, 465
suppressed conscience, 465
Volunteers, 194–198
children's emotions and, 244–245
comfort levels, 196–198
encouraging, 241–246, 249
first visits, 242–243
parents as, 194–198, 242–243
regular, 195, 197, 200, 245–246
special events, 243–244
in multidimensional classrooms, 241–242
Vygotsky, Lev, 47–53
adult guided development, 47–48, 80
critical analysis of, 50–51
emotions management, 53
and Piaget, 47, 48, 50, 51
private speech, 49–50, 53
role of peers, 51–52
scaffolding, 48–49, 50–51
zone of proximal development, 48, 50

W

Waiting, and transition time, 231–233. *See also* Transition time
Wait time, as listening technique, *306*
Weather, activities for, 221–222
Webbing, 190
Websites, and parental communication, 290
What About Discipline? (Stone), 108
Windows of opportunity, 74, 75
Winning, as losing, 87
With-it-ness, 130–131, 375–376. *See also* Guidance; Teaching
Working in the Reggio Way: A Beginner's Guide for American Teachers [Wurm, 2005].), 13
Writing guidebook sample, for parent handout, 524–525
Written notes, and parental communication, 288–289

Y

Young Children (NAEYC), 127, 128, 156
York, Stacy, 487

Z

Zan, B., *19*, 44–45
Zone of proximal development, 48
and private speech, 48
and scaffolding, 49
and teacher-directed instruction, 48